PRESIDENT GARFIELD

From RADICAL *to* UNIFIER

C. W. GOODYEAR

SIMON & SCHUSTER

New York   London   Toronto   Sydney   New Delhi

Simon & Schuster
1230 Avenue of the Americas
New York, NY 10020

First Simon & Schuster hardcover edition July 2023

SIMON & SCHUSTER and colophon are registered trademarks of Simon & Schuster, Inc.

For information about special discounts for bulk purchases,
please contact Simon & Schuster Special Sales at 1-866-506-1949
or business@simonandschuster.com.

The Simon & Schuster Speakers Bureau can bring authors to your live event.
For more information or to book an event, contact the Simon & Schuster Speakers Bureau
at 1-866-248-3049 or visit our website at www.simonspeakers.com.

Interior design by Ruth Lee-Mui

Manufactured in the United States of America

1 3 5 7 9 10 8 6 4 2

Library of Congress Cataloging-in-Publication Data has been applied for.

ISBN 978-1-9821-4691-7
ISBN 978-1-9821-4693-1 (ebook)

To Chip, Elizabeth, and Adelaide,

For all their hard work.

———•◦•———

To Ellen,

For loving the result.

"Time is the only healer—with wisdom and justice at work."
—President-Elect James A. Garfield, January 25, 1881

Contents

PROLOGUE

"Fortune brings in some boats that are not steered."

—Shakespeare's *Cymbeline*, as quoted in Garfield

diary entry for August 17, 1878

Rain drums Chicago's gridded streets on the early morning of June 9, 1880. Decorations sag and calcium lights hiss; warm, glowing lobbies lure celebrants inside as the night air is washed of the tang of fireworks. Then peace rules the city, with only newfangled electric lampposts—exuding soft light and a soothingly industrial *thrum*—left holding out against the black and the quiet.[1]

This brief calm falters before dawn, when a murmuring crowd packs the entrance of the Grand Pacific Hotel on Jackson Street. A band soon arrives to beat out patriotic tunes—thereby spoiling an ambush: the weather is unseasonably dismal, the hour unreasonably early, but hundreds have defied both to escort the new Republican nominee for president on his journey home. [2]

His attempt at escape fails almost immediately. At eight-thirty, a distinctively large head (two feet in circumference) is seen bobbing under a side-exit, and the mob catches up to it within a half-block. Thus overtaken, James Garfield can only politely surrender to popular will. His hat lifts to reveal a kindly smile. Eyes like summer lightning invite the people to come along, if they'd like.[3]

They do, in a human tide—its noise, the pumping lyrics of "See, The Conquering Hero Comes" and less rhythmic swells of cheers. The candidate at its center has been buffeted by thousands of congratulations in the last eighteen hours.[4]

Upon finally reaching a train station, Garfield climbs onto a car festooned with flags. He shelters within until nine o'clock sharp—a time that is marked by engines firing, wheels chugging, and the car's back door creaking open. Then, as a witness recorded:

> Gen. Garfield yielded to popular demand and appeared on the rear platform, where he was greeted with a succession of cheers from a thousand pairs of patriotic lungs.

His outline recedes into the rain, leaving behind a depot of soggy supporters who are exultant despite the weather and their wetness. Their happiness had been well-stoked since yesterday, when Garfield yielded to a far more pressing demand from a larger audience. "I am not a candidate, and I cannot be," he had repeatedly told a convention packed with senators and generals, governors and congressmen.[5]

Editors now opine the Republican Party (so dreadfully divided) had little choice but to force Garfield to accept the nomination for president anyway. "He was so aggressive, and yet so conciliatory."[6]

Under bluer skies and across a nation now stretching unbroken from Atlantic to Pacific, millions of citizens learn the rough, remarkable outlines of a life driven by those traits. James Garfield's story had begun in a setting so rudimentary as to be alien to most Americans in this mechanized age: a one-room log cabin on the Ohio frontier.

Erudite readers would describe his reported upbringing as almost Dickensian. Garfield's father (indistinguishable "from the other plodding farmers" of early Ohio) had not survived their harsh surroundings for long—leaving his widow and four children to fend for themselves on a lonely homestead. "Mrs. Garfield . . . managed to support herself and the family on the little farm left by her husband, and James, from his earliest years, was obliged to aid . . . in the general work about his home," describes one northeastern outlet. "James had a tough life of it as a boy," another in Illinois summarizes.[7]

Other columnists take pains to specify the toils of the nominee's childhood. Early years splitting firewood, plowing, and working a carpenter's bench had ended when he ran away for the Twainish exploit of piloting a canal boat. But brawls and a bout of malaria evidently set the teenager straight: Garfield enrolled in nearby schools—paying for one by working as its janitor. Readers from Manhattan, New York, to Manhattan, Kansas, peek over their papers to tell their children to never complain again.[8]

Then, a climb that packs enough color to defy the black-and-white of print. The canal boy is baptized; he emerges as a tall, sandy-haired teacher, caning students in a firelit winter classroom; he roams summer roads as a lay preacher; an almond-eyed student passes by, catching his attention; he turns twenty-six and is a married college president—idolized by hundreds of farmers' children flocking for instruction; he is a state senator, swapping peacetime political capital for a wartime army uniform; he is raring to fight as civil war engulfs America, telling voters a "government actually based on the monstrous injustice of human slavery" must not be allowed to exist; he leads congregants and students up frigid Kentucky slopes to hunt rebels; a general's stars bloom on his shoulders— the youngest to bear them in the U.S. Army; he crusades into the Deep South, sheltering runaway slaves in camp against orders; he becomes the youngest congressman in America at thirty-one and one of its most progressive. Then seventeen years fly by in a paragraph, and he is minority leader of the House—an unassuming, unparalleled survivor of an age's worth of legislative battles.[9]

Many of Garfield's political triumphs are lost to readers in that acceleration. He had been the youngest participant in America's radical revolution and remains perhaps the last still politically alive; he had chaired

committees governing the country's military, budget, census, and currency; he had trimmed many millions in federal spending; he had single-
handedly investigated a president, swindled an Indian tribe out of its
ancestral lands, and even established a new wing of government: the first
Department of Education. ("Shall we enlarge the boundaries of citizenship, and make no provision to increase the intelligence of the citizen?"
he'd dared Congress during that particular fight.)[10]

His speeches on these topics and more, as later compiled by a colleague, would be found to "present an invaluable compendium of the
political history of the most important era through which the National
Government has ever passed."[11]

Garfield has also seemingly found time for impressive activities
outside the Capitol. Republicans as varied as William McKinley, James
Blaine, and Benjamin Harrison court his stump services. Statesmen jaded
by a lifetime of sappy speeches have reported their cynicism cured by a
single Garfield performance. "It was eloquent, but it was far more than
that;" one would write with wonder:

> It was *honestly* argumentative; there was no sophistry of any sort; every
> subject was taken up fairly . . . indeed, every person present, even if
> greenbacker or demagogue, must have said within himself, "This man
> is a friend arguing with friends; he makes me his friend, and now
> speaks to me as such."[12]

Reports of the new nominee's other extracurriculars dazzle other observers. Garfield is multilingual—and ashamed to have let his German, in
particular, get rusty recently. He has built a legal career in parallel with his
political one, only to see it also reach incredible heights: attorney Garfield
has won cases before the Supreme Court. Whenever time allows, he also
writes articles for *The Atlantic* and *The North American Review*. His most
recent editorial in the latter had run the year before—insisting, against
rebuttal, that it had not been a mistake to grant Black Americans the

vote, and that ongoing attempts to suppress that right only amounted to national self-sabotage:

> Such a conflict will not only retard the advancement of the negro and delay the restoration of national harmony, but it will inflict immeasurable injury upon the social and business prosperity of the South . . . Reviewing the elements of the larger problem, I do not doubt that [Black] enfranchisement will, in the long run, greatly promote the intellectual, moral, and industrial welfare of the negro race in America; and, instead of imperiling the safety of our institutions, will remove from them the greatest danger which has ever threatened them.[13]

An even more exceptional piece from Garfield's pen ran in the *New England Journal of Education* a few years earlier; an original proof of the Pythagorean theorem. The editors had attached a note verifying Garfield's work, calling it "something on which the members of both houses can unite without distinction of Party."[14]

As Garfield's train clips out of Illinois, Democrat reporters use less flattering episodes of his long career to paint him as the epitome of a Washingtonian swamp creature. ("He is the most corrupt man in America!" an ex-cabinet secretary thunders.) Reprinted in graver tones is the allegation that Garfield helped rig the previous presidential election, before brokering an era-ending compromise to paper the crime over:

> Hayes could plead that he did not steal the Presidency. He was the fence . . . Garfield was one of the principal robbers.[15]

Yet other Democrats cannot help but add to their opponent's resume. "I look upon him as the ablest Republican on the legislative floors of Washington," one confesses to a reporter. Others compliment Garfield's possession of that rarest of political qualities—genuine friendliness to everyone,

no matter their party or the issue at hand: "He was so generous an opponent, so warm and free and liberal in his relations to his political foes."[16]

It was, all told, an impossible record to succinctly review. "Such an accumulation of honors had never before fallen upon an American citizen,"
a senator would later say of Garfield's resume.[17]

The sitting president agrees—even ranking Garfield's name highest
in the national pantheon. "The truth is no man ever started so low who
accomplished so much in all our history," Rutherford B. Hayes scribbles
in the White House. "Not [Benjamin] Franklin or [Abraham] Lincoln
even."[18]

Garfield's engine is a dark line splitting Indiana's verdure from the clouds
that ceiling them. Whenever it stops, voters peer through rain to see lingering evidence of Garfield's strenuous upbringing for themselves. Taller
than everyone in sight, the candidate is also built like a "country Samson."
A friend says Garfield cannot even pick up a book without revealing a
bull-like strength. Another thinks the same about his gait, inadvertently
"redolent of woods and fields rather than of drawing-rooms."[19]

Citizens at South Bend see the Samson analogy, sadly, only holds
from the neck down; Garfield's "massive forehead" has little hair left
above it. This baldness is balanced somewhat by a lush, earthy beard, but
this cannot offset the large cranium. Whenever Garfield covers it up, the
impression to amused spectators is that of "a hat walking away with a
man," rather than vice versa.[20]

At Ligonier, Garfield greets girls bedecked in red, white, and blue. At
Butler, he beams through the "first ordeal in baby-kissing." The celebrations grow discordant as his train nears the hallowed land of Ohio. A
band *blarps* "not very sweet music" at Elkhart. A cannon at Goshen blasts
off in more tuneless salute.[21]

Elsewhere, though, Republican leaders hear unfamiliar notes of harmony sounding in the ranks. "You see," one explains to a reporter, "we had
either to take the Devil or the deep sea. We happily went between, and

took up a compromise man." "It seems to me that Garfield was the only way out of a dilemma," another agrees cheerily. "It is another evidence that Providence governs in the affairs of this nation, and comes to its relief in its darkest hours as frequently before."[22]

At first glance, America does not look to be in a dark spot at all. Many of its luminaries say things are demonstrably as bright as ever—the path ahead, glinting with yet more promise. James Blaine calls this but a continuation of the progress that has defined the country's last decade and a half, progress that has been "not only unprecedented but phenomenal": a once-enslaved race now enjoys citizenship; immigration is pumping the republic's population up by a million souls annually; a hundred thousand miles of railway bind its thirty-eight states and ten territories together, helping products both grown and manufactured reach port in record volume; companies have bemoaned "painfully large" profits; telegraph lines click loudly in every place of business, while men like Thomas Edison and Alexander Graham Bell work in near-solitude on technologies designed, in theory, to draw Americans even closer to one another.[23]

But on nearer inspection, the sheen rubs off to reveal a foundation of disparity beneath. While Black Americans theoretically enjoy equality, many (especially in the South) know exercising such rights is practically an impossible—if not fatal—endeavor. "The old master class is today triumphant, and the newly-enfranchised . . . little above that [state] in which they were found before the rebellion," Frederick Douglass laments. In defiant evidence of this, many who once fought to destroy the Union on behalf of slavery now sit as its legislators.[24]

And yes, national wealth is stacking high—but overwhelmingly in the accounts of a few. This has produced a new, terrifyingly powerful class of citizen, the so-called "robber barons." Andrew Carnegie and Jay Gould have already joined it; the empires of Morgan and Rockefeller (run on the more liquid stuff of capital and oil, respectively) are just beginning to grow. Such men are also stamping out dissent among menials. The first-ever nationwide strike occurred three years ago.[25]

But perhaps the period's strife is most prevalent in America's politics. Division abounds: the sitting president is widely considered illegitimate— not only by Democrats relitigating his election but also by fellow Republicans. The (professedly) wittiest ones call him "Rutherfraud." Others boast of boycotting the White House during his regime. Yet the disdain Republican senators hold for President Hayes dims in the glare of their hatred for one another. Fifteen years of peace and political dominance have done to the party what war and generations of Democrats never could. Vividly named blocs ("Stalwarts" and "Half-Breeds") spent the last administration clashing with the same spirit of the Montagues and Capulets. [26]

Little of substance divides them. Each Republican faction is defined more by a pugilistic, bird-of-paradise of a leader than policy; each run machines that trade places on the public payroll as rewards to cronies; each wallows in corruption ("like a rhinocerous in an African pool") while politely feigning interest in cleaning up government. "As for politics, we seem to be in a backwater period," Henry Adams sighs.[27]

Such disparities have, at least, been good fodder for humorists. One has used them to lend the era a name. Mark Twain calls this the "Gilded Age"—wherein, more than ever, not all that glitters in America is gold.[28]

Only Garfield seems to have navigated all the strife without much issue; he has certainly witnessed more of it than almost anyone. His House tenure measures as almost a record-breaker, and from an increasingly powerful perch in that body he had participated in almost every major American political event since the Civil War: presidential administrations, constitutional amendments, economic catastrophes, an impeachment, election crises, Klan violence, and more had come and gone. Garfield served as one of the Republic's few constants throughout it all. [29]

The secret to his success was no secret at all. In a profession with the lamentable tendency to attract show ponies instead of workhorses, and a period favorable to partisan grandstanding, Garfield had embraced undramatic efficiency in the driest fields of lawmaking imaginable, obsessively tending to the vital, oft-neglected inner clockwork of American

government. "Gentlemen . . . I believe in work," he explained to one audience. It was an advantageous belief: in Garfield's experience, congressmen who prioritized political theater over creating sound policy rarely
accomplished much in the end—for themselves or the country. This was
especially true of those angling for the White House; Garfield has lost
good friends to what he dubs the "Presidential fever . . . [which] impairs
if it does not destroy the usefulness of its victim." It struck him as an
awful disease—capable of reducing a valuable statesman into just another
ineffective politician, with the mere thought they could be president one
day.[30]

Having thus tacked away from the prevailing political style, Garfield
can now laugh in Capitol coatrooms at the president's expense while remaining the administration's most trusted legislative ally. He considers
himself a civil service reformer, but also doles out patronage to allies and
chides clean-government activists for using "too much proclamation" in
criticizing machines. He is just as Janus-like about the South's never-
ending mess. "Outrages" against Black Americans could not be tolerated;
then again, neither could the federal government break constitutional
limits to try to stop them.[31]

Most jarringly, though, Garfield has stayed on good terms with everyone in Washington. Stalwart bosses think him a "most attractive man
to meet," as do reformers. The Half-Breed chief is an especially dear
friend. Lower-ranking Democrats even treat him—the leader of their
opposition—as a confidante. As one would admit:

> It happened once that I—a young member—was called upon to close
> on the Democratic side a debate, which Mr. Garfield was to close
> the next morning on behalf of the Republicans . . . I was extremely
> anxious to make a reply which would do credit to myself and not dis-
> grace my party; and I went to Garfield that night and pointed out my
> dilemma . . . Like the man that he is—like a brother, I might say—he
> told me what he was going to say, the whole time of his argument, and
> thus gave me the benefit of twenty-four hours' study in which to reply

to him. You can understand my admiration, my love, my anxiety for that man.[32]

Cynical colleagues have taken all this as proof of something wrong with Garfield. Frederick Douglass has diagnosed him with a missing backbone. Ulysses Grant and Stalwart senators second the opinion. "Disquieting tendencies in respect both to persons and principles," a reformist legislator would agree. Even sympathizers of Garfield call him a political weather vane, sure to spin unpredictably in foul weather.[33]

Garfield would turn these complaints back on their issuers. It is holding blindly to fixed opinions, and reflexively attacking those with different ones, which is the refuge of the weak and naive. "To be an extreme man is doubtless comfortable," he has written. "It is painful to see so many sides to a subject." His agony would only intensify whenever fellow Republicans again wasted time persecuting one another over trifling bits of partisan dogma. "It is the business of statesmanship to wield the political forces so as not to destroy the end to be gained," Garfield once lectured a reformer.[34]

As for the charge of being too nice, Garfield could only confess to a fault in personality. "I am a poor hater," he admitted on one occasion. A New York academic recalls getting this impression from a crackling hearthside conversation with the minority leader:

> Having settled down in front of the fire . . . we began to discuss the political situation, and his talk remains to me one of the most interesting things of my life . . . One thing which struck me was his judicially fair and even kindly estimates of men who differed from him. Very rarely did he speak harshly or sharply of anyone, differing in this greatly from Mr. Conkling, who . . . seemed to consider men who differed from him as enemies of the human race.[35]

This trait, of all things, is what won Garfield the presidential nomination he claims to have not even wanted. Deadlocked between declared candidates, the Convention had rallied to him as a figurehead who might rescue Republicans from their own divisions. Initial reactions indicate it had done so. "His nomination will produce perfect unison," a Supreme Court justice predicts to a journalist, "because he has helped everybody when asked, and antagonized none."[36]

Garfield's train continues bearing him east, eventually reaching his homeland. "The course of the train after striking Ohio soil has been through a series of ovations difficult to describe," writes one passenger. Well-wishers at Toledo seem as if they would physically carry Garfield to the White House "if he had only said a word."[37]

The next day Garfield is strolling sun-dappled Cleveland. Around him, again and everywhere, is proof of the history he has witnessed: almost all the buildings in eyesight are older than him. After arriving in town, Garfield had been reminded of a particularly rustic episode from his youth by a passing banner. It read: "He who at the age of 16 steered a canal boat will steer the Ship of State at 50."[38]

But when a friend predicts just such a victory ahead, Garfield is back to business. "Say, rather, the work has just begun."[39]

At two o'clock he is in a coach trundling down a hot dirt road through a bower of blossoming trees. This is Ohio's Western Reserve—a bucolic corner of America that, like its political idol, seems to embody "in thought, as in action . . . the median line between the overflowing East and ever-welcoming West."[40]

Brick farm homes dot its rippling land, and in their doorways hang Garfield's portrait. Their owners had been his flock in worship, his students in antebellum, his soldiers in war, his voters in peacetime. One would, in old age, remember Garfield as "my ideal . . . of all that is manly, brilliant, and good—a Sir Galahad, our knight."[41]

The carriage soon rolls into his first seat of power: Hiram College. Here Garfield's climb to influence over the Reserve began. Its commencement ceremonies are scheduled for this afternoon; its former administrator is still planning to attend.

•   •   •

Before they start, Garfield visits the home of his father-in-law. Therein he reunites with Lucretia—his wife, and (to borrow his expression) the "earthly source of all my joys." Their love is true but had not always been so. "Crete," ever-serene, had quietly endured a great deal during their early years together: her husband's months away from home, his emotional neglect, the death of their firstborn—and even, secretly, an affair. But she had held on, and Garfield had atoned, and neither can now imagine life without the other. Picturing her face is what allowed Garfield to withstand the ambush of his nomination. "She is unstampedable," he likes saying.[42]

The commencement speaker tells the packed auditorium at Hiram of a man "who was at one time a fellow-student with a number of persons present . . . With respect to the future we cherish the larger hope. I introduce to you Gen. Garfield."

Garfield can offer only a few words to the graduates walking in his footsteps:

> While I have been sitting here this afternoon . . . it occurred to me that the best thing you have . . . is perhaps the thing you care for least, and that is your leisure—the leisure you have to think in, and to be let alone; the leisure you have to throw the plummet with your hands . . . the leisure you have to walk about the towers of yourselves, and find how strong or how weak they are, and determine which need building up, and how to shape them, that you may be made the final being that you are to be.[43]

Thus, in trying to speak on leisure, the next president of the United States betrays that he does not really know what it is.

He never would. The hardest work of Garfield's life remains ahead—not only winning the presidency but using it to try cobbling his party and country back together. By doing so, Garfield earns another arduous distinction: he becomes the second president to be assassinated.

Its spectacle grips the nation. Wounded by gunshot, Garfield takes eighty agonizing days to die. His condition keeps his countrymen united in anxious vigil. Perhaps more remarkably, the partisan faction perceived as being responsible for his shooting (by perpetuating the period's toxic, rancorous politics) is ostracized; American voters use Garfield's death to chart a course to calmer public discourse and cleaner government.

The arc of a remarkable life is thereby eclipsed by how it ends. Future historians would be drawn to studying Garfield's murder, its impact on the nation, and the lingering question of what the man could have achieved, instead of what he already had.

In his final hours, Garfield seemed to worry this would be the case. He looked up from his deathbed to ask a friend:

Do you think my name will have a place in human history?

An affirmative answer then appeared to relax him. "My work is done," Garfield said aloud before passing on.[44]

Little could he have imagined the places his name would hold for centuries to come—not just in history, but the ongoing lives of his compatriots and the land itself. Americans would name their children in honor of the martyred president; an Apache chief would even change his own to do so. Thousands of Garfield streets, avenues, and boulevards would be built, as would hospitals, schools, towns, and entire counties also bearing his name. Mount Garfield would be scaled by climbers in both the Rockies and the Appalachian Trail. A sculpture of him would stand guard in Congress's Statuary Hall, while yet another was to occupy a roundabout on the Capitol's southwest corner.[45]

Other pieces of his legacy found purchase in obscurer parts of America: *Lupinus garfieldensis* still grows wild and snow-white on northwestern peaks; Johnny Cash recorded a single about the slain president; a more indirect (and incongruous) tribute to Garfield has come in the serialized form of a lazy, orange cartoon cat.[46]

A theme of reconciliation threads his life together. Garfield spent his early years as a bright country boy endeavoring to make sense of the country he had been born to; his middle ones, as a progressive soldier-statesman trying to build a more righteous, peaceful America out of the ashes of civil war; his very last months, succeeding in doing so—in great part, ironically, by being killed.

That he reached the presidency at all is miraculous, considering where he started. Garfield was born in a log hut in a primeval forest, on the fringes of an adolescent republic that was starting to stretch apart at the seams.

Part I

THE WILDERNESS

1

"Sweet are the uses of adversity"

—Shakespeare's *As You Like It*, as quoted in
Garfield diary entry for September 28, 1878

In January 1829, Abram Garfield emerged from a shack in Orange, Ohio, swiveled west, and started toward what passed for civilization on this frontier. He did so alone—flouting what his neighbors, miles off, considered common sense. The snow smothering their land was deep enough to trap horses. The roads beneath were in poor condition, while wolves still roamed the woods beside them. Yet Abram walked off alone anyway. Friends would not have expected different. "No man dared call him a coward," one would remember.[1]

Indeed, defiance ran deep in Abram's bloodline. "In the cross I conquer" had been the Garfield motto in medieval England, and upon crossing the Atlantic the family had colonized coastal Massachusetts, fired the opening shots in the Battle of Lexington, then moved deeper into the continental interior as the United States entered adolescence. Male Garfields tended to grow strong and strong-willed; as Abram left Orange, old men in Worcester, New York, could still remember his grandfather, Solomon, carrying a two-hundred-pound millstone for two miles without stopping for a breather. Garfield women, meanwhile, had to be tough enough to tolerate such stubborn men.[2]

Abram embodied his heritage as he walked. Standing a whisker under six feet tall, with a shock of tawny hair and ocean-colored eyes, he crossed miles of woodland that had yet to be tamed. Only rarely did the surrounding trees ("rich-grained maples, towering hickories, and giant sycamores") yield before a homestead of the kind Alexis De Tocqueville had recently seen being abandoned across a still-wild Midwest. "Among these abandoned fields, these day-old ruins," the Frenchman wrote, "the ancient forest does not delay growing new shoots." On reaching the village of Newburgh Heights near nightfall, though, Abram could observe enduring signs of settlement: fenced pasture, homes built from planked wood rather than log.[3]

Yet such structures did not totally ward off the dangers of frontier life, and within one waited the tragic cause for Abram's return. Stepping through a doorway, he reunited with his wife, Eliza, and their children— now reduced by one. The youngest, two-year-old James Garfield, had died without warning the prior afternoon. Now back beside his wife, Abram offered her the only comfort he could: "The Lord gave, and the Lord taketh away, and blessed be the name of the Lord."

Eliza would later recall resisting this advice. "I almost frowned on my Maker," she said of her grief. "But I made up my mind to live a different life."

One awaited in Orange. Within the fortnight, the Garfields had buried James, crammed into an oxcart, and trundled off to Abram's cabin to face the future together.[4]

Though Eliza would refer to her family's new setting as the "wilderness," it had a formal name—the Western Reserve, an archaic title befitting a region stuck in the past. Despite forming the northeastern corner of Ohio at the turn of the nineteenth century, Lake Erie's jagged shoreline had signified nothing to New England's early colonists if not the distant west, and, shortly after the Revolution, the United States allowed

Connecticut to retain rights to settle that territory. Thus, it went onto maps as the Connecticut Western Reserve, though other nicknames reflecting a grounded view of what awaited pioneers there (and in broader Ohio) also entered use: "the back country"; "the vast interior"; "the howling wilderness."[5]

Few dared brave it at first. Even the earliest American surveyor of the land (a Yale graduate named Moses Cleaveland) did not remain for long. He mapped the Reserve, negotiated with local Indians, then headed back east, never to return and leaving behind a settlement bearing his name. The trials of those who stayed proved the wisdom of this choice. "None but the courageous could have endured the privations of the early days," a Reservist would one day write.[6]

The first American citizens to inhabit the Reserve became hardscrabble homesteaders—the men among them often going shoeless to conserve precious leather. Their wives made gritty breads in mud ovens, using "bear's meat instead of beef" as stuffing. Their dwellings were rickety cabins that had quilts for doors and greased paper rather than glass for windows. It is, therefore, unsurprising that early Reserve families often awoke to find animals sharing their home. Nor could the weather be kept out: storms of spectacular variety blew off Lake Erie—lightning in summer, blizzards in winter, and sometimes both at once, in localized phenomena called thundersnows.[7]

By 1801, only a few hundred people called the Reserve home. Despite being the closest region of Ohio to the crowding American coast, it would also become the last to be meaningfully settled by white men.[8]

True to form, they gradually arrived in force anyway. The circumstances prompting this were already in motion at the turn of the century; commerce and populations had flourished along the Atlantic, most demonstrably in Manhattan. Professionally engineered turnpikes plowed into northeastern forests in the early nineteenth century, and as an observer noted, once such a road "is opened through the woods . . . the country which was before a trackless forest becomes settled." Like the first footprints planted in a snowdrift, such efforts made it easier for others to follow.[9]

After the War of 1812, New York gubernatorial candidate DeWitt Clinton dusted off the idea of building a waterway connecting the Hudson River to Lake Erie. Critics balked at the colossal price tag of "Clinton's Big Ditch" (six million dollars, or nearly a third of all capital in New York) but voters picked Clinton. A historian would describe the triumph of his infrastructure idea as a rare instance of "long-range planning in a democracy." Construction began on the fittingly titled Erie Canal in mid-1817, amid boasts by Governor Clinton that it would "convey more riches on its waters than any other canal in the world."[10]

Upon completion in 1825, it proved him right. The Erie Canal surpassed 375 miles in length, permitting uninterrupted travel across the Empire State. In the judgment of a foreigner, it was "simple as a work of art, prodigious as a commercial artery." Property prices doubled; the government recouped costs quickly via tolls. Better yet, all New Yorkers (from true-born Manhattanites to fresh immigrants like the Carnegies of Scotland) could use the Erie Canal to relocate to the Midwest.[11]

This did not mean a canal boat ride was pleasant. Dirty, crowded, and mind-numbingly slow, the Erie's vessels failed to impress passengers. "In taking notice of this mode of conveyance," wrote one tourist, "it is merely to guard my countrymen from traveling much by canal in the States."[12]

Even in the Reserve, a hundred or so miles away from the Erie Canal's terminus, development began to appear. Printed newspapers reached the region by 1818, as did steamboats from the canal boomtown of Buffalo. The latter invention entranced the Ohioans. Their leaders decided to try building their own canal before New York's had even been finished. After several surveys, they selected a route that ran from Cleveland to a spot on the Ohio River bordering Kentucky. It was a bold plan (proposing a bisection of the state) but work began on July 4, 1825. In implicit acknowledgment that this venture was not an original idea, Ohio let New

York's governor Clinton ("so interested in all canal projects") lift the first shovelful of earth.[13]

Millions more followed, as raised by rougher men across three hundred miles of undulating terrain. This work went on at a relentless pace for several years: laborer teams spent winters felling forests with handheld axes, then digging the thawed soil in spring. Though the men earned good pay for their troubles (in cash, as well as whiskey) they still found their lot hard to endure. "I am cold, wet and sleepy," one wrote. "My head aches so that I am almost insensible to everything around me." But for those workers who could retain their own ambition while helping realize that of Ohio, there remained much fortune to be made.[14]

Abram Garfield was one such man. He first moved to the Reserve after marrying Eliza Ballou in 1819, and after a few years of hardship common to the region, viewed the prospect of a job on the Ohio Canal as a fine one. Good with his hands and even better with other workingmen ("[he] could take a barrel of whiskey by the chime and drink out of the bung-hole," one reminisced), Abram found work on the waterway as a superintendent. Little time passed before he aimed higher—joining friends in a contract to build their own canal section. This venture worked out "first rate."

Alas (like many risktakers) Abram took too much heart from his initial success. He contracted to build three further sections in Tuscarawas County in 1827, only to see his costs crush his earnings. As Eliza recounted (in an accidental pun): "We sunk a good deal in the Canal."[15]

So, in relocating to Orange, the Garfields were moving on not only from the death of their youngest, but also their mixed fortunes in a modernizing Ohio. Their new cabin would certainly offer them a simpler way of life: Abram had built it with help from a half-sibling, Amos, using rough-hewn logs for walls, chipped tree trunks for flooring, mud as a mortar. Upon completion, the single-room dwelling spanned a mere twenty by thirty feet. A loft offered a sleeping perch for the youngest Garfields; the rest would make do on the ground before a fireplace. Outside lay fifty acres of hills cut through by a stream. The nearest neighbors were miles away.[16]

But the Garfields treated their new situation as an opportunity for renewal, rather than a depressing retreat into the woods. Abram quickly converted the property to their needs. Orchards of plum and apple trees cropped up about the cabin. Fences were ringed around future wheat fields.

Eliza did not let sorrow interrupt her duties, either. Though James ("darling Jimmy") had been her favorite, after his loss she doted on the kids still with her—Thomas, Mehitable, and Mary. "Our family circle had not been broken," she would recount.[17]

It even grew. A new Garfield arrived in Orange at two o'clock on the morning of November 19, 1831. He made an impression from the moment of his appearance (particularly on poor Eliza, given the newborn's weight of ten pounds). The baby's size, hay-colored hair, and pale blue eyes made him a dead ringer for his father, and both parents agreed he seemed "promising." That such a child had come to them after their setbacks elsewhere only added to his significance. "We felt that our loss was partially made up," Eliza wrote the boy decades later.

> Although my suffering was so intense, I in a manner forgot my pangs . . . you know not how proud your parents were of you.[18]

In this spirit, the Garfields named their son after the one they had lost—James, now "transplanted into the Paradise of God to bloom forever." The baby's father took to perching him on one knee to read to him from the Bible, one of the few books around.[19]

Homes like theirs, and scenes like this, had already begun to vanish in this part of the Reserve by 1831. With the entire Ohio Canal opening the prior year, rickety wooden boats were ferrying people and transformative forces alike deeper into the region—per one historian, carrying "the world to the wilderness." Brick buildings were rising in Cleveland, while land along the Canal grew many times more crowded, even in Orange.[20]

Similar developments, repeating across the Midwest, would ensure that James Abram Garfield would be the last American president to begin life in a log cabin.[21]

Yet for every mile the Republic grew toward the Pacific, it sowed future troubles. The nation's expansion was not only adding to its great crimes against native peoples, but also building pressure on an ideological fissure that had lurked in its foundation since 1776. By Garfield's birth, two incompatible American systems—slave and free, southern and northern—remained in a westward race for dominance; each believed it equaled survival.

Evidence of one's superiority (beyond the moral) was becoming harder to ignore. Northern industry was ascendant—its factories mechanizing, its capital accumulating, its workers at liberty to demand higher wages or seek new paths of profession, and the products of their labor circulating throughout the wider country. Meanwhile, the South remained trapped in feudal agrarianism—its enslaved Black population digging the same crops, on the same land, for generations with northern-made shovels.[22]

That such societies still coexisted was, essentially, due to the continued dependence of southern gentry on slavery for wealth and political power, and their undying readiness to threaten secession should its future come into question. Such warnings had been raised since the country's founding. "Great as the evil [of slavery] is," one of the Founding Fathers had sighed, "a dismemberment of the Union would be worse." This view prevailed as the United States expanded.[23]

By 1831, the reigning agreement governing the future of American slavery was the so-called "Missouri Compromise." It dictated that a line of latitude (parallel 36°30' north) be used to determine under which system any new states or territories would join the Union. Its negotiators had imagined this simple rule would serve as a "final settlement" to the trouble. Yet statesmen on both sides during its creation expressed certainty that a decisive, inevitable clash had only been postponed. John Quincy Adams called the controversy over the Compromise a "title page to a great tragic volume." A Georgia congressman had made a more sanguinary prediction during its consideration: "You have kindled a fire which all the waters of the ocean cannot put out, which seas of blood can only extinguish."[24]

Nonetheless, more self-aware slaverymen had sensed the enormity of their sin and that of the nation in accommodating it. "Indeed, I tremble for my country when I reflect that God is just; that his justice cannot sleep forever," wrote Thomas Jefferson.[25]

Ohio joined the Union as a free state, and its development reflected that. And yet, even as the frontier's dangers began draining out of the Reserve, tragedy again struck the Garfield family.

On a crisp morning in 1833, smoke cut through the sky over the Orange homestead. Forest fires were not uncommon in the region, so Abram knew full well how to fight this one. By evening, the fire had been turned away, and Abram came back to Eliza with safe fields—plus a persistent cough—to show for his efforts.[26]

After two days, though, Abram had turned deathly ill. A local doctor induced a blister on his throat (ostensibly to tap "every particle of inflammation in his body") but such medicine only aggravated the condition it was meant to treat. Abram stood up a few hours later, rasped about saplings Eliza needed to look after, then returned to bed and died against a wall he had raised.[27]

Abram's passing was not the Garfield family's first recent brush with death, but a more devastating one could not be imagined for them. It brought difficulties upon them that, at the time, only the loss of a father could. Around the Orange cabin sprawled a half-tilled property that remained under mortgage, its fields now without a man to work them. Eliza found that even her sorrow after the first James's demise did not compare to her new one. "Death again entered our humble dwelling and took from me my dear husband," she wrote many years later. "I was almost heartbroken."

Nonetheless, only days after burying Abram ("the companion of my bosom"), she set out with an ax to finish fencing the pastures that now belonged to her.[28]

Physically speaking, Eliza could scarcely have differed more from her late husband. Where Abram had been large and muscular, she stood tiny and stringy. Those who characterized Garfield men as big, hulking animals used smaller creature comparisons for Eliza. She was "birdlike," or even a "small, lithe, compact, sinewy, and nervous . . . 'French pony breed'" of American.[29]

But grit steeled that frame. Though grievously wounded twice in a handful of years (first by the death of her favorite son, then after being "perfectly happy" again, Abram's) Eliza would persevere on behalf of her remaining children. "I will not say anything about myself," she would one day deflect when asked about what she did to get by.[30]

Fortunately for future historians, others were around to witness her actions. To relieve the homestead's debt, Eliza sold off much of it, leaving just enough to feed the family. Once Abram's last planting of wheat had been harvested, his widow then replaced the crop with simpler ones like corn and potatoes. A few sheep were brought in to provide wool that Eliza spun for money. When neighbors or relatives came by to offer adopting the kids into their own homes (a common courtesy toward widows on the frontier) she always rebuffed them. "She was a very brave little woman," Thomas, her eldest boy, reflected a half-century later.[31]

Her courage was of the traumatized and, therefore, most admirable sort, for Eliza would never be the same following Abram's death. "You all know I have had a hard time since your father died," Eliza wrote her children many years after the fact.[32]

And yet—at least while the children were young—she cast a cheery veneer over this inner sadness. The kids would long remember her singing to them in the firelight, in a high, happy voice that carried into their dreams.[33]

By necessity, the children also pitched in around the home. "We all had to work, every one who could lift a pound," Mehitable, seniormost of them, remembered.[34]

The only one who could not help at first was the youngest. He remained active, though—always climbing out of his crib, along the property's fences, or into the loft his father had built. "He was never still a minute at a time," Eliza later said.[35]

Garfield, like most, would never be able to remember his earliest years beyond fleeting flashes of memory. As an adult he could recall tussling with siblings in front of the fire, the wall behind alight with dancing shadows, "in which I traced a thousand fantastic figures of giants on fiery steeds and hosts embattled for war." Another boyhood recollection had Garfield plucking idly at a cheap cornstalk fiddle.[36]

And yet, the same thing stayed conspicuously missing from them all. Childhood bullies ensured Garfield would never forget Abram's absence, and as an adult he would never quite get over it. As General Garfield of the U.S. Army was to write in wartime Washington:

> To some men the fact that they came up from poverty and single-handedness is a matter of pride . . . but on the whole, reviewing it all, I lament sorely that I was born to poverty . . . Let no man praise me because I was poor and without a helper. It was in every way bad for my life . . .[37]

Alone among his siblings in not being able to work after Abram's death, Garfield would also be the only one left with no memories of his father. While serving as chair of the House Appropriations Committee, Garfield would make a great effort to fill this void—with the help of archivists, obtaining one of Abram's old pay stubs. This lone scrap of handwriting and the remembrances of others would be all Garfield ever had to remember his dad by—a man to whom he owed so much and so little, so like and unlike him.[38]

2

"Many can brook the weather that love not the wind."

—Shakespeare's *Love's Labour's Lost*, as quoted in
Garfield diary entry for January 15, 1868

Cleveland neared cityhood toward mid-century. Its merchants raised warehouses to accommodate the commerce pouring into town; a "magnificent" hotel was established to do the same for its growing upper class. Land speculators fought rivals off turf that, not too long before, no one wanted. Historians would credit Cleveland's transformation in this period to the enterprise carried by Lake Erie and the Ohio Canal.[1]

The rest of the Reserve's growth stayed humbler for the time being. Crop fields kept supplanting old-growth forests. Hewing such spaces out of the wilderness required exhaustive work. First, trees would be cleared with hand axes and controlled burns. Later came the stone-picking—a task assigned to children on account of their nimble hands. Teams would comb through the dirt, plucking out any rocks and leaving fine, tillable soil behind. It was among the most painstaking of the labor needed to farm the frontier: even a pebble left in the soil might mar a mis-swung scythe. The Reserve's kids would go home with their nails worn to the bed, blood oozing from fingertips rubbed raw by thousands of bits of stone.[2]

Fortunately, by the time Garfield reached working age (the late single digits) Orange had little stone-picking left to do. A different assortment of tasks instead beckoned in the ocher fields carpeting its hills. Garfield's first working winters would be spent splitting tinder and stacking straw, his springs by more woodcutting and some carpentry. He hoed during summers, then toward the fall would start to draw hay. This latter job made for the easiest one of the year. But, as a visiting farmhand wrote, the Reserve's August climate still made it arduous: "The thermometer rose to 100 and over . . . even if one works without a shirt and drinks water constantly, it is almost unbearable."[3]

The variety of these tasks did not translate to any skill at them for Garfield. No matter which job he took on around Orange, dangerous episodes of clumsiness followed. Relatives were around to witness these: one cousin barely dodged a misplaced ax-swing; another had a distinct memory of seeing Garfield fall from a barn onto a woodpile. Thomas once watched his younger brother topple under a waterwheel, momentarily presuming him dead. But then Garfield emerged on the other side—soaked, yet saying he was happy to have seen the mill's mechanism from within.[4]

It was a telling reaction to nearly being killed—one which, in Thomas's view, fit into a broad, irritating pattern. Whenever hoeing alongside his elder brother, Garfield always lost focus after a few swings. "He would let his mind wander off . . . cut off the corn every time," an elderly Thomas would bemoan to an interviewer. The same habit struck when Garfield was alone; he would come back from walks hurt, having become "lost in thought" and neglected to watch his step. "A new thing, however unimportant," remembered another friend, "always attracted his attention." Simply put, Garfield's mind had already begun to drag him away from farm work. "He was always anxious to know all the whys and where," Thomas diagnosed.[5]

It was therefore almost fortuitous (for everyone) that Garfield hurt himself so often. He would recall his subsequent periods of recuperation with fondness years later, as well as the supportive presence by his side throughout them:

Mother takes care of, borrows books for me, and I sit with the battered foot bolstered while I read all the newspapers, the History of
Connecticut, "Putnam and the World," and all the battles of the Old
Revolutionary Fathers. I am well again, working with the carpenter . . . [and] again I cut my foot and Mother takes care of me another
few weeks.[6]

Chances for intellectual enrichment remained fleeting on the Reserve,
though not because of any disregard for it by locals. They had brought
with them from New England a veneration for education. Yet as with so
many other aspects of life on the Reserve, school was often subordinated
to more pressing household needs. During Garfield's youth, most Reservists his age only studied in winter—the season when little work needed to
be done, provided the firewood was stacked high enough. "The struggle
of making a living was great and the services of children . . . invaluable," a
Reserve historian has rationalized.[7]

In accordance with this, Reserve schoolhouses were spartan things.
Communities placed them in ugly parts of the landscape to deprive pupils of any prettier sights than their reading. Inattentive scholars could
expect beatings; a hearth smoldered feeble-red against the cold. All told,
Reserve schools made for deprived places, boiled down to the essentials
and bleached free of what most kids considered fun. A graduate supposed
this was the point:

> This privation helped pupils to self control and led to industry. Maybe
> it did, but the author believes it took much joy out of life . . .[8]

For a youngster growing up in a household stabilized by both parents,
this might have been the case—the Reserve's schools making for dreary
places, time served therein the childhood equivalent of a prison sentence.
But for Garfield, it instead served as a reprieve from the other obligations
of his home life. "At school very pleasant," Garfield wrote in one of his

first diary entries. The next day he duplicated this sentence, tacking on more "very's" for good measure.[9]

The family noticed this proclivity and was happy to support it. "Whatever else happens, James must go to school," was supposedly Eliza's motto as soon as her youngest child began to show his true colors. The other kids complied with the order—taking turns carrying their little brother for several miles to his classroom.[10]

Eliza supported his education in other ways, too. Once Orange township grew to a size sufficient to require its own school, she donated part of her property for the building, thus buying favor from teachers and cutting commute times for her offspring.[11]

Other obstacles persisted. These included the old issue of seasonality: all too often, spring arrived to find Garfield working the fields rather than studying.[12]

Nor did injury offer him much relief after a while. Garfield made short work of the small library Eliza gathered for him to pore over while injured. "He [soon] had read everything he could get," Thomas later remembered. The result was that well into adulthood, Garfield would be able to recite these books' excerpts down to the page number.[13]

And, of course, Garfield's wounds could not keep him out of commission forever. Inevitably they healed, forcing the boy back to the work he did not care much for.

By late spring 1848 (in the tradition of teenagers), he had begun considering more permanent escapes from his surroundings. Fortunately, one was at hand—observable, even, on the horizon.

For a young Reservist seeking adventure in antebellum, the region's waterways beckoned as realms to find it. Both Lake Erie and the Ohio Canal were bustling by mid-century—teeming with boats crewed by tough men who enjoyed a folk-hero status in a region built upon their trade. "What the cowboy was to the youth of the mid-twentieth century," an industrial scholar has written, "the boatman was, perhaps, to the Ohio youth of the mid-nineteenth century." A boy named Thomas Edison would soon be wandering the dockyards of Milan, Ohio, memorizing work songs hollered by passing canal men.[14]

In early 1848, while chopping wood, Garfield could glance up to see their ships dotting the teal fringe of Lake Erie. He could still picture the view decades later: "The blue expanse seemed to me a region of enchantment and the great vessels the only means of going into that region."[15]

His first attempt to join one went poorly. After giving Eliza the slip to hike to Cleveland alone, Garfield found a ship that had left its gangplank unguarded. He hurried aboard to beg the captain for a job. Alas, all Garfield got in reply was "such swearing and cursing as . . . it had never been my lot to hear." He fled with "the loud jeers and laughter of the men" ringing in his ears.[16]

Chastened, Garfield made his next approach with far greater care. He scouted a stretch of the Canal in April, then returned a few weeks later to observe a boat launch. At the end of May he dared a test run to Cleveland on a friend's boat. Garfield then asked a cousin named Amos Letcher for a full-time place on a vessel Letcher half-owned, named the *Evening Star*.

"What kind of work do you want?" Letcher later remembered asking. "Anything to make a living," Garfield said. Such an attitude won him an offer to become the *Evening Star*'s towpath driver—a role that would put Garfield in closer company with the animals pulling the boat than its crew, but one that he did not hesitate to accept.[17]

His time aboard passed in the soft hues of adolescent summer. Dirt towpaths, leafy canalbanks, smokestacks puffing gentle columns of smoke into July skies—the *Evening Star* spent months snaking languidly past hundreds of miles of such scenery, across an industrializing Midwest. Its holds emptied, refilled, then emptied again with the raw material of economic revolution: copper ore and smelted iron, jagged heaps of stone coal and lumber.[18]

Its youngest crewman stayed beside the vessel's pack animals, clad in heavy oilcloth. His duties consisted not only of prodding the beasts, but holding his own in the canalman's pastime of fistfighting. Garfield used his brawn against opponents twice his age—winning, as he would recall as a congressman, "much prestige with the rough men along the canal." More remarkably to them, he refused to hit a downed adversary. This meant foes sometimes got off the ground apologizing for having given the teenager trouble.[19]

Perhaps Garfield might have stuck with them, had his lack of coordination not interfered again. Walking alone one night on the *Evening Star*'s dimly lit deck, he tripped into the canal. It was a dangerous mistake: despite dreaming of a boatman's life, Garfield had not yet learned to swim.

He seized a line trailing off the *Evening Star* but felt the rope unspool. It only caught tight at the last possible moment—right as Garfield's head went under. After drifting for a while, the boy hauled himself back aboard to discover the rope had snagged in a crevice on the stern and "there knotted itself."

This struck him as the unlikeliest of escapes. Garfield later explained that it felt genuinely miraculous in the moment:

> I sat down in the cold of night and in my wet clothes and contemplated the matter . . . I believed there was just one chance in a thousand for a rope . . . to get into a crack and knot there . . . my thoughts turned upon home and mother . . . Next I thought of her earnest, constant prayers which I had heard from a child [sic] and I believed that Providence had saved my life . . . I thought He had spared me for my mother and for something greater than canaling.[20]

Garfield was already second-guessing this epiphany by next morning, but then came another lucky break. A few days after Garfield fell in the canal, as the *Evening Star* passed Cleveland for the fourth time that summer, he became shaky and feverish. It was a giveaway precursor to malaria; Garfield was kicked off the boat to get healthy.[21]

He reached home at nine o'clock that evening. At its doorway, he overheard Eliza in mid-prayer for his safe return. Once she said an amen, he lifted the door latch to reunite with her, then collapsed into bed, ready to accept her care again.[22]

Garfield would hardly get up for three months, a period in which Eliza (shrewdly) made the most of her captive audience. Having opposed his departure for the canal in the first place, she could not bear the thought of him doing so again. So Eliza pressed an idea to her son as he sweated out his fever—that, should he qualify for a teaching certification, he would be able to work year-round: summers on the canal, winters in the classroom. Eliza even offered the family's life savings to send Garfield back to school to earn the necessary certificate. It was a perfectly crafted suggestion— one designed by Eliza to strike, javelin-like, at Garfield's incipient doubts about his future.

It hit home. "The suggestion seemed to be just," Garfield would later tell an interviewer. To another audience, he was to recall reaching a more ambivalent verdict. "I resolved to attend school one term, and postpone sailing until autumn."[23]

His hedging did not last. Garfield resumed his education at a religious school in the village of Chester. Its reputation was not sterling—even among current students. "From what I can learn of that school it ant [sic] much," one woman wrote a friend considering the "Geauga Seminary."[24]

But Garfield thought the place a revelation. One of his first letters home revealed he felt enthralled at the vistas reopening before him:

"I like the school better every day and I think I am learning fast . . . Nothing hinders us from learning if we wish to."[25]

The only possible hindrance remained that of money. By the end of Garfield's first term, the funds Eliza and Thomas entrusted to him were practically gone.[26]

Thus given an excuse to return to the canal, Garfield opted instead to work as a field hand—staying close to home as well as school. He spent the summer earning a dollar a day until August 2, when another attack of clumsiness got an again-injured Garfield literally carried off the job.

Fortunately, by that point he had earned enough to reenroll at Geauga as long as he continued working part-time. "You need not trade off my rifle unless you get a good chance," Garfield wrote home a fortnight into the new semester.[27]

Garfield found all his fellow students "very friendly," but may not have noticed one paying particularly close interest to him. Lucretia Rudolph was not the outgoing sort, anyway. But she kept a dark, sharp eye on the gregarious boy in her classes. He radiated goodwill—whether interjecting excitedly as a teacher explained fluid mechanics, or daydreaming at his desk (reminding Lucretia, with his tousled blondish hair, of a drowsy lion).

Crossing a yard one afternoon in Chester, she lifted her hat to see Garfield beaming at her before walking off. He was bound somewhere else, for now.[28]

As much as Garfield enjoyed the Geauga curriculum, he found a source of greater enrichment outside the classroom: he joined a debate society (the Zetelethian) after arriving in Chester, and in doing so entered an invigoratingly gladiatorial arena of intellectual activity. "Had a very interesting time," he noted following one of his first debates. "Interesting times," he repeated the next night.[29]

Indeed they were. Turbulent events were spoiling Geauga's students for topics to discuss. Their country's triumph in the recent Mexican–American War had allowed it to "negotiate" an extortionate settlement—including a stretch of prairie reaching all the way to the Pacific. This "Mexican cession" represented the second-largest expansion of American territory to that point in history. Some Democrats still wanted to absorb the losing nation totally, but their "All Mexico" crusade died at the hands of other congressmen with other concerns at heart. "Ours is the government of the white man," Senator John Calhoun of South Carolina reminded his countrymen.[30]

Many Whigs cast the war from its outset as a conspiracy to benefit a handful of white men, in particular: southern slavers desperate to expand their domain. But after failing to prevent the conflict, Whigs could only lament what effect its spoils would have on the Republic's old, unsettled issue. "Mexico will poison us," Ralph Waldo Emerson predicted.[31]

It certainly tainted the Missouri Compromise. Whigs and northern Democrats supported a proviso to ban the extension of slavery into lands won in the Mexican war, only for the measure to be repeatedly stifled. Talk of a new grand bargain began brewing in corners of the Senate by 1849, but pessimism about any lasting concord persisted. "Slavery and freedom are conflicting systems," Senator William Seward would soon warn. "Their antagonism is radical, and therefore perpetual."[32]

The Reserve had famously strong opinions on this subject. "All its instincts were intensely antislavery," an observer summarized. This was evident in the region's politics: the Reserve's congressman was the silver-maned Joshua Giddings, esteemed among Whigs as "master of us all in anti-slavery matters," and a deliberate offender of the House gag rule forbidding mention of "the peculiar institution."[33]

Giddings's constituents shared his zeal. Touring through the Western Reserve, Frederick Douglass even remarked that "it was pleasant to see our cause look popular for once." The region's overt antagonism to slavery was complemented by local subversion of the practice, too: the Reserve has been estimated to have contained more stops on the Underground Railroad than any comparably sized part of the country. This made the region, per one writer, the "Mecca of the slave escaped from bondage."[34]

Some Reservists were abolitionist to the point of militancy: John Brown grew up there, but was, while Garfield attended Geauga, on his way to spilling blood for the cause in other parts of America.[35]

•   •   •

Thus, in the summer of 1849, the debate societies at Geauga had much to chew over. Slavery did not provoke much difference of opinion among the students, but all its derivative questions incited discussions that fascinated Garfield. He copied down the resolutions that caught his attention most forcefully. "Would it be policy for a republican government to require anything more than suitable age and residence to become members of the elective franchise?" was one evening's topic. Ten nights later came a more inflammatory one: "Are the negroes naturally inferior to the whites?"[36]

Even between friends sharing the musty halls of Chester, such subjects sparked fireworks. Garfield watched one classmate quit the group in a rage after the "inferiority" debate. A more ominous question (concerning the "propriety of disunion") disbanded the entire Zetelethian. Garfield spotted the irony in this. "Society divided the society," he wrote wryly that night. "I joined the new one."[37]

Garfield managed to stay remarkably upbeat throughout this discord. He even seemed to relish the heated rhetoric it raised from his fellows. The more provocative the topic in question, the more captivating the exchanges it sparked, and the more intrigued Garfield became with them. "I love agitation, and investigation, and glory in defending unpopular truth against popular error," he wrote before one such discussion.[38]

Notably, he did not take the "agitation" personally and, when possible, took pains to ensure others did not either. "I am tinctured with the sanguine temperament," the teenager wrote with satisfaction in August 1849. Given a chance to lead debate a few weeks later, Garfield chose to argue that "Competition ought to give way to Cooperation."[39]

Yet he tacitly acknowledged that this attitude had limits. Days after the "cooperation" debate, he listened to a preacher argue that war had never solved any difficulty. "I am not decided on that," the young man wrote afterward.[40]

Garfield made a lasting commitment the following spring. Having secured a part-time teaching job between semesters, the young man found the practical business of running a classroom dull. "School as usual," served as his default diary entry in these months—as slotted around reports of more interesting debates in the town hall about current affairs ("Is the glory of America greater than her shame?"), as well as the occasional scrap with a pupil ("He [the student] caught a billet of wood and came at me"). More often, though, his classroom stayed peaceful; a card proclaiming "study hours" proved an effective inhibitor of most bad behavior.[41]

This gave Garfield the space to consider higher things. Between lessons, he picked up a book of poetry (the safe haven of many a moody adolescent) and wrote of feeling above the "mean and groveling scenes of Earth."[42]

A few days later, Garfield watched a friend get baptized and felt "considerably roused on the subject." The next morning he went into the water himself. "The cause is prospering," he wrote at week's end. "Truth is mighty."[43]

Garfield's enthusiasm echoed the peculiarly warm, liberating nature of the church he had just joined. Its adherents didn't even like the idea of giving their denomination a specific name—out of concern that doing so might erect yet another barrier in the already-divided world of Christendom. They preferred simply being called Christians. "Or," as Garfield later conceded, "the Disciples of Christ."[44]

Other aspects of the Disciple movement were equally unintrusive. A convert had only to profess their faith, confess their sins, and accept baptism to join it. They would rise from the water remarkably free to reach their own views on Christian doctrine. The closest thing Disciples had to an instructive principle was a motto intended to spark dialogue and minimize conflict among their kind: "We speak where the Bible speaks, and we are silent where the Bible is silent." In a similarly inclusive spirit, any given Disciple was technically as capable as any other to speak on matters of scripture—for the movement lacked a hierarchical clergy, its founders having blamed "priest-craft" for all the petty dogmatic divisions of other denominations. The Disciples instead trusted congregants to serve as their own ministers and preachers, like religious minutemen.[45]

It is impossible to ignore how well such a faith—inclusive, open-minded, and empowering—complemented the character of its newest convert. But Garfield's joining of them was preordained in other ways. His parents became Disciples after the death of the first James. Though the youngest Garfields could not convert to the faith as children (Disciples only trusted adults' abilities to consent to baptism), their mother's adherence to it surely made an impression.[46]

Nor were Disciples rare in the Reserve. The region was considered the "principal theater" of the denomination—its rugged terrain, freethinking people, and dearth of cities ("fountains of iniquity," per one of the Disciples' founders) making it fertile ground for the faith. So affirms the account of a Reservist Disciple after an icy baptism in an Ohio creek: "Very cold; though our hearts were warm and rejoicing."[47]

Rejoice Garfield did, through winter and into brisk springtime. He returned to Geauga with a spiritual enthusiasm to add to the one he already held for classroom study—just as a tributary might strengthen a larger river's current. "O! How much wisdom of God is shown forth, even in the flower," Garfield declared after a botany lesson. He also dabbled in the classics. "*Felix sum*," he wrote experimentally as summer neared.[48]

The debate hall remained a happy realm for him—perhaps too happy. A freeman lectured the Geauga students one night about slavery, but Garfield's subsequent diary entry indicates he felt more taken by the speaker's style: "The Darkey had some funny remarks and witty too."[49]

A touch of anxiety did mar his mood near the end of June, when he was picked to address the school's exhibition ceremony. But the day came and went, and Garfield passed through this crucible feeling as if a tremendous threshold had been crossed. The possibilities beyond looked both infinite and unimaginable:

> The ice is broken. I am no longer a cringing scapegoat but am resolved
> to make a mark in the world. I know without egotism that there is
> some of the slumbering thunder in my soul.[50]

He did not know where, exactly, to try making this mark, but pre-emptively ruled out one field of labor. A few days after his exhibition performance, Garfield attended a political rally held by the Whig candidate for governor, and quickly decided the entire process of running for office was unseemly. "Perfectly disgusted with the principle," the teenager journaled that evening.[51]

3

————·————

"The means that heaven yields must be embraced
And not neglected."

—Shakespeare's *Richard III*, as quoted in Garfield

diary entry for November 24, 1878

The Compromise of 1850 moved through Congress in piecemeal, its backers working with the nervous delicacy of surgeons at an operating table. Its terms certainly read tortuously: for example, slavery would be allowed to continue in Washington, D.C., but the slave trade would not. As for the land taken from Mexico, only California would be admitted to the Union as a free state. The rest was to be organized into territories lacking "any restriction . . . on the subject of slavery." Such provisions risked attack from both parties, and so were shepherded across the floor with utmost care. Once Congress approved the last component of the new Compromise, however, scenes outside the Capitol instantly turned boisterous. Drunken shouts of "The Union is saved!" echoed in the streets. "Settled forever," murmured soberer spectators about the same old problem.[1]

Yet each party now creaked with structural damage incurred in the passage of this deal. Support of it had been determined by the sectional identities of congressmen instead of their partisan ones. Southern

Democrats seethed that they had won mostly desert to somehow cultivate into plantation land; northern Whigs, meanwhile, commenced abandoning their party in droves on account of a particularly loathsome component of the Compromise: the passage of the Fugitive Slave Law, which empowered slave catchers to work with impunity across the North. Thus, "instead of stilling controversy, the measure would bring home to the free states the most objectionable features of the 'peculiar institution.'"[2]

The horrific spectacles of Black citizens (former slaves or not) being abducted south sharpened the political sentiments of white northerners. Whigs became Free Soilers; Free Soilers converted to abolitionism; abolitionists became militant. "I am a peace man," Frederick Douglass declared to a New York audience. "But this convention ought to say to slaveholders that they are in danger of bodily harm if they come here." John Brown instructed supporters how to inflict it: "Let the first blow be the signal for all to engage; and when engaged do not do your work by halves." Representative Joshua Giddings of the Western Reserve stated he would rather have the "ashes of my own hearth slaked in my own blood and the blood of my children" than comply with the Fugitive Slave Law.[3]

Giddings brought this sanguinary attitude forth in speeches to his constituents. During one such performance in October 1850, the congressman unknowingly addressed his successor on the subject.

"He spoke quite fluently," James Garfield reflected afterward. But the young man was not ready to take Giddings's side on the issue at hand: "I could not help but consider that the cause for which he was laboring was a carnal one. Not fully settled on that."[4]

Garfield had not actually resolved his opinions on much of significance yet. He was trying, though—and in the style of converts, studying what elders in his newfound faith believed. Though the Disciples were opposed to a formal ecclesiastical hierarchy, one of their founders (an aquiline-faced Virginian named Alexander Campbell) had happily become the closest thing the movement had to a leading voice. From a school in the

Appalachians called Bethany College, Campbell oversaw the education of younger Disciples. Via a periodical named the *Millennial Harbinger*, he kept followers of all ages tethered to his guidance on spiritual matters— matters that, alas, had become tainted by politics.[5]

Charged (by himself) with keeping a unifying religion unified, Campbell was clinging to an eroding middle ground on the matter of slavery—a topic that was in the Bible, and therefore not one the Disciples could avoid discussing. Yet he lacked the temper to keep this dialogue under control. Any prominent Disciple dissenting with Campbell about slavery too vocally might open the next *Millennial Harbinger* to find themselves called out and (most acidly for an evangelical) tarred as a "very good miniature Pope."[6]

Garfield, however, seemed eager to follow the lead of his faith's most prominent member. He subscribed to the *Millennial Harbinger* and hastily assumed Campbell's opinions on current affairs: a good Christian could not take part in politics—it would be "serving two masters to participate in the affairs of a government which is point blank opposed to Christians (as all human ones must necessarily be)." Likewise was it unchristian to fight for said government; Garfield read a pacifistic Campbell speech and deemed it a "profound work." He hesitated, however, before taking Campbell's side on that most contentious of subjects. Only after reviewing essays on slavery's place in the Bible did Garfield concede that the "simple relation of master and slave is NOT UNCHRISTIAN."[7]

If only Garfield could have met the man he would become: not merely a voter but a leading statesman; not just a soldier but a major general; not simply an abolitionist, but such a fervent one that it spurred him into politics and war in the first place. One can imagine the mutual embarrassment.

Garfield left Geauga because of tension between Disciple students and the Free Will Baptists running the school, and spent the next couple seasons working. He again got a job running a district classroom, only to find that such work hardly paid a living wage. He supplemented his income by threshing oats, "hauling saw-logs" after class, and quarrying lime. Ongoing lyceum debates gave Garfield mental workouts to balance these physical ones ("Resolved, that the plow has been, and is of more utility to man, than the printing press and pen combined").[8]

Discouraged by low enrollment, Garfield soon quit his teaching job entirely and used his subsequent free time to savor disappearing parts of the Reserve. He climbed a hill one afternoon and, at its summit, beheld a rolling sky studded by clouds floating "in the depths of the blue cerulean." Descending back to civilization, Garfield boarded a canal boat bound for Cleveland, then realized en route that he was traveling a section of the waterway his father had built. He took the wheel for a while.[9]

It was not long before his eyes shifted to the future again. On August 23, Garfield left Orange with cousins, traveling east through orchards heavy with ripening fruit. After a few hours of travel the group saw their destination on the horizon—a glinting metal dome. It marked where the Disciples of the Western Reserve had been flocking throughout the last year: the town of Hiram, and the school they had built in its center.[10]

Tension with other congregations was not the only reason the Reserve's Disciples had created their own school. "It was a time, too, of general educational awakening," a local wrote wistfully. "There was a rustling in the air, a going among the mulberry trees . . . calling people away from clearing the woods."[11]

Nor were local Disciples interested in their denomination's prevailing place of higher education anymore. To be sure, some yet craved "to sit at the feet of our beloved and mighty Brother A. Campbell of Bethany College, Va." But that campus no longer seemed hospitable for Western Reservists; southern students outnumbered northerners there, and so while Bethany technically banned all arguments about slavery, in practice only "criticism of the barbarous institution" was forbidden. Campbell had also begun advising adherence to the Fugitive Slave Law. "He was not sufficiently anti-slavery to suit the constituents of Joshua Giddings," an observer in the Reserve wrote.[12]

They broke ground on their own institution in 1850. Hiram was the perfect setting; the township lay close to Cleveland but remained insulated from the urban hustle-and-bustle. "No stagecoach wheels rolled within five miles of the place," one of the arriving Disciples wrote.[13]

The school would not subtract in any way from Hiram's rusticity: it consisted of a three-floor brick building, perfectly colored to blend in with the autumn reds and browns of adjacent oak and maple groves. Its name (the "Western Reserve Eclectic Institute") took inspiration from the setting as well as its intended educational philosophy. "A thing is called "eclectic" that claims the right of freely choosing from all sources," a historian would clarify. Locals would simply call the new school the "Eclectic."[14]

Students arrived in September 1850—at first on foot, and then, in winter, on sleighs that hissed over thick snowbanks. Some later admitted feeling disappointed by their first glance of the Eclectic itself. Its lustrous dome, visible from miles off, was on closer inspection mounted atop an unimpressive building ringed by grass stubble. Yet the first cohort of pupils was a cohesive group (almost all "sons and daughters of farmers and mechanics") and few could complain about cost; a full Eclectic term's room, board, washing, and tuition came out to only twenty-two dollars.[15]

The boy destined to be the Eclectic's most famous graduate enrolled a year after it opened. Garfield's arrival on campus somehow became an incident to remember among those of his peers who witnessed it. The image of a six-foot-tall, broad-chested, not-quite-twenty-year-old walking into Hiram imprinted in their minds with lasting crispness. Many would long remember the young Garfield's honey-colored hair, beneath which kindly blue eyes glinted with good humor.[16]

They were looking back with gratification. Garfield would one day talk with evident pleasure and empathy about the students he encountered at Hiram: "untutored farm-boys and farmer-girls, [who] came here to try themselves, and find out what manner of people they were." But another classmate recognized greater equivalence between Garfield and the school itself. "Both were in the formative period; both were full of strength and enthusiasm; but both needed growth and ripeness."[17]

One difference did hold between Garfield and most other Eclectic pupils that semester; though tuition was low, he still could not afford it. He accepted a position on the school's janitorial staff to earn his keep—sweeping floors, making fires, and ringing bells to signal class time. "My first distinct recollection of him [Garfield] is as he stood in the hall grasping the bell rope," a classmate reminisced. Other alumni would remember (with distinct displeasure) that Garfield rang his bell at five o'clock every morning.[18]

As it was with that bell, so it proved with all Garfield's work at Hiram. One of his first memories of the Eclectic would be overhearing pupils reciting geometry. Their expertise left the newcomer "regarding both teacher and class, with a feeling of reverential awe," and determined to catch up. Garfield vowed to "nerve myself up to the task of studying again," and proceeded to get up a great amount of nerve in short order; the next day, he enrolled in a Greek class that was, by his estimate, at least a term ahead of him.[19]

Instructors tried to deter the young man from taking on too much work, too quickly. "He had studied a little of Latin grammar, but had done nothing in the way of translating. I had no class to suit him in," Garfield's new classics teacher later recounted. At being told this, however, Garfield had immediately insisted he would not only join but "overtake the advanced class," so long as the instructor agreed to hear his recitations after-hours.[20]

Garfield persevered solo when such oversight was unavailable. "I have today commenced the study of geometry alone," he journaled in October. "In about two hours I got the definitions and 8 propositions and the scholiums and corollaries appended."[21]

He had learned to enjoy arduous study during the previous two years, but a new scholastic thrill galvanized him at Hiram—that of competition.

Classmates noticed. "He had a great desire and settled purpose to conquer, to master the lesson, to prove superior to every difficulty, to excel all competitors," wrote H. W. Everest. Corydon Fuller guessed Garfield simply did not sleep; his light always stayed on far into the night, and the class bell always pealed out before dawn.[22]

Even more noteworthy, though, was how amiable Garfield remained outside the classroom with those he tried to surpass inside it. "With this desire to conquer," Everest elaborated, "there was found the most generous and exultant admiration at the success of another." This endearing edge to Garfield's drive endured even in adverse situations. "Very warm," he scribbled near midnight after losing a debate held in the local lyceum hall.[23]

The topics the Eclectic's student societies discussed were as foreboding as those Garfield had fielded at Chester. One asked them to debate "that we would hail with joy the day when . . . the American Union should encircle the whole American continent." ("Warm time," Garfield journaled after.) Another October evening's resolution proposed that the "signs of the times portend the speedy dissolution of the American union." "I spoke on the Negative," Garfield recorded. "Warm time."[24]

Another debate held a few weeks later ended discordantly. "We had a miserable lyceum this evening and a poor question," Garfield said afterward, without elaborating on what went wrong. He nevertheless admitted feeling responsible for the session going awry. "I shall hereafter be more careful to regard the feelings of others," he resolved.[25]

He evidently succeeded. By term's end, Garfield was not only the Eclectic's top-ranked student, but also (per a classmate) a "universal favorite" among students. His valedictory speech consolidated both places of influence:

> Fellow Students—The time has at length arrived when our connection with this institution and with each other, as seekers of knowledge, is about to terminate, at least for a season . . . Side by side we toiled up

the steep ascent upon whose beetling summit stands the fair temple of knowledge. All hearts beat in unison; mind communed with mind, affections were blended and strengthened.[26]

Again, his winter was spent teaching less esteemed company in a district school. Garfield diagnosed in his latest group of students "some cases of—perhaps I may name it—intellectual dyspepsia. I am as yet baffled to find a cure for it." His annoyance grew as the off-season rolled on and none his remedies worked. He was left agonized for a classroom with "every scholar eager to learn."[27]

Garfield fished for commiseration in letters to new friends. Corydon Fuller received an especially revelatory screed. "Oh!" Garfield wrote. "That I possessed the power to scatter the firebrands of ambition among the youth . . . and let them see the greatness of the age in which they live, and the destiny to which mankind are rushing." Failing that, Garfield confessed to Fuller, "I intend to keep it predominant in my own breast, and let it spur me forward into action."[28]

Ahead, for now, was only a return to the Eclectic, "with all its associations . . . a beacon light to cheer me on." But, looking up one night, Garfield let his thoughts spiral off into the starscape, thinking literally in light years:

> Corydon, I had another reflection . . . It is a philosophical fact that light occupies eight minutes in passing from the earth to the sun . . . May there not be a spot far off in the immensity of space where it will take months, yea, years for the light to travel? . . . thus the steeds of imagination carry me.[29]

Those "steeds of imagination" pulled vigorously at the young man during the next two years. "Studying very hard," he wrote that spring. "Good times." Most students would have pled otherwise were they in his shoes: on a typical school day, Garfield might recite Greek, Latin, a hundred and twenty further lines of Sallust's *Jugurthine War*, thirty from Virgil, and another few pages of Greek before joining a mathematics class. Hard labor served as the breaks in this punishing schedule. Garfield kept a janitorial job at the Eclectic and spent the summer doing carpentry.[30]

He was just as diligent about staying in the good graces of classmates. Garfield and Fuller founded a new society called the Philomathean, and, with its topics staying pertinent to current events ("Resolved, that the discovery of the gold mines of California are, and will be, a benefit to the United States"), Garfield continued pouring oil over troubled waters between participants. Blunders on this front were recorded, learned from, adapted to:

> Today I have learned a practical lesson, which I hope to profit by in years to come. . . . A word may make an enemy which volumes cannot win back. . . . Hence, if our actions or words are injurious or offensive to anyone we should discontinue them.

Younger speakers accordingly thought Garfield "very wise," relishing even a single conversation with him.[31]

His closer confidantes at Hiram heard many more. Garfield grew especially intimate with Corydon Fuller, bonding over similar academic interests and a shared need to work part-time jobs to afford school. Relatedly, they each found satisfaction in outperforming wealthier classmates ("whose bills were paid without any exertion on their own part").[32]

Almeda Booth also became a comrade. A stern and stern-faced instructor at the Eclectic, "Miss Booth" was regarded as the best teacher in the school and possibly the smartest person in the Reserve. Garfield considered her a fine intellectual foil and a maturing force. "I have looked up to her as a near and dear elder sister," he would say, "and she, perhaps, has looked upon me as an impulsive, ambitious, and warm-hearted elder brother."[33]

One more friend at the Eclectic, Charles Wilber, was exposed to

Garfield's rising ambitions but tried tamping the flames down. "Well James, either your Cauldron is not large enough else your fire is too hot . . . there is certainly something the matter with you." But Wilber's advice came too late; by that fall, the Eclectic's teachers invited Garfield to join the faculty, part-time. His janitor's broom went away for good. The next term's catalogue listed him as both a student and instructor.[34]

While climbing the ranks at the Eclectic, Garfield had periodically returned to Orange to feel a gulf widening between him and his family. "My folks live in a world differing from the one which I inhabit," he wrote sadly in the summer of 1853. Their drift apart had become irreversible by then; Garfield's siblings were older and rooted to their lives as farmers. He stayed preoccupied with schoolwork around them, despite realizing this made him appear "cold or absent-minded." In fact, though Garfield's family noticed his mind was often elsewhere, they did not mind it much. Thomas was amused to hear his younger brother sleep-talk in math problems.[35]

Their figurative distance became matched by a literal one that October. Thomas wanted to relocate to Michigan in search of better farmland, while Eliza had decided to move in with daughter Mary at the nearby village of Solon. The family reunited at their old cabinsite for one final meal before selling the property. Garfield considered the event a send-off not only to his brother, but also the life they had all once shared:

> We shall in all human probability never all thus again be together . . .
> Our old Home . . . is sold, and the old familiar scenes of my boyhood
> will be desecrated by the hands of strangers who know [not] the striv-
> ing of soul, the throbbings of youthful ambition, the laying of plans,
> and building of bright fabrics visionary and wild for the future that
> cluster around and consecrate the memory of the place.[36]

He was not severing all connections with his kin—only conceding, for now, that they were on distinct tracks. His now appeared to be leading out of the Reserve entirely; while Thomas was heading west to farm,

Garfield had begun looking east for enlightenment. His diary mentioned a "wandering thought . . . of making a writing tour in the southern states next fall and winter, and then . . . enter[ing] Yale College."[37]

In merely reflecting on this plan, Garfield felt an upswell of gratitude to those who had put him in a position to pursue it. "Mother," he wrote to Eliza, "I can never repay you and him [Thomas] for the kindness and love you have always bestowed upon me." He decided he would try, though; noticing Eliza's wrinkling brow, Garfield made a private promise "to render the decline of life peaceful and happy to her."[38]

Garfield would also reimburse Thomas in the future, albeit more literally—from Congress, writing out checks to an elder brother still struggling on a far-off farm. "Our paths were always more and more diverging," Representative Garfield would say of his siblings.[39]

Restlessness forced Garfield to take a holiday in November, 1853. "Finding a necessity of stirring around," he boarded a night train to Buffalo, then took another car in the morning for the Canadian border. Lake Erie became a flat, perfect glass plane on his left. Pine flavored the air, mist lending its scent a soft, wet texture.

Soon Garfield was beside Niagara Falls, beholding a "liquid world begirt with rainbows, tumbling from the skies . . . as though the heavens themselves were molten seas and falling to the earth." He jotted these observations down and dispatched them to Hiram—to a student, Lucretia Rudolph. "I know not why I have written," Garfield's note ended, "only just I felt like it and did so."[40]

She had flitted closer and closer to him during the previous few years, like an approaching comet. Lucretia had been just another classmate of Garfield's at the seminary; upon transferring, like him, to the Eclectic (where her father was a trustee) she began serving as a background character in his diary.[41]

They had an extended encounter at a Geauga reunion in May 1852.

"We recounted the scenes of the past," Garfield wrote afterward. By spring 1853, both were studying a more distant past together—Garfield the classics teacher, Lucretia one of his pupils. A class photo has the pair side by side, staring inexpressively into the camera.[42]

Yet their courtship was marred from the start by awkwardness. Playfulness dotted Garfield's and Lucretia's notes, but each approached the other cautiously in person. This was natural for Lucretia, who always exuded coolness to the world. Doe-like yet inscrutable behind a pair of dark eyes, she struck people as somehow both naive and wary. "Undemonstrable in the extreme . . . Gentle, patient, unobtrusive almost to timidity," was one friend's first impression of Lucretia. "I remember thinking her a little diffident," another would reminisce. Those who pierced Lucretia's veneer, however, found the woman within "intellectual, educated, sober, dignified . . . in reality what she pretends to be."[43]

Garfield, on the other hand, was in flux—friendly but restless, well-intentioned but still finding his bearings in life. His fundamental uncertainty extended not just to his own future, but to whether Lucretia would be a valuable addition to it. "She has a well-balanced mind," Garfield observed in one diary entry, nevertheless lamenting he could not detect "that warmth of feeling . . . which I need to make me happy." Their in-person meetings did little to dispel their mutual uncertainty. Lucretia described a kiss from Garfield as "coldly received and not returned."[44]

They continued to correspond, though, chasing teasing embers of warmth in each other. Intellectually they were perfectly matched. One topic was of especial interest—at least to Garfield. He asked Lucretia if her mind "ever inclines to chase the tossing bubbles of ambition." "I wish it did more than it does," she replied.[45]

They continued discussing this subject into the New Year. Garfield divulged powerful opinions on it:

We all shrink with horror from the effects of ambition, and some almost conclude that the thing itself is wrong—but it seems to me that it is necessary to success in every department of life. It is to the man what the fire is to the steam engine . . . It *urges* one to *action*. So, let it burn. Restrain it only by the laws of God.[46]

His engine was finally primed to haul him out of the Reserve in spring 1854. The college question had been settled; Garfield had written a trio of New England institutions for information about enrolling. Yale's reply read coldly, its dean's "aristocratic face" apparent in his handwriting. The letter from Brown also gave off an ivory tower pomposity. Only the note back from Williams College seemed to reciprocate Garfield's interest: "We shall be glad to do what we can for you." This sealed the deal. Garfield was heading for Williamstown, Massachusetts.[47]

His dismissal of another school—Bethany College—had been revealingly thorough. "I am the son of Disciple parents, have always listened to their preachings, have become one myself," Garfield had mused. This, he decided, raised the danger that attending Bethany would lead him to "look at the world and all its belongings from one standpoint."[48]

His other qualm with Campbell's school revealed that he had finally begun to hold a firm stance on something. "It [Bethany] is too pro-slavery in its views," Garfield wrote.[49]

He packed his bags for Massachusetts on June 23. "It matters not to the society in which I am now to move, if I was an orphan boy, and battled the world alone," Garfield wrote himself during a break.[50]

His actions during the following week, however, betrayed an awareness that his boyhood had not been a lonely struggle at all. Tearful farewells were given to Eliza and Almeda Booth, then Garfield decided to see the Orange cabin for one last time. A two-hour visit with Lucretia added an indecisive entry to these farewells; the couple agreed they loved each other, but also "determined to let our judgement rule on the matter . . . to correspond and write freely our thoughts."[51]

Then Garfield boarded a creaking stagecoach for Cleveland. That night he was on a steamboat puffing across Lake Erie. Lightning danced overhead.[52]

His surroundings and mood brightened in tandem as he got farther east. The Hudson was a blue carpet unfurling beneath Garfield; a setting sun ("large and golden") trimmed its riverbanks with warm reds.[53]

Downriver, Garfield met with Fuller and together the two Ohioans explored a bustling Manhattan. Passing one street market, they noticed a strange, curved bolt of color hanging in one fruit stall. Garfield asked the shopkeeper what it was. Fuller was on hand to record the answer:

> The man at first seemed to suspect the question to be a joke, but finally answered that they were bananas.

Moving on, Garfield made a remark his friend would long remember:

> He [the shopkeeper] thinks we are exceedingly green, not to know what every street urchin here knows; but . . . I have long since determined not to let an opportunity pass for learning something, simply because I must expose my ignorance in so doing.[54]

4

"There's in him stuff that puts him to these ends."

—Shakespeare's *Henry VIII*, as quoted in Garfield
diary entry for December 7, 1878

Garfield found more novelties to behold in Williamstown, starting with the setting; the high, forested Berkshire hills reminded him of bearded wise men. New England's buildings looked equally venerable. "To one who has seen cities rise from the wild forest in the space of a dozen years . . . many reflections are awakened by the look of antiquity that everything has around me," the transplanted Midwesterner wrote. Another sight was more frightening than fascinating: Garfield's classmates would now be privileged scions of the Eastern elite. He fretted about being left in their dust.[1]

Garfield dug into old habits to avoid such a fate. Pleasantly introducing himself to the other scholars, he discreetly tried to "calculate their dimensions." This analysis led him to conclude that of his forty-two new peers, thirty-seven "shall stand behind me within two months." Similar reconnaissance of Williams's student debates convinced Garfield he could beat the competition there, too. "The olden fires that have had no need to blaze much . . . begin to flame up again," the young man journaled. He elaborated on this feeling to Fuller:

Oh Corydon, those fires that we so often have felt. . . . I lie here alone on my bed at midnight tossing restlessly. . . . I feel that there are but two tracks before me—to stand among the first, or die.[2]

He still endeavored to befriend those he wanted to surpass. Other undergraduates at Williams did not initially know what to think of Garfield; he had joined their ranks as a junior—an old junior, at that—and radiated a western crudeness. "The garb of a country tailor lent no grace to his angular, bony, and muscular frame," one urbane classmate sniffed. Another recalled Garfield simply "looking like a backwoods-man." This visual was reinforced by the tawny beard Garfield had begun cultivating.[3]

Yet his blue eyes still struck those around him as "mirthful." When given the chance, Garfield played along with their stereotyping—caricaturing himself as an Ohio country boy lost in a crowd of Eastern sophisticates. "Look-a here . . . I ain't none o'your orators. These literary folks talk as if they had done everything and made everything," Garfield said in a discourse titled "Speech of the Backwoodsman." Even the imperious president of Williams College, Mark Hopkins, could crack up at these performances. "He [Hopkins] would sit there doubled up in his armchair with his long thin legs twisted into a knot [when Garfield debated], and would almost go into convulsions of laughter," remembered one observer.[4]

This good humor served a purpose, however. Garfield's passing bits of self-deprecation hooked listeners in on time to hear bursts of potent oratory. "His massive figure, commanding, self-confident manner, and magnificent bursts of fiery eloquence won and held the attention of his audience," recalled a peer. In hindsight, several of Garfield's classmates would describe him as their class's greatest debater.[5]

More exceptionally, he did not refuse any of their company. "He never held himself aloof from the society of intelligent and vivacious sinners, while enjoying the fellowship and communion of the saints," wrote a friend. "No one thought of him as a recluse," President Hopkins would one day agree. "Not *given* to athletic sports, he was fond of them." Garfield explained in another discourse that he simply found too much to learn from mixed company:

> The cloistered monk . . . may become a prodigy in critical erudition, but it needs the contact of mind with mind to develop the orator, to bring out those powers which enable the thinker to sway the masses by the power of his own thought.[6]

Further contact of this sort ended in spring 1855, once Garfield was elected the Philogian Society's president (disqualifying him from participating in debates). He was also chosen by his peers to become an editor of the *Williams Quarterly*. It was the perfect start to what would be a perfect electoral career. Garfield would never lose an election of any sort.[7]

He did not let these first victories go to his head, however. Underclassmen hoping to get published found Garfield more hospitable to their pitches than other, snootier *Quarterly* editors.[8]

It was beginning to pay closer attention to national politics. Tensions in that realm had been escalated by yet another broken pact over slavery between America's parties; Democrats used their congressional majorities in 1854 to pass the Kansas–Nebraska Act, finishing off the Missouri Compromise. No longer would a line of latitude determine whether new American lands would be slave or free. Instead, a territory's citizens would settle the matter for themselves—in what the act's sponsor, a northern Democrat named Stephen Douglas, dubbed "popular sovereignty." The senator's introduction of this legislation reflected the refusal of his southern Democrat peers to let the Union maintain the status quo. One of them had said it would be better to have Nebraska in hell than in the Republic as a free state, as the Missouri Compromise would have mandated.[9]

Outrage flared across the North with an intensity sufficient to kill a major party; split on whether to support the Kansas–Nebraska Act,

Whigs simply couldn't stand one another anymore. Northern senators of the party resigned in protest of the legislation, while southern colleagues accused them of "wild fanaticism" for doing so. Douglas also adopted a dismissive tone—joking about being able to navigate back to Illinois "by the light of my own effigy."[10]

Douglas's legislation sent other Americans to Kansas, to settle that territory's "popular sovereignty" by force. Slaverymen got there first—stuffing ballots, passing laws that made criticism of the institution punishable by death, and even patrolling Kansas's borders to turn back any immigrating abolitionists.

Some still managed to sneak through. John Brown did so by convincing the border ruffians that he and his sons were just surveyors. The guns in their baggage escaped notice.[11]

Garfield watched Kansas bleed from Williamstown. One night in November 1855, he attended a speech by a visiting abolitionist editor whose presses had been cast into the Missouri River, "his life threatened for speaking and writing his sentiments in reference to Slavery and the Election outrages in that Territory." Garfield left the lecture invigorated, his opinion on the topic suddenly honed to a knife-point:

> I feel as though a great, united effort should be made, and that effort should have but one aim and that should be the suppression of Slavery in every newly acquired territory. . . . I feel like throwing the whole current of my life into the work of opposing this giant evil.[12]

He began using his places of authority at Williams to comment on current affairs. Garfield published a poem skewering Democrats in the *Quarterly*. In another speech to fellow students, he even appeared to sketch the vaguest blueprint of a political philosophy:

> There are two classes of men, whose spheres of thought, feeling in action, are in perfect contrast with each other—the *Utilitarian* and

the *Idealist* . . . But in this, as in all of man's extremes, wisdom chooses the golden mean—the harmonious blending of these two characters.[13]

It was a bold position to stake out—and an impossibly precarious one to hold for long. Inevitably a statesman is buffeted to a point of personal equilibrium between the poles. Garfield's would be settled over a lifetime, in a protracted contest between his pleasant, optimistic nature and the discordant events whirling about it.

He wandered New England between semesters. On one adventure, Garfield discovered "hundreds of stranger Garfields" in southern Massachusetts. But he could see why his own branch of the family had moved on. Daniel Garfield's stony acres near the Connecticut border made for a depressing sight.[14]

Garfield also used these trips to hone the key Disciple skill of preaching—something any member of the denomination had the right to practice, and which he felt increasingly drawn to. "I cannot resist the appeals of our brethren for aid while I have the strength to speak to them," Garfield explained to Fuller. It did not hurt that the congregations paid well (up to five dollars per appearance).[15] It was also a fine way to get comfortable addressing larger public audiences.

The winter between 1854 and 1855 found Garfield earning money in a more familiar way—by teaching, this time at a school in Vermont. Its headmaster had recently been a local named Chester Alan Arthur.[16]

In fall 1855, Garfield managed to return to Hiram—his heart brimming with the "bright hope" at seeing Lucretia again. Their correspondence during his year at Williams had drawn the pair closer. Nicknames had even been swapped. She had begun to go by "Crete" in his letters, and Garfield was now her "Dearest."[17]

Unfortunately, this hard-won affection evaporated on contact. Garfield no sooner reunited with Crete than felt the "most dark and gloomy cloud" envelop him—its source, the emotional awkwardness still marring their interactions. The woman Garfield had gotten to know in writing was witty, kind, overflowing with fondness; the one he met back in Ohio seemed devoid of warmth, with not "one ray of light struggling through the gloom." "It seems as though all my former fears were well founded," he wrote despairingly. "She and I are not like each other in enough respects to make us happy together." The void between them suddenly appeared insurmountable—all the more so because the lovers thought they had bridged it.[18]

Hope rekindled in the waning minutes of Garfield's trip. He visited Crete a final time before heading back to Williams, during which she let him read her diary. Its pages glowed with the passion Garfield had been anxiously searching for. "From that journal I read depths of affection that I had never before known that she possessed," he wrote afterward. A resurgent confidence in their love practically propelled him back east. Crete felt the same revival of passion, and the day after Garfield left she wrote a letter crediting the visit (and another power) for their breakthrough: "Dearest James, I can see only the guiding of a Providential hand in all your visit to Ohio. . . . Did my heart ever know such happiness before? Such a pure deep joy? Never, *never*."[19]

In the next spring, Garfield declared to Crete he was "already in spirit, your husband, and you my darling wife," which implied that the distance between them had closed for good.[20]

"How would you like, dearest, to become, not exactly a Trojan Helen, but a Trojan Lucretia?" So teased another letter Garfield sent Crete during his last few months at Williams, as he weighed next steps. It made a pun of an offer he had received to teach in Troy, New York. Even better bids were coming in from other institutions.[21]

Yet one was calling out for him with special force. "Brother Hayden thinks you are *morally* bound to come back here," Almeda Booth had written Garfield from Hiram.[22]

The truth was that the Eclectic had meandered its way into a succession crisis. Amos Sutton Hayden was its inaugural president and, since

Garfield left for Williams, had managed to extend an initial five-year term into an indefinite one. Sadly, Hayden had proven to be a better preacher than administrator; worse, he did not distinguish much between the roles. By 1856, his managerial style was grating on pupils, teachers, and trustees alike. "In many respects Mr. Hayden's administration had been eminently successful," an Eclectic graduate later wrote. "But it soon became apparent that his growth in the qualities of leadership was not increasing with the growth and widening influence and patronage of the school."

Dissenters cast out feelers for replacements in early 1856. Several landed on the same name. "I think the moral obligation resting upon him [Hayden] is quite as strong to give up the management [of the Eclectic] to you," Booth's letter to Garfield continued conspiratorially.[23]

It was an easy case to make. The Eclectic needed a vigorous leader well-suited to the task of expanding the fledgling institution. The young, popular ex-janitor, student, and teacher who had left for a prestigious New England college seemed ideally fit for the role.

Garfield nonetheless played coy with the idea. He received letters intimating the Eclectic's presidency would soon be his should he return to the school to teach (a formal job offer from the trustees topping off this correspondence), but he replied to the outreach tepidly, teasingly. "I have said and still say (in all love to Bro. H[ayden]) if he is to remain the principal permanently I will not go there," Garfield wrote one informant. But genuine reluctance also bubbled in his thoughts. Returning to the Eclectic would, after all, be going back to a place he had outgrown, while partaking in a succession plot rubbed Garfield's conscience the wrong way.[24]

At the same time, ambition still burned within the young man, and he must have realized a path to influence would be far easier to forge at the Eclectic than the other schools available. He also truly loved the place and its people—particularly a pair of women there: Crete and Eliza. Thinking about his mother still yanked on Garfield's heartstrings:

In reviewing the varied scenes of my short yet eventful life, in examin-
ing the tangled web of circumstance . . . I can see one golden thread
running through the whole—my Mother's influence upon me.[25]

Garfield ultimately decided to accept the Eclectic's offer condition-
ally: "I would go there for *one year*—but for the present . . . not engage for
a longer time than that." He was just as evasive to friends about the larger
role allegedly in play. "I do not know the origin of the rumor concerning
the presidency of the Eclectic," he wrote Corydon Fuller.

I presume there is nothing in it . . . though perhaps I might echo the
sentiment of Sam Houston. "If the Presidency is thrust upon me, I
shall do as I please about it."[26]

It was a view he'd assume about a different presidency, a few decades
later, to much the same result.

Garfield was influential at the Eclectic before he even set foot back on
campus; his reputation among its scholars and other teachers had already
been sterling prior to his departure for Williams. "He handled large
classes . . . with conspicuous power," one recalled. "He took captive the
members of his classes . . . His pupils and fellow-students had a great deal
to say about him, as well as much to write in their letters."[27]

On returning to Hiram, he picked up where he left off—taking on
as much work as possible throughout all parts of the community. "I am
delivering a course of fifteen lectures a day on Grammar in the evenings
and teaching my six classes a day," Garfield told Eliza. He preached on
Sundays to fill out the weekends. "I don't *intend* to do as much next term,
but I have a very poor faculty of getting rid of work, and I presume I shall
do all that is piled on," he pled that November to Corydon Fuller. Again,
Garfield made sure to enjoy the company of those around him, and this
time found a receptive audience in his students; pupils treated him not

only as an esteemed instructor but a confidante. Garfield was the rare teacher comfortable throwing a reassuring arm around tearful, homesick boys. "Some were poor; . . . some wanted courage and self-reliance; some tended to despondency," one later wrote. "Mr. Garfield found them out."[28]

A pair of Garfield's former students had since become teachers themselves: James "Harry" Rhodes and Burke Hinsdale. He tucked them tighter underwing after returning from Williams.[29]

Hinsdale formed what can only be described as an especially ambitious bond with his former instructor. During one period wherein he was "struggling with the hard questions of life," Hinsdale received a letter of advice from Garfield that he would treasure for many years:

> God has endowed some of his children with desires and capabilities for a more extended field of labor and influence . . . Tell me: do you not feel a spirit stirring within you that longs *to know, to do and to dare* . . . They are the voices of that nature which God has given you, and which, when obeyed, will bless you and your fellow men.

Hinsdale could not help but notice that Garfield's last word ran over an image of the U.S. Capitol stamped on the stationery. [30]

Hayden resigned from the Eclectic in June 1857 with predictable piety. "Other important duties in the Kingdom of God press upon me," the principal announced. A council of teachers was appointed to fill his duties in the interim: H. W. Everest, James Rhodes, and Almeda Booth each took a spot on it. They elected a fourth member, James Garfield, as chairman.[31]

"There appears to have been some hesitancy in making him principal in name," remembered Hinsdale. There was: accusations of a Garfield-for-President conspiracy simmered in corners of the Eclectic. He protested his innocence. "I had never by word or action manifested the least desire to gain the Presidency of the Eclectic," Garfield informed Fuller. "However, the Trustees were urging me to take charge of the school."[32]

This Garfield essentially did, despite the technical authority of the board. "He was principal in fact," Hinsdale wrote. Local press coverage echoed this view of the arrangement when it was announced:

> The Teachers of the Hiram Eclectic Institute elected Prof. Jas A. Garfield, Chairman, (or nominal head of the school).[33]

The following summer, once Garfield officially became the Eclectic's head, it was reported as if the prior arrangement never existed:

> Professor Garfield occupied the position of principal for the last year . . . and has proved himself well fitted for the post.[34]

As a result, the date the first Garfield administration began would long remain a matter of opinion in Hiram.

5

⸺ ◦ ⸺

"He that commends me to mine own content
Commends me to a thing I cannot get"

—Shakespeare's The Comedy of Errors, as quoted in
Garfield diary entry for January 29, 1878

Life at the Eclectic liberalized with its change in regime. A visitor roaming campus in summer, 1858, would have heard piano music carrying faintly on the warm breeze, and passed students playing games on bright, leafy lawns. The tall, bearded figure of the school's principal (hardly older than the students) moved freely about the fun. He could be seen smacking a wicket-ball for six, then joining a side in rugby. Garfield was also an enthusiastic contributor to the chess craze sweeping Hiram—defying grumblers in the community who called the game unchristian. "I am not of the number of morbid moralists who shudder at any amusements," Garfield wrote frankly in his diary. The half-keg of beer in his basement testified to this well enough.[1]

Such scenes defined Garfield's leadership of his alma mater. He was intent on infusing youthful vigor into a place that had been terribly stifled by what one resident called the "odium theologicum." Historians of the Eclectic recorded an almost barometric shift in school culture ("The ecclesiastical way of looking at things somewhat receded with the retirement of Principal Hayden"), while the Eclectic's roster started to mark the enrollment of more pupils from other denominations. "Brother Hayden's efforts were mainly directed toward gathering Disciples here—[but] it seems to me that Disciples will come here anyway," Garfield explained to a friend. "Our special efforts should be directed toward the community in general."[2]

Even as enrollment climbed into the several hundred, Garfield managed to bestow individual pupils with depths of attention they would cherish for years to come. He etched "carpe diem" into their textbooks and slipped handwritten good-byes into the hatbands of departing pupils. One day, a boy named Charles Henry approached Garfield for advice on an oration for commencement. After delivering the address as instructed, Henry felt himself being lifted off the ground behind stage. His source of propulsion turned out to be an ebullient principal Garfield, who was saying: "Old boy, you did well . . . I am proud of you." As Henry wrote in old age:

> Looking back over a bridge of years, through storms and toil and smoke of battle, that was one of the happiest moments of my life. His praise was dearer to me than all; his approbation was worth years of toil to secure.[3]

As it was with Henry, so it proved with generations of those enrolled at the Eclectic. Away from farm and family, indulging in education, they found principal Garfield young enough to relate to, accomplished enough to admire, personable enough to befriend. "He came in contact with from one hundred and seventy-five to three hundred students a term," a former student calculated. "Mr. Garfield was the standard by which they measured men."[4]

Garfield did not neglect his burgeoning obligations as a preacher, either. Outside of classes, he tended to Disciple congregations across the

Reserve. He baptized people, married them, and on occasion gave their eulogies. "In short he did, on occasion, everything that is required of a minister of the Gospel," a friend remembered.[5]

He also went above the usual pastoral call of duty. When an especially pompous agnostic came to town, Garfield took up the man's challenge to publicly debate whether life was created by the "laws of spontaneous generation." Hundreds attended, ultimately declaring the local principal the winner. [6]

Garfield hardly had time to savor such victories. "I have been busier this winter than in any period of my life," he wrote near the end of his first year running the Eclectic. Neighbors marveled at his industriousness: "He 'threw' off, without fatigue or fretting, work enough to wear down and out half a dozen ordinarily strong men."[7]

Yet some anxiety did stick to Garfield. The cause was not his workload per se, but some negative gossip now circulating in Hiram, like bubbles in a stirred drink, at his rapid rise to the top of the school and local community. Conservative Disciples resented his secular approach to running the Eclectic; dissidents within it (the sourest of whom, Norman Dunshee, had been on the board that first took over from Hayden) spoke of Garfield's campus popularity as a carefully arranged personality cult.[8]

It was impossible to tune out. Walking around the Eclectic, Garfield imagined he could practically overhear Dunshee "write over every act of mine 'For Ambition's purposes.'" The disgruntled teacher soon started causing even more trouble on campus, once Garfield made the controversial decision to block abolitionists from holding a rally there.[9]

He had wanted to keep politics (particularly that of any "overheated and brainless faction") out of the school, but this had become practically impossible under current conditions; since destroying the Whig Party in spectacular fashion, the topic of slavery had only further pervaded America's electoral and social landscape. Free Soilers had united with northern Whigs to form a new party—the Republican Party—whose first pick for the presidency, John Frémont, let them campaign on the delightfully alliterative motto "free soil, free speech, free men, and Fremont." But alas, James Buchanan won the White House instead. Republican despair only deepened when the Supreme Court then decreed that an enslaved man named Dred Scott could not be considered emancipated just because his master had taken him to a free state. The language the court used in this decision essentially ensured Black men in America "possessed no rights which a white man was bound to respect."[10]

Such developments further polarized not just the country's politics, but parts of society heretofore insulated from the slavery debate. Several Christian denominations had already split along sectional lines, and Disciples on the Western Reserve were now agitating to do the same. They passed resolutions announcing that "every Christian should use his influence" to rid the United States of slavery and that those who disagreed had no right to identify as Christian. In refusing to let the Eclectic be dragged into such a debate, Garfield caught heat from both sides. "I stand between two fires," he wrote a friend. "One party of my friends blame me as being too cool on the slavery question; another for being too hot."[11]

Garfield's effort to preserve his school's neutrality belied a hardening personal opinion. Upon first being roused against slavery at Williams, he had concluded the practice could only be curbed "gradually—and when that will be done, God only knows. In the mean time, men ought not to go wild on the subject." With the entire country having since done so, Garfield's own restraint ebbed as well. As he wrote Corydon Fuller:

Who can read the doings of the present Administration and Congress—and not feel his whole soul aroused at the enormities and cursedness of slavery?[12]

An uptick in runaway slaves from the South reaching Hiram only heightened Garfield's animosity for the monstrous institution they had escaped. Meeting one intelligent young girl, he "could not [help] but feel the enormity of a system which should enslave such as she." Another fugitive slave came through town a few months later. Garfield gave this one money, plus the advice "to trust to God and his muscle."[13]

That Garfield had cash to donate reflected a welcome change in his fortunes. "A few weeks ago I cleared up the last of my college debts and am now, for the first time in several years, free pecuniarily," he wrote Fuller in early 1858. He had ideas on how best to use this freedom. "Teaching is not the work in which a man can live and grow. . . . I think there are some other fields in which one can do more." Lawbooks began to dot Garfield's reading lists.[14]

A little more than a year later, though, he had set his sights on another profession. Garfield entrusted this plan to Harry Rhodes, who had enrolled at Williams:

> If I do not take the law the next best course seems to me to [be] an educational and political one—the latter (polit.) to be reached through the former (Educ.). Should this be the chosen plan I know of no place, where—everything counted—we could do better than here.[15]

Garfield's control of the Eclectic had already cleared a usable path to politics. It ran through one of the school's trustees—Harmon Austin, a man whose influence spanned the Reserve. Austin was a farmer and served as the Trumbull Agricultural Society's president; he was also a loyal Republican and chaired the party's local District Committee. He was an ardent Disciple of Christ (as his trusteeship of the Eclectic indicated) and his favorite preacher was none other than the school's principal. "Your sermons [have] done me more good than anything I have heard in many weeks," Austin had written Garfield in October.[16]

He expressed predictable disappointment when Garfield disclosed an interest in leaving the pulpit for politics. "I cannot but feel that it is a *burning shame* for one possessing such *rare abilities* . . . that you should for one moment indulge the idea of leaving a field of labor for which you are so admirably fitted," Austin wrote in reply.[17]

Precisely how Garfield changed Austin's mind is not clear. But an interesting incident passed between the two; Austin's niece got a job at a school in Portage County, only to find she lacked the proper accreditation to teach there. Austin asked if Garfield might award her such a certificate without the requisite examination. ("*I would take it as a very special favor to me if you could bring that about.*") Garfield responded the next day with a filled-in, backdated license.[18]

Austin's tone regarding Garfield's ambitions soon changed markedly. In May, he wrote Garfield about having "many things to say . . . that I cannot commit to paper."[19]

Amid all this, Garfield got married—almost as an afterthought, and a resigned one at that. A familiar emotional distance had opened again between him and Crete; her efforts to call attention to it sputtered over the embarrassing length of their engagement (four years). "Those boys and girls at Hiram have no right to claim all your attention, and I shall complain if you allow them to do so," read one such attempt. "My Dear Jimmie . . . I can't quite grow reconciled to your running off," opened another of Crete's letters. "Will you not write me as frank a letter as this?"[20]

He complied. "I do love to be with you," Garfield confessed, "but there is a restless and unsatisfied feeling about a good deal of the time." His private musings echoed the same indecision:

> Marriage comes again with all its necessitous and hateful finalities to perplex me. I seem to myself . . . to have lost the muscle of my will.[21]

Garfield conquered these feelings by fall 1858, but this did not impress his betrothed. Barely suppressed ambivalence is hardly an encouraging trait in a fiancé; Crete felt her heart almost break "with the cruel thought that our marriage is based upon the cold stern word *duty*." She hoped this would change, though—even making a joke of Garfield's indecision by sending him an invitation to their November wedding. His journal for that night, however, documented the event in a revealingly passive tense:

> Was married to Lucretia Rudolph by Pres. H. L. Hitchcock of Western Reserve College[22]

Things at the Eclectic moved swiftly in May. Norman Dunshee was fired—his duties handed off to Harry Rhodes, due to return from Williams College. Dunshee decided this must be the doing of Garfield ("prince of slaveholders and plotters") but the board held its nerve.[23]

The accused expressed surprise at these developments. "I not only did not counsel it [the firing] but did not expect it," Garfield told Rhodes. An objective review of his correspondence would indicate otherwise.[24]

Once Dunshee was gone, Garfield sent another query to Rhodes: "Shall I run for State Senator or Representative—either or neither—this fall?"[25]

In August, circumstances aligned to force Garfield's hand. He heard that the top Republican to represent Portage and Summit counties in the state senate had passed away, and hardly had time to process this before a party delegate reported that "leading citizens" wanted principal Garfield to run in the deceased's place. After checking with other school officers (finding "it compatible with my duties to be absent the required time"), Garfield allowed his name for consideration under three preconditions:

> 1st, I should [make] no pledges to any man or any measures.
>
> 2nd, I should not work for my own nomination other than to let my [friends] know my name was up.
>
> 3rd, I ran at their instance not mine.[26]

His professed reluctance was not strong enough to keep him from the convention. Garfield attended it, but salvaged some pride by not directly

soliciting delegates for support. They nominated him in four ballots anyway. "I presume that my youth and early life have had some favorable
influence on the result," Garfield wrote after returning home.[27]

These looked likely to be helpful in the election, too. An article reporting on Garfield's political debut took hold of a peculiar quirk of his
past:

> At the age of eighteen he was in the employ of the Ohio and Penn-
> sylvania Canal.[28]

Garfield fielded more questions about slavery than canal life while campaigning. The *Anti-Slavery Bugle* treated him to a particularly blistering
interrogation on the topic. "He believes the Fugitive Slave Law of 1850
unconstitutional but holds that the master has a constitutional right to re-
claim his slaves," it noted. Similar snipes harried him along the campaign
trail; Garfield seemed determined to chart a middle course between his
party's blocs on the major issue of the hour.[29]

The results spoke for themselves. Garfield not only won his race but
outperformed the Republican ticket. "I never solicited the place nor did
I make any bargain to secure it," he reminded friends. Harmon Austin
predicted greater victories ahead. "He [Garfield] is bound to rise; he will
be in Congress before five years."[30]

Before the year was out, another Western Reservist sparked much trouble
elsewhere: John Brown led supporters in a raid on the Virginian hamlet
of Harper's Ferry—his plan, to loot its arsenal then lead a slave rebellion
into the Alleghenies. "I know these mountains well," Brown explained to
a skeptical Frederick Douglass.[31]

His ensuing application of the plot was just as harebrained. The first
casualty of Brown's attack was a Black bystander; within two days, a force
of Marines had subdued Brown after a siege. He was hastily sentenced
to death.[32]

· · ·

"I have no language to express the conflict of emotion in my heart," Garfield scribbled on December 2. John Brown's hanging had been scheduled for that day and, as the hours passed, the Eclectic's principal felt his thoughts—involuntarily, rebelliously—drift to the doomed abolitionist. "I do not justify his [Brown's] acts. By no means," Garfield told himself. But the longer he thought, the more vivid the scene in his mind became, and soon Garfield was picturing a lonely old man walking the gallows under guard "because his heart beat for the oppressed." The principal closed his reflection on Brown's fate in tones of pure veneration: "Brave man, Old Hero, Farewell. Your death shall be the dawn of a better day."[33]

Garfield's temper flared from sadness into righteous anger over the following week. "Now as of old, 'Without the shedding of blood, there is no remission' of so great a sin," he wrote an associate. His words, intentionally or not, mirrored Brown's final ones.[34]

6

"Let's carry with us ears and eyes for the time,
But hearts for the event"

—Shakespeare's *Coriolanus*, as quoted in Garfield
diary entry for March 20, 1878

Few of the politicians Garfield met in Columbus impressed him. "They are not as gods," he soon decided. Only one specimen seemed likely to plead an exception to the rule; Garfield met Ohio's outgoing governor Salmon Chase, whose domed head barely fit the ego crammed within. Allies had learned to work around it. "Chase is a good man, but his theology is unsound," one lamented. "He thinks there is a fourth person in the Trinity."[1]

Garfield reached a similar conclusion. Admiring Chase's politics, he detected an unhealthy amount of ambition wafting off the man.[2]

He felt purer esteem for another new acquaintance: Jacob Dolson Cox, a fellow state senator from the Reserve. The two hit it off so finely that they decided to room together. "I find Mr. Cox very much of a man," Garfield declared. Cox, meanwhile, characterized his new friend as a jovial bear—"big and strong," fond of a rib-cracking hug or roaring "over a bit of fun or a comic passage in an author . . . while he would shake you up to his own key of enjoyment in the thing that pleased him."[3]

But discordant sounds were bouncing about Garfield's thoughts. He attended the new governor's inauguration and felt his heart leap in sync with the accompanying cannon salutes. On seeing Garfield get to work in the statehouse, spectators christened the newcomer quite the artillery piece himself. "Mr. Garfield will prove one of the twenty-four pounders of the Senate," one predicted.[4]

Threats of the use of weapons had become common in American legislatures in the prior few years. It was another indicator of the ongoing erosion in national discourse. Southern representatives, made paranoid by Brown's raid, challenged Republican peers who criticized slavery to duels. In the Senate, a Democrat had beaten Charles Sumner to near-death after a particularly torching speech against the institution. Southerners spanned through a kaleidoscope of dismissals in its aftermath: Sumner was faking his injuries; Sumner had tricked his assailant into striking; Sumner deserved a thrashing anyway. Even facts about political violence were malleable (or insignificant) under the force of the country's polarization.[5]

In Columbus, Garfield defied it, and in so doing confused his colleagues. To be sure, his physical place in Ohio's senate (on the left of the chamber) symbolized his ideological one. Garfield, Cox, and another lawmaker formed what the press came to call the "Radical triumvirate" for their perceived extremism; he coined a reciprocal nickname for moderates that hit them where it hurt ("emasculated Republicans").

Simultaneously, though, Garfield remained personally pleasant with those he found politically revolting. He led a delegation to Louisville, where he cordially invited southern legislators back to Ohio for a much-needed goodwill dinner. The slavers hardly knew what to make of this Northern ambassador: "Though he is eminently *Black* Republican in his politics, he nevertheless is white Republican in his manners and good breeding."[6]

Garfield's overtures to the southerners proved just as bewildering to abolitionists back home. "Not being a politician we are unable to appreciate the reason why 'the strong barriers of party prejudice' which separate the advocates of slavery from the defenders of free labor, should on this, or any other occasion, be 'overwhelmed and swept away' by any influence whatever," one wrote.[7]

They need not have worried. Garfield had little intention of letting good feelings blunt righteous policy. When an "emasculated Republican" introduced a bill restricting Ohio from ever sending "military expeditions to other States" (a measure sold as a "'soothing syrup' panacea for the South"), Garfield loudly led the opposition:

> The fears of Virginia lie not in the power of John Brown and his handful of men, but her terrors are the terrors of conscience that tells her of crimes against human liberty; terrors that . . . no legislation of Ohio can reach.[8]

Such piety might have led Garfield's foes to wonder if he had mistaken the Senate floor for a church pulpit. After all, he still tended to the faithful, and the press described Garfield as ready to address any flock. "Senator Garfield delivered a very touching discourse yesterday morning before the convicts in the chapel of the Penitentiary," read one dispatch from Columbus in March 1860.[9]

Whenever else Garfield's name graced newsprint, it did so in a vivid variety of guises. Local papers regularly profiled "Senator Garfield," "Prof. Garfield," or "Rev'd Mr. Garfield"—sometimes switching titles in the same article. One column mentioned another profession:

> The life of Hon. James A. Garfield, of the Portage Senatorial District, is a remarkable illustration. . . . Twelve years ago he was [a] driver upon the tow-path of the Ohio Canal.[10]

He continued blending duties back at Hiram. Despite his new obligations in Columbus, Garfield hung on as the Eclectic's principal and remained a favored preacher. He even started to let students accompany him to political meetings. Charles Henry followed Garfield to an event with only nine attendees, afterward asking why bother addressing such a small crowd. "That is the way to get larger audiences, Charlie," Garfield replied smilingly.[11]

He did not show nearly as much patience toward his wife. Crete was the only person in Garfield's orbit who paid for his hyperactivity—the only obligation he felt comfortable dropping, like a discarded juggling pin, upon taking up the added burden of office. She tried to stay close when he first left for Columbus:

> You will write to me often, very often—twice a week, certainly? Tell me all about yourself, your success, your impressions of all that interests you, and sometimes let your heart turn to your little loving wife.[12]

Alas, Garfield only inclined his thoughts back to Crete occasionally, and then with hardly any affection at all. "I shall try to make life for you and myself as pleasant as possible," he scribbled from the Senate floor on one occasion—only to cut this dispiriting line off as legislation came up. In an even weaker moment, Garfield said off-hand to Crete that he considered their marriage a mistake.[13]

The pain bit deep, and Crete gritted against it out of a fear of just making things worse. "I crush back the tears just as long as I can," she wrote her husband, "for I know they make you unhappy."[14]

The domestic tyrannies of the era meant she had little other choice; a neglectful, loveless marriage was something American women in the 19th century had little recourse for. But Crete still stubbornly took encouragement from the love that lit up her husband's letters every so often. "I very much miss your kind attentions," he wrote her while in bed sick. Another cause for optimism came on July 3, 1860, in the form of a blonde baby girl. The Garfields named the child Eliza Arabella ("after her two grandmothers") but soon started calling her "Trot" after a favorite Dickens character. The bond between father and daughter seemed equally strong.

"How much the fact of our little Trot's existence has added to the horizon of our lives," Garfield would soon write.[15]

Nevertheless, he remained fixed on the same vector as before. The day after Trot's birth was an auspicious date, and her father used it to give a political speech in the town of Ravenna. The topic was the nation's potential disunion, which Garfield called unlikely:

> Is there any one of all these States that would break the bond of the Union. . . . And if there were, would not the thirty-two remaining sisters throw their arms of affection around the erring one and bring her gently back to the sacred circle of home?[16]

Then, blind to the irony, Garfield took a trip over Lake Erie with friends. "My love to 'Trot' and all," he dashed to Crete while sailing away.[17]

The second-ever Republican nominee for president was, everyone admitted, an odd-looking man. But Abraham Lincoln's ugliness was apt. Skeletally thin and prone to wearing a stovepipe hat that only made him look more so, he won top billing in a party frankensteined together from disparate factions: Free Soilers, abolitionist "Jacobins," and Democrats alarmed by southern secession talk all identified as Republican in 1860. Frederick Douglass described the thin connective tissue binding them as follows:

> The Republican Party is . . . only negatively antislavery. It is opposed to the political power of slavery, rather than slavery itself.[18]

Lincoln conducted his campaign accordingly—assuming the moderate position on slavery he had always projected and using folksy anecdotes to disarm quibblers. Many Radicals, for example, disliked Lincoln's refusal to endorse a repeal of the Fugitive Slave Law. But others who studied "Honest Abe" closer decided "that he is in his heart an abolitionist."[19]

Democrats suspected the same. Such was the sectional distrust saturating the country's politics that Lincoln's foes could not (or would not) distinguish between his views and those of the Republican extreme. Even southern moderates decided Lincoln's ascent to the presidency would herald a chaotic abolition of slavery, and they could not stomach such a prospect. Southern states collectively tried to make it impossible; Republican candidates would not even be allowed to appear on the region's ballots that November.[20]

A week after Lincoln won anyway, southern states started organizing conventions for secession. The future Confederacy's soon-to-be vice president would tell a crowd in Georgia that their breakaway nation's "foundations are laid, its corner-stone rests, upon the great truth that the negro is not equal to the white man; that slavery . . . is his natural and normal condition."

South Carolina sent delegates to Washington to negotiate for a handover of federal garrisons in the state's borders. Hundreds of its militia took positions overlooking an island fort in Charleston Harbor.[21]

"We are three months into a revolution," Senator Garfield wrote from a wintry Columbus in February. "And yet no militia are called out, no troops levied, no streets barricaded, no bloodshed." Indeed, the delay between the election's results and what the losing side called its consequences confused many Americans. Either the secession rhetoric coming out of the South was a mass tantrum over election results, a bargaining ploy with the incoming administration, or a bona fide bid for disunion. Uncertainty permeated even the pinnacle of government; Buchanan was eager to hold the country (and himself) in an indecisive stupor until his successor arrived.[22]

While campaigning, Garfield had seemed only half awake to the real potential for war. "I move that we give three cheers for the unspiked gun," he said rather flippantly in an August flag-raising ceremony at Hiram. He fired off similar rhetoric months into the "secession winter." A high (or low) point came when he introduced a measure penalizing treason against

Ohio—a bill with the rare distinction of being both legally dubious as well as redundant.[23]

But he sobered as disunion began to look more likely, its impetus more obvious. "I do not now see any way this side of a miracle of God's which can avoid civil war," Garfield wrote in January. "Indeed, I cannot say that I would wish it were possible. To make the concessions demanded by the South would be hypocritical and sinful." He elaborated on the intolerable sin in question a few weeks later:

> May it not be an economy of bloodshed to tell the South . . . that dis-
> union seals the doom of slavery, that if the South forms a government
> actually based on the monstrous injustice of human slavery it will be a
> Cain among the nations of the earth?[24]

The sight of President-Elect Lincoln passing through Colum-bus bucked Garfield up. He could practically hear Republican spines straighten at the thought that this man's inauguration might herald war. Garfield could not help but express excitement at whatever righteous conflict (political or literal) might follow, and what yields might come to those who helped win it: "This really is a great time to live in if any of us can only catch the cue of it."[25]

He already sensed how to do so. Garfield told Crete that she could soon expect to find him and his colleague Jacob Cox drilling with mus-kets outside the Columbus statehouse.[26]

Part II

THE WAR

1861–1865

7

"There is a tide in the affairs of men,
Which taken at its flood, leads on to fortune."

—Shakespeare's *Julius Caesar*, as quoted in
Garfield diary entry for January 4, 1878

Fort Sumter vanished under an acrid puffball of fire, smoke, and fragmenting artillery shells on April 12, 1861. Shore guns kept peppering the outpost for two days; President Lincoln's great offense had been to try resupplying its garrison, which after months of standoff was down to nibbling pork rinds. The resulting rebel bombardment ended up being more flash than sizzle (the only Union casualties came during a fumbled cannon-salute surrender) but it nonetheless blew apart the nation's peace. Lincoln called out the militia to end an insurrection that could obviously not be quelled peacefully.[1]

This message carried the first notes of a tune that Lincoln would hold throughout the conflict to come. It pled that the Union had not entered this war by choice or to settle slavery's fate, but simply to keep itself intact. Such a stance delicately skirted the internal divisions of loyal states; Republicans and a good number of Democrats bought in to it. Even Stephen Douglas jumped into line behind his old rival. "Every man must be for the United States or against it," the northern Democrat declared after visiting President Lincoln. Radicals alone dared predict that the shots fired on Sumter had, in fact, mortally wounded slavery. [2]

"I am glad we are defeated at Sumter," Garfield scrawled after hearing of the surrender. "It will rouse the people." The news certainly jolted him awake: the state senator could now perceive how the entire conflict before the Republic would pan out. "I can see nothing before us but a long and sanguinary war," he informed Crete. To Rhodes, Garfield confessed seeing further:

> I can see no possible end to the war till the South is subjugated . . .
> The War will soon assume the shape of Slavery and Freedom. The world will so understand it. [3]

These were bold predictions to make so early in the Civil War. For months to come, the northern consensus held that the Union would swiftly crush this upstart Confederacy "as an elephant would trample a mouse." Garfield's contrarian view of events lured him into deciding that he needed to find an important part to play in them. "The more I reflect on the whole subject," he wrote in another letter to Crete, "the more I feel that I cannot stand aloof from this conflict. My heart and hope for the country are in it." [4]

Luckily, ways to pitch in abounded. Only days after Sumter's fall, the North hosted what would go into history books as the "Uprising of the People." From city to city, county to county, "came mass meetings, speeches by prominent citizens, lawyers, ministers, priests, military officers, veterans of the War of 1812 and the Mexican War." Neighborhoods raised funds to equip soldiers or support their families. Local sewing circles started knitting battlefield bandages. In Manhattan, an aristocrat named Theodore Roosevelt, Sr., would soon launch a landmark initiative to give financial advice to enlistees. "It is a great luxury to feel I am at last doing something tangible for this country," he wrote. [5]

Thus, from the Civil War's very first days, there were myriad

opportunities for a patriotic northerner to serve the Union—particularly
for influential community men like Garfield. Already, he had received letters from students (current and former) asking how he planned to assist
the war effort, and how they could best do so, too. One practically declared a readiness to follow his principal's lead into any field imaginable:

> Mr. Garfield, you have for a long time seemed to take especial interest
> in my success. . . . I have thought, too, often, how I could compen-
> sate you in some slight degree for the much happiness you have given
> me . . . my only offering is . . . a desire to be of service to you.[6]

Of all the available avenues for national service, one beckoned most
obviously. The Union's standing army was in poor condition—its soldiers
spread thin across lonely outposts throughout the far west, their numbers
(and arsenals) withered by low peacetime funding and southern defec-
tions. Yet with the whole country now whooping to war, these gaps in the
ranks were rapidly being filled by civilian volunteers. The president could
see as much from a glance at his correspondence; Northern governors
were pledging more manpower than the government knew what to do
with. Other notes to Lincoln came from the enlistees themselves:

> I have but one son of seventeen summers, he [is] our only child . . .
> [but] We are ready to volunteer, to fight for the integrity of the Union.[7]

These rough-and-ready soldiers would require capable men to rally
and lead them—a task the army's professional officer caste had neither
the time nor patience for. Particularly audacious northern civilians would
need to step into these roles themselves instead, meaning certain volunteers would be commanding their own volunteer regiments. The glory
won by such heroics would be twofold: someone marshaling their own
neighbors into battle would be serving not only their country, but also
their local reputation. Interpretations varied as to which these men preferred. As a veteran would write:

> In no episode of American history have there been greater opportunities for men of high character . . . to wield a strong and controlling influence over large numbers of their fellow citizens than were given to the officers who organized and commanded the Volunteer regiments of the Union Army.[8]

Experienced soldiers had well-founded doubts about such officers; it was hard to put faith in a commander who had bought a uniform yesterday, and whose grasp of military strategy came mostly from borrowed library books. A stereotype soon formed of a small-town politician buckling on a sword, rushing to the frontlines, then hurrying home to trade their brief, dubious service for higher office—as a gambler might cash in a hastily won stack of chips. A name was attached to this caricature: "'Political general' became almost a synonym for incompetency, especially in the North," a historian would judge.[9]

Yet from the instant Garfield learned of the attack on Fort Sumter, he set himself on becoming just such an officer. Nor was Garfield the only politician in Columbus to do so; he and Jacob Cox had a confidential conversation "over the prospects of the country and the future of our own lives." Recognizing that joining the army would benefit both causes, the pair then divvied up books on battlefield tactics and Napoleonic history—dabbing the finishing touches on an image of two would-be political generals getting to work.[10]

On April 17, Garfield addressed hundreds of enlistees in Columbus. Then he hurried back to the Reserve to rouse his constituents to war. "Old and young are ready to do battle for their country," read an after-action report of one of these barnstorming performances. Another scrap of coverage indicated that the Eclectic's principal was, again, mixing his ecclesiastical duties with political ones:

> Garfield goes forth, like an apostle of Liberty . . . proclaiming the Gospel which demands equal obedience to God and resistance to tyrants.[11]

To Crete, he divulged the hope of taking on another job in future. "If I should go to Congress we would move there for the Winter (isn't this a fine specimen of unhatched chicken?)" It was another bit of evidence that Garfield considered her a passenger in life.[12]

And yet, his ambitions soon stalled out. Opportunities for commissions came and went, and Garfield bungled all of them. Rallying newly enlisted troops in Columbus, he heard a rumor that Governor Dennison intended to make him a full-blown brigadier general (quite the debut rank for a twenty-nine-year-old amateur). But Dennison disabused him of that idea—a blow that was followed, in brutally quick succession, by news that a regiment Garfield helped raise had picked another man as its colonel. Hiram friends informed him he was angling too nakedly for a high rank; Governor Dennison then told Garfield the only commission left available would be a lowly lieutenant colonelcy.[13]

Garfield went home brooding—or, as he tried to spin it for friends, "greatly perplexed on the question of duty." A rank of lieutenant colonel struck him as a mediocre one to swap his senatorship for. Suddenly, Columbus looked like it might be an arena where Garfield could be most useful to the Union cause: his treason bill (once buried in the "jeers of Democrats") had sailed through the senate against only eight dissenting votes; Governor Dennison had also tasked Garfield with passing war legislation and importing war matériel from Illinois and Indiana.[14]

Distant concerns of family also pressed in. "Then the little dear Trot is creeping about the floor!" Garfield beamed in one letter to Crete. "Do you think she will remember me when she sees me?"[15]

Summer arrived, and Garfield marked the occasion by politely notifying the governor that he would refuse the remaining commissions. Sympathetic press lent him cover. "Duties in another calling has induced this declination . . . not disinclination on his part to serve the country," offered the *Western Reserve Chronicle*. But, unbeknownst to many, Garfield considered this a conditional retreat:

I have finally decided, as you doubtless heard, to decline the appointment tendered me by the Governor . . . but I made this compromise
with myself: "There are plenty to take the place now. But if there shall
hereafter be more levies . . . I can go then, with the full approval of my
own judgment and that of my friends."[16]

The country's necessities changed abruptly on July 21, 1861, along a lush
sliver of land in upper Virginia. United States troops advanced toward
rebel positions near Manassas in the expectation of imminent, easy victory. Representatives even followed the soldiers in carriages stacked with
picnic baskets—expecting to behold, through viewing glasses, a theatrical
sweeping away of the outnumbered traitors.[17]

Their alarm at subsequent events need not be imagined. Union
forces broke before a fierce rebel counterattack, fleeing like partridges
scared up from brush. A cohort of Congressmen pulled out their own
guns to turn back the rout but might as well have tried to sweep the sea
back with brooms.[18]

Secretary of State William Seward read of the catastrophe through a
haze of cigar smoke—a telegram's awful text ("Save Washington and the
remnants of this army") sending him sprinting to the White House. The
next day Lincoln formally asked to be provided with many, many more
soldiers.[19]

The disaster of Bull Run prompted both Dennison and Garfield to re-
approach the subject of the latter's commission. "Can you take a Lieut.
Colonelcy?" the governor wrote the senator. "I am anxious that you should
do so." An intermediary promised Garfield that Dennison would "do the
best he can for you" to make accommodations for further promotion. Garfield took his time before asking the governor when to report to camp. "I
have concluded to go," he informed Crete a few days later.[20]

•   •   •

Dry, dusty steppes of parade ground; camps billowing with flies; a tiny desk crisscrossed with shadows cast by candlelit netting; mineral-tinted groundwater that turned out to be a potent laxative; these became the landmarks of Garfield's world during the hot, hazy late summer of 1861. He initially commanded a regiment of one—himself—but began scratching names onto his roster with speed.[21]

A single sermon at a Hiram church netted sixty enlistees. Within a few days an entire company had been formed out of Garfield's Eclectic students, past and present. Other Western Reservists joined the rush. "'Why?' it may be asked," a veteran of Garfield's regiment would reminisce. "Because Christian fathers and mothers wanted their boys to enlist under the young professor of Hiram."[22]

Mistakes made in packing lists were swiftly corrected: linen sheets, picked out and thrown away, as were ornate pistols gifted by doting parents; reveille at six o'clock struck the enlistees, at first, as "aimless barbarism." Games of cards and checkers helped days pass. Dusk would be welcomed with campfire songs, until drums beat out taps "which means for soldiers to put out the lights."[23]

Garfield again served as a distant figure of kindly authority for his boys—supposedly the best shot in camp, but more inclined to oversee training from afar on horseback. Whenever the enlistees needed a break from their drilling, Garfield would form them into a square and (as one private recollected) "give us a speech on some moral subject." They venerated him and, among civilians, were known to reference the fact that Garfield once worked on the Ohio Canal.[24]

He had, by personal estimate, never been two-thirds as overworked. By the end of November, however, he had a full regiment—the Forty-Second Ohio—to show for his efforts, and informed Crete he had earned the rank of colonel.[25]

Garfield's notes to her had been sparse since his commissioning. "I know that you are very very busy," one of Crete's replies begged, "but not so busy that you *cannot* write." But such complaints barely registered to her husband against more interesting, pertinent letters flowing in from political confidantes—like the following from Rhodes, still at the Eclectic:

> We are to be ruled by military men for the next twenty years. . . . The object and aim of your life is to subordinate all things to political advancement.[26]

Garfield replied to another correspondent that he was, for now, simply having a grand time "tearing down the old fabric of my proposed life, and removing its rubbish for the erection of a new structure." But, while finally leading his regiment out of camp on a gorgeous Sunday, he carried proof of lasting local foundations that would await his return; a sabre gifted by the community glinted off Garfield's waist, mirrorlike in the white December sun.[27]

8

"There is no soul, more stronger to direct you than yourself."

—Shakespeare's *Henry VIII*, as quoted in Garfield

diary entry for January 11, 1878

He reached Louisville, Kentucky, alone, to see General Don Carlos Buell's massive Army of the Ohio stuck in stasis. This had become an embarrassingly common posture for Union forces across all fronts; the brash northern overconfidence preceding Bull Run had since collapsed into paralyzing hesitation, and Radical Republicans were now practically bouncing off the Capitol's walls in their frustration at the war's lack of progress. They heaped blame on every leader possible. "Lincoln means well but has no force of character," one Radical complained to a diplomat.

> He is surrounded by Old Fogy Army officers more than half of whom are downright traitors. . . . I began to doubt whether this accursed rebellion could be put down without a Revolution in present Administration.[1]

General Buell, conversely, saw plenty of reason to take his time fighting through Kentucky. Conquering the border state was an intimidating

assignment: its incongruous topography both restricted military campaigning and reflected the mixed allegiances of its people (its "slave soil
hemmed and wedged by free-soil strips"). At the very bottom of Kentucky (and Buell's anxieties) was a massive rebel army ready to turn back
any Union force reaching for Tennessee. So, Buell was perfectly happy to
build his force in Louisville during the winter of 1861. He presented this
idleness as a bit of strategic genius:

> Thus far I have studiously avoided any movements which to the
> enemy would have the appearance of activity or method.[2]

Yet this could not be sustained forever; Buell's ultimate objective was
vital to the Union cause, and the President desperately wanted him to
commence offensive operations. "I hope to have God on my side," Lincoln quipped, "but I must have Kentucky." Buell thus had a vague intent
to lurch down from Louisville in early 1862. But a shadow lay over these
plans; the rugged eastern arm of Kentucky needed to first be cleaned of
rebels. To neglect this would be to leave the Army of the Ohio's flank
exposed to counterthrusts once it decided to break camp.[3]

No one on Buell's staff wanted the assignment. One can appreciate
why; among career army officers, it is usually best professional practice to
stay near a general of good rank and reputation. Nor could a cold Appalachian bushwhack have sounded like fun. Luckily, one of the subordinates
to whom Buell offered the mission knew of a fresh volunteer regiment
from Ohio that would be better-suited to securing east Kentucky.[4]

On the night of December 16, Garfield entered Buell's quarters and was
asked to draft a campaign plan for the capture of east Kentucky. It did
not matter that he had been in uniform for only a few months and never
seen combat. Garfield stayed up all night wrestling with the assignment,
and in the morning presented his work to a satisfied general. He would be
entrusted with not just the Forty-Second for this adventure, but supple-
mental units of Kentuckians and other Ohioans.[5]

He hopped aboard a boat to follow his men, who were already put-
tering down the Ohio River into east Kentucky. The Forty-Second's first
views of the territory were not encouraging. "We had not supposed that
within so short a distance of home there was any such wilderness as this,"
one would write.[6]

Garfield had detected as much from a glance at its maps in Louisville. To Crete, he projected pleasure at being trusted with an offensive
campaign through such a land while so many other officers still dawdled
in camp:

> When I reflect that this movement covers an area of 6000 square
> miles and has no railroad or telegraphic lines, and think how soon the
> winter will be upon us in all its severity . . . I feel that my hands are
> very full indeed . . . But after all, I must confess that I am pleased with
> the prospect of work.

Writing Rhodes, however, Garfield's pen let out a little tremor: "The
work will be positively enormous."[7]

So, too, was his adversary in this land—quite notoriously so. In a just world,
Brigadier General Humphrey Marshall would have been known solely by
his record. He had fought valiantly for the Union in Mexico and graduated from West Point alongside the men leading each side of this conflict.
But, alas, Marshall was also built like an elephant. This gave all Americans something to distinguish him in a war already brimming with famous commanders. Northern press tagged Marshall as the "rotund rebel
of Kentucky" and, less alliteratively (and imaginatively), "that obese traitor."
Marshall's soldiers made the counterpoint of venerating his size. Yet one is
left to wonder how the Confederate general must have felt, puffing at the
head of a column, to hear such praise rise in song from the trailing ranks:

> Humphrey Marshall, he's our boss.
> Big as Hell, brave as a hoss.[8]

Big and brave or not, Marshall represented a potent threat. Reports that he was roving east Kentucky with as many as six thousand men (plus cavalry and cannon) had helped prompt Buell to dispatch Garfield's force to secure the region.[9]

It landed there inelegantly on December 17—one of the Forty-Second's steamboats, springing a leak and beaching near the village of Catlettsburg. Wet Ohioans waded ashore to join a gaggle of drunk locals eager to share "blood-curdling accounts" of the "invincible Humphrey Marshall."

The last of their humor dispelled, Garfield's men turned to salvage their most problematic cargo: 150 unbroken pack mules. "Does any veteran of the Forty-Second live . . . who has forgotten that afternoon with the mules?" one would write more than a decade later.[10]

The path ahead of the Forty-Second was demarcated by a river—the Big Sandy, a strand of water that winnowed south around the slopes of east Kentucky like an artery around muscle. Its course made the severity of the mission before Garfield's men evident: the Sandy River Valley was a giant basin carved from shale, its rims thorned by stony peaks; its floor was crammed thick with the hardiest trees on the continent. "Poplar, oak, cherry, walnut . . . in every valley, cove, and mountain-side."[11]

The Forty-Second Ohio forged through it all, using trails along the Big Sandy's banks, as the river and its tributaries fluctuated too much in depth to be navigated by boat. But these footpaths were also too small for the men to use properly; they could not march abreast, and soon dark rectangular shapes dotted the way behind them—mess chests, discarded to lighten the load. Wagons creaked over knolls, only to come frighteningly close to flipping over the other side.[12]

Garfield caught up with some of his boys on December 21, at a cluster of hovels called Louisa. There, he saw that this region was "terribly broken up in its social and commercial relations," just as it was geographically. ("Poor, illiterate, and provincial beyond belief" read a less tactful estimate of the locals by one private.) Entire families shared a single book—the Bible—that none could read a word of. One man boasted of having "twice seen a steamboat," but neither he, his wife, nor any of their twenty-one children could grasp what a railroad was. They had heard George Washington was in the war, "but upon which side they could not tell." A member of the Forty-Second Ohio wondered at how America could send missionaries abroad when such ignorance existed inside its borders.[13]

But the northerners demonstrated barbarity themselves. A flurry of squawks and oinks broke their camp on the night of the twenty-third, after they had hunkered beside a farm.

The next morning, after learning his men had stolen livestock, Garfield publicly scolded them and paid the aggrieved farmer for his losses. The event signposted a bleak beginning to the campaign, and the enemy had hardly been encountered at all.[14]

Things brightened in every way at the end of December, when the Forty-Second reached a juncture of a Big Sandy tributary that permitted resupply. Another regiment joined them, by which point the weather ("for a week past . . . cold and rainy") finally warmed. The Yankees started drilling in sunlight again.[15]

The practice came right on time, for rebels had finally been detected—albeit only fleetingly throughout the surrounding gulleys. Potshots had been made at Union scouts; one of Marshall's officers was apprehended on December 27; a spy told Garfield that the southerners were digging trenches down the valley, past a village named Paintsville. The colonel spent part of New Year's Day outlining the situation for his wife:

> I dare hardly hope that I shall capture a whole army. . . . I cannot tell you how deeply alive to the scheme in hand are all the impulses and energies of my nature. I begin to see the obstacles melt before me and the old feeling of succe[e]ding in everything I undertake gradually taking quiet possession of me.[16]

Marshall's defenses, however, did not sound as if they would be melting away anytime soon. To obliterate them, Garfield begged General Buell for the single offensive element his brigade lacked—artillery. "Send me four small howitzers, with shell and shrapnel, if possible," he wrote. "I can get them here by boat and haul them with our mule teams." Garfield had, in fact, requested heavier firepower several times since the start of the campaign. Buell had denied them all—knowing that the last thing an offensive force fighting up and down muddy hills needed was cannon to tow around. He repeated this wisdom to Garfield as a long-suffering teacher might a struggling student. Infantry, Buell predicted, will prove "more efficient than the enemy's artillery."[17]

Garfield had to take the general at his word. The Forty-Second and their partner units trekked further down the Sandy's tributary on January 1, toward what was assuredly a well-equipped and thickly entrenched enemy. "The advance was difficult and slow," reads one surviving account, "the [wagon] train not being able to make more than five or six miles a day, and sometimes a considerably less distance." The souring weather was to blame; heavy rain was once again dicing the Sandy Valley with muddy streams of runoff.[18]

The Union force began to judder over bumps of rebel resistance, like a coach hitting cobblestones, the nearer it got to Paintsville. Losses were minimal, but a captured enemy confirmed Marshall had concentrated his host just past the settlement ahead, behind fixed positions. Another piece of intelligence drew Garfield's notice on January 6: a trio of circuitous, tree-lined roads led toward the enemy's position—one through its center, the other two around the flanks.[19]

Garfield arranged his men across these paths and choreographed their procession to Paintsville. One column moved in on the village's east on the afternoon of January 6. Two hours later, a second one did the same on the west. A final procession moved down the centermost road shortly afterward. These three prongs converged the next day in an abandoned town. The last reported sighting of Marshall's men had been of but a few flashes of gray cloth, hustling south.[20]

At dusk, sparks danced on the horizon. They drew the notice of Garfield's scouts, and as the soldiers edged toward a point three miles outside Paintsville, wooden parapets loomed out of the darkness. Mercifully, the fortifications were empty. Tiny campfires sputtered beyond, casting weak light over abandoned food tins and rifles. Once Colonel Garfield reached the hilltop ramparts of this "Fort Marshall" at eight o'clock, a full moon was casting further illumination onto what had happened there: thousands of frozen footprints shone in the snow, leading off into the frigid dark.[21]

Garfield sat down in what had recently been Marshall's quarters. He sent a dispatch to Buell explaining the situation and his intent to pursue the rebels wherever they had run to. "I shall not need any artillery," he now agreed.[22]

Garfield's first brush with Marshall, though passing, had dispelled an illusion that had been cast by the fog of war. Early reports leaking out of east Kentucky (describing an intrepid Confederate roving its hills with a mobile, well-equipped force) were actually out of touch with reality. Encounters with Marshall's men had exposed this well enough to Sandy Valley locals. One described the rebels as "ragged, greasy, and dirty"—fewer in number than rumor suggested, and even more deficient in firepower. Many shouldered flintlocks or even squirrel guns rather than modern rifles. Though Marshall did truly possess cannon, these only weighed down his force.[23]

Hunger and sickness had been a heavier burden on the southerners. Marshall himself was ill with the mumps and, confessedly, did not want to fight in east Kentucky any longer. Locals did not seem sympathetic to the Confederate cause.[24]

His misery had been exploited, then magnified by the exchange at Paintsville. Per Marshall's beleaguered view of events there, a leviathan-size Union army was now charging down the Sandy Valley. News of another approaching northern force was all Marshall had needed to hear to order a retreat to a town named Prestonburg. Heaving down there (after having his provisions at Paintsville set ablaze) Marshall made a self-pitying whine to himself:

> I sometimes wonder, why I undergo all this exposure and Hardship?[25]

His tormentor had resolved not to let it end just yet; Garfield was moving in pursuit. "I fear we shall not be able to catch the enemy in a 'stern chase,'" he wrote Buell, "but we shall try." Garfield later explained to Crete that he did not want to accept a half-victory:

> I was unwilling that he [Marshall] should get away without a trial of our strength.[26]

Garfield hunted the rebel commander relentlessly during the next few days. His force sustained the chase through sleepless nights, sleety rain, and cold campsites kept free of any fires ("I wanted to keep the enemy ignorant of our position"). At last, they caught sight of Marshall's troops near the end of a broad gulley run through by a creek ("Middle Creek") and Garfield spent predawn on January 10 putting his soldiers into position around the gap. A crackle of gunfire shivered the pines at one o'clock; the Battle of Middle Creek was met.[27]

Garfield watched it unfold from the vantage point of a hilltop log church. The layout of the skirmish below him was simple; Marshall's force had encamped along a southwestern ridge, while the Unionists held the northernmost crest beside Garfield. He sent cavalry to ride through the valley—a maneuver that drew fire from (thereby revealing) the Confederate positions. Garfield immediately ordered his Hiram boys and the Kentucky companies to storm across the valley, over Middle Creek, and into Marshall's gunline.[28]

The northerners practically sprinted over the open ground, then found cover at the foot of the Confederate hill. Above them rose an "almost perpendicular" slope choked with brambles. Then it became a volcano; smoke wafted from the ridgetop as Marshall's men opened fire. Even the rocks and twigs around Garfield, on the other side of the valley, chipped with enemy rounds.[29]

Slowly, however, the northerners taking the rebel hill realized nothing was hitting them. Howitzer shells screamed above the treetops; the bark over the Ohioans' heads was stripped clean; so many rebel bullets were being shot, in fact, that locals would find hundreds in the topsoil for years to come; nevertheless, Marshall's men struggled to hit the one target that mattered. "Had the casualties been proportionate to the amount of power burned," one of Garfield's men would write, "the Union force at least would have been annihilated." A post hoc analysis would reveal the causes of this discrepancy: Marshall's men were shooting downhill, with low-caliber guns, at a small number of enemies crouching behind trees. Conversely, Garfield's men could look uphill to see rebels bunched together behind sparse cover.[30]

A lopsided exchange continued for hours, before both sides retreated at dusk. The northerners had only suffered one fatality. They went to sleep "confident of victory."

Then, at eight o'clock, a distant blaze lit up the night.[31]

At dawn the Yankees beheld its source: Marshall had again incinerated all his stores and run away. Garfield's soldiers picked over what the enemy left behind, then tramped back to friendly territory.[32]

The cold concerned them no longer. "Tired, footsore, [but] I have never seen a happier day than the day after the battle," one of the U.S. soldiers recalled years later. A different emotion warmed Garfield as he scratched out his account for friends at home to enjoy: "I can never tell you how full of love and pride my heart is toward our Hiram boys."[33]

•   •   •

The North soon swelled with greater pride for him. The one-year mark of the war was nearing, and thus far the conflict's lack of progress had drummed down Union morale. This, plus the scarcity of other significant action in the winter of 1861–1862, meant a victory of any size was destined to be hailed in the North like rain after a drought.[34]

And so, once word of Garfield's victory trickled down from east Kentucky, it was flung around the country by an exultant northern press. Outlets in Michigan, Connecticut, and Washington, D.C., were among the few to report it dryly. The farther that news of the engagement flew, however, and the more often it was retold, the more warped its events became. Massachusetts and Indiana readers received an account so dramatic and lengthy that it would be retold as truth for decades; it spoke of a Union colonel joining his student-soldiers as they charged the traitor hill. "Go in boys," Garfield had reportedly cried. "Give them *Hail Columbia!*" He supposedly led the assault in his shirtsleeves—having ("with a wild shout") flung his officer's jacket into a tree in a fit of patriotic passion. A Californian paper described rebel camps beyond Kentucky as quaking at the thought of facing such a fanatical Unionist. *The New York Times* christened Garfield the North's "Praying Colonel." A profile gracing its front page repeated the shirtsleeve story.[35]

A journal in Boston described him most imaginatively: "Col. Garfield stands five feet nine . . . and is withal what the ladies have always called 'a handsome man.'" Moreover, "Rev. Mr. Garfield" was such a zealous Disciple of Christ that he had purportedly been known to beat up those who dared interrupt his sermons. The paper got one detail of his background correct, though:

> In his early days of boyhood . . . he ran away from home and became a driver on the canal.[36]

The most sustained adulation for Garfield resounded in the Reserve. Its press spent weeks rehashing his triumph in Kentucky. By the end of January, they still boasted that a lone local volunteer officer had proven himself "worth a dozen such 'Military men' or 'West Pointers.'" At Hiram, Harry Rhodes read all such coverage with delight, then wrote to its subject. The story of Garfield throwing his coat into the tree seemed particularly ludicrous, but Rhodes saw utility in it: "Although from your letter I am led to the conclusion that . . . the above story is fiction . . . it will do you a great deal of good in the popular estimation."[37]

Flipping through letters from other officers, Garfield noticed his reputation rising in professional army circles, too. Even George McClellan, Lincoln's top general, extended personal congratulations to Garfield for his "handsome achievement against forces superior in number and having the advantage of three pieces of artillery."[38]

Historians would put the clash at Middle Creek, by virtue of timing, in a far loftier position than its size merited. "And the battle, though relatively small, was the first real Union victory of the War," reads one such account.[39]

The Battle of Middle Creek served as the figurative high point of Garfield's campaign in east Kentucky. Its low point arrived shortly thereafter—ironically, once the region's rivers started to rise. The Big Sandy filled with rain to the point that its tributaries became unnavigable, cutting Garfield's brigade off from resupply. Marching to the mouth of the river, he confiscated a civilian steamer and piloted it personally down the treacherous waterways—past treetops peeking out of the swirling currents and through near-capsizals. At last, he docked in camp with fresh rations and, as news of this latest exploit left the region, the nation's press again turned laudatory:

> We would like to be informed of some honorable work that Col. Garfield can *not* do.[40]

He soon discovered it. Garfield woke up one morning in the second half of the month and saw wheat stacks, fences, and even whole houses floating by his window—the Sandy Valley's streams having now completely burst their banks. Soldiers bobbed around camp in troughs; steamboats chugged past to dock on horse-posts.[41]

Then, as the waters finally receded, the northerners fell sick. Once-healthy men began to drop dead. "Four battles would not be so disastrous to us," Garfield wrote Crete, before becoming badly ill himself. Burying Hiram boys added to his agony. He divulged as much to Crete:

> I declare to you there are fathers and mothers in Ohio that I hardly know how I can ever endure to meet. A noble young man from Medina County died a few days ago. I enlisted him, but not till I had spent two hours in answering the objection of his father, who urged that he was too young to stand the exposure. He was the only child . . . I would rather fight a battle than to meet his father.[42]

As if to offset this misery, Garfield vented the anger he was starting to feel at the condition of the broader war. He read of dawdling by McClellan in Virginia; of imprisoned Confederates being permitted to keep their slaves; of Lincoln restricting northern generals from freeing slaves in the South. Righteous fury thus interspersed Garfield's writings:

> If the severest vengeance of outraged and insulted law is not visited upon those cursed villains who have instigated and led this rebellion it will be the most wicked crime that can be committed.[43]

And yet, in another note, Garfield expressed a faith that the Union's struggles in fighting this war might serve a greater cause in the long run:

> But out of the very weakness and timidity of our leaders I draw the hope that God has willed it . . . Let the war be conducted *for the Union* till the whole nation shall be enthused, inspired, transfigured with the glory of that high purpose. Let all the deeds of valor add their glory to that purpose, all the blood of noble men that die in the fight hallow it, all the love [of] the people for the fallen ones sanctify and exalt

it . . . they will love the Union more than slavery and slay the python because it[s] slimy folds roll toward the cradle of our infant Hercules (for the Union spirit is yet an infant with what it is to be).[44]

A spring thaw came and Garfield used it to give "Sir Humphrey" one last whipping. Intelligence reached camp that Marshall was using an opening on the Virginia border to raid the Sandy Valley. Garfield gathered a force on March 14 for a counterattack. It infiltrated the rebel-held pass on March 16 under the cover of a snowstorm. The exchange that followed would be compared by the northerners to a turkey shoot; it ended when Marshall's men resorted to instinct and fled.[45]

"They [the southerners] evidently left in the greatest haste," one of the Ohioans jotted down after the engagement. "After taking what articles we wanted, the cabins were burned and we left." Garfield and his men returned to base clinking with trophies—rebel swords and guns, knives made from scythe blades, love letters intended for belles back down South. Garfield took Marshall's notes for himself.[46]

He picked up a better reward upon returning to base: confirmation of his promotion to brigadier general, heretofore only rumored. "I have never said a word in reference to it in way of expressing a desire for it," Garfield had assured a friend after hearing of it. Now, though, he accepted the star with mixed feelings: joy at the honor, grief for the divorce it portended. "It makes me very sad to think of being separated from the 42nd," Garfield told Rhodes.[47]

He was directed to escort his regiment back to Louisville. "The work of Gen. GARFIELD and his Brigade, in the Sandy Valley, was now done," a regimental historian would later write. "No enemy was left within reach; the whole of Eastern Kentucky was protected and tranquil."

The Hiram boys packed up camp alongside their commander (now the youngest general in the whole U.S. Army) and, as they tramped aboard boats taking them back upriver, struck up in happy song.[48]

9

During the next week, Garfield followed after General Buell's Army of the Ohio from Louisville to Nashville, then finally southwestern Tennessee. Buell was himself racing to catch up to another general; Ulysses Grant had camped on a muddy riverbend and was waiting patiently for rendezvous. Alas, their reunion was marked by disaster. Buell's men approached Grant's location on April 6 to the thundering sound of cannon fire. Up ahead, a dazed William Tecumseh Sherman was yelling, "My God, we're attacked!" Grant, years later, struck a sheepish tone while admitting he had not thought such a thing possible:

> The fact is, I . . . had no idea that the enemy would leave strong intrenchments to take the initiative.[1]

An enduring, almost wickedly terse name would be given to this clash by a small log church near it—Shiloh. Survivors would ironically remember the fight as a hell on earth. "Flashing streaks of fire" lit up its surrounding forests; fighters spotlighted in these reports looked "ludicrously like the figures of demons." Confederate battle screams added to the sense of pandemonium.[2]

Garfield arrived at Shiloh when it was nearly over (at half past one on the morning of April 7), then spent two days marching over what he (quite accurately) described as the "most horrid carnage that any American battlefield ever presented." It had not yet entirely finished—occasionally a shower of shells flew at Garfield's men. One round even zipped past his head and pulped another officer. Nevertheless, the battle's outcome had been decided—the ambushing rebels, turned away at great cost—and so General Garfield's role at Shiloh would mostly be that of observer and chronicler. "The horrible sights I have witnessed on this field I can never describe," he repeated in another letter to Crete. Garfield did manage to mention he had seen that phenomenon of awful battlefields: "the best and worst in generalship."[3]

"It was a case of Southern dash against Northern pluck and endurance," Ulysses Grant later admitted. The general also acknowledged receiving a great epiphany:

> Up to the battle of Shiloh I, as well as thousands of other citizens, believed that the rebellion against the Government would collapse suddenly and soon . . . [but afterwards] I gave up all idea of saving the Union except by complete conquest.

While Grant assumed this outlook, Garfield (who had predicted a protracted, costly civil war since its beginning) spent weeks burying Shiloh's dead.[4]

Thus kicked off his season of discontent. The muddy armageddon of Pittsburg Landing around Garfield yielded, by the end of April, to an expanse of bogs puddling between there and Mississippi. "The great army here has been slowly advancing toward Corinth;" he wrote in mid-May, "but the weather has been so very bad." Even in good conditions this movement would have proceeded at a crawl: Buell's and Grant's men had to build heavy log pathways over what felt like an infinite bayou. "[W]oe to the man or beast that was unfortunate enough to step or fall off these roads," a private wrote. "Some of the mules that fell off . . . were never found." The northerners could be forgiven for thinking little lived here but alligators.[5]

Their destination hardly seemed better. "Corinth was a wretched place—the capital of a swamp," a veteran remembered. That it might have been, but Grant, at least, also saw the city as a lever that, if pressed, would exert pressure on the broader Confederacy. "If we obtained possession of Corinth the enemy would have no railroad for the transportation of armies or supplies," he later explained. Indeed, once Garfield reached the city limits, he could hear trains trundling in the distance. "Hitherto . . . a symbol of peace and enterprise," the young general wrote, "[now] the harbinger of the most humble barbarism and strife."[6]

It would be a different strife than any he had witnessed thus far. Where the Sandy Valley campaign was a string of running engagements, and Shiloh had been a face-to-face bloodbath, the battle of Corinth would be a drawn-out siege. Union forces dug earthworks and began pittering away at the city from afar. Garfield's world became a monotony of scratched observation lenses and wispy impact clouds popping on the horizon.[7]

Garfield described them under candlelight in his letters home. "We stand under arms from 4 o'clock in the morning till broad day light," read one of his notes to Hiram at the end of spring. "This we have done for nearly a month."[8]

He used this time to reflect on the broader war. The more he did so, the more he decided it was being fought incorrectly. Months of campaigning through the Confederacy had taught Garfield that new, more aggressive martial philosophies were needed to conquer what was obviously an unrepentant land of rebels. "In one thing, I fear we are mistaken," he mused. "We have believed in a suppressed Union sentiment in the South." Garfield now had plenty of anecdotes to invalidate this assumption. He had accepted the hospitality of fellow Disciples in the Sandy Valley, only to learn that they supported the Confederacy. "It is one of the painful facts of the rebellion that nearly all the most cultivated and enlightened people in this country . . . are on the side of rebellion," Garfield had written afterward. At Nashville he saw mansions belonging to that "enlightened" class being guarded by U.S. soldiers who had to endure public haranguing for their troubles.[9]

Garfield thus doubted the wisdom of continuing to treat the occupied South with restraint—as the Union still insisted its armies do. This policy even covered the most outrageous type of Confederate property; Northern officers trying to confiscate slaves from civilians, as John Frémont had done the previous summer, could expect their orders to be revoked by Lincoln and their commissions put in jeopardy. The president was still presiding over a fractious northern coalition and remained on guard against any notion that this war was abolitionist in purpose.[10]

Down near Corinth, however, Garfield could see that preserving the Union's sovereignty and ending slavery were not exclusive; accomplishing the former demanded completion of the latter. "The fact can no longer be denied," he wrote, ". . . the Union can never live in these States except upon the 'broken body and shed blood of slavery.'"[11]

As Corinth's siege dragged on, Garfield flashed a bit of hunger to shed rebel blood, himself. He feared the enemy might flee the city without facing battle; the apparent reluctance of his commanders to force such an engagement made him question their dedication to prosecuting this war with the requisite aggression. The thought of staying in their company (really, under their thumb) filled Garfield with despair as summer came. "I begin to feel that I am losing great opportunities for growth," he wrote home.[12]

Only half coincidentally (for, to a certain extent, such a move had always been anticipated) a friend pointed out an escape route. "I hope very much you will be relieved from the Army by September," Harry Rhodes wrote Garfield. "If you are you will be spontaneously sent to Congress." The Reserve's reigning representative was no longer Joshua Giddings, but a freshman named John Hutchins, who, it turned out, was a poor inheritor of the mantle. More interestingly, a redistricting had occurred since Hutchins's election—meaning he would technically not be running as an incumbent.[13]

Garfield could practically sleepwalk his way into this new House seat if he wanted. He had taught and ministered to generations of the Reserve's people, then led hundreds of them off to war. Stories of his ongoing service still intermittently featured in Ohio's newspapers. His run would be among the easiest of all imaginable political contests.[14]

And yet, Rhodes knew that having a volunteer general return home to run for office risked branding him as someone who had only launched a military career to bolster his political one—an impression Garfield was loath to give. Rhodes therefore phrased the suggestion of Congress carefully; it would be a "better theatre" for service than the army. "So long as you are swallowed up in the great indistinguishable mass of an immense army you will have no special will of your own," he wrote in a follow-up to Garfield. "Yours it is to obey."[15]

Garfield approached the suggestion warily. A cautionary parable came to mind; a friend of his—William Hazen—had (allegedly) abandoned the front lines at Shiloh to lobby for a promotion at headquarters, to disastrous reputational result. "I am sorry to tell you that he has fallen in the estimation of many of his best friends here," Garfield told Rhodes. "He may come back with stars on his shoulders but . . . many will have fallen from his reputation." Garfield shuddered to think of the same fate befalling him.[16]

But his coyness dissipated as Corinth's defenses crumpled. "I cannot but feel an interest in what you say in reference to Congress," Garfield admitted at the end of May, after the rebels successfully escaped the besieged city (as he had feared they would). He had one unyielding condition about entering the race, however: keeping Hazen's recent mishap in mind, Garfield made clear he wanted it to look as though running for Congress was not his idea. "If the people of the District should see fit to elect me of their own choice I shall be gratified," he told Rhodes. "I will take no steps whatever in the matter, and will only think of the thing—in the very improbable event of its being spontaneously tendered to me in my absence." Garfield's guidance was unnecessary: his friends, having assumed this answer would come, were already "feeling about quietly" in the Reserve's political circles.[17]

This gave the general time to ponder the arc and motive force of his military career:

> I believe I entered the service with patriotic motives . . . I cannot for a moment think of taking any course which even by inference throw a shadow of suspicion upon those motives as being for political or demagogical purposes . . . the whole year's work would be misconstrued. I would rather be reduced to a residuum of 100 pounds.[18]

Coincidentally, he had begun to shed weight from camp fever. Garfield made light of his sickness—joking to Crete that he could do with losing a bit of flab.[19]

After Corinth fell the rebel army escaped, and the southern kaleidoscope once again shifted around Garfield. The bayous of Mississippi gave way to the dazzling verdure of Alabama's Tuscumbia Valley. Plantation land sprawled as far as the eye could see—its hills, crowned by splendid colonnaded mansions. Though Garfield's force was not here to fight but occupy, there remained hostility to confront: Southern belles snarled at the sight of Union-blue uniforms, and pointedly crossed the street to evade the shame of walking under the American flag. Local farmers boasted to the Yankees that their crops were bound for hungry Confederate armies.[20]

They failed to mention that they were not the ones working the fields. Garfield noticed, though; for the first time, he could study slavery firsthand:

No one who sees the splendor and luxury of these wealthy planters'
homes can fail to see that the "Peculiar Institution" has great charms
for the rich, and yet no one can fail to see that it is the poor man's bane.
We pass these fine plantations and see the slaves toiling for masters
and masters' sons who are in the rebel army fighting us, and we let
them stay at their toil.[21]

This latter point pained Garfield to no end. Hating slavery, he was
bound by army policy from interfering with it. He repeatedly retold one
heart-rending incident in letters home: a few days before Garfield's arrival in Tuscumbia, another regiment had marched through the valley and
been approached by slaves begging to be freed. "Take us with you, we will
work, we will do anything for you," the runaways had said. But the U.S.
officer in command had simply pulled out a pistol and forced them back
to their toil. "The poor slaves went back to suffer not only their terrible
bitter disappointment, but all that is in store for them in consequence of
this expression of their wishes," Garfield wrote, aghast.

One night shortly afterward, a group of slaves came to sing for him
in camp. "Poor fellows!" Garfield bemoaned to Crete. "How can they sing
songs? . . . We seem to be as much their enemies as their masters."[22]

The general's notes to confidantes on the Reserve soon hit higher
pitches of urgency. Campaigning in Alabama had let him see not just to
the civil war's end, but the surely greater challenges that would confront
the Union afterward. Considering them made him readier than ever to
abandon the military for national politics. As he expounded to Harmon
Austin:

It seems to me that the successful ending of the war is the smaller of
the two tasks imposed upon the government . . . There will spring out
of this war a score of new questions and new dangers. The settlement of
these will be of even more vital importance than the ending of the war.

I do not hesitate to tell you that I believe I could do service in Congress in that work and I should prefer that to continuing in the Army.

Then Garfield clarified his preferences:

Should the people, of their own motion . . . choose to nominate me for
Congress—I should esteem it a mark of high favor.[23]

Around this time, Garfield received an order from a commanding
general to search his camp for a runaway slave, then return the fugitive
to their master. "I had the honor to be, perhaps, the first officer in the
Army who refused to obey such an order," Garfield would reminisce as a
congressman.[24]

He could already see from correspondence that Austin was working fe-
verishly to gin up a "spontaneous" movement for his nomination. A telling note had reached him from a local Republican official: deliberations
of potential House candidates were being made, "and *your* name comes
up among others for consideration." The note's balance begged Garfield
to officially enter the race:

You have a stronghold in the confidence of the people . . . I write thus
presuming you are willing to occupy any post where duty calls you.[25]

But Garfield would not drop his façade. "I wrote him [the official] in
answer as I have written before," he told Rhodes, "that I must leave the
matter wholly to my friends." Those very friends now worried project-
ing only tepid interest in the House seat risked backfiring; Republican
delegates in the Reserve wanted to hand "General G" the nomination,
but only if he would surely accept it. They hinted that if a verbal expression saying as much was impossible, a tacit physical one would do; maybe
Garfield could return home for a few weeks?

Such suggestions were passed on to the general, who still replied in
a neurotically noncommittal manner. "Well, James," Rhodes wrote exas-
peratedly. "I am sure you will do well to come part way home and see to
some things."[26]

Crete felt anxiety radiating off Garfield over the matter. "I don't know but *politics* is to be the death of you yet," she wrote her husband.[27]

At least his duties in Alabama had become easier. Instead of having to worry about military maneuvers, Garfield was assigned the leisurely task of leading the jury in a court-martial of another Union officer.

Outside these courthouse proceedings, Garfield sampled luxury he had scarcely imagined possible. He stayed with the wealthiest man in town, who was more than happy to treat a Yankee officer to southern hospitality. Garfield slept in linen sheets, dined on roast pork, and even indulged in an indoor shower every morning ("Doesn't that astonish you!" he wrote Crete). Unfortunately, his patron was also eager to reveal the source of this opulence. Garfield suffered a tour of the man's plantation outside town—and an introduction to the ninety-five slaves who worked it.[28]

The excursion did not impress Garfield as his host intended. Garfield wrote afterward only of gaining new insight into the terrible illogic binding slaver society together:

> I do not wonder that the Slave aristocracy is so fascinating to a man of wealth. . . . Herein lies the great vicious self-deception of their social system. They pursue such a course with their slaves, and render it manifestly true that the mass of their Blacks are wholly incompetent to direct the business of their own lives—then they point us to their slaves and say with an air of triumph, "These people are infinitely better off here than in freedom, we are religiously bound to take care of them."[29]

Garfield did not have much time to make further observations. He did not even make it to the end of the court-martial—the illness he had started to suffer at Corinth came back with a vengeance in Alabama. Headaches, fevers, awful nausea, and bowel issues hit hard; Garfield's skin and eyes turned jaundice-yellow; dozens of pounds dropped off him in a matter of weeks.[30]

He tried to make light of his symptoms, but soon could joke about the matter no longer: toward the end of the month, Garfield had to be carried into court on a stretcher. Sick leave was duly granted him on July 30. It arrived at a miraculously convenient time; Rhodes wrote a letter the very next day pleading for Garfield to demonstrate at least some public interest in the House race back home:

> James, I have no doubt that you will be nominated if you consent to run . . . You must decide *immediately*.[31]

The last half of August found the sickly general in a farmer's cabin on a quiet nook of the Western Reserve. His wife and daughter joined him, and for the first time in nearly a year (and in a sense far longer) they finally spent quality time together. Trot had crept deeper into his affections during their time apart—though she was now mistaking other men's portraits for his. Crete's letters back, infrequent and sometimes resigned in tone, left even more to be desired.[32]

In the cabin, though, these wounds healed alongside Garfield's physical ones. The yellow faded from his skin; he put back on some of the forty-three pounds he had lost during the previous month; family reconciled. "I know now . . . our love is perfect, and all is peace," Crete would write Garfield after the vacation. "I trust in you most entirely." He felt much the same. "Everything conspired to make the visit dear to me," Garfield was to reply.[33]

It was an apt choice of words; the cabin had been picked by Harmon Austin, and it happened to be within an hour's ride of the Republican nominating convention, which happened to coincide with the general's vacation. In a similar burst of good fortune, a flurry of fawning local press kicked up around Garfield while he recuperated. Some stories mentioned citizens wanted him to take up another job:

The name of Gen. Garfield is prominently named among voters . . . as a candidate for Representative in the 38th Congress. Without in any way making any invidious distinction . . . we can say that Gen. Garfield has shown qualities both in civil and military life, which prove him possessed of the requisites for a successful and valuable public man.[34]

Garfield pretended not to notice the attention. Another Republican delegate wrote to the cabin asking if he intended to accept the House seat. Garfield's reply signaled a half-baked idea of working as both military commander and congressman for a while. Then, in reflexive self-correction, he deployed a familiar smokescreen:

I take this occasion today that my proposed nomination is not of my own seeking. I should consent to accept if only . . . its being the spontaneous wish of my fellow citizens.[35]

Garfield wrote his mother on September 2. "They are holding the congressional convention for this district today at Garrettsville," he mentioned in an off-handed manner. "I have done nothing about it and I really don't much care about it." He supposed, happily, that he was the only contender not attending the convention.[36]

Of course, even from miles off, he towered over the proceedings. The delegates could not so much as open their papers without reading an editorial instructing them to pick the man "who could run a steamboat by night and whip rebels by day."[37]

Congratulations poured upon Garfield's cabin that afternoon. "It was a spontaneous act of the people," he would crow about the nomination to one well-wisher.[38]

10

"Who should study to prefer a peace
If holy churchmen take delight in broils?"

—Shakespeare's *Henry VI, Part I, as quoted in*
Garfield diary entry for May 13, 1878

Garfield hardly had a week to celebrate before receiving orders from the
secretary of War to report to Washington. With the Republican nomination in hand, his election as the Reserve's House representative for the
next Congress was practically assured. But he was also still a general, for
now, and as such he remained a cog in the Union war machine, yoked to
bigger gears. "I have no idea what post is to be assigned me," Garfield
wrote Burke Hinsdale before his departure for Washington. He strolled
with Crete at the train depot until the whistle blew, gave a goodbye kiss
to Trot, and then was flying off alone to the mid-Atlantic.[1]

His first glimpse of the capital would not have been a cheerful one.
Washington was, by late 1862, nearer to a gargantuan military encamp-
ment than a city. Thousands of dirty troops loitered the District with
nowhere to go, no offensive to join. "They drop down anywhere," wrote
Walt Whitman, "on the steps of houses, up close by the basements or
fences, on the sidewalk . . . and on them as they lay, sulkily drips the rain."

Shadow-blues and mud-browns anchored Washington's wartime color palette—even the drinking water looked like cloudy ale. Passing flickers of officer's lace broke up the monotony, as did the white stonework of a renovating Capitol building and an unfinished Washington monument.[2]

Garfield would spend this trip mostly above the muck, in the refined company of cabinet members. He had a burgeoning reputation as a prodigy of American public life to thank for this: recently the youngest general in the U.S. army, at thirty-one Garfield was now slated to become the youngest member of Congress. Secretary of War Edwin Stanton wanted to take Garfield's measure, while an old acquaintance—now–Secretary of the Treasury Salmon Chase—seemed awfully interested in reconnecting. The two received Garfield swiftly after his arrival and struck their guest as a mismatched pair of power brokers: Stanton, dark-bearded, "slightly inclined to corpulence"; Chase, six-foot-two and virtually hairless beyond a pair of luxuriant eyebrows. Meeting their gazes exposed deeper differences in nature. The secretary of War studied people with a hypercritical, bulldoggish glare; Chase, however, had aquiline eyes that always seemed to be scanning for higher places to roost.[3]

A more iconic profile rounded out Garfield's welcome: Abraham Lincoln. "I soon saw the Secretary of War and the President," Garfield wrote home. "They told me to rest a few days and . . . if there were any field I would prefer, they would give it to me if they could."[4]

The Treasury secretary proved even more accommodating. Garfield had barely settled into a shabby hotel before Chase basically kicked in the door to whisk him away. "Mr. Chase and his daughter Kate have insisted that I shall stay with them while I remain in Washington," Garfield scribbled to Crete on September 27. "I have a delightful room and am much better pleased." His contentment only grew over the following weeks, as Secretary Chase dueled Garfield in late-night chess games and escorted him to the District's most exclusive parties.[5]

Between such excursions, Garfield examined the national leadership up close. The verdicts he had reached from the front lines were confirmed;

the Union's war was being waged idly, by generals either too risk-averse or ambivalent about the rebellion to fight it forcefully. "A command in the Army is a sort of tyranny," Garfield had theorized in Tennessee, "and in a narrow mind engenders a despotic spirit which makes him sympathize with slavery and slaveholders."[6]

Now, Garfield only needed to peep over the Potomac to see further reason to distrust northern commanders: George McClellan had apparently just enabled a Union defeat at the Second Battle of Bull Run by refusing to support General John Pope. It was enough for Garfield to draft a brief eulogy for the Union: "Died of West Point." He expressed bafflement that Lincoln could tolerate such incompetence:

> I think we are passing through a most fearful time, and the most fearful aspect by far is the painful weakness and uncertainty of the Administration.[7]

Garfield's host applauded him for catching on so quickly. Secretary Chase's pursuit of the Republican nomination in 1860 had ended (like myriad White House bids) with his appropriation by the winner to reconcile a wing of their shared party. Ever since, he had been the Lincoln cabinet's most errant member, led astray by stubborn personal opinions, as well as visions of his own future administration.

Secretary Chase generously shared his discontent with his guest. He said Lincoln's cabinet was a farce, that "it is a misnomer to call it a Cabinet" at all. Chase invited Stanton over and together the two department heads despaired before Garfield at not being "allowed to use bold and vigorous measures" in fighting the rebellion. A Chase administration, for example, would have already had General McClellan shot dead for ineptitude.[8]

Compliments broke up Chase's complaints. "I would rather have you for Secretary of War than any other man I know," he told Garfield. One morning, the general opened a paper and was surprised to read a glowing profile of himself in it. The Treasury secretary smilingly admitted to arranging the piece.[9]

Such treatment worked wonders. "Chase is, I believe, by far the strongest man in the Administration," Garfield decided, "and he seems to be thoroughly imbued with a moral and religious sense of the duties of the government in relation to the war." The Treasury secretary recorded a mutual feeling of admiration toward Garfield in his diary:

> This fine officer was a laborer on a canal in his younger days . . . A large part of his regiment, he said, was composed of students from his college.[10]

Alongside Chase's sweet talk and gossip, Garfield also absorbed a new field of study from him. Though the secretary had known virtually nothing about monetary and financial policy before joining Lincoln's cabinet, this had not stopped him from revolutionizing both fields in the year and a half since. From atop the Treasury department, Chase had presided over a historic growth of the federal debt, the creation of a national bank system, the implementation of a protective tariff, and the flooding of the Republic with a new, fiat money intended to finance the northern war effort. Gold-backed dollars remained most Americans' currency of choice, but citizens were obliged to accept Chase's so-called greenbacks for transactions, too. Market rates reflected how bitter such medicine tasted—within months, three gold dollars could be exchanged for four paper ones. Chase framed his invention as a necessary evil, but his reluctance did not go so far as to stop him from printing his face on the notes. "The engravers thought me rather good-looking," the secretary supposedly pleaded.[11]

Personal time with Chase therefore exposed Garfield to a new and engrossingly complex universe of public policy. It promised to be not only interesting but useful; Garfield sensed expertise in financial legislation would be vital to navigating the nation's peacetime order, whatever that looked like:

I think, if we ever survive the shock of war, the great currency question will be revived with new interesting features resulting from our huge national debt which now amounts to seven hundred millions and will be nearly doubled before the war closes.[12]

He further foresaw that this terrible war would need to be followed by a generation of hard choices and "great cheapness."[13]

The House offered Garfield more colorful topics (and people) for study. While Chase wrangled with dollars and cents in the executive branch, others of his breed of Republican—the Radical Republicans—agitated Democrats, the administration, and one another alike in Congress. This came fairly naturally; Radicals were the most progressive wing of the country's most progressive party, and in the tradition of such movements often had the organizational discipline of a herd of cats. Simultaneously, though, their shared vision of how to prosecute the war had been unyielding from its onset. "Free every slave—slay every traitor—burn every rebel mansion, if these things be necessary to preserve this temple of freedom," one summarized.[14]

Yet mere preservation of the Union was not really the goal. Across many unguarded moments, Radicals admitted their objective was instead to revolutionize the Republic—or, at least, reform it into true compliance with its founding ideals. By the Lincoln administration, as moderate Republicans warmed to abolishing slavery, Radicals were already arguing for full racial equality. Replies pleading for pragmatism fell on deaf ears. "The radical men are the men of principle," one Radical loftily boasted. "They are not your slippery politicians . . . the liberation of mankind or the welfare of the people, are not to be detached by your higgling."

"Conservatives and traitors are buried together," another replied to appeals for moderation.[15]

This was the caucus Garfield could look forward to joining in the next Congress—and within which he could, hopefully, serve as fresh blood.

A glimpse at the Radicals' House leader suggested that this was sorely needed; dragging a clubbed foot around the Capitol, his face "dented with processes of thought acting on experience," Thaddeus Stevens was a melted candle of a man. The nation's oldest congressman and its most sarcastic (a truly withering statesman), he dropped insults on Democrats and moderate Republicans like stones on flightless birds. Those complaining of Stevens's meanness, his place in the pockets of the railroad industry, or his gambling won no apologies. "Congress is composed of men, not angels," the Radical chieftain liked to say.[16]

Yet ideological purity clung to him like a halo. As a young man, Stevens had used his savings to buy a slave's freedom instead of lawbooks for himself. When abolitionist women begged the "Great Commoner" for a lock of hair, he would—in an abundance of generosity—fling his whole toupee their way.[17]

And of course, like all Radicals, Stevens lamented this president's reluctance to focus the war against the institutions and people responsible for starting it. He wrote out his disappointment right before Garfield reached the District:

> Whether we shall find *anybody* with sufficient grasp of mind, and sufficient moral courage, to treat this as a radical revolution, and remodel our institutions, I doubt. It would involve the desolation of the South as well as emancipation . . . a re-peopling of half the Continent. This ought to be done but it startles most men.[18]

Thus, Stevens and Garfield had much in common as far as political views went. They also shared a sense of welcome astonishment in September—when the president issued a preliminary version of his Emancipation Proclamation.[19]

Lincoln drafted it in a language that Radicals habitually struggled to interpret—that of restraint—and borrowed logic that had heretofore been exploited only by certain generals and pieces of legislation: if slaves

were truly property rather than people, then surely the Union could confiscate them just as it might any other war matériel. Bypassing the shortcomings of preceding measures, the Emancipation Proclamation thereby
decisively declared every slave in Confederate territory to be, from January 1, 1863, "thenceforward and forever free."[20]

Critically, though, Lincoln kept his political balance—framing his
measure as strictly one of "military necessity." By freeing the Confederacy's slaves, he professed an intent to draw rebel armies' attentions to
their home front, rather than achieve a social agenda for the Union as a
whole. The Proclamation's fine print verified this: slavery would still be
permitted in border states and Union-occupied swaths of the South "as if
this proclamation were not issued."[21]

Garfield seemed to look past such nuance. "The President's heart is right;
God grant that he may have the strength to stand up to his convictions,"
he wrote Crete. By the New Year, Garfield was chafing to return to front
line duty, so that he could "help in carrying out" the Emancipation Proclamation.[22]

Off-handedly, he marveled "that a second-rate Illinois lawyer should
be the instrument through whom one of the sublimest works of any age
is accomplished."[23]

Garfield did not wait much longer before getting his wish. After what had
felt like a revoltingly protracted layover in Washington (three months) he
was finally ordered to report to Murfreesboro, Tennessee. This gave him
just enough time to momentarily flash through his family's orbit back at
Hiram.

The visit was sorely needed. The gratification Crete felt during their
cabin retreat had since drooped back into discontent. Garfield had left for
Washington without taking her, and having appreciated his presence, she
could hardly bear the thought of returning to lives apart. The depth of her
hurt embarrassed her. "I am sorry that I cannot be more patient, but it is
because I love you so well," she wrote her husband in December. "Indeed

you do not know how earnestly I long to be with you again—to be held close, so close to your big heart." Garfield's ill-considered descriptions of fine ladies he met in the District did not help things. Nor did Trot's pining for him. "Just now she is turning over the leaves of a book," Crete reported, ". . . and only this moment whispering 'papa come home.'"[24]

Garfield had, in reply, flitted between empathy and exasperation. "I cannot tell you how full of gratitude is my heart that your soul goes out so strongly towards me," he wrote from Washington. But this enthusiasm, too, faded as Crete continued longing for his company from afar. Near the end of his layover in the capital, Garfield could only again extend to his wife a vague hope "that we can live happily and joyfully together, and never so much as now."[25]

He doubled down on this while heading to Tennessee. "I most firmly believe that the days of our darkness have passed away," Garfield wrote Crete after leaving her side yet again. "Let us rejoice together and be glad in the new light of love and peace."[26]

And yet, he had enjoyed himself too much in Washington. Assuring Crete of his faith in their marriage, he had already violated its most sacred bond. His sin would lie dormant for now.[27]

11

"Defer no time; delays have dangerous ends."

—Shakespeare's *Henry VI, Part I*, as quoted in
Garfield diary entry for January 8, 1878

Evening fell on January 25, 1863, and Garfield was hunched in a wagon careening south on an icy road that shot ramrod-straight to Murfreesboro, Tennessee, as rebels swarmed down the nearby Nashville Pike. Fortunately, the brigadier reached terra firma unharmed except for a fresh coating of dust. On hand to welcome him was none other than his new superior officer—Major General William Rosecrans, commander of the Army of the Cumberland. Despite being sick, Rosecrans spent the next three days chattering to the newcomer like a hyper-caffeinated parrot. "We sat up till two o'clock, notwithstanding his illness and my frequent remonstrances that he should go to bed," Garfield wrote blearily on January 27. "We discussed a great range of questions of war, government, and religion. I find him [Rosecrans] a man of very decided and muscular thoughts."[1]

Here, at last, gleamed that species of army officer which Garfield thought so endangered in the stilted, medal-laden ranks churned out by West Point. Rosecrans's reputation was one of unhindered aggression; he had seized Murfreesboro after routing Braxton Bragg and now seemed poised to march into southeast Tennessee, itself a "back door to the Confederate heartland." Even the gory deaths of subordinates right next to Rosecrans could not break his focus from an engagement. "Never mind, brave men must die in battle; we must seek results," he had quipped on one such occasion.[2]

Even in camp, Rosecrans appeared incapable of sitting still. Seemingly always sifting through his pockets for a watch, he tended to pull out tangles of rosary beads and clinking crucifixes with it. Garfield was further intrigued to discover that Rosecrans was the rare Catholic who distinguished cursing from sinning. "Gentlemen, I sometimes *swear*, but I never *blaspheme!*" Rosecrans would explain to audiences confused by the discrepancy.[3]

Garfield also expressed surprise at how attached Rosecrans became to him. Their late-night chats had made an impression; though a few divisions were "fishing" for a new brigadier, Rosecrans asked Garfield to instead serve as his chief of staff. "I am almost alone in regard to counsel and assistance in my plans," Rosecrans explained. He only had himself to blame for this professed lonesomeness; his last chief of staff had been decapitated after the general ventured too close to the action—a loss that Rosecrans, splattered in brains, had promptly sanctified "as a Christlike sacrifice to help win the battle."[4]

Garfield's hesitation could therefore be understood. But his reservations did not concern his physical well-being. Garfield instead worried that being Rosecrans's aide would not let him sufficiently serve the Union cause. "If by his chief of staff, he does not mean merely a chief clerk, but an adviser, a kind of alter ego . . . I could do more service there than in any other [place] in the army," Garfield wrote in meditation. He gave equal consideration to a less noble facet of the dilemma: "Would the army and country think so?" Weighing these dual aspects of the offer (patriotic and political), Garfield fell back on a pecuniary turn of phrase. "By taking that position, I should make a large investment in General Rosecrans, and will it be wise to risk so much stock in that market?"[5]

As one might while evaluating an investment, Garfield turned to the secretary of the Treasury for advice. "I am considerably embarrassed by the proposition and hardly know what to say about it," he wrote Chase, while also expressing an admiration of Rosecrans's fighting spirit. ("He is sound to the bone on the great questions of the war.") The secretary replied that it would be smart for Garfield to stick by such a commander.[6]

So, Garfield accepted the job and relished the thought of being busy with meaningful work again. "I shall no doubt often regret that I am not in command of a division; but I shall nevertheless go to work thoroughly," he told Crete.[7]

Reporters touring Murfreesboro in spring 1863 tended to encounter a "tall, deep-chested, sinewy built man," perched behind a pigeonholed desk in Rosecrans's headquarters. His "expansive forehead" shone out at them, as did the blue-gray eyes beneath. Yet Garfield's warmth belied this intimidating appearance. He gave hearty handshakes to journalists while complimenting their writing, exuding a "distinguished personage" to all callers.[8]

One sight nevertheless dismayed him during this stint of camp life; around Murfreesboro, crowds of slaves freed by the Emancipation Proclamation were crowding under the protective skirt of the U.S. Army. Once there, however, they had nothing to do with their liberty but mill about, hungry and idle. "Thousands have been abandoned by their masters," Garfield wrote ruefully. "It is one of the saddest pictures I ever witnessed to see these only innocent people in the South should *per necessitatem* be the greatest sufferers."[9]

He and Rosecrans tried devising solutions but had few resources to spare. Worse yet, some fellow officers identified as "proslavery," while others who agreed with the necessity of crushing the institution still felt no compassion for the slaves themselves. Garfield was again reminded of the awful civic challenges that would come upon the Republic after its military ones ended. "The Negro question is becoming one of very great practical difficulty," he wrote with a telling choice of adjective.[10]

Rosecrans, a Unionist Democrat, likely spared less thought for these issues than his abolitionist chief of staff. But, characteristically, this did not stop Garfield from enjoying "Old Rosy's" company. They even attended mass together. "I can understand the Latin . . . I hope you are not alarmed by my becoming a Catholic," he gibed in a note to Eliza.[11]

The two generals also took walks together. On these strolls, gunfire sometimes rang in the distance, despite no combat being reported.[12]

Frustratingly, the sounds of battle got no closer during these months and it became apparent the nervous energy that once propelled Rosecrans was now dragging him into indecision. He focused his hyperactive attentions on reinforcing Murfreesboro rather than preparing any offensive campaign. Supplies requisitioned from Washington piled up in camp, making it resemble a "citadel." Rosecrans's abrasive style of talking to dissenters (whether below or above him in the command chain) made him the sourpuss king of this castle.[13]

By late spring, the administration had had enough; Rosecrans had rested in place for nearly half a year and, once an example of martial pluck, now stuck out as the army's laggard. His ongoing demands for resupply no longer won sympathy in Washington. "Everything has been done and is now being done for you that is possible," read one reply from the Department of War. "Your complaints are without reason. You cannot expect to have all the best arms." The president also reached the end of his rope, but those who had risen alongside Rosecrans in the ranks expressed less surprise at his sudden inactivity. "As a subordinate I found that I could not make him do as I wished," Ulysses Grant would reflect.[14]

Garfield, however, was taken off-guard. Having first categorized Rosecrans as an officer who "strikes forward into action with the utmost confidence," by June he realized he might have made a mistake "investing" in the general by becoming his aide. Worse yet, Rosecrans's hesitation appeared to be spreading around Murfreesboro:

Now I write to tell you that I have given up all hopes of either dying or fighting at present. . . . Just on the eve of our [rumored] movement there seemed to fall down upon the leading officers of this army as suddenly as a bolt from the blue a most determined and decided opinion that there ought to be no immediate or early advance. Officers who to my certain knowledge were restless and impatient . . . became suddenly conservative and cautious.[15]

Garfield's agitation with this eventually reached the point where he decided to try budging the Army of the Cumberland himself. A poll was conducted of its other senior officers about a movement in the middle of June; Garfield took charge of tabulating the results.[16]

Few of those he surveyed had high opinions of him. An impression had spread among the brigade commanders that Garfield epitomized everything wrong with the volunteer officers that cropped up in the army during this war. One peer thought a mere handshake with Garfield conveyed the message "vote early, vote right." "As I have said before," another would state in his memoirs, "Rosecrans had no idea of the use of cavalry, and Garfield . . . who became an 'Old Man of the Sea' on Rosecrans' shoulders, was everlastingly meddling."[17]

The poll Garfield ran validated the latter point. Fifteen staff officers were asked if they supported an advance to Chattanooga against Braxton Bragg's rebels; all fifteen said no. Garfield tallied these responses, then attached a postscript (several times longer than the actual results) entombing them in a landslide of data, intelligence, and editorialization explaining why he thought them wrong. "For these reasons," Garfield signed off, "I believe an immediate advance of all our available forces is advisable." It took him several days to draft this screed and, after handing it in, he claimed to honestly not know what the outcome would be. It did not seem to trouble him that his opinion had not been requested.[18]

Its effects became clear on June 24. Without much warning, the entire bulk of the Army of the Cumberland—tens of thousands of troops, horses, mules, cannon, and wagons—lurched up off the packed-dirt campgrounds of Murfreesboro. Garfield barely had time to write Crete before it moved out. "I send you love and a thousand kisses to Trot," he scribbled.[19]

Garfield's own departure was interrupted by the ferociously musta-chioed form of Major General Thomas Crittenden. "It is understood, sir, by the general officers of this army, that this movement is your work," Crittenden spat. "I wish you to understand that it is a rash and fatal move, for which you will be held responsible." This venom was impotent, though; the Army of the Cumberland lumbered southeast at one o'clock.[20]

It picked up astonishing speed. Rosecrans's force left Murfreesboro in a flurry of snaking thrusts made through driving summer rain, while Bragg responded to the advance as if he had assumed the Yankees would truly stay encamped forever; the Confederates retreated as Rosecrans's columns jabbed down from all directions. The only thing hindering the Army of the Cumberland from running the rebels down was the rain-softened ground, which gave way like wet sponge cake. "My clothes are as stiff with Tennessee mud as my fingers are with chill," an officer wrote. Such conditions gave Bragg barely enough time to get the bulk of his men to Chattanooga by early July. The bridges and railroads they hurried over were dynamited to ensure the northerners couldn't follow.[21]

This closed what went into history books as the Union's Tullahoma cam-paign, one "perfect in its conception, excellent in its general execution." The raw numbers support such a conclusion; despite adverse weather, Rosecrans had pushed the enemy lines back eighty miles in eleven days and captured nearly two thousand prisoners. Even southern newspapers somberly described the advance as masterful.[22]

Perhaps this would have won Rosecrans (and his chief of staff) more celebrity had it not occurred at almost the exact same time as two more glorious campaigns led by other major generals: Ulysses Grant seized Vicksburg, Mississippi, and all thirty thousand of the rebels occupying it on the fourth of July; meanwhile, up in Pennsylvania, George Meade turned back Robert E. Lee near a village named Gettysburg. These victories outshone anything else achieved not only that summer, but throughout the war. "Though the war was destined to continue for almost two more bloody years," a historian would write, "Gettysburg and Vicksburg proved to have been its crucial turning point."[23]

A key feature of these battles distinguished them from the Tullahoma campaign in the moment; whereas Grant and Meade had managed to put huge rebel armies out of commission, Rosecrans ultimately failed to apprehend Bragg's force. Officials in Washington held this against him. "Lee's army overthrown; Grant victorious," Secretary Stanton telegraphed Rosecrans almost mockingly. "You and your noble army now have a chance to give the finishing blow to the rebellion. Will you neglect the chance?"[24]

Rosecrans nevertheless shared what glory he had reaped, allocating much to one subordinate in particular. "All my staff merited warm approbation for ability, zeal, and devotion . . . but I am sure they will not consider it invidious if I especially mention Brigadier-General Garfield, ever active, prudent, and sagacious," he declared in an open letter.[25]

Little did Rosecrans suspect his chief of staff was composing another memo for a more private, powerful audience—Salmon Chase. "I have for a long time wanted to write you . . . to say some things confidentially on the movements in this department," Garfield opened confessionally to the secretary of the Treasury. Then he poured forth; the months-long delay in Murfreesboro had been spent "in idleness or trifling"; Rosecrans had "seemed blind to the advantages of the hour"; he, Garfield, had been the only one agitating for an advance against Bragg, but when movement at last came, rain made it impossible to catch the rebels. Garfield felt obliged to relieve himself of responsibility for the blown chance of vanquishing them:

I shall never cease to regret the sad delay which lost us so great an opportunity to inflict a mortal blow upon the center of the rebellion . . .
Officially I share his [Rosecrans] counsels and responsibilities even
more than I desire, but I beg you to know that this delay is against my
judgment and every wish.[26]

This letter was Garfield's way of selling off his "investment" in Rosecrans. Chase replied appreciatively and secretly kept the receipts.

In early September, the Army of the Cumberland at last reached the destination the administration had been cheering it on to—Chattanooga, a
city striated by both the Tennessee River and railway lines. A rebel loss
here would mean yielding the belly of the Confederacy to Union attack.
The Atlantic, Gulf of Mexico, and Ohio and Mississippi rivers were all a
day's train ride from Chattanooga. Garfield anticipated a fierce clash for
it. "We are all across the river and are closing in on the rebel army," he
wrote excitedly on its outskirts.[27]

One can only imagine his disappointment when Bragg again got
away on September 8. The rebel commander had heard from scouts that
the choice boiled down to either accepting siege or fleeing to fight another day. He chose the latter option—and, before executing it, gave some
of his scouts instructions to get captured.[28]

The bait almost worked. Rosecrans ventured hungrily over the Georgia
border on September 10, lured by reports from rebel deserters that Bragg
was in full flight. Soon Rosecrans's columns were winding into gulleys
crowded with cedar and short-leaf pine, blackberry brambles and honeysuckle. Also in these woods (and almost as lost) were Bragg's forces—but
whenever the rebels spotted the Yankees, they hesitated to shoot. Eventually the Unionists, like deer lined up for too long in a hunter's scope,
sensed something vaguely amiss.[29]

•   •   •

On September 19, after more than a week of building tension, the armies bumped together and began blasting each other to bits. At last, Rosecrans had his decisive battle, which would be named for the sluggish, rocky line of water that it ran across—Chickamauga.[30]

The clash hosted perhaps the most chaotic fighting yet seen in the Civil War. This owed as much to the confusing landscape as the bewildered participants; both sides could hardly see a thing through the thick undergrowth. Soldiers popped out into cathedral-size spaces buttressed by trees, only to discover (too late) that they now stood forty yards from enemy cannon. Similar scenes repeated throughout the many ravines, forests, and creeks crisscrossing this nebulous corner of the Georgia–Tennessee line. [31]

The fighting's muddled nature meant Rosecrans stayed in the thick of it, with Garfield at his side. Helping the general retain control over the scattered Army of the Cumberland taxed Garfield like nothing ever had before. It provided him a new personal standard to measure exhaustion by, which few things in Congress would ever beat.[32]

He could not complain about the workload, though. After all, the battle probably wouldn't have happened had he not first needled Rosecrans to leave Murfreesboro.

Rosecrans and his command staff spent the opening night of Chickamauga huddled in a widow's cabin. They hardly slept a wink—stress ate at them, as did the brisk winds whistling through the shack's floorboards. Every now and then Garfield would get up to comfort the owner's children. Come dawn, however, the tensest officer in the hut was its highest-ranking. Rosecrans looked even edgier than usual—his cigar jutted awkwardly out of a steel-tight jaw, through which he expressed regrets for fighting on a Sunday. He made the morning's mass extra long, as if in penance.[33]

Whatever blessing Rosecrans sought did not come about. At noon, a correspondent in his staff awoke to an "infernal" screaming of shells and the alarming sight of Rosecrans making the sign of the cross. Every other Union soldier in sight was scrambling madly in the direction of Chattanooga like stampeding cattle ("the whole road . . . filled with flying soldiers").[34]

The panic had been sparked by a remarkably miniscule error in the battle arrangement. Mistakenly perceiving a hole in his ranks (an impression Garfield may have neglected to correct) Rosecrans moved a division from his right flank to his left, thus accidentally creating a gap instead of plugging one. Confederate general James Longstreet marched his troops right into it, throwing the entire Yankee line into disarray.[35]

The stream of fleeing troops carried reporter Charles Dana to Chattanooga at four o'clock. There he was surprised to come across a shaken-looking Rosecrans. The general had beaten him to the city and seemed certain the Confederates were but moments away, too. It was enough for Dana to conclude that the battle had been worse for the Union than Bull Run. Garfield, however, was nowhere to be seen.[36]

Precisely why Garfield remained at Chickamauga while his commander left the field would never be agreed upon—the story changing in fact and implication based on the teller. One man would remember Garfield trotting into Chattanooga the next day, saying simply that he had been parted from Rosecrans in the chaotic retreat. But to a closer friend—Jacob Cox—Garfield elaborated: during the panic, Rosecrans and he had both heard exchanges of fire on the Union's left flank, indicating that organized fighting was still continuing. Unfortunately, Rosecrans seemed too dumbstruck to react to this development. "He rode silently along, abstracted, as if he neither saw nor heard," Garfield recounted to Cox. Embarrassed, the chief of staff volunteered to investigate the noise himself. Rosecrans gave his assent "listlessly and mechanically," and so Garfield rode off, following the sounds of gunfire.[37]

Rosecrans would recall things differently. He was to remember instructing Garfield to head for Chattanooga to rally U.S. forces against a Confederate attack upon the city, at which point Garfield had been the one to hesitate—overwhelmed by Rosecrans's many orders. The major general thus decided to switch assignments. Garfield would check on the left flank, while Rosecrans went to secure Chattanooga personally.[38]

Irrespective of which man future audiences would believe, the visuals in the moment universally damned one in particular. Fighting raged on at Chickamauga; Garfield galloped toward it as his commander trotted away.

Garfield's ride was spectacular. Bullets whizzed past him, as did the faces of rebel soldiers shocked to see a Union general galloping by. One of the orderlies escorting Garfield was killed, but the general kept following the rising noise of battle. His horse took a wound but loped on. "How I escaped death I do not know," Garfield would later write.[39]

His bravery was ultimately rewarded by the sight of General George Thomas's men holding off the rebel advance from a hilltop—the final bastion of resistance across the tattered remnants of the Union battle line. Garfield stayed with them through the night. At some point, he telegraphed to headquarters from this position that Thomas was "standing like a rock" against a flurry of Confederate attacks. Come dawn, the assault had ebbed, and Chattanooga was temporarily saved.[40]

Thomas and Garfield won terrific plaudits for their actions. The former's steadfast defiance of the rebel advance transformed him overnight into a military celebrity—the famous "Rock of Chickamauga," a title lifted from Garfield's telegraph. Meanwhile, Garfield's dash across the battlefield also reaped generous attention. "Gen. Garfield Runs the Gauntlet" blared headlines, in a phrase that one colonel borrowed in his official map of the action. ("The place where General Garfield ran the gauntlet," he wrote next to an "x.")

General Thomas Wood also incorporated Garfield's ride in his summary of the fighting—albeit as a club to knock the conduct of their commander:

> After the disastrous rout . . . General Garfield made his way back to the battle-field (showing thereby that the road was open to all who might choose to follow) and came to where my command was engaged.[41]

Criticisms from Washington were less circumspect. Rosecrans's rumored behavior at Chickamauga appeared to exemplify everything that had gone wrong with the Army of the Cumberland as a whole. The president was overheard saying that Rosecrans had acted "like a duck hit on the head." Edwin Stanton snidely marveled at the velocity and distance of the general's flight from the battlefield.[42]

But perhaps the cabinet verdict on what to do about Rosecrans was settled by Salmon Chase. The secretary of the Treasury unfurled and read aloud to Lincoln a lengthy, withering letter detailing Rosecrans's hesitations in camp ahead of the Tullahoma campaign. Chase (prone to thespian tendencies) ended the reading with a flourish: "That letter was written by Rosecrans' professed friend . . . James A. Garfield."[43]

October's end found Garfield heading north out of Chattanooga, carrying with him official accounts of the Battle of Chickamauga to present in Washington, as well as a gracious farewell bulletin from Rosecrans:

> Brig. Gen. J. A. Garfield has been chosen by his fellow citizens to represent them in the councils of the nation. His high intelligence, spotless integrity, business capacity and thorough acquaintance with the wants of the army, will render his services, if possible, more valuable to the country in Congress, than with us.[44]

Despite these kind words, Garfield endured a brutal examination by the secretary of War on a layover and sheepishly confirmed to Stanton that Rosecrans had fled Chickamauga in a daze. Once Garfield got to Washington, he discovered he had been promoted to major general. Briefly he juggled the idea of continuing to serve in uniform:

> I laid the matter before Lincoln, Stanton, and Chase, and they all said that . . . they would not dare risk a [Congressional] vacancy nor did they feel it would be safe to lose my military experience from the next House.[45]

Thus practically begged to leave the army (by the highest advisers imaginable), Garfield resigned his commission. It was a smooth transition back to political life; he had barely removed his army coat before appearing next to Secretary Chase at a rally in Baltimore.[46]

An attendee heard Garfield tell the crowds why he had accepted an army commission in the first place:

> For the last two years he had felt it was time to work, and he had endeavored to perform his share of the labor.[47]

During those two years, family had served as little more than a fleeting, faraway distraction for Garfield. In December 1863, though, it turned into a wellspring of awful grief; he and Crete hardly had time to celebrate their reunion and the arrival of another child—an almost box-headed boy named Harry—before their first fell deathly ill with diphtheria. A bedside vigil commenced.

"I will write you again," Garfield told Harmon Austin on December 1, "when the light of our home goes out." When it did at seven o'clock that evening, he barely stuck around long enough to attend Trot's burial. Then Garfield was Washington-bound—so tangled in grief that Crete feared he might never come back to Ohio.[48]

He managed to keep it together for a political speech before departing the Reserve. An audience member was impressed:

So cheerful . . . so eloquent . . . only fifteen years ago he was a boat driver.[49]

But this veneer cracked in Washington; meeting Secretary Stanton's children, Garfield was tearfully reminded of his departed daughter. He attempted an old cure. "I try to be cheerful and plunge into the whirlpool of work which opens before me," he wrote a friend.[50]

12

"I never did repent for doing good
Nor shall I now."

—Shakespeare's *The Merchant of Venice*, as quoted in
Garfield diary entry for September 18, 1878

The day after Trot died, hundreds of Garfield's soon-to-be colleagues huddled before a renovated Capitol. The building's curved rafters would no longer jut into the sky like an exposed ribcage: its years of repairs finally ended at noon, when a colossal "Statue of Freedom" was loudly bolted to the apex; a hundred cannon blasted in patriotic salute; sarcastic cheers echoed from nearby jailhouses. Heedless, the stooped forms of senators and congressmen shuffled off to get back to work.[1]

The U.S. Capitol was at last fixed, but, in contrast, the figurative edifice of the Confederacy had obviously, irreversibly cracked. The past year had been filled with bloody catastrophe for rebel armies. Officials in Richmond now assumed the strategy of a weary boxer—hoping to just endure enough battlefield beatings until the Yankees finally tired of fighting ("If we can only *subsist* . . . we may have peace").[2]

From the North, though, it looked as if the rebellion might stove in at any moment, and so the Union's leaders had commenced discussing how to cobble the states together again. The president wanted to approach this task with the utmost magnanimity: amnesty, Lincoln thought, should be granted to nearly any rebel who had had their fill of treason, so long as they swore a new oath to the Constitution. Similar generosity must be extended to southern voters: if just 10 percent of any rebellious state's voters made a loyalty vow, Lincoln believed their new government could be put on track to rejoin the Union.[3]

At the same time, his charity had limits. High-ranking Confederates could not be forgiven so easily, and it must also be left to Congress as to whether southerners could assume any legislative seats they were elected to. Furthermore, the South would need to accept that slavery was over. "I shall not attempt to retract or modify the emancipation proclamation; nor shall I return to slavery any person who is free by the terms of that proclamation," Lincoln decreed. Those conditions out of the way, he moved to test his vision of Reconstruction on Louisiana.[4]

Witnesses marveled at the president's liberality. "It was impossible to discover in Mr. Lincoln a single sentiment, I shall not say of revenge, but even of bitterness in regard to the vanquished," wrote an observer. "The policy of pardon and forgiveness . . . appeared to his mind an absolute necessity." Yet the faint notes of radicalism in Lincoln's plan also indicated to some that the president possessed exceptional executive tact:

> The art of riding two horses is not confined to the circus . . . [Lincoln] has for some time been riding two political horses, and with the skill of an old campaigner, he whips them—the radical horse "a leetle ahead."[5]

Yet many Radicals (unhappy with being only "a leetle ahead") fretted that the president's heart was again interfering with better judgment. A 10 percent threshold certainly seemed to be a low passing grade for southern loyalty. "The idea that the loyal citizens, though few, *are the State* . . . I have not been able to comprehend," Thaddeus Stevens protested. Other Radicals did not share Lincoln's faith that the wartime legality of the

Emancipation Proclamation would hold up in peacetime. "I think it safer to *make it law*," one declared.[6]

They sketched up alternative blueprints for reunification, of which one plan—as outlined by a piece of legislation called the Wade–Davis Bill—gathered the most momentum. If passed into law, Wade–Davis would require a full 50 percent of a state's legal voters to swear loyalty to the Union before it could rejoin. It also altered the phrasing of the oath in question; Southerners taking the vow would need to swear they had never fought (nor helped others fight) the Union.

A bemused President Lincoln reviewed this so-called "ironclad" oath of the Wade–Davis Bill and *tisk-tisk*ed. He and his party's progressive wing obviously read from different parts of the Bible:

> On principle, I dislike an oath which requires a man to swear he *has* not done wrong. It rejects the Christian principle of forgiveness . . . I think it is enough if the man does no wrong hereafter.[7]

Thus, the deck for the Thirty-Eighth Congress was stacked for all sorts of brawls. The field for deciding them would be the House of Representatives, wherein Radical power was concentrated. It made for a gloomy arena: hundreds of congressmen hunched behind oak desks in a space lit by the flickering of a thousand lamps.[8]

Yet the mood of the chamber brightened noticeably that December. Day in and day out, its viewing gallery audibly giggled at the same sight: a tall, "rather boyish" looking freshman ambling up the aisles, his arms threaded around the tubbier waists of older legislators. James Garfield never seemed to notice his exhibits of friendship amusing hundreds at a time that winter.[9]

He had no cause to mind the laughs, anyway. Within a day of reaching Congress, Garfield had won friends in high places and begun clearing out a spot for himself, too. He voted Schuyler ("Smiler") Colfax in as speaker, then had his military laurels swapped for legislative ones; Garfield was invited to a select council to organize the House, then joined the Military Affairs Committee, a premier council in wartime. He began playing second fiddle to its chair, Robert Schenck, and soon the two decided to rent a home together.[10]

It was a mutually advantageous friendship, if an odd-looking one: Garfield's vim and youth were offset by his roommate's lack of either quality. "Crippled, grim old Schenck," was how one writer described the chairman, and it was an apt portrait. Portly and slow, Schenck carried a right arm that had been paralyzed by shrapnel at Bull Run. He liked using his remaining hand not so much for work as stacking poker chips, and, in fact, was already on his way to becoming an international authority on five-card draw. His book on the subject would open with a biblically wry (and resoundingly Republican) pearl of wisdom:

Put not your trust in Kings and Princes: Three of a kind will take them both.[11]

Schenck's hobby did not lend itself to legislative attentiveness. Fortunately, Garfield proved happy to take up whatever committee duties were distracting his housemate from the card table, and therefore got to do as much lawmaking as a freshman representative could dream of. A week after arriving in the House, Garfield was staying up late drafting the Union's new conscription law himself.[12]

He also got opportunities to excuse Schenck's absences from the House. Once Garfield blamed illness. On another occasion, he confessed the military affairs chair was preoccupied with a meal of "bivalves and other shellfish." It being Good Friday, the joke was funny enough to make the *Congressional Globe*.[13]

Garfield quietly needed the laughter. Grief over Trot's death still chafed under the surface, even as he tried to distract himself with work. "I count the days back when our precious little Trot was with us . . . But they sweep on like the rush of a river," he mourned in a note to Crete in December.[14]

Crete reported, as if in reminder, that their newest child, Harry, was sprouting baby teeth. "I am more than anxious to live with him enough to feel that he is a part of my life," Garfield promised.[15]

More than a few representatives proved immune to Garfield's charms. Perhaps inevitably, the House's eldest and prickliest member did not get along with its youngest and most jovial. Garfield tried to make light of this: "Old Thad[deus Stevens] is stubborn and quite foolishly mad because he can't lead this House by the nose as has been his custom hitherto."[16]

Dislike from Democrats bothered him even less. Garfield's pedanticism on the floor gave them a nickname for him: "The learned gentleman from Ohio." He demonstrated a capacity for fiercer rhetoric, though. When Representative Alexander Long invoked the whole House's fury by declaring his support for recognizing the Confederacy, Garfield dressed him down in a sermon-like speech that airily likened Long to Benedict Arnold. Radical editorials praised Garfield for being as effective "fighting traitors in the House as the rebels on the front."[17]

He spent the war's remainder doing so with an enthusiasm that jarred enemies, colleagues—and, eventually, biographers—alike. To be sure, Garfield stayed "smooth, ready, pleasant" outside the Capitol. But those who encountered him on the House floor might have assumed the spirit of John Brown had passed on to another Western Reservist. One Democrat labeled Garfield "as wild a radical as ever sat in Congress."[18]

He provided good fodder for such stories—telling the House on one occasion that rebel leaders could not be allowed to inhabit the nation they had betrayed. The rebuilt Union needed to exile such men, "as God and his angels drove Satan and his host from heaven." Nor could their offspring be allowed to inherit their earthly holdings:

Landed estates, Mr. Speaker, are inseparably connected with the peculiar institution . . . if we want a lasting peace . . . we must take away
the platform on which slavery stands—the great landed estates of
the armed rebels of the South. Strike that platform from beneath its
feet . . . and divide it into homes for men who had saved our country.[19]

Counterpoints about the cruelty of punishing Southern sons for
their fathers' sins did not slow Garfield one iota. Nor did he spare much
thought for trifling issues of legality:

What is the Constitution that these gentlemen are perpetually fling-
ing in our faces whenever we desire to strike hard blows against the
rebellion? It is the production of the American people. They made it,
and the creator is mightier than the creature.[20]

This aligned with his caucus's opinions on that founding document.
As one cabinet officer grumbled, Radicals tended to be "humanitarians
and not constitutionalists." In further compliance with this stereotype,
Garfield expressed a fealty to higher law regarding the cause closest to
Radical hearts:

Mr. Speaker, it has long been my settled conviction that it was a part
of the Divine purpose to keep us under the pressure and grief of this
war until the conscience of the nation should be aroused to the enormity of its great crime against the Black man, and full reparation
should be made.

We entered the struggle, a large majority insisting that slavery
should be let alone, with a defiance almost blasphemous. . . . Slowly,
and at a frightful cost of precious lives, the nation has yielded its
wicked and stubborn prejudices against him . . . Like the sins of mankind against God, the sin of slavery is so great that "without the shedding of blood there is no remission." Shall we not secure the favor of
Heaven by putting it away completely?[21]

No doubt Garfield's vexation on the subject was heartfelt. He was greatly troubled to find that he was (at first) the only Military Affairs Committee member to favor immediately equalizing the pay of Black soldiers with white ones. When he eventually fell behind a plan for a sliding scale, Garfield defensively flourished his Radical credentials. "I have never been anything else than radical on all these questions of Freedom or Slavery, rebellion and the war," he insisted to a friend. "I have had neither inclination nor motive to be otherwise."[22]

At the same time, the twin features of his political persona were oscillating, like prongs on a struck tuning fork. Behind closed doors he laughed too agreeably at other congressmen's jokes; on the House floor, he seemed too willing to be a disruptive iconoclast—his waywardness sometimes carrying him into Democrats' traps. Representative Long, for example, pounced when Garfield dismissed the Constitution as an insignificant hurdle to the Radical agenda.[23]

Eventually, after one particularly defiant floor episode, the secretary of the Treasury took Garfield aside. "I was very proud of your vote the other day," Chase told his mentee, "but I want you to bear in mind that it is a very risky thing to vote against your whole Party."[24]

Garfield received a stronger reminder of this upon returning to the Reserve for reelection in summer 1864. "There is a little white squall ahead of me," he wrote. This was an understatement; in fact, Garfield's renomination by local Republicans seemed in jeopardy.[25]

The gust had blown off a larger storm whipped up between Radicals and the president on the national stage. The former's Wade–Davis Bill had squeaked past both houses of Congress, but upon receiving it Lincoln simply pigeonholed the offensive legislation until the congressional session expired—a pioneering use of the "pocket-veto." Radicals seethed at their hopes for Reconstruction being thus thwarted. The measure's authors decided the president's offense merited public redress. They penned a manifesto accusing Lincoln of "executive usurpation," then published it in the *New York Tribune*.[26]

Upon getting back to the Reserve, Garfield was surprised to hear many constituents believed he was the secret writer of the hyperaggressive manifesto in the *Tribune*. Garfield stiffened—less at the nonsense rumor than the realization that some of his voters were "that breed of cattle . . . so devoted to Mr. Lincoln as to be blind to his faults."[27]

He was determined to correct this, even if it cost him reelection. On the day the Reserve's Republicans met to nominate their House candidate, Garfield was asked if he had indeed written the anti-Lincoln screed in the *Tribune*. He gave a "short, emphatic, and decisive" rebuttal to the assembly. No, he had not authored the thing—but, yes, he agreed with its contents. Garfield also promised to criticize Lincoln or any other president in future, if his conscience demanded it; if that didn't sit well with the delegates then they should not send him back to Congress. Garfield then "strode haughtily out of the hall"—hearing behind him a roar erupt from the audience.

The cries were not of outrage, but for his renomination; Garfield's outburst had impressed rather than aggravated his constituents. He would be returning to Washington for his second House term—having both demonstrated his "independence" and, perhaps, learned the peril of using it too freely.[28]

Ohio's governor could hardly believe that a politician could survive lecturing their voters like that. He said any electorate "that would allow a young fellow like Garfield to tweak its nose . . . in that manner deserved to have him saddled on it for the rest of his life."[29]

Garfield could not have missed the irony of Salmon Chase, of all people, advising him to avoid causing party trouble. After all, Chase had already launched a palace coup. "I think a man of different qualities from those the President has will be needed for the next four years," the secretary had written in November 1863. Alas, everyone knew whom he had in mind, and so the secretary of the Treasury's latest run at the presidency stumbled. Leading moderates accused him of financial misconduct. Even sympathetic citizens failed to fall into line behind the secretary's candidacy.[30]

The rest of the cabinet chuckled about Chase's ambitions. "There never was a man who found it so easy to delude himself," they said. The mirth ran to the top of the administration. "[Lincoln] seems much amused at Chase's mad hunt for the Presidency," John Hay wrote. "He laughed on & said he was sorry the thing had begun."[31]

It took a while for Garfield to agree that Chase was fooling himself. He continued serving for some time as a loyal friend: Garfield fought those "most shameful" House charges against the secretary's "good name," even leading an investigative panel that dispelled them. He also accepted a spot on Chase's presidential campaign committee.[32]

Yet Garfield could not forever ignore political reality or the country's lack of interest in a Chase administration. "It seems clear to me that the people desire the re-election of Mr. Lincoln," he confessed in February 1864. Republican unity suddenly appeared more important than Radical command of the party. Soon Garfield had the depressing privilege of returning his mentor's advice—advising the secretary of the Treasury to withdraw from a futile campaign that "could only distract the Party."[33]

Yet Chase's bid continued, and Garfield watched on with macabre fascination. The secretary's evident obsession with the White House marked the first case of what his mentee now christened "Presidential fever." Garfield would later say Chase's contraction of this illness was the "great mistake of his life and from it resulted almost all the blunders of his life." Its symptoms horrified Garfield: infecting prominent statesmen like Chase, it plagued them with dreams of obtaining the presidency— distracting dreams that led nowhere, only atrophying the sufferer's ability to make useful policy until they were a spent force.[34]

The president had reached a similar diagnosis; Secretary Chase was obviously suffering from "mild insanity" about winning the White House. Lincoln soon put him out of his misery. Chase submitted a resignation in protest of a patronage dispute, only to be shocked when the president accepted it.[35]

●   ●   ●

Adjusting his political bearings in mid-1864, Garfield also decided to set his personal life straight. Letters had revealed his family was still glaringly absent one member (i.e., himself) and at risk of being so permanently. "He [Harry] loves to be petted," one note from Crete told Garfield of their son. "He is getting to know your picture," she assured. "He would soon learn to love you were you with him."[36]

But Garfield had to unburden himself of something first. A recent rumor circulating among friends that he had labeled "wickedly and maliciously false" (a denial Crete believed) was, in fact, true. He went to Hiram in June and confessed to having had an affair with a New York widow in Washington in 1862.[37]

The correspondence between Garfield and Crete in this revelation's aftermath are but the tumbling scraps of an immense emotional fallout. Garfield found solace in self-pity. "I still believe I am worthy to be loved after all the books are balanced," he wrote while traveling back east. "I believe after all I had rather be respected than loved if I can't be both. . . . I can't be the latter without the former." Crete, for her part, now appeared ready to comply with her husband's evident wishes to be left alone for good:

> I pledge you anew my heart and my hand to aid you in carrying out any arrangement which shall help you most in the work you will try to do.[38]

Yet somehow, within days, her stubborn love for him started to rise again out of the ashes. "'Love you': of that be the surest of anything in the world," Crete wrote Garfield. His reply grasped eagerly for forgiveness: "More than ever I am glad to read your good sensible loving words, which put my own silly weaknesses to the blush."[39]

A reminder of all they had endured together came the next month, on what would have been Trot's fourth birthday. Her parents spent it apart but wishing they had not. Come September, Garfield was begging Crete to "rest your whole weight upon my love—which I assure you is no longer a weak or bruised reed."[40]

She tested it during election season. Back on the Reserve to campaign, Garfield felt her slip a note into his hand. On it was some math Crete had performed—calculations comparing how long they had been married versus together in person. The disparity glared off the paper: the Garfields had been married for nearly five years, but been in one another's presence only twenty weeks.

As Garfield later remembered of this moment:

> I then resolved that I would never again go to Washington to a session of Congress without taking her.

To another journalist, he seemed to wonder that Crete had put up with his many shortcomings for so long. "I have been wonderfully blessed in the discretion of my wife," the congressman would boast. "She is unstampedable."[41]

Garfield was back in the legislative swing of things the next January. "Mr. Speaker," he said to a packed House, "we shall never know why slavery dies so hard in this Republic and in this Hall till we know why sin has such longevity and Satan is immortal."[42]

Luckily, Garfield's histrionics did not jeopardize the measure at stake; on January 31, 1865, a Constitutional amendment to outlaw slavery passed the House by the combined votes of Radicals, moderates, and a handful of Democrats. Immediately following the House's vote, euphoric scenes broke out in the streets outside the Capitol. Charles Douglass detailed them in a note for his father, Frederick: "I wish that you could have been here . . . such rejoicing I never before witnessed, cannons firing, people hugging and shaking hands, white people I mean, flags flying over the city . . . I tell you things are progressing finely."[43]

Garfield also felt ecstatic. He had cast a vote in favor of the amendment, and afterward extolled its passage as the death of American slavery. "I wish you could have been here," he wrote Burke Hinsdale. Garfield was thrilled not only by the history made but the immediate future it necessitated—the president's rumored negotiations for a Confederate surrender were now certain to fold, meaning the rebellion would likely end in a bloody, decisive clash. "The peace bubble has burst," Garfield crowed happily.[44]

It did not occur to him that this might have been the outcome that the president was fishing for all along.[45]

Garfield's opinion of Lincoln changed almost instantly on the morning of April 15, 1865. The prior night the congressman had traveled up the Atlantic for a business trip. As Garfield's train rattled north, curtains had lifted back in Washington on a performance of *Our American Cousin* in Ford's Theatre. He reached Manhattan near midnight, then awoke the next day to shuttered businesses, deserted avenues, and news of the president's murder.

Ambling around New York, the man destined to be America's second assassinated president ruminated on the tragedy that had befallen the first. He made an uncharacteristic confession to his wife: "Could I have you and our precious boy in my arms I could almost let the world and its work go—without a thought or care for them."[46]

Come the fourth of July, however, Garfield was telling crowds of constituents in Ravenna that the nation's work was not yet done. Though hostilities had ended, the Civil War's terrible purpose had not been met by the country:

> In the great crisis of the war, God brought us face to face with the mighty truth, that we must lose our freedom or grant it to the slave. In the extremity of our distress, we called upon the Black man to help us save the Republic . . . we made a covenant with him, sealed both with

his blood and ours, and witnessed by Jehovah that, when the nation was redeemed, he should be free. . . .

What is freedom? . . . Is it the bare privilege of not being chained—of not being bought or sold, branded and scourged? If this is all, then freedom is a bitter mockery, a cruel delusion, and it may well be questioned whether slavery were not better."[47]

Such rhetoric flowed over the Reservists from a composite Garfield. He was their reverend, principal, general, and Congressman, at once and at only thirty-three. In Washington, men already spoke of him as "one of the readiest debaters and most impressive speakers in Congress."[48]

Now, under a blazing summer sun, he outlined a more ambitious goal for the entire country to tackle next. True equality of race needed to be enshrined across the United States. Garfield expressed dismay at the consequences of failure on this front:

The nations of the earth must not be allowed to point at us as pitiful examples of weak selfishness . . . our duty must be so done that the eternal scrolls of justice will ever bear record of the nobility of the nation's heart. Animated, inspired, generous, fearless, in the work of liberty and truth, long will the Republic live, a bulwark of God's immutable justice.[49]

Then—as if staggered by the colossal workload he had just assigned the nation—Garfield fainted. Friendly hands caught him before he hit the ground.[50]

Part III

THE HOUSE
1865–1880

13

"Now join your hands, and with your hands your hearts,
That no dissensions hinder government."

—Shakespeare's *Henry VI*, as quoted in Garfield

diary entry for October 4, 1878

On waking, Garfield blamed his collapse on sunstroke. Yet its cause could just as easily have been his fatigue after a long, sweltering summer of political turmoil, or his anxiety at what further strife awaited the new Congress. His nerves had not cooled by autumn. "No political struggle in this country has been so fierce as that which we shall see in the 39th Congress," Garfield said in September. "We are in imminent danger of losing half the value of the war by unwise management of the elements out of [which] the restored Republic is to be built." It was an apt, succinct description of things: disarray had flared up among the Union's leaders about what to do now that the Civil War had been won; the "elements" Garfield vaguely inclined his head toward were, indeed, badly jumbled.[1]

The biggest unsorted pile lay in a ruined American south. The last wisps of gun smoke blew off that region to reveal a territory depleted by its own war effort as well as northern campaigns on land and sea. Much of the southern industry that existed in antebellum was gone; the currency of the rebelling states had become worthless; their governments had been destroyed, with parts of their society regressing all the way to the barter system. Southern families now used thorns in place of pushpins, berry juice instead of ink. Many also missed their men. About a quarter of southern white military-aged males were dead.[2]

But the poorest in the land—poorer even than the lowliest whites— were its ex-slaves. Neither property anymore, nor yet equal citizens, they held a precarious place in the postwar South. Observers feared they would soon essentially slip into slavery again, "forced to submit to the harshest terms by their former masters."[3]

They wisely congregated in population centers where the U.S. Army had concentrated its troops. In the presence of these occupiers (some of whom shared their race) Black citizens felt more secure. The alternative was scary to consider; it was "legally and practically anarchy" throughout the rural South, filled as it was by some who had not yet given up the war, and more who resented its result.[4]

At the same time, the U.S Army's protective bubbles in the South were already collapsing. Its troops wanted to go home and had justification for doing so—the war being over, their enlistment terms met. Peace-keeping did not strike many as a good reason to postpone returning to regular life. "Going home is the uppermost in the soldier's mind," one private wrote his wife in May 1865. Thousands of Union soldiers swiftly deserted back north.[5]

That was fine with politicians in Washington already eager to trim the army (and, indeed, the federal government) to a fiscally responsible peacetime size. The nation's debt now stood at an intimidatingly novel and gigantic size—the billions—while a new protective tariff ringed its economic borders like a moat. Furthermore, many Americans regarded the currency used to fund the war as illegitimate, even though millions of these free-floating greenbacks still circulated freely throughout the country.[6]

This perilous tangle of affairs had only been made more so by the mer-curial man unexpectedly charged with fixing it. Andrew Johnson had coal-black eyes and a face uncreased by laugh lines, and acquaintances saw that behind these features smoldered a soul "destined to conflict." The rare Southern Democrat to stay loyal to the Union in the Civil War, Johnson spent the conflict breathing fire on his treasonous countrymen. "Show me the man who makes war on the government . . . and I will show you a traitor," then-Governor Johnson of Tennessee scrawled in a rage at the conflict's beginning. "If I were President . . . by the Eternal God I would hang them."[7]

Born dirt poor and made an indentured servant as a boy, Johnson had come through life with dents on him; maybe a weakness for drink, but certainly a tendency to delusions of grandeur. He provided evidence of both as vice president: drunkenly stumbling through his inaugural address, and when later lecturing a Black audience, taking up the cloying mantle of white savior—accepting he was the African race's "Moses," vowing to shepherd them "through the Red Sea of war . . . to a fairer future of liberty and peace."[8]

Radicals therefore had reason to discreetly welcome Johnson's unexpected rise to the presidency: a kindred spirit, in ideals and attitude, would at last occupy the White House. "By the Gods," one breathed, "there will be no trouble now in running the government."[9]

Yet it came, albeit slowly, trickling out of the White House in the spring and summer like water through a cracked dam. The first leak sprang on May 9. Free of oversight until Congress reconvened that winter, the president unilaterally granted recognition to a state government in Virginia. Vacationing Radicals could only assume the best of a man they still considered an ally: "I see the President is precipitating things. . . . It would be well if he would call an extra session of Congress. But I despair of resisting Executive influence."[10]

This deference gave way to dismay by month's end, when Johnson issued a pair of proclamations further unveiling his own surprisingly lax philosophy of Reconstruction. The first provided amnesty to a wider swath of rebels; the second set up another southern state government under a plan that would grant the vote to the recently rebellious, but not to ex-slaves. Radicals now gauged one another's willingness to seize the wheel from this obviously wayward president:

> Can't we collect bold men enough to lay the foundation for a party to take the helm of this government, and keep it off the rocks?[11]

Two dueling visions of the Republic's future course became apparent. The president's rested on a foundational belief in white supremacy—one shared by many of his countrymen, north and south alike. It turned out Johnson had loathed slavery not for its chattelization of Black Americans, but for how it aggrandized rich whites at the expense of poor ones. "I have been their slave instead of their being mine," he sputtered to an appalled Frederick Douglass.[12]

More ignorant statements passed Johnson's lips. "No independent government of any form has ever been successful in their hands . . . they have shown a constant tendency to relapse into barbarism," he replied on official presidential letterhead to the idea of Black citizenship. He further insisted (apparently with a straight face) that giving former slaves the vote would bring unprecedented tyranny to America.[13]

Congressional Radicals, still in recess, shuffled their papers in preparation to set Reconstruction on a more enlightened path that December. A devastated South represented an exceptional chance to build a better Republic out of the ruins of war—one that this idiotic, accidental executive must not be allowed to squander. "There is a feeling that the South is now at the mercy of the North, and that . . . the opportunity is at hand to quell definitely, once for all, the temper of oligarchical pride which worked such disaster to the Republic," wrote Georges Clemenceau. The Frenchman, working as a foreign correspondent in New York, would find the spectacle of the Union rehabilitating a conquered foe instructive for his future.[14]

Of course, the Radicals intended to teach not just one class of American a lesson, but elevate another. They planned to accomplish the things

Johnson, Democrats, and a number of Republicans dreaded: universal civil rights; the Black vote; even the redistribution of the South's most valuable asset into more deserving hands. Thaddeus Stevens counted 400 million acres of southern plantation land belonging to the region's richest 10 percent. He hoped to hand much of this property to those once enslaved on it, in forty-acre parcels.[15]

Achieving all this would hinge on keeping the South in what Radicals considered its present state: out of the Union, and its populace therefore without the privileges enjoyed by their northern countrymen under the Constitution. The caucus further believed that Congress alone could dictate when such a status might change. Stevens warned the president as much in a letter:

Reconstruction is a very delicate question. The last Congress (and I expect the present) looked upon it as a question for the Legislative power exclusively.[16]

Unsupervised as he was in Washington that summer, Johnson responded to such lectures by doubling down on his bad behavior. Thousands of high-ranking ex-rebels were soon making "all avenues of approach to the White House," then emerging from the mansion with freshly printed pardons. "They kept the Southern President surrounded by an atmosphere of Southern geniality, Southern prejudices, Southern aspirations," wrote Whitelaw Reid. "They asked him if he was going to let Massachusetts Abolitionists lead him now and control his own Administration, while his own native South lay repentant and bleeding at his feet."[17]

Reid would soon tour the South to realize it was not so penitent a land, after all. Virginian men boasted they would have won the war if it had stayed a "fair fight." Louisianians jeered a federal agent who was "fortunate to escape with no more pointed expression of the public opinion concerning his office and duties." In Tennessee, loyal and disloyal citizens alike spoke of a "duty to help set back the upstart niggers" presuming to expect equal rights. "Every few nights, I was told, a negro was shot in some of the back streets," Reid recounted.[18]

The president waved all such reports of disquiet away, calling them the work of a biased press "endeavoring to create the impression that there exists in the South disaffection and dissatisfaction."[19]

Garfield had been adding up the country's troubles well enough from Ohio. They hung on his horizon like a mesh of lightning clouds. He resorted to habit in anticipation of meeting them that winter. "I am trying to do a good deal of reading to prepare myself for the struggle which will be upon us," he reported to Corydon Fuller. "I look forward with great anxiety, not unmixed with alarm, at the signs of the times."[20]

He regarded a prospective political clash more somberly than he had only a few months before. This attitude owed itself to a changed man and his changing times. The starch in Representative Garfield's collar had softened during the rough-and-tumble of his first term, and with the Civil War finally over, the deepening of fractures in its winning coalition rightfully worried him. Garfield felt an instinct resurge that had been dormant for a while, one that had first arisen in the Western Reserve's lyceums years ago: a desire to keep everything civil between allies.

He hurried to assume the best of his caucus's emerging foe. "If President Johnson means by his present policies merely to . . . discover the state and temper of men and things in the revolted states, it will do us good," Garfield wrote. He squinted until the president's actions took favorable shape:

> Indeed, the [Southern constitutional] conventions that have already been held under his orders have done much to open the eyes of loyal men to the sublime impudence of those villains who look upon their long career of treason and blood as . . . in a high degree meritorious.[21]

As might be suspected, friendship underlay this wishful thinking. Back when he deployed to Tennessee with the Army of the Cumberland, then-General Garfield met then-Governor Johnson and they had struck up an "intimate acquaintance."[22]

Yet Garfield remained convinced the Union needed to be rebuilt thoroughly and deliberately, in accordance with Radical wishes—so as to avoid mistakes made in haste, as well as give the government time to test the South for residual treachery. He told his constituents as much. "In regard to reconstruction," an audience member of a Garfield speech related, "the speaker was in favor of taking observations. . . . He was an unbeliever in sudden political conversions." The Reserve's congressman had not stopped playing preacher on the stump.[23]

He nevertheless implied an anxiety that at least one soul was beyond salvation. "I fear that President Johnson is going too fast on the road to-wards reorganization. I fear it leads too far into rebeldom," Garfield told a friend. "I agree with you, that it would at least be decent to wait [to Recon-struct] until the grass is green on the graves of our murdered patriots."[24]

He took solace that Congress could refuse to seat any legislators sent by Johnson's southern regimes. Garfield also promised to hold the line if the president tried forcing such a fight: "So long as I have a voice in public affairs, it shall not be silent until every leading traitor is completely shut out of all participation in the management of the Republic."[25]

He did, however, guard his tone with a closer friend on a more divisive topic. Jacob Cox had made a fine transition from the army back to politics—just as he and Garfield planned back in Columbus once the war broke out. Yet after becoming the Republican nominee for Ohio's governorship in mid-1865, Cox felt compelled to clarify his views on the proper place of Black Americans in a postwar Republic. He drafted a bombshell of an essay in late July, then (as if unaware of its explosiveness) sent out copies to major newspapers.[26]

His screed went into record as the "Oberlin letter." On impact it blew another crack in the Union's old war coalition; Cox openly broke from the Radicals, saying suffrage would not be a boon to Black Americans in the South at all, but rather a curse—for whites would never let them enjoy

it in peace. Nor did Cox rush to blame such a reaction. After all, he offered, "the only basis of permanent nationality is to be found in complete
homogeneity of people." Any attempt to force equality between the races
would therefore only kick off "a strife for the mastery." Cox had no doubt
this would ultimately result in Black Americans being "reduced to hopeless subjection, or utterly destroyed." Better for everyone, the candidate
suggested, that ex-slaves be shepherded to a slice of the country where
they could "work out their own salvation."[27]

A summer storm of controversy followed—punctuated by Democratic laughter and Republican moans. "Unwise and indiscreet," Harmon
Austin said to Garfield of Cox's letter.[28]

Garfield, however, approached his embattled friend with sympathy and
even esteem—a gesture made especially remarkable by the gulf of opinion
between them on this most contentious subject. "Though I cannot agree
with all the positions you take I most thoroughly admire the bold manli-
ness of your letter," he wrote Cox.[29]

Then Garfield politely pushed back against his friend's propositions.
Segregation by Black southerners would be "hopelessly impracticable."
Moreover, any social strife instigated by legislating racial equality in
America did not mean the idea was unworthy. "I agree with you that 'it
is folly to resolve that the lion shall lie down with the lamb,'" Garfield
conceded:

> [But] The only question is what will bring peace—and strengthen
> and perpetuate the Union and the guarantees of liberty. I was sorry
> you discussed homogeneity as necessary to peace . . . one of the worst
> copperheads in Congress made an elaborate speech last Winter taking
> the same ground and arguing that abolition would bring inevitable
> ruin to the negro race or to the Republic.[30]

Cox appreciated Garfield's overture but held the counterpoint that he
was not the one being unreasonable—Radicals were. Democrats would

glide to victory if they could tar the entire Republican party as a gang of insatiable racial equalists; the American public was not nearly so progressive as Radicals assumed. "On that issue, if made, you will be beaten," Cox predicted to Garfield before his letter's publication. But cordiality won out again: Cox closed with "my best regards . . . and don't fail to let me hear from you soon."[31]

Garfield also stayed in pleasant disagreement. He vowed to keep Ohio Radicals from bailing on Cox at the polls and, accordingly, worked the stump. Representative Garfield told voters in Ravenna he "would give the Blackest negro that ever lived the right of suffrage," before (discordantly) giving a "glowing tribute" to Cox. An audience in Warren heard another two-note performance:

> Gen. Garfield . . . declared that he dissented from Cox's theories, but for the sake of the party he would support him for Governor.[32]

He struck a more mournful tone in private. "I am exceedingly sorry that Gen. Cox published his long letter. I fear it will split the party," Garfield lamented. "But we must try to keep it together."[33]

The congressman maintained this attitude regarding his family life, too. Despite reconciling with Garfield after his affair, Crete was back to complaining that his visits home were "so unsatisfactory, so short, and so crowded with work, that I scarcely know how to endure the disappointment." Harry, too, was pining for him. ("How badly did he feel when you left this morning.") When another child arrived in October—a new James—Garfield's heart must have quavered at the idea of this one also never knowing his father.[34]

No sooner had Garfield returned to Washington in December than he picked out a home big enough to fit them all—fully furnished for the sum of $135 a month. "You will only need to bring silver and bed linen," Garfield wrote his wife. Crete packed excitedly.[35]

Another important woman in her husband's life would be joining them. "You have no child that loves you more than I do—or would go farther or do more to make you happy," Garfield had written his mother the prior year. "It has all my life been my great desire that I might have a comfortable home, where I could make you comfortable." It was the least he could do to bring Eliza with him to Washington, given all she had done for him back in those Western Reserve woods, now mostly gone.[36]

Garfield accepted none other than the president's hospitality in the District. "He [Johnson] sent for me day before yesterday and . . . we tried to look over the whole field of difficulties before us," Garfield told Burke Hinsdale on December 11. The congressman used equally inclusive language to describe his meetings with fellow Radicals. "I have advised all our people . . . to proceed on the presumption that the President is with us on all the great questions," Garfield mentioned after a caucus.[37]

One freshman representative could only scratch his head at this optimism (or was it bona fide ignorance?). Rutherford Hayes duly recorded an unflattering first impression of his fellow Ohioan. "General Garfield, a smooth, ready, pleasant man—not very strong."[38]

Powerful men in town were nevertheless queuing up to help him, and Garfield savored this attention. "It has been very gratifying . . . to find so many of the leading members of the government and of Congress expressing kind and complimentary sentiments in regard to me."[39]

These patrons spanned all three branches of American government. President Johnson and his secretary of the Treasury, Hugh McCulloch, represented the executive interest in Garfield's political career. Meanwhile, a familiar benefactor peered down on him from the peak of the American judiciary: Salmon Chase had landed nimbly after leaving Lincoln's cabinet, becoming chief justice of the Supreme Court. Fantasies about his own administration still sometimes broke Chase's focus from the bench.[40]

The closest observer of Garfield's budding career, however, was the man best-placed to nurture it. House Speaker Schuyler Colfax was prone to grin at everyone, but he now beamed with peculiar pride at Garfield. The young Ohioan's hard, if occasionally overzealous work in his rookie term had endeared him to Colfax. Nor had Garfield's stump appearances in the Midwest gone unappreciated—including by a few women from Colfax's homeland of Indiana. "The ladies all talk of you so lovingly," Colfax jested in a note. He ended this letter with a telling sign-off: "My love (paternal, of course)."[41]

Colfax's professional and personal affection bore fruit for Garfield as the speaker arranged committees for the Thirty-Ninth Congress and asked Garfield for his preferred assignments. Garfield's subsequent request to be freed from the Military Affairs Committee came as a complete surprise. "Well," the speaker replied, "that is the most remarkable thing I have ever heard."[42]

It shouldn't have been. Though the next Military Affairs Committee was slated to perform vital work in demobilizing the army (dozens of other congressmen were fighting for a place on it) Garfield thought a financial committee assignment would be even more influential. His wartime studies convinced him of this, as did Secretary McCulloch and Chief Justice Chase. Garfield parroted their suggestion to the speaker; finance, he told Colfax, "is to be the great question of the country."[43]

Garfield got his wish—becoming, in only his second House term, the second-ranking member of the Ways and Means Committee. Years later he oozed satisfaction at the impeccable timing of the placement. It had occurred, Garfield boasted, "just at the time we were beginning to handle those great dry questions of detail about tariff, taxation, and the public debt." He viewed such a byzantine realm as a child might a candy store.[44]

Garfield bagged an excellent literal spot in the House, too—drawing a seat directly behind Thaddeus Stevens and near the floor. Soon he was writing familiar-sounding letters to Crete from this vantage point. "The upper and nether millstones are grinding me again . . . it really seems as though the crush of work was heavier than ever before." But the rewards of such labors apparently took the pain away:

I have received very gratifying evidence of my standing with the leading men here . . . I hope to make a successful winter of it, though our way is full of breakers.[45]

Within the week Garfield had reason to curse his good standing with everyone. Radicals asked him to publicly defend their Reconstruction plan; at the same time the president begged for his help getting legislators from Tennessee seated in the House. "The crush of work not only continues but increases," Garfield wrote ruefully. Looking ahead, he now saw a legislative sea lined not just with breakers, but monsters: "Scylla" on one side, "Charybdis" on the other.[46]

During Ways and Means Committee meetings, Garfield could look up from his work to acquaint himself with a New York Republican named Roscoe Conkling. They were a passing study in contrasts: Conkling, flame-haired and always clad in a migraine-inducing mist of colors (his presence in Congress, that of a "bird of paradise in a barnyard of duskier fowl"), Garfield in mute midwestern fashion and balding. Friends described each as suffering from opposite yet equally inhibiting faults of personality. Conkling basted opponents in acidic insults that stung for years; Garfield loathed offending anyone for an instant.[47]

After avoiding taking a side for more than a month, Garfield finally tried to coast between President Johnson and the Radicals on February 1, 1866—or, rather, bridge their positions. His House speech on Reconstruction started ominously for the faction that requested it: Garfield repudiated his caucus's belief that southern states had, by rebelling, successfully left the Union and thrown away all their constitutional protections. Instead, he split the difference—arguing that the South's failed attempt at secession left the region neither fully in the Union nor entirely excluded from it. He picked out one rebellious state to illustrate this theory:

Now, Alabama may violate a law of Congress, but she cannot annul it. She may break it, but she cannot make it void. . . . Alabama let go of the Union, but the Union did not let go of Alabama. We have held her through four years of war, and we hold her still.

Thaddeus Stevens hauled himself up to interrupt Garfield's heresy before it did more damage:

If the gentleman from Ohio will permit me. . . . Some of the angels undertook to dethrone the Almighty, but they could not do it. And they were turned out of heaven because they were unable to break its laws. Are those devilish angels in or out of heaven?

Garfield's answer came out quick and saber-sharp:

It was the Almighty who opened the shining gates of heaven and hurled them [Satan's devils] down to eternal ruin. They did not go without his permission and help. And if these States are out of the Union it must be because the sovereign people of the Republic hurled them out[, which did not happen]. . . . I am glad the gentleman interrupted me, it happily illustrates my position.

Then, having so far cut away from the Radicals, Garfield tacked back to their waters—agreeing Congress alone could dictate the course of Reconstruction. Garfield laid out its proper path: "They [the South] must give us proof, strong as holy writ, that they have washed their hands and are worthy again to be trusted" before fully rejoining the Union. Nor could the Republic stop at simply ending slavery. It would be dangerous to leave other iniquities between the races intact:

Mr. Speaker, I know of nothing more dangerous to a Republic than to put into its very midst four million people stripped of the rights of citizenship, robbed of the right of representation, but bound to pay taxes to the government. If they can endure it, we cannot. . . . I say that the inequality of rights before the law, which is now a part of our system, is more dangerous to us than to the Black man whom it disfranchises. It is like a foreign substance in the body, a thorn in the flesh; it will wound and disease the body public.

Garfield did not fail to be diplomatic toward his dissenters—or, rather, one particularly powerful one. "Let us not endanger the future because the President's policy in the past has not been all we could desire," he told the House. Garfield even suggested Johnson had been justified in acting alone while Congress remained out of session. Now, though, the Radicals needed to graciously relieve the president of the burden of rebuilding the Republic.[48]

Press reviews were split. The *New-York Tribune* called Garfield's nuance brilliant. ("His definition of the present status of the rebel States . . . bristling with fine points, and of great oratorical merit.") The Cincinnati *Enquirer* disagreed. For all of Garfield's pedantry, he—like all Radicals— still did not seem to know or care how American laws worked.

Mr. Garfield may be a scholar; he may comprehend "what constitutes a State" as thoroughly as the poet. . . . He may be able to wade the Ohio in low water and flounder in the fish ponds of our territorial subdivision. . . . But when Mr. Garfield gets into mid-ocean he is somewhat over his depth.[49]

Garfield explained to friends that the only thing he had been fishing for was a ceasefire between factions who should, by all rights, still be allied ("In my speech I tried to take ground for both him [the president] and Congress to stand on"). Garfield privately called each side blameworthy. Johnson was blindly falling "into the hands of our enemies." "Stevens and his followers," on the other hand, were too ready to take a course "which, if continued, will destroy the Republican Party."[50]

Garfield stashed away these anxieties in public though. "On the main points of the problem," he sunnily told one reporter, "I believe there is far less difference of sentiment than is generally supposed."[51]

The president made him look foolish less than two weeks later. Johnson vetoed the measure Garfield's address had technically concerned and insisted Congress had no right to exclude legislators sent to it by his southern regimes. This lost Johnson his lone Radical ally. "The President has at last declared war," Garfield wrote resignedly the following evening. "He has left the true men of the country no choice, but to fight him." Crete sent a letter to Harmon Austin brimming with concern for the situation: "Affairs here look dark just now. . . . James is very anxious over the result."[52]

In fact, Garfield felt the national mood to be exactly like that during the Fort Sumter crisis. He bemoaned that the coalition which had won that conflict was now fractured for good:

> I have done what I could to hold the Union party together, and have counselled a firm but conciliatory course. . . . I fear we must not only fight the old enemies of the Union party, but the President with them.[53]

Johnson, meanwhile, had resorted to telling White House tourists that the Radicals were conspiring to overthrow his government. A witness wondered if he was drinking again.[54]

14

"'*Tis not enough to help the feeble up,*
But to support him after."

—Shakespeare's *Timon of Athens*, as quoted in
Garfield diary entry for May 16, 1878

The next Radical broadside struck the president with dizzying speed. In March, Congress passed the Civil Rights Bill of 1866, making good on what the caucus had always threatened to do alone if necessary—extend full citizenship and legal equality to Black Americans "in every State and Territory." Advisors urged an affronted Johnson to sign it. "The thing, itself is desirable," implored one. "But, aside from that, I am persuaded that it would go far to harmonize the feelings of men who should never have differed."[1]

Alas, Johnson was not built to seek out harmony, nor did he think Black citizenship "desirable" in the slightest. He vetoed the Civil Rights Bill and attached a rambling message questioning if Blacks held the "requisite qualifications" to be American citizens. This burnt many of the president's remaining bridges in Congress. House Radicals, having expected no better, then moved to override him entirely on April 9.[2]

Garfield got home that night in a festive mood. He jotted a post-action report to an army friend:

> I am glad to tell you that I have just returned from voting for the Civil Rights Bill which we have passed over the President's veto 121 to 40, a thing unprecedented in American history.[3]

Hope even kindled in him that, like one of those unruly district school students Garfield had spanked so long ago on the Reserve, the president might have just profited by his humiliation.[4]

Seeing signs to the contrary, the Radicals then took a bolder step. To ensure equality of citizenship would not be clawed down in the future, they proposed a Constitutional Amendment enshrining the principle for good. This monumental amendment (the fourteenth) passed Congress in June. Johnson's attempts to stymie it seemed almost pathetic to the legislators. ("His message was about as appropriate as though it had contained the bill of fare for his breakfast, his latest tailor's account, or his opinions upon the cause of thunder.")[5]

Tuning out the president's interjections, Garfield and other Radicals only worried the new amendment did not go far enough. Certain components had been diluted to appease moderates. The clause banning ex-Confederates from voting in national elections only until 1870 particularly vexed Garfield. "If it had disenfranchised rebels perpetually," he ruminated, "or . . . forever prohibited the leaders from holding office, I think it would have been a stronger and better proposition."[6]

Bothered by this neutered provision, Garfield also expressed concern for the absence of another. What better way to safeguard Black citizenship, he told the House, than to equip that race with voting rights? ("The sword, the spear . . . that best befits a man for his own defense.") But, voicing that most encouraging sign of a maturing statesman—a willingness to "take what I can get"—he joined in voting the Fourteenth Amendment into law.[7]

•   •   •

Other legislative business pressed in close. Questions of financial policy (jangling in Garfield's ears like so many sacks of coins) honestly captured his attention better than the chore of steamrolling a president. Perhaps predictably, he sought out middle ground on some of these subjects. Import tariffs, for example, "should be so high that our manufacturers can fairly compete with the foreign product, but not so high as to enable them to drive out the foreign article, enjoy a monopoly on trade, and regulate the price as they please."[8]

He saw no room for balance on another fiscal topic. The idea of a permanent paper dollar in America chilled his blood:

> The manifold evils resulting from a state of such things cannot be computed. . . . Let us not continue to practice this conjurer's art, by which sixty cents shall discharge a debt of one hundred coins.[9]

On April 15, the speaker heaped another assignment onto Garfield's plate. The occasion was the anniversary of Lincoln's death; Colfax knew no better man to commemorate it for the House than Garfield. He tasked his protégé with preparing a eulogy of the late president in fifteen minutes.

A friend nevertheless called the ensuing speech "one of the most felicitous things . . . in our Congressional history." "It has been considerably complimented," was all Garfield allowed afterward.[10]

Around the same time, another friend also called on Garfield by surprise to ask him to perform a more singular service for the whole nation. Emerson White knew of no one in Congress better equipped to take on the task he had in mind: to establish a federal authority supporting American public education.

White had indeed picked out an ideal ambassador for his cause from afar. Not only had education been a transformative force in Garfield's life, but he had also served as a school administrator in Ohio, and now possessed the necessary political chops and personal relationships to carry bills of his own through Congress. Still, White must have been astonished at how forcefully his counterpart took hold of the proposal. He had hardly given his pitch before Garfield asked for a draft of the measure. White obediently and hastily drew up a bill proposing a federal "Bureau of Education."

Garfield and the draft took mutual possession of each other from that point onward. He practically ran to place it before the House. A bipartisan special committee, swiftly formed, mostly rubber-stamped the plan White sketched out in the Garfield home. One key change was made, however; the committee—headed by Garfield—decided the new authority should be named a "Department."

This rang as a mighty title for what was, per the fine print, a modest proposal; if Congress went along with Garfield's pet project, America's first Department of Education would pop into being as little more than a few statisticians based in Washington—its purpose, to gather educational data from states for distribution among the country's teachers, academics, and lawmakers. A lone commissioner (retained for a few thousand dollars a year) was to be entrusted with overseeing such work.[11]

Yet Garfield's speeches defending the measure showed he thought its potential return to be boundless. He made the novel argument that improving the education of citizens was the wisest expenditure a government could make. "A tenth of our national debt expended in public education fifty years ago would have saved us the blood and treasure of the late war," Garfield told the House in June.[12]

Nor did he neglect to underline present needs. "One third of a million people are being annually thrown upon our shores . . . a large per cent of whom are uneducated," he said. A greater number of disadvantaged Americans could be found down South:

> Shall we commit the fatal mistake of building up free States, without first expelling the darkness in which slavery has shrouded their people? Shall we enlarge the boundaries of citizenship, and make no provision to increase the intelligence of the citizen?[13]

Sadly, Congress answered such questions with a wavering yes—striking Garfield's proposal down by two votes. This would have been its end, were it not for Garfield's friendships with well-placed peers. He ran around the chamber to rally them. Representative James Blaine later said this outreach had the whiff of desperation to it:

> I was good natured, or weak enough, at the request of my persuasive
> friend from Ohio to yield the floor . . . to move a reconsideration.[14]

This gave Garfield enough time to make necessary adjustments to his bill. A week and a half later, he had ("with great difficulty") secured enough votes for its passage ("by a tight squeeze").[15]

Garfield's prize would be heaps more work that would bury him semi-regularly throughout the rest of his political life. The Department of Education he had founded was destined to sputter along like a leaky ship—hamstrung by poor command from within and congressional attacks from without. "Ever since I secured the passage of the first bill we have had to struggle for the life of the Department," Garfield would sigh to one of its employees.[16]

Yet he would repeatedly step in to bail it out. When one commissioner bungled his duties, Garfield ousted the man. Fiscal vultures in Congress routinely circled the "useless" Department of Education in search of funds to strip; Garfield always batted them off. "I am not one of those who seek to pluck out the eyes of the nation," he chided one flock.[17]

Congressional Democrats never stopped trying to eliminate the department entirely, under darker justifications than mere public economy. As Fernando Wood of New York complained about Garfield's creation:

> We have already established a department called the Freedman's
> Bureau . . . to support hundreds of thousands of lazy, idle negroes at
> the expense of the Government, and the object of this Department of

Education is to educate those negroes . . . people who will not work, people who are supported out of the public Treasury by appropriations of Congress for illegal and improper political purposes.[18]

These attacks took their toll. Garfield would live to see his department busted down to a bureau, which it would remain until more than a century later—when a new administration would give a resurrected Department of Education a cabinet seat. Garfield's speech for his measure's passage appeared to acknowledge that his initiative's importance would become apparent with time. "It is an interest that has no lobby to press its claims," he told the House. "It is the voice of the children of the land, asking us to give them all the blessings of our civilization."[19]

Though few would ever credit Garfield as a forefather of American public education, his correspondence must have lent him quiet satisfaction. "The operations of the Department of Education, which you were instrumental in establishing, are watched here with great interest," reported a diplomat in England. "I don't believe you will ever do a work more beneficial and fruitful," one educator wrote Garfield.[20]

Simultaneously, he managed to accomplish something quite advantageous for himself. The opportunity had also come via a visitor to Garfield's home—a stouter, snuff-chewing one named Jeremiah Black. Black was a Democrat lawyer with distinguished service in public and private practice. Having been attorney general in the Buchanan administration, "Judge" Black was not popular with Republicans (let alone Radicals). The disdain was mutual; shortly into the Lincoln administration, a friend asked if Black had qualms about changing parties. "A very serious one," he deadpanned. "I believe in a hell!"[21]

But the warmth coming off Garfield did not feel infernal to Black. The two, both Disciples of Christ, met in Washington during the Civil War and an unlikely affection quickly blossomed. The judge's family basked in it. As Black's daughter reminisced: "Each drew out what was best in the other . . . they laughed and joked like school boys. . . . How could they help being fond of each other when they were both so large of heart and brain?"[22]

As Garfield would one day retell it, Black paid a particularly welcome visit in early 1866, saying he had heard of something Garfield told the House about the proper limitations of military law. He wondered if Garfield would be willing to repeat the point in a courtroom. "Well," Garfield recorded as his reply, "it depends on your case altogether."[23]

What he then heard impressed him. "It is a new case and one of intense interest," Garfield informed another friend.[24]

This turned out to be a criminal understatement of things. Black had asked Garfield to join one of the most important pending legal cases in the country—one due to be decided in the Supreme Court. Its origins lay in the Civil War, but its verdict would lastingly shape the Reconstruction yet to come.

In 1864, a posse of Indiana Democrats styling themselves the "Sons of Liberty" plotted to storm Union arsenals throughout the state, then march south to join the Confederate war effort. Fortunately, the Sons were apprehended before acting on this scheme, and a panel of Union officers quickly found them guilty on a blitz of charges before condemning them to death. Yet this sentence was blocked when one of the prisoners petitioned for a last-minute writ of habeas corpus, questioning if a military tribunal could legally operate in a jurisdiction in which civil courts remained open.[25]

Their case (named after the petitioner, Lambdin Milligan) then ricocheted up through American courts, picking up notoriety and significance along the way. Republican press shrugged off the "villainous" men's demands for due process ("Thus to all northern traitors"), while Democrat columns oozed with compassion for them. By the time Milligan and his posse were due before the Supreme Court, they had become a partisan cause célèbre and hired a leading Democrat attorney—Jeremiah Black—as their representation.[26]

Yet Black had evidently decided he needed help. Upon hearing the judge outline his argument, Garfield happily offered to provide such assistance. "I believe in that doctrine," he would remember telling Black. "I believe in English liberty and English law."[27]

It was, nevertheless, a confusing stance for a congressman of his politics to assume. Garfield took criticism for wading into the case on the prisoners' behalf, from constituents and fellow Radicals alike. As one columnist expounded:

> It is a profound mystery why Gen. Garfield . . . should be found using all his eloquence, and the influence of his position in favor of treason and traitors. . . . This, Gen. Garfield has done in advocating the liberation of Milligan and his associates from the Penitentiary. . . . Every one is astonished, and the question asked, whenever the subject is talked about, is, 'What in the world induced Gen. Garfield to do such a thing as that.' "[28]

Garfield had a rebuttal ready. In future, he would describe representing Milligan as a matter of principle—one pure enough to overcome petty matters of party identity:

> I knew when I took the Indiana case that I would probably be misunderstood, but . . . I was willing to subject myself to the misunderstanding of some, for the sake of securing the supremacy of the civil over the military authority.[29]

But the strength of this position is weakened by a neglected thread of correspondence—one that would only be pulled on years later, after diligent historical digging. Almost a year before being approached about the Milligan case, Garfield had received a note from Black. "Get a card printed," it instructed. "Something in this form:

BLACK AND GARFIELD
Counsellors at Law
Washington City
Supreme Court and Other Courts of U.S.[30]

A collaboration between the two had thus been on the books, so to speak, for a while. A reason why Garfield might have welcomed such a partnership (then fuzzied its timeline) can be found in that most awkward of adult subjects: money.

He had become starved for it by the Civil War's end. Garfield's family was then growing at the steady, alarming rate of one addition every two years (a daughter, Mollie, would arrive in 1867), and he had resolved to house it, plus his mother, in both Hiram and Washington. His congressional salary could not comfortably cover such expenses, and early attempts to supplement it had not gone well; Garfield speculated in real estate in 1865 only to find the market confounding. "I fear I shall come to you *'property poor'* as they say," he had written Crete after one disappointing investing trip. Experiments with leasing mineral rights yielded no better returns. Thus, Garfield finally met a topic he could not master: fluent as he was in public finances, he would never get a steady grip on his own.[31]

And yet, money woes were not, like a dull textbook, something he could simply ignore. "I feel a little like a slave working in the mines for his freedom," he wrote in 1865, "and have . . . the feeling that the pursuit of wealth is not the noblest thing in the world."[32]

This conclusion could only have been reinforced by the behavior around Garfield in Washington: current events had conspired to make it easier than ever to monetize American public office. Steel and railroad companies, enriched in wartime, were now showering elected officials with millions in stock in exchange for pro-business attitudes; opportunities to front-run treasury debt transactions abounded; on a grander scale, the federal government (now fattened into the "Yankee Leviathan" by war spending) offered congressmen a plethora of patronage jobs to dole out.

Harry Rhodes marveled that Garfield hesitated to join the rush: "Were I in your boots . . . I wouldn't fleece the government, but if I could not make a fortune with your chances . . . then I'd hang my harp on the willows."[33]

The legal collaboration with Black saved Garfield from having to resort to such unseemly measures. He expressed relief to Crete at being able to partake in a somewhat honest side-hustle: "The Judge . . . thinks we can reap large mutual advantages from such a partnership."[34]

Garfield still tried to hide the financial motivations informing his legal debut. He would, in future, repeat an erroneous account of its origins, and, furthermore, point out he took no compensation from the Milligan case anyway. As he told one reporter: "Now, these men were paupers . . . I never have seen the men, never have had any relation with them, never have received a cent in any way."[35]

Yet a cascade of not just cents, but thousands of dollars, would thereafter flow to Garfield because of the Milligan case—its source, future clients eager to retain an attorney (and a congressman, at that) with Supreme Court experience. So, too, would Black profit from Garfield's participation; after all, what better way to enter a highly politicized case than with a bipartisan legal team? Surely only the most righteous of causes could prompt a Radical to defend treasonous Democrats.

Garfield certainly gave such an impression once Milligan's case reached court. He embraced his share of the legal work with zeal and, by all accounts, the talent of an experienced lawyer rather than a novice (for this was his first-ever case). The novel task of drafting a brief gave way before his usual habits. "I sat down and worked two days and two nights, with the exception of four or five hours sleep," Garfield reported later. Black was impressed with the final product. "Don't you change a word of that," the attorney instructed.[36]

Garfield delivered his text unedited on March 6 before the Supreme Court. Its fundamental points were (to quote the argument itself) "not personal." "I desire to say in the outset that the questions now before this court have relations only to constitutional law," Garfield opened. He proceeded to contradict himself on this front (saying "nothing in the calendar of infamy" surpassed his clients' accused conduct) but spent his performance using constitutional, historical, and even poetic precedent to emphasize his fundamental point that the Sons of Liberty had been deprived of due process. No one in America (not even the "guiltiest of its citizens") deserved such treatment.[37]

Credit for the case's outcome must be owed to Garfield's more experienced co-counsels. The Supreme Court handed down a unanimous ruling in Milligan's favor, then left a majority opinion to be published in winter and Radicals to seethe in the meantime.[38]

It was a terrific setback for their cause; the legality of military courts still operating in the South had suddenly been thrown into question, and Johnson quickly used the Milligan verdict to justify suspending all pending trials of southern civilians before ongoing military tribunals. Thaddeus Stevens decried the outcome as "perhaps not as infamous as the Dred Scott decision . . . [but] far more dangerous in its operation upon the lives and liberties of the loyal men of this country . . . [it] has taken away every protection in every one of these rebel States from every loyal man, Black or white, who resides there."[39]

A few Radicals now raised the idea of impeaching the Supreme Court. Stevens, however, made the novel suggestion of instead targeting the president, "from whom all evils flow."[40]

The Western Reserve's congressman entered reelection season again facing headwinds billowing out of his constituency. Garfield had, only two years before, been waylaid by charges of excessive radicalism; now he was being accused of having Confederate sympathies. He could only marvel at the ferocity (and dubious logic) being uncorked in Radicals by the Milligan verdict. "The papers [are] insanely calling for the abolition of the court," Garfield bemoaned to a friend. But he expressed confidence that his productive, progressive legislative record would speak for itself.

"If a plain honest course of hard work will not secure the approval of the people, I prefer to be beaten," Garfield wrote.[41]

Supportive letters soon sprinkled the Reserve's papers. "When . . . men approach you and declare that Garfield defended the Indiana conspirators, tell them it is a false accusation," one exhorted. "He never did defend them, nor justify, nor apologize for them." Another pointed out that Garfield "never saw or consulted with the prisoners . . . nor has Gen. Garfield ever received any [fee], nor does he know that he ever will."[42]

The candidate simultaneously reburnished his Radicalism on the campaign trail. "I believe that we shall never be right in this country until we declare that every son of man of proper age, and not convicted of any crime, shall have an equal voice in saying who shall rule him," Garfield told Toledo voters. He appeared on stage next to Representative James Ashley, who had already drawn up impeachment articles for the president.[43]

Old friends carried him over the finish line. He attended Eclectic alumni reunions (he was still, technically, the school's president) while Harmon Austin and Harry Rhodes rushed to far-flung townships as Garfield proxies. He was made the guest of honor at a veterans' convention, while at another rally a trooper of the Forty-Second Regiment generously knocked out a heckler. Most campaign events proved less eventful.[44]

Each of the 126 Republican delegates at the Reserve's nominating convention voted to send Garfield back to Congress. He would trounce the other party's candidate in the general election by more than ten thousand votes. A Democrat columnist distilled Garfield's victory into three words: "Hard to beat."[45]

His own future resecured, Garfield reviewed the broader political landscape on New Year's Day 1867. He saw a pathway for national reconciliation opening ahead—and, somehow, reason to think the country might proceed down it. "In reference to Reconstruction, I feel that if the Southern States should adopt the [Fourteenth] Constitutional Amendment within a reasonable time, we are morally bound to admit them," Garfield wrote Burke Hinsdale.

His recent imbroglio with his own caucus tempered his optimism, however, while Radical talk of impeaching the president also weighed on Garfield's thoughts. He realized he had a better grip on political reality than other Republican hardliners:

> If we could succeed in an impeachment it would be a blessing— probably—but it is perfectly evident that with the Senate constituted as it is we cannot effect an impeachment. Still . . . impracticable men are determined to push the insane scheme of making the attempt and setting the country in a ferment.

Garfield now distinguished himself from his caucus. "I am trying to do two things," he admitted to Hinsdale. ". . . be a radical and not a fool, which if I am to judge by the exhibitions around me is a matter of no small difficulty." Writing on, he expressed a hope that the country's other political pole might at least come to its senses: "I wish the South would adopt the Constitutional Amendment soon and in good temper."[46]

Instead, almost all the southern states refused to ratify the Fourteenth Amendment. This provided Radicals a final bit of proof that the region was not repentant for the late war, nor sufficiently loyal to rejoin the Union. Prior evidence of this during the election season had been altogether more horrifying: hooded men in Texas shot Black people for calling whites by their first names; a secret society called the Black Horse Cavalry killed enough Unionists in Louisiana that judges there refused to travel alone anymore. "One thing has definitely been proven," the French journalist Georges Clemenceau summarized from Washington. "The whole region has become impossible as a dwelling place for those who believe in the Union."[47]

The South's refusal to comply with the amendment represented an opportunity to change this. The generosity of moderates had been exposed as misguided; Radicals could now justify enacting an unvarnished form of Reconstruction. In February, they did—forcing through legislation that dissolved Johnson's southern governments, returned the region to military rule, and set paths to statehood hinging not only on ratification of the Fourteenth Amendment, but on the adoption of Black suffrage. Johnson reflexively vetoed the measure (citing ex parte Milligan while doing so) but Congress overrode him again.[48]

Garfield could only hail this as a necessary step that Radicals had been forced to initiate. "The Fourteenth Amendment did not come up to the full height of the great occasion; it did not meet all that I desired in the way of guarantees to liberty," he told the House, "but . . . They [the Southern governments] have deliberated; they have acted; the last of the sinful ten has at last, with contempt and scorn, flung back into our teeth the magnanimous offer of a generous nation." He hailed the onset of Radical Reconstruction ("It puts the bayonet at the breast of every Rebel murderer in the South to bring him to justice"), then warned the president of the price of continuing to pout: "Mr. Speaker, I want this Congress to give its commands to the President. If he refuses to obey, the impeachment-hunters need make no further search for cause of action."[49]

To better muzzle Johnson, Congress passed the Tenure of Office Act. Now the president could not even fire his own appointees without Radical permission.[50]

Garfield found distraction from these fireworks in the drier legislative duties which interested him so. "We are now working day and evening on our Tax and Tariff bills and I am giving my whole energy to these subjects," he wrote in February. Not so secretly, Garfield hoped to control the writing of all such laws soon.[51]

He also arranged higher offices for his friends. A postmaster job in Warren stood vacant; a tax assessor for his congressional district needed to be assigned; David Swaim, an army friend of Garfield's, also wanted a better assignment in the ranks.[52]

This last request brought Garfield before someone he had not seen since the Battle of Shiloh. The congressman visited Ulysses Grant—asking the general to find an appropriate position for Swaim. It was as pleasant an interaction as the two future presidents would ever share.[53]

15

"*Who has a book of all that monarchs do,*
He's more secure to keep it shut than shown."

—Shakespeare's *Pericles*, as quoted in Garfield

diary entry for December 5, 1878

The summer of 1867 found Garfield on the trip of a lifetime. Urgent advice from a doctor ("to get away from work and have rest") had instead been interpreted as an order to embark on an odyssey. Garfield set his sights on the Old World and resolved that his wife must accompany him there—the children, left with their grandmother. "In my present state of health I need Crete more than they," Garfield reasoned.[1]

He saw to one nagging bit of business before crossing the Atlantic; Garfield had decided that evidence of his affair with Lucia Calhoun must be destroyed for good. Crete expressed understandable doubts ("I cannot but feel it would be better to let the fire of such lawless passion burn itself out"), but her husband went to see Calhoun in New York anyway, ultimately achieving his mission: he and Calhoun's illicit love letters would never be seen again. "You cannot be so much relieved in heart and mind as I am," Garfield wrote Crete.[2]

A few days later, the couple were together on a ship steaming east out of Manhattan. Crete was retching as soon as the deck began to pitch, but her husband remained impressed by her resilience. "A better sailor than I expected," he journaled approvingly.[3]

A "delicate, hazy" purple nimbus tinged the horizon on July 24. Then the Garfields were skirting Ireland. The waters swashing their ship's bow turned pea green—the passing landmass, resembling a long band of lichen. Ahead rose the pale cliffs of Wales, and within a day Garfield and Crete were disembarking along the clanking dock works of Liverpool. The congressman felt himself admiring the industrial strength on display. ("A most remarkable exhibition of skill and energy.") The couple got to their hotel and Garfield soon settled on smaller facets of English life to scrutinize. "I was struck with the fact that the brick[s] were from half an inch to an inch thicker than ours."[4]

He spent the next month taking in grander sights from better angles: Westminster Abbey, the Tower of London ("so full of sad and strange history"), the British Museum ("The Elgin Marbles disappoint me"). But the high point of these excursions came during a visit to the Houses of Parliament, where Garfield was given the privilege of sitting alongside Members and Lords as they debated.

Differences in style caught his notice (politicians here hesitated a lot), but Garfield was happy to observe deeper ideological parallels between British and American statecraft:

> There seems to be as much of the demagogical spirit here as in our Congress. Underneath the absurd wigs . . . there is still a constant reference to the demands of the people.[5]

A trip to a squire's manor tempered this admiration. The nobleman's pristine estate, thoroughbred horses, paired guns, and hearty disdain for politics ("especially the liberal side of it") convinced Garfield that differences did, in fact, exist between their nations' ruling classes. Garfield was compelled to write Eliza—and through her, his children in her care:

I do not pass a day without being thankful that I and my children were born in a land where royal blood and great wealth are not needed to make men noble in the eyes of the world—but where the works that men do, and the principles they adopt, make them noble or ignoble.

When the boys get old enough . . . I want them to know that though I have for two evenings sat on the steps of the British throne, and heard speeches from Dukes and Earls in the House of Lords and admired much that is great and wise and good in the firm old government and laws of England . . . I thank God that my boys may be men, esteemed in their native land for their worth rather than their birth.[6]

Eliza may have been reading a profile of Garfield that had come out in a Western Reserve paper only a few days prior. It told readers his life was a parable of that uniquely American ideal of self-improvement. Nor had Garfield's climb finished:

Many a poor boy will take courage as he beholds him [Garfield] gradually rising from a mere canal driver to the House of Representatives, and, we trust, from thence to the height of political fame.

The article tacked on an excerpt from one of Garfield's letters discussing his upbringing. "Poverty is very inconvenient," he had acknowledged, "but it is a fine spur to activity, and may be made a rich blessing."[7]

He caught up on current events in his homeland upon reaching France. "There is passion enough in each village of the U.S. to run a steam engine," Garfield wrote ruefully from Paris in October.[8]

The excitement's cause was the now-familiar one—Johnson fighting the Radicals—and, again, Garfield found fault in both sides from afar, while still holding out hope for the future: "The folly of the President and the unwisdom of Congress have conspired to make the situation complicated. But I draw upon my great faith [in] our country."[9]

The Garfields were sailing home in November. Poor Crete heaved off the bow while her husband admired an oncoming New Jersey coastline tinseled in amber foliage.[10]

He was not ashore long when off-season election results reached his ears. "A great political reaction had [sic] manifestly set in, and our Party is terribly beaten," Garfield wrote. "I have come back to Washington with a heavy heart, and with a gloomy winter full of storm and tempest before me."[11]

The congressional season indeed set in cold and bleak. While the Garfields had been idly strolling European capitals, the House Judiciary Committee in Washington had been rustling desperately for something to impeach Johnson over. This inquisition proved self-fulfilling; the scrutiny it put on the president helped pressurize his erraticism to the point of eruption. Johnson at last tried to fire Secretary of War Edwin Stanton in August, violating the Tenure of Office Act and handing Radicals a somewhat viable impeachment charge.[12]

The president's squirming also threw moderate Republicans behind the revolutionary step of removing him. "Before July, the majority of our Party were against it," Speaker Colfax informed Garfield. "Now they are solidly for it." But Garfield wished otherwise. He could not shake a fear that any strike against the president would just bounce back on its proponents. He mourned that an "exciting and unfortunate" contest was inevitably coming anyway, "which cannot fail to damage the Republican party."[13]

This sadness at his party's immediate prospects mingled with resentment at a surprising reduction in his own. For a while, Garfield had assumed that for the Fortieth Congress he would be made chairman of the mighty Ways and Means Committee. Nor was he the only one to think so; press correspondents profiled Garfield as a shoo-in for the post. "The latest general impression is that General Garfield will be Chairman of Ways and Means," decreed the *New-York Tribune* on November 23. "This is the choice Committee of the House. . . . A great part of the legislation of Congress will be upon the subjects which come into the province of this Committee."[14]

It was a nice affirmation—not only of Garfield's entitlement to the job, but also his foresight in specializing in financial policy. He projected apathy while secretly salivating over the great responsibilities about to fall to him:

> It looks as though I should be Chairman of Ways and Means, but I do not know. I am glad to tell you I have not spoken to Colfax on the subject and have made no efforts to secure it . . . [yet] if I should be at the head of W[ays] & M[eans] it will be the most arduous and responsible work and the severest trial of my life.[15]

Yet his House patron disappointed him. Speaker Colfax tasked Garfield with supervising the Military Affairs Committee—giving the Ways and Means chairmanship instead to Garfield's curmudgeonly ex-roommate Robert Schenck. At hearing this, Garfield indulged in a rare outward eruption of anger. ("It greatly disgusts me," he fumed to a friend.) He had spent nearly six years studying financial policy—the last two as a leading contributor to the Ways and Means Committee. The secretary of the Treasury even considered him the best-read man in Congress on the field! In contrast, the closest Schenck ever came to studying money had been through glimpses at his poker chips.[16]

The speaker expressed sympathy but little remorse. "I was sorry to disappoint Garfield, whom I love, and who had set his heart on being Chairman of Ways and Means," Colfax later wrote. But the speaker needed to defer to even higher laws than friendship: per House tradition, tenure mattered more than expertise or competence, and Garfield could not be an exception to this rule. Nor did Colfax think Garfield had much right to feel sorry for himself; the Ohioan was still burning a hot path up the legislative ranks. "Garfield is Chairman of Military Affairs, which for his third term is better than I got at that stage," the speaker pointed out to a friend.[17]

Garfield regained his composure—taking comfort not only in his still-high place in the House ("Of course the place I am in is important"), but the surprise other representatives expressed that he had not been given

Ways and Means. He also retained his stubborn faith that hard work inevitably reaped reward. Garfield repeated this belief to Harry Rhodes, as if in rededication: "There is no life-work that has not drudgery . . . its rough and terrible and for that I am thankful it is so; for out of that drudgery comes success and happiness."[18]

Garfield was not present when the House voted to impeach Johnson in February 1868, but he returned to the Capitol in time to watch the Senate trial. It quickly dulled him. Garfield might have been the only man bored by the first attempted ouster of a president, describing it as a biblical flood of self-important rhetoric. "We have been wading knee deep in words, words, words . . . and are but little more than half across the turbid stream," he wrote in April. The river evaporated into an interminable downpour by May—an "endless shower of words, words, words."[19]

Garfield thought this deluge might just drown the case—its source, ironically, being the congressmen running proceedings. They sounded more interested in holding the political spotlight than advancing their argument. Garfield supposed that, if given a choice between speaking and losing the case, or keeping silent and winning it, his caucus-mates would promptly launch into a six-hour sermon.[20]

But their words had apparently been of some use; Garfield now thought that the president was determined to continue defying Congress illegally—and that the impeachment charges were both righteous and had some chance of success. "It seemed to me it [impeachment] would be manifestly an interminable contest," Garfield admitted in a speech. "But now, at last, the President . . . left us no choice."[21]

An old friend was presiding over the Senate trial set to determine whether that was true. He reached the same conclusions as Garfield about the prosecution's conduct. "Too much speaking by half," Chief Justice Salmon Chase jotted down in the center of an overcrowded, overheated Senate.[22]

•   •   •

Warning lights had been blinking throughout the Senate trial that Johnson would likely be acquitted. Moderate Republicans, already skeptical of the validity of the impeachment charges, expressed worry for what Benjamin Wade, President *pro tempore* of the Senate, would do in the White House should its current occupant be evicted. Wade ("a man of violent passions, extreme opinions") struck many as a Radical mirror-image of Johnson.[23]

There were also issues with the trial's supervisor; Salmon Chase did not disguise his doubts about the case well. "The whole business seems wrong," the chief justice opined to a friend. He cast off the last of his judicial impartiality in May; eagle-eyed Washingtonians saw the chief justice and undecided senators stepping into cabs, chatting on street corners, huddling in parlors.[24]

Most illustrative of the frailty of the Radical case, however, was its enfeebled champion: Thaddeus Stevens looked as if he was only being kept from the grave by his determination to dump Johnson in a political one first. He insisted on being carried to the Senate trial every day to oversee this work, anyway. Hardly audible from a few paces away anymore, Stevens's voice ("hollow and sepulchral") still whispered iron Radicalisms into being:

> What good did your moderation do you? If you don't kill the beast, it will kill you.[25]

Those outside Stevens's caucus echoed such thoughts in a far more upbeat tone. "Radicalism will not only be dead, but will rot if they [the impeachers] fail," a conservative wrote happily.[26]

The final verdict was both narrow and crushing; the Senate came one vote short of removing Johnson. In the painful aftermath of this verdict, Garfield was not the only one to blame it on the trial's judge. But the loathing Garfield directed at Salmon Chase had a particularly deep bitterness to it, made intense by the respect he once held for the man. "I have no doubt he [Chase] is trying to break the Republican party and make himself President," Garfield complained to Harry Rhodes. "It is treachery for personal ends and deserves the contempt of all good men." Still, it hurt ("like shedding my blood") to cast away an old mentor.[27]

But, like all pain, this one bore Garfield lessons. He chalked Chase's latest errancy to a resurgence of "presidential fever." Another warning against political hubris came in a note from his mother, Eliza, a few weeks later: "The love of power has ruined many a man, and I awfully fear you will be drawn into the vortex before you are aware of it."[28]

Garfield swore not to be. He continued to fret, though, about what impeachment's collapse meant for the course of the country. "It will not only be a total calamity to our Party," he had predicted before the verdict, "but will be most disastrous to our friends in the South."[29]

Indeed, though the full aftershock of the trial's failure would take time to register, its initial brunt finished off the most important Radical; Thaddeus Stevens died in August. Before doing so, he wrote an epitaph for his gravesite, conceding his life's work remained incomplete:

> I repose in this quiet and secluded spot, not from any natural preferences to solitude, but finding other cemeteries limited as to race. . . .
> I have chosen this that I might illustrate in my death the principles which I advocated through a long life, equality of man before his creator.[30]

Pacing through the Capitol later that year, another Republican congressman confessed to a friend that he welcomed Thaddeus Stevens's death—even calling it "an emancipation for the Republican Party." For too long, the Radicals had been allowed to hold reasonable Republicans captive to their "hot temper," the costs of which had been exemplified during the late impeachment misadventure. Now, like the toppling of an ancient tree in an old-growth forest, Stevens's demise had opened a hole in the political canopy. A sprightlier generation of House Republicans could aim for it—and, on breaking through, perhaps reach greater heights.[31]

The man told his companion that only three Republican representatives could fill that void. One was William Allison of Iowa. "James Garfield is another."

A long pause. On tenterhooks, the congressman's friend asked who the third potential successor to Stevens could be.

James Blaine gazed up wolfishly at the Capitol rotunda. "I don't see the third," he admitted.[32]

16

"Men prize the thing ungained more than it is."

—Shakespeare's *Troilus and Cressida*, as quoted in
Garfield diary entry for September 26, 1878

To recapture the White House, the Republican Party fell into lockstep behind the most famous man on the continent. Ulysses S. Grant once would have made for the unlikeliest of presidential contenders; less than a decade before, he had been a broke shopkeeper with a drinking problem who (per his father) "had failed in everything." Yet, as with many men throughout history, war turned out to be Grant's salvation, and by 1868, he enjoyed a near-mythological status across the Union as its savior. Northern schoolboys studied his life in textbooks. Crowds respectfully removed their hats as his taciturn face zipped by on a streetcar. Such reverence only increased in pitch the closer admirers got to Grant; they encumbered the general with gifts of cigars, liquor, Treasury bonds, and even fully furnished homes. He accepted such favors without protest or much of a perceptible outward response.[1]

Few yet suspected that behind Grant's stony visage rested a similarly boulderlike mind—dull and heavy, possibly prehistoric but practically impossible to budge. Even after he agreed to run for president, it sounded to some as if Grant was asking to be left alone: "Let us have peace," he said again and again. Republicans duly appropriated this phrase into a campaign slogan.[2]

Voters proved they liked the candidate more than his party. Though Grant captured the presidency decisively, Democrats won ground in the House of Representatives. Southern unrest further muddled the outcome: the violence afflicting that region now looked less like a passing squall than a harbinger of persistent, organized political bloodshed. White gangs broke up Republican meetings in Louisiana; up to two hundred Blacks were killed by one such mob in St. Landry Parish. In other parts of the South, Republican officeholders, including a congressman, were assassinated. The military commanders Johnson appointed to keep peace lacked both the manpower and inclination to do so. One said if Black southerners cared for their safety they should just keep away from the polls.[3]

It all gave leading Republicans in Washington much to contemplate. As one would reflect in a memoir: "The result was not comforting to the thoughtful men who interpreted its true significance and comprehended the possibilities to which it pointed."[4]

Garfield had done his duty that campaign season. Despite not exactly admiring Grant's wartime leadership ("It is very hard for you and me to forget Shiloh, eh?" Garfield wrote another veteran), he dutifully flapped the party standard on the stump—telling voters the election of 1868 represented a referendum on the late Civil War and its results. Should Democrats triumph at the polls, "the three hundred thousand [Union] men who have died in the struggle will have died in vain."[5]

He appeared to prefer talking about the public money—sounding, to one observer, like discussing the nation's finances relaxed him somewhat. Regarding Reconstruction (that most monumental consequence of the Civil War) Garfield used the past tense, as if it were a finished work that could be looked back upon with pride:

The burned and charred timbers and broken foundations of the old
Rebel States were not fit material to work into the great temple of liberty. We dug down to find the solid rock of loyalty. . . . We had found
that whatever might be the color of a man's skin . . . he should be made
a part of the great political structure. On that broad basis Congress
reconstructed the South . . . the work with which you charged us two
years ago has been completed, except in the States of Virginia, Mississippi, and Alabama.[6]

Garfield still promised justice for any who might try to undo such
progress. "If you persist in forming Ku Klux Klans in the South," he
warned a Democrat heckler, "we propose to use the bayonet."[7]

Upon Grant's victory, though, Garfield expressed little confidence
about the next administration's policies. "I have no doubt there will be
many changes when Grant takes the reins," he said. "How general and
sweeping these changes will be, I cannot, of course, form any opinion at
this time." Garfield did, however, know that such refurbishment would be
necessary for the survival of republicanism. With its original legislative
purpose ("demolish[ing] not only the institution of slavery but the party
which maintained slavery") fulfilled, the party was now in need of a new
governmental philosophy:

This work [ending slavery] developed a peculiar kind of talent, very
efficient in its object. It was of the *destructive*, not the *constructive*
kind. As soon as our party came into power we needed ability of the
constructive kind . . . to build, to maintain, and support the administration of the government.[8]

The new vice president hinted that the new regime would not be opposed to perpetuating certain Radical policies, though. Schuyler Colfax
told voters the administration he was joining did not intend to repeat the
mindless "executive opposition" of its predecessor.[9]

•   •   •

Colfax's promotion to the vice presidency gave his party a chance to clean House, so to speak. The speaker's chair lay vacant; Republican representatives needed a new leader. Garfield could only mumble flattered gratifications when many colleagues called him just the man for the job. Yet he declined to commit himself to the contest. His hesitance was heartfelt; becoming speaker would lift Garfield away from the dense, dry minutiae of running committees—a prospect that would have appealed to most of his associates, but sounded to him quite hellish:

> Many of my friends have been kind enough to urge me for the Speakership, but . . . I still feel I can do more effective work on the floor than in the Chair.[10]

Furthermore, the new administration looked like it would be determined to set sound fiscal policy and rein in the greenback dollar. Garfield had long imagined contributing to this work; he also still daydreamed of becoming chairman of Ways and Means. A chance at being productive in such legislative arenas appealed to him more than the purely procedural power of the speakership.[11]

Luckily, a colleague had his priorities precisely the other way around.

While Garfield was being spoken of as the west's candidate for the speakership, the east's was James Gillespie Blaine. Washington had never been stalked by a purer political animal. Wisp-thin and coal-eyed, Blaine arrived from Maine in 1863 as an original specimen of a new breed of American statesman.[12]

Indisputably a genius (Blaine went off to college at only thirteen years old), he had decided long ago to devote his intellect almost exclusively to the art of charming the common man. He had taught in schools, he had edited a newspaper . . . but these served as mere testing grounds for Blaine's true discipline—the laserlike projection of his charisma. By the time he inevitably entered politics, he had already become a generational talent in making strangers think themselves his intimate friend. A favorite trick was asking random constituents about their children or their work or a local stud horse he had read about, all of which he happened to remember off-hand. "How in the world did he know I had a sister Mary, who married a Jones?" exclaimed one man, evermore a loyal "Blainiac."[13]

It required monomaniacal focus. How much so is illuminated by an incident later in Blaine's life, as he and an ally beheld an approaching stagecoach:

> "I suspect that carriage is coming for you," said a friend. "Yes," said Blaine, "but that is not the point . . . there is a man on that front seat whom I have not seen for twenty-seven years, and I have got just two minutes and a half to remember his name in." He remembered it.[14]

By the time Blaine entered the House, his ability to conjure affection from passersby had already become legendary. This trait would earn Blaine a nickname for the ages: in Washington's parlors, he would be called the "Magnetic Man."[15]

Yet, like all magnets, Blaine repelled as well as he attracted. His inner ambition burned hot, at a temperature those not charmed by him found off-putting. "Aggressive, artful," was how they described his maneuvering from afar; up close, they recoiled as he laced entreating arms about their waists. Through the smarm, they perceived a soul that "touched on all sorts of subjects . . . with illumination, if not penetration."

The best description of Blaine ever offered by such skeptics would be given by President Grant:

> A very smart man, and when I say that I do not mean talented, but smart.[16]

Smart enough, apparently, to know how to see off a rival. Ever since entering the House simultaneously, Garfield and Blaine had been friendly—the former, because he was naturally friendly to everyone, and the latter, because he had carefully weighed the benefits of being so. Secretly, Blaine first took Garfield's unaffected pleasantness as idiocy. "He [Garfield] is a big, good-natured man who doesn't appear to be oppressed by genius," the Maine representative snarked.[17]

Yet once both won consideration for the speakership in late 1868, Blaine acknowledged Garfield's abilities in a letter to him that expertly blended flattery, straight talk, and the tantalizing prospect of payoff:

> My Dear Garfield . . . It is my impression that the general conviction among members is that the Speaker should be taken from the East in consideration of the fact that the office for the last five years has been [held by the] West. . . . This fact would prevent you having that strength if a candidate—which your eminent position in the House and before the country would justly entitle you to expect—and I infer from this . . . you will probably not allow your name to be used. If not, I desire your most active sympathy and support for myself.
>
> Of course, I make no claim upon you except that which springs from sympathy of views, identity of age, contemporaneous service in the House, and an unbroken and cordial friendship for the past six years—I am sure that it would be of advantage to you to have someone in the chair *on whose friendship you can rely.*"[18]

The implied ransom of committee power practically leapt off the page. Already disinclined to try for the speakership, Garfield hurriedly agreed to Blaine's offer, thus securing the place for the friend who had promised to reward this support handsomely.

Then, however, Garfield received a lesson on his counterpart's nature. Having delivered his side of their deal, he struggled to get the newly minted speaker to do the same. He repeatedly sent his calling card to Blaine's quarters only to have it returned with the apology that the speaker wasn't in. The regrets became difficult to believe; seeing Vice President Colfax sneak into Blaine's offices finally dispelled them. Garfield fired off an angry note to the so-called friend he helped elect; maybe Blaine was exactly who his enemies said he was:

> Your manifest unwillingness to see me has given color to some rumors . . . which I should not otherwise have thought of for a moment.[19]

This flushed the speaker out of hiding. "Your letter pains me for it implies that you think it possible for me to show you a discourtesy," Blaine replied. "*I never got your card.*" He then stacked Garfield's plate high. For the Forty-First Congress, Garfield would not only chair a financial committee (Banking and Currency) but, almost unprecedentedly, he would informally run another designing the country's next census. Blaine further flattered Garfield by putting him on the elite five-person Rules Committee (out of "warm and unbroken personal regard"). His side of the bargain finally fulfilled, the speaker projected magnanimity:

> I have acted in the most perfect good faith . . . to do what would be most agreeable to you personally and most advantageous for you.[20]

Thus closed (albeit shakily) the first act of what would be one of the most subtly influential political relationships of the American postwar era—a period still taking shape, which both congressmen wanted to help define. Much bound Garfield and Blaine together: their drive; their concurrent arrival in the House; their reputation as public prodigies; their interest in a post-Radical Republican order; the smiles forever fixed on their faces. Much distinguished them: the fantasies each had about their political futures, the way each applied their intellect, the reasons each greeted strangers warmly.

They would move forward in parallel—influencing each other's movements, but never entirely falling into the other's orbit nor entering a collision course, hurtling through the political void together. Only one dared believe the presidency lay ahead; the other knew well the danger of entertaining such fancies.

Few Americans would appreciate the lasting influence the pair exerted together on the nation. As an acquaintance of both Garfield and Blaine wrote in a later period:

> Their entrance upon the stage was of as much latent significance to the Republic as to themselves. Men with much in common that was brilliant and great, they yet presented great contrasts . . . from this friendship flowed influences and consequences largely shaping the destinies of the Republic, perhaps never to be fully understood outside of a small circle.[21]

Blaine and Garfield's committee transaction represented but a single deal in a cascade of far shadier ones that befell the American government in this era. Their number was novel; their source, not quite—for since the Republic's founding, the country had lacked a professionalized civil service. Most public employees instead owed their jobs to a recommendation made to the White House by their local congressmen. America's bureaucracy had thus implicitly prized political loyalty from its inception. It had not taken long for this to be reflected in its operation. As a historian wrote of the late Washington administration's civil service: "By many avenues, intrigue and faction crept in."[22]

They only metastasized with the growth of government. By the end of the Civil War, the federal bureaucracy was the country's largest employer, with more than 50,000 offices on-hand to be doled out. Their occupants enjoyed existences mostly free of work and worry. A lack of competitive tasking or term requirements meant civil servants only needed to stay on the right side of their political patron to keep their post. Nor did they need to fret about income: in addition to their official pay, American bureaucrats were often (legally) allowed to skim funds from the public they served. A clerk in Boston, for example, could gather "a very large fortune" by pocketing fees off immigrants applying for citizenship. Top customs officials could take cuts of fines on goods arriving in American harbors.[23]

By 1868, this "spoils system" of public administration had industrial-ized. The dispersal of patronage by congressmen attained a new scale, coalescing around an efficient series of steps: local party organizations would get a man elected; he would appoint organization men to plum public jobs; the cronies would contribute to their patron's reelection (through the application of funds or force); thus the graft spun on under its own power.

The popularization of such practices did not go unnoticed by outraged citizens; a new political movement based on cleaning up the American civil service arose after the Civil War. "At present there is no organization save that of corruption, no system save that of chaos; no test of integrity save that of partisanship; no test of qualification save that of intrigue," moaned one such "reformer."[24]

Conversely, another figure arose in each party's ranks to supervise the stealing. A fittingly mechanical name was attached to the patron-age rings ("machines") while the men who managed them were called "bosses." A profile of the prototypical Reconstruction-era political boss reads as follows:

> The primary function of the boss was to organize, centralize, and uti-lize political power. He was selected for his ability to manage machine members and locate jobs for partisans, to strike bargains and alliances with opponents, to discover a man's price, to wring the last nickel of an assessment out of a federal judge or a rural postmaster . . . the boss must also have no hesitation about stuffing a ballot box, sending a group of "the boys" to threaten or rough up voters, about fixing a pri-mary, manipulating public funds, or removing battalions of political opponents from public office when profitable.[25]

Sometimes congressmen served as bosses themselves. More often, they delegated the job. But (provided they were attached to a machine) representatives and senators in Washington always served as the primary wrangler of public jobs for their loyalists, grist for the mill.

• • •

In squabbling over one such office, James Blaine kicked off a feud that would haunt him for many years to come. In 1866, he had helped put together a bill that created a lucrative post for a specific army officer, only for another representative to oppose that clause on the floor. As their exchange spiraled off into ugliness, Blaine dealt the other congressman an outburst of breathtakingly florid brutality:

> The contempt of that large-minded gentleman is so wilting, his haughty disdain, his grandiloquent swell, his majestic, supereminent, turkey-gobbler strut has been so crushing to myself and all the members of the House. . . . The resemblance is great. It is striking. Hyperion to a satyr, Thersites to Hercules, mud to marble, dunghill to diamond, a singed cat to a Bengal tiger, a whining puppy to a roaring lion.[26]

The attack hit Roscoe Conkling where it hurt. All men have their vices and the New Yorker's happened to be vanity—rarely did Conkling step out without his hair curled into a corona of orange-yellow locks, his wardrobe arrayed in harmonized hues, his aides set into file behind him like a line of worshipful pageboys. Blaine's tirade thus gave voice to what many in Congress had long been tittering about.

Like any good barb, one of Blaine's lines would never leave its target's hide; cartoonists would hereafter draw Conkling as a debonair turkey. The New Yorker—feathers badly ruffled—told friends he could never forgive the inventor of such an insult.[27]

Garfield used patronage about as much as he did life's other indulgences. Never one to pass up the occasional cigar or drink, he also sporadically arranged sinecures for friends in his congressional district. That was simply the norm of holding a House seat; one had to bat for one's supporters in Washington and doing so included making sure they got first dibs on good government jobs. This expectation is illustrated by a letter sent to Garfield by a member of his old regiment after he made it to the House:

Anyone who used to belong to the 42nd must be helped to anything he wants. You are our member of Congress. We look to you to push our advancement.[28]

He did—although less from a desire to rent political favor, but to make good on obligations of duty and friendship. Veterans of the Forty-Second received top consideration whenever a patronage job fell into their ex-commander's power to bestow, although he felt comfortable denying them, too. Likewise, if an influential friend from the Eclectic (like Harmon Austin) could use a favor from some official in Washington, Garfield would gladly act as middleman.[29]

Garfield did particularly well by a loyalist with feet in both worlds: he got Charles Henry (an Eclectic student turned Forty-Second soldier) appointed as a post office agent. This seems to have been the closest Garfield got to playing dirty with local patronage: Henry would one day (in a memoir chapter titled "Mailbags and Politics") recall using the job to become a "political intelligencer for General Garfield." Readers are left to wonder if any letters opened before their proper destination.[30]

But Garfield had no machine and relied on no bosses to preserve his power. The Reserve's pastures, forests, and villages lacked enough jobs or people to sustain such operations. Nor would its congressman have approved of such a thing—having heard the birth cries of the reform movement and sympathizing with them. Already, Garfield had become one of the first representatives to require competitive examinations for his district's applicants to West Point.[31]

Two favors nonetheless slipped past his guard. The first was ostentatious; in past recent years, Garfield had tired of renting homes around Washington. Such transience did not reflect well on a congressman of increasing influence. A quick crunch of the figures only added to Garfield's annoyance; buying a District house a few years before would have come out cheaper for him than renting all this time! He wrote out a new resolution in the summer of 1869:

I have resolved not to bring my wife and children here as boarders anymore.[32]

And yet, despite Garfield's lucrative legal practice (which would put him again before the Supreme Court the following year) he had not gathered nearly enough money to buy a home in Washington by himself. Fortunately, an old friend stood ready to subsidize this extravagance; whereas Garfield had helped David Swaim retain a high rank in the peacetime army, Swaim now seemed eager to help him purchase a home. Together, the two men found a lot on I Street (near the White House), and Swaim gave Garfield a loan to build it. This advance would be repaid on lenient terms, over many years, in a mix of both cash and the personal affection of a powerful politician.[33]

The second gift Garfield accepted was less flashy, yet more dangerous. He had actually taken it about two years before—cash-strapped from his European vacation, Garfield met a colleague who seemed almost frantic to share an investment opportunity in a business with a French-sounding name. In fact, both salesman and company had weird monikers: Oakes Ames, Credit Mobilier. Precisely what transpired during Ames and Garfield's encounters would become a point of contention. A pair of points never entered dispute, though: what Ames tried to sell, and that Garfield left the meetings with money.[34]

By midsummer of 1869, though, those facts lay in Garfield's past like unexploded land mines. He certainly seemed ignorant of their danger; walking past the skeletal frame marking his family's future home in Washington, Garfield perceived the emerging foundations of lasting happiness. As he scribbled to Crete after one such stroll:

I go every day to the little spot of earth where we are planting a home and think of what it will be to us if life and prosperity are spared to us. I have spent several hours half-dreaming. . . . I watched the bricks as they were laid, and felt how sweet it would be when all our little darlings should be in happy and safe shelter under its roof.[35]

He also took time to savor associations of his past. Harry Garfield would remember seeing nostalgia swell up in his dad at the most mundane of times:

> Two figures were always in the back of his head, 42 and 56. In other words, the 42nd Regiment and the Class of '56 at Williams [College]. Occasionally I would meet him at the Capitol after school and walk home with him. How many steps to the next corner? 42 or 56, or some combination or fraction of the two, would be discovered for the answer.[36]

Other numbers occupied the remainder of Garfield's free time and thoughts. He ran his Census Committee into the ground—keeping its unfortunate members in Washington during the summer recess for tedious deliberations on new figures to quantify, old metrics to eliminate, and outdated census verbiage to correct, while other congressmen were permitted to enjoy their vacation. "Very unheroic work," Garfield wrote to Jeremiah Black. But he reveled in it; colleagues even accused him of going "mad on the subject of statistics." Such assessments were corroborated by Garfield's pedantic lectures on the topic to the broader House:

> Since 1850, in spite of its losses, the republic has doubtless greatly increased in population and in wealth. . . . The time for reviewing its condition is most opportune. Questions of the profoundest interest demand answers. Has the loss of nearly half a million young and middle-aged men, who fell on the field of battle or died in hospitals or prisons, diminished the ratio of increase of population? Have the relative numbers of the sexes been sensibly changed? Has the relative number of orphans and widows perceptibly increased? Has the war affected the distribution of wealth, or changed the character of our industries? And, if so, in what manner and to what extent?"[37]

Other congressmen rolled their eyes at Garfield's insistence that they attempt to ground their debates in figures, measurements, and data, but Henry Adams asked his brother to entertain Garfield at their family's ancestral home in Massachusetts, anyway. They had experience grading political horseflesh; Adams thought Garfield showed promise:

> Garfield will talk about a railway-schedule with you, for his devilish census, which is a bore. So get ready to help him, for he may help you some day. We may never come up, but he probably will swim pretty strong.[38]

Garfield's honors had already accumulated to the point that he received an invitation to speak to the Spencerian Business College in June 1869, on the "elements of success." He told the assembled students he had but one: an obsession with self-improvement. The alternative of trusting one's final place in the universe to chance struck him as weak, wishful, lazy:

> No, young gentlemen, things don't turn up in this world unless someone turns them up. Inertia is one of the indispensable laws of matter, and things lie flat where they are until by some intelligent spirit (for nothing but spirit makes motion in this world) they are endowed with activity and life.

Nothing, not even the most unfair adversities, could hold back a hard worker. Garfield drew upon his life to underline this point—even splashing in a coy reference to his long-ago fall into the Ohio Canal:

> Young gentlemen, let not poverty stand as an obstacle in your way. Poverty is uncomfortable as I can testify; but nine times out of ten the best thing that can happen to a young man is to be tossed overboard and compelled to sink or swim for himself.[39]

It was an ironic turn of phrase. Though Garfield's speech ended with a tribute to the egalitarian nature of the nation the students were to inherit (its society, like "the ocean, where every drop . . . is free to mingle with all others"), he had begun to push another class of American out of his frame of view. His legislative focus now rested fully on duller, cleaner issues like currency and the census rather than fixing the South; likewise, Garfield had chosen the site of his Washington townhome, in part, because it was not so "infested with Negroes" as other neighborhoods.[40]

17

"Virtue itself turns vice, being misapplied;
And vice sometimes by action dignified."

—Shakespeare's *Romeo and Juliet*, as quoted in
Garfield diary entry for April 11, 1878

Further proof of the wisdom of Garfield's focus on fiscal policy could be found throughout New York City by this point. All along Wall Street, the Union's wartime needs had revolutionized a nascent American financial sector. Hundreds of millions in securitized federal debt, a protective industrial tariff, and a new national bank system: such policy innovations had helped the number of bankers in Manhattan increase tenfold between 1864 and 1870. The New York Stock Exchange now had its own building, while citizens could actively buy and sell Treasury bonds. Certain names were rising above the banking rank-and-file; John Pierpont Morgan was on his way to becoming Wall Street's "financial gorgon."[1]

Salmon Chase deserved much credit for this development, but perhaps the most significant of his economic inventions was one for which he felt the greatest reluctance. Even as secretary of the Treasury he had believed "no more certainly fatal expedient for impoverishing the masses" existed than creating a fiat currency. The needs of the Civil War forced

Chase to go ahead with printing many millions of free-floating "green-backs," anyway. By thus shifting America onto multiple types of dollar, the secretary enabled a particularly dangerous kind of financial activity: domestic currency arbitrage.

Businessmen waded enthusiastically into this market—trading gold dollars for paper ones and vice versa as their values oscillated. Some had legitimate reasons for this activity. (Customs duties, for example, still required payment in gold.) Yet many were simply speculating—hijacking war news, political gossip, and old-fashioned gut instinct to ride the shifting prices of each American dollar to profit. The work of "gold gamblers" hardly lent itself to popular esteem during the Civil War; those with bearish positions on the greenback would loudly cheer the market impact of Confederate victories. The currency traders were promptly booted from the New York Stock Exchange for prioritizing profit over patriotism.[2]

Unperturbed, the gamblers built their own trading room and consecrated it to their commodity of choice. A gold-colored fountain graced its center, topped by a gold-leaf dolphin spitting water into a basin, within which swam goldfish. Lacking other inspiration, the traders christened their new home the "Gold Room."[3]

By 1869, the Gold Room's floor remained packed by men using Chase's greenbacks to guess where Grant's monetary policy, European markets, and trading momentum might send the market. Transmitters flashed updates to hundreds of brokerages around Manhattan. Their inventor (a twenty-something named Thomas Edison) supervised his machines from above the floor, crowded as it was with traders "behaving like a pack of howling coyotes."[4]

It had become easier than ever for amateurs to join the melee. Margin loans were readily available to almost anyone; a man with $500 could theoretically execute million-dollar trades, hundreds of which were being made daily in the Gold Room by late summer 1869. One visitor thought the avarice had surpassed biblical heights:

Gold, gold, gold was the cry. The rich man Dives in the Gospel never shouted so pitifully for a drop of water as the thirsty ones did yesterday for the yellow ore.[5]

Garfield had long kept his eye fixed on the greenback side of these transactions—and with fear, not greed. The inherent instability of a free-floating currency frightened him, as did others' embrace of it. "I see the tide of error and insane clamor for paper money rising higher and higher," Garfield wrote before Grant's inauguration. Watching capital start flowing from America's rural banks (like those on the Reserve) to "great moneyed centers . . . for the use of gold and stock gamblers, but not for legitimate business" only added to his belief that greenbacks were having a narcotic effect on popular judgment. "The spells and enchantments of legendary witchcraft were hardly so wonderful," he said in one House speech.[6]

The magic would soon wear off. At eleven o'clock on the morning of September 24, 1869, after weeks of spiking gold prices, a courier reached the Gold Room from the office of James Fisk. He yelled out a purchase order that prolonged the previous week's increasingly absurd exuberance for the metal—which had all been spearheaded by Fisk. A ship-size man who left a wake along Wall Street to match, the former carnival barker had spent the prior decade becoming the epitome of a piratical New York capitalist: he had sold smuggled southern cotton to the northern military, swindled Cornelius Vanderbilt in cattle deals, and even used his winnings to procure a Manhattan opera house, complete with attached apartments. This latter purchase allowed Fisk to enjoy the singing, then the singers, in that order. "As devoid of shame as the desert of Sahara is of grass," opined the Reverend Henry Ward Beecher.[7]

But once Fisk began hoarding gold in early September 1869, Wall Street paid even greater notice to him than usual, for Fisk (and his business partner, Jay Gould) had apparently befriended the metal's market-setter:

the president of the United States. Grant had repeatedly been seen accepting the traders' hospitality during the prior months—even sitting in the owner's box at Fisk's opera house. And so, when Fisk began snapping up gold, other brokers assumed he was operating off inside information from the White House itself. Fisk and Gould nourished these rumors. "They not only bulled gold . . . but talked freely of the warrant which they had from Washington," recalled one speculator. "The highest official of the land was quoted as being with them."[8]

Reality finally broke back in to the Gold Room just before midday on Friday, September 24. A telegram arrived from Secretary of the Treasury George Boutwell, ordering the sale of several millions in government gold; it seemed the president was not in Fisk and Gould's corner after all. This realization hit with immediate force. "Possibly no avalanche ever swept with more terrible violence," wrote one observer. The bells of Trinity Church started pealing at noon. Before the echoes died out, the gold price had already fallen by almost 15 percent.[9]

Glee became panic. Brokers "flapped about the floor like headless chickens, bewildered as to who owed how much to whom." As tickers plunged (so forcefully that some telegraph wires melted) rumor spread that Fisk's clique had made out like bandits. Mobs of speculators hundreds-strong poured out into downtown Manhattan, claiming "Judge Lynch" owed Fisk and Gould a visit. New York militiamen fanned out but couldn't stop one rioter from socking Fisk on the nose.[10]

Back in an emptied Gold Room, technicians took comfort that they had never bought into the mania themselves. "Shake, Edison, we are O.K.," one assured the other. "We haven't got a cent."[11]

But the pall cast by "Black Friday" quickly spilled over into the country proper. With dollar values jumbled, few consumers knew "what to ask or give for goods," making the nation's total economic loss "of course incalculable." A resulting depression in America's agricultural sector wrought especial devastation in the agrarian Midwest.[12]

In Cleveland, a banker shot himself. James Garfield had been one of his friends. "Wall Street gambling is guilty of his death," the chair of the House Committee on Banking and Currency wrote. "But the great criminal is irredeemable paper currency, which is every day opening hell on our people." By Monday, back in New York, all but one of the fish in the Gold Room's fountain had died.[13]

"And now we come to [by] far the most important and interesting question of all," asked the New York *Sun* in October. "*Was Gen. Grant concerned in the gold speculation?*" In the weeks following Black Friday, as the economy regained its footing, it transpired that Fisk and Gould's boasts about allies in Washington had not been bluster after all; not only had a Treasury official apparently invested with them, but the president's secretary and even his brother-in-law, Abel Corbin, held reported stakes in the gold ring. This only added to the suspicion building on Grant personally. Even Republican newspapermen asked the president to publicly deny involvement, "in order to relieve yourself entirely from all responsibility for the acts of others." He did so but many remained unsatisfied.

Indeed, Democrats welcomed the fiasco. It had introduced the American public to the idea that President Grant was criminally stupid, or maybe even stupidly criminal. Some Republicans couldn't help but worry this might truly be the case. As one wrote:

> Every one in public assured every one else that the President himself was the savior of the situation, and in private assured each other that if the President had not been caught, this time, he was sure to be trapped in the next.[14]

It was under this cloud that Congress handed authority for investigating Black Friday (and its ringleaders' rumored ties to the White House) to the House Committee on Banking and Currency. This effectively gave its chairman control over the president's fate.

•   •   •

By inheriting command of the "Investigation into the Causes of the Gold Panic," James Garfield came under an abrupt barrage of public attention and private pledges of assistance. Little of either was informed or objective. Democratic papers expressed doubt that Garfield ("the mere tool of the money ring") would lead a trustworthy inquiry, while Henry Adams expressed confidence that he would catch the guilty parties. ("It is not so hard to see what they are as how to get at them.") Garfield was not so sure, and he made only the vaguest guesses as to where the work would take him. "The investigation will lead us to examine the dens of the Gold Room, some of the offices of the Sub Treasury at New York, and perhaps . . . the parlors of the President," he predicted to Burke Hinsdale.[15]

He traveled to New York to tour the Gold Room—collecting trading slates, noting the timing of etched price swings, eavesdropping on conversations to learn trader lingo. "It is very difficult and disagreeable business," he confessed to a friend, "but I suppose I must undertake it." Summonses went out to witnesses of all stripes by mail and telegram. Garfield also requested the correspondence of government figures implicated in the accusations.[16]

Finally, Garfield asked that his committee be moved to new accommodations. Its existing ones bordered both a restaurant and a men's room. The odors of each risked distracting the congressmen from their work.[17]

Garfield won plaudits for his preparedness when the actual hearings began in mid-January. As an eyewitness reported:

> General Garfield had, as is common with him, thoroughly mastered the subject, and brought all his legal ability to bear, for the purpose of extracting the truth from unwilling witnesses.[18]

Some put on better shows than others. Fisk, for example, barreled before the committee "with the life and uproar of a steamtug" on January 22, a diamond flashing from his breast "like a headlight from a locomotive."

He questioned what gave Congress the right to intrude into his affairs, but Garfield interrupted: "We have only availed ourselves of your celebrated financial abilities," the congressman reportedly said, "to assist us in unravelling an ugly public transaction." Thus defused, Fisk relived the panic with heedless relish, punctuating "his utterances with grotesque actions . . . and several times the Committee were convulsed with laughter."[19]

After hours of questions, the trader invited the congressmen to stop by his opera house sometime. Garfield is recorded as giving a noncommittal answer:

> Thanks, Mr. Fisk, for your kind offers . . . a first-class actor was lost to the world when you became the "business-manager."[20]

Far less entertaining was Jay Gould. He and Fisk traveled as a pair to Washington to testify back-to-back before Garfield's committee. They did everything together, in defiance of conspicuous dissimilarities: Gould was slight, shriveled ("a sickly scarecrow," per one biographer), and, in further contrast with Fisk, eternally inexpressive. Few familiar with Gould's past could blame him. He had been born poor, lost a parent and multiple stepparents, then beat a lonely path through his profession of choice by brainpower and will alone.[21]

In this, Gould resembled Garfield. But if the latter struck those around him as an amiable avatar of the American dream, Gould embodied a more predatory vision of it. "There was a reminiscence of a spider in his nature," an acquaintance recalled. "He spun huge webs, in corners and in the dark."[22]

The testimonies of Fisk and Gould made clear that the president was in trouble. Grant had evidently been the target of a far-reaching influence campaign conducted by the traders. Its intent had been to co-opt the president into helping corner the gold market—either by giving his intimates stakes in the scheme, convincing Grant that high gold prices would be good for the economy, or (as a last resort) spreading the impression on

Wall Street that his allegiance had been thus bought. Hence the generosity openly showered on the president by Fisk and Gould, the financial theses Gould had mentioned to Grant in private settings, and the gifts of cash and gold foisted upon those in the president's personal circle.[23]

Garfield's investigation also clarified that Fisk had been the operation's boisterous (and clueless) front man, while Gould did all the planning. This fact had not stopped "Diamond Jim" from insisting to Garfield's committee that Julia Grant—the president's wife—had invested with the gold conspirators. Fisk demanded she also be hauled in for questioning.[24]

This catapulted the committee dangerously close to where Garfield had predicted it might end up: in the White House foyer, grilling a president.

With the First Family entering the crosshairs of his inquiry, Garfield felt the burden of public responsibility fall heavily over his shoulders. The hearings had opened up an "abyss of wickedness"; Garfield, having led the plunge into it, was aghast at the scandal already dredged up by his investigation. "Its developments are among the most frightful exhibitions of rascality I have ever seen." More vexing to him was the utter unreliability of the witnesses. Their testimonies formed a Gordian knot of conflicting timelines and accusations of complicity—ones even correspondence records could not reliably untangle. Fisk claimed Assistant Treasurer Butterfield had been placed into his government job by the ring; days later, Butterfield claimed no connection with the conspirators whatsoever. Letters given as evidence went dismissed as forgeries.[25]

Inundated by such inconsistencies, Garfield inclined instinctively toward a rosy view of the biggest name connected to Fisk and Gould:

> Thus far the President stands untouched, though it is uncomfortable to remember that he has accepted the hospitality of such people as Fisk and Gould.[26]

Samuel Cox, Democrat of New York, tried to push the committee to meaningfully ponder the question of Grant's innocence. He motioned at the beginning of February to have Garfield "respectfully request of the President . . . whether he desires to be heard before the Committee, or otherwise, with reference to said evidence" implicating the First Family. The committee unanimously approved this request—including Garfield. Faith in the president's innocence aside, he felt committed to "letting the chips fly as they may."[27]

Shortly thereafter, though, Garfield scribbled an addendum:

> My position is a very difficult one and if I get through [this Committee] without breaking bones that ought not to be broken, and break those that ought to be broken, I shall have accomplished a success that I hardly dared to hope for.[28]

Grant reacted to Garfield's investigation as he had to Gould's advances: glacially. Steadiness was, after all, a foundational part of the president's personality, letting him grind through life with deliberate force. Attempts to influence his course had to be undertaken with great care. Only gentle flattery and nudging had any chance of changing Grant's trajectory on anything; overt attempts to shift it typically met crushing defeat. Even friendly advice about Cabinet appointments could be misinterpreted by Grant as rude intrusions.[29]

Thus, the initial efforts of the gold ring to control him had gone poorly. The president had slowly wised up to the fact that Gould was trying to manipulate him. After this epiphany, Grant ordered Secretary Boutwell to sell a trove of Treasury gold. Alas, this move came too late to avert a panic, save the president from having associated with Gould and Fisk, or prevent the real implication of others close to him. Of particular mortification was a letter the First Lady had sent her sister-in-law, warning that Abel Corbin (Grant's sister's husband) needed to have "nothing whatever to do with [Gould]. If he does, he will be ruined." This implied foreknowledge of the market mayhem.[30]

So, hoping to avoid any further humiliation of his kin, the president let Garfield know that none of the First Family would be interested in appearing before the committee. A figure from Garfield's past conveyed this refusal; Jacob Cox, now secretary of the Interior, told Garfield the "feelings and nerves" of Grant's female relatives would not fare well under public questioning. The president provided a different excuse for himself. Garfield relayed this back to the committee:

> The President desired me to express his thanks to the committee . . .
> and to say that he preferred not to see the testimony, nor to make any
> suggestion or statement in reference to it, during the progress of the
> investigation.[31]

It was a polite stonewalling tactic that satiated the committee's Republicans and outraged its Democrats. Samuel Cox tried to forcibly summon the president, "so that we might all join in the justification of his personal integrity," but Republicans united to insist the committee lacked the power to do such a thing. Another member tried amending Cox's motion (to simply "request" that Grant appear) but this, too, hit partisan deadlock. With that, after another week and a half of testimony, the fact-finding period of the House's Gold Panic investigation ended.[32]

Responsibility for drafting its majority report fell to the committee chairman. "One of the hardest undertakings I have ever had," Garfield commented of this task, "but I think it will do a great deal of good for the country."[33]

Garfield reported his findings on March 1. They read evocatively for a government document—casting the Black Friday plot as "an unworthy copy of that great conspiracy to lay Rome in ashes and deluge its streets in blood," its perpetrators "the debauchees of the Opera House." Nor did the report skimp on the affair's more tedious details: the inner functions of the Gold Room, hour-by-hour price movements on the trading floor, the means through which Gould "pretended that the President was a convert" to his scheme. Yet hints of ambiguity flavored the report, too. On the first page of its summary, Garfield conceded the "peculiar character of the operations to be investigated, and the secrecy with which they were carried on, made it difficult for the committee to find the clue to many transactions." And on the final one, signatures from the committee's two Democrats were missing.

This abstention was, primarily, because Garfield's summary concluded that the "wicked and cunningly devised attempts of the conspirators to compromise the President of the United States or his family utterly failed." Generously eliminating Abel Corbin from this circle, Garfield claimed his investigation otherwise found nothing to validate Fisk's "groundless and wicked" assertion that Grant family members held gold stakes, or that the president had done anything "inconsistent with that patriotism and integrity which befit the Chief Executive." While acknowledging the guilt of other implicated individuals (including Fisk, Gould, and Corbin) Garfield put the lion's share of the blame upon his old nemesis, the greenback dollar:

> So long as we have two standards of value recognized by law, which may be made to vary in respect to each other by artificial means, so long will speculation in the price of gold offer temptations too great to be resisted, and so long may capital continue to be . . . used in this reckless gambling which ruins the great majority of those who engage in it, and endangers the business of the whole country.

This was one of the few majority conclusions the Committee's Democrats endorsed. Having been prevented from interrogating the president, they wrote off the remainder of the investigation as a half-hearted partisan effort. As Samuel Cox dissented:

Whatever value this examination has for future legislation one value it has not. It has not enabled the committee with unanimity to speak fully of the connection of the highest government official with this extraordinary movement in gold.[34]

But Cox's protest lay buried at the back of Garfield's 500-page publication, while the majority opinion graced its front. Newspapers weighted each accordingly. From the front page of *The New York Times,* to those of the *Washington Evening Star* and *Chicago Tribune,* Garfield's verdict headed bylines and columns. Where Cox's featured, editors culled it into a trailing paragraph or two.[35]

As a historian of Black Friday has written, "Garfield's clean bill of health convinced most Americans that their President was an honest man." But, in private and throughout political spheres, the affair gave the first hint that other deficiencies lurked in President Grant's character. Upon the release of Garfield's report, a Republican journal echoed its conclusion that the president made "only one error [in Black Friday] . . . accepting the hospitality of, and entering into conversation with," unscrupulous men like Fisk and Gould.[36]

Yet for a significant minority of fellow Republicans, Grant's lapse of judgment augured worse tidings for the rest of the administration. Among these skeptics was Henry Adams:

> That Grant should have fallen, within six months, into such a morass . . . rendered the outlook for the next four years—probably eight—possibly twelve—mysterious, or frankly opaque.[37]

Adams actually saw right through this opacity. He and his emergent reformist brand of Republican recognized that Black Friday was but another indicator of rising corrupting influences in American government. "For the first time since the creation of these enormous corporate bodies," Adams wrote of Fisk and Gould's partnership, "one of them has shown its power for mischief, and has proved itself able to override and trample on law, custom, decency." Whitelaw Reid soon reached a similar conclusion: "All Administrations, I suppose, are more or less corrupt . . . the depth of corruption this one has reached is scarcely suspected as yet." Within such men as Reid and Adams lay the seeds of future Republican schisms.[38]

It was not that they considered the president guilty of corruption. Rather, they viewed him as an abettor of it—either lenient or naive to the sleaze festering in his government. Adams would later call Grant's rise to the presidency "alone evidence enough to upset Darwin," but also put much of the shame of Black Friday on what he considered the House's half-hearted review of it: "The Congressional Committee took a quantity of evidence which it dared not probe, and refused to analyze."[39]

The New York *Sun* did its best to rationalize the committee chairman's supposed complicity:

> Garfield is a gentleman of high tone, fine attainments, and of more intellect than falls generally to the average Congressman. His great trouble lies in the fact that he endeavors continually to square his sense of duty with his party obligations . . . he continually vibrates between what he ought to do for himself and what he is forced to do for his organization, and ends in an injury to both.[40]

But Garfield appeared to harbor no such doubts—either about his own conduct, or that of his committee. He barely noticed them being expressed by others. "It is very well received by Congress and the country," he wrote a friend about the reactions to his Black Friday report.[41]

President Grant seconded this opinion; in June, Garfield told a friend that "the President expresses himself under a good many obligations to me for the management of the 'Gold Panic Investigation.'"[42]

Nevertheless, there were still limits to Garfield's influence—limits he encountered anew once his investigation closed. Enjoying the president's gratitude and a partnership with Speaker Blaine, he nevertheless watched his own pet initiatives get bogged down in Congress. His census reform bill, for one, struggled to get traction in the Senate. Garfield blamed its eventual demise on a "want of proper study of the measure in that body."[43]

Even in the House, though, Garfield's technocratic legislative style could provoke suicidal levels of boredom from his colleagues. "Mr. Speaker," pleaded one Democrat dazed by a financial bill of Garfield's design, "in looking over this House today and seeing the number of vacant seats . . . the conclusion has been forced to my mind that in the judgment of this House the bill reported by my colleague, the learned Chairman of the Committee on Banking and Currency, is dead-born."[44]

Such exchanges reminded Garfield how exceptional his interests were in Washington. "I look up in the midst of the turmoil and vexations of political life almost every day," he wrote around this time. "I can understand why the Carpenter of Nazareth frequently went to the mountain apart."[45]

Garfield hardly paid attention to the Fifteenth Amendment's passage— certainly not as much as he had the Thirteenth's and Fourteenth's. He was not the only Republican to do so. The new amendment was hailed as the necessary capstone to Reconstruction (making male suffrage a constitutional right throughout the nation), but congressional Republicans had in recent elections learned the dangers of going, as Schuyler Colfax put it, too far "ahead of the people." The result was a vague, limited amendment vulnerable to nullification via poll taxes and literacy tests, notable more "for what it does not than for what it does contain."[46]

Garfield's constituents invited him to a celebration of the Fifteenth Amendment's passing into law. The congressman was forced to send along his apologies, but made sure to mention his interpretation of the occasion:

> I greatly regret that my official duties here will not permit me to be present . . . but allow me to say . . . I regard the adoption of the 15th Amendment to the Constitution as the triumphant conclusion of the

great struggle between freedom and slavery in this country . . . we have reached that grand plane of equality before the law which opens before every man in this country such a career as his own worth will prepare for him.[47]

Garfield's largest remaining point of concern about Reconstruction regarded whatever quantifiable results of the process would be revealed by the next census. "The chains have been stricken from the limbs of four millions of slaves," he mused. "What effect their enfranchisement will have on the wealth of the nation and its social and material prosperity are questions of absorbing interest."[48]

18

"O! It is excellent
To have a giant's strength; but it is tyrannous,
To use it like a giant."

— Shakespeare's *Measure for Measure*, as quoted
in Garfield diary entry for July 24, 1878

American voters understandably expressed greater interest in clean government as the year continued. Grant met this rising tide slowly, as he did many things. It was not that the president did not notice bosses cronyizing the federal bureaucracy; Grant complained he could barely open his paper without having to arrange patronage for some obscure loyalist. Instead, he simply couldn't be moved to consider reform important or practical. Insistence that it was only annoyed the president; Republican reformists were nothing if not dissidents, and Grant did not like dissidents. "He was kind and indulgent to those who looked up to him as a superior," one Cabinet Republican recalled. "He was the reverse to those who did not." The party's sycophantic bosses argued that neither they nor the president had anything to apologize for. "Of course, we do rotten things in New York," tutted Roscoe Conkling, now a senator for the Empire State. "Politics is a rotten business."[1]

After steering the president to as soft a landing as possible in the Black Friday investigation, Garfield spoke favorably of reform—but argued Congress deserved blame for ongoing abuse of the patronage, not Grant. "The fault, lies here, fellow-citizens of the House of Representatives," Garfield declared in March. "We go, man by man, to the heads of these several departments, and say 'here is a friend of mine; give him a place.'" He bit back when other congressmen called reform impractical. For an example of effective, politically expedient reform, Garfield would proudly point out how the Department of the Interior (headed by his good friend Jacob Cox) had cracked down on machine operations. "No man, so far as I know," Garfield boasted, "has been appointed to service in that bureau except on a strict competitive examination."[2]

But Garfield's brag about his friend came too soon; as a reformer in Grant's cabinet, Cox had already found himself the administration's black sheep. His professionalization of the Department of the Interior had been thorough (Cox instituted competitive tests for appointees, fired inept staff, and even denied his own brother a job), but consequently attracted the ire of the machines.[3]

A boiling point came in 1870, when party bosses tried shaking down Cox's clerks for "voluntary" donations. Cox banished the extortioners, who brought their grievances to the president, who took the whole fiasco as his secretary's fault. "General Cox thought the Interior Department was the whole government," the president later rued, "and that Cox was the Interior Department." Cox's defense that he had "fought fraud with such vigor as I could," only offended the president for its insinuation about the broader administration. The secretary offered his resignation, then read that it had been accepted on October 6—and noticed that the administration was blaming his departure on personal problems.[4]

Garfield refused to take such reports at face value and listened to gossip circulating in Washington about why his friend had really quit the cabinet. "I am greatly distressed at the rumors in regard to the cause of Gen. Cox's resignation," Garfield told Lyman Hall. "If it is in consequence to the pressure of that corrupt set of manipulators who wish to make our civil service a blackmail office, it will hurt the Administration worse than any single event." His concerns were both personal and political: Garfield hated seeing Cox humiliated, but—eyeing midterms—also knew that if Grant had indeed caved to the bosses it would burden the whole party ticket.[5]

Garfield wrote Cox for answers. The ex-secretary's reply confirmed the rumors:

> The fact is precisely as the public generally understands it . . . I had made up my mind to fight without flinching and when I saw symptoms of [a] lack of backing at headquarters, to tender my resignation . . . Since then the effort has been *painfully* made to produce the impression that personal and family reasons were the only ones given by me.[6]

Garfield urged Cox to publicize his side of the story if he had not done so already. "It is a clear case of surrender on the part of the President to the political vermin which infest the government," Garfield wrote. "You should publish the correspondence and let the country know the whole case." Somehow Garfield did not think this exposé would harm the president. In fact, he felt revealing the truth of Cox's ousting might serve as some kind of grand wake-up call that would make Grant repent. "Both he [Grant] and his Administration may yet be saved from the effects of this criminal blunder," Garfield told Cox. "But the only effective remedy is an unmistakable rebuke from the party that elected him."[7]

The result was all confrontation, no resolution. Cox handed his incriminating letters to the press within days, only to kick off a terribly timed spat in the Republican ranks. Reformist publications pilloried "General Grant's Unconditional Surrender" to the bosses; Grant's advisors replied by escalating ad hominem attacks on Cox. Thus, the schism only made the party's divisions starker. As one reformist newspaper challenged its readers:

Who is more capable of saving the Republican party from defeat two years hence—General Cox, who demands civil service reform, or General Grant, the promoter of such abuses?[8]

Unnoticed in the clamor was Garfield's role in prompting it. Now he could only inch forward with more wariness about the extent to which machine politics had infiltrated his party. Garfield even spotted their tendrils in his closest House ally; visiting Blaine's home one evening, Garfield had an epiphany that the speaker "believes the Civil Service Reform a humbug."[9]

Nor did Garfield fail to grasp what the affair revealed about Grant. He gave a speech later that year at the Army of the Cumberland's reunion in honor of General George Thomas. Garfield's keynote stressed that the "Rock of Chickamauga" had known better than to accept gifts from sycophants. Newspapers noticed the implication and wondered if the president (a "Gift Enterprise Manager") would, too.[10]

Garfield returned to Ohio to, ironically, face charges that he had also exploited his office. His I Street house struck certain voters as an extravagant splurge; Democrat papers were asking "how a man can become so rich in a few years' salary of a Congressman." Garfield chalked this scrutiny up as part and parcel of the electoral cycle. "I am treated as a very respectable and moral man for about one and three quarter years and then . . . I am everything that is bad." Garfield was forced to open his books to political surrogates, explaining his legal work and the debt he assumed to build the house. Such clarifications were necessary for voters stirring against public graft.[11]

In fact, Garfield's finances were tight enough to make him refuse a good political opportunity. Rutherford Hayes, exhausted of being Ohio's governor, had asked Garfield to "make the sacrifice" by taking his place. But Garfield declined. "I am too poor to accept the position," he explained; accepting a thousand-dollar pay cut to go from congressman to governor would ruin him. He begged Hayes through intermediaries to run again.[12]

Other letters asked Garfield to reconsider, but, whenever caring to respond, he would cite a less embarrassing reason for remaining in Washington:

> My position in the next House will probably be more important than any I have held hitherto and all my friends here think I ought not, by any means, to leave Congress.[13]

Reformist Republicans stayed home for the 1870 midterms, professing to find it hard picking "between the very vicious principles of the Democrats, and the very vicious practices of the Republicans." This ambivalence helped the Republican Party lose its two-thirds control of Congress and convince Grant to change his tune on reform; the president now admitted patronage "does not secure the best men, and often not even fit men, for public place," and announced the creation of the Civil Service Commission to advise him on future reforms.[14]

Of course, Republicans were not the only ones to blame for their party's setback. Democrats had also worked hard to depress turnout, through vicious practices of their own.

"It seems as though the old Spirit of Secession and Slavery is transformed into that of robbery and murder," Garfield wrote in March 1871. It was an elegant description of a gruesome truth about the American South; that Grant's presidency had not brought it harmony at all. The violence that marred the midterms made this indisputable. Frederick Douglass offered a superior assessment of the situation:

> A rebellion is upon our hands today far more difficult to deal with than that suppressed but not annihilated in 1865. . . . Ku Kluxism . . . now moves over the South like a pestilence that walketh in darkness and wasteth at noon-day.[15]

Indeed, exploiting a shrinking, restrained U.S. Army, aggrieved white southerners, and a preoccupied Republican Party, the Klan spent the months leading up to the election of 1870 terrorizing southern country-sides with impunity. "The sheriffs do not arrest them," a correspondent attested, "or, if they do, juries do not convict them." It was actually more dangerous to testify in such cases than be a defendant in one. In Mississippi, five of the main witnesses in one case were slain, convincing the survivors "it is sure death to testify before the Grand Jury." The South's senior-most remaining Republicans warned the president that time was not on their side; Klan-led voter suppression had helped Democrats win in Georgia, Florida, and Alabama, and "if Alabama can be carried by intimidation & fraud so can every other state South."[16]

This crisis played well to Grant's nature. It drew his attention southward—to a region overrun by men flouting his authority, murdering innocents, and in spirit undoing the war that made him. This roused the president to action. Reading aloud reports from South Carolina to his cabinet, Grant deployed cavalry to the state and pledged further troops for North Carolina. An inspired Senate arranged an investigation into Klan violence in 1871, interviewing victims and members alike. The details it unearthed ("sickening, horrible details," as Garfield described to a friend) prompted many Republicans to "again appeal to the power of the nation to crush, as we once before have done, this organized civil war." It was a remarkable development: having already deployed soldiers to keep peace in the South, Grant now discovered that many supporters wanted to empower him to wage war in it again.[17]

Other factions swore to oppose such a thing. Democrats branded the president "Kaiser Grant," while reformist Republicans (starting to identify as "Liberals") had their own reasons to oppose giving the president new authorities. "These are momentous changes," pouted one Liberal. "They not only increase the power of the central government, but they arm it with jurisdiction over a class of cases of which it has never hitherto had, and never pretended to have, any jurisdiction whatever."[18]

Furthermore, Liberal Republicans were questioning the wisdom of continued federal intervention in southern affairs. Senator Carl Schurz spoke for a rising number of northern Republicans who had grown tired of worrying about the old Confederacy:

> We desire peace. . . . We desire the removal of political restrictions and the maintenance of local self-government to the utmost extent compatible with the Constitution as is. . . . We desire the questions connected with the Civil War to be disposed of forever, to make room as soon as possible for the new problems of the present and the future.[19]

Nevertheless, the party's mainstream would not yet abandon the South, and so Republican congressional leaders were left to craft a legislative response to the Klan in the absence of overt instructions from Grant. After spending an evening at Blaine's to brainstorm a path ahead, Garfield left the speaker's home restless, yet again noticing "ugly signs of disintegration in our party."[20]

Garfield did himself a disservice by describing the Republican split so passively, for he was helping force it. Appalled to read of the "terrible necessities of the Union people in the South," Garfield also expressed alarm at the proposed solutions. In February 1871, Representative Ben Butler introduced a bill authorizing the president to suspend habeas corpus, oust certain southern officeholders, and purge suspected Klan supporters from local juries—an array of powers that Garfield thought tested the "very verge of the Constitution." It seemed so extreme as to be self-defeating; the "most violent and revolutionary" measure, if passed, would surely just run aground in the courts. And yet, Garfield acknowledged "something ought to be done to repress" the Klan. Caught between two opposing instincts (the radical and the pragmatic) Garfield helped smother Butler's measure.[21]

But the president would not abandon the fight. Grant summoned the Forty-Second Congress to convene almost immediately after the

Forty-First ended, putting the House opposition to aggressive Klan legislation on skates. During the new Congress's opening days, Garfield
called for appointing another investigative committee and adjourning the
House until December. This failing, he emphasized that Grant "has not
informed Congress that there is any lack of legislation to enable him to
keep the peace." Then Grant did just that—personally asking Speaker
Blaine to focus the House exclusively on "providing means for the protection of life and property" in the South.[22]

As this new legislation took shape (greatly resembling Butler's original proposal) Garfield's distress flared. "I have never suffered more per-
plexity of mind, on any matter of legislation, than on that we are now
attempting concerning the Ku Klux," he wrote.[23]

His confusion did not reflect a reticence about whether to support
the bill or not—Garfield instead appeared thrown off balance by the
strength of his own opposition to it. Practical anxieties about the measure
(its "double danger of having our work overthrown by the Supreme Court
and of giving the Democrats new material for injuring us on the stump")
melded with awkward ideological ones. ("It seems to me that this will
virtually empower the President to abolish the State Governments.")[24]

Of course, that was arguably the act's purpose; local authorities in
parts of the South had proven themselves incapable of preventing Klan
violence, and at worst were complicit in it. "This organized conspiracy
is in existence in every County of the State," warned North Carolina's
governor. "It is believed that its leaders now direct the movements of the
present Legislature." Nor did the act's supporters share Garfield's concerns about its legality. This was especially true for the recently arrived
Black members of Congress: Representative Joseph Rainey said he did
not care for a constitution "which fails to shelter beneath its rightful
power the people of a country." Garfield had said much the same thing as
a rookie representative.[25]

His newfound interest in preserving states' rights was, however, itself
a practical decision. In explaining his "painful anxiety" about the anti-
Klan legislation, Garfield called the bill "plainly outside of the line" of

constitutionality but more often cited a fear for the "political reaction . . . this new step towards centralization will produce." The Republican Party hardly seemed cohesive enough to endure such whiplash. Garfield had pledged to Harmon Austin to do all he could "to resist extreme and injurious legislation," and the anti-Klan proposal, as it stood, apparently ticked both boxes.[26]

He weighed alternative suggestions on how to calm the American South. The idea of building a federally subsidized railroad through it seemed a particularly "efficient measure of Reconstruction . . . [which] would do much to make the Southern property-holders feel that they were to be treated as equitably as other sections." Looking beyond the Klan bill's constitutional issues, Garfield further wondered whether its most muscular components would even solve anything. "I doubt whether legislation is the cure for the troubles in the South," he wrote an Ohio editor. To another ally, he repeated the same sentiment with the same crucial verb: "doubt."[27]

He took heart that at least some good had been accomplished by the past efforts of Radicals. When one of Congress's Black members (a representative from South Carolina) addressed the House on the Klan crisis, Garfield discreetly celebrated the speaker's presence in the Chamber:

> His Grammar and Pronunciation are better than an average of congressmen. . . . What a sight for the ghost of Calhoun to look down upon.[28]

On April 4, Garfield unfurled the banner of opposition and rallied Republican dissenters against the anti-Klan legislation as it stood. As the *Chicago Tribune* reported that evening:

> The three speeches of note today were those of Morton, in the Senate, and Garfield and Butler in the House. . . . Morton and Butler favored extreme measures for the South. Garfield set forth the views

of moderate Republicans, and argued with much power against those features of the pending bill which refers to suspending the *habeas corpus* and the use of military forces.[29]

It was, indeed, a spirited performance. Garfield planted his resistance to the bill on the need for a proper balance of governmental powers in the Republic; just as the Civil War had "vindicated and secured the centripetal power of the nation," so must Congress "see that the centrifugal force is not destroyed, but that the grand and beautiful equipoise is maintained." He proposed amendments that would do so—ones lessening the president's ability to suspend habeas corpus, safeguarding the civil rights of any southerners detained under the legislation, and narrowing the circumstances under which the government could intervene in Klan-plagued states.[30]

The following day, the measure was amended in accordance with these points, and, thus modified, earned enough support to pass the House. It received President Grant's signature on April 20, and Garfield declared victory to Harmon Austin:

> We have had a long struggle over the difficult question, the suppression of the Ku Klux outrages, in the South. We are in great danger, of pushing our jurisdiction too far. . . . I felt it necessary to resist the Bill in the form it was first presented . . . but I am glad to tell you that most of the very points that I made against the bill, was adopted by the House. . . . The speech which I made may not be a popular move, but in some respects it is the most important I have ever made.[31]

Hate mail provided Garfield with proof of his speech's unpopularity, at least in the still-radical elements of the Republican base. He fell back to citing the politics of necessity. "I have worked earnestly from the start to get a bill that would be effective to suppress the outrages," he patiently told one correspondent, "and at the same would not break down when it reached the Courts."[32]

Those closer to Garfield assured him of the righteousness of his actions. Cox reminded him that their party's future depended on appeasing at least a handful of the "intelligent, well-to-do, and controlling class" of southern whites, lest they vote Democrat forever. Cox congratulated Garfield for realizing this. "Don't be disturbed about being charged with lack of back-bone!"[33]

Nonetheless, Garfield would waver somewhat on the significance of his stand. To one friend, he boasted of his opposition to the Klan bill. "It was a perilous thing, to resist the current, at the time I did; but the resistance was successful," Garfield declared.[34]

But by the summer (once Grant began using his new powers—powers that Garfield doubted the wisdom and ultimate efficacy of) he was questioning if the grander flow of events could be shifted at all:

> After such a review, I . . . feel my fast-growing conviction strengthened that politicians and parties are in the main but sticks and bubbles whirling along on the great current . . . whose movements we may modify a little, but which we neither create nor control. The ship of state rights herself, and drives on, whether it be a sleepy Palinarus or a wakeful pilot who holds the helm.[35]

President Grant used the authority given him by the Ku Klux Klan Act as wakefully as one could expect—deploying federal troops and lawyers from the newly created Department of Justice to clean out renegade southern provinces. Soldiers in North Carolina apprehended hundreds of alleged Klansmen there. A similar crackdown occurred in Mississippi. Only in the western counties of South Carolina (after reading Attorney General Amos Akerman's report that two-thirds of the white men there were likely Klansmen) did Grant play his trump card of suspending habeas corpus. More than one thousand citizens were imprisoned for violating the Ku Klux Klan Act by November. More would have been apprehended had they not fled the state.[36]

And yet, Grant's vigorous application of the Ku Klux Klan Act also suggested the impermanence of its results. "No such law could be enforced by a state authority," wrote one southern Republican, "the local power being too weak." Another agreed that Grant's actions proved only "steady, unswerving power from without" could keep peace in the South.

But this infusion of federal power had been a close call in the first place, and even then, as one scholar has noted, it "pushed Republicans to the outer limits of constitutional change"—a difficult place to occupy long-term. The act's strongest provision had been drafted accordingly; the president's ability to suspend habeas corpus would expire within a year. Nor did Attorney General Amos Akerman, one of the act's most important enforcers, expect anything resembling it to follow:

> The real difficulty is that very many of the Northern Republicans shrink from any further special legislation in regard to the South. . . . Even such atrocities as Ku Kluxery do not hold their attention as long as we should expect.[37]

19

The carriage rolled west, its wheels crushing sagebrush that stretched out blue-green and infinite toward the Rocky Mountains teething the horizon. This prairie's magnificence was rivaled only by its rugged, almost unfathomable scale; the rig jostled through valleys that looked five miles long but were in fact fifty, fording streams that looked shallow but were revealed upon entry as axle-deep. One evening, after days of such travel, a support strut on the carriage finally shattered, forcing the passengers to doze on buffalo hides in the scrub.

The most important of them did not mind the delay. James Garfield found himself, quite literally, starstruck by the vista and concluded God had been in a kind mood when He created western Montana.[1]

Garfield's trip in August 1872 represented a welcome reprieve from his mounting responsibilities in Washington. Snoozing in the aromatic Montanan sage, Garfield officially ranked among the nation's most powerful Republicans. James Blaine had appointed him chairman of

Appropriations—holder of the "purse strings of the nation." Pundits hailed the promotion:

> The Speaker, in providing an agent for the prompt and able discharge of public business, could have made no better choice, and but few of equal merit.[2]

Garfield had lived up to these expectations. He passed almost all the year's major Appropriations bills through the House by April, while taking an unusually hands-on approach to the typically detached job of dispensing federal funds; when an unfamiliar field demanded public money, Garfield strove to familiarize himself with it via late-night research trips to the Library of Congress. "Few public men in Washington keep up literary studies," read one flattering profile written during this time. "General Garfield is one of the few. No one more constant in attendance at the Capitol than he; no one more laborious on Committees." A given workday might see him visit the White House, the Department of the Treasury, the Interior Department's Post and Patent offices, then I Street to share whatever knowledge he had acquired that day with his family. Harry would remember his father coming home laden with southern sugarcane that had been presented for subsidy consideration:

> We were given a vivid picture of the process from the time the sugarcane was cut until it appeared as the finished table product that we knew . . . We knew its succulence, but Father did not intend that our knowledge should stop at the portal of the palate.[3]

Journalists reporting on Garfield's movements often felt obliged to comment on a specific feature. "What a head that is! . . . It seems as big as any two to be found in the neighborhood." "A striking physical presence," noted another correspondent, ". . . with a large head, a flowing auburn beard, a clear eye, and an air of vitality, health, and bodily well-being about him."[4]

•   •   •

If only the same thoroughness was being practiced by other leading Republicans. Instead, patronage battles and melodrama still split the party's
ruling cadre by early 1872. Garfield heaped out blame for it; glancing at
a wintry White House, he assumed President Grant was attempting to
prove "with how little personal attention the Government can be run." A
look at the other side of the Capitol was hardly more encouraging. "The
Senate has done nothing in the way of legislation," Garfield told Burke
Hinsdale. "Their time has been devoted almost wholly to politics." He
believed the real power in Washington now lay with the Senate bosses,
and that "such men as Cameron, Chandler, Morton, and Conkling are
not likely to confer any permanent honor on anything they touch."[5]

Garfield was particularly eager to steer clear of that final name. He
had even begun to avoid giving stump speeches in New York state, for fear
of getting "mixed up in any Conkling scheme."[6]

The president's closeness to such men made Garfield doubt the
wisdom of renominating him. Nor was he the only Republican to do
so. Liberal discontent had reached the point that they had decided to
try unseating Grant—choosing Horace Greeley, founding editor of the
New-York Tribune, as their presidential nominee. Gaff-prone and eccentric, Greeley did not strike establishment Republicans as a potent foe. "So
conceited, fussy, and foolish that he damages every cause he wants to support," one said about the Liberal champion. But Greeley's bid (pledging
clean government and cutting bait from the South) catered to awkward,
emerging truths about the electorate. His mistake was phrasing these
sentiments indelicately. "Root, Hog, or Die!" represented all the advice
he had for Black Americans complaining about their safety in the postwar Republic. Asked about the Klan problem, Greeley shrugged. "Not as
much violence occurs in Texas as in New York City," he said. Such clumsiness convinced most Republicans to play it safe. "That Grant is an ass,
no man can deny," said one, "but better an ass than a mischievous idiot."[7]

Garfield refused to take the Liberal threat so lightly. It would be one
thing, he thought, if Greeley's campaign was "as weak as it is ridiculous."

But, returning to the Reserve, Garfield encountered many constituents "infected with Greeleyism." The bug even afflicted him a little; Garfield confessed to his journal that the Liberal platform was, "in some respects, the most admirable political declaration I have known." He soon shrugged this admiration off, though—sensing, behind Greeley, a Democratic attempt to sabotage the Republicans from within.[8]

At the same time, Garfield felt no real enthusiasm for Grant's candidacy, nor did he sense it among other Republicans. Siding with the president and bosses against reformists and ex-rebels, he settled it was "true that no party ever rises to any moral height above that which it had at its creation; but that, on the contrary, its tendency is downward."

As though to fight this fate, Garfield privately reserved the right to break from Grant in the future, "whenever it is clear that we can do better for the country by so doing." It was under this cloud that Garfield was tasked by Congress and the president to go to Montana to complete an errand for the administration.[9]

Heading west, Garfield effectively traded his front-row view of one American conflict for that of another. He crossed its frontlines in Kansas—his train passing desiccated buffalo skeletons and valleys quilted by fields of wild shortgrass and tracts of fresh farmland. "They tell me this grass disappears when the prairies are cultivated; that it seems to die out in the presence of our agriculture," Garfield wrote. In Utah he met the men transforming the plains so. The drunker his stagecoach driver, the smoother the ride.[10]

Such people and the ones they were displacing were why the Appropriations chair had come to Montana. The territory's newspapers hailed his arrival on August 19: "Hon. James A. Garfield arrived at Helena on Sunday and left this morning for the Bitterroot Valley, to remove the Flathead Indians to their new reservation."[11]

An ugly scene awaited Garfield, repeating *ad infinitum* across the Republic's postwar frontier. The Bitterroot's Salish people ("Flathead" was an unfortunate, erroneous misnomer) were facing down hordes of white settlers in their ancestral lands, while the president—drawing on a prior treaty made under duress, that his government had not honored anyway—was ordering the tribe to vacate.

The Salish had heretofore been superhumanly restrained in their dealings with the Republic to their east as well as its citizens. "Their assertion that no one of their tribe ever killed a white man, remains uncontradicted," read one federal report of the time. And yet, Garfield trundled into Montana's Bitterroot Valley in August 1872 to find its invading whites armed to the teeth anyway, "a good deal alarmed, and . . . apprehensive of hostilities." On him lay the duty of averting any possible bloodshed—by getting the Salish to walk away.[12]

How he did so can, and must, be summarized by an outsider only in brief. Only the modern-day Salish are qualified to relate the tragedy of their ancestors' relocation in the voice and depth it deserves and has so rarely received; previous Garfield biographies have told varnished versions of it, systematically neglecting tribal histories that offer less flattering perspectives of an important American statesman. In the interest of correcting the record, this author feels obliged to redirect readers to the excellent work of Salish historians for the full scope of this story.

Nevertheless, a basic recounting of events can be presented here: Garfield spent the better part of a week huddled in a hot buffalo-hide tent, struggling to secure the written consent of a trio of Salish chiefs to move their people to a northern reservation called the Jocko. "Somewhat tiresome" negotiations, war dances, and riding excursions only secured him the agreement of two.[13]

Options dwindling, and feeling "bound to do all in my power to save these noble Indians from the mistake they will make if they refuse," Garfield deliberately circumvented the opposition of the third chief, Charlo. He concluded Charlo would eventually decide to relocate his followers as more whites continued reaching the Bitterroot, anyway, and so wrote a letter advising Secretary of the Interior Delano to have the government proceed as if "all is now in a fair way for satisfactory settlement [in the Bitterroot]."[14]

Despite admiring his counterparts' "aristocracy of personal prow-
ess," Garfield assumed by thus disregarding their will he was nudging the
Salish toward their best possible destiny in America—one of industry,
safe distance from whites, and even suffrage (which he predicted would
be Indians'"salvation"). In practice, however, he was making a crucial contribution to their genocide.[15]

The Department of the Interior would act in accordance with Garfield's guidance to ignore Charlo's refusal—even forging the chief's name
on its articles of agreement with the Salish. The subsequent publication
of this forgery, per one Montanan official, "created the impression that all
trouble was over . . . and a large white emigration poured into the Bitterroot." The remaining Salish suffered greatly in the following years; Chief
Charlo would understandably refuse to ever trust federal promises again.
("For your Great Father Garfield put my name next to a paper I never
signed.") And yet, it did not matter; an army escort forcibly removed the
Bitterroot's last Salish in 1891.[16]

By that point, Garfield was dead and American history had already
cast him as a heroic martyr. The Salish, however, would rightly immortalize him as a great villain of theirs.

Garfield's trip out of the Bitterroot was just as stunning as his journey
there, carrying him through alkaline deserts and auburn fields, as well
as a hilly detour or two. These blended into a dazzling and inescapably
cruel landscape. Garfield watched wolves hunt antelope out his carriage
window. Passing through one gulch, he noticed a scorched pine tree towering along the roadside. His driver explained that its branches had been
used by vigilantes to hang bandits, and that purpose sealed the tree's fate,
for trees on which men are hung always die. "Man is the master of this
world," went a local saying, "and when his spirit goes out, something has
to go with it."[17]

Once back in Washington, Garfield would trade this and other pearls
of wisdom from this voyage. "The most discouraging trait in their character was a lack of acquisitiveness," he told one audience of the Salish.[18]

In his ongoing work as Appropriations chair, he would continue to mourn the continued hardships of all American Indians—but mostly through the detached, callous lens of public expenditure, as applied to cultures he did not understand. "The passage from barbarism to civilization is difficult," Garfield would write while evaluating further funding for Indian subsidies. "The savage is cheaper than the semicivilized man."[19]

While heading back east by stagecoach and rail, Garfield had no reason to anticipate that disaster (of a cataclysmic, party-shaking sort) awaited in Washington, poised to snare him personally. The country actually learned of it before he did: as Garfield trundled through Wyoming, Colorado, and Kansas, *The Sun* devoted the front page of its September 4 issue to an explosive story. "The King of Frauds," blared its banner. Trailing subheads outlined a scheme of "colossal bribery . . . princely gifts to the Chairmen of the Committees in Congress." *The Sun* identified not only the congressmen in question, but the entity behind the scandal. It had a strange name that readers struggled to pronounce.[20]

Garfield heard the news on September 8, after he reached Fort Leavenworth. His gaze drifted to the company dominating the headlines plus his own alleged entanglement with it. "The Credit Mobilier story . . . is one of the vilest and boldest pieces of rascality in the way of wicked journalism I have ever seen," he wrote after getting a grip on the story. "I think this is independent of the fact that my own name is so unjustly involved in the lie." This was a wishful assumption, built on faulty memory.[21]

20

"Defend your reputation, or bid farewell to your good life forever."
—Shakespeare's *The Merry Wives of Windsor*, as quoted
in Garfield diary entry for September 11, 1878

The outcry engulfing Washington had its roots in what carried Garfield to Montana, and, indeed, necessitated his trip there: the nation's railroads. In the space of a decade, the industry had risen to a central place in American society—an ascent that began in the Civil War, when the Union realized how crucial an interconnected continent would be to its future prosperity and peace. Millions of square miles spread invitingly beyond the Mississippi, while on the far-off Pacific coast lived people of worryingly tenuous attachment (political or otherwise) to the government in Washington. Thus enticed and anxious for the frontier's potential, the Union united public and private interests to conquer it—anointing several rail companies to bridge the Great Plains. The firms were pledged considerable government support: millions in federal bonds, land grants surpassing the size of entire states. It was, at first glance, an extraordinarily generous arrangement, one that Republicans (as the era's dominant political faction) received credit and blame for. "For this excess of liberality," wrote a House dissident, "the grantees owe no gratitude to the Democratic Party."[1]

The incentives appeared to have had their desired effect. By the close of 1868, the Republic had a mile of railroad for every 876 inhabitants (a world-leading ratio) and its line building only gained momentum into the following decade. This boom carried auxiliary industries along with it. (As one cabinet Republican of the era pointed out, American railroads were subsidized not only "for business which required them, but for the business they were expected to create.") More than a third of all American iron mined in this period ended up in rails, while new trades cropped up alongside the tracks, creating supply chains that flowed back toward the Atlantic—cattle herds filled the Great Plains, to stock the meatpacking plants of the upper midwest, which kept eastern cities well-fed. Railroads enabled and interconnected them all.[2]

Garfield monitored this growth from Congress. To him it rang as terrific progress, of both a commercial and national sort:

Talleyrand once said to the first Napoleon, that "the United States was a giant without bones." Since that time our gristle has been rapidly hardening. Sixty-seven thousand miles of iron track is a tolerable skeleton even for a giant.[3]

But in the course of cultivating this skeleton, the railroads had been forced to get creative in winning notice from their public benefactors; they had learned the hard way that congressmen suffer brutally short attention spans. "Congress was needed as midwife," one industrial historian has written, "but Congress was distracted by the tug and haul of a thousand demands." To dispel these distractions, the railroads had resorted to throwing cash, stock, and campaign contributions at "our friends of influence." This approach proved somewhat effective—in the words of one lobbyist, turning congressmen as incompatible as James Blaine and Roscoe Conkling into "gentle steeds."[4]

Yet such gifts did not dispel all the railroads' challenges. A central one lingered; their work sat at an awkward intersection of public utility and private commerce, in an industry for which no demand existed yet (the far west lacking regular train riders). Not being government entities, the companies were expected to live or die by free market principles; burdened by regulations that came with government subsidies, they struggled to raise the private capital necessary to grow. ("No one cared to hazard large sums on a dubious enterprise for uncertain returns.") The executives of America's early intercontinental railroads therefore needed to employ other means to carry their businesses to term.[5]

One figure distinguished himself in this activity. His name was Oakes Ames, and from the Civil War onward, he split his time between serving in the House for Massachusetts and doing the same for the Union Pacific company. Ames preferred to think of this as a confluence of interest rather than a conflict of it. On the House's Pacific Railroads Committee, he heard companies grumble about the commercial difficulties of laying track across the continent—work that was, after all, of national interest. After a year of what Ames generously called "patient deliberation," he opted to "assume the herculean task" of helping the Union Pacific and American government better serve each other. Exactly how he did so tested even the loose ethics of Reconstruction-era politics; Ames dealt himself and other congressmen stock in a construction contractor subordinate to the Union Pacific, called Credit Mobilier.

Credit Mobilier was to a certain extent unexceptional. It aided the Union Pacific as other subcontracting entities did other railroads; helping the railroad company's directors limit their liability during the exceptionally risky construction phase of the business. However, as these contractors' shareholders were also often the managers of the railroad companies, it is unsurprising that they frequently lined their own pockets. In the style of fraudulent businesses, Credit Mobilier drastically overbilled its client (Union Pacific, and thus indirectly the American government), pinched on what it delivered, and bought the loyalties of anyone who could either accelerate or stop the scam.[6]

Ames thought there to be nothing wrong with this. As far as he cared, "progress and profit" had always gone hand in hand, and if the Republic wanted to bridge the continent, it needed to sufficiently incentivize the men who took the risk of doing so. Thus excusing the operation, Ames spent the latter half of the 1860s convincing fellow congressmen to buy Credit Mobilier shares and become invested (literally) in the Union Pacific's growth.[7]

Ames lured representatives from throughout the Midwest and New England to take Credit Mobilier stock. Writing a coconspirator in 1868, he declared victory. "I don't fear any investigation here . . . I have used this [stock] where it will produce most good to us, I think."[8]

Still, Ames knew that having more friends in Congress could only help the cause. It was around that time that he and Garfield held their private meetings.

During the following few years, the Union Pacific kept plowing across canyons and mountain ranges, from Nebraska through Utah Territory. Wherever picks failed to break frozen earth, dynamite sufficed. In continuing to extend government support to this expansion, the Credit Mobilier shareholders on Capitol Hill were indirectly paying themselves handsome dividends—as high as 80 percent on their stock.[9]

Ames took the railway's success for his own. "The road was constructed . . . mainly through his exertions and sacrifices," Ames's own memoir would purr. Yet, just as America's railroads matured in the early Grant administration, so too did the reform movement, and inevitably talk of fraud in the industry swirled.[10]

In New York, *The Sun* finally broke the full Credit Mobilier story on September 4, 1872. Flubbing the scandal's finer details, the paper's headline still framed its significance sufficiently: "Congressmen who Have Robbed the People, and who now Support the National Robber."[11]

Ames would never comprehend the outrage that followed *The Sun*'s scoop, nor the denials and embarrassment of fellow stockholders around Capitol Hill:

It is difficult to account for the excitement that at once ran wild through the country according to any rules of reason or morality. The members of Congress whose names were involved seemed to have been terror-stricken. The fire thus kindled broke forth in a flame.[12]

Garfield did not feel the heat at first. His actions after returning east instead suggest bafflement; in Kansas, he journaled of being "dragged into some story which I do not understand, but see only referred to in the newspapers." During the next few days, Garfield reached out to another member of *The Sun*'s list (now–Vice President Schuyler Colfax) seeking clarity on what precisely they had been accused of. He then issued a public denial that he had subscribed to or taken ownership of any Credit Mobilier stock.[13]

Nonetheless, as his confusion persisted through September, Garfield received a series of letters from his legal ally and fellow Disciple, Jeremiah Black. They made it obvious, with mounting urgency, that Black had something important to say about the accusations. "I take it for granted you will let me see you," he wrote before Garfield's initial statement hit the press. "Say nothing [further] without seeing me first," he demanded after it. Black wrote sharply because he remembered what Garfield ostensibly could not: that Garfield had accepted money from Oakes Ames back in the late 1860s, and that it had been understood to represent Credit Mobilier dividends, taken from stock Ames held on Garfield's behalf.[14]

Critically, Black's story cast his friend as an unwitting pawn in the swindle—Garfield had supposedly been misled by Ames about the nature of Credit Mobilier, returning the dividend money once Black told him of the rumors surrounding the company:

> You regarded O.A. [Oakes Ames] as a perfectly upright man—an example of solid integrity—had no suspicion that he had private interests . . . much less that he was a ring-leader in any fraud. . . . He offered you some stock in Cred. Mob.—offered to sell it to you at par . . . you were not the instrument of his corruption, but the victim of his deception.[15]

Black did not speculate on why his friend could not recall these events. Nonetheless, he lent Garfield a defense that the rest of Congress's Credit Mobilier shareholders could have only envied. Henry Dawes, chair of Ways and Means, was carefully claiming that he never bought stock that he did not pay the proper value of. Vice President Colfax said bribery would not have been necessary for him to support Union Pacific subsidies ("You might as well say that a Methodist would have to be bribed to advocate Methodism").[16]

These obfuscations would all backfire on their issuers. Garfield did not have the same problem as these men, but he was not exactly safe either: though Black's version of events cleared Garfield of corruption, it also made him guilty of gullibility—of being a naive tool to cannier, crooked interests. This was a weak excuse in Grant-era Washington.

Only a presidential candidate as inept as Horace Greeley could fumble a godsend like Credit Mobilier. Reform was the most potent element of his platform, and the scandal could not have been better-timed to validate its righteousness to voters. Yet the contradictions of the contender and his Democrat-Liberal coalition proved too difficult to reconcile; Greeley got crushed by Grant in November, at the polls as well as in spirit. "I have been assailed so bitterly that I hardly know whether I was running for President or the penitentiary," he complained. Greeley died less than a month later—not long after his wife, but before the Electoral College had time to ratify his defeat.[17]

Yet the reform movement and the related uproar over Credit Mobilier outlived Greeley. This meant Republicans could not afford to ignore either issue, despite keeping the presidency and retaking ground in Congress. Few appreciated this better than Garfield: "A two-thirds majority is always dangerous. If our party will have the wisdom to temper their victory with prudence . . . we may be able to steer clear of disaster."[18]

In accord with what prudence demanded, on December 1 Garfield visited James Blaine to ask the speaker to organize a House inquiry into Credit Mobilier.[19]

Blaine needed no convincing. Unlike many House Republicans, he had been too sly to fall for Ames's stock pitches. But the public still doubted Blaine's innocence in the affair, and, as speaker, he could not neglect the political well-being of the larger caucus, and so, had already decided to launch an investigation into Credit Mobilier. "We shall be the biggest fools on earth if we fail to take the initiative," the speaker told his Appropriations chair.[20]

Together, the two chatted until dusk. Then Garfield returned to I Street to speak with Jeremiah Black. Garfield held another talk with Oakes Ames later—professedly, to fact-check his memory of their previous ones.[21]

On December 2, addressing the charges leveled against an array of representatives (including himself), Blaine told the House an inquiry was needed to determine if any representative "was bribed by Oakes Ames in any matter touching his legislative duty." Then, with a stirring flourish of bipartisanship, he surrendered the speaker's chair to a Democrat. A remarkably balanced panel of two Democrats, a Liberal, and a pair of Republicans took shape, to be chaired by Luke Poland of Vermont—a man trusted on both sides of the congressional aisle. ("I suspect, from his tone and manner, that he once was a Methodist minister of the best type.")[22]

As though in gratitude for its creation, Poland's committee closed off its opening hearings to the public and let Blaine skip ahead of the witness queue. The speaker submitted his one-page testimony in writing on the morning of December 12, answered two questions, then exited stage left. He had handled his part brilliantly. Even Democrat columns gushed that they had "*always* admired James G. Blaine."[23]

No other witness performed so smoothly, least of all Oakes Ames. The committee's central interview subject couched almost all his responses to questions in damningly evasive language. "I do not recollect what account he gave," he pleaded when invited to grade another witness's description of Credit Mobilier. "I think so," Ames offered when asked if the company kept a secretary. His clumsiest dodge came when Poland requested a timeline of Ames's stock transactions: "One of the things I can never do is remember dates."

One might assume such statements would disqualify a witness. Yet somehow, Ames still managed to go through a list of accused congressmen and tell the committee with confidence whether each man accepted Credit Mobilier shares. Garfield, apparently, had not: "I agreed to get ten shares of stock for him and hold it until he could pay for it. He never did pay for it or receive it."[24]

Most would have taken this as a welcome exoneration. But Garfield bristled at its insinuation. "He stupidly says he agreed to get it [the stock] for me," Garfield grumbled. "His statement would have been exactly according to fact if it had said he proposed to get it for me." Apparently, Ames's memory was so defective that he could not even stick to the narrative he and Garfield had agreed on a few nights prior.[25]

Not that Garfield would immediately correct it. He had decided to bite his tongue in public about Credit Mobilier, defying baited headlines like "General Garfield, You are Wanted," so he could hone his story. He had since settled that Ames had indeed offered him shares and reserved them while Garfield considered the investment. Somewhere around the same time, Ames had also given him a few hundred dollars—not as a dividend payment, but rather a friendly loan between colleagues. Then, upon subsequently hearing rumors about Credit Mobilier, Garfield had purportedly decided to refuse the stock and repaid Ames. All in all, this read as a sanitized version of Black's story, its details tweaked into as generous a narrative as possible for Garfield.[26]

He provided it to Poland's committee on the morning of January 14, 1873, then went home to continue insisting his innocence to his diary:

> I am too proud to confess to any but my most intimate friends how deeply this whole matter has grieved me. While I did nothing . . . that can be construed into any act even of impropriety much less than corruption, I have still said from the start that the shadow of the cursed thing would cling to my name for many years.[27]

He did not have to look far to see this validated. "Gross exaggerations and wicked falsehoods" were running rampant in the press. "He [Garfield] took the bribe of Oakes Ames just as others took it," insisted *The Sun* a month after their first scoop.[28]

In reflex, Garfield rejected that he had done anything regrettable, and even, to one ally, denied receiving a stock pitch from Ames.[29]

But Garfield kept these errant defenses private; only friends got the privilege of hearing him complain that he had done nothing anyone could justly criticize. "It [the Ames transaction] was a simple accommodation from one man to another," Garfield elaborated to Harmon Austin. "My conversation and conduct have been entirely consistent with this view of the case."[30]

Oakes Ames soon flourished even more inconsistency. During his first round of testimony, he had claimed his stock deals with other congressmen did not equate to bribery—Ames said bribing friends made little sense. But their subsequent rejections of any association with Ames or Credit Mobilier wounded him.[31]

Unwilling to suffer having himself and his work so thanklessly thrown under the bus, Ames decided to provide more illuminating evidence to the Poland committee on January 22. Thereafter, he carried written records and a professedly sharper recollection of things into the hearing room. The press correctly identified the emotion at play. "Oakes Ames has recovered his memory with a vengeance," quipped the *Evening Star*.[32]

Ames still hedged his way through these appearances ("I have stated it as I remember it; I may be mistaken") but now produced enough hard evidence to make verified liars out of many whom the inquiry had already heard from, including himself. Ames's records turned out to be filled with transactions categorized by congressmen. Though their organization left much to be desired (being recorded in a manner somehow both deficient and convoluted), Ames augmented these notes with receipts as well as refreshed memories. Among his most dramatic changes of heart regarded Garfield. Ames now said Garfield had not only proposed buying Credit

Mobilier shares but also taken ownership of them, along with a dividend payment of three hundred and twenty-nine dollars.

Not that Ames could prove this, nor would he bindingly commit himself to its truth. Asked if the dividend payment might have been a loan, as Garfield insisted, Ames replied, "Not to my knowledge," before later allowing (repeatedly), "I may be mistaken." Nor had Garfield's name been crossed out in Ames's crimson record book (indicating his deal had not been settled), and neither could Ames stick to a story of how, exactly, Garfield received the alleged payment.[33]

While not entirely improving on his prior performance as a witness, Ames nevertheless succeeded in bringing the names of others back into deeper question. "He is evidently determined to drag down as many men with him as possible," Garfield told his diary.[34]

Unfortunately, conditions now made it harder for Garfield to reenter the fray. The Poland committee's hearings had been forced open for the public, and, having already spoken his piece to the committee, Garfield was loath to do so again before an excited gallery. "The condition of panic into which the public mind is thrown makes it nearly impossible either to speak or listen with calmness," he wrote Burke Hinsdale. The scrutiny and mockery had already been hard to endure; after Ames's latest testimony, a Democratic columnist issued a new edition of the Republican dictionary. Garfield's alibi informed one entry:

> Innocence = Interviewing Geo. F. Train and Oakes Ames . . . and thinking they would pour money into his lap without anything expected in return—James A. Garfield[35]

So Garfield opted to not re-testify. "If the people will believe . . . a man blackened all over with contradictions and fraud as against my statement I cannot help it," he announced with finality to Harmon Austin. Garfield also revisited Jeremiah Black, who confirmed that "nothing in the case" indicated the committee could find him at fault.[36]

He needed to break his silence again at some point, but now was clearly not the right time. "I am waiting with what patience I can for a moment of calm when men will hear," Garfield wrote on February 17.[37]

He tried to find solace in congressional work in the meantime—a relief the speaker generously helped provide. As ambitious as James Blaine might have been, he nonetheless had a heart, and by 1873 the Appropriations chair had earned a spot in it. Just as Poland's hearings started reflecting poorly on Garfield, Blaine (in one biographer's words) "went out of his way . . . to show esteem, regard, and consideration for Garfield," even letting Garfield serve as speaker for certain debates. Democrats observed, with an incorrect use of the plural, "that the friends of GARFIELD are maneuvering to give him an improved standing."[38]

Correspondence would have confirmed this observation. "Your Father is much attached to General Garfield," the speaker's wife had written their son.[39]

Though Garfield believed the Poland committee would acquit him, the panel instead took Ames's new testimony as basically the truth—concluding that Garfield had accepted Credit Mobilier shares as well as three hundred and twenty-nine dollars of dividends. "This sum was paid over to Mr. Garfield by a check on the Sergeant-at-Arms," asserted Poland's report.

Yet the committee recommended disciplinary action against only two of the accused congressmen—Ames, naturally, and James Brooks of New York, who had cashed in on tens of thousands' worth of railroad securities. Poland concluded the remaining statesmen had not "been affected in their official action in consequence of their interest in Credit Mobilier stock." Historians have found this a peculiar verdict ("By some baffling twist of logic it concluded Oakes was guilty of offering bribes . . . but no one was guilty of accepting them"), but the public reaction at the time was less incredulous than one might expect. After all, as one journalist remarked, "investigator and investigated were in a boat together in Congress."[40]

Yet Garfield had begun getting battered in the House. Floor opponents now had something solid to club him with, and, as if dazed by Poland's surprise verdict of his guilt, Garfield kept blundering into their attacks. In February, he challenged Ben Butler over expense privileges, but the Massachusetts representative fired back: "I want no quarrel with the gentleman from Ohio. *De mortuis nil nisi bonum* [say nothing but good about the dead]." Laughter rang out, while Garfield dropped mutely into his seat ("pale as death, fairly gasping for breath"). Similarly, right after Poland's report hit the printers, Garfield made the boneheaded move of saying congressmen with legal claims against railroads should not be allowed to vote on related legislation. Samuel Randall of New York made the obvious counterpoint. "There should be no question as to whether men who were saved by railroads, as you were yesterday, should be allowed to vote on measures affecting them." An observer described Garfield again slinking down. "The old adage 'a burnt child avoids the fire,' does not hold good in his case."[41]

Whitelaw Reid wrote Garfield with well meaning but blunt advice:

> Frankly and in all friendship, I think you are in an ugly fix . . . you got into it in all innocence, and have only wounded yourself in floundering about trying to get out. Stop floundering. Don't say a word. Shut your mouth and keep it shut.[42]

Yet this was impossible for Garfield. He was an elected official, after all, and the committee report had not offered him the public redemption he had been counting on. His correspondence now told him the Western Reserve was showing signs of profound unrest. "People have been asking," Burke Hinsdale wrote from Garfield's old power base of Hiram, "whereunto shall this thing grow?"[43]

Preoccupied as they were with the Credit Mobilier panic, Garfield and his allies overlooked two other scandals he became ensnared in around the same time. The first sprouted from his legal career, which had always threatened to complicate his public one; the prior spring, Garfield had been offered five thousand dollars for a few days' work assessing a type of pavement being pitched to Washington by the DeGolyer company for the District's sidewalks. He accepted, prompting subdued celebrations from corporate counterparts. "The influence of Gen. Garfield has been secured," one director wrote the other. "He holds the purse strings of the United States . . . all the appropriations for the District must come through him." The DeGolyer company obviously knew it had bought Garfield's political influence rather than his legal expertise.[44]

Garfield lived up to these expectations. Finishing his legal review briskly, he then personally endorsed the product to Washington's Board of Public Works—a body that depended on Garfield's Appropriations committee for funding. At best a conflict of interest, at worst a bribe, this transaction slipped neatly under the public radar. Awareness of it would leak out slowly (during the course of years rather than days) and so Garfield deferred its fallout, delaying a blow that may well have finished off his political career if delivered immediately.[45]

The second scandal Garfield neglected was less shameful but attracted greater outcry in the Reserve than Credit Mobilier. He only realized this upon returning home.

Garfield arrived in Cleveland on March 8, 1873, and almost immediately wrote Crete of hearing "the thousand echoes which the Credit Mobilier explosion has made." They reverberated across the Reserve: local conventions were adopting resolutions urging Garfield's resignation. Garfield saw "false and unjust" commentaries filling most every newspage. Before long, he realized that the wrath had little to do with Credit Mobilier. "The District is in great roar over the Salary Bill," he scribbled with surprise.[46]

During the closing days of the Forty-Second Congress, an Appropriations bill had passed with a clause boosting salaries across the federal government, including for elected officials. Advocates of this raise contended increasing pay for public servants might make them less inclined to defraud taxpayers in the future. Yet the finer details of the legislation cheapened such arguments: it had been written to be retroactive to the last Congress, enabling representatives to draw salaries from time already served. Such naked self-dealing stirred widespread disgust. "Outside of the criminal classes there has seldom been a more melancholy exhibition of the weakness of human nature," wrote George Boutwell. American voters (now lamentably skilled at naming scandals) dubbed it the "Salary Grab." While the shrewdest representatives (like James Blaine) had tiptoed around the outrage by simply not accepting their backdated salaries, Garfield could not dodge the matter so easily; as Appropriations chairman, he had technically overseen the legislation.[47]

His constituents, being mostly the descendants of frugal New Englanders, appeared exceptionally riled up by it. "The Credit Mobilier seems to be almost forgotten in the midst of this new storm," Garfield wrote. But the outrage was also obscuring his actual involvement in the Salary Grab. He had, in fact, fought the retroactive pay raise repeatedly, until the Committee of the Whole tacked it to the year's most important Appropriations bill. Unwilling to jeopardize the funding of the government, Garfield had grudgingly allowed the legislation to pass—a triumph of practical committee leadership that now risked kneecapping him politically.[48]

The Reserve's newspapers had not detailed the depth of his opposition to the Salary Grab; even Garfield's longtime friends did not seem to fully appreciate his innocence. Nor could they agree on what he should do now. "Hinsdale writes me a long letter saying I must come home," Garfield mused in April after returning to Washington. "Harmon Austin thinks I had better not come yet. Halsey Hall says come and so it goes."[49]

Garfield ultimately opted to collect his thoughts before directly confronting his constituents' anger. Correctly detecting more fury at his Salary Grab role than the Credit Mobilier scandal, he prioritized his defenses appropriately. "I do not propose to be stampeded nor born down in the tempest of clamor now raging," he promised an ally.[50]

·   ·   ·

Garfield's only reliable source of stability in these months was his wife. Crete remained, as ever, the most resilient presence in his orbit. Among the first letters he received after the Credit Mobilier story broke had been one from her, promising everything would be all right. She stayed resolute as this prediction proved quite wrong. "Darling . . . I am sure you will get into the sunshine again. But you know I love you all the same. Through sunshine and through storm." Busy as Garfield was, he had by now become grateful, as he had once not been, for their partnership. He voiced this sentiment on Crete's birthday, overlooking his troubles to celebrate her arrival into his life and all they had accomplished together:

> I thank the giver of life, and all the happy fates, that brought you into being forty-one years ago today. When I think of the separate paths we wandered so long, before knowing each other, I bless each bush and tree that veered those paths until they met and brought us together. . . . How strange it is, that marriage can be considered a bond—a shackle! To me it is liberty, love, life.[51]

"This is the birthday of the best woman I have ever known," Garfield journaled that evening. It is unlikely he shared this opinion with his mother—still cooped up with her son's family on I Street. "We are all very well and enjoying life as well as Mortals can," Eliza wrote that winter.[52]

Garfield eventually wrote his way out of trouble. He spent the spring drafting two essays for his constituency. The first explained his role in what he called the "salary question"; the second did the same for Credit Mobilier. Garfield finished writing the former in the Reserve, only to see that even Hiram buzzed with "mean slings." "It is cold, dismal weather," Garfield wrote, "and the task before me is more dismal still."[53]

He managed to tackle it diligently. Garfield's letter on the Salary Grab came out as a meticulously crafted document. It dissected the raise's legislative history to prove he had "resisted [it] at every stage" until one-seventh of the government's funding became hostage to backdating congressional pay. "In a word," Garfield summarized, "I was called upon to decide this question: is the salary amendment so impolitic, so unwise, so intolerable, that in order to prevent its becoming a law the whole bill ought to be defeated?" Garfield had decided it was not—a choice he now hinted at regretting. "Doubtless I have made my full share of mistakes . . . my vote on this bill may have added another to the list."[54]

To supplement this near-apology, Garfield drew again on his deep local network—incorporating friends' edits while also letting them know he had not accepted his retroactive pay. "But I do not wish this fact made public . . . I am not willing to appear to have been driven to measures by mere clamor," Garfield elaborated in one note. However, he told enough allies of this secret that it leaked before he issued his letter. This allowed him to confirm in his statement ("with great reluctance") that he had put the money "beyond the reach of myself or my heirs." It was reputational maneuvering of the kind Garfield professed to be bad at. [55]

His Credit Mobilier response was even more thorough. That letter came off the presses as a thick ream of corporate history, committee testimony, attempted reconciliations of conflicting accounts, and expressions of outrage at the selfishness of other congressmen. But its core message remained the same: that its author had been wrongly lumped in with the misdeeds of other, greedier politicians. "If there be a citizen of the United States who is willing to believe that, for $329, I have bartered away my good name," Garfield's essay concluded, "these pages are not addressed to him . . . I address those who are willing to believe that it is possible for a man to serve the public without personal dishonor."[56]

The phrasing of Garfield's twin letters betrayed that for all the material things these scandals threatened, he most feared the danger they posed to his reputation. "Ten years ago you called me from another field of duty and honor," Garfield reminded voters in his Salary Grab letter, ". . . [ever since] I have conscientiously sought to serve you and the country with the best of my ability." Likewise, in his note on Credit Mobilier, he asked his constituency to consult the "public records for a vindication of my conduct."[57]

Citing a reputation diligently built across decades, Garfield secretly wondered if he had, by accident and within a few months, demolished it. His diary entry for April 21 (the day the Salary Grab explanation hit the presses) was that of a man agonizing for his legacy:

> This is the date of my letter to the Dist. I wonder what my boys will think of it, twenty years hence. I wonder what I will, if I am alive. Perhaps all this trouble may look very small and be laughed over. Perhaps not. For it may mark the decline and fall of my political power.[58]

Taking a train ride through Pennsylvania, Garfield dozed, dreaming of broken idols and thunderstorms.[59]

Then the weather turned. Editorials that had been blasting Garfield for months quieted in early May; their bruised target was left "somewhat at a loss to know what it means." At first, he dared not assume the danger passed—maybe he had simply entered its eye. But Garfield discarded this caution as the weeks went by with no sign of further storm. "This has been a golden day," he wrote mid-month, "and better than weather or any external condition . . . my soul is emerging from the shadows which this late winter of scandal and outrage has thrown upon me."[60]

Garfield would enter that rarest of political company—surviving not one, but two great scandals of his era at once. The letters explaining his part in each had satisfied most supporters and refuted enough critics. "There is certainly nothing in all this to destroy confidence in General Garfield's integrity or usefulness," decreed a reformist publication in response to his Salary Grab letter. "He has not shared personally in the plunder, and he has too many years of usefulness and honor behind him." Luke Poland only asked why Garfield's Credit Mobilier explanation had not been offered earlier to his investigative committee.[61]

The Western Reserve's voters also absolved their representative of any wrongdoing. He had done his best to prove his innocence to them, and they still trusted his word over that of anyone else. "I receive on all hands strong commendation for the thoroughness and fairness of the article on Credit Mobilier," he told Harmon Austin. "I really think that the pamphlet settles the questions with all sensible people."[62]

The stain lingered on the age. Credit Mobilier offered Democrats, Liberals, and historians alike a new buzzword for the corruption continuing to define America's postwar political system. Writers would deem it "the signature scandal of the Gilded Age." Senator John Ingalls would likewise commemorate Reconstruction as a time "of moral typhoid which follows great wars, an era of profligacy, of Credit Mobilier." Henry Adams used Credit Mobilier as an example of how American capital and government were still combining to fleece the public at an industrialized, continental scale:

> Who, then, constituted the Credit Mobilier? It was but another name for the Pacific Railroad ring. The members of it were in Congress; they were trustees for the bondholders, they were directors, they were stockholders, they were contractors; in Washington they voted the subsidies, in New York they received them, upon the Plains they expended them, and in the Credit Mobilier they divided them.[63]

The year's other scandal left a similar taint. As one of the president's biographers has judged, "the 'salary grab' wasn't Grant's handiwork, but as with Credit Mobilier, it became identified with his tenure."[64]

Garfield fared remarkably well in comparison; implicated in both outrages, he was able to escape not only their political fallout, but their public one, too. A Democrat editor felt inspired to lend the congressman a new nickname: "the Artful Dodger."[65]

In a fine bit of poetic timing, the American railroad industry came apart in the fall of 1873. The cause was a collapse of the market dominoes it had set up in the first place; a European economic downturn slashed demand for American grain. This caused domestic prices to plunge, right when railroad directors began questioning the loans and mileage they'd accumulated in the good times. They could not rely on bond sales for further capital—Credit Mobilier had spoiled investor confidence in corporate leadership. Then, on September 18, 1873, a "financial thunderbolt": Jay Cooke's investment house collapsed. The realization that a titan like Cooke (the "modern midas") could go under sparked a financial panic that would take more than half a decade to run its course; within months all domestic economic activity had been suspended in some form. "I stay in my office, not knowing what to do," admitted one New York industrialist. The so-called "Panic of 1873" kicked off the longest period of uninterrupted economic contraction in American history.[66]

It hit the South especially hard. The region's industrial base remained brittler than the North's, and the Panic ensured this would remain the case for the foreseeable future. The Texas and Pacific Railway buckled before almost any track had been laid. Frederick Douglass's Freedman's Bank failed, causing millions of dollars in savings deposited by Black Americans to disappear. Nor was agriculture spared: cotton's price folded in half, causing land values throughout the South to drop precipitously. Such a depression would have been difficult for any ruling party to survive. This was doubly true for the remaining Republican governments of the South; amid the prior year's great scandals, Reconstruction had once again begun to sputter. [67]

This was most evident in Louisiana. In April 1873 (as Garfield was writing his Salary Grab letter), the Supreme Court ruled against a coalition of New Orleans butchers who were suing the state for violating their Fourteenth Amendment privileges. In disagreeing, the court's majority gelded the amendment—deciding its privileges and immunities clause only applied to a citizen's federal rights (like access to waterways), not the more important ones vested by states. Such phrasing effectively ruined the amendment's ability to provide full citizenship for Black Americans in the south, as the Radicals had drafted it to do.[68]

Almost concurrently, Klansmen killed an assembly of more than one hundred Black and white Republicans, who claimed to represent the lawful government of the settlement of Colfax, Louisiana. The atrocity's very site had a bleak significance: Colfax was the namesake of Vice President Schuyler Colfax, and it had been built in Grant Parish, named for the president. He reacted furiously. "The so-called conservative papers of the State not only justified the massacre," Grant seethed in a Senate message, "but denounced as federal tyranny and despotism the attempt of the United States officers to bring them [the perpetrators] to justice."[69]

Marshals rounded up the killers for prosecution under a precursor to the old Ku Klux Klan Act, but the Supreme Court would again disappoint—ruling that only states, not individuals, could be prosecuted for violating Fourteenth Amendment rights. The murderers walked free, another disastrous legal precedent having been set, and another nail having been put in Reconstruction's coffin.[70]

Garfield had broken from his own political troubles to study the South's woes again—if only briefly and from a distance. His jumbled deductions speak for themselves: in January, the day before his first Poland committee hearing, Garfield advised the House "against seizing the [Southern] State Authorities but in favor of a careful investigation of the official facts furnished up by the President."[71]

By May, he changed his mind—journaling, after the Colfax massacre, that "our Reconstruction in Louisiana is manifestly a failure, and I fear we shall be compelled to take military control of that state." Surely, though, he knew this was not in the cards anymore.[72]

"I close this volume which records the stormiest year of my life," Garfield told his diary on his forty-third New Year's Eve. It had been a bad one for both man and country: behind the onset of economic and social malaise, Garfield perceived a broader crisis of institutional confidence sweeping America. He expounded on this to a reporter:

He [Garfield] looks upon the panic as rather the result of a morbid condition of the public mind than as the consequence of an unhealthy condition of business. . . . A collapse of the overgrown fabric of railroad speculation, he thinks, could not have been averted, but . . . the public, rendered morbidly suspicious by the exposures and scandals of the last Winter, transferred their distrust from the field of politics to that of business.[73]

Garfield had felt the glare of this suspicion firsthand and, resenting it, nonetheless anticipated encountering more as he tried to return to performing useful public business. "I have not achieved much," he journaled, "but I have climbed to the heights where the winds blow furiously and cold." Maybe further up the slope, at least, waited an opportunity for greater productivity.[74]

A friend's intervention kept this hope alive. James Blaine retained the speakership for the Forty-Third Congress and decided to allow representatives who had been caught with Credit Mobilier stock to keep their committee chairmanships. Such stability made sense for Blaine: as speaker, he needed reliable legislative lieutenants, and as an acquisitive politician, he wanted to keep friends close. Taking his old spot atop the Appropriations committee, Garfield expressed appreciation—even admiration—for the gesture:

After all this noise and gossip . . . Blaine has done the manly thing in standing by the old leaders of the House. The so-called Credit Mobilier Congressmen occupy all the old places.[75]

What Garfield attributed to strength, the country considered shamelessness. *The New York Times* said the House's failure to punish Credit Mobilier stockholders proved "the Congressional standard of morals is not high enough to condemn it."[76]

21

"He reads much,
He is a great observer, and he looks
Quite through the deeds of men."

—Shakespeare's *Julius Caesar*, as quoted in
Garfield diary entry for February 26, 1878

The following few years passed quickly and drearily. It was the time for necessities, for the preservation of capital (financial as well as political), and it would be remembered by those who survived it as a leaden blur of "declining markets, exhaustion . . . a lowering in value of all kinds of property including real estate, constant bankruptcies, close economy in business and grinding frugality in living." An especially deep pall fell over Washington. In the first winter following the Panic, Garfield thought the capital's social scene had lost all gaiety. Nor did public life seem happier; Congress now needed to slog through the thankless politics of austerity.[1]

Though all agreed the economy required repair, the means some Republicans came up with to perform it ran against others' hard-money dogma; Senator Thomas Ferry proposed a measure boosting the number of greenbacks in circulation up to $400 million. Gold standard devotees (including Garfield) considered this an unacceptable reversal of the hard-won progress made against fiat currency since the Civil War. The bill passed Congress anyway. "At last we have been borne down by the inflation tide," mourned Garfield in March 1874. "The House by this backward slip has lost nearly all we gained in the direction of specie payments in the last seven years." But then President Grant vetoed the "inflation bill" after a sleepless night thinking it over, flouting the advice of almost all his counselors. Garfield paid a visit to the White House to express gratitude in person. "He [Grant] has met the issue manfully," Garfield told Burke Hinsdale. "I feel like forgiving him for a multitude of blunders in view of this veto."[2]

Despite lacking the ability to single-handedly stop offensive legislation, Garfield had reached the heights of congressional influence that let him control how else Congress responded to the Panic. The nation's downturn had put substantial pressure on the government to chop spending; as Appropriations chair, Garfield wielded the cleaver. "My position in the House is I think stronger than ever before," he wrote in February. Washington insiders noticed and accorded the House's old workhorse more attention:

> Gen. Garfield . . . the wife of the Congressional family . . . has been growing all this Congress. The three Appropriations bills he has already passed save $10,000,000 to the taxpayers; and the fourth bill saves $4,000,000 more, judiciously pruned.[3]

Waste waited to be trimmed across the government; from the Treasury to the army to Congress's administrative staff, payrolls looked bloated to Garfield. He steered his committee accordingly—downsizing departments by the hundreds and budgets by the millions. A particularly withering eye was cast at the government's Indian Peace Commissioners: "I begin to doubt the efficiency of that Board to accomplish much . . . I fear they are an expensive luxury." Nor could wounded veterans dodge Garfield's penny-pinching. "I have every reason to believe that nearly twenty per-cent of all the names on the Pension rolls are those without sufficient warrant," he reflected in March. Garfield even tried stripping $25,000 earmarked for the Little Sisters of the Poor—arguing the charity's overt Catholicism made it ineligible for federal funds. Other congressmen expressed shock that someone could be so cold-hearted, attributing it to religious prejudice by the Disciple of Christ chairing the Appropriations committee.[4]

Such cuts were in keeping with the times. More than ever, Americans distrusted the swollen, scandal-plagued government that had emerged from the Civil War. Garfield channeled this sentiment as he pruned the federal ranks. Yet there was still one initiative he wanted the government to keep funding—civil service reform. He argued for this in June, when other representatives wanted to stop funding competitive examinations for clerical applicants:

> The simple question before the House now . . . is whether we will try any longer to do anything to better our civil service . . . [or] if we simply mean to trade and make merchandise out of the offices of the United States. . . . Now, I do not believe in most of the things that have been done in this matter of civil service examinations. Much of it is trifling. . . . But let us try, try on; and let us appropriate the small sum of $25,000 to keep trying . . . to better the civil service of the United States.[5]

Alas, this was a lonely pitch by Garfield—and close to being a hypocritical one. Since surviving Credit Mobilier and the Salary Grab, he had doled out more places on the public payroll to Western Reserve loyalists. Garfield felt obliged to do so—grateful as he was for the "splendid, manly friendship" they showed by sticking with him in his recent hour of need. One man was given top billing for control of a mail route, on account of Garfield considering his family "good people . . . [who] have been my true friends during all the storm." He also arranged for his ex-student Charles Henry to be promoted in the post office department. Comparable largesse was bestowed on the Western Reserve's newspapermen. Democrats did not fail to notice the pattern:

> The *Sentinel* of Ashtabula County is warm for Garfield, but its editor, Mr. Howells, obtained through him the appointment of Consul to Quebec. The *Telegraph* of Ashtabula is all for Garfield, but its editor, Mr. Reed, is Collector of the port of Ashtabula. The *Telegraph* of Lake County is for Garfield, but its editor is Postmaster at Painesville. The *Republican* of Geauga County, is for Garfield, but the editor's brother is Postmaster at Chardon.[6]

Slashing budgets, fighting a running battle against inflation, supporting reform while securing patronage for friends—Garfield appeared to find this work rather unfulfilling. "He has a hungry brain, and a wonderful constitution," read one flattering profile of Garfield in this period. "This has been the method of his busy life." But, in private, the congressman admitted the ordeals of 1873 had jaded him, sapping the happy energy that once propelled him through public life. It was harder to pick up the pen; harder to find satisfaction in crafting a concise bill or giving a good House speech anymore. "I am habitually graver . . . than I was before the storm struck me," Garfield confided to Burke Hinsdale.[7]

His next birthday was a somber occasion:

> Today completes my 43rd year. I have passed all the dates which superstition had fixed in my mind as the limit of my life. . . . While my life has been a busy one, I feel keenly that I have accomplished but little.[8]

What little recognition Garfield received for his ongoing endeavors could have passed for mockery: a new wing of Washington's insane asylum opened that winter, named after the Appropriations chair who allocated it funding. He politely toured it for an hour, perhaps identifying a bit with the patients.[9]

• • •

"The people have gone crazy," Garfield fumed after the 1874 midterms, in which Republicans surrendered their House majority for the first time since before the Civil War. The party's southern losses were especially pronounced: two-thirds of the region's House seats went Democratic, while Republican governments fell in Alabama, Arkansas, and Texas.[10]

But Garfield eventually recognized that this setback had good explanations after all. "I am satisfied that Grant made a great mistake in not reorganizing his Cabinet," Garfield journaled. "He has done more than any other President to degrade the character of Cabinet officers by choosing them . . . because of their pleasant personal relation to him." Looking south, Garfield also decided old Radical talking points had stopped resonating with the electorate. "I have for some time had the impression that there is a general apathy among the people concerning the war and the negro," he wrote. "The public seems to have tired of the subject, and all appeals to do justice . . . seem to be set down to the credit of partisan prejudice."[11]

Garfield voted with other Republicans to pass the Civil Rights Act of 1875 (banning racial discrimination in American hotels, train cars, and theaters) before Democrats could assume control of the House. He also, conversely, criticized Grant's use of troops to force illegitimately elected Democrats out of the Louisiana state legislature. "Thousands of negroes have been murdered and no adequate punishment has been meted out to the murderers," Garfield conceded. "Yet in the midst of this exciting, perilous situation, Sheridan [Grant's commander] has acted so impudently . . . as to turn the tide of public indignation against him and the Administration."[12]

Looking ahead, Garfield thought the Republican losses proved they had to move on from Grant (whom he now considered a millstone around the party's neck), as well as what he loosely phrased as "a good many other things."[13]

Nor was Garfield the only Republican putting thought toward what would be required to win the next presidential election. With Grant having no appetite to run for another term, a flurry of would-be successors began jockeying to take the party's nomination for 1876. At the front of this pack (to the surprise of few) galloped James Blaine. Almost as soon as he lost his speakership when House Republicans went into the minority, Blaine's offices were flooded with letters from voters in miraculous quantities asking him to consider a White House bid. "We were literally swamped with them," swore one aide.[14]

Preening, Blaine made a show of being carried along with the tide. "Now there's Blaine. Damn him!" one Democrat said to another as the man in question strolled by. "But I do love him." Republican senator Carl Schurz reacted differently—exemplifying the disgust many felt for Blaine's saccharine style of politics. Walking beside Blaine in Lafayette Square, the prudish Schurz froze to feel an arm slip over his shoulders, with a casual, "Carl, you won't *oppose* me, will you?"[15]

"He was born to be loved or hated," another congressman would reminisce of Blaine. "Nobody occupied a middle ground as to him."[16]

Garfield had known of Blaine's White House ambitions for years. His only grievance with them had been their annoying tendency to block vital committee work. "I regret to say that having a Speaker in the Chair who is a candidate for the Presidency makes it more difficult to get on with the public business," he complained in early 1874. "He [Blaine] is anxious to oblige so many people that he gives the floor to all sorts of subjects rather than Appropriations bills." With a path to the executive office now wide open, Garfield knew his friend would not miss the opportunity to rush down it. Yet he also discerned something Blaine was apparently blind to: "The worst danger Blaine has to contend with is the fact that he is so widely known as an active candidate for the place."[17]

Garfield decided to throw in with his friend's bid anyway. "I wish Blaine were less of a politician," he sighed to Burke Hinsdale, "but I believe he would make a good President." The personal contrast Blaine would offer with the current executive would certainly be welcome; Garfield had attended a dinner with both Grant and Blaine the prior May, only to be reminded of how dull and downright weird the former could be. Grant told Garfield he avoided foods most citizens enjoyed, and admitted hating dogs just as they seemed to hate him. Then the president asked Garfield if animals were insane or could become insane. As Garfield diplomatically recorded of this chat:

> Learned some curious facts concerning the President's tastes, which throw some light upon his character.[18]

When yet another administration scandal broke (this time implicating Secretary of War William Belknap) the president talked it over with Garfield, showing off another fundamental trait. "His imperturbability is amazing," Garfield marveled. "I am in doubt whether to call it greatness or stupidity."[19]

Then, there was the ongoing failure to clean up the civil service; Grant's acquiescence to the Senate bosses appeared to be getting meeker and meeker. A pair of them were even preparing presidential runs of their own, solidifying Garfield's decision to back Blaine's bid:

> Mr. Blaine is by no means my ideal of statesmanship. I believe, however, he would give us an honest and brilliant Administration . . . much better than we could expect from [Senators Oliver] Morton or [Roscoe] Conkling.[20]

He proceeded to pitch in enthusiastically as a campaign lieutenant. On a trip through Chicago, Garfield held a powwow about the race with the editor of the city's *Tribune*, who let slip gossip about Blaine; rumor had it the candidate had, as a young man, impregnated a lady and then married her out of duty before meeting his current wife, Harriet. Garfield trusted only Blaine and his own spouse with this potential bombshell. Crete wanted to believe it: "My opinion of Mr. Blaine would be rather heartened than otherwise by the truth of such a story: for it would show him not entirely selfish and heartless."[21]

Yet she struggled to see anyone better suited for the presidency—other than her husband, that is. "Is it not possible that in this vast Republic enough really noble and good men can be found to at least take the lead in the management of affairs?" she asked. The broader field left many Americans similarly disenchanted: Roscoe Conkling and Oliver Morton had staked their ground as proud heirs apparent to Grantism—warts and all.[22]

Blaine could have locked up the anti-Grant vote had he been any less polarizing or his ambition at all tempered. In the chamber, House Democrats asked when Republicans would finally "bow down before his Majesty from Maine."[23]

Garfield reserved doubts that they ever would. He knew (from experience) that those who openly aimed for the presidency tended to self-detonate on course to it. History provided a better template for success:

> But few men in our history have ever obtained the Presidency by planning to obtain it: in most cases it is got as the result partly of accident and partly by the popular sentiment . . . seizing hold of a man who had not done much about it himself.[24]

Also observing the scramble, John Hay (Lincoln's former assistant) couldn't believe a decade had passed since a truly honorable man held the White House. He said that, for 1876, he merely wanted "a man on one ticket or the other for whom I can vote without nausea."[25]

One soon presented himself. In Columbus, Ohio, Rutherford Hayes was barely a year into his third term as governor, staving off advances from Republicans wanting to nominate him for the White House. His denials packed terrific force. "If other fools, forty in number, rush in, I shall not," he shot at one petitioner. Such was Hayes's style; amber whiskers and superficial mildness masked inner stubbornness. His resume resembled that of an average rank-and-file Republican politician: Hayes had fought in the Civil War, entered Congress, then left Washington for the placid political waters of his home state. Even those who liked Hayes found little thrilling about the man. Chattier Republicans described him as inexpressive and dull. But he was neither. Hayes had both a sharp mind honed at Harvard Law School and a proven fighting spirit; no fewer than three horses had been shot out from under him in the Civil War, while Hayes himself had been wounded several times—once with such apparent severity that newspapers reported his death.[26]

He hung on to his political principles with comparable grit. At the close of the Grant administration, Hayes jotted them down as follows:

I hate the corruptionists . . . I doubt the ultra measures relating to the South, and I am opposed to the course of Gen. Grant on the [potential] 3rd term, the Civil Service, and the appointment of unfit men on partisan or personal grounds.[27]

In short, Hayes hoped the Republican Party would abandon much of what Grant stood for. Yet in compliance with his nature, Hayes kept these opinions and their strength mostly to himself. He agreed to run for president only passively—telling admirers to "let availability do the work." Accordingly, as dissatisfaction with more aggressive nomination contenders built throughout 1875, more began talking of Hayes as a palatable, if bland, alternative.

"A third-rate nonentity, whose only recommendation is that he is obnoxious to no-one," scoffed Henry Adams about Hayes. Yet that might just be a strength in the clash ahead.[28]

Blaine prepared fireworks to keep attention fixated on him. That was how he functioned politically: happily stoking division, as long as the light coming off it allowed him to look heroic in the glare. The most brazen and splendid of these displays came in January 1876, when Blaine decided to publicly rehash the painful legacy of Andersonville prison, where thousands of U.S. troops had died from malnutrition and exposure.[29]

He struck this match after a Democrat moved to end suffrage restrictions on southerners still disenfranchised under the Fourteenth

Amendment. Blaine put forth a countermeasure that would grant amnesty to all ex-rebels except Jefferson Davis, whom he charged with personal responsibility for Andersonville ("a prison house the ideal of Dante's Inferno and Milton's Hell").[30]

Sectional animosity erupted again with a fury. "The effect was instantaneous," wrote one historian. Former Confederates in the House responded to Blaine's provocation by insisting that nothing deplorable had ever happened at Andersonville, that its northern prisoners merely died of homesickness—in fact, it was the Union that had committed atrocities against detained southern boys. These counteraccusations stirred angry rebuttals of their own, feeding outraged debate.

Some recognized that this was precisely the outcome Blaine wanted; Democrat Samuel Cox of New York accused him of "raking up again the embers of dead hates . . . which will never elect him to the Presidency if he lives a thousand years."[31]

So, too, did certain Republicans think the Magnetic Man had gone too far this time. "It seems almost as if Blaine had virtually killed himself as a candidate, as I always thought he would," one wrote afterward. "He will die of too much smartness at last."[32]

Far better received during this drama was the speech of Blaine's apparent lieutenant. Garfield spent the day after the ex-speaker's initial provocation rebutting the House's Andersonville apologists. The differences in his and Blaine's rhetorical styles soon came to the fore; Garfield rose "determined first of all to keep my temper," and delivered a methodical oration that ran nearly two hours—as extended by motion from Democrats relieved to be addressed rather than berated. The tail of Garfield's speech still carried a potent sting:

> For the sake of three hundred thousand heroic men who, maimed and bruised, drag out their weary lives . . . do not ask us to restore the right to hold power to that man who was the cause of their suffering—that man still unshriven, unforgiven, undefended.[33]

The Democrats' amnesty bill failed, and though reporters hedged on whether the Andersonville controversy helped "Mr. Blaine's prospects for the Presidency," all agreed Garfield came out of it well:

> General Garfield's speech today was exceptionally good . . . until the Speaker interfered to prevent it, he was repeatedly applauded both on the floor and in the galleries.[34]

Garfield, in reflecting on the episode, decided Blaine had indeed "lost something by being aggressively personal."[35]

Only a few months later, the ex-speaker reaped what he had sown. A blemish from Blaine's past came into better light after the Andersonville imbroglio; despite avoiding entanglement in Credit Mobilier, Blaine had allegedly once accepted money from the Union Pacific in a secret (ludicrously profitable) bond transaction. His squirms only wiggled up more of the loose talk. "I begin to think they may damage his chances for nomination," Garfield wrote as the rumors wormed into the Capitol.[36]

Blaine took the audacious step of giving a speech dedicated to refuting them on the House floor—only for a railroad executive to declare he could produce receipts. Blaine promptly stole these ("Holy Moses! He's got me memorandy," the witness cried as the minority leader escaped), refused to surrender them to an investigatory committee, and read cherry-picked excerpts to the House a week before the Republican convention.[37]

This did not salvage Blaine's reputation. The age's corruption had now splattered him, too, after years of expert dodging. Even Garfield (describing the House scene as "electrical") felt his faith in Blaine jolted at this series of events. "He certainly is not the highest type of reformer," Garfield judged. "Hardly a reformer at all."[38]

Garfield also felt a mounting worry for his friend's well-being; Blaine's usual abundance of energy had seemed a bit manic recently.[39]

•   •   •

Only a few days later, as bunting unfurled around Cincinnati for the Republican convention, a blazing Sunday sky irradiated Washington. Blaine stepped out to walk his family to church—clad in a dapper coat unsuited to the heat but perfect for his personality.

It was only a mile-long stroll, but at the end of it, the minority leader started to sway. "His head hung heavily forward, and his gaze seemed bent vacantly on the ground at his feet," a witness reported. Then Blaine grabbed his temple, before falling into his wife's arms, unconscious. Garfield returned to I Street with his own brood, after attending a Disciple service, to find a letter informing him of the news. He rushed to the minority leader's bedside.[40]

Garfield had long recognized the danger in Blaine's relentless pursuit of the White House: "He cannot do or say anything . . . which is not studied in view of his being a candidate for the Presidency." Now sprawled comatose in his parlor, Blaine proved he could not even pass out without sending tremors through the political world—none good for him. Devotees fretted for his life while enemies conjectured. Some of the latter insisted this was just another ploy for attention. ("Blaine feigns a faint," read one alliterative Democratic headline.) Others saw a conflicted conscience taking its toll. "He was in the coils of his own corruption, like Laocoon in those of the serpent," wrote a reformist.[41]

Observing his friend's crumpled form, Garfield knew this to be no ruse. Whether heatstroke or a nervous breakdown, the cause did not matter; Garfield just wanted his friend to live. He returned to I Street for intermittent (often futile) rest. "Could sleep but little last night on account of my anxiety for Blaine," Garfield jotted down one morning.[42]

As the minority leader flitted in and out of consciousness, updates came in by telegraph from Cincinnati. A wire had been strung directly to Blaine's home—tethering its owner to word of what should have been an electrifying triumph.[43]

The convention heaved with Blaine's vacillating health. This was a shame, as otherwise the gathering had augured well for him; Conkling's bid had sputtered, on account of the boss's inability to control delegates hailing from beyond New York, the hub of his web of power. "They seemed to regard him as frigid, repellent and exclusive," conceded a friend. "And this was, except to his intimates, true of him."[44]

Nor could Oliver Morton, Benjamin Bristow, or Don Cameron pick up much steam as candidates. Hayes, on the other hand, inspired widespread regard but little zeal. Cincinnati was essentially his hometown, yet even here mentions of the governor drew only shrugs of approval. Still, none appreciated Hayes's lack of charm better than the man himself, and from afar he inertly glimpsed agreeable paths ahead at the convention.[45]

Blaine's deputies showed no such restraint. Their passion struck other delegates as delirium—an impression cemented into history by Robert Ingersoll, an agnostic orator, in a speech sanctifying his idol's gallant blows against the House's ex-Confederates and those accusing the ex-speaker of corruption. Ingersoll's only god, it seemed, was Blaine. His climax rang out over the hall:

> Like an armed warrior, like a plumed knight, James G. Blaine marched
> down the halls of the American Congress and threw his shining lance
> full and fair against the brazen forehead of every traitor to his country
> and every maligner of his fair reputation.[46]

Forevermore, among adversaries and admirers alike, Blaine would be the "Plumed Knight"—reflecting, again, his power to be loved and loathed for the same reason.

But his sudden illness hamstrung his nomination, already enfeebled as it was by stubborn charges of corruption. As one Republican wrote, regardless of what triggered Blaine's collapse, "the White House is no place for a valetudinarian, a dyspeptic, or a nervous invalid." This sentiment gave anti-Blainites time to scramble behind an alternative. Through six rounds of voting on June 16, Blaine slowly built on his lead—but another candidate's count also ominously rose with each vote; in the seventh came a thrilling combination in that challenger's favor—nearly three hundred delegates switched to Rutherford Hayes, giving the governor just enough votes to take the nomination.[47]

It was the narrowest of victories but most Republicans expressed satisfaction. "Mr. Hayes was not the first choice of his party, but it was thoroughly united by his nomination," reported a journalist.[48]

Garfield was at Blaine's side the moment it became clear the minority leader would be defeated—when New York's delegation voted solidly for Hayes. Garfield saw his friend take news of this development without flinching, then write out a concession.[49]

Perhaps, while scribbling, Blaine considered the man who had delivered his candidacy its ignominious deathblow: not Hayes, but Roscoe Conkling, commander of the New York delegation. That senator had an incredible capacity for holding a grudge; all this, for being compared to a turkey a decade before.

Garfield knew Hayes better than most in Washington. The two were senior Republicans from the same state, who had entered the army and Congress at the same times and for similar reasons. Hayes had even tried to hand off his governorship to Garfield. Yet none of this had made them close; after all, Hayes was hardly capable of being close to anyone, a fact Garfield knew all too well:

> Governor Hayes . . . is a good, sensible man, but I question whether he would run as well in other states as a man of wider reputation.[50]

It was a diplomatic way of suggesting the governor lacked what other men called charisma.

But once the nomination went Hayes's way, Garfield realized he could use their not-quite-intimacy to be of especial help in the campaign ahead, and that the nominee's outsider status might appeal to an electorate disenchanted with the status quo. Two weeks after Cincinnati, Garfield sent Hayes a note offering advice for his acceptance letter. "Far more than in any year of our history, the campaign will turn upon your exposition of the platform," Garfield confided. He counseled Hayes to plead devotion to the gold standard and clean government. "The President who will devote a term to that reform," Garfield elaborated to his diary, ". . . will stand among the foremost benefactors of his country." He also offered Hayes his energies for the campaign ahead:

> I feel great confidence in your success. But I do not shut my eyes to the fact that we have a very hard and close contest before us.[51]

Garfield's apprehension had much to do with the Democratic nominee. Not to be outdone in blandness, in June the Democrats nominated Governor Samuel Tilden of New York for the presidency. Tilden was many things, but an exciting man he was not. Small and salt-and-pepper-haired, he had trudged through Albany's cyclonic politics aloof, eccentric, and alone—his natural state of being. He had studied at Yale but withdrew because its food disagreed with him; he once drafted a list of single women whose company he tolerated, but eventually decided it would be better for everyone if he went through life by his lonesome. "Given the opportunity, he preferred to quantify human problems and relations," a historian wrote.[52]

Such profound dispassion lent itself well to the law. By the late 1860s, Tilden was one of America's most prominent corporate attorneys and had amassed a fortune representing railroads. This helped him transition fluidly to public life, despite lacking many real friends. He measured out as the least objectionable kind of Democrat: northern, pro-Union, and doggedly reformist. It was he who had kicked the infamous, bejeweled Boss Tweed out of Tammany Hall and into a jail cell. In sum, Tilden represented excellent bait for voters tired of Grantism—craving change, yet reluctant to support a Democratic Party still tainted by treason.[53]

Hayes reciprocated Garfield's courtesy and anxieties. The governor dispatched a confidential reply, confirming the editorial advice had been useful:

My Dear General: My "letter" is ready, and will I hope be satisfactory to you . . . Now for the campaign.[54]

He had strong opinions on how it needed to be waged: Tilden's façade of decency had to be knocked off, and the man beneath lashed to the misdeeds of his party. "Our main issue must be it is not safe to allow the Rebellion to come into power," Hayes wrote Garfield in a follow-up. The governor was here signaling the opening of a Republican campaign designed to rouse dormant war spirits once again. It was a cynical strategy that came to be called "waving the bloody shirt"—but, sadly, the Republican Party had no better banner to rally under. And though Hayes felt ambivalent about Grant's southern policies, he knew sectional grievances needed to be stoked if Republicans wanted to keep the presidency. "*We must choose* our own topics," Hayes insisted to Garfield in August. "The danger of giving Rebels the government, is the topic people *are most interested in.*"[55]

It was a good sign for Garfield that Hayes felt comfortable confiding in him so. The governor had been genuinely flattered by Garfield's offer to campaign vigorously ("No time is to be lost," Hayes agreed). Certainly, other congressional Republicans did not seem quite so supportive: Blaine had absconded for Maine, set on taking a senatorship as a consolation prize to the presidency; meanwhile, Conkling sulked in New York, snubbing Hayes's written requests for help, claiming to be too preoccupied with illness to leave his rooms let alone his state.[56]

As promised, Garfield spent the campaign season mostly outside his district. He tramped as far as Presque Isle, Maine, but a stone's throw from the Canadian border. Papers there hailed him as a comrade of the local political idol:

During the recent session he proved one of Mr. Blaine's most powerful allies. . . . Gen. Garfield is a man of commanding presence and fine voice, and is one of the most able of the Republican orators of the country.[57]

Nor did Garfield neglect the Midwest: he stumped across Indiana on behalf of gubernatorial candidate Benjamin Harrison; in Ohio, he swore to do all he could to help William McKinley—one of Hayes's former army aides—win his first House election.[58]

Regardless of where Garfield went, he kept his message to voters constant: this election would be a referendum on the Civil War, on Reconstruction, on the postwar Republican order. Garfield even said the same in the House. It was a reemergence of his old, eloquent Radicalism, returning as war rhetoric infused American politics once again:

> With all my heart I join in the gentleman [Rep. Lamar of Mississippi] in rejoicing that—*the war-drums throb no longer and the battle-flags are furled*,—and I look forward with joy and hope to the day when our brave people [are] one in heart, one in their aspirations for freedom and peace . . .
>
> But such a result can be reached only by comprehending the whole meaning of the revolution through which we have passed and are still passing. I say still passing; for I remember that after the battle of arms comes the battle of history . . . And those who carried the war for union and equal and universal freedom to a victorious issue can never safely relax . . . until the ideas for which they fought have become embodied in the enduring forms of individual and national life. Has this been done? Not yet.[59]

Garfield also spent time researching Hayes's biography. He discovered much to respect and even relate to. "I find my heart warming up towards Hayes very much, since I find how true and thorough he was in student life and habits," he journaled. "It is a joy to speak for a man whose stuff and spirit one can wholly and cordially approve of."[60]

And yet, stopping by the governor's handsome childhood home, Garfield also took careful note of the contrasts in their lives. He entrusted these observations to Crete:

He [Hayes] had this advantage over me: that he was never oppressively poor. I have this morning seen the house where he was born . . . a far better house than my mother or I ever had until I built ours at Washington.[61]

Refreshed on the importance of proper beginnings in life, Garfield spent the final stretch of the election reconsidering his family. He had provided his children with privileged lives in Washington—ones befitting his own status as one of the District's most remarkable men. Alongside his ongoing political and legal careers, Garfield had recently added other feathers to his professional cap. He contributed an article to *The Atlantic*, and, only a couple months afterward, managed a yet more impressive feat: after "some mathematical amusements and discussions," Garfield sketched out an original proof of the Pythagorean Theorem, publishing it that April in the *New England Journal of Education*.[62]

Yet Garfield noticed that his industriousness (the force that had brought him so far in life) was not transferring to his offspring. He privately lamented that they "do not seem to have that hunger and thirst for knowledge that I always felt when I was a child." When Garfield took his eldest sons to the dentist, he was bemused to hear both Harry and Jim needed to have teeth filled. "It is surprising that at their age they should have this work done," he journaled. "I have lost but one tooth."[63]

By the fall of 1876, Garfield had decided his children might benefit by growing up less comfortably. On October 31, he put a deposit down for a hundred acres of farmland in the village of Mentor, Ohio, barely ten miles from the shoreline of Lake Erie. The property hardly looked bountiful (it was somehow both swampy and gravelly) nor was it cheap. Yet its new owner thought these facts lay beside the point. "As a financial investment, I do not think it very wise," Garfield admitted upon assuming the mortgage. "But as a summer home, and [for] teaching my boys to do farm work, I feel well about it." An added, unspoken, benefit was that relocating to Mentor would let Garfield escape being gerrymandered out of his House seat by the now-Democratic Ohio legislature.

Garfield also saw some irony in this splurge. "So, at last, I am to be a farmer again," he wrote upon returning to Washington.[64]

A sadder feeling of déjà vu arrived to ruin the moment. "Neddie," Garfield and Crete's third-born son, caught whooping cough before the Mentor purchase closed, just ahead of the election. A telegram summoned Garfield from the trail to the unconscious boy's bedside, only for the child to die a few days later. "It required all my courage to hold up the hearts of the children, even though aided by the better courage and faith of their dear mother," Garfield wrote the night of Neddie's passing.[65]

Eliza, a practiced chronicler of death in the family, played her role well as ever. "Our dear little Eddie . . . is transplanted into the paradise of God to bloom forever," she wrote her sister. It was the same expression she had used to send off James Ballou Garfield (the first James Garfield) nearly half a century before.[66]

Garfield left his son's graveside to campaign hard throughout the election's closing days. Whisked before crowds measuring in the thousands, he had more at stake in the election to come than any Republican bar Hayes—with Blaine elevated to the Senate, Garfield would be speaker if their party were to regain the House majority. Yet warning signs flashed in early November: New York friends told Garfield that state was likely to go for the Democrats. "If it fails us," he wrote, "the Presidency will hang upon a thread." A timely glance at history reminded Garfield that no party had ever kept the White House in an economic downturn—that, like clockwork, "the cry of hard times has [always] been followed by a change of Administration."[67]

And so, by the evening of November 5, Garfield held on to only the faintest hope that his party might eke out a presidential victory. He felt far surer the result would be the closest of his lifetime.[68]

22

"Diseases desperate grown
By desperate appliance are relieved"

—Shakespeare's *Hamlet*, as quoted in Garfield
diary entry for October 17, 1878

While Hayes and Tilden each took pride in being clean political operators, their parties suffered no such constraints of conscience. In the South, violence broke upon Black and Republican voters throughout the summer. "If you can find words to characterize [this] atrocity and barbarity . . . your power of language exceeds mine," South Carolina's governor wrote a friend. Meanwhile, across the North, the Republican National Committee shook down thousands of bureaucrats for forced contributions, lining them up like steer at an abattoir. "The federal officials have been bled dry until I am ashamed to ask for more," one boss reported to headquarters.[1]

And yet, on November 7, Americans awoke under drab skies to cast their ballots in relative peace. Tilden even mingled with voters in Manhattan, his ember-red corsage glowing against the morning gray. Hayes could not muster such courage. He instead holed up with his wife, Lucy, to accept returns by telegram.[2]

The Republican soon had good reason to keep a low profile. As night fell, news flashes cast an ever-grimmer portrait of events for his party. Though Hayes and Tilden each received more votes than any previous presidential candidate, the South and a few key northern states seemed to have gone for the Democrat. It was not exactly a crushing defeat for Hayes, but it did measure out as a decisive one—a loss he had actually prepared for. "I shall find many things to console me if defeated," Hayes had assured a friend prophetically.[3]

Sure enough, as midnight passed, the defeated Republican calmly trod upstairs to join his wife in bed. Tucked between the linens, they wondered what a Democrat president might bring upon the Republic. "Both of us felt more anxiety about the South—about the colored people especially—than about anything else," Hayes later recalled of this chat.[4]

Garfield had lost his chance at the speakership, but also dwelled on the nation's loss (and the South's) rather than his own. "It now appears we are defeated by the combined power of rebellion, Catholicism, and whiskey, a trinity very hard to conquer," he reasoned. "We shall have a hard, uncomfortable struggle to save the fruits of our great war." He went to bed as the nation's presses whirred out headlines heralding a Democrat triumph.[5]

Not every Republican felt so prepared to take the defeat lying down. Stopping by a Fifth Avenue hotel at midnight, one in particular—Daniel Sickles—found an embarrassing aura of surrender permeating the party's headquarters in New York. Its chairman, Zachariah Chandler, had vanished with a bottle of ostensibly medicinal whiskey; Sickles limped over what felt like acres of barren carpet. Reaching Chandler's desk, he flipped through telegraphs from battleground states—double-checking the election was indeed lost.[6]

Paunchy with a dense, dark, mustache, Sickles had already made himself infamous as a man unafraid (proud, even) of taking extreme measures if the moment demanded them. As a congressman in antebellum Washington, he had shot his wife's lover (the district attorney) dead in the street before pleading temporary insanity. It was the first time such a defense had been pulled off in America. But, post hoc, Sickles did not stick to it. "Of course I intended to kill him," Sickles admitted to friends. "He deserved it."

The murderer-cuckold later became a Union general. While galloping across Gettysburg, he was clipped in the leg by a Confederate cannonball, shredding the limb below the knee. Sickles had the bones collected in a tiny coffin and sent to museum curators. For years to come, he brought friends to pay respects to the shards on display.[7]

Now, leafing through dispatches at party headquarters, Sickles sought a path that might offer his party a way out of its current calamity. He quickly "reached the conclusion that the contest was really very close and doubtful, but by no means hopeless." The truth was a bit stickier. In fact, Sickles realized that four states (Oregon, Louisiana, Florida, and South Carolina) had not yet called their results, and that should they unanimously declare for Hayes, the Republican would still lose the popular vote, but take a one-vote electoral college majority—and therefore, by the slimmest margin possible, the presidency. Better yet, the southern states in play still had Republican governments. This left the door open for some partisan sleight-of-hand.[8]

Moving as quickly as his leg allowed, Sickles drafted orders for operatives in these states. Chandler had gotten too drunk to be a good editor, so Sickles was instead assisted by a party boss named Chester A. Arthur. Arthur—a crony to Senator Conkling—was not one to balk at hardball. "He looked at the world through slightly closed eyes, as if most things were comfortably out of focus," one historian has written.[9]

Reviewing Sickles's text, Arthur nodded in assent (a familiar gesture), so the directive shot out over telegram wires:

```
WITH YOUR STATE SURE FOR HAYES, HE IS ELECTED. HOLD
YOUR STATE.[10]
```

Encouraging replies came back soon. Satisfied, Sickles shuffled off for bed.

• • •

Hayes awoke "master of myself and contented and cheerful" a few hours later. He had lost the presidency but was determined to take the defeat well. Yet the same could not be said of his party: though almost all the morning papers announced a Tilden victory, Zachariah Chandler was telling anyone in earshot, "Hayes has 185 votes and is elected." The candidate bridled at such recklessness. "I don't think encouraging despatches [sic] ought to be given to the public now, because they might mislead enthusiastic friends," Hayes told reporters. "I do heartily deprecate such despatches."[11]

His scorn ebbed as allies flocked with rumors of Democrat vote suppression in the South and assurances he was the rightful winner of the states in question. "You are undoubtedly elected next President of the U.S.," read a telegram on November 12. "Desperate attempts are being made to defeat you . . . but they will not succeed." These convinced Hayes to scrap for an office he now believed rightfully his.[12]

Garfield once more reacted in parallel with Hayes. On election night, both accepted defeat and fretted for the South; by the following afternoon, each realized all might not be lost. "It would be strange indeed if Hayes should carry it by one [electoral college] majority," Garfield wrote. He returned to I Street to find the "chill and sorrow" of Neddie's death still hanging over the household. The next day an urgent message arrived. Garfield's campaign duties had been extended by the president himself:

> I would be gratified if you would go to New Orleans to remain until the vote of Louisiana is counted. General Kellogg requests that reliable witnesses be sent to see that the canvass of the vote is a fair one. Answer. U.S. Grant[13]

The country was lucky to have Grant at the reins for this particular crisis. The president had a talent for quashing disorder. What's more (like most), Grant did not feel affection for Hayes; the president had sensed how much his anointed successor detested his policies. So the Republic would have as dutiful and objective an executive as possible as it navigated the uncharted waters of a disputed presidential election. Grant ordered troops to the southern states in dispute to ensure the "proper and legal boards of canvassers are unmolested in the performance of their duties." "Either party can afford to be disappointed by the result," he elaborated to William Tecumseh Sherman, "but the country cannot afford to have the result tainted by the suspicion of illegal or false returns." The nation was now not only in danger of picking an illegitimate president, but also of fostering a widespread perception that one had been so chosen.[14]

Hoping to avoid either outcome, Grant decided to dispatch trustworthy Republicans to the contested states, as he heard the Democrats were doing the same with their own loyalists. Soldiers could be counted on to keep the peace, but only what the president called "representative and fair men of both parties" might instill political calm.[15]

Despite his implication in Credit Mobilier and the Salary Grab, as well as the DeGolyer pavement affair, Garfield ranked as one of these esteemed statesmen again. "Now that Mr. Blaine goes to the Senate, Garfield is generally looked upon as the most influential man on the minority side of the House," commented one Republican editorial. "Serious mistakes have been made by General Garfield in his public career, but many consider him in culture, intellectual power, and legislative experience, as having few equals in Congress."[16]

The president evidently agreed, and, furthermore, intuited that regardless of how each state was called, Congress would be the ultimate arena where this election would be decided. That made Garfield's inclusion in this fact-finding phase critical. Grant asked him to personally follow up on reports of fraud in Louisiana "so as to be ready to debate the case in the House." "Agreed to go," Garfield wrote after receiving this assignment.[17]

By midnight he was aboard a train bound southwest from Washington. Before departing, Garfield sent a note to Burke Hinsdale reflecting on the frightening novelty of the national crisis:

The deadlock in the returns of the Presidential Election raises a new and dangerous question, at the precise point where our institutions are weakest, and wholly untried . . . we are left to the patriotism, the good sense, and the justice of a small number of men.[18]

He did not bother mentioning he was one of them. His train continued rocking across pale southern vistas—forests dusted with snow, cotton fields, the frosty silhouettes of Louisville and Nashville. Garfield had last seen them as a general in a conquering army.[19]

He had heard many things about New Orleans over the years, most of them unflattering. Garfield's Forty-Second Ohio had deployed there after he joined Buell at Shiloh. What the soldiers had written of their new surroundings described a vibrant city that was pushing its luck:

My dear General . . . New Orleans is a great city and is a modern Sodom, if there is one. . . . If it should become necessary to destroy this American Paris, no miracle is necessary. The city is lower than the river banks and heavy rains about the headwaters would bring it to pap.[20]

Now finally glimpsing New Orleans for himself, however, Garfield was smitten. "The thing that strikes a northern man most forcibly is the wonderful vegetation which abounds everywhere," he wrote. Ferns sprang from cracks in the pavement, while in the garden of his host (a veteran of the Forty-Second, who had evidently decided Sodom wasn't so bad) Garfield beheld an unimaginable bounty of fruit and flowers: pear, plum, banana, and fig, alongside honeysuckle, jasmine, and twenty types of rose, all within a single acre of land. Manmade structures also drew his interest—the steam-powered waterwheels heaving water toward nearby Lake Pontchartrain, the "curious" French Quarter buzzing with an equally curious, foreign-sounding people.[21]

Yet the scenery could not distract him from noticing and describing the nastier aspects of local society. "You would naturally think that people ought to be very good who live in such a place," Garfield hinted to his kids. "But . . . it is unfortunate the people here are not so beautiful as their trees and flowers." He was more explicit with Crete; Louisiana's whites, Garfield wrote, "smile in the morning and commit murder at night."[22]

His political work in the state brought this to his attention. Not long after arriving in New Orleans, Garfield and the other Republican delegates set about investigating the rumors of Democrat election misconduct. They did so with a mind to congressional battles to come; Louisiana's election authority (the state's Returning Board) was a widely mistrusted institution. Its membership was entirely Republican (illegally so) and in disputed races they had always favored their own party, often with tortuous reasoning—a track record that congressional Democrats would surely exploit when it came time to certify the election. Thus, the visiting Republican delegates in Louisiana hoped to gather other evidence of Hayes being the rightful winner of the state.[23]

Garfield took charge of studying events in West Feliciana Parish—a swampy region a hundred miles northwest of New Orleans. Its returns reeked of foul play: the parish registry counted 406 white and 2,218 Black voters, but only twenty citizens had cast a Republican ballot in the prior election. Garfield pored over testimony gathered from residents, suspecting a "fair count of the lawful vote of this state will give it to Hayes," but resolved to let the proof speak for itself.[24]

All told, he studied forty-nine depositions and in doing so pieced together a bleak mosaic of violence orchestrated against Republicans by local Democrats. A state senator abducted and shot dead; a prominent Black Republican, dragged by horse for four miles, "where his body was found mutilated the following morning"; an old man murdered before his family. West Feliciana's coroner had even fled his home after receiving threats from Klansmen to end inquests into the killings.[25]

Garfield spoke with some of the witnesses to test their narratives for himself and found them truthful. One story hit exceptionally close to home; that of a Black woman who claimed to have watched white Democrats kill her husband. Garfield took her story to heart—for the woman

shared a name with his own widowed mother, to whom he repeated the
tale:

> When I reflect that the poor outraged woman . . . bore the name of
> Eliza, it added to my indignation at the Party and the people that
> tolerate such a system as that which makes such a case possible. No
> coroner's inquest was held; no arrests were made; no effort was made
> to find out and to punish the murderers.[26]

Here, at last, Garfield could study the repression of Black southerners
firsthand. Before, their suffering during Reconstruction had been a depressing abstraction for him—something to be dolefully read in congressional reports and newspapers, distantly lamented but not fully felt. The
bloodshed Garfield personally studied in Louisiana, however, seemed
to finally grant him a visceral disgust. His emotional distance from the
South's injustice had been closed by a few conversations with its victims.

Learning that other Republican delegates had also found comparable
misconduct in other parishes, he readied to depart Louisiana—certain
Hayes deserved its votes and that the fight to allocate them correctly
would be "very fierce," anyway. With a presidency up for grabs, Garfield
doubted either party would bother viewing the accumulated evidence
through any lens other than that of partisanship. As he wrote Crete before departing:

> The trouble is . . . passion has so blinded the eyes of men, that many
> will not see the plainest statement in reference to this case.[27]

The delegates headed for Ohio to brief Hayes. A full moon hung over
their train; prairie fires whipped beside the tracks as Garfield elaborated
to Hinsdale about all he had learned in New Orleans:

> I know of nothing in modern history so destructive of popular gov-
> ernment, and so shocking to humanity, as the conduct of the rebel

Democracy during the four months that preceded the late election in Louisiana . . . [which] I can illustrate by supposing that the Democrats of Ohio had by armed bands and occasional murder kept so many of Republicans of the 19th District from voting . . . [that] the majority of votes cast in the District had been for Tilden.

Then Garfield's thoughts wandered into reconsidering the broader South. His distance from Black southerners was suddenly regained; Garfield expressed pity for all southern people, with evident exasperation for some new way to instill harmony between them:

They [white southerners] have many reasons for dissatisfaction—but none for the fickle, mercurial, and barbarous spirit which they carry into politics. . . . The future of the Negro is a gloomy one unless some new method can be introduced to adjust him to his surroundings. His labor is indispensable to the prosperity of the South. His power to vote is a mortal offense to his late masters. . . . If he votes against them, as he almost universally endures to do, he will perpetuate the antagonism which now bears such baneful fruit. I am tangled in the meshes of this strange problem.[28]

The delegates steamed on to Washington. Along the way, Louisiana's Returning Board announced it had invalidated enough Democrat ballots to flip the state to Hayes by a few votes.[29]

As things went in Louisiana, so too did they go in Florida and South Carolina: Republican-packed Returning Boards revised returns to favor Hayes. Their excuses for doing so raised bipartisan eyebrows. Florida's Board threw out votes from Democratic precincts because clerks took a dinner break while counting ballots, allowing the Board to declare Hayes the state's winner by only 926 votes. Three of South Carolina's election officials were Republican candidates in the elections they had been charged with policing. Even more distasteful activity occurred behind the scenes in Louisiana, when the chair of the Returning Board surreptitiously offered the state to Tilden for a million dollars.[30]

This all gave the nation's Democrats grounds to contend that they, in fact, were the ones being cheated out of a presidency. Some leading Republicans conceded the point. "The doings of the Louisiana returning-board are, to say the least, suspicious," admitted Senator Carl Schurz. Grant coolly told his cabinet that he, too, couldn't say for sure which candidate had won.[31]

Democrats did not accept the situation so serenely. Their change in mood had been literally audible in the weeks after Election Day: "Tilden and Reform" served as the campaign's rallying cry, but as results drifted into dispute and Republican Returning Boards set to work, it switched to "Tilden or fight," then "Tilden or blood!" Democratic voters proposed an armed march on Washington to put the rightful man in the White House by force. Some Republicans mocked this rhetoric, but Grant took the threat seriously enough to boost troop numbers around the capital in late November.[32]

Thus, by the time Garfield returned on December 5, Washington looked much as it did in the secession winter of sixteen years before: the Potomac was lined with soldiers; the broken silhouette of the unfinished Washington Monument marred the city skyline; evening headlines spoke of armed mobs patrolling southern capitals.[33]

The historical parallels were hard to miss down there, too. "To me it seems that if the spirit of liberty still survives the issue is Tilden or Civil War," wrote a Democrat back in New Orleans. "Will the Northern Democracy fight?"[34]

Signs indicated they might: a bullet shattered Hayes's window one night. Meanwhile, Grant received death threats through the mail. These prompted the president to order a metal walking stick—taking his security, quite literally, into his own hands.[35]

For now, though, the only fighting in Washington would be of the legislative variety, as dished out between congressmen trying to seize the

White House via procedural warfare. Certifying electoral college results had been a formality to this point in American history. Yet Congress's reconvention on December 4 revealed the existing rules had room for creative reinterpretations. As a representative later summarized:

> The Senate was Republican, the House Democratic. The all-absorbing, war-threatening questions were: Had the President of the Senate, by virtue of his office, the right to count the electoral votes? Did the Constitution invest him with discretionary power to decide what were and what were not the electoral votes of a state? Must both Houses of Congress acquiesce in counting the votes of a state before they could be counted? . . . Peace, unless one or the other party surrendered its claim of victory, seemed out of the question. No middle ground appeared possible. The horrors of another civil war loomed up before the affrighted vision.[36]

The parties each assumed constitutional arguments that best served their agenda. A stalemate settled over Capitol Hill, leaving Garfield in a uniquely vulnerable position on its front lines. Now head of the House Republicans, he had to hold firm against an irate majority flirting with treason. "My position here is one of unusual responsibility and difficulty," Garfield explained tersely to Charles Henry.[37]

This was putting things lightly. On Garfield's first day as Republican leader, a Democrat openly advised caucus mates to hoard muskets. A quieter warning was raised to Garfield directly. A journalist overheard it:

> Mr. Morrison, the Democratic leader, had, while in New Orleans, predicted to Gen. Garfield that people would be cutting each other's throats within a hundred days . . . today he walked over to Gen. Garfield's seat and . . . said "You remember the prediction I made in New Orleans." Garfield replied that he did, but that he hoped Mr. Morrison had changed his mind by this time. "On the contrary," said Mr. Morrison, "I . . . believe it more firmly now than ever."[38]

Garfield did not flinch before such rhetoric. Less theatrical than Blaine, less caustic than, say, Roscoe Conkling, and personally convinced Hayes deserved the presidency, Garfield was well-equipped to calmly endure the Democratic majority's fury, as the delicate situation demanded. He even spotted opportunity in it. "The Democrats went into caucus and attempted to impeach the President. This will damage them and help us," Garfield wrote the evening of December 7. He also thought he saw a seam in their coalition.[39]

This was only visible in the House, where a few observers noticed the Democratic caucus did not seem cohesive. Older southern members were "noticeably cooler" whenever impeachment or insurrection threats arose. "Most of the conciliatory talk appeared to proceed from them," wrote a witness. Such behavior prompted Garfield to wonder if some Democrats might be lured into letting Hayes take office. His curiosity grew when a Tennessee representative took him aside to say that if Republicans presented "good ground to stand on, fifty Democratic Congressmen would stand by Hayes."[40]

Not long afterward, other southerners invited Garfield to speak on the topic. These were vague, sporadic prompts, but by December 13, he considered them sufficient to write Hayes for guidance.

In Columbus, the candidate had stayed quiet, refusing to wade into the tussle over whether he would be the next president. His only connection to events on Capitol Hill was through the mail, which stacked high. "There are too many cooks at Washington," he grumbled while leafing through one pile. Yet Garfield's letter caught Hayes's curiosity:

> My Dear Governor, I did not intend to nix your silence so soon but there are some elements here which seem to be moving in a hopeful way, and if any good can be accomplished, it must be attended to soon.[41]

Blending courtesy with urgency, Garfield reported that certain southern Democrats who "have seen war enough" had indicated an openness to supporting Hayes's confirmation. "Just what sort of assurances the Southern members want is not so clear," Garfield admitted. Nonetheless, he supposed that should Democrats "dissatisfied with Tilden and his more violent followers" become convinced that Hayes would support a "liberal and generous [southern] policy," then they might switch sides—creating not only an end to the presidential crisis, but also, perhaps, a population of southern whites who would protect the "Constitutional rights of the Negro" without federal supervision:

> I think one of the worst things in our past management of the South has been the fact that we have not taken into our confidence . . . men whose interests are identified with the South and who will help to divide the white people politically."[42]

Garfield did not let himself get totally carried away with this prospect. "I do not think anybody should be the custodian of your policy and purposes," he assured Hayes, while welcoming anything "in the way of suggestion" the candidate could offer.[43]

One might assume Hayes's distaste for deal-making would lead him to prohibit any pact with wavering Democrats. Yet his reply to Garfield indicated otherwise:

> My Dear General, I am exceedingly obliged for your letter. Your views are so nearly the same as mine that I need not say a word.

Hayes then added supplementary words—clarifying his plans for the South had been clear the entire campaign and he would not elaborate further on them. "*There is nothing private*," he emphasized. It was a cautious, cautionary expression of interest.[44]

Garfield duly spent December testing the Democratic coalition. He took backroom meetings with southerners as the congressional stalemate continued, hearing assurances they cared "more for the peace and growth of their country than for the old quarrel" and might support

Hayes under certain conditions. But doubt still tainted these talks. "I am not sure these men can be trusted," Garfield mused after one discussion. He also kept in mind that only Hayes could make promises for his administration.[45]

And yet, Garfield saw little reason to curb the conversations; around Washington, people were saying this was the last peaceful holiday the country would see for years. Hearing such chatter, Garfield kept engaging with Democrats fishing for a deal ("studying their advances . . . with some suspicion of its good faith"). He confessed to a friend that he felt obliged to hear out all ideas for how to solve things peaceably:

> I have no doubt that whichever man is inaugurated President, will go in with a cloud upon his title . . . But the behavior of a great nation, in the administration of its laws, at a critical moment, is more important than the fate of any one man or Party.
>
> We have reached a place where the road is marked by no footprint, and we must make a track what will be fit to follow after we are dead. It is only at such times that the domain of law is enlarged, and the safeguards of liberty are increased.[46]

The climate certainly did not lend itself to clarity. A heavier than usual curtain of ice, snow, and fog fell over Washington ahead of Christmas—a veil pierced only intermittently, by sleighs and pedestrians slipping through the sleet.[47]

Garfield would not be able to wander the District freely for long. Shuttling between private talks concerning one way to break the presidential crisis, he was suddenly yanked into deliberations over another—for, in January, a handful of Republican senators crossed party lines to form a bipartisan Electoral Commission to bindingly adjudicate the election results. Garfield utterly loathed the idea. He spouted off about it to Hayes:

I have no words strong enough to describe my indignation. . . I don't believe one half of one percent of our Party had any doubt of the justice and fairness of your election, and of the right of the President of the Senate to declare it.[48]

The commission proposal struck him as an admission otherwise, as well as a foolish forfeit of the Republican institutional upper hand in exchange for the "uncertain chances of what a committee . . . will do." He also considered it illegal. Garfield's conferences with southern Democrats had been aimed at resuming the usual vote count in Congress; the commission, on the other hand, attracted praise for skirting the "fine points of Constitutional law involved in the dispute."[49]

Garfield did not find this laudable in the slightest. "A compromise like this is singularly attractive to a class of men who think truth is always halfway between God and the Devil, and that to split the difference would be partisanship," he grumbled. Hayes agreed—calling the commission a "surrender, at least in part, of our case."[50]

As it turned out, a devil of sorts had helped create the commission—making it not a forfeit by Senate Republicans but a betrayal by one in particular; Senator Roscoe Conkling had decided Hayes had not won the White House. He sneered to see Democrats agree but hesitate about what to do next, and asked if they intended "to act upon the *good boy* principle of submission." Given no clear answer, Conkling joined friends in negotiations with Democrats. In late January, reading off cream-colored, gold-edged paper, hair coiffed "with studied carelessness," the senator declared only a bipartisan commission could dispel the "mists which have gathered in our land." Critics guessed Conkling could have shaved hours off the oration by focusing less on his appearance while giving it.[51]

Garfield did his best to kill the measure. He badgered Senate friends, including Blaine, to oppose it. When the commission bill passed that chamber anyway, Garfield launched a last-ditch defense in the House past the point of his voice giving out. His address (lengthy like Conkling's but lacking the New Yorker's panache) lasted until nearly midnight on January 25. Sleepless observers admired it from packed galleries:

> Gen. Garfield's speech, as a composition in English and as an argument, was equal to any yet delivered in this debate, and in some respects, passed all others. It was impressively delivered, was free from turgid ornament and theatrical effect, and yet a crowded gallery remained till 11 o'clock [PM] to listen to it with close attention.[52]

The commission idea still coasted through the House, courtesy of the Democratic majority. Grant signed it. "The country is agitated," his approval message read. "It needs and desires peace and quiet . . . between all parties and all sections." The president was also speaking for himself— having begun daydreaming about an impending exit from politics.[53]

Few of the commission's details were left to chance. Neither party wanted it any other way. ("I may lose the Presidency," Tilden conceded with remarkable grace, "but I will not raffle for it.") Five representatives, five senators, and five Supreme Court justices were slated to serve on the Commission, where they would vote on how to award each state's votes. They would be drawn in equal share from the parties, with one specific justice—David Davis—serving as a neutral swing vote. All of the commission's congressional members would be directly elected from the House and Senate.[54]

It still came as a shock when House Republicans nominated their leader, Garfield, as a commissioner—even to him. Democrats were less pleasantly astonished, thinking Garfield had played a big enough role in the crisis already. One column argued that he should not be allowed to adjudicate an election "made doubtful by frauds which . . . [he has] conspicuously abetted, protected, procured and defended."[55]

House Republicans remained insistent on the issue, while Democrats dithered. A few worried rebuffing Garfield might make Republicans

boycott the commission altogether. He thereby ended up being confirmed, albeit by the fewest votes of anyone selected from the House. As
one spectator recorded of the Democrats' dilemma:

> There was some talk about refusing to accept the decision of the
> Republican caucus as final in the case of Gen. Garfield . . . but the
> [Democratic] party-leaders frowned upon this incipient movement to
> disturb the *entente cordiale*.[56]

Perhaps they should have kept their guard up. As a historian has
noted, Garfield's appointment "emphasized the political character of the
Commission," and while debating it, Democrats failed to accord proper
attention to the fate of a more important commissioner: the panel's
agreed-upon swing vote, Justice David Davis, was nominated to the Senate by Illinois Democrats the night before the commission became law.
Davis (hefty in weight and principle) thought this violated his impartiality, so he yielded his commission spot to Justice Joseph Bradley, an out-
and-out Republican. His party took heart. "The Commission seems to be
a good one," Hayes wrote once its membership finalized.[57]

It assembled on January 31 in the chambers of the Supreme Court,
which required refurbishment for the task ahead. The commissioners
were too numerous to fit into the Justices' usual seats, so a long, narrow
table was placed in the room's center. Steel pens and thick sheafs of paper
lined its edges. Reporters toured the space before proceedings began: "For
the next week or two, this affair of walnut and pine will be the central
point of the political system of the United States."[58]

Harper's Weekly illustrated the scene: Garfield was depicted at its far
end, his gaze fixed on the material spread before him. Alone out of all his
new colleagues, he had decided to privately record the conversations to
follow.[59]

Everything kicked off the next afternoon. A joint session of Congress
convened in the House Chamber at one o'clock, under the gaze of a few

hundred lucky citizens. "Strange as it may seem," wrote one, ". . . not one person in 10 is met who had more than a remote and glimmering idea of the manner of its execution." Indeed, while the commission's creation had cooled threats of war, the country's confusion had only spiraled since Election Day. Dueling governments, Republican and Democrat, had installed themselves in the disputed states, certifying competing slates of electors in the process. The Electoral Commission had much chaos to cut through.[60]

It began doing so at three o'clock in the afternoon—once competing certificates for the election results of Florida came up for counting. The Senate secretary bundled up the documents and dropped them off to the Electoral Commission. "Here is a new wheel put into an old machine, and yet the cogs and pinions seem to fit perfectly," recorded someone tracking the exchange. "The Commission takes up the novel task of making a President as quietly as if it were an every-day affair."[61]

The lack of commotion did not, in fact, mean the commission lacked for tension. Quite the opposite: Garfield found its silence painful—the audible ticking of other commissioners' pocket watches, ominous. The stress also had an uncomfortable personal edge for Garfield; Jeremiah Black, his old legal associate, had taken vigorous control of the Democratic case. It rested on convincing the commissioners that they had the power to venture "behind the returns"—essentially, to bypass the decisions of state authorities and themselves determine which candidate got how many votes in each state. It was an aggressive argument, as well as a weird one for a Democrat to make. Republican lawyers assumed the equally incongruous counterview that going "behind the returns" would be an unconscionable violation of states' rights. In pursuit of the presidency, both parties were ready to forsake principle.[62]

The stakes were also high enough to shake Garfield's relationship with Black. For the first time in their friendship, politics disrupted it. "I fear Judge B[lack] is falling into the loose and garrulous ways of an old man," Garfield wrote. Arguments closed on February 5, and the commission then entered private deliberation. "On the whole," Garfield wrote the following evening, "I have never spent a day in closer and severer intellectual work."[63]

The debate could not have been that arduous. By February 9, the commission had not only decided whether to go "behind the returns," but also which candidate deserved Florida's votes. The verdicts were reached by the same miniscule margin—eight to seven in favor of the Republican side, the vote split precisely across party lines. At this, everyone realized how the entire election would be decided, and as Theodore Smith chronicled, "a roar of Democratic anger . . . shook the capital and reverberated throughout the country." Prior promises to respect the commission's ruling went out the window. "As well expect chastity in a brothel, honesty in a den of thieves, or shame from a charlatan," raged one Democrat.[64]

Yet, as earlier in the crisis, the Democrats diverged about what to do next: a few in Congress scrambled to block a resumption of the vote count, while others at home sent death threats to Justice Bradley, the commission's supposed swing vote. Tilden, for his part, began booking a trip abroad. [65]

The attacks against Garfield were restricted to published ones on his character. Some sounded like flattery:

> There was a time when the best men of both parties had a high respect for Mr. Garfield . . . a hard student, and a man of untiring industry, but he is pompous, arrogant, and overbearing.[66]

He accordingly showed few outward signs of fatigue as the commission continued working: returning home at night, Garfield would kiss Crete, transcribe the day's deliberations as best he could recall, then move on to other activities—like joining a game of cards with other congressmen, playing with his children, or even finishing off a piece for an upcoming issue of *The Atlantic*.[67]

•   •   •

Its topic collided awkwardly with current events. Titled "A Century of Congress," Garfield's article was intended to be a brisk review of the first hundred years of American legislative history, as written to honor the auspicious date of the nation's centennial.

Though the anniversary had not turned out to be a happy one, Garfield's essay came out surprisingly sanguine—drawing a clean line from musty colonial conventions of the seventeenth century to the bustling modern Congress. Upon reaching this point, the author could not resist critiquing the condition of contemporary lawmaking. "As a result of the great growth of the country," Garfield offered, ". . . Congress is greatly overloaded with work." The antebellum heroics of Webster or Clay had become impossible to duplicate; the era's complexity meant collaborative committees were now needed for what herculean personas and lone-wolf lawmakers could once pull off alone. "No one man can even read [all] the bills, much less can he qualify himself for intelligent action upon them," Garfield admitted. Nor could congressmen speak as unguardedly on them anymore. "The telegraph . . . will tomorrow morning announce at a million breakfast tables what has been said and done in Congress today." Garfield did not know whether such technology would lend itself, in the long run, to Congress's ability to function.

Of all the "dangerous innovations" of the era, though, Garfield said one needed urgent correction: Congress had accumulated too much control over the federal bureaucracy, reducing it to a "vast corrupting power . . . in running the machine of party politics." The result was not just an unethical framework for government operations, but a thoroughly inefficient one. Political cronies made for poor civil servants; congressmen neglecting lawmaking to award them such roles anyway "greatly impairs their own usefulness as legislators." Garfield did not mention he had exploited such a system in the past. Instead he simply announced through *The Atlantic* that curbing patronage represented "one of the highest and most imperative duties of statesmanship."

Yet Garfield reassured readers the key to success in the American legislature remained unchanged from a century prior. The approach he outlined sounded familiar to friends:

> In Congress, as everywhere else, careful study—thorough, earnest work—is the only sure passport to usefulness and distinction . . . six thousand two hundred and eighteen men have held seats in Congress; and among them all, thorough culture and earnest, arduous work has been the leading characteristics of those whose service has been most useful and whose fame has been most enduring.[68]

Finishing up his edits, Garfield continued voting with the Republican bloc of the Electoral Commission. Once Louisiana's votes were confirmed for Hayes (again, by a one-vote margin) he felt free to let friends know a favorable presidential outcome was "almost a certainty." The only remaining trouble lay in what congressional Democrats might do out of desperation. "They vote for the longest time, and the longest recess[es], and the most frequent adjournments," Garfield wrote.[69]

He also weighed the risk of assassination—in part due to a fear that, should he be killed, his commission place might fall to a Democrat, throwing the presidency back into jeopardy. But Garfield ultimately dismissed this prospect. "I have taken no stock in this [threat] . . . and only mention [it] . . . to show how much feeling prevails." He imagined he could hear raw gusts of passion whistling through Washington like a breeze.[70]

On February 26, Garfield received a nondescript invitation to drop by Wormley's Hotel that evening. The sender was Stanley Matthews—a Republican judge close to Hayes who had also gone to New Orleans as a party delegate. It had been another day of obstruction in Congress; Democrats had filibustered for three hours, postponing the counting of votes from Rhode Island. "Every inch of ground is being contested," Garfield complained. But Wormley's was only a few blocks from I Street, and so he trekked over anyway, ducking under the awning at the stroke of nine.[71]

Despite being the smallest luxury hotel in Washington, Wormley's was the most expensive and widely considered the finest. Brilliant light and music poured from its windows every evening. Few regulars could recall anyone leaving "hungry and dry." Perhaps more noteworthy than the hotel's hospitality was its owner; James Wormley, despite being a Black man in Reconstruction-era America, had built a thriving business through a myopic fixation on service and the bottom line. He did not hesitate to host men who thought he should not be able to vote, provided they paid for the privilege.[72]

This would make the purpose of Garfield's visit ironic. Entering Wormley's, he spied not only Matthews, but a coterie of other familiar faces huddled in apparent consultation. Beneath a pall of cigar smoke sat William Dennison—the man who had, as wartime governor of Ohio, gotten Garfield an officer's commission and thus launched him to national fame; nearby stood Senator John Sherman ("cool as an iceberg, as usual, and silent as a sphinx"). Opposite these Republicans loitered congressional Democrats: representatives Ellis and Levy of Louisiana, plus Watterson of Kentucky, all men whom Garfield had watched fight for Tilden on the House floor.[73]

But the reason for this odd gathering and the request that he join it remained unclear—that is, until a Democrat took Garfield aside and began reading a list of conditions off a slip of paper. This prompted Garfield to realize "there had been former consultations, and that a compact of some kind was [being] meditated."[74]

Indeed, there had been and was. Since the Electoral Commission began its work under the pale, coffered ceiling of the Supreme Court, a new crop of Whiggish Southern Democrats had become agitated at their own party's conduct. The rhetoric being thrown out in response to the almost-certain prospect of a President Hayes had assumed an apocalyptic tone. Promises of a new civil war were still being made; a few Democrats had even introduced legislation for a new election.[75]

Amid such histrionics, a handful of more level-headed Democrats had again reached out to well-connected Republicans—offering to undermine their party's futile, embarrassing, dangerous congressional filibuster in exchange for concessions from the next administration. Stanley Matthews had heard them out and let the exploratory talks morph slowly into quid pro quo negotiations. By late February, the group had begun to discuss terms so grand that Matthews's counterparts insisted he rope in "strong Republican leaders like Sherman, Garfield, Morton, and others," to ensure their pact had teeth.[76]

Now Garfield listened to its conditions. At least the men surrounding him did not lack for vision: Matthews had committed the Hayes administration to removing federal troops from Louisiana and recognizing Democratic governments in the disputed states—in effect, folding up Reconstruction. The Democrats had extended a similarly grandiose set of vows. Garfield transcribed them with thinly disguised disdain, "among them that civil and political rights . . . be guaranteed to the [Southern] negro; that there should be no political prosecutions, that . . . [Louisiana Democrats] should elect at least one Republican Senator, etc." Trailing off, Garfield did not bother noting that the Wormley Democrats had also offered to make him speaker of the House.[77]

None of this cut against Garfield's ideological principles. In the last few weeks alone, declarations of the need for a new southern policy had crossed his lips and flowed from his pen. Garfield had even hosted confidential talks of his own with wavering Democrats—not just to break the certification impasse, but also with the ambition of cultivating a generation of southerners who could be trusted to respect the "Constitutional rights of the Negro" without federal supervision.[78]

Yet the scene at Wormley's grated Garfield's sensibilities, which were better attuned to current political reality than those of anyone else in the room. Things had changed since December: the vote count had commenced and the Democratic filibuster, while a nuisance, stood no chance of ultimately blocking Hayes from becoming president. War threats did not frighten Garfield so much as remind him of infantile tantrums ("The Democrats are behaving very badly"). Garfield also knew, firsthand, that Hayes did not want anyone embellishing his views on the South.[79]

He felt compelled to share his disapproval with the room:

I spoke for a few moments, stating that nobody had any authority to speak for Governor Hayes, beyond his Party platform and letter of acceptance. . . . For myself, I had no doubt that the new Administration would deal justly and generously by the South—and the whole nation would honor those Southern men who are resisting anarchy and thus are preventing civil war; but neither they nor we could afford to do anything that would be or appear to be a political bargain.[80]

Noticing the impact of this faux pas ("Matthews did not like my remarks"), having spoken his piece ("to prevent any misunderstanding so far as I was concerned"), Garfield then spun on his heel and departed ("not caring to be present longer"). Upon reaching home, he recorded all he had witnessed—something no other attendee of the Wormley conference thought to do that night.[81]

The gathering Garfield escaped would become one of the most widely misconstrued (and notorious) in American history. He had been wise to flee; as awareness of the Wormley meeting spread over the following years, many attached sinister retroactive significance to it—pinpointing it as the moment Reconstruction was surrendered in exchange for the presidency. Months into the Hayes administration, even Republicans were referring to it as "almost too infamous for belief." W. E. B. Du Bois (later writing with the added perspective of years and race) labeled it "a bargain . . . so raw and obvious that it must not yet be submitted to public opinion." Other historians would immortalize the secret summit as the Compromise of 1877, only to debate whether it accomplished anything.[82]

For all this hyperbolic analysis yet to occur, Garfield had read the room at Wormley's correctly within minutes. As he surmised, no one present could commit their party to any terms other than those already in inexorable motion on the national stage. The next day, Garfield saw further evidence that the prior night's events meant little: congressional Democrats continued filibustering "with all their might."[83]

Hayes himself would later confirm Garfield's intuition—that he had been aware of the Wormley's meeting, but its Republicans "took upon themselves the responsibility of giving assurances without consulting me." That said, Hayes admitted the men displayed "knowledge of my views and temperament" in their discussed terms.[84]

He left Columbus on the afternoon of March 1, president-elect in all but title. Hayes had metamorphosed over the winter from a congenial loser into a man certain of his victory and its righteousness. Nonetheless, standing under a spring sun and backdropped by a hissing locomotive, he voiced polite uncertainty about what awaited ahead—neither the White House nor national peace were yet secure. "If I am called to the work to which Abraham Lincoln was called sixteen years ago," Hayes announced, "it is under brighter skies and more favorable auspices." Then, to the gently undulating notes of "Auld Lang Syne," Hayes's train chugged out for the Atlantic coast.[85]

Meanwhile, in the Capitol, Garfield stood sleepless amid the noisy reality of finalizing Hayes's win. Democrats howled from atop their desks as Vermont's votes came up for counting. A few waved pistols but dared not pull the triggers. At one point, Louisiana Democrat William Levy (a face Garfield spotted at Wormley's) revealed he and some other southern members would end their part in the obstruction, due to:

> assurances from prominent members of the Republican Party, high in the confidence of Mr. Hayes, that . . . he will be guided by a policy of conciliation towards the Southern States; that he will not use the Federal authority or the army to force on those States governments not of their choice.[86]

It formed another crack in the Democratic line, but Garfield did not pay it much notice. "The filibusterers were more determined than ever," he wrote. The mayhem carried on until just after four o'clock the next morning, when Wisconsin's votes were counted. "It is done," one Democrat wrote acidly. "And fitly done in the dark."[87]

• • •

Hayes received the news as his train rocked past Harrisburg, Pennsylvania. "I hear you; don't wake everybody in the car," the new president-elect chided the messenger. They pulled into Washington's Baltimore and Potomac station several hours later, just as Congress's Republicans collapsed into beds across town.[88]

Grant would remember this day as one of his happiest. "The change was not so apparent to the world," his son admitted, ". . . [but] with us, he was all animation." The president had only two things to confer with Hayes about before leaving Washington: first, Grant had decided southern voters were "clearly opposed . . . [to] the further use of troops in upholding a state government." He talked with the president-elect about the issue at the White House, then ordered those army soldiers still deployed in the South to return to their barracks. The region's last Republican state governments would soon collapse; the last support struts had been kicked out from under Reconstruction.[89]

The next evening, Hayes and Grant met in another acknowledgment that the crisis was not quite over. The former took his oath of office in secret and ahead of schedule. This meant Hayes's public inauguration two days hence would be a charade—albeit not in the way Democrats still suggested it was.[90]

He nonetheless managed to make an impression with it. The new president's address from the Capitol's East Portico on March 5 outlined an ambition to forsake the policies of the previous eight years. In one breath pledging to support equal rights in the South, Hayes used his next to promise "to use every legitimate influence in favor of honest and efficient local self-government." Such double-speak would be practiced by many presidents for the next century. Hayes asked only "cordial cooperation" from white southerners as he returned the federal government to the "just limits prescribed by the Constitution and wise public economy." He barely avoided apologizing for Reconstruction—only saying its "immeasurable benefits . . . will surely follow, sooner or later."

Shifting from sectional concerns to administrative ones, Hayes turned more forceful and less patient. Regarding the civil service, he called for a "reform that shall be thorough, radical, and complete." He claimed to not care which party's operations might be the worst affected for it. "He serves his party best who serves his country best," Hayes said.

In short, the Inaugural revealed its author wanted to invert the executive strategy of his predecessor: Grant had appeased his party's bosses and policed the South; Hayes intended to do the opposite.[91]

Garfield watched the address from a few feet away. Reporters thought he looked "heavy, ministerial," but inwardly Garfield might have been the most serene man in Washington that day. He had played a more comprehensive role in the settlement of the disputed presidency than anyone else: personally investigating the election violence in the South; the party line in Congress; being elevated to the elite, extraordinary council trusted with picking the next president; and finally joining, then abandoning, a conspiracy to ensure the imminent administration would reign peacefully.[92]

Now, relief was Garfield's dominant emotion and he extended it to everyone in sight. Hearing Hayes declare war on party machinists, Garfield admired the new executive for speaking "clearly and forcibly." To Grant (chief enabler of Republican bossism), he offered a paradoxical feeling of forgiveness. "No American has carried greater fame out of the White House," Garfield would write reverently that evening.[93]

Seeing Hayes drop to kiss the Bible, Garfield saw the president's lips land somewhere in Psalm 118. A biographer would guess they settled on the following:

The Lord is on my side; I will not fear; what can man do unto me?[94]

Senators Conkling and Blaine glowered from behind the man who had taken the Republican nomination from them. Nor did they neglect each other: a passing laugh from Blaine drew a self-conscious look out of Conkling.[95]

But they were in the same boat. Hayes had just used his inaugural to herald a campaign against the wellspring of their power—patronage. Sharp-nosed political observers were already scenting the Senators' bitterness.[96]

Garfield was not ignorant of this brewing spat (Blaine had already asked him to try changing Hayes's mind about reform) but the minority leader refused to let it ruin this glorious occasion, the peaceful transfer of executive power. "There were many indications of relief and joy that no accident had occurred," Garfield chronicled that night, ". . . for there were apprehensions of assassination."[97]

While Blaine and Conkling seethed at their diminished place in the political order, certain other Americans resigned themselves to having none. "The negro will disappear from national politics," predicted one northern outlet as the last federal troops stood down in the South. Frederick Douglass expressed "a sense of alarm" at Hayes's conciliatory course, but also an understanding of it. "What is called the President's policy," he said, "might rather be considered the President's necessity. Statesmen often are compelled to act upon facts as they are, and not as they would like to have them."[98]

Samuel Tilden returned to bachelorhood in New York, surprisingly satisfied with losing the White House. "I can retire to private life," the Democratic candidate wrote, "with the consciousness that I shall receive from posterity the credit of having been elected to the highest position . . . without any of the cares and responsibilities of the office." He would take his pride in winning the popular vote to the grave—his sarcophagus inscribed: "I Still Trust The People."[99]

In 1887, President Grover Cleveland would sign the Electoral Count Act into law, expressly to ensure the fiasco of a decade prior could never repeat. Hereafter, Congress would have to be in session at one o'clock on the afternoon of January 6 following every presidential election to formalize the results; representatives and senators would have limited authority to challenge certificates submitted by states; the vice president would serve as presiding officer but, likewise, not have the power to invalidate election returns.

"Should another Presidential crisis ever confront the country, this new law will be found of vital importance," predicted the *San Francisco Examiner*.[100]

23

"Give every man thine ear, but few thy voice.
Take each man's censure, but reserve thy judgment."

—Shakespeare's *Hamlet*, as quoted in Garfield
diary entry for May 29, 1878

Any observer with a shred of political sense could tell Hayes did not enter the White House with a strong mandate. His win had been the thinnest possible under the Constitution, resolved behind closed doors between party power brokers, along partisan lines amid threats of civil war, then secured by a secret swearing-in. Upon the actual start of his administration, congressmen had already bestowed the new executive with nicknames winking at his dubious claim to the job. Democrats only recognized "Returning Board Hayes" as "a *de facto* President." Republicans accorded the man more respect, but called him "Rutherfraud" among friends who could be trusted to laugh at the pun.[1]

A shrewder president, lower-minded and better-versed in the ways of Capitol Hill, might have recognized that this did not exactly add up to a winning hand. But Hayes had campaigned on his precise lack of such traits. Like many Washington outsiders, he was proud to plead ignorance to the established rules of the game. Scoffs of realists during the election had only stoked his determination to prove them wrong. "I shall show a *grit* that will astonish those who predict weakness," Hayes vowed.[2]

He acted on this pledge promptly, commencing his regime heedless for what others would consider political reality. Rather than use cabinet selections to buy favor on Capitol Hill, Hayes tapped a string of cold, charisma-free reformists who could be counted on to cut off patronage from their own party. Against congressional dissent, the president played hardball—refusing to communicate further with the Senate if his nominations were snubbed. As if to further confound anyone looking for signs of prudence, Hayes tapped a southern Democrat to run the post office, and an Indianian landlubber for secretary of the Navy. "Why, the durned thing's hollow!" the latter supposedly said upon touring one of his department's ships.[3]

Nor did Hayes second-guess his instincts about the South. He hesitated only over the timing of his retreat from it—pulling soldiers out of South Carolina at the end of March, and from Louisiana not long afterward. As if to give a once-over to the former Confederacy before washing his hands of it, the new president took a summer tour through some of its states.

His statements given along the trip were those of a man insistent on seeing what he wished. "After thinking it over," Hayes told a group of southern Blacks, "I thought your rights . . . would be safer if this great mass of intelligent white men were let alone by the general government." Ex-rebels muttered this president was surely the best since Washington.[4]

"Received everywhere heartily," Hayes wrote upon his return to the White House. "The country is again one and united! I am very happy." His positivity persisted into the fall. "My official life in the Presidency has so far been successful . . . and happy. The country does seem to be coming back to the ancient concord," read the diary entry marking his birthday.[5]

Hayes did not celebrate the occasion, nor his presumed success, as his predecessor might have done—with a drink. No sooner did the First Family move into their new residence, than Grant's alcohol had been locked away. The only liquor to enter White House grounds for the next four years would have to be smuggled, either in secreted flasks or spiked fruit. Attendees at state dinners would wonder why so many fellow guests seemed so fond of oranges.[6]

Garfield noticed within weeks what the president took almost a year to appreciate: that the administration had taken damage within moments of leaving port, having scraped against Republican rocks in Congress. "I see signs already of an outbreak in our ranks," Garfield wrote within days of Hayes's inauguration. Checking in on the Senate, he found that embitterment against the president was rife in that chamber, too:

> It is clear that below the surface of approval there is much hostile criticism and a strong tendency to believe that Hayes' policy will be a failure.[7]

Indeed, wounded in varying ways by Hayes's reckless actions on the cabinet, patronage, and the South, Senate Republicans were already spoiled for reasons to make this belief a reality. They whispered the president had forgotten which party he belonged to. "Ingratitude," was a word thrown around more loudly in Senate cloakrooms. "Administrations do not make Parties," Roscoe Conkling soon snarled portentously to a big audience. "Parties make Administrations."[8]

Garfield did not exactly feel heartened by the president's opening moves, either. He expressed the same unease at the cabinet situation as other Republicans. Hayes's choice of Carl Schurz to lead the Department of the Interior struck Garfield as "unfortunate and unwise." That of Senator John Sherman for the Treasury made little sense either. The notion of appointing a Southern Democrat stirred only further incredulity. "Hayes is thinking of putting a Rebel in his Cabinet," Garfield pondered. "It would be either a disastrous failure or a great success." And yet (as implied in that assessment) Garfield remained willing to lend Hayes that which precious few other Republican legislators would by the end of March: the benefit of the doubt.[9]

His was a patience borne from older, impersonal frustrations. For all the president's assertiveness, Garfield understood the country needed new courses on administrations-old problems, and he still trusted Hayes's ideological compass on them, if not his methods of following it. "In the main the President's purposes are right," Garfield told one friend. To other unconvinced Republicans, Garfield acknowledged their worries, only to keep counseling tolerance—asking Blaine simply to "give the [new Southern] policy a fair trial."[10]

He could not ignore, though, that the way ahead on this front looked as hazy as ever. "I fear Party lines cannot be obliterated by generosity," Garfield journaled after talking with another Republican. "I hope I may be mistaken." Having watched several presidents fail to fix the South, he could only assume a wishful uncertainty about whether Hayes might do better. Rheumatic aches in his shoulders now reminded Garfield how very long he had served in Congress, in great part fretting over but a single section of the Republic.[11]

Another familiar problem proved harder for Garfield to wish away. Leading the House Republicans, he now controlled more patronage than ever—and found the appointment power excruciating. While Conkling and Blaine fumed over having loyalists iced out of the cabinet, Garfield struggled to elude hordes of supplicants starving for any spot on the federal payroll. No sooner had the administration begun, than they began scouring Washington in packs numbering in the dozens, hunting the minority leader through the capital. "They had scented my coming and were lying in wait for me like vultures for a wounded bison," their quarry wrote after one ambush. "All day long it has been a steeple chase."[12]

I Street offered him no refuge; the office-seekers simply staked out Garfield's address. A few especially bold ones knocked on the door as late as ten o'clock at night, with an impudence that astonished the owner. It was enough to further satisfy him that President Hayes deserved leeway from Congress. "If we could return to the policy of the Fathers and make the country know that offices were not Party rewards," Garfield wrote, "it would be a great step." The status quo struck him as literally unworkable. He could hardly sit down for five minutes without being interrupted by some man begging for a government job.[13]

Fending off the ambitious crowds, the minority leader weighed a promotion of his own: the cabinet shuffle had left one of Ohio's Senate seats vacant—a spot most assumed Garfield would fill. Events on March 9 made this seem certain: a poll of Ohio's state legislature identified him as the race's front-runner. The Reserve's newspapers assumed the matter settled and printed fond, premature homages to Garfield's House career:

> Reluctant as we may be to spare him from the House, his just claim
> for the Senatorial successorship can hardly be refused. We know no
> man of equal fitness for that place.[14]

Unfortunately, the president had different ideas: inviting Garfield to Pennsylvania Avenue, Hayes asked him to remain minority leader, citing the administration's desperate need for reliable House leadership to help pass its agenda. Garfield ultimately decided to comply with this request. It was a stunning display of goodwill, and Garfield made sure everyone knew it was, by telegramming an explanation to a friendly legislator in Columbus, making his withdrawal (and its noble reason) a matter of public record:

> The President requests me to remain in the House, where he thinks
> I can at present be more useful in the work of pacification which his
> Administration has undertaken.[15]

Terse though it was, Garfield's withdrawal drew widespread attention, unused as the American political world was to seeing a statesman deviate from self-interest on request. Democratic and Republican editors alike praised it. "Mr. GARFIELD was, as a member of the Electoral Commission, very instrumental in securing the Presidency for the man who was not elected," noted the *Cleveland Plain Dealer*, managing to fit in a barb at Hayes. Republican Representatives expressed relief that their leader would remain in place, while headlines from coast to coast described "Gen. Garfield's Self-Sacrifice" to the public.[16]

The man echoed this phrasing to friends. "You have seen before this that I have made the sacrifice and consented to remain in the House," Garfield wrote Charles Henry. "I thought it was hardly just . . . but the President was so urgent about it that I thought I had better be more generous than the rest of them [congressional Republicans]." He had genuinely wanted to go to the Senate. That chamber (dignified, anti-populist, lordly) suited his nature far better than the House of Representatives in which he had served so long and dutifully. But Garfield had decided he "could not refuse [Hayes] without selfishness." That quality was already in abundance around Washington; he secretly wondered if, by practicing the opposite trait, he might just distinguish himself. "I cannot believe that, in the long run, a man will lose by self-sacrifice," Garfield told Harmon Austin.[17]

The yields of this attitude appeared by year's end. On December 25, a letter arrived at I Street from the president—asking Garfield to stop by the White House for a chat, also offering "to call at your house if you prefer." It was unusually deferential, almost friendly behavior from an executive not known for such qualities. The postscript tacked on as much warmth as Hayes could humanly muster:

"P.S. A Merry Christmas to you and yours—H."[18]

The Hayes administration proceeded predictably. During the summer of 1877, an investigation the president commissioned into the nation's customhouses published its findings in installments, revealing (in damning, dripping detail) just how much corruption had festered across the basic of-fices of government during the prior decade. The most flagrant example could be found in New York City, the busiest port in the nation. About 75 percent of the country's customs duties were assessed at Manhattan's customhouse. Its staff were political appointees, and until 1874 their leaders had the legal authority to personally pocket a cut of fees or fines imposed on imports. By assuming appointment control over these jobs in the Grant administration, Senator Roscoe Conkling converted the continent's largest place of business into a cog in his political machine. In 1877, it reaped more than a hundred million dollars of duties—revenue the New York custom-house's chief collector, Chester Arthur, still took care to split between the government, his clerks, and loyal bosses, as he had for years. A gorgeously mutton-chopped conductor of the spoils system, "The Gentleman Boss" ran his establishment as honorably as possible, extorting importers with effi-cient courtesy. Even reformists agreed Arthur ran a tight—if sleazy—ship.[19]

The president, though, saw nothing worth salvaging. While his com-missioned inquiry recommended Arthur's staff be trimmed by only 20 percent, Hayes decided the rot ran too deep for half-measures. By mid-summer, he was preparing a scorched-earth campaign on behalf of reform, with the New York customhouse looming as a prime target. His opening move was to issue an executive order forbidding all federal employees from the "management of political organizations, caucuses, conventions, or election campaigns," also exempting them from forced donations to any machine. The president followed up in September by tapping a re-formist New York aristocrat named Theodore Roosevelt, Sr. as Arthur's replacement—alongside substitutes for two other top customhouse of-ficers. His selections went to the Senate for approval, thus commencing what Senate bosses would cast as a "systematic and inexcusable warfare" against their kind.[20]

Conkling took up the sword to defend his empire. Hair bobbing, eyes flashing, during a party convention in Rochester he gave an internecine call to war for the ages—branding Hayes and reformist Republicans an awful mix of pious, predatory, and effeminate:

Who are these oracular censors so busy of late in brandishing the rod over me and every other Republican in this State? . . . cracking their whips over Republicans and playing school-master to the Republican Party and its conscience and convictions? . . . Some of them are the man-milliners, the dilettanti, and carpet-knights of politics. . . . Their vocation and ministry is to lament the sins of other people. Their stock in trade is rancid, canting self-righteousness. They are wolves in sheep's clothing. . . . They forget that Parties are not built up by deportment, or by ladies' magazines, or gush.[21]

Conkling's speech announced the crippling of the administration. In moving so tactlessly against the bosses, Hayes had drastically underestimated how integral machine politics had become in the national party structure. By the close of the Grant administration, Conkling was no longer a mere senator. Along Capitol Hill, he went by "Lord Roscoe"—a title nodding both at his influence and elegance. Clad ever in a dazzling array of polka-dotted ties, checkered kerchiefs, pointed shoes, the Lord commanded his own Republican faction devoted to Grantism. They called themselves "Stalwarts," to make clear that they would not compromise their beliefs nor apologize for them. Another bloc, headed by James Blaine, opposed them in the Senate—but Blaine could never fall in line behind Conkling. The Stalwarts called the Plumed Knight's followers "Half-Breeds" to make their deviancy clear. Yet, in the manner of their chief, the Half-Breed Republicans liked reform as long as it didn't apply to themselves.[22]

Hayes lumped these bosses into one intolerable morass. Blaine a "scheming demagogue, selfish and reckless," would "gladly be wrong to be President." Conkling, for his part, seemed a hateful dandy. Disdaining each, the president believed he could override both. Only when his customhouse nominees ran aground in the Senate (as opposed by Half-Breeds and Stalwarts alike and held up in a committee under Conkling's control) did the president at last realize there was a "very decided opposition to the Administration, in both Houses of Congress, among the

Republican members . . . the objections extend to all my principal acts." This epiphany did not make him consider changing course.[23]

He clung to this attitude beyond the point that its shortcomings became clear. "In the language of the press, 'Senator Conkling has won a great victory over the Administration,'" Hayes admitted as Roosevelt's bid stalled out that December. "But . . . I am right, and shall not give up the contest."[24]

Roosevelt sympathized but, trapped in senatorial limbo, sensed the greater reform cause would also be in terminal stalemate during this administration. He wrote as much to his son, Theodore Jr., at Harvard:

> The "Machine politicians" have shown their colors. . . . I feel sorry for the country however as it shows the power of partisan politicians who think of nothing higher than their own interests, and I feel for your future. We cannot stand so corrupt a government for any great length of time.[25]

Thus the stage was set for a thoroughly unproductive presidency, defined by a trio of unyielding egos of the same party who hated one another. Conkling maintained Hayes was really a disturbed old woman with no claim to his office; Blaine did not step inside the White House for essentially the rest of the term; the president insisted he was happy to have not given either man a foothold in his cabinet, let alone his agenda. To have done so, Hayes said, would have invited the "intrigues and obstructive acts of personal ambition" into his White House. It did not have room for anyone's but his own.[26]

Garfield watched it all from the House with bemusement. Familiar with men on all sides of the fracas, he instead focused on matters immediately before the House of Representatives. The peculiar duties of minority leadership meant Garfield had little choice but to do so; his own legislative flock, outnumbered by Democrats, could ill-afford to endure the divisions ripping up the rest of the party. As one historian described the role of a Republican leader trapped in congressional minority:

He must criticize Democratic measures, expose Democratic mistakes, use his powers of oratory and parliamentary management to hamper or defeat their measures . . . he must utter every word with a view to its probable effect on the fortunes of the Party.[27]

A few Republicans dared wonder whether one of the rumors circling from the last election were true—that Garfield might receive enough votes from Southern Democrats to be made speaker. "I sincerely hope we can make you Speaker," freshman representative William McKinley told him later in the spring.[28]

But Garfield sensibly retained the skepticism he first felt back at the Wormley summit. When it came time for the House to pick its speaker, he won every Republican vote and lost every Democratic one. Unbothered, Garfield returned to I Street, shooed away office-seekers until nine o'clock, then read some Caesar. Upon reaching his birthday that November—his first since becoming minority leader—he marked the milestone by pledging to take a selective, economical approach to the efforts ahead:

I am 46 years old and have passed the recognized meridian of life—for effective working power, especially for new work . . . For the future, I suppose I must draw upon what I have accumulated in the way of intellectual stores to make up for failing enterprise, and vital energy.[29]

It was a good outlook to cling to, given political conditions. During the ensuing term, Garfield's legislative leadership would be cautious and undramatic—conducted with an eye to preserving the practical integrity of his caucus as opposed to its ideological one. Fearful of forcing House Republicans into a referendum on an unpopular, divisive president, Garfield stalled his faction from forming a caucus for about half a year. As he rationalized a few years later:

When Hayes came in there was a tremendous row in our own Party. . . . I held the role then of trying to protect our Party from

splitting. . . . The tendency of a part of our Party to assail Hayes and
denounce him as a traitor. . . . was very strong and his defenders were
comparably few.[30]

In muting anti-Hayes theatrics within the caucus, Garfield suggested
he belonged to the former group. Nonetheless, in conversations with journalists, he continued to give credit to concerns with the administration—
more regarding the topic of reform than that of the South, and out of
practicality instead of principle:

> I think it [Hayes's reform orders] has given us more of a backset than
> the Southern policy, and awakened more distrust. . . . This feeling
> does not prevail alone among machine politicians, but is often ex-
> pressed by the best class of Republicans. If it gains ground, Hayes will
> break down.[31]

He remained just as circumspect about conflicts with the House majority. Old hands could not help contrasting Garfield's method of legislative combat with that of his melodramatic predecessor. "As the Republican
leader in the House, he [Garfield] has been more conservative and less
rash than Blaine," wrote one witness. "Blaine's tactics were to continually
harass the enemy by sharp-shooting, surprises, and picket-firing. Garfield . . . [waits] for an opportunity to deliver a pitched battle . . . when
the fight was a fair one, and waged on grounds where each Party thought
itself the strongest."[32]

Garfield put tremendous preparation into these engagements. His
children remembered columns of books forming in the I Street home
during this period—ammunition for forthcoming House battles. Visitors assumed the stacks to be load-bearing. They lined the entry hall, the
living room, the dining room, and even (most conveniently) the bathroom, wherein books lay corded up like kindling wood. Each tome bore
dog-ears and annotations that flagged scraps of information for sorting
between fifty topic-specific pigeonholes in Garfield's office. Whenever

he decided to bring this collection to bear, the effect was that of an ava-lanche. "There is a common-place saying in the reporters' gallery," a writer explained, "that when Garfield chooses to cram on a subject, there is no man in Washington who can stand before the deluge of facts with which he will overwhelm all opposition." Fleeing the scene did not guarantee escape. "Find out what the damn fool is saying now," pouted one victim in the House's lobby to errand boys, as the minority leader droned on about tariff theory.[33]

But Garfield kept a polite, friendly tone to his part in such exchanges. A Williams classmate stopped by to watch him, noticing the "old cordial, effusive, affectionate manner remained."[34]

This is not to say all House Republicans approved of these traits. Many in Garfield's own party took his meticulousness as pedanticism, his determination to acknowledge other views as proof of a lack of his own, his avoidance of protracted legislative battles the behavior of a man afraid of them. Though far from the oldest man in the House, Garfield was em-pirically the most experienced—having served continuously since 1863, a tenure bested by only one other, less eminent representative. Yet a glance at his evolution over this period, from Radical to moderate, seemed to confirm that a slipperiness lurked in his character. "Disquieting tenden-cies in respect both to persons and to principles," a senator summarized from afar during this period. "His will power was not equal to his per-sonal magnetism," recalled another. House critics agreed: "A man of great ability, with good impulses and an honorable ambition, he [Garfield] too often surprises his friends and mars his own prospects by yielding in the very midst of a contest." Certainly, Democratic columnists did not re-ciprocate Garfield's restraint. Monikers like the "Reverend James," and "DeGolyer Garfield" proliferated—winking at how the minority leader's image of rectitude clashed with his record of accepting money from un-clean sources.[35]

Garfield could not plead ignorance to all these charges. Friends often wrote with advice on how to be more aggressive. Even flattering columns called him passive.[36]

Accepting the feedback, however, he refused to adapt to it—to seek out more scraps with Democrats or confine himself forever to a single perspective on the evolving problems confronting a changing America. "It is important to every man to have the advantage of another man's view from another standpoint than his own," Garfield expounded to Hinsdale. "It enables him to see stereoscopically rather than to see surface only."[37]

Nor would he stoop to being vicious, even when opponents did. "I think there is danger I [am] getting too spiritless in regard to personalities," he admitted to his diary, "but the fact is . . . I never feel that to slap a man in the face is any real gain to the truth."[38]

On the rarest of occasions, Garfield proved himself willing to take the gloves off, to great effect. When a bill that would have derailed the nation's destined return to the gold standard came up in November 1877, he marshaled opposition to it—delivering an address that managed the rare feat of changing votes among representatives. "He was at his best," recalled an enamored McKinley. "Those of us who were so fortunate as to hear him cannot efface the recollection of his matchless effort." New York's papers would crown Garfield's speech the most important of the congressional session—a verdict justified when, halfway through the Hayes administration, greenbacks finally hit parity with the gold dollar.[39]

A couple years later came a more dramatic demonstration of the same principle. The Forty-Fifth Congress expired in March 1879 without having passed sufficient funding for the government. Democrats had burdened Appropriations legislation with unrelated provisions ("riders") intended to curb federal poll watching in the South, which the president refused to sign into law. "The practical object of the 'so-called' Democrats is very plain," a judge wrote Hayes as the debacle unfolded. "They want to kill with impunity so many negroes as may be necessary to frighten the survivors from the polls of the South."

The resulting standoff sparked the first government shutdown in U.S. history. Hayes summoned a session of Congress to fix the mess. He also promised to veto any funding legislation containing the offensive provisions.[40]

Garfield, positioned as he was in the Democrat-controlled House, took command of the Republican response. He distributed forceful rules of action among his caucus in early March and paid visits to Hayes to ensure the president would keep his nerve. A few days later, the minority leader fired off an opening half-hour attack against the Democrats. Arms waving, forgoing his notes, "rushing up and down the aisle . . . pounding of books and desks," Garfield spoke with genuine, expressive anger—channeling, some thought, his best Blaine impersonation.[41]

His fury, he explained to the House, was not at the loathsome ideology on display, but rather the Democrats' decision to hold the country hostage in pursuit of it. Never before had a House majority deprived the government of funding in an attempt to extort a policy change. Garfield could hardly believe this one was now doing so—he could tolerate many types of politics, but not the "revolutionary" one of fiscal sabotage:

> Mr. Chairman, I have no hope of being able to convey . . . my own conviction of the very great gravity and solemnity of the crisis which this decision . . . of the Committee of the Whole has brought upon this country . . . The program announced to the American people today is this: that if this House can not have its way in certain matters not connected with Appropriations, it will so use or refrain from using its voluntary powers as to destroy the Government. . . .
>
> Gentlemen, we have calmly surveyed this new field of conflict; we have tried to count the cost of the struggle, as we did that of 1861 before we took up your gage of battle. . . . On this ground we plant ourselves, and here we will stand to the end.[42]

As Garfield sat down, sheening with sweat, Republicans buried their leader in handshakes and backslaps; Southern Democrats scurried to admit to journalists that the shutdown had not been their idea, and that they were "troubled at the attitude in which the Party has been placed by General Garfield's speech."[43]

Typically skeptical Republicans were impressed. "It was full of which his [Garfield's] speeches generally lack . . . fire, earnestness, and courage," McKinley gushed to Hayes. "The Democrats indicated they had not expected . . . quite so defiant an attitude," another onlooker wrote. Indeed, Garfield's performance set a bold attitude that his party would keep up for the rest of the shutdown. Hayes was to issue several successive vetoes of rider-laden Democratic spending bills, until acceptable legislation emerged in June.[44]

Yet while huddling with other senior House Republicans after his impassioned keynote address, Garfield asked openly if he had been too "radical" in his delivery. "He was afraid that he had offended someone," a colleague remembered, incredulous.[45]

It was Hayes's opposite inclination that prompted Garfield to give up on him, too. "I am almost disheartened at the prospect of getting anything done by the President," Garfield wrote near the one-year anniversary of the administration. Hayes's executive flaws had become irrefutable by then. The president's forceful reform efforts had only stoked widespread resentment among rank-and-file Republicans. Making rounds in the House, minority leader Garfield found almost zero representatives who identified as an ally of the administration. Meanwhile, with Democrats uniting their party around the notion of Hayes's illegitimacy, and Black rights continuing to deteriorate, Garfield realized the administration's southern policy "has turned out to be a give-away game." Appeasement had clearly reaped no reward, Garfield wrote, "while they [Southern Democrats] have spent their time in whetting their knives for every Republican they could find." Concluding that placating the South had been an error, Garfield drifted away from a course he had helped bring about.[46]

The president still continued to show signs approximating affection to him. Invitations to White House dinners arrived intermittently at I

Street, penned on immaculate card ("My Dear General, I would be glad to see you if *perfectly* convenient this evening . . ."). These gave Garfield chances to psychoanalyze the president, difficult as this task proved to be. "Among the curiosities of his mind . . . is the fact that he sees no fun in Pickwick, Don Quixote, and Gil Blas," Garfield assessed. More seriously, he found the president remained impervious to any criticism. "It seems to be impossible for a President to see through the atmosphere of praise in which he lives," Garfield wrote.[47]

This struck Garfield as more than ignorance on the part of Hayes. "I am forced to the conclusion that he is too small for the place," the minority leader wrote a friend in the state department. To Harmon Austin, Garfield elaborated:

He [Hayes] has that worst infirmity, the fear of being influenced by men of his own Party who are larger than he. The result is that he shuts himself up and does not avail himself of the help which every President needs.[48]

Garfield certainly had no such weakness himself. Despite having a personal distaste for Conkling (describing the senator as a "great fighter, inspired more by his hates than his loves; [he] desires to have followers rather than friends"), Garfield accepted conferences with the Stalwart boss in deference to his legislative influence.[49]

Blaine, for his part, sent incessant, dictatorial requests that Garfield deliver stump speeches in Maine: "Your first speech will be on Saturday last day of August and every day of ensuing week"; "You must reach Portland Friday evening this week." The Plumed Knight evidently could only communicate through commands. Yet Garfield heeded them politely—ready as he remained to help the greater Republican cause. In return, Blaine made reciprocal campaign appearances in the Reserve.[50]

"It is the business of statesmanship to wield the political forces so as not to destroy the end to be gained," Garfield told a friend. It was a barely disguised critique of the president.[51]

•   •   •

As predicted, exhaustion came more easily to Garfield during these years. Whenever in need of solace, he turned to Crete, with an appreciation expressed biblically. "You are 'the shadow of a great rock in a weary land,'" Garfield wrote his wife while away on a legal case:

> "All roads lead to Rome" says the old proverb. In the directory of my life, all roads lead to Crete. Even when I am going away from you, I remember I am travelling on a circuit which ends in your arms, and so the car wheels sing of you as they hurry me on.[52]

Following this track often led him to the Mentor farm, which had supplanted the I Street home as the Garfield family's terra firma.

The children especially liked it. By the time their father became minority leader, they numbered five, as assorted into three blocs: "the boys," eldest sons Hal and Jim; Irvin and Abe, the "little fellows," barely out of toddlerhood; and Mollie in-between.[53]

The first of these clans was the most difficult to manage. Hal was caring and serious to a fault—troubled by chronic nightmares and, on waking, in need of reassurance they would not come to pass. Jim had an opposite problem. Impulsive with a fiery temper, he constantly battled his surroundings, be they objects or people. Garfield dubbed his second-eldest son the family's cotton plant. "*It has more enemies than any other plant,*" he explained to the boy. "[Yet] If it lives through the many dangers which beset it, it becomes the hardiest . . . the mightiest vegetable on earth." Mollie was easier to keep happy. At Mentor, she preferred to plink away at a piano in the main house.[54]

Garfield, in the habit of fathers fixated on work, played the favored parental role of benevolent schoolmaster. Coming home in the evenings (at I Street, from Congress, at Mentor, from the fields), he was just as comfortable horsing around with the kids as he was helping them with homework. Games of croquet went interspersed with trivia at the dinner table. "Memory furnishes no record of dull moments," Hal remembered.

Rarely did Garfield have to bring any discipline to bear, and as Hal put it, "there was never anything stern about this discipline. We knew that obedience was necessary."[55]

Only Jim's behavior ever suggested otherwise. "I took him into the woods and flogged him severely," Garfield wrote after one episode of defiance, saddened he had resorted to "pounding goodness into a child." Fortunately, political duties kept Garfield from having to tangle with the complicated minutiae of child-rearing too often.[56]

Crete had no such luck. At least the equal of her husband in intellect, she was deprived of an outlet for it by her era. Family management instead took tyrannical control of her days. She read to the children in the evenings, nursed them whenever illness struck, and supervised farm improvements whenever Garfield was away—which was most of the time. The workmen she was left to deal with alone added to her burdens:

> I often notice where a little headwork would help them to accomplish a good deal more without adding to the labor, but . . . men have so much contempt for a woman's ideas, especially men without culture.[57]

Sideways glances at the political world ("I can see nothing to make Mr. Hayes desire that the Presidency should be decided for him"), and downward ones at literature, were her only breaks. Mostly these sufficed. Nevertheless, every now and then, Crete felt the constraints forced on her gender by the age and vented to her husband about the injustice of it all. But her complaints rarely lasted long:

> It is horrible to be a man but the grinding misery of being a woman, between the upper and nether millstone of household cares and training children is almost as bad. To be half-civilized with some aspirations of enlightenment and obliged to spend the largest part of the time the victim of young barbarians keeps one in a perpetual ferment. Now, I will stop, and complain a while of *things* or of one thing. . . . The drain seems to be out of order.[58]

Much work went on around the Mentor farm during these years, taking well after its new owner. The original cottage was converted into a larger two-and-a-half story structure. Beds of hugonis roses put a bright frame of color around the main home, while tillage, pasture, and pristine Reserve woodland cut up the rest of the property. Garfield took great pleasure in the abundance of labor on offer throughout it. "You know I have never been able to do anything moderately," he wrote Burke Hinsdale during his first spring at Mentor. To another friend, Garfield gushed about the "luxury of going to bed tired and lame from manual labor."[59]

He found room for more cerebral activities, too. Presented with copious tracts of field, he used them to run scientific trials on various fertilizers. "I shall be glad to give you the results next harvest," Garfield wrote Harmon Austin. Reports of these agricultural experiments (and others) yielded mockery from Democrats. "Garfield will not accept the invitation of the Massachusetts Republican convention to deliver a speech," wrote the *Cleveland Plain Dealer* in late 1878. "He is busy grafting potatoes on pear trees."[60]

Eliza Garfield stayed close by. Whenever her son left the farm to hit the campaign trail, she harped on him from afar: "I assure you that I feel very lonesome and if I was not so busy I should be homesick . . . don't let Politics get the better of your good judgment."[61]

She occupied the uppermost floor of the main house at Mentor during the summers, "in a Mecca of comfort," staying glib with reporters coming to profile her son.[62]

Halfway through the Hayes administration, everyone was keen for it to be over with. Republicans joked that if the incumbent ran against nobody, then nobody might just win. Hayes felt no impulse to test the theory. He had vowed to serve only for a single term, and little about his tenure made him want to extend the sentence. "I am now in the last year of my Presidency," Hayes wrote when that threshold passed, ". . . and look forward to its close as the schoolboy longs for the coming vacation."[63]

The dueling factions of his party each had champions in mind to succeed him: Half-Breeds believed no one other than the Plumed Knight could repair the "tomfoolery" of the current administration. The Stalwarts' messiah, on the other hand, finally returned from exile in 1879: having circled the globe, Ulysses Grant landed in a crowded San Francisco harbor to find many Americans now missed him. Once ashore, the former president signaled he would not mind being returned to power. "He now seeks to grab the government of the United States—a thing unprecedented—for a third term," remarked a Democrat. To court the support of those Republicans who could not bear the thought of either man as president, a meeker contender entered the ring—Secretary of the Treasury John Sherman. One can only admire Sherman's imagination; an infamous lack of political touch had already earned him the moniker the "Ohio Icicle" from the press.[64]

His candidacy for the White House inspired meaner comparisons. As one detractor wrote:

> Herodotus says that some of the Asiatics were in the habit of having connection with dead women. I presume the supporters of Sherman feel a similar enthusiasm.[65]

Garfield knew each contender personally but had qualms with them all as candidates. Atop all of Grant's baggage, Garfield considered the very idea of a three-term president to be a disastrous one. In the past, he had called it the "ghost . . . [that] has haunted our Party."[66]

Something equally intangible was off about Blaine. "I like Blaine—always have—and yet there is an element in him which is disagreeable," Garfield wrote in the spring after hearing his friend scheme about the nomination. He gave the least consideration to frigid old Sherman. "The day has been intensely hot," Garfield wrote Crete one summer night in Washington, "[then] Senator Sherman came . . . and that was the only touch of coolness I have had."[67]

The lack of interest turned out not to be mutual. As Garfield weighed the budding presidential field, Sherman was trying to cobble together something resembling a movement for his own candidacy. To look authentic, it needed to begin in his home state. Yet Ohioans had just as little passion for Sherman as anyone else. "He has not got the hearts of the people and never had," Garfield mused. To compensate, the secretary hoped to win the allegiance of more popular Buckeye politicians. This interest led him, in 1879, to extend a sub-rosa offer to Garfield: in exchange for support of his presidential campaign, Sherman would help elevate Garfield to one of Ohio's vacant Senate seats.[68]

Garfield was circumspect about the proposal. "I shall make no trades with Sherman or anybody else," he insisted to Harmon Austin when the idea first arose. Secretly, however, he could not help but consider doing just that. Garfield had never gotten over passing on the Senate to better serve this administration, and he could not muster any enthusiasm for leading the House under another. "Perhaps I can wield more influence here [the House] than I could in the Senate," he wrote Charles Henry, "but . . . the prospect of continued hard work in that turbulent body is wearysome to me."[69]

Garfield also worried if he passed on the offer, Sherman might angle for the Senate spot as a fallback to the presidency. Though the secretary lacked popularity among voters, Garfield knew he possessed something perhaps more effective among the partisan elite—patronage. "He has the whole power of the Treasury Department in his hand," Garfield wrote, weighing a putative matchup. "This is an unfair advantage and not altogether in accordance with the principles of civil service reform."[70]

Such calculations ultimately brought Garfield around to compliance. "My course towards Sherman's candidacy for the presidency would depend, in part, upon his conduct towards me in the pending [Senate] contest," he told an intermediary. Accordingly, Sherman stood aside as Ohio's legislature gathered to tap a new senator-elect in January. The secretary's loyalists would try to spin his abstention nobly:

> A contest between Sherman and Garfield for the Senatorship would have been a battle royal—it would have been the greatest contest in the history of Ohio . . . and would have left bitterness of feeling

and party dissensions; to avoid these results, and for the party good, Mr. Sherman peremptorily refused to stand for the election.[71]

Even had Sherman tried to take the seat, the outcome would have likely been the same. By the prior November, more than half of Republican legislators in Columbus had already decided to vote Garfield to the Senate. Elected Republicans across the state practically identified themselves by their respect for him. "[I am] Heart and soul a Garfield man," one legislator declared to a friend. "Nine-tenths of my constituents are for Garfield and if I live I will cast my vote for him," promised another from northernmost Adams County. Such admiration saturated the entire state;[72] journalists touring Ohio could tell which man its citizens revered most. "Ask, 'who is likely to represent your county in the Legislature?'. . . [the answer is always] 'Some man that is in favor of Garfield,'" wrote a frustrated Democrat.[73]

Nonetheless, Sherman's withdrawal certainly made things simpler. Republicans in Columbus made Garfield senator-elect within a half hour of convening on January 6. He had not even needed to visit Republicans in Columbus to request their votes—defying a tradition that cut against his personal sensibilities. "To have broken the bad custom of 40 years, which led candidates to go on the ground and personally solicit votes . . . is a matter of very great gratification," Garfield wrote Harmon Austin.[74]

Glee at the result itself also bubbled close to the surface. Charles Henry broke news of the election to his old principal, at which point, as Henry later recalled:

He threw his arms around me, lifted me from the floor and swung me around with his old time boyish way . . . the Senate that he never logrolled for was his Elysian Field for six years ahead.[75]

But Garfield had considerably less enthusiasm for the presidential candidate he was now lashed to. Sherman quickly began inundating him with awkward, insistent requests for private chats and a public declaration of support. The senator-elect complied—albeit with a reluctance that would have alarmed a cannier politician than Sherman. Garfield's eventual endorsement came out feebly:

> I have no doubt that a decisive majority of our Party in Ohio favors the nomination of John Sherman. . . . I think they ought to present the name of Mr. Sherman to the National Convention and give him their united and cordial support.[76]

Commentators noticed this letter read like a hostage note. "SHERMAN has sought to apply GARFIELD's popularity to his own uses, but personal popularity is non-transferable," observed one. But the secretary seemed to feel differently—so pleased with Garfield's support, that he soon asked the senator-elect to attend the Republican Convention as his campaign's floor manager. "On many accounts I would be embarrassed to go," Garfield mentioned to a friend, ". . . [but] I do not wish to shirk the responsibility, nor appear to be negligent of Sherman's interests."[77]

Incapable of refusing work put before him, he decided to agree to the secretary's request.

Yet after word of Garfield's appointment to senator-elect first reached Washington, it had become apparent to some that another role could be available. One evening in January 1876, a congressional delegation led thousands of Republicans through the District to celebrate the minority leader's win in front of his home on I Street. Garfield stepped outside to a storm of congratulations, and the teasing, opening bars of "Hail to the Chief." Then the rain came.[78]

Presidential speculation trails anyone who inhabits Capitol Hill long enough, but, recently, it had ambushed the minority leader with embarrassing frequency. Newspapers raised the prospect after House speeches;

inbound mail from voters intermittently asked if he would consider a run; on his regular visits to the sitting President, Garfield even heard Hayes suggest the White House could be in his future somewhere.[79]

He bristled at all such suggestions, having learned from the mistakes of friends like Salmon Chase and James Blaine. "I have so long and so often seen the evil effects of the Presidential fever upon my associates . . . that I am determined it shall not seize me," Garfield wrote after batting off the suggestion again in early 1879.[80]

Certainly, both presidential ambitions and political dysfunction were running high in Washington by the twilight of the Hayes administration. Though the president had managed the nation's finances well, almost little else of public utility had been achieved in his regime. Hayes shared responsibility for this. Mark Twain, observing the deadlock, joked that if Congress had been around when God said, "Let there be light," nothing would have happened.[81]

Yet a glance at the men elbowing to succeed Hayes made many citizens believe the Republican party (and the nation) was poised to regress rather than simply stall, falling back as it now was on flawed political personalities from the past. "As for politics," Henry Adams observed, "we seem to be in a backwater period."[82]

And so, as the spring came, more than a few Republicans cast about for agreeable alternatives and soon found themselves arriving at the same doorstep on I Street.

Garfield struggled with what to tell these callers. They included a midwestern governor and a party boss, who separately expressed the same view; that the party convention would split irreconcilably between Half-Breeds, Stalwarts, and reformers. This would force the party "to take up some other man" who might offer an acceptable path between the factions—a role none fit better than Garfield, reluctant as he seemed to be to accept. "I told him I would not be a candidate, and did not wish my name discussed in that connection . . . that I was working in good faith for Sherman and should continue to do so," Garfield recorded as his response to one. To another, he dropped his guard—saying:

[I will] act in perfect good faith towards Mr. Sherman, and do nothing that would in the slightest degree interfere with his chances for success. At the same time, I would consider such suggestions . . . within the limitations just mentioned.[83]

Evidently the presidential nomination would, in fact, be acceptable, but only if no other man could be found to assume it and it came to Garfield organically. This stipulation did nothing to daunt his visitors. They left to consult with allies after the minority leader's conditional rebuffs.

Having never known an administration to be productive, Garfield did not view the suggestion of his own with enthusiasm. He took terrific comfort in its improbability. "I should be greatly distressed if I thought otherwise," he wrote after receiving another pitch to run for president. "There is too much possible *work* in me to set so near an end to it all."[84]

Part IV

THE PRESIDENCY
1880–1881

24

"He is a tried and valiant soldier."

—Shakespeare's *Julius Caesar*, as quoted in
Garfield diary entry for April 27, 1878

Despite having almost burned to ash in recent memory, Chicago was well-prepared to host the Republican National Convention by May 1880. Party delegates arrived to find local elites even speaking fondly of their city's infamous Great Fire. Its effect had apparently been gentrification by incineration: where rickety tenement districts once sprawled beside Lake Michigan, now iron-and-stone hotels loomed high. Land prices held far above pre-fire levels; developers clapped one another on the back for outlasting the lean times; on Chicago's bookshelves, histories of the blaze contained chapters titled "Some Wholesome Effects of Adversity."[1]

It was therefore a fitting place for Grant and Blaine to try again for the presidency. Each man had endured a gloomy few years—the former, on a world tour made by boat, train, and (least pleasant of all) camel. Venice, the former president opined, would be pretty if only the streets were drained; meeting emperors in Asia and Europe had merely reminded Grant how much he missed executive power.[2]

Blaine resented having never known it. Both contenders knew by experience to play coy with the nomination in 1880 ("Horses cannot drag me into it," the senator told a friend), but allies of each flocked to Chicago in the thousands anyway.[3]

The result was mayhem that completely clogged the city by June 1. Under rose-wrapped portraits of Grant, Half-Breed banners, and the odd, outnumbered image of Sherman, Chicago's sunny avenues became too crowded for all but the burliest men to move down. "The Black mass of humanity fills all the open spaces in the hotels," wrote one reporter. "It looks like one huge body, with a thousand arms to be sure for gesticulation and a thousand throats for cheering, but still one body."[4]

Shouted sales pitches for "Blaine Lemonade" promised relief from the heat, but the concoction tasted weak, artificial. Clouds of cigar smoke and a "Babel of brass bands" smothered attempts at conversation. Convention tickets were sparse, free rooms even sparser. Landlords pondered whether to try cramming seven guests to a bed.[5]

More than a few national correspondents felt outmatched by such scenes. "The din and confusion is indescribable," admitted one.[6]

Mercifully, the one place of adequate size for the convention was its designated arena—the Inter-State Exposition Building, another new arrival on Chicago's skyline. Its glass-and-brick domes had inspired an observer to dub the structure a "Crystal Palace" during construction. The nickname stuck even though the finished interior invited closer comparison to Grand Central Terminal. On the morning of June 2, 1880, it buzzed with droning packs of Republicans that were slated to play informal-if-crucial roles in the convention. From galleries about the elliptical space, they would overlook a pit occupied by party delegates and render loud judgment on events therein.[7]

It had mostly filled by noon. There went Roscoe Conkling strutting toward the chairman's platform—arm-in-arm with Chester Arthur, a seventy-strong column of New Yorkers trailing behind. Their appearance on the Palace floor drew cheers from admirers and grudging praise out of enemies. "A handsome man is Mr. Conkling," conceded a writer for the

Chicago Tribune, then noting the "foppish Venetian point" in the senator's goatee and the "cold, gray-blue, selfish eyes" piercing out above.[8]

Others looked on these features with real admiration. To many Black Republicans present, Grant signified their race's best, perhaps final chance at justice in America. White delegates saw them treat Conkling accordingly:

> The sable Grant men of the South, who believe Grant to be their political savior, look upon Conkling as his prophet, and they worship him as a demigod.[9]

Across the aisle sat leading Half-Breeds. They had the same problem as Conkling's Stalwarts for the contest ahead—that of a polarizing candidate. Journalists still ranked Blaine among the "best loved and most hated of public men," and in Chicago, like everywhere else, his supporters' passion equaled the loathing of his enemies. Even Shermanites (stuck to a candidate with the personality of an ice cube) scoffed at appeals to switch to Blaine's side. "His rivals are desperate," Harriet Blaine consoled their daughter.[10]

They actually were—so much so, that Stalwarts had already been caught playing dirty. Word had circulated that the convention chairman, Senator Don Cameron, wanted to force the party to pick its nominee by unit rule, wherein each man would have to vote for the candidate who held a majority of their state delegation's support. This would have significantly eased Grant's nomination had Stalwarts done a better job keeping their mouths shut. In a meeting on the evening of May 31, Cameron quashed a motion by Half-Breeds and Independents acknowledging each delegate's right "to cast and have counted his individual vote," then outright denied an appeal.

This confirmed the Stalwarts were planning to procedurally rig the convention. Anti-Grant men around the table stood in a rage. Such tyranny, one said, "would have been a disgrace to the most despotic government of Europe or Asia, of this or any age." But the Half-Breeds flashed some medievalism, too: one threatened to throw Cameron out a window.[11]

• • •

A last-minute deal helped avert such unpleasantness—a compromise anyone trailing James Garfield could have tracked the progress of. Upon learning of the unit rule standoff, Garfield quietly went around Cameron to suggest a solution to the chairman's puppet master. "I called on Senator Conkling and suggested a temporary Chairman might be agreed on by the opposing forces and thus avoid a contest," Garfield journaled on the night of June 1. Alas, Lord Roscoe "did not appear willing to take much responsibility for his followers." Garfield joined anti-Grant committeemen to pick an alternative chair anyway. They settled on Senator George Hoar of Massachusetts, an independent, but (unsurprisingly) the Stalwarts still would not yield to Cameron's removal.[12]

Shuttling between threat-filled backrooms, Garfield played it calm and conciliatory, as he had since arriving in Chicago. The anxiety he once felt for the "loose talk" about his own possible presidential candidacy had since turned into a peculiar mix of detachment and resignation. Garfield had decided to (as he'd told callers at I Street) "act in perfect good faith towards Mr. Sherman" and strenuously disavow attempts to change that. Yet he would not run too hard from circumstance; if presidential lightning happened to strike him, so be it. In the meantime, Garfield would do what came naturally: be considerate, diplomatic, and, above all, flexible to further developments.[13]

Asked to address an anti-Grant rally at a baseball park, he declined; when a friend's brother couldn't find a place to sleep, Garfield let the man split his bed. And as the Republican convention threatened to come apart before it began, Garfield bluffed to reporters about the meeting with Conkling. "The purpose was solely to adjust differences as to methods in organization," Garfield said cheerily to one writer. "No result was actually reached, though we think good progress was made in that direction."[14]

Conkling soon lent these words truth—bidding Chester Arthur, dog-like, to go let the other factions know Hoar would be an acceptable chair as long as the unit rule would be left for the convention to settle. Biographers of the men involved in this resolution would identify Garfield as its catalyst. But, approached by a journalist again on the morning of June 2, he deflected credit:

> General Garfield and Governor [William] Dennison . . . said at once, when they heard of the compromise, that it must be accepted. They declared the Committee would have been fully justified in proceeding to extreme measures last night, while Cameron remained defiant . . . [but when] he agreed to yield the vital point over which the contest arose, it was the duty of the opposite party to meet him in a spirit of conciliation, and do everything in its power to prevent a division in the Party.[15]

Eager as Garfield appeared to be to avoid attention, his head still glared out from the smaller, fuller-haired ones carpeting the Palace floor on June 2. This made it easy for spectators to keep an eye on him—as a surprising number were now doing. The convention's early dysfunction had led many to begin grooming dark horses, and few suggestions drew better initial reception than Garfield. A chat with the man cemented the good impression. "General Garfield is, as is well known, a conversationalist of peculiar charm and remarkable power," jotted a convention-goer who had the pleasure of a personal encounter.[16]

Some of the interest in him was secretly artificial. Wharton Barker (one of the men urging Garfield to run) had seeded the galleries with "reliable men" to cheer whenever the senator-elect appeared on the floor or his name was announced.[17]

Concerns were also raised, but none appeared disqualifying in light of those of the men already clawing for the nomination. One attendee said his issue with Garfield's DeGolyer fee was that it had been so small; a smart representative would have taken a bigger bribe. Others wondered whether the Ohioan's geniality masked a nature too feeble for the role of party figurehead. "Garfield is not disagreeable . . . but I think he is too weak a man," a delegate mused.[18]

Garfield had worries, too. Prepared as he now was to accept a presidential nod under the right conditions, he feared the public would think he desired it—just as he had feared, back in the Civil War, that voters would believe he wanted to leave the army for Congress. "You can hardly imagine the embarrassment I have been in from the moment of my arrival here by the number of delegates . . . openly expressing the wish that I was the Ohio candidate," he wrote Crete. "So much of this [gossip] is said as to put me in constant danger of being suspected of ambitious designs; but I think I have been so prudent as to thus far disarm most of the suspicious ones. . . . I shall do nothing and ask nothing, far better pleased to have nothing but the knowledge that many desire me."[19]

Indeed, journalists wandering the Palace on June 2 described Garfield as active and dutiful on behalf of Sherman. Nor did the secretary suspect otherwise. Despite hearing talk of Garfield as a possible dark horse, Sherman had tasked the minority leader not only with serving as his floor manager, but also formally nominating him at the convention.[20]

But here, too, Garfield retained some wiggle room for himself. Despite telling a reporter in Chicago he had Sherman's nomination speech ready to go, Garfield (deprived of both time and inspiration) had not even begun writing it.[21]

His window to do so closed with a bang just after one o'clock; Chairman Cameron rapped a gavel made from Lincoln's doorframe onto a desk at the front of the Palace. He then gave the hammer to Hoar, putting the convention in independent hands as it started down the boring path of committee selection. Stalwart snipes sometimes interrupted the tedium. "Bad blood was brewing," jotted an observer.[22]

The dreariness lifted, momentarily, when it was announced that Garfield would join the Rules Committee. The applause at his inclusion sounded like the second-loudest (and first genuine) cheer of the day in the hall. Its subject was seen smiling—flirtatiously so, in the opinion of a gallery member.[23]

•   •   •

1

The image of a six-foot-tall, broad chested, not-quite-twenty-year-old walking into Hiram imprinted in their minds with lasting crispness. James Garfield as a retired canal boy and determined student.

2

"'All roads lead to Rome' says the old proverb. In the directory of my life, all roads lead to Crete." James Garfield and Lucretia Garfield, circa 1853.

3

"I cannot stand aloof from this conflict. My heart and hope for the country are in it." General Garfield, the rare Union commander determined to punish the rebellion and raise Black southerners to full equality.

4

"There will spring out of this war a score of new questions and new dangers . . . of even more vital importance than the ending of the war." Fighting through the South convinced Garfield how crucial and difficult Reconstruction would be, and that he needed to help shape it on the national political stage.

5

"A striking physical presence, with a large head, a flowing auburn beard . . . and bodily well-being about him." Representative James Garfield, a progressive-turned-compromiser, the only statesman capable of being friendly with everyone in Washington.

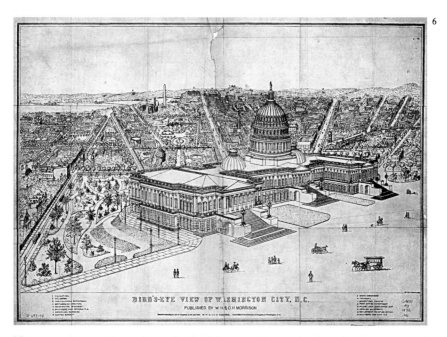

6

The nation's capital mostly as Garfield knew it during his lengthy Congressional career, between 1863 and 1881.

Behind Grant's stony visage rested a similarly boulderlike mind—dull and heavy, possibly prehistoric but practically impossible to budge. Ulysses Grant, eighteenth president of the United States.

Washington had never been stalked by a purer political animal. Senator James Gillespie Blaine, the "Magnetic Man," idol of the Half-Breeds.

His hair curled into a corona of orange-yellow locks, his wardrobe arrayed in harmonized hues, his aides set into file behind him like a line of worshipful pageboys. Senator Roscoe Conkling, "Lord Roscoe," ringleader of the corrupt Stalwarts.

Amber whiskers and superficial mildness masked inner stubbornness. Rutherford B. Hayes, nineteenth president of the United States.

An affection for high living, a yearning for camaraderie, and a moral spine just pliable enough to yield to both. Chester Arthur, a Conkling crony who redeemed himself after inheriting the presidency from Garfield.

"Such an accumulation of honors had never before fallen upon an American citizen." President Garfield—party unifier, reluctant executive, and ideological enigma—at his apogee.

13

"She is unstampedable."
"Crete" Garfield as First Lady.

"It has been a delightful day at Lawnfield, as the papers insist on calling our place." Garfield's farm bustled in the election of 1880.

Blaine had crossed two-thirds of the station's waiting room when a bang erupted behind him, followed by another. President Garfield is shot.

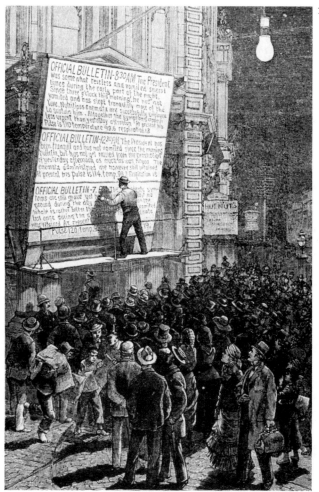

*A new national pastime: gathering before giant bulletin boards
to read the latest updates dispatched from
the president's sickroom.*

"Garfield dies—if he dies—a martyr to the spoils." The president's death served as a rallying cry for healthier American public discourse and the depoliticization of the federal bureaucracy. Here is he is portrayed being wounded while trying to chart a route to "good government."

Metal-studded oak doors and buttressed balconies lent the building a passing resemblance to a huge castle turret. But churchlike elements also draw the eye. President Garfield's final resting place, beside Lake Erie.

The convention's second day opened to high temperatures, and so the sound of fluttering handfans echoed off Palace rafters throughout the morning. As clocks struck eleven o'clock, an opening prayer was given, and at the "amen," Conkling rose as if summoned by it. Swaddled in snug gray-blue (and looking a bit baffled) the senator bore an unfortunate resemblance to a flustered pigeon as he insisted on adjournment until evening.[24]

His flight attempt had nothing to do with the heat. The Stalwarts' failed unit rule maneuver had solidified resistance to Grant instead of bypassing it, leaving Conkling and his flock no immediate floor tactic left but sabotage ("in the forlorn hope of gaining by the delay," an observer guessed).[25]

But Conkling received an entirely undesired interruption in the middle of his motion—a roar of cheers that cut him off. He spun around to see it was the audience loudly reacting to Garfield's arrival on the floor. Looking convincingly startled by the noise himself, the minority leader offered a slight bow of recognition to the gallery. A bystander (taking the cue off Roscoe's face) judged that having the spotlight thus stolen "was a novel experience for Mr. Conkling."[26]

Conkling had good cause to keep an eye on Garfield that day. The Rules Committee had made the Ohioan its chairman the night before—putting him, practically speaking, in charge of settling the unit rule controversy. Garfield had not exactly been ambiguous about his opinion on it. "It is wholly un-Republican for one man to cast another man's vote," he had been overheard saying in a hotel lobby. He provided better editorial fodder to another reporter:

> I think that if the unit rule does not prevail it will be everybody's fight; if it does it will be everybody's funeral.[27]

The Half-Breeds in the Palace seemed to have taken these quips to mean Garfield would help hasten a Stalwart defeat. A Blainite objected to Conkling's motion for a recess, parrying snide ripostes in the process ("I shall not enter with the gentleman the field of irony and sarcasm, in which he is so expert"), before another moved for Garfield to introduce his committee's majority report—the adoption of which would secure individual balloting. Shouts of "podium" broke out.[28]

But Garfield declined his marks. Against calls to take the stage, he opted to stand on his chair to speak; invited to rout the Stalwarts immediately, Garfield also took the middle ground—his Rules report was apparently ready, but courtesy was owed to those committee members disagreeing with it. "Good faith requires this certainly," he intoned, "that if the minority is not ready with their report they ought to have time."[29]

A veteran reporter taking in the scene was struck by the strange nature of the man suddenly at its epicenter:

> It is difficult to describe Garfield. He is a highly intellectual man, but he don't look it . . . he looks like a man with the courage of his own convictions, but that is just what he don't fully possess. In a controversy he frequently tries to please both sides. He has vigor and dash, but he is apt, after he has carried the enemy's works and placed his feet on the parapet, to reflect a moment, and then retire and call off his forces. But . . . on a chair near the centre of the delegate-floor, he received an ovation of which any man might be proud.[30]

The result merited pride too. Half-Breeds, left with empty floor time, gave Conkling his recess. An atrocious winner, he took this surrender with a taunt—lauding the Blainites on the "momentous, the critical, the portentous results" of their obstruction.[31]

As the convention went into recess, the secret winner of the proceedings thus far hastened to his hotel through crowds rippling with what was already being called the "first wave of the Garfield boom" outside the Palace. Half-Breeds spoke well of him under flags featuring Blaine's face. A few idle Grant supporters sneered at his "attempt to carry water on both shoulders." But the overall sentiment on the streets was strikingly positive. "The most popular man in this Convention by all odds is General Garfield," wrote one surprised journalist.[32]

In a message sent that day to his closest confidante—his wife—Garfield confessed feeling less shocked. But he predicted events would soon bring his popularity back to earth:

Since I wrote you yesterday morning, the signs have multiplied that the Convention is strongly turning its attention to me . . . I should think there was something in it, but for the [unit rule] contest I am to have with Conkling. If I win that fight, it will be likely to embitter him and his followers against me. If I lose it the Convention will lose interest in me. . . . I take to myself the lesson I lately wrote to Hal, and say, I will do my whole duty as I see it, and take the result as an indication of what is best. . . . I am happy in expecting no lightning to strike me, but am gratified that so many here think it will.[33]

The convention returned to its work before this note reached Crete. Again, Garfield's committee report was asked for, and once more he mounted his chair, igniting cheers that carried on for more than a minute. When they faded, he made a statement some considered expertly inoffensive. But as it closed ("That is all I have to say"), clapping rose again from the balconies.[34]

The next day brought his and Conkling's differences into sharper relief. Both men entered the Palace late: Conkling with theatrical slowness and "all his stage airs"; Garfield a few minutes after, less dramatically but to similar reception. Barker had suggested that Garfield begin delaying his arrivals, and, noticing the compliance, concluded that the congressman truly desired the nomination.[35]

The Palace was back down to a tolerable temperature that morning. Conkling added to the coolness with a new resolution:

Resolved. As the sense of this Convention, that every member of it is bound in honor to support its nominee, whoever that nominee may be; and no man should hold a seat here who is not ready to so agree.

This was a baited hook. No Republican could object to the resolution's phrasing other than the abnormally independent, or those loath to
let Conkling look gallant, even for an instant. Three such men belonged
to West Virginia's delegation. They voted accordingly, thus playing into
Conkling's hands—he moved for their exclusion from proceedings on
account of insufficient Republicanism ("the delegates . . . do not deserve
to have, and have forfeited their votes in this convention"). The Appalachians reacted by loudly questioning the right of the Blaines and Conk-
lings of the party to expel them:

> In the name of God; has it come to this, that one who has battled . . .
> in behalf of Republicanism, when it cost something more than it did
> in the State of New York or in the State of Maine, cannot freely ex-
> press his opinion in a Republican Convention?[36]

It briefly looked as though it had. Delegates piled their disapproval
on the dissenters. Then Garfield caught the eye of Hoar, rose upon
being recognized, and in doing so again donned the mantle of party
peacemaker. "I fear this Convention is about to make a grave error," he
intoned, and at this "there was great cheering, cheering from all those
who felt that the right thing would now be said in the right place, and
the Convention extricated from the meshes of Mr. Conkling's soph-
istry." [37]

Garfield obliged them. He used semantics to turn back the larger
convention—pointing out the West Virginians had said they still expected to support the Republican nominee in the fall, whomever that
might be. To prosecute them further was therefore, for now, a pointless
distraction from party unity as well as the business at hand. "If these
gentlemen had arisen . . . and said 'I will not vote for your nominee' then
the question would be a pertinent and entirely different one," Garfield
reasoned. "Is every delegate here to have his Republicanism inquired into
before this Convention will allow him to vote?" A surge of "nos" formed
the reply. Then he turned to flatter the West Virginians:

One of them . . . for twenty long years, in the midst of slave-pens and slave-drivers, has stood up for liberty with a clear-sighted courage and brave heart equal to that of the best Republican that lives on this globe.[38]

Rounds of applause served as Garfield's punctuation. They closed his every sentence and fell in anticipation of the next, to an effect some compared to a thunderstorm. It ended gently: Garfield said he hoped the "distinguished gentleman from New York will take pleasure in withdrawing the resolution, and let the Convention proceed with its business." A reporter judged that Conkling's expression "did not raise any strong presumption that pleasure was quite the word to use," but the senator knew when a skirmish was lost. Conkling decided to let his resolution die a slow death; once again, his attempt to sway the convention had instead reduced the Stalwart playbook to one of delay.[39]

The senator, pallid and sullen, turned over a scrap of paper, then began to write. Nothing in public life had taught him that goodwill or nobility existed in it, except as gestures to either serve or screen the base interests of those making them. Conkling himself embodied this. The coiled locks crowning his head, the airy lavender corkscrews of his writing, the bows he gave to ladies gifting him roses on the Senate floor—all feigned gentility by a statesman who considered the abuse of power an integral part of politics. Anyone claiming otherwise could only be an idiot or, worse, the craftiest of liars.[40]

Conkling's note made clear which one he believed Garfield to be. Adding a looped "R.C." as a mark, he instructed a minion to pass the sheaf to the minority leader. Garfield received the following message:

New York requests that Ohio's real candidate and dark horse come forward. We want him in our seats while we prepare our ballots.[41]

An indirect retort came from Garfield later that day, when he at last unveiled the Rules Committee's majority report recommending the convention use individual voting in the balloting to come. Then, to more cheering, Garfield gallantly asked his committee's Stalwarts to give their rebuttal ("they ought to be heard, and I have no doubt they will be").[42]

That night's session turned out to be the most acrimonious thus far. A speaker said Grant and Blaine's names too close to each other, thereby sparking a petty battle over which could stir the most applause. Conkling conducted the Stalwart shouting with a handkerchief. One hefty woman mounted the stage to lead the Half-Breed reply—eclipsing poor Chairman Hoar, "and, to the rhythmic swaying of her body, chanted 'Blaine, Blaine, James G. Blaine.'" Sherman delegates threw confetti, but in doing so only cast the finishing touches on the image of a diminished party:

> The continued roaring, which lasted three-quarters of an hour . . . showed to what a pitch and passion the once cool and dignified Republican Party had come.[43]

Garfield was indistinguishable amid the ruckus, which lasted past two o'clock in the morning. Forces were rallying to him, too—albeit less noisily and more productively. The West Virginian delegates sent a letter voicing gratitude for his earlier stand against the "tyranny of machine politicians" (and promising to soon provide "more *substantial* evidence of our appreciation of your generous and patriotic act"). Meanwhile, bylines classifying "MR. GARFIELD AS A PEACEMAKER" were being set over accounts of his defense of the party dissenters, for placement beside columns describing a convention otherwise in a "disgraceful condition of disorder."[44]

Crete somehow sensed the shift in her husband's fortunes from Mentor. "I begin to be half afraid that the convention will give you the nomination, and the place would be most unenviable with so many disappointed candidates," she wrote. "I don't want you to have the nomination merely because no one can get it, I want you to have it when the whole country calls for you as the State of Ohio did last Fall."[45]

Yet proceedings in the Palace indicated to many that only more dead-lock lay ahead. "Thus it may eventuate that, after worrying each other out with ballot after ballot, some hardly represented man would get the majority of the Convention," predicted a syndicated column. "Some think the person is Garfield." Debate over the nature of the Ohioan's friendliness ("bordering on weakness") appeared to be delaying his coronation as the dark horse.[46]

As if to validate such concerns, Garfield spent the evening session trying to think of a parallel for its chaos in history: maybe, Paris during the Revolution.

He refused to fill in its details to Crete afterward—instead, just describing how he endured it:

> For any man to have kept his head upon his shoulders is no small matter. If I have succeeded better than most, it is largely due to the fact that I always see before me: your calm, sweet face, counselling wisdom, prudence, and truth.[47]

A little past seven o'clock on Saturday night, James Joy of Michigan crossed the convention stage. The time had come for nomination speeches, and in having Joy do the honors for Blaine, Half-Breeds thought they were correcting upon their idol's past presidential run; one of the senator's errors in 1876 (besides that ill-timed breakdown) had been letting allies get carried away with themselves. It was critical to play things calmer this time—a point lost so far in Chicago, but which Joy, a no-nonsense industrialist, could deliver while also locking up Midwestern votes. In Washington and the meantime, Blaine made a show of getting on with work as usual.[48]

Yet Joy's first sentence in Chicago set the tone for a dismal oration. "I shall never cease to regret that circumstances . . . impose the duty upon myself to make the nomination of a candidate to this Convention," he apologized, in maybe the worst opener to an endorsement ever uttered.

Joy labored through the remainder in nervous near-silence. Audience members either could not hear him or quickly stopped listening. The text was nearly as damaging as its delivery, though parts read with self-awareness ("If . . . words of mine are important for the candidate . . . they will benefit him but little"). Joy's coup de grâce against his own side came at the end of the speech—when he nominated "James S. Blaine," to a split second of confusion before other Half-Breeds realized his error. "G., you fool!" they cried. But, the damage done, they shifted to discussing if Blaine's candidacy might survive his nomination.[49]

At least Joy was allowed to finish. His speech ran long, prompting calls of "time" to ring out. It was then that James Garfield rose to move for an extension, saying he was "sure no man will object" to letting Joy finish. This polite intervention was received well—even by Half-Breeds praying for a swift end to the misery. Someone afterward observed that "General Garfield . . . has managed all through the Convention to say the right thing at the right time."[50]

A subsequent speaker decided to improvise his own stage, leaping atop the Palace's press table. An ensuing barrage of applause poured unbroken on the elevated form of Conkling for ten minutes. The senator bore it in silence—head bowed, comfortable in the clamor. "The scene was a striking one," an onlooker wrote.

As the noise finally died, Conkling began his nomination speech with a poem dedicated to its subject:

When asked what state he hails from
Our sole reply shall be
He comes from Appomattox
And its famous apple-tree.[51]

The performance that ensued was Conkling, distilled; graceful in its flourishes, brutal in the blows it struck for its speaker, his movement, and the politics he represented. Winning this election (to "decide . . . whether the country shall be Republican or Cossack") required unrepentant Republicanism. "The supreme need of the hour is not a candidate who can carry Michigan," Conkling declared, with a withering look at Joy. "The need is of a candidate who can carry doubtful States. Not . . . of the North alone, but also doubtful States of the South." Only Grant could accomplish such a feat, his "fame . . . earned not alone in things written and said, but by the arduous greatness of things done"—done through what Conkling vaguely referred to as "common sense." Nor would elaborations be necessary with Grant back in control of the party. "We shall have nothing to explain away," Conkling promised. "We shall have no apologies to make."[52]

If the senator only offered a few, right then, he might have won his idol the White House again. Instead, Conkling let the audience stoke his worst qualities. "Never were sneers more grossly ill-advised," a historian has judged. Half-Breeds and independents jeered throughout the performance and the senator obnoxiously made a show of savoring the hatred, even sucking a lemon as hisses of "machine" rose up from the audience.[53]

He also used the third-term concerns around Grant to insult those Republicans who held them. "Nobody now is really disquieted by a third term except those hopelessly longing for a first, and their dupes and coadjutors."

To Conkling's disciples, this was him at his best, bringing the "force and fire of a philippic" to bear for their vision of Republicanism. To those still on the fence, less heat would've been welcome. "Mr. Conkling has the weakness of all positive men long successful in the practice of mere force," one reflected. "He does not perceive the value of toleration . . . the race is not well galloped unless he splatters the other jockeys."[54]

The next one was still figuring out how to saddle his steed. Garfield had puzzled for weeks over how on earth to convincingly nominate Sherman at the Convention—even going as far as to visit the secretary's home to beg for pointers. Garfield later grumbled that this trip had been fruitless:

I asked him [Sherman] to suggest frankly what he considered the strong points of his public life . . . he left that wholly to my judgment, but suggested that the chief characteristic of his life from boyhood up had been courageous persistence in any course he had adopted.[55]

Thus uninspired, Garfield had arrived in Chicago without a speech ready, and to the Palace on Saturday with only a handful of loose points in mind. His plan had become to supplement Sherman's legislative record with the "suggestions of the hour," and thereby half-improvise a nomination speech. The clamor created by Conkling's performance at last gave Garfield the creative spark he badly needed ("the idea of carrying the mind of the Convention in a different direction," he would later explain to Crete).[56]

As the audience noise at last dwindled, he walked up the Palace aisle to a resurgence of cheers, and, reaching the press table, jumped atop it, near a dark crease left by Conkling's shoe. Sweeping nautical analogies had dotted the prior nomination speeches; now Garfield also ad-libbed maritime language, but to opposite effect:

> *Mr. President.* I have witnessed the extraordinary scenes of this Convention with deep solicitude. Nothing touches my heart more quickly than a tribute of honor to a great and noble character; but as I sat in this seat and witnessed this demonstration, this assemblage seemed to me a human ocean in tempest. I have seen the sea lashed into fury and tossed into spray, and its grandeur moves the soul of the dullest man; but I remember that it is not the billows, but the calm level of the sea from which all heights are measured.[57]

Thus commenced a speech aimed not at exciting its audience but stilling them. "Gentlemen of the Convention," Garfield began, "your present temper may not mark the healthful pulse of our people. . . . Not in Chicago, in the heat of June, but at the ballot-boxes of the Republic, in the quiet of November, after the silence of deliberate judgment, will this question be settled." The Palace obeyed Garfield's call for calm. "He was not much interrupted by applause, as he requested that he should not be . . ." wrote a reporter.[58]

Garfield used the quiet to loftily review the party's past glories, rather than those of any single member of it. Only by the combined efforts of all Republicans had they slain the "demon of Slavery," nurtured the explosive growth of American industry, and restored to the country "a currency as national as its flag." But, Garfield said, these past Republican triumphs paled in comparison with those still ahead, as long as the party kept cohesive. "How shall we accomplish this great work?" he asked the convention. "We cannot do it, my friends, by assailing our Republican brethren. . . . The coming fight is our Thermopylae. We are standing upon a narrow isthmus. If our Spartan hosts are united, we can withstand all the Persians that the Xerxes of Democracy can bring against us."

Garfield introduced the Leonidas of his metaphor not by name, but nature and accomplishment:

> We want a man whose life and opinions embody all the achievements of which I have spoken. We want a man who, standing on a mountain height, traces the victorious footsteps of our party in the past, and carrying in his heart the memory of its glorious deeds, looks forward prepared to meet the dangers to come. We want one who will act in no spirit of unkindness towards those we lately met in battle. . . . You ask for his monument. I point you to twenty-five years of National Statutes. Not one great, beneficent law has been placed on our statute books without his intelligent and powerful aid. He added in formulating the laws to raise the great Armies and Navies which carried us through the war. His hand was seen in the workmanship of those statutes that restored and brought back "the unity and married calm of States." . . . He has stood in the blaze of "that fierce light that beats against the throne;" but its fiercest ray has found no flaw in his armor, no stain upon his shield.

Only with his final sentence did Garfield put a name to this heroic profile:

> I do not present him as a better Republican or a better man than thousands of others that we honor; but I present him for your deliberate and favorable consideration. I nominate John Sherman of Ohio.[59]

Garfield then stepped down onto a convention floor trembling once again with enthusiastic stamps and cheers. Hoar declined to gavel the scene quiet—betraying his approval for the applause by letting it outlast any that had come before. The chair would one day describe Garfield's speech as "one of the greatest oratoric triumphs I ever witnessed," a sentiment that was already being repeated in the Palace as Garfield found his seat. "These words were needed by the Convention," an attendee wrote. Another was impressed that Garfield made Sherman sound half-viable as a candidate.[60]

Over in Washington, a ticking noise heard through the secretary of the Treasury's door betrayed he was following events at the convention by telegraph. Sherman would deem Garfield's address a "specimen of brilliant eloquence rarely surpassed," and leave copious space in his memoirs for particularly flattering excerpts of it.[61]

Yet many in the Palace did not recognize dull old Sherman in the speech at all—instead believing it to be a better portrait of the speaker. Even more agreed that Garfield had been better-served by the performance than the candidate it nominated. "It's a very good speech," one man chortled, ". . . two words for Garfield to one for Sherman." Whether this was intended or not remained up for dispute. "Garfield honestly did his best for Secretary Sherman . . ." countered one reporter, "and yet the General is so popular here . . . that the chief effect of his speech has been to increase the talk and speculation as to the possibility of his being made the nominee if the situation were different."[62]

Conkling could only curdle with embarrassment. Garfield's speech had cut through the technical brilliance of the senator's preceding one, casting light on the petty, divisive spirit it had been built around. "One was the effort of an angry and reckless partisan; the other the appeal of a cool-headed, sagacious political leader," read one review.[63]

To add insult to injury, ladies in the galleries now questioned openly if Conkling was, in fact, the most attractive man in the Palace. Garfield brought brainpower, rustic charm, and (handsomest of all) inner nobility into consideration:

> There is a grace and elegance in the person and manners in Conkling . . . but the figure we now see before us [Garfield] is rough-hewn in form and rugged of feature . . . His eyes are a cold gray, but they are often—yes, all the time, in this speech—lit brilliantly by the warm light of worthy sentiments, and the strong flame of a great man's convictions.[64]

A pair of throwaway nominations to independents formed the night's final business. As Conkling stood to leave, a passerby asked how he felt. With Garfield's nautical expression still hanging over the Palace (no longer a "human ocean in tempest"), the senator replied that he felt seasick, then escaped.[65]

Garfield spent the Sabbath refusing supplicants. "I shall be happy if let alone by this Convention," he wrote Crete. But though convention business was officially suspended for Sunday, a veritable cross-section of the Republican faithful made pilgrimages to Garfield's room anyway, beseeching that he permit being nominated.

Some callers (like Benjamin Harrison) were old friends; others strangers. Yet none could get Garfield to betray a hint of interest in the presidency. "No, my name must not be used," he told one. "I am going to nominate John Sherman . . . my name must not be used." A reporter tracked these processions, and how they ended, and wrote that while the "General himself says positively he cannot honorably be a candidate . . . This makes his friends more strenuous than ever that he should be announced as a candidate."[66]

He even had to deny the popular will in church. At a Disciple service with Charles Henry, Garfield was noticed by congregants and invited to preach. But he politely declined the pulpit.[67]

The next day proceeded into stalemate, as all expected. Applause again greeted the late arrivals of Garfield and Conkling, but once Chairman Hoar allowed voting to start, excitement promptly left the building. Hallways hushed; music stopped; messenger boys silently flitted across the Palace floor. "No more, in short, of that froth that floats on the vexed sea of a National Convention," wrote one audience member.[68]

The sea instead froze: the opening ballot gave Grant just over three hundred votes, Blaine a little under that number, while Sherman barely broached ninety. Twenty-seven further rounds followed that day—the final one, placing each main candidate within five votes of what they earned in the first.[69]

One of the only thrilling moments came on the second round, when a lone Wisconsinite voted for Garfield. Wharton Barker smiled (he had instructed the delegate to do so) as the galleries stirred. "The name of Garfield seemed to make the audience tremulous," wrote a reporter. "A block of votes going to him then would have created a tremendous excitement." Benjamin Harrison crossed the Palace floor to publicly congratulate the man who had privately rebuffed his request to run yesterday.[70]

Garfield took the handshake. By adjournment at ten o'clock that night, his delegate count had reached a grand total of two.[71]

Walking to the Palace the next morning with Charles Henry, Garfield accepted a leaflet from a passerby. He unfurled it to read a piece of scripture hailing the "stone which the builders refused." Entering the Palace, he heard yet another round of applause, and a song that also augured well:

I dreamt I dwelt in marble halls

With vassals and serfs by my side

And of all who assembled within those walls

That I was the hope and the pride[72]

The avalanche of goodwill that had built above and around Garfield during the past week at last dislodged on the thirty-fourth ballot. The Wisconsin delegation's chair said his state would cast two votes for Grant, two to Blaine, and then, with a yell, "SIXTEEN VOTES FOR GENERAL JAMES A. GARFIELD!"[73]

With this shout, the Palace's balconies ("men, women, and boys") took to their feet and cheered. Garfield got up, too—not to add to the uproar but stand against it. *"Mr. President,"* he started, before being cut off by the chair.

"For what purpose does the gentleman rise?" demanded Hoar.

"I rise to a question of order," Garfield replied. ". . . No man has a right, without the consent of the person voted for, to announce that person's name, and vote for him, in this convention. Such consent I have not given—" Hoar, unamused, rapped Garfield quiet.[74]

The senator was not about to let Garfield ruin this for either of them. He had arrived at Chicago believing "it would be unwise to nominate either General Grant or Mr. Blaine," and, in an unguarded moment, mentioned the one candidate delegates might unite behind (though only if locked in a room for a protracted period) was Garfield, a good friend of his. Circumstance had since conspired to put the whole convention into precisely such a scenario.

So Hoar felt fine shutting Garfield up on a technicality. "The gentleman from Ohio is not stating a question of order," the chair ruled, before ordering the clerk to start the next ballot. "I recollect the incident perfectly," Hoar admitted years later. "I interrupted him [Garfield] in the middle of his sentence. I was terribly afraid that he would say something that would make his nomination . . . or his acceptance impossible, if it were made."[75]

Other states threw votes to Garfield throughout the next round. "It seemed to have flashed upon every one in the house at once that Garfield had been chosen for the compromise," a journalist in the galleries wrote. When Indiana was called, Benjamin Harrison announced nearly all his delegation would vote for Garfield. This helped nearly triple the dark horse's delegate count in the span of a ballot, while Sherman's and Blaine's eroded.[76]

Telegrams shot out from the floor to let these candidates know. The secretary of the Treasury was spotted pacing in Washington, seams visible in a glacial face.[77]

The color on Garfield's fell as the thirty-sixth ballot commenced. He said nothing as Connecticut allocated almost all its votes to him—simply resting a "deathly pale" head on one hand. Admirers mistook this for stoicism. "He . . . held his massive head steadily immoveable . . . [with] an appearance of extra resoluteness," wrote one. In fact, the underlying feeling was shock; Garfield, ready as he had been to accept a spontaneous nomination, found the reality of it hard to endure. It was also (literally) an exceptional experience. "He was being struck with Presidential lightning while sitting in the body which was to nominate him." After all of Iowa's delegates put their votes in for Garfield ("The turning point of the day," a journalist judged) other delegates crowded near, grasping for him with handshakes strong enough to test his shoulder-socket.[78]

Silence finally failing him, Garfield started saying whatever he could to either avoid the inevitable—or, at least, further demonstrate he did not want it. He asked a delegate if it would be all right to leave, only to be told it would seem prudish. To another, Garfield said he would prefer being "shot to death" than have anyone suspect him of desiring the presidency. "You must not desert Sherman," he pleaded to other Ohioans.[79]

Just then, a telegram arrived from Washington ordering them to do so. The secretary of the Treasury had finally realized that he would not be president. He tapped out a message to Chicago instructing supporters to switch to Garfield, then left his office to feign to reporters he always knew the "cat would jump that way." Inwardly Sherman wondered if Garfield truly had.[80]

Blaine, a nimbler political feline, did a far better job landing on his feet. Garfield received a telegram from the senator during the thirty-sixth ballot that read with impeccable timing and chivalry:

Maine's vote this moment cast for you is with my cordial concurrence. I hope it will aid in securing your nomination and assuring victory to the Republican Party.[81]

Half-Breeds could now vote their conscience. The subsequent announcement that all but one of Ohio's votes would go to Garfield (himself the solitary holdout) met great noise—applause, plus the groans of benches, chairs, and tables in the Palace being stood upon.

Garfield apologized to a Blainite ("I am very sorry this has become necessary") and, swiveling to a reporter, deployed clumsy chitchat before dropping the pretense:

I wish you would say [in your article] that this is no act of mine. I wish you would say that I have done everything, and omitted nothing to secure Secretary Sherman's nomination. I want it plainly understood that I have not sought this nomination, and have protested against the use of my name.[82]

Soon a mob jammed in, interrupting Garfield as Wisconsin gave him what he claimed not to want.

He looked dazed amid the crush of congratulatory backslaps, handshakes, and telegrams. "Won't you telegraph my wife?" Garfield was heard saying. "She ought to know of this."[83]

One of the messages Crete received from her husband that afternoon left to her judgment whether the terms they had recently discussed were now met:

DEAR WIFE. IF THE RESULT MEETS YOUR APPROVAL, I
SHALL BE CONTENT. LOVE TO ALL THE HOUSEHOLD.[84]

A row of cannon blasted outside the Palace at about two o'clock, shaking windows along streets named for past presidents. The big-headed, disheveled figure of Garfield was then seen hurrying out, through the crowds and away from the pursuing melody of "Hail to the Chief." He fought through the throngs ("good-naturedly," per a description) before hopping into a stagecoach with a few others and pulling a felt hat down over his eyes. The vehicle took off into deeper Chicago, chased by shouts of, "God bless you, General!" and "Bully boy, Garfield!"[85]

Inside the carriage, dusty and rumpled, Garfield looked more like he had just won a fight rather than a presidential nod. Charles Henry noticed a strange look—both pensive and dumbfounded—take over his old principal's face. "He seemed like a man benumbed," Henry thought.[86]

Garfield let this expression slip only once after returning to his hotel room; among the six-hundred-odd telegrams he opened throughout the next few hours was a short one from Hal and Jim, off at school in New Hampshire. ("Have received news. Very glad and send our hearty congratulations.") These simple words were enough to bring tears to Garfield's eyes. Recovering, he then confessed to a reporter that among his apprehensions at being nominated was, yes, a concern for what the "hostile attitude assumed by Conkling" might mean for the fight ahead.[87]

He turned a freshly minted "Garfield for President" badge in his hands. It was crimson red, as were the massive floral bouquet spelling "Garfield" back in the Convention Hall and the ribbons now streaming off delegates' chests.[88]

The Stalwarts in the Palace had stayed deathly silent during the Garfield boom, alone in refusing to give in to it. "Unmoved," "glum," "black as a thunder cloud"—so read descriptions of Conkling's men as the convention swung for its dark horse. At least they died hard; while other

Republican factions gradually rallied to Garfield, the Stalwarts to their candidate until the bitter end.[89]

"All of these [men]," an elderly survivor would eulogize, "for thirty-five ballots, stood like the rock of Gibraltar, faithful to their idol, and went down with their colors nailed to the mast." They would thereafter identify as the "immortal 306," and spend the rest of their lives dedicating books to one another, and hosting reunions, and striking coins with Grant's face and Conkling's signature on them, and, when their name started being disproven, "mark the deep gaps that the dread Reaper has left in our lines" in a roll kept of "distinguished dead."[90]

Such was the devotion of Grant's political soldiery, and so it is unsurprising that the Stalwart rank and file was in no mood to pitch in with Garfield in Chicago following his surprise victory. In the recess after his nomination, they milled around the Palace promising "all sorts of disasters" as long as other Republicans continued to "pile insults" on their kind.[91]

Their leaders also held the line. Grant abstained from sending Garfield any congratulations and, when asked for an opinion of the new nominee, offered what first passed for a compliment then, on review, as a wicked barb: "Garfield has always been right."[92]

Conkling could not disguise his contempt at all. Of all the humiliations Garfield's presence in Chicago brought him the prior week, the harshest came on the very last ballot—when Hoar declared the dark horse had enough votes for nomination, then asked the Stalwart floor leader in front of the whole convention: "Shall the nomination be made unanimous?" Conkling's whispered assent sounded "funereal" to those who could hear it. Later cornered for comment, the senator found his voice again—offering a line that was, regrettably, "quite too sulphurous to be recorded in the public press."[93]

Such behavior appeared to confirm a convention result that all attendees had feared, and that the choice of Garfield had, in part, been aimed at avoiding: a party too beset by internal divisions to win in November.

Common sense suggested a solution. It was well known that a Stalwart heart, no matter how wounded, could be swiftly healed by the awarding of a lofty enough title (as one Grant delegate had yelled earlier during the convention, "What are we here for except for the offices?"). Though the highest in the land had now been deprived them—stolen by the dark horse—another remained available.[94]

Garfield had never thought highly of the vice presidency, regardless of administration or occupant. The office had only ever been useful to him as a yardstick for utter political uselessness. "Of all the stupid places in public life," he said during the Grant administration, "the Lieutenant Governorship of Ohio and the Vice Presidency of the United States head the list."[95]

But a purpose for it was finally at hand on the afternoon of June 8. While still receiving journalists, Half-Breeds, and independents at the Grand Pacific after his nomination, Garfield let other Ohio delegates fan out to lure a New York Stalwart into the vice presidential slot, and thus erect a veneer of party unity. This proved tough sledding: the banker Levi Morton was ready to accept the post—at least until he scurried to Conkling for approval. "If you think you will be happy in the association, accept," the boss advised icily.

Morton backtracked while Conkling baited the trap for other stragglers. "Mr. Morton has declined," he told another suspected waverer. "Perhaps you would like the nomination for Vice-President?" The Stalwart said he wouldn't object to it. "I hope no sincere friend of mine will accept it," Conkling replied at this failure of loyalty.[96]

Secretly, in another part of Chicago, one of them considered doing so anyway. Despite what millions of Americans thought (for much mud had been thrown on his name by the White House's current tenant) there was decency hidden under Chester Arthur's swooping whiskers and oval frame. It had always been there, albeit buried beneath more evident traits: an affection for high living, a yearning for camaraderie, and a moral spine just pliable enough to yield to both. A friend recalled that, as a child in Vermont, Arthur was good at directing other boys as they built miniature dams out of mud, only standing just far enough away to keep his own hands clean.[97]

A career that began in civil rights law and military service in New York had tapered off into the cozy confines of Conkling's postwar power structure. Arthur rose through the Stalwart ranks quickly, putting his cut of the spoils to use along the way. Starting his days in fine, fuzzy tweed, he liked to throw on darker attire in the afternoons; by dusk the "Gentleman Boss" would typically change into a tuxedo that kept his folds hugged tight. He did not stay nearly as attentive (or close) to his wife, the socialite Ellen "Nell" Arthur. The customhouse collector instead spent his nights tinkering with machine business over brandy until the early morning.[98]

In the second half of the Hayes administration, Arthur's good fortune fell apart: the president finally managed to oust him from his prized customhouse role in 1878. Then, in January 1880, came a more rattling blow: Nell caught a fatal case of pneumonia while Arthur was again away on business. He would forever regret how he lived before Nell's passing, and he did not know how to do so after. "Honors to me now are not what they once were," Arthur told a friend.[99]

Except, it seems, the vice presidency. Arthur was shocked to be offered the job by the Ohioans. His expertise lay in rigging elections as a boss, not winning them as a candidate—he had never even run for office before. Meanwhile, other Republicans were already hailing Garfield's nomination as a Waterloo for the Stalwarts. "My mind enjoys inexpressible peace at the breaking up of the machine," one reformer soon expounded to a journalist in New York.[100]

That said, Arthur was not built to say no to a chance at higher office, let alone one so chic as the vice presidency. New York's delegation (in Conkling's absence) agreed to present him to the convention for it. Then Arthur had to go seek out his Lord's blessing.[101]

He finally found Conkling in a Palace backroom. They met in its middle—not noticing a journalist tucked in one corner, quiet with pen ready:

ARTHUR: I have been hunting everywhere for you, Senator. . . the Ohio men have offered me the Vice Presidency.

CONKLING [in indignant tones]: Well, sir, you should drop it as you
would a red-hot shoe from the forge.

Arthur's eyes then gleamed with what the silent observer took for
resentment. "I sought you to consult, not—" the ex-collector started
again. But these words teased defiance. "What is there to consult about?"
Conkling interrupted. "What, sir, you think of accepting?"

The issue forced, Arthur almost apologetically stood up for himself:

ARTHUR: The Office of the Vice President is a greater honor than
I ever dreamed of attaining. A barren nomination would be a
great honor. In a calmer moment you will look at this differently.
CONKLING: If you wish for my favor and my respect you will
contemptuously decline it.

But, to Arthur, the exchange indicated there was little to begin with.
He told Conkling he would accept the offer to run alongside Garfield,
causing the senator to wheel off "in a towering rage." Arthur gave a con-
trite look after the departed boss, then also made his exit.[102]

It would be a short-lived separation; Arthur and Conkling's ties ran
too deep to be cut by a quarrel, no matter how sharp. The two not only
shared the same politics, but also (after Nell's death) a home on the corner of Fourteenth and F streets in Washington. Neighbors called it the
"Morgue," presumably because Republicans went there to be dissected by
Conkling the mortician, Arthur his assistant.[103]

The convention reassembled and an Ohioan delegate declared his
"desire . . . to see the Republican Party of this nation a compact, united,
vigorous and triumphant Party," before moving to make it so "by putting
on the ticket, with General Garfield as the head, General Arthur." The
convention obliged this request on the first ballot.[104]

At eight o'clock that night, the party's two nominees reacquainted
themselves in the parlor of the Grand Pacific—Arthur congratulating

Garfield, Garfield returning the compliment and saying that he "hoped the contest now was free from bitterness." Arthur replied that he "did not believe . . . there was the least bitterness of feeling entertained by anybody."[105]

Hundreds of well-wishers marched past during the next few hours, shaking the pair's hands so frenziedly as to tangle Garfield's arms and dislocate one of Arthur's fingers. The injured digit's ring needed to be filed off. Another trinket stayed on Arthur throughout the reception, though—a Grant-for-President badge, glinting off an overlooked lapel.[106]

Near midnight Hoar arrived to give both nominees an official send-off. The chairman told Garfield of the "unanimity of pleasure" the party felt upon selecting him, who "represent[ed] not only the distinctive principles and opinions of the Republican Party . . . [but] also its unity;" Garfield's response mentioned that he never held the "slightest expectation . . . my name would be connected with the nomination," before also garnishing the altar of party harmony:

> I have felt, with you, great solicitude concerning the situation of our Party during the struggle; but, believing that you are correct . . . that substantial unity has been reached in the conclusion, it gives me a gratification far greater than any personal pleasure your announcement can bring.[107]

Barnstorming back to Ohio the next day, Garfield said little further. The cheers of tens of thousands; the sappy tributes given to him ("the noblest man that ever lived") by governors, mayors, and generals at each stop; the cannon salutes, the banners with his name; the gifts of voters (babies for kissing, rose bouquets for holding, a custom knife for who knows what); that elderly man telling restrainers he would "see Garfield or hell," the grips that nearly yanked Garfield off his train—nothing got the next president to stop his outward deflections.[108]

Against incessant congratulations, he repeated, "Thank you, sir, if it is a victory." Garfield politely informed the crowds of Toledo that he could not give them a full address. Those in Elyria heard only a few more sentences:

> Fellow citizens of my native county and of my State . . . I cannot at this time address you in a speech, other than to say I know all this demonstration means your gladness at the unity and harmony and good feeling of the great political party . . . For all these things I thank you, and bid you good night.[109]

Throughout the entirety of this homecoming, in the privacy of Garfield's car, friends from Hiram, the army, and politics "endeavored in vain to divert his mind from the train of solemn, if not sad, reflections which seemed to engross it."[110]

Half-Breed and independent Republicans around the country, meanwhile, collectively clutched their pearls at the great concession Garfield had already made to Conkling. Their excitement at his nomination wavered at Arthur's for opposite reasons: the "friends of Mr. Blaine, who furnished the bulk of the vote for Mr. Garfield," feared the implied battle for future spoils; reformists expressed angry surprise that, as president, Garfield might invite such competition at all. Even impassive Secretary Sherman showed pique—calling the choice of Arthur a "ridiculous burlesque," the man's only distinction being "that he was discharged from an office he was unfit to fill."[111]

Luckily, more saw the merit of it. "The lion and the lamb had lain down together," a senator wrote of events at Chicago. Stalwart voters also interpreted the final ticket as well as possible; "I regard the nomination of General Arthur as a high compliment to Conkling . . . it was a kind and liberal act of the anti-Grant men to go in for him under the circumstances," a Stalwart official told one reporter. On the other side of the party spectrum, President Hayes also inferred what he wanted from the result: Garfield's nomination "was the best that was possible," Arthur's a "sop thrown to Conkling . . . emphasis[ing] the completeness of his defeat," a bone thrown "from sheer sympathy."[112]

Blaine assumed indifference, nodding politely at Arthur's "wide acquaintance with the public men of this country"; in secret, he predicted defeat, but preferred the party losing with Garfield over it winning with Grant. He also knew the political wisdom of hedging one's bets. The Plumed Knight would help in the battle ahead in case it went unexpectedly well.[113]

Pragmatic reformers also preached patience. E. L. Godkin wrote in *The Nation* that Republicans "not unnaturally disgusted" by Arthur's selection should rest assured it would not amount to much:

> There is no place in which his powers of mischief will be so small as in the Vice Presidency . . . It is true General Garfield, if elected, may die during his term of office, but this is too unlikely a contingency to be worth making extraordinary provision for.[114]

In a Boston library, another man also adjusted himself to the surprise ticket. Dealt a bad hand in life, he had thus far played it atrociously. Despite only nearing mid-age, he could already look back on failures in preaching, the law, publishing, and marriage, across which he had inflicted enough woe to fill many lifetimes. His sights were now fixed on practicing politics—the Stalwart kind, which promised contributors what the man had always wanted so terribly: a place of influence.

His time in Boston had been spent writing a speech endorsing Grant. He knew it would earn him handsome reward—a belief that Garfield's surprise nomination did not change much. Necessary edits made, the man boarded a ship to Manhattan and set out on a collision course—not just with another boat downriver, but, also, the fate of the nation. He sensed this. "When I left Boston for New York," the man would later recall from behind bars, "I felt that I was on my way to the White House."[115]

25

"I call to mind your gracious favors
Done to me, undeserving as I am"

—Shakespeare's *The Two Gentlemen of Verona*, as quoted
in Garfield diary entry for December 16, 1878

"General Garfield is no stranger to the American people. His reputation is national." So pontificated a Republican editor in Topeka the day after the nomination. Nevertheless, a sketch of the candidate had been put out for display in that town anyway—one large enough to require illumination by train headlight and attract throngs of curious citizens through the evening. As Kansans crowded in to familiarize themselves with Garfield, few realized a village in their own state had already been named in his honor nearly a decade before.[1]

Similar scenes repeated from Key West to the Hudson Valley, Kalamazoo to San Francisco. Between celebratory cannon blasts, millions of ordinary Republicans recognized Garfield's name but realized they needed more acquaintance with the man himself. After all, his reputation had been earned in that kind of political service that mostly occupied bylines rather than headlines, and within which Garfield had vaguely channeled, as Blaine would describe it, "the liberal and progressive spirit of Republicanism without being visionary and impractical." This had cloaked him in broad, agreeable cover. "I don't know how any man could have been chosen who, on the whole, walks so well in that safe *via media* . . . of the Republican Party," remarked a New Yorker.[2]

Next morning, papers filled in the requisite physical details (six foot tall, strong build, "an unusually large head, which seems three-fourths forehead") beside those biographical ones so crucial to presidential contests. It emerged that Garfield had been raised by a widow "without fortune" in Ohio's backwoods. Early schoolmates said he swept floors, rang bells, and borrowed to afford his education, all the way to Williams. Simultaneous service in preaching, education, and state politics followed—and, when war came, dashing military heroics across snowbound Kentucky slopes and the killing fields of Shiloh and Chickamauga. His congressional career was better known, but context on how Garfield led it carried new charm: citizens now learned of his late-night research ventures into the Library of Congress ("his arms full of books borrowed"), his complete lack of pretension. "He dresses plainly . . . cares nothing for luxurious living, is thoroughly temperate in all respects save in that of brain-work," reported an acquaintance.[3]

And atop it all apparently rested that rarest of political traits—a genuine kindness that Garfield extended to all who approached, regardless of party. "No man keeps more cordial relations with his political antagonists, and no man has warmer or more numerous personal attachments."[4]

At the same time, the overall arc of *achievement* read more strikingly; the Garfield story, one columnist opined, was that of an American who had "carved his own pathway, unaided and alone, from the lowest rank in life to the proudest position to which an American citizen can aspire."[5]

This narrative's political strength was being tested before its subject even got home. As Garfield's train crossed into Ohio, old men in New York applauded the notion his life "embodied in his life and career—from the poor boy on the farm to the lofty distinction of his Presidential candidacy—the very genius of American civil institutions."[6]

Europeans read the result differently. "A curious commentary on the uncertainty of party politics in America," observed a London paper, before presenting Garfield as having "commenced the battle of life for himself . . . [as] a day labourer." A Parisian cabled that the French had a better grip on Garfield's early profession of choice, plus its potent symbolism:

> They are unable to comprehend the machinery by which the dark horse was suddenly shoved to the front. . . . They content themselves with giving biographical sketches of General Garfield. . . . They have seized upon the fact of General Garfield having originally been a boatman to fish a pendent to Lincoln as a rail-splitter.[7]

Republicans in America noticed this detail, too, with glee; their campaign material would practically write itself. "In 1860 it was Honest Abe, the rail-splitter," opined the *Chicago Tribune*. "In 1880 it is General Garfield, the wood-chopper and canal-driver." Even the president (a most difficult man to excite) felt thrilled for the propaganda opportunities now before the party. "The truth is no man ever started so low that accomplished so much in all our history. Not [Benjamin] Franklin or Lincoln even," Hayes wrote. "Let it be thoroughly presented—in facts and incidents, in poetry and tales, in pictures, on banners, in representations, in processions, in watchwords and nicknames."[8]

Garfield spotted the first of these efforts once his train reached Cleveland—a flag held aloft, its inscription predicting, "He, who at the age of 16 steered a canal-boat, will steer the ship of state at 50." It was an inauspicious comparison to reach for: Garfield had only worked a towpath for a few months.[9]

Once Garfield got to Mentor, reformist friends began insisting he stay there. Their letters read as though the nominee were actually a wayward toddler in desperate need of supervision. "My Dear General, you got away from Chicago much earlier than I expected," Whitelaw Reid tutted. "First of all, I beg of you to make no promises to anybody . . . please don't make any journeys or any speeches . . . There is no place where you can do so much for your supporters, and be so comfortable yourself, from now on until November, as on your farm." The president would pile in with stricter parenting. "Rule 1st, absolute and complete divorce from your inkstand," Hayes ordered. "You will see the sense of *writing no letters to strangers*, or to anybody else *on politics*." Both feared that an unattended Garfield might run off to make nice with those Republicans still pouting about his nomination—namely, Conkling and the Stalwarts.[10]

Lord Roscoe had last been spotted fleeing Chicago in a complete tantrum. Boarding a train out of town after Arthur's betrayal, he had called Garfield a gutless worm, a "trickster of Mentor," then disembarked to see his loss to the worm being cartooned as a train-wreck itself. Conkling soon said he would prefer to spend the campaign season in jail instead of helping Garfield—a position all Stalwarts, freed of the convention's tumult, coalesced around. Nothing about the nominee indicated trustworthiness for them: not his sunniness (so odd to New Yorkers), not his public record, and certainly not his conduct at Chicago. The nominee's evident backstabbing of Sherman informed a new entry in the Stalwarts' vocabulary: "Garfieldesque." They settled on avoiding becoming his next victim by holing up in their state, lassoing errant allies (particularly that rather porcine one, Arthur), then gumming up party machinery. This would permit the wringing of concessions in exchange for "any vigorous campaign."[11]

Meanwhile, Grant detached himself more than usual from the world. Secretly dismayed by his defeat, the general told Conkling he felt "weary of constant abuse . . . [from] former professed friends," then headed out to holiday in a West now becoming rather free of Indians.[12]

Part of Garfield also wanted to abstain from any active work—to, just as Hayes would instruct, "sit-cross legged and look wise" until November. Doing so would let him keep playing the role of reluctant candidate and adhere to the ambivalent public approach to job-seeking he had relied on for his entire career. But other instincts (and husbandly duties) led him astray. Garfield still owed his party an acceptance letter, which he needed papers from I Street to draft, while Crete also had a list of furniture she needed him to retrieve from Washington.[13]

"The events of the past week seem to grow more and more unreal," Crete told her husband. "But I suppose I shall grow accustomed to it all after a while." She had, after all, learned "to travel fast and think faster ever since I have known you, to keep even within seeing distance." Garfield assured his wife—and Reid—that he would "make the trip [to Washington] as quietly and quickly as possible."[14]

Alas, once in the District, Garfield got carried away by good intentions. He attended hundred-man banquets, received serenades from veterans' groups, and received callers heartily, amid indiscreet visits paid to all sorts of Republicans about town. He might have even met Conkling had Garfield not first accepted a carriage ride with Carl Schurz—Hayes's secretary of the Interior, a reformist tsar who looked like a scarecrow and whom Stalwarts treated as one. News of this excursion sent Conkling into hiding at Wormley Hotel, where Garfield's notes begging a meeting could be easily ignored amid the cigar-smoke.[15]

Arthur also declined an invite to meet Garfield in Washington. "After the organization of the [Republican National] Com.[mittee] I will be glad to cooperate in any way that may be desired," he wrote from Manhattan.[16]

Blaine, conversely, expressed no such reservations about being of help. He and Garfield had been friends for their whole congressional careers— a bond the latter had felt fluctuate with its perceived value to the former. This had never been cause to end it, though. Enjoying Blaine's company and penchant for gladiatorial spectacle, Garfield also accepted the Magnetic Man for who he was at heart: a transactional soul, whose dream had always (quite nakedly) been to barter his way into the White House. Garfield rarely took the "reckless" or "selfish" conduct that resulted personally, instead ascribing it to presidential obsession.[17]

Yet on first seeing Blaine after the events in Chicago, Garfield found these "childish" symptoms all gone—a change in the senator made particularly appealing by the simultaneous Stalwart pout. The two friends held a "full, long, and cordial talk" in Washington about campaign matters. Garfield left the District only wishing they had the time for another.[18]

As he sat down at Mentor to begin his acceptance letter, Garfield sent out notes thanking those reformists who had already offered input on it. Then he fired off two further letters—one to Blaine expressing gratitude for their talk in Washington ("there were many things I wanted to say to you, and still more which I wanted you to say to me"), and one to Arthur regretting that they had not met at all.[19]

Their responses also differed. Blaine replied almost at once from vacation. He moved with good speed for a gout sufferer—leaping out of an Appalachian spring to shoot back point by point guidance on how, precisely, Garfield needed to posture on political issues. Blaine closed by predicting overwhelming victory and voicing a warm "Love to Mrs. Garfield."[20]

Arthur never gave so indulgent a reply—not to Garfield's first letter, nor subsequent ones. Garfield wrote his ticketmate repeatedly into early July for advice, even offering to host Arthur at Mentor. But the interest was not reciprocated. At times pleading ("Can't you please come and see me by and by[?]"), at times apologetic ("I hope you will not consider me importunate in my invitations to you to visit me"), Garfield's overtures to his prospective vice president stirred only crisp, telegraphed dodges and counter-invitations to New York.[21]

When Grant heard of this outreach, he smirked. He had won the White House twice, and "no one ever offered him a suggestion about his letter of acceptance, and he never thought more of it than any other letter he had to answer." The Stalwart embargo on Garfield was now in full effect.[22]

Their snubs gave the candidate something else to bring up to Blaine, who soothingly replied that the Stalwarts did not deserve fretting over. "A little time must be allowed for pouting and petting," the senator advised. "But they cannot in the end afford to scuttle a ship on which they are passengers." Garfield complained to Blaine that the figurative sea was troubling him, too. All the letters flooding into Mentor made it almost impossible for him to step outside, "much less study the great questions of the campaign which will soon confront me."[23]

They were a mosaic of the novel and tragically familiar, spanning out in all directions of the compass.

In northern and eastern cities, demand for civil service reform had only swelled in the last administration. It remained a "passionate cause which the ethical would not let sleep," both despite and because of Hayes's struggles to enact it. Perhaps no president except Johnson had ever sabotaged their cause so well in Congress; the Democratic House now had a spoilsman leading its reform committee (a figurative fox in charge of the chicken coop) while Republican Half-Breed and Stalwart senators still sank Hayes's nominees out of spite. In short, as a reform historian has condensed, "Congress was not disposed to do its share of the work."[24]

Meanwhile, after nearly seceding again in the last presidential election, the South was solidly Democratic. Few means were available for the federal government to stop the ongoing reversal of Reconstruction there—and fewer Northern Republicans than ever thought it would be wise to try. President Hayes, his conciliation policy a failure, now could only feebly point out southern racial outrages to Congress. But Frederick Douglass noticed most of those on Capitol Hill now treated old sectional issues as faux pas:

> Under the fair-seeming name of local self-government . . . moral difference(s) between those who fought for the Union and liberty, and those who had fought for slavery and the dismemberment of the Union, was fast fading away. The language of sickly conciliation, inherited from the Administration of President Hayes, was abroad.[25]

Other animosities were, conversely, gaining political prominence. A pair had peculiar relevance to the railroad industry—the first centering upon the growing friction between American capital and labor: the nation's first-ever nationwide strike erupted in 1877. After the unrest had been quelled by federal troops, moguls still thought their kind needed further government protection in the form of a tariff kept high enough to fend off foreign competition over price and wages. Thus, to paraphrase one writer, Uncle Sam was weighing whether to become a nurse to giants. The election of 1880 was primed to be a referendum on what balance the industrialized republic wanted between forces of owner and worker, protectionist and free trader.[26]

The second point of anger spanned racial and class tensions. Out in the plains, American railroads had begun hiring Chinese immigrants as a source of cheap labor. By 1880, this practice had been successful enough to attract tens of thousands of such workers from abroad to the Pacific states, kindling white grievance. The Caucasian working class bemoaned livelihoods lost; histrionic novels like *Last Days of the Republic* cast the migrants as a foreign invasion, destined to sweep east and end with the "Imperial Dragon of China" flying over a conquered Washington; congressmen, senators, and presidents alike now regularly courted fears on the stump about the "Chinese Question." Republicans saw, in the working conditions Chinese laborers accepted without complaint, a possible return of slavery to the United States.[27]

Against this confusing backdrop of issues, Democrats made a curious presidential pick. General Winfield Scott Hancock represented an improvement on the Samuel Tilden blueprint—even less vulnerable to bloody shirt attacks (he had fought for the Union) and, incredibly, even more bland. A friendly editor could only present the general as a "good man weighing 250 pounds." Others labeled him "Hancock the Superb" on account of frontline gallantry but found little else to make a moniker of: no elected office, few examples of personal belief, nothing either agreeable or disagreeable.[28]

He was, in a word, vanilla—a flavor of candidate that would be of great appeal in the campaign his party hoped to run. While the GOP would be reduced to merely casting Hancock as a Trojan horse or empty mask, Democrats could tar Garfield as the epitome of a failed, corrupt Republican establishment that had now misruled the nation for decades.[29]

The blemishes of Garfield's personal past added texture to this narrative. An early Democratic cartoon sketched him as a jockey literally saddled by bags labeled "Credit Mobilier" and "DeGolyer," as well as a top-hatted, befuddled Chester Arthur. A number began appearing in the real world in ink and chalk: "329," a reference to the amount Garfield allegedly accepted from Oakes Ames. It would confront Republicans in frightening frequency and location throughout the election: for regular citizens, on barn sides, fences, and sidewalks, while members of the Hayes cabinet would find the figure written on their mail, their napkins, and (most alarmingly) their bed posts.[30]

A few ironworkers even brought the figure to Garfield's doorstep—arriving at Mentor with scrips of paper reading "329" tucked into their hats. He ignored the slight, instead treating its perpetrators to a speech on the virtues of their profession. Then Garfield shook their hands and thanked them for the visit.[31]

"Perhaps it is better that the tempest blew upon me six years ago and got me immuned [sic] to inclement weather," he confided to a friend.[32]

In fact, his entire family put up well with campaign pressures. Each Garfield felt them—even Hal and Jim, attending boarding school in rural New England. Their father's first letter after the convention urged them to stick "steadily to your work . . . not allowing your heads to be turned by any of the events passing around you. . . . Don't say anything about my nomination that indicates any feeling of exultation or pride." He need not have worried, for the boys found the attention unbearable. Sycophantic classmates laced arms around theirs and called them nicknames. As Hal reported back:

> I despise them all. . . . One fellow said I suppose if your father is elected you will stop study[ing] and bum it out in Washington. I told him . . . it should be all the more reason for studying hard.[33]

The intrusions were more overwhelming in Mentor. The farm was overrun within days of its owner's nomination—even branded a rather redundant new name by the press: "Lawnfield." Hundreds of tourists invaded daily via a railroad line along the property's northern border. They marched through Garfield's wheatfields, clambered over his fences, and, on reaching the front lawn, treaded it brown.[34]

Courtesy demanded these hordes be met with kindness. Spending his mornings sifting through mountains of mail (campaign correspondence, mixed in with voter requests for his foot size, parenting advice, farming tips, or horse), Garfield would often walk on his porch near noon to address the day's intruders on whatever topic came to mind.[35]

This unassuming gesture quietly revolutionized American campaigning. As Blaine later remarked:

> Never before, in the history of partisan contests in this country, had a successful Presidential candidate spoken freely on passing events and current issues. To attempt anything of the kind seemed novel, rash, and even desperate.[36]

Garfield, however, later explained that he was just being polite. "I could not play dummy on my own doorstep," he protested, "when my yard was filled by voters from all parts of the country, hurling speeches at me on all subjects." He typically treated such visitors with addresses peculiar to their cause. Industrial workers heard Garfield call capital "only another name for crystallized labor saved up"; Indiana merchants listened to him praise how all American labor now stood on the "solid basis of specie values," the keystone of capital stability. A German delegation heard more interesting doublespeak. To them, Garfield started praising immigration—European, at least—in English ("From the Teutonic races, from the Latin . . . the best elements mingle here, and like any other alloy of metals, it makes a stronger mixture than any one of the parts alone") before doing the same in their native tongue by reciting a verse of German poetry, then adding a personal *"wilkommen alle"* to close it.[37]

Nor did the rest of his family neglect their visitors. Little Abe could often be seen swinging in cherry trees over their heads, plucking fruit from the branches. Mollie presented a neater look, her collar bearing a gold broom-shaped brooch—signifying, she said, a "clean sweep for Ohio." Garfield clasped her close and said she was worth "more to me than a dozen Presidencies!" Over her father's shoulders, Mollie admired another person staying near him that summer—Joseph Stanley Brown, Garfield's longtime House aide.[38]

Eliza helped attend the reporters her son let into the home proper. "She is about as old as Cleveland . . . her widowhood has lasted forty-seven years!" one marveled. "She recollects her husband jumping into the woods with his ax to open a space for their cabin." As the man admired her, Eliza quietly stacked logs at his feet and struck a match to them—its light flickering over eyes that had first opened in the Jefferson administration. Another writer thought Eliza did not appear terribly thrilled with her son's nomination.[39]

Perhaps only Crete showed greater patience. Many of the uninvited guests at Mentor expected not only a speech from its owner, but a meal from his wife, too. She complied but staged a crafty rebellion—confiscating all chairs from the reception areas, leaving out only refreshments of cookies and lemonade. This helped keep the callers moving along. Those who paid attention to her while passing by saw an "expressive and harmonious" face, capable of both smirks and shyness. Her husband praised the character beneath to anyone who would listen. "I have been wonderfully blessed in the discretion of my wife," Garfield told one journalist. "She is one of the coolest and best-balanced women I ever saw . . . she is unstampedable."[40]

He proved less so. Writing hundreds of letters, spontaneously lecturing strangers, retelling his life to writers on the veranda, and hearing artists grumble about his head size ("It's a buster")—Garfield sometimes found it too much. He would throw on a slouch hat and flee into his fields to perform a refreshing bit of non-campaign work. Riding through the property, he noticed tree branches, corn stalks, and even fence posts were now missing—casualties to the crowds hungry for any piece of him.[41]

An acquaintance expressed worry about the potential of an assailant lurking in the crowds, but Garfield (after a momentary silence) shrugged. "Well, if assassination is to play its part in the campaign, and I must be the sacrifice, perhaps it is best."[42]

He also suspended preference over what people called his farm. When Whitelaw Reid gifted him a stack of stationery emblazoned "Lawnfield," Garfield felt obliged to start using it. "It has been a delightful day at Lawnfield, as the papers insist on calling our place," the candidate journaled one night. "The moonrise was unusually brilliant."[43]

On July 12, Garfield's acceptance letter finally left Lawnfield a balanced thing, as circumstances required. Strong language masked softness on substance across the key issues: the national government needed to "exercise all its Constitutional authority" to ensure "every citizen, rich or poor, white or Black, is secure in the free and equal enjoyment of every civil and political right guaranteed by the Constitution and its laws," lest "social and industrial forces . . . continue to be disturbed." Protecting both American "labor and capital" necessitated a tariff high enough to stave off foreign competition as well as bring revenue into the Treasury. Finally, patronage abuse by party machines demanded correction. That said, to "select wisely, from our vast population, those who are best fitted for the many offices to be filled requires an acquaintance far beyond the range of any one man." Implementing reform therefore had to be a congressional duty, not a presidential one—but, if Garfield might make a suggestion, a fine place for lawmakers to start would be setting term limits on federal posts.[44]

Now it was the reformists' turn to call Garfield spinally challenged. "The unworthy phrases in which Mr. Garfield's ideas are concealed or his old-time professions recanted betray a want of backbone," one wrote. Chiding letters arrived at Lawnfield from friends who thought they knew Garfield better than to surrender to the machines. "I thought you yielded a little too much," John Sherman's read. The secretary of the Treasury suggested Garfield's desertion of the great cause might make the North vote Democrat that winter. Schurz flew in with sharper criticism—hurt that he, apparently, had been the one taken on a ride in Washington. He told Garfield the acceptance letter was a "great disappointment to very many great men who hailed your nomination with joy and hope." Hayes, too, was aghast at Garfield's apparent bid "to trim, to talk so equivocally as to have the benefit of opposing nobody."[45]

Garfield could only shake his head. His issue was not with reform, only its ongoing absence in any significant, lasting sense. Hayes's attempts to clean the American government had relied on the club-like use of executive power, politically destructive and ephemeral in result; any future president could easily reverse the progress already made. Garfield politely replied to administration friends criticizing his letter that he was simply hoping to wage their shared battle in a more efficient manner once in the White House. He thanked Schurz for the "frank and faithful criticism," praised Hayes's "singularly pure record," while citing a personal one unmatched in "real reform." To Burke Hinsdale, Garfield divulged a clearer vision for how he would achieve it in office:

Earnest as Pres. Hayes's efforts have been—he has made the mistake of mostly antagonizing Congress and trying to effect a reform without legislative aid. I would shift the line of battle . . . presenting in a message a well-considered plan of civil service [reform], urge[ing] its adoption by Congress as law. Its chief features should be: (a) For the minor offices including clerks—a fixed term, say four years.

(b) A carefully drawn provision, enumerating the grounds in which such officers shall be removed.

(c) A provision that protects the officer from removal on other grounds . . . This plan would bring all the reform sentiment of the country to bear upon Congress, and would, sooner or later, result in a law, which would greatly narrow the field of uncertainty that now makes the life of an appointee so miserable. Again, it would be very dangerous for a[ny] new Administration, or a new Congress to repeal such a law and reintroduce the doctrine of spoils.[46]

It was a novel idea—the American executive conducting popular will like a current, zapping legislative blockages to dust from the White House. One day, another president would take similar inspiration to build the "bully pulpit." But by the end of July 1880, reformers had accepted it as a tepid but tolerable stance on their cause by Garfield—acceptable if only for want of a better alternative. "I can see no single object to gain from bringing Hancock in," Henry Adams confessed. "Whether Garfield can carry New York and Indiana, is, however, the real question."[47]

Indeed, with the South practically preordained to vote as a monolith for Hancock, Garfield's campaign would hinge on switching that pair of northern states Republican. His prospects for doing so (especially regarding the former) hung on how the Stalwarts read his letter. If they saw weakness in it, too, then perhaps they might return to the fold—lured by the scent of spoils.

Whereas reformists read Garfield's acceptance letter with disappointment, and the Stalwarts did so with hungry curiosity, Blaine must have studied it with pleasure. The greatest force in the document arose about the Chinese question, exactly as the senator suggested—and with the same phrasing he had provided Garfield. Blaine had advised a "servile class assimilating in all its conditions of labor to chattel slavery must be excluded from free immigration" (and told the nominee "clothe the proposition in your own language"). But Garfield had clearly found the senator's word choice too good to leave in the editorial dustbin. His official position on the Chinese migrant crisis thus parroted Blaine's informal one—that "any form of servile labor" must not be introduced to the Republic "under the guise of immigration."[48]

For all their volume, reformists were only getting murmurs of agreement off Garfield, if not quibbling, gentle rebuttals. The Stalwarts had refused to consult with the nominee at all. Blaine had spoken sparingly, in a saccharine pitch, and now heard a near-perfect echo carry out over the country.

•   •   •

Garfield had to be virtually hauled out of Lawnfield by train in early August. "I am very reluctant to go," he grumbled privately. "It is an unreasonable demand that so much effort should be made to conciliate one man." But, on a sunny Tuesday morning, he managed to look happy while blessing a nearby veteran's memorial ("Ideas are the only things in the universe really immortal"), before boarding an engine bound east.[49]

Garfield had reluctantly decided to visit Conkling in New York. The organizational condition of the party gave him little choice: Stalwarts had sulked their way into a choke hold over the Republican National Committee, shoehorning one of their own—former senator Stephen Dorsey—into the job of committee secretary. Though a chair of Garfield's choosing (Marshall Jewell) officially held top job, in practice committee hierarchy had since devolved considerably: Jewell, a reformist windbag, felt outclassed by Dorsey, a swarthy, keen practitioner of the spoils system. Jewell confessed to Garfield he could hardly keep up. "Dorsey's running it himself I guess," he wrote, "or all creation's running it, I don't know which."[50]

Among the few things Dorsey and Jewell had agreed on was the need for a Garfield-Stalwart détente before any real electioneering could get done. Dorsey wrote the nominee that such a rapprochement would be "imperative" to capturing New York and therefore the election. Jewell concurred: "With that we can win; without it we certainly cannot."[51]

Garfield weighed this advice against contradictory appeals from Reid and Hayes, as well as his own fear that further overtures to Conkling might be a final straw for reform voters. "They have not broken from us, and as the case stands, will not . . ." Garfield replied to Dorsey. "Is there not a danger that my visit to NY will positively alienate many of that class? This is the one question that gives me pause."[52]

A couple days of therapeutic barley-threshing helped him get over it. At the end of July, Garfield came back from his fields sore and ready to keep testing the reformers' patience with him, just as he was testing his own with the Stalwarts.[53]

•   •   •

Such stamina served him well throughout dozens of stops along the train journey that followed. His engine skated along the Lake Erie shoreline, then, at Buffalo, curved south to bisect a New York caught in the lively throes of summer. At each town, thousands of well-wishers offered up colorful greetings and gifts to the passing candidate—bouquets, fruit baskets, cotton "in various stages of manufacture," welcome speeches ripe with the burgeoning Garfield mythology:

> I would prefer for President of the United States . . . the patient, persistent, noble man, who when but a boy of seventeen cut 200 cords of wood in one winter.[54]

He added chapters to its lore along the way. At Poughkeepsie, German canal workers saluted the man who had famously also worked a towpath. *"Wie geht's, mein Herr!"* Garfield replied, wringing a rough hand. *"Wie geht's!"* [55]

Arthur hopped aboard—meeting Garfield for the first time since Chicago—as did Benjamin Harrison and congressman William McKinley. Each of these presidents-to-be gave bows or speeches off the train car as it wove through the Hudson River Valley.[56]

Out the window rolled a vista of upturned faces ("so many thousands . . . to estimate the mass is wholly vain"). These beamed up at Garfield all the way to his destination of Manhattan's Fifth Avenue Hotel. As police escorted his carriage to this building, John C. Frémont hosted a quieter gathering in another part of the city. The first ever Republican candidate for president told friends he felt "well satisfied" with Garfield. A quarter century before, Garfield had said much the same about him.[57]

Entering the Fifth Avenue Hotel through a side entrance, Garfield encountered the man he had most wanted to be there—James Blaine. The senator normally did not like being anywhere near New York, let alone in the heart of it; Blaine was persona non grata in Conkling country. But Garfield's notes during the previous few days had sounded desperate, temptingly so. "My dear friend," the first had read, "you must stand by me . . . I want to go over the ground with you . . . I want to know how large a force C[onkling] has behind him and just what the trouble is." A second telegram Garfield sent read more needfully: "You must not fail me." Blaine's presence at Fifth Avenue proved he never would.[58]

Only at twenty minutes past eight o'clock did Garfield throw a bone to the throngs gathered outside the hotel. He stepped onto a balcony to give an avenue full of waving citizens a fast, hoarse, "Thanks for your kind congratulations, and your presence." That was all. He ducked inside, as the gathering, though disappointed, offered up more applause.[59]

Somewhere beyond, a man moved through the masses in clothes that had been slept in since his arrival from Boston. He would soon find his way into the hotel lobby and, for the next few days, pass around loose-leaf copies of a speech ("Garfield against Hancock") to any Stalwart who would take them. He imagined that everyone, including Arthur, was impressed by it, and that soon Garfield would be reading the typescript with gratitude.

In fact, no one in the foyer could understand the man much, in writing or conversation. "He was the laughing-stock when he was not an annoyance to everybody about the room," a witness would later testify in court.[60]

A few floors overhead, Garfield soon flashed frustration, too. It turned out Conkling was not even in the Fifth Avenue Hotel, nor, apparently, did he plan to be. Only later would the senator be revealed to have been in Coney Island the whole time (closer to a less political type of circus), leaving cronies to the unpleasant business of brokering a deal with the presidential candidate. It was another insult to add to a mounting pile of them; even the Stalwarts in the hotel looked embarrassed and annoyed by Conkling's behavior.[61]

While other party chiefs like Blaine and Sherman paced Fifth Avenue's gilt hallways, a tense silence held between the Stalwart lieutenants and Garfield in a suite on the afternoon of July 5. How it then broke would one day become a matter of fierce dispute—much like a few other secret summits Garfield joined in his career, recalled oppositely by its participants.[62]

The Stalwarts would insist that the hush was followed with a complete capitulation by Garfield, as extracted by their lead negotiator in the hotel—not Arthur, but a small, courtly skeleton of an ex-congressman named Thomas Platt. Lightbulb-headed and wire-lipped, Platt would one day be known to New Yorkers as the "Easy Boss" of their state's Republican machine, prone to idly beam as victims did all the talking.[63]

Platt would claim things went exactly that way with Garfield. A slight lean by the Easy Boss in that suite ("We cannot afford to do the work, and let others reap the reward") and the candidate allegedly gave way with no resistance—professing he, too, had gripes with Hayes and would run his administration differently, as long as the Stalwarts helped him win it. "If this was done, he assured us that the wishes of the element of the Party we represented should be paramount with him, touching all questions of patronage," Platt was to testify.[64]

Emphasis was apparently placed on "all." As the Stalwarts told it, Garfield offered them control over the selection of New York's future district attorneys, marshals, and even (to what must have been a prickle in Arthur's muttonchops) the staff of Manhattan's customhouse, provided he won the White House in November. A few Stalwarts heard further terms; in an aside with Levi Morton, Garfield supposedly said that if the banker took charge of the campaign's finances, he could expect to be made the next secretary of the Treasury.[65]

The hotel's doors swung open, not along Fifth Avenue, but the adjacent Twenty-Third Street at dawn on August 7. This departure time and location allowed Garfield to evade another voter crush, but his exit did not entirely escape notice. Waiting reporters wrote that he looked at ease under his dark slouch hat, and the traveling party around him seemed relaxed, too. It boasted a few noteworthy additions, including Platt.[66]

Morning wires went out from Manhattan speculating what a growing number of Stalwarts considered a fact: that, behind closed doors, a compact had been made between presidential candidate and party spoilsmen. Headlines affixed a name to it: "The Treaty of Fifth Avenue."[67]

Garfield hopped aboard a ferry, then a train, as Conkling came out of hiding to hear its terms. The boss got them from Chester Arthur and was then ready to declare himself, if not happy, then resigned to be of help in the campaign. "If you insist," Conkling airily decreed, ". . . I shall carry him through." "He really thinks he is the Savior of the Situation," a witness marveled.[68]

Perhaps he was, though; on Garfield's trip home the yields of Stalwart support were already evident. The Easy Boss accompanied him and had arranged for their train to cross New York's southern counties (vital electoral territory, Platt assured) and sent ahead telegrams rousing the "faithful" to prepare a proper reception. The crowds out Garfield's window were, accordingly, the biggest he had yet seen in New York. "Fellow-Citizens, you are altogether too much for me," the candidate told one gathering. Another day would pass before Garfield reached home, cradling evidence that the attention had really been too much—a hand swollen and angry-red from an avalanche of shaking.[69]

At least it had been put to good use. The next day's mail would present Garfield with positive coverage of the New York trip, and even a kind note from President Grant (now ready to return east, feeling a "very deep interest" in the success of the Republican ticket).[70]

But before getting a chance to see these, Garfield used his sore hand to scribble out a diary entry that indicated a different understanding of what had transpired on Fifth Avenue:

> Very weary but feeling that no serious mistake had been made and probably much good had been done. No trades—no shackles—and as well fitted for defeat or victory as ever.[71]

A closer look at Garfield's behavior while leaving New York should have let the Stalwarts know he did not feel in hock to them. Presented with a chance to meet Conkling, Garfield had declined, settling "it is probably best" for the two to keep avoiding each other.[72]

He felt the opposite about Blaine, who had once again proven to be excellent company ("the prince of good fellows," Garfield told his diary). [73]

As summer ended, the campaign season proper began, in inescapable tides of political song, literature, stump-speaking, marching, and propaganda that swept the nation—waves that seemed (more often than not) to be carrying canal boats.

Inspired by the Fifth Avenue entente, Jewell and Dorsey had kicked the Republican National Committee's printing presses into full production at last. Their output made up in volume for what it chronically lacked in originality. Along with millions of reproductions of Garfield's House speeches came ballads like "Boatman Jim," "Our Boatman," "Jim Garfield of the West," and "Plow Boy of Ohio"—their lyrics pasted over more popular folk tunes, their choruses often hitting the same sappy sentimental notes as another.[74]

Official campaign biographies read little better. Their titles, viewed side by side, betray a shared inspiration and a collective shortage of it: "From the Log Cabin to the White House," "From the Towpath to the White House," "From Canal Boy to President." Only in poetry did a few Republican writers distinguish themselves: though many stuck with the campaign's prevailing imagery ("With Garfield at the helm! All hands aboard! No laggards now!"), a few themed their work around the fights their nominee had seen at Chickamauga and Shiloh, or even the hard-money issue.

Whenever a rascal strove to pass,
Instead of silver, money of brass
He [Garfield] took his hammer, and said with a frown,
The coin is spurious—nail it down![75]

Print was also used to pillory the Democrat—"a weather (Han)cock," as one Republican song skewered him. Dorsey and Jewell issued a booklet titled "A Record of the Statesmanship And Political Achievements of Gen. Winfield Scott Hancock." But it came out empty—filled by blank pages, the last of which bore only a single word that let readers in on the joke: "*Finis*."[76]

Little metallic log cabins jingled on Republican collars coast-to-coast, paying homage to a Western Reserve shack that last stood almost half a century before. Other products (sold by companies rather than committees) soon offered sordid ways to celebrate Garfield's ascent: Garfield-branded whiskey, confectionary ("Our Candy-date"), and even "Tow Path Fine Cut" chewing tobacco.[77]

Meanwhile, Stalwart soldiers literally marched to fight for Garfield. Some did so in uniform, like the hundreds-strong "Legions," "Brigades," and "Boys in Blue" who paraded around American cities in formation throughout the late summer, in units named after Grant, Conkling, Garfield, or Arthur. Others went about their duty in discreet business attire; across New York, tens of thousands of small-town postmasters, tax collectors, police chiefs, and courtroom officers moonlighted as gears in the Stalwart machine—caucusing, money-raising, vote-buying. Reformists could hardly visit the state without noticing, in horror, that every village and passing train car appeared to have an official more in Conkling's employ than the government's. In the fall of 1880, such men were leased out to Garfield.[78]

Some ensured New York's private workforces would also do their part at the polls. Names of the state's leading corporations were typed up for use as target lists. An ancient, arthritic Stalwart would one day boast of making "every manner of argument to persuade the laboring man" in this campaign.[79]

More upstanding friends of Garfield went to work elsewhere. Burke Hinsdale wrote his former principal's official campaign biography (a tome stump speakers relied on "like a preacher with his Bible") then redeployed to Indiana to rally thousands of that state's Disciples of Christ to vote one of their own into the White House.[80]

Another class of voter was carefully targeted, too. Frederick Douglass had the usual qualms about Garfield as a candidate. "For that place [the Presidency] I wanted a man of sterner stuff . . . defeat with Grant was better than success with a temporizer," the old abolitionist later wrote. "[Garfield] did not, to my mind, have in his moral make-up sufficient 'backbone' to fit him for the chief magistry." But Douglass said otherwise to hundreds of Black New Yorkers in October 1880, drawing attention to the nominee's other, more admirable traits:

> That deep-chested, three-story-headed man, James A. Garfield, must be our President. . . . I know him, colored man; he is right on our question, take my word for it. . . . He has shown us how man in the humblest circumstances can grapple with man, rise, and win. . . . He has built the road over which he traveled. He has buffeted the billows of adversity, and tonight he swims in safety where Hancock, in despair, is going down.[81]

Chester Arthur worked hard to push Hancock's head underwater. Until the Fifth Avenue meeting, he had been jammed in the most awkward spot of any politician on the continent—married, on paper, to both a boss and a presidential candidate yanking him in opposite directions. During what must have been a quiet fishing trip with Conkling upstate, he had struggled to smooth things over. "Arthur's constant effort was to make everybody else happy," the senator reported afterwards to Levi Morton. "No wonder we all like him."[82]

Once party harmony was established, though, the Gentleman Boss put the ruthless streak of his character to work. Flattering friends like Henry Ward Beecher and Mark Twain into stumping for the Republican ticket, Arthur swiveled to subject Stalwart subordinates in decidedly harsher treatment: loyal judges, cops, lighthouse keepers, dockworkers, museum curators, and construction workers were inundated with demands for campaign donations. Branded "voluntary," the requests were anything but. Those Stalwart officials who did not fork over as much as a fifth of their salaries were told their names would be added to a roll for distribution to department heads for retribution. Pleas for mercy garnered none. "*Push things*," Arthur instructed underbosses.[83]

They did, shaking loose hundreds of thousands of dollars into party coffers, wherein they joined other streams of revenue: Levi Morton's fundraising efforts had only just begun to rake in donations from New York's financial elite. Secretary Dorsey was overseeing shakedowns in another corner of government while, secretly, keeping dollops of the funds for himself. The scale and source of his thieving would in due time shock even the most jaded sensibilities in Washington.[84]

Yet the visible political hyperactivity was already adequate for American humorists to work with. Indiana was depicted as a state composed solely of tree stumps, each bearing a politician, mother, or infant giving a political speech. *Puck* issued a cartoon showing uniformed Stalwart senators from New York, Illinois, and Pennsylvania marching after a grab bag bundled with "offices." A Democrat columnist in Philadelphia breathlessly reported the results of a recent scientific experiment:

> A prominent Republican who examined several mosquitoes the other day, was greatly shocked at the discovery that none of the insects carried Garfield flags.[85]

Decades hence, his kidneys on the brink of killing him, the Easy Boss would croak with pride at the work his Stalwarts put into that election of 1880, despite the traitorous administrations it led to: "No equally exhaustive and 'red-hot' canvass was ever before made."[86]

Garfield was not as uninformed nor uninvolved in it as his captivity at Lawnfield suggested. Packing wheat off to Cleveland for sale (200 bushels, 90 cents apiece); playing croquet behind the house; speaking from his porch and engaging more baffling visitors behind the scenes (a grilling by one "Susan B. Anthony" about women's suffrage taking the cake); amid it all, Garfield regularly checked in with committee contacts on "how the Departments generally are doing" for those forced contributions, urging proceeds be split fairly across battleground states. He tried to convince his New York allies to avoid the coastal American habit of overlooking the Midwest. "Success in Indiana will be an immense help to NY and all other close states," Garfield told Arthur.[87]

In return for his attention, Garfield heard gripes about cabinet secretaries blocking collections ("Schurz['s] attitude will cost us $100,000+") and vague reports of methods *entirely outside* committee business being used in Indiana. *"There is only one question about carrying Indiana,"* Dorsey wrote via an intermediary, *". . . and that is the question of money."* Another committee man even invited Garfield to help on that front, which forged a path that would become well-trodden by future presidential candidates. "Can't you capture a few first-class millionaires, and clip them in for loose change?"[88]

Garfield was perfectly ready to comply. He took a meeting with an old frenemy, Jay Gould ("We had a conversation on the campaign. I think he will help"), and vaguely recalled knowing an upstart oil tycoon that had holdings in Indiana—named, Garfield half-remembered, "Rockafeller." "Do you know his state of feeling towards me?" Garfield wrote a friend. Advised that hosting John Rockefeller at Lawnfield might poke the Pennsylvanian working-class "like a knife," Garfield settled for accepting the oilman's money. He was the first candidate to ever invite the industrial mega-rich (a class growing in wealth, shrinking in size) into presidential politics. And, as a Rockefeller biographer has put it, Garfield was also the first to consider the electoral danger of doing so.[89]

He could still be stiff to the robber barons if needed—an impressive feat for any politician to pull off with donors of any sort. When Gould dared probe, for example, whether a large enough contribution might buy him the right to name Supreme Court appointees, the candidate fired back, "I do not care enough for the Presidency to assume its functions under any bonds but my conviction of duty." Gould overcame the rebuff to become the campaign's top donor, alongside other capitalists like "Rockafeller" and Levi Morton. The channel remained open.[90]

Garfield's secret courting of such men and nodding at bureaucratic shakedowns ("Do all you can to raise the *sinews of war*," he wrote one collector) risked appalling the reformists he claimed to identify with. But it once again exhibited his distaste for impractical dogma. The Hayes administration's executive orders to limit campaign donations and participation by government officials were, Garfield told a friend in July, simply pinning the "badge of political disability" on men who could otherwise be of use in a party struggle. This one held the highest stakes of any election since the war: Republicans were facing off against ex-traitors and Democrat spoilsmen who had already reconquered the South, and had nearly taken the presidency during the last cycle. Having presided over a congressional minority, Garfield could recognize when conditions did not lend themselves to refusing help or hindering potential allies. Maybe things would look different once the White House was secure.[91]

Reformist Republicans remained amenable near the close of the campaign. Hayes even invited Garfield to join a reunion of the President's regiment at William McKinley's home. Their train left Lawnfield on August 31—along, Garfield noticed, a section of the old Ohio Canal. He then realized it had been thirty-two years since he first walked it.[92]

A trio of events injected drama into the campaign down its final stretch. None ruffled Garfield much, least of all the first—a mid-September failure in Maine's local elections. Blaine, on the other hand, was mortified by it. The senator had tramped up and down his state's rocky coastline for weeks, giving five speeches an evening and seeing normal indications of imminent victory. Instead, Maine narrowly elected a Democratic governor and booted one of its Republican representatives from the House. Blaine's ensuing depression swiftly gave way to conspirative outrage: only fraud could have done this—probably by bribery and possibly by illegal immigrants. Rumor reached him of hordes of Canadians scurrying over the border to vote Democrat, before vanishing back into the pines. Blaine transmitted these claims to Lawnfield.[93]

Garfield was smarter than to believe these fairy tales. He thought Republican apathy seemed a more likely culprit in the loss—that, and perhaps

Mainers getting justifiably weary of "Blaine and his autocracy." Democrats made as much of the debacle as possible; some in Pennsylvania marched with flags calling "Garfield's Canal Boat Swamped," complete with artistic re-creations of such a scene. But as money started arriving from alarmed Republican industrialists and Garfield heard Blaine had truly "worked like a Trojan," he decided the fiasco "may in the long run prove the salvation of our campaign . . . I find every Republican setting his teeth more firmly and resolving to work more vigorously in consequence of it."[94]

Blaine thought another lesson had been learned; that northern Republicans did not want to hear anything about the South anymore. "Fold up the bloody shirt and lay it away," Blaine yelled aloud to his staff, waving a cane about. "It's of no use to us. You want to shift the main issue to protection. Those foolish five words in the Democratic platform, 'A Tariff for Revenue Only,' give you the chance." And so, the Republican Party drifted further from the dimming lodestar of civil rights and toward the brightening one of business.[95]

The end of September brought the second exciting development, this time at Garfield's doorstep: Ulysses Grant himself arrived in the village of Warren, Ohio, to give a campaign speech and project party unity. Though carefully choreographed, it still represented the first time in living memory (and possibly ever) that a former president had taken the stump for a successor. Grant spoke for seven minutes to thirty-five thousand Ohioans before yielding to an even more surprising guest—Roscoe Conkling.[96]

The senator had debuted on the campaign trail only a week before, in a characteristically long, self-indulgent speech in New York. That four-hour address had sounded mostly like an airing of Stalwart grievances, dotted by expressions of how uncomfortable Conkling felt. It named Garfield once, and only then after urging of Conkling by the audience, and that endorsement had not exactly come out forcefully:

> Some service with him in Congress has made me well acquainted
> with General Garfield. That he has the intelligence, experience and

habits of mind which fit a man for the Presidential office, I think I know. . . . That he is competent to the duties before him, there seems to me no reason to doubt.[97]

Conkling's Warren performance came off even worse; the senator did not mention Garfield at all, despite being in the candidate's home constituency. Though Grant did not name the nominee either, Conkling's rudeness was made more jarring by how long he spoke (two hours) and how much trouble had been made to accommodate him: ever-fussy, the senator had let it be known ahead of time that he would not deign to treat his voice to the chilly Ohio outdoors. As Garfield haggled through Arthur ("Will he speak from a covered platform closed on three sides?"), Warren's citizens had built a wooden wigwam to shelter the senator.[98]

Still, he refrained from mentioning Garfield by name in his speech. As he and Grant then piled into coaches for a stop by Lawnfield, their audience applauded, then murmured at the "impudence" just shown. The giant hut in Warren now loomed as a monument to Stalwart pettiness.[99]

Garfield, true to form, did not show signs of minding. Grant, Conkling, and their attendants alighted at Lawnfield to find the candidate ready with fruit, coffee, and hearty greetings ("How are you, Senator?"). Garfield shuffled Eliza out to meet the distinguished guests, then stood back as Grant commandeered the parlor for another reception. "I had no private conversation with the party but the call was a pleasant and cordial one all around," Garfield wrote as the Stalwarts later departed into a stormy night.[100]

They did so believing they had just ratified the "Treaty of Fifth Avenue" with a new "Treaty of Mentor." None seemed troubled by the fact that only one of them (Senator John Logan, of Illinois) had thanked Garfield by name during that gathering in the nominee's home. Grant and Conkling once again neglected to do so.[101]

That may have been the last straw; offense had silently been taken. Garfield ruminated further on the Stalwarts' visit in the days after it ended, eventually concluding they were "more concerned in running Grant in

1884 than they are for carrying Republicans safely through the contest in 1880." Conkling, specifically, was a "singular compound of a very brilliant man and exceedingly petulant spoiled child." And yet, as neither aspect could be split from the other, both required placation for the moment.[102]

Two days after the Stalwarts' Warren rally, Garfield sent another telegram to Blaine from Lawnfield: "Don't fail to come here from your Jefferson meeting and spend the night with us." The Plumed Knight was already on a speaking tour through Ohio, praising Garfield at every opportunity.[103]

The final exciting twist of the campaign was actually a good omen for Garfield in disguise. On October 20, a Democrat tabloid said it had discovered an old letter from him to a union rep named "H. L. Morey," of Lynn, Massachusetts, discussing Chinese immigration in the West. Its contents were packed with political poison—opining that the "question of employees is only a question of private and corporate economy, and . . . companys [sic] have the right to buy labor where they can get it cheapest."[104]

This damning excerpt ran the next day in papers from Massachusetts to Louisiana to Michigan. Democrat editors used it to brand Garfield as something between a race traitor and corporate stooge—a furtive ally of "unrestricted Mongolian emigration" to American shores, an accomplice of industrialists trying "to re-establish slavery in the United States." Handwriting experts rushed to pronounce that only a consummate forger could have copied Garfield's scrawl so well. "Denial is worse than useless," solemnly decreed the chair of the Democratic National Committee.[105]

Garfield thought otherwise. At a glance, he could identify friends not seen in decades; now accused of confessing secret immigration sympathies to a "Mr. Morey," he instantly knew he had never done so. He smelled a last-minute ruse concocted by the Democrats ("in their desperation") to frighten Pacific Coast whites into the Democratic fold. A few days' investigation revealed this to be the case. Though the Morey Letter bore an official House letterhead, its other flaws—inconsistencies in Garfield's handwriting, a stamp that didn't exist at the date provided, and the fact no

"H. L. Morey" or union existed in Lynn, Massachusetts—marked it as a blatant sham. Within the week, Garfield had published a comprehensive rebuttal that asked for "able detectives . . . [to] haul the rascals down." Within another, a man was on trial for forging the thing, as reported by the same papers that had first testified to the letter's veracity.[106]

The Morey Letter was the earliest attempt to manufacture, from whole cloth, what America's future political pundits would call an "October surprise"—a hubbub that shakes a presidential race during its closing stretch, throwing candidates and voters alike off-balance. Botched timing and execution by the Democrats saved Garfield from this one, as did the mercifully simple ways Americans in the late nineteenth century received news. One day's newspaper columns described Garfield's guilt; the next, his innocence, as tapped out across telegraph lines.

The Garfields nevertheless considered the debacle a new low in American politics. The candidate tutted at every facet of the letter—the attempt to forge his handwriting, "very clumsy," the opinions expressed, "stupid and brutal." His wife vented to their children about it. "I don't believe there was ever such contemptible meanness practiced by any Party as has been practiced by that wicked old Democratic Party since your papa was nominated," Crete told Harry.[107]

Carriage rides out of Lawnfield offered an escape from the venom now tainting the campaign in its close, closing weeks. Crete and Garfield roved through the forests near Orange, every passing foot of which reminded the latter of some long-ago childhood escapade—field accidents, barn raisings, walking back sick from the Canal. Only the odd Republican or Democrat party flagpole, peeking out over autumnal woods, kept the Garfields tethered to their time and place on the earth.[108]

Oddly, none of the Pacific papers thought to ask the real victims of the Morey Letter—the Chinese immigrants—for their opinions on it. Once it was obvious the document was a fake, white westerners returned to sullenly watching them file into sun-drenched quarries, pits, and railroad depots. "Three thousand Mongolians working at the lake, where two thousand white men once thrived, is a sad thing to contemplate," decreed a Nevadan editor at the end of October. Democrats pivoted to saying Garfield might let the Chinese steal suffrage one day, too.[109]

As Election Day approached and winter started dusting the lands around Lawnfield in frost, the Garfields received another unusual delegation: a gospel chorus from Fisk University, an all-Black institution in Tennessee. The visitors joined the candidate, his wife, and a handful of neighbors over refreshments in the front parlor. At one point they stood to sing hymns of the kind Garfield had first heard in southern fields, when the U.S. Army's policy was still—to a younger Garfield's chagrin—to leave slavery alone. As a general, he had listened to these songs with impotent anger; now he did so in silence while on the cusp of the presidency.[110]

He had lately decided that the well-being of Black Americans was the most difficult conundrum in national history. It had vexed him and his party for a generation, now. As the youngest man in Congress, Garfield boasted of having "never been anything else than Radical on all these questions of freedom and slavery, rebellion and the war. I have had neither inclination or motive to be otherwise." Ever since, with many other Republicans, Garfield's passion had ebbed against incessant southern unrest, ideological concerns about the balance of governmental powers, and mounting obstacles of legal, political, and economic variety.[111]

Upon becoming minority leader, Garfield was basically the last Republican on Capitol Hill to have witnessed the entire arc of Reconstruction firsthand, in full: from the passage of the Thirteenth Amendment to those secret deals in the disputed election of 1876. He embodied it, too. Shutdown battles with Democrats aside, Garfield had been mostly reduced to defending Black rights in print—contributing an article to the *North American Review* in 1879 arguing, against rebuttal, that giving Blacks the vote had not been a mistake nor should it be reversed. He had also pointed out how that right was often practically a hollow one, anyway:

Much as the negroes of the South have accomplished since emancipation . . . Open violence, concealed fraud, and threatened loss of
employment, in many parts of the South, have virtually destroyed
the suffrage and deprived the negro of all the benefits which it was
intended to confer. Hitherto, these outrages have been justified . . .
on the grounds that they were provoked by the interference of the
national authorities with local self-government in the South. But during the last two years, there has been no ground even for this poor
excuse.[112]

An irony escaped Garfield's notice as he wrote; he drafted this piece
in a home he had deliberately built in a neighborhood Black Washingtonians avoided. His separation was therefore quite total by the time of his
presidential nomination, both intellectually and physically.[113]

The campaign risked changing that. Watching a veteran's parade
from that Fifth Avenue balcony, Garfield had reminded the crowds that
though millions of white men once betrayed the Union, "in all that long
and dreary war we never saw a traitor in Black skin."[114]

Now the Fisk singers' concert in the Lawnfield parlor stirred stronger
emotions. As the last song ended, tears ran down the faces of other guests.
Garfield did not weep, but, walking over to his fireplace, broke the silence
to thank his visitors and urge them onward. He prescribed to them his
latest panacea for racial injustice in America—the same one that had,
now-famously, cured the type of hardship he had been born to:

Now, friends, the earthly savior of your people must be universal education; and I believe that your voices are preparing for the coming
of the blessing. . . . I hope and believe that your voices are heralding
the great liberation which education will bring to your lately-enslaved
brethren. You are fighting for light and for the freedom it brings; and
in that contest I would rather be with you and defeated, than against
you and victorious.[115]

But only several days later, and a few feet away, Garfield altered his tune and regained his distance in front of another Black delegation. He advised that their race "let it be understood that you are ready to work out your own material salvation by your own energy, your own worth, your own labor. All liberty can do for you is give you a fair and equal chance within the limits of the Constitution . . . this equal chance and nothing more." He closed by saying he thought highly of his Black colleagues in Congress, that he would continue to perform "whatever can justly or fairly be done" to help their cause. Finally, Garfield stood forward to shake each of his visitors' hands. The gesture signified both recognition and dismissal.[116]

In a few months, Garfield was to come across a piece of poetry printed in his calendar:

Habitual evils change not on a sudden
But many days must pass and many sorrows.

He would copy it into his diary—beneath, scribbling that the verse "might be applied to the Southern question. Time is the only healer, with justice and wisdom at work."[117]

No other answer appeared available to him. A lifetime of thinking, tinkering, and fighting had led Garfield to shrug and surrender the Republic's most stubborn problem to the solution of all things.

In November, peace wreathed the country like a fog. "A lull along the whole line of battle," Garfield wrote on the first of the month. The next morning he arranged for the plowing of a new garden, went to Mentor to vote at two o'clock, then on the way home stopped by the cheesemonger's to settle bills.[118]

At the same time, a young Theodore Roosevelt, Jr., took a break from his honeymoon to ride into inner Long Island. Upon returning to his spouse for more tennis and card games, he reported, "I drove over to Norwich to deposit my first vote for President—for Garfield."[119]

• • •

Friends packed Lawnfield that evening. "Waiting for the *news*," one wrote in the hearth light, stepping around tobacco spit pooling on the floor. Word of the results also came in dribbles. At eleven o'clock in the evening, reports arrived that New York was officially for Garfield! This boded well for the other states to come. The family served dinner at midnight as the returns stacked up—the meal turning more festive with each bulletin. "At 3AM we closed the office," Garfield wrote, "secure in all the northern States except NJ [New Jersey] and the Pacific States."[120]

In front of a New Jersey laboratory, a mile-long stretch of streetlights blinked on. Thomas Edison had ordered an assistant to flip *that* circuit if the telegraph chattered with news that Garfield was the next president. When it did, the aide complied, activating the first-ever incandescent elections display in American history.[121]

Fifty telegrams awaited Garfield when he awoke at eight o'clock. Within hours their number had soared into the hundreds. Their recipient plucked out one from Hayes, reading it with new sanguinity toward the author. "The President is very happy," Garfield wrote afterward, ". . . whatever his critics may say he has given the country a very clean Administration." Quickly, though, the mail torrent began to look unmanageable and Garfield started to fret. "Two or three thousand letters have now accumulated. And the flood seems to be rising."[122]

They told him that his had been a narrow but resoundingly legitimate victory. Garfield's miniscule popular vote margin over Hancock (a few thousand votes) was offset by a healthy electoral college advantage of 59, won by decisive turnout in that crucial pair of swing states, New York and Indiana. Had Blacks been allowed to the polls, the solid South might even have cracked. But control of the next Congress would rest on a knife-edge: Republicans could look forward to a sliver-like majority in the House, and a perfect balance of parties in the Senate.[123]

Most of the nation nonetheless sighed in relief that the fiasco of the previous presidential contest would likely not recur. To be sure, some Democrats loudly alleged fraud and called for Congress to intervene as it had in 1876. But, as one Republican columnist judged, the country would avoid "revolution . . . because the voice of the people is so overwhelming that conspirators will fear to disregard it." Seventy-eight percent of registered voters went to the polls—a new record.[124]

The weeks and months after the election would pass quietly for its victor. Garfield wanted nothing less. Presidency secured, he now needed to decipher what the American people wanted him to do with it. Once more, it was time to study the currents of popular will. "Lincoln said in his homely way that he wanted 'to take a bath in public opinion,'" Garfield wrote to Burke Hinsdale. "I think I have a right to take a bath before I do much talking."[125]

He and Crete would break up this soak with sleighrides. It was the earliest deep winter to hit the Reserve in forty-nine years—since the one Garfield had been born in. "A curious fact," he wrote his eldest sons.[126]

Hancock went to bed at seven o'clock on election night saying no one should wake him. Ten hours later, his wife did—with bad news. "It has been a complete Waterloo for you," she reported.[127]

He briefly pondered rumors that five thousand Democratic ballots had been seen bobbing down the Hudson but decided he didn't want the presidency that badly anyway. The general was not blessed with much political sense (he had made a huge gaffe on the tariff a few weeks before) but retained enough to know Garfield was in for a rough go ladling out the spoils. "He would not exchange positions with Garfield for any earthly inducement," Mrs. Hancock later said.[128]

In the Delmonico's restaurant of lower Manhattan, Stalwarts celebrated under the warmth of gaslight and victory. Ulysses Grant sat near Jay Gould, Thomas Platt (now a senator-elect) close to J. P. Morgan. The real place of honor, though, was set aside for Secretary Dorsey. Tributes to his campaign work littered the restaurant—gigantic models of Indiana's and New York's coats of arms woven from live flowers, moss, and grasses. Staff said they had never served so ornate a dinner.

The keynote was delivered by a rosy-cheeked Chester Arthur. His speech's disjointed delivery and content made the audience guess the next vice president had enjoyed rather too much wine:

> Gentlemen, . . . It is greatly gratifying to me to be one of this distinguished gathering, met here to do honor to Senator Dorsey. . . . It was my fortune to know something about the service Mr. Dorsey rendered to the Republican Party. . . . I don't think we had better go into the minute details of the campaign, so far as I know them, because I see reporters present, who are taking it all down . . . if I should get going about the secrets of the campaign, there is no saying what I might say to make trouble between now and the 4th of March.

It was a drunken wink that perhaps the election result had not been so rightful after all. But the Stalwarts clapped and laughed on heedlessly. The administration ahead looked to be one of plenty.

Roscoe Conkling was not in attendance, but a mention of his name wrought loud cheers from the floridly decorated tables of Delmonico's.[129]

The Blaines celebrated with better judgment, having apparently been blessed with foresight. All the way back in October, the senator and his beloved wife, Harriet, had adopted a new habit—spending part of their mornings in bed together, picking Garfield's future cabinet for him.[130]

In late November, Blaine received an invitation to be the first to join it. All Garfield wanted in exchange was a promise the senator would abandon his presidential dreams—at the very least, until 1888. Blaine solemnly vowed to do so. Within the fortnight he had picked out his consolation prize. "The more I think of the State Department, the more I am inclined thereto," he wrote the president-elect. That was fine with Garfield, who had already decided Blaine would be a brilliant chief diplomat.

Harriet was even happier with her husband's promotion. "Socially, you know, it is the best position," she told their son.[131]

No sooner had he been promised the role, than Blaine began giving Garfield copious advice on things quite outside the arena of foreign affairs. "You are to have a second term, or to be overthrown by the Grant crowd," he predicted to the president-elect. "If they succeed in doing it your Presidency will have been a failure, taking its place in history as no better than Hayes'." Blaine warned Garfield that defying this grim fate would require careful handling of what the senator defined as the Republican Party's three blocs, the first of which he named ("for convenience of designation") after himself:

> Now the Blaine Section is all *yours* . . . They are all now Garfield['s] without rebait or reserve "waving demand and notice."

Blaine identified another party faction as the "Reformers by profession." He could not mask his disdain while describing them for Garfield:

> They are to be treated with respect, but they are the worst possible political advisers, upstarts, conceited, foolish, vain, without knowledge of measures, ignorant of men . . . noisy but not numerous, pharisaical but not practical, ambitious but not wise, pretentious but not powerful. They can be easily dealt with and can be hitched to your Administration with ease.

Blaine said the final group, the "Grant Section," merited more respect, if only for its dangerous contents ("all the desperate bad men of the Party, bent on boot and booty . . . who accept your Administration because they cannot help it, and are looking . . . longingly to the restoration of Grant . . ."). Patronage needed to be kept from such men, lest they use it to sabotage the administration.

Blaine returned to his old, pleasant self after this dire warning. He sent good wishes to Crete—saying her opinion on cabinet decisions meant more than Garfield's. "The advice of a sensible woman in matters of statecraft is invaluable," he insisted to the president-elect.[132]

Garfield largely agreed with Blaine's assessment of things. His only addendums were that both Stalwarts and reformers had done valuable campaign work, and so "reasonable pains should be taken to retain them." Even here, cautioned against inviting a malignant presence into his administration, Garfield felt bound to meet it halfway. He concurred on the value of a female opinion in politics, but, unfortunately, Crete sided entirely with the senator's view of the situation.[133]

It deteriorated rapidly once Levi Morton told Garfield he had decided to accept the role of secretary of the Treasury. The president-elect expressed surprise that Morton felt entitled to it ("This was not my understanding and seems wholly inadmissible"); the banker was just as taken aback by being refused. In an instant, Stalwarts shook themselves out of their celebrations; perhaps those treaties of Fifth Avenue and Mentor should have been put in writing.

During the next few months, the Stalwarts would lean upon Garfield repeatedly—in writing, in person, and in increasingly heavy tones, demanding their terms be met. "I need hardly add that your Administration cannot be more successful than I wish it to be," Conkling wrote the president-elect after a visit to Lawnfield, ". . . nor can it be more satisfactory to you, to the country, and to the Party than I will labor to make it." But whenever Garfield showed signs of wavering—of compromising—Blaine would come in to warn his friend that dealing Conkling into the cabinet would be the presidential equivalent of ingesting strychnine.[134]

Blaine was even urging the president-elect to make a preemptive strike. If Garfield did not wipe out the Stalwarts, they would put his administration in an early grave. But this purge needed to be conducted carefully:

> They must not be knocked down with bludgeons. They must have their throats cut with a feather.[135]

•   •   •

One night after the New Year, Garfield fell asleep to abruptly find himself aboard (what else?) a canal boat with Arthur, floating on to "some great ceremonial" ahead under a deluge.

As the downpour grew, Garfield abandoned ship and swam ashore. Once safe on solid ground, he turned to see his vice president sinking under the surface. A friend restrained Garfield from diving back into the water; trying to rescue Arthur would apparently be fatal. It was then that Garfield thought of himself, for the first time, as president-elect. He sprinted naked into the stormy night before collapsing ill in a cabin to receive the care of an old Black woman.

Then Garfield awoke dry and (mercifully) clothed in Lawnfield. Heavy ice was slipping off the roof outside, no mail had come, and Crete was out shopping. "The 'days go on,'" he wrote, "but very slowly when she is away."[136]

26

"I've touched the highest point of all my greatness"
> —Shakespeare's *Henry VIII*, as quoted in Garfield
> diary entry for December 29, 1878

Gales howl over Washington in the early hours of March 4, 1881, and come daylight, miles of avenues are reburied in ice and torn streamers. Last night, the District had seemed to be flying enough flags to swaddle the planet in red, white, and blue. Now they lay tattered—the most brilliant Inauguration display ever, reduced to colorless scraps in a capital shrouded in gray.

But as the sun rises, the city's elements blend beautifully. A vista emerges that might as well have been daubed onto an Impressionist canvas. Snow sputters into hail, drizzle, then snow again. Dashes of color bleed into the morning: lavender drips off rain-bleached American flags, onto streets already flecked calico by people treading the slush underfoot. Laughing Texans pass glum Yankees, southerners bump into plainsfolk. Sidewalks, windows, and two-and-a-half-story viewing scaffolds fill the area along the avenues between the White House and the Capitol steps, dark faces adjoining white.[1]

Huge iron arches staple Pennsylvania Avenue. There are thirty-eight in total—each honoring a state in the Union, as ordered according to date of admission. The White House's columns cut dark bars through the haze, making the manor look like a prison for poor President Hayes, his term of hard labor about to be commuted. A few blocks away on G Street, each redbrick window of Riggs House is studded by a decorative metal shield.[2]

One protects Garfield. He is alone as he hunches over a typescript and feels so. He has approached his address in the usual obsessive manner—forgoing sleep over the last few months in favor of dissecting the inaugural speeches of his predecessors, probing for points of emulation or improvement. All but Lincoln's have been dreary reading. "Doubtless mine will be also," Garfield wrote.[3]

In a frantic bid to avoid this fate, he ditched all his drafts just days ago. Now the president-elect reviews a fresh one, its last sentence dashed out at two-thirty this morning.[4]

His focus is broken by the unsettling sight of a weeping U.S. senator. Through tears, William Allison of Iowa begs Garfield to pick another secretary of the Treasury; "certain forces" had made Allison desperate to forgo the job. Garfield did not need to guess the unnamed power—Senator Conkling had been in the room only a night ago, ranting something about the Treasury being owed to the Stalwarts. Nor is Allison the first cabinet selection to resign in such fashion. Levi Morton had refused the Department of the Navy in a similar, slightly drunker way a few nights before. Conkling was alarmingly proficient at getting powerful men to cry.[5]

The president-elect sees that he needs to let Allison flee before it is too late. "Though this disconcerts me," he writes to himself, "the break had better come now than later."[6]

At a little past ten o'clock, he is in the back-left seat of a gilt, four-horse carriage en route to the Capitol, trundling under the metal archways that straddle Pennsylvania Avenue. Beside him sits Hayes. For the next hour, the two bearded Ohioans cross a wilderness of celebration—hills made from viewing stands, forests made of banner-strewn telegraph poles and lampposts. Garfield achieves the tricky feat of acknowledging every cheer while not neglecting the president, either.[7]

Hayes, knowingly or not, is repeating the same thing over and over. "Out of a scrape," he murmurs. "Out of a scrape." Some commenters see poetic justice in his administration's end. "Mr. Hayes came in by a majority of one," a columnist jokes, "and goes out by unanimous consent."[8]

Democrats still do not see it as a laughing matter. Delaware's House of Representatives has just passed a resolution, along party lines, reminding the nation that the outgoing president is illegitimate, and that his successor had been "one of the chief actors in the perpetration and consummation of this great fraud."[9]

Tiny sunbursts flash in the Senate Gallery as Chester Arthur is sworn in. The glitzed fezzes and uniforms of ambassadors form a few. But those drawing the most notice come off the Garfield women of the humble Midwest: Eliza's halo of snowy hair ("for almost every hair . . . a wrinkle"); the gold pin under Crete's mousey face; the ribbons trailing off young Mollie's hat.[10]

The senators below are a dark ocean, in which Roscoe Conkling's height and cherry-red lapel ribbons mark him as an island, his coiffed mane wisping up like smoke off a volcano. He slopes away from James Blaine as if by magnetic force, and ahead, in interest, as Arthur is placed within a heartbeat of the presidency.[11]

Garfield walks onto the Capitol's East Portico at half past twelve, arm-in-arm with Hayes and following Frederick Douglass, marshal of the District and maestro of the day's events. The abolitionist, flinty and venerable, does not feel enthralled by either man behind him, but while shepherding them through this revered ceremony, he suddenly recognizes silver linings:

I felt myself standing on new ground, on a height never before trodden by any of my people; one heretofore occupied only by members of the Caucasian race.[12]

Garfield takes in this scene as he removes his hat. East rolls the largest Inauguration crowd the District has ever hosted—its people sticking like dark snow to every tree branch, ledge, balcony, rooftop, and scrap of earth in sight. A solitary streak of unblemished marble peeks out from the mass; Horatio Greenough's *Enthroned Washington* is pointing skyward, reminding its subject's inheritor to heed the invisible audience.[13]

Garfield's address begins as a review of national progress. He reminds his listeners that almost a hundred years has passed since the adoption of the first written Constitution. In that time, the population governed by the document increased almost twenty-fold, its area of jurisdiction about fifty times. The first American century has been "crowded with perils, but crowned with the triumphs of liberty and law," as epitomized by the Republic's triumph over "the supreme trial . . . civil war." That conflict had been necessary: "blood and fire" had cured ills that had been allowed to linger too long in the national soul. Those cancers are now gone; the wounds have scarred; Garfield declares that the country is tired of picking at them.

Sacredly preserving whatever has been gained to liberty and good government during the century, our people are determined to leave behind them all those bitter controversies concerning things which have been irrevocably settled, and the further discussion of which can only stir up strife and delay the onward march. . . . This decree does not disturb the autonomy of the States, nor interfere with any of their necessary rights of local self-government, but it does fix and establish the permanent supremacy of the Union.

Then, a riff that starts Radical, but ebbs into notes sounding out the common good: Garfield says the Civil War midwifed the greatest political revolution in American history, "the elevation of the negro race from slavery to the full rights of citizenship . . . No thoughtful man can fail to appreciate its beneficent effects upon our institutions and people. It has freed us from the perpetual danger of war and dissolution. It has liberated the master, as well as the slave, from a relation which wronged and enfeebled both. It has surrendered to their own guardianship the manhood of more than five millions of people, and has opened to each one . . . a career of freedom and usefulness."

Within a few paragraphs, Garfield points out that those paths remain obstructed in the South. He almost apologizes for his frankness—saying it is required by the immense gravity of the offense in question:

> It is alleged that in many communities negro citizens are practically denied the freedom of the ballot. . . . To violate the freedom and sanctity of suffrage is more than an evil; it is a crime, which, if persisted in, will destroy the government itself. . . . If in other lands it be high treason to compass the death of the king, it shall be counted no less a crime here to strangle our sovereign power and stifle its voice.

Yet he does not prescribe retribution for it, as such rhetoric from another might foretell. Instead, the president-elect benignly pledges ("so far as my authority lawfully extends") to help all Americans receive the protections promised them by the Constitution. In fact, in the "practical" struggles of these Black citizens in the South, he diagnoses a greater threat to the Union entire. Garfield's answer for this is discrete, pointed, sharp:

> But the danger which arises from ignorance in the voter cannot be denied. It covers a field far wider than that of negro suffrage and the present condition of the race. It is a danger that lurks and hides in the sources and fountains of power in every State. . . . For the North and South alike there is but one remedy. All the constitutional power of the nation . . . and all the volunteer forces of the people, should be

summoned to meet this danger by the saving influence of universal education.

Tens of thousands listen to Garfield in the slush. A few Black audience members have tears on their face. At times, the sun peeks past the clouds. "Nature seemed inclined to be apologetic at this moment," an onlooker writes.[14]

The president-elect breaks other new ground. He endorses the creation of a canal monumentally grander than the one he knew as a boy—one to link the Atlantic and Pacific oceans across Central America. Existing plans are admittedly vague. Garfield, characteristically, says he does not want the Republic lashed to any "narrow policy" for now. In a non sequitur, he flips to attacking strange religious practices reported from Utah:

The Mormon Church not only offends the moral sense of mankind by sanctioning polygamy, but prevents the administration of justice through the ordinary instrumentalities of law.

Garfield closes on a more familiar talking point—reform. He asks Congress to safeguard both politicians "entrusted with appointing power," as well as incumbent bureaucrats, "against intrigue and wrong" by attaching term limits and official codes of conduct to civil service. At this, Conkling smiles. He had heard fledgling presidents carp such foolishness before.[15]

After Garfield takes his oath, his first act as president is to kiss the most important women in his life—first Eliza, then Crete. Even Douglass feels moved by the gesture: "Nothing so unaffected and spontaneous and sacred could awaken in the heart of a true man other than sentiments of respect and admiration."[16]

At two o'clock, boys huddle under their mother's shawls down Pennsylvania Avenue, whining about the cold and that such a thing as Inauguration

Day even existed. A cry of "they're coming" (cued by a shimmer of bayonets on the skyline) lures the tiny grumblers out in time to see a coach
roll by with Garfield and Hayes in the backseat, the two men's titles transformed.[17]

Garfield wields his top hat skillfully, raising it every few seconds into
raw, chilly air, showing tourists that "the newly made Executive is developed in baldness as well as dignity."[18]

The face beneath is pensive, and folks guess why. Some suspect Stalwart sabotage ("He has built up and torn down a dozen Cabinets in the
last three months"). Others think Garfield is reviewing something other
than his surroundings—times long past, and places that do not exist anymore:

> Perhaps he saw the little log cabin where he was born, the humble
> canal-boat, the school-house, the college, the battle-field, the chamber
> of the Nation's legislators, and, last of all, the White House, the acme
> of the honorable ambition of every American.[19]

Past and present had already been linked by a shout of "low bridge!"
from the sidewalk earlier in the day. It served another reminder of old
canal days. Garfield had smiled at the warning and ducked to avoid a collision that might well have damaged the structure in question.[20]

As daylight fades over the festivities, a few incidents in the afternoon
attract particular notice: General Winfield Scott Hancock appears near
Garfield in a review stand alongside the White House—forced by his
rank into the unenviable spot of celebrating his own defeat, in front of
the mansion denied him. A hearse somehow joins the military parade
passing below.[21]

The next secretary of State is seen sneaking into 1600 Pennsylvania
Avenue to congratulate its new tenant in person, and reacquaint himself
with it. Like an ascetic monk thumbing prayer beads, Blaine has obsessively tallied each passing day since he last entered this hallowed center

of American power. By his count, that was almost thirty-seven months ago.[22]

Over in the blue room sits a canal boat made from red, white, and blue flowers. At five, the president it honors hosts his first official reception. "I congratulate you Mr. President," Mark Hopkins of Williams College said to his former student. Garfield grips his old mentor warmly, replying, "You are more President than I."[23]

Correspondents in the city scrutinize the new president's address for meaning, as one might a prophecy. Their appraisals make it clear that Garfield managed to make most people think he sympathized with them. Northerners judge he plans to treat the South "with a sternness" not unlike Grant's. Southerners divine the opposite, praising Garfield for being wise enough to water down the old Republican Black suffrage spiel with cautions for a democracy "darkened by illiteracy."[24]

A border state editor splits the difference, seeing no partisan color in the speech at all. But that did not detract from its quality; clearly, the new president "knows where he stands, knows what his duty is, and means to do it though the heavens fall."[25]

As rain indeed falls that night, Garfield smiles through the first Inaugural Ball held under electric light. Hundreds of pounds of turkey and beef tongues and gallons of oysters and coffee are quaffed down. Tickets go for five dollars; guests of all color and class are in attendance but don't mingle.[26]

It had been a matter of intense gossip whether Crete (in a wine-colored dress) and Garfield would dance, but the new First Couple refrain. Instead, they receive mumbling processions of well-wishers through the night. Gilbert and Sullivan tunes bounce off a floor polished to a mirror shine. Had the president glanced to his feet, he would have seen a bearded face staring up at him; had he stepped outside, and looked up, he would have seen it again—this time, traced in the twilight by silver-tailed rockets.[27]

·   ·   ·

The president returns to the White House to find Senator William Windom ready to fill a cabinet role another man had fled from in frightened tears that morning. "After a full hour's talk, offered him the Treasury," Garfield writes. "Very weary." He joins Crete in bed as the capital's lights flicker for him.[28]

Two hundred feet up a half-built Washington monument (due for completion by the end of this new administration) a banner waves. Fireworks in the shape of a golden tree, now Niagara Falls, make the phrase on its fabric legible from the ground: "W. and G." The letters stand for the last initials of the first president and his newest successor.[29]

Hayes is already leaving town by rail. Outside Baltimore the following day, the former president's car clips two others—closing his protracted political trainwreck with a brutally quick literal one.[30]

27

"A very little thief of occasion will rob you of a great deal of patience"

—Shakespeare's *Coriolanus*, as quoted in Garfield

diary entry for March 23, 1878

The administration began as all do: with an empty cabinet and a country ruminating about imaginary arrangements of its spots. Campaign debts—financial and political—had been tallied over the winter, for use by columnists to guess how the president might split the spoils across his party's factions. Yet the scope of his obligations made this hard. Half-Breeds had nominated Garfield, Stalwarts had elected him, and reformers had stayed grudgingly by his side throughout. "If all reports are true," sighed one verdict, "President Garfield's Cabinet will contain about one hundred and twenty-five persons." The possibilities were pruned down as the inauguration neared, but once Garfield's cabinet was finally revealed, so many leading Republicans had already been linked to it that those who never had expressed embarrassment.[1]

Its composition marked it out as an authentic work of its author, clearly as obsessed with placating everyone as ever. Any Republican could find a selection to admire and another few to fault. The attorney general would be Wayne MacVeagh—a Pennsylvanian reformer with an awful middle part and equally ugly attitude to political bosses. Balancing him would be Postmaster General Thomas James, the reluctant Stalwart of the cabinet. A midnight abduction had been necessary to peel James away from Conkling to even interview for the place. Blearily, he had accepted the job, but rumor said James still wore a Grant campaign badge under his coat collar.[2]

In another bid for party unity, Garfield practiced some presidential nepotism—asking Robert Todd Lincoln, sole surviving child of Abraham, to serve as secretary of War. Lincoln, an ordinary Chicago attorney, knew his credentials to run anything larger than a law partnership began and ended with his last name. But such a name carried peculiar power nonetheless—especially for a president trying to stitch a tattered Republican Party back together. So Lincoln accepted, albeit feeling the honest grip of impostor's syndrome on his heart, never to leave. As an older man, he would smile and say no one had ever really wanted him for anything in life. "They wanted Abraham Lincoln's son."[3]

As if reminded of another group in need of placation, Garfield lassoed a southerner into his cabinet—and an ex-Confederate at that. William Hunt of Louisiana assured everyone it had been grudging service on his part. Reporters graciously depicted the next secretary of the Navy as the "greatest man in the South who never believed in the scheme of Southern Empire." With that, the fact of a former rebel being handed oversight of an armed services branch did not attract much notice.[4]

The same could not be said for the "Premier of the new Administration," as Blaine was presented in print—a man "too well known to need much description." His selection to run the State Department stirred little surprise and much attention. It had become the gambler's favorite of all possible nominations, one of the few the press predicted confidently after the New Year. Some let it shape their view of the rest of the cabinet. "Taken all in all, the hand of Blaine in the formation of the group, with one single exception, is plainly visible," wrote a Democrat.[5]

The intent of its actual architect was obvious, though; whether he could accomplish this with such a group remained in doubt. "The Cabinet announcement demonstrates Garfield's pliability," read one column. "It is a patchwork which has not patched a peace." "An incongruous mosaic . . . incapable of cohesion, and certain to disintegrate," a senator would quietly agree.[6]

Roscoe Conkling wavered over whether to shatter it immediately. The senator's winter had been made particularly bitter by the president-elect's refusal to give the Treasury to a Stalwart. Ensuing efforts to remind Garfield of his campaign promises had failed, leading Conkling to assume the worst. His notes to the president-elect turned almost threatening; his private rants, conspiratorial. "Was it only to find out what I would like, and then do just the opposite," Conkling would spit to a friend, "that this man Garfield called me to Mentor?"[7]

The truth was likely more mundane. At those Fifth Avenue and Mentor summits, Garfield had probably offered to "consult" Stalwarts on patronage—a term that meant a different thing in their language than that of the rest of the English-speaking world. After November, the Stalwarts expected to be deferred to like creditors, not treated like allies. The president-elect expressed real surprise at their feelings of entitlement, even despite Conkling's poor manners in the campaign and Blaine's warnings that "Stalwart" was a synonym for "snake in the grass." "I will not tolerate nor act upon any understanding that anything has been pledged to any party, state, or person," the president-elect asserted after refusing to make Levi Morton secretary of the Treasury. Even so, he had spent the months ahead of his inauguration trying to come up with some other way to conciliate Conkling.[8]

His pick for secretary of State made this futile. Ever since James Blaine called Conkling a turkey on the House floor, the two had built what was, at once, one of the pettiest and most important political rivalries in American history. Its silliness had grown in parallel with their power. By the time each man entered the Senate, and built a faction of the party around themselves, each had also reached the profoundly childish point of pretending the other did not exist. Whenever forced to cite one another during floor proceedings, they would instead attribute the quote anonymously. This let the senators evade having to refer to each other as a "gentleman."[9]

Garfield's selection of Blaine to run the Department of State broke this charade. Conkling could not ignore the insult, telling other senators it only made sense as a "premeditated attempt to humiliate him." Combined with being deprived of the Treasury, it was enough to convince Conkling to further lower his expectations for this administration.[10]

Yet he refrained from entirely giving up on it. Another campaign vow of Garfield's rang faintly in his ears—that control of New York's federal offices would be left to the Stalwarts, as it had been back in the halcyon days of the Grant administration. This was an alluring enough prospect for Conkling to hold out hope. Moreover, not having to see Blaine in the Senate every day would honestly be welcome. Conkling thus let it be known that he would not obstruct any of the cabinet nominations, with one qualification: he would have to pinch his nose once Blaine's came up, "to escape the stench that such an appointment must cause in the Senate."[11]

To better air out his nostrils, Conkling would venture out on buggy rides with Chester Arthur from their home on Fourteenth Street, trotting under Washington's budding cherry blossoms and past tulip bulbs pushing through the dirt. "I have helped elect Garfield," the senator would grumble, "but I can have no voice in his Administration." Whether the vice president, sitting shotgun, ever took offense to the insinuation is not known.[12]

Over in the White House, looking about a full cabinet for the first time, Garfield saw only harmony. In the scene around the central table—the figure of Lady Justice perched at its end, even the off-setting facial hair of the cabinet (Hunt's silver-plumed goatee, Windom's fleeing hairline)— everything in sight attested to balance. "Though not an ideal Cabinet, it is a good combination of *esse et videri* [to be and to seem]," Garfield wrote himself.[13]

But he knew not to preside over it for too long at a time. For chemists

and political peacemakers, the rule is the same—combustible elements
are best kept apart. Garfield's cabinet meetings would be concise. Blaine
would remember the president reaching decisions quickly, at least "when
all had been heard."[14]

These prompt dismissals helped Garfield's cabinet realize it shared a
common problem. The secretaries would leave White House grounds
to find themselves, one and all, top prey for that endemic predator of
Washington—the ambitious jobseeker. Local reporters saw a new generation of it crop up before the inauguration:

> The "office-seeker" is one of the peculiarities of the streets of Wash-
> ington. One meets him at every turn—around the steps and doors of
> the hotel—in the Departments, at the Capitol—he is everywhere; and
> it is sad to see the eagerness with which he clutches every ray of hope;
> how he longs and prays for the looked-for vacancy.[15]

John Hay compared them to frogs. Back in the Quincy Adams administration, a local had instead been reminded of the "locusts of Egypt."
But a better analogue would have been the cicada—for office-seekers
were a cyclical pest, emerging en masse every four years to blitz politicians in town with the same noise, again and again: "Please look at my
papers."[16]

They were a seasonal reminder of the extortionate price the Republic
still paid for having an unreformed civil service. The federal bureaucracy
had ballooned in size since the first administrations, but the way places in
it were allocated remained decided by political appointment, rather than
professional ability. Most every agent, diplomat, tax collector, judicial clerk,
and postmaster on the federal payroll owed their jobs to the endorsement
of a patron in Washington (usually a congressman, senator, or secretary)
as given to the president for approval. This system was the bedrock on
which Stalwart and Half-Breed machines were built, and its perpetuation
meant every president's first business was to sort through thousands of

applications of men either seeking a government job, or fighting to hang on to one. "There is a great deal of talk about Party services," a witness to one such rush wrote, "and very little about civil service."[17]

By the start of Garfield's administration, each intersection in the District attested to his predecessor's failure to fix this. Office-seekers spilled out of the parlors of overbooked hotels claiming "to have rendered yeoman service for the successful candidate." Some were men fresh from college; others were wizened has-beens (even former congressmen) desperate for a petty office to save them from undignified poverty. They mingled all over Washington—joined by almost all the country's marshals, the lawmen having abandoned their posts to ensure they would keep being paid to hold them under the new regime.[18]

It was the greatest rush on the patronage Washington had ever witnessed. Its intensity earned this wave of office-seekers a new nickname in the spring of 1881: "the 'orifice'-seekers." They lived up to it; senators were spotted walking down the Capitol steps with a different man prattling an application into each ear.[19]

Like any pest, the jobseekers were pathetic in small numbers but scary in large ones. No department was safe from them. They packed every hall in every public building, in a clamor that sounded to clerks "like the sound of beasts at feeding-time." A closer listen would have revealed that the applicants were forcing proof of their political loyalty (letters of endorsement, or copies of campaign speeches for Garfield) into the unwilling hands of the secretaries themselves.[20]

Like the broader patronage system, here was another governmental norm that had lived past its due; the gap between any American and their leaders remained only a matter of geography. If one wanted an audience with any statesman (even the president) they just had to drop by the right office and wait.

Staring out a White House window on the morning of March 8, the president found his view of Pennsylvania Avenue blocked by a thicket of strangers that had sprouted on the front lawn. He spent the day clearing

them out with firm, friendly handshakes. By evening, Garfield was exhausted. "The fountains of the population seem to have overflowed and
Washington is inundated," he wrote. He had accepted, by personal estimate, several thousand job applications that day in the East Room.[21]

It served as a dismal introduction to what the business of the presidency had been reduced to. Garfield's first weeks in office would be little
more than a blur of greeting office-seekers and trying to sort worthies
from thousands of the dishonest or insane; for every postmaster tear-
ily begging to be retained, there was a caller introducing themselves as
Julius Caesar. Such specimens filled the White House's anterooms daily,
demanding Garfield's assistant Joseph Stanley Brown let them meet the
president. The loyal aide said he finally knew "what it meant to be thrown
into a den of wild beasts as were the ancient martyrs."[22]

Shutting the mansion's doors offered only a stopgap solution; the federal bureaucracy still needed staffing, and the White House had to stay
open to the public. Plus, a few office-seekers reportedly managed to slip
past security anyway. One supposedly did so by curling his hair distinctively, then bluffing to the guards: "Make way, I am Senator Conkling."[23]

Papers reported that Garfield spent up to seventeen hours a day
receiving such men. Even Democrats worried what this boded for his
well-being. "Such a disgraceful scramble has never been seen in Washington," one wrote, "and is likely to prostrate Garfield if relief is not soon
afforded."[24]

Garfield agreed. He could not recall feeling so tired before, and in the
papers constantly unfurled in his face by strangers, he felt reminded of
highwaymen drawing pistols.[25]

Being held up in such a manner (literally and figuratively) deepened
doubts Garfield had long held about the value of the presidency for both
its occupant and the country. While serving in Congress, he had decided
even a longing peek at the White House could prove fatal to a legislator's usefulness; otherwise-brilliant friends like Salmon Chase and James
Blaine had let such glances lure them from policymaking into selfish,

ceaseless, fruitless political posturing. Nor had Garfield known any recent president to have been effective in office, either. So he had rightly shuddered when callers to I Street first tried to talk him into running for the job. "There is too much possible *work* in me to set so near an end to it all," Garfield wrote afterward.[26]

Enduring the awful scramble on the patronage within his own administration only confirmed to Garfield that the presidency was truly anathema to productivity. "My God," he muttered aloud at one point. "What is there in this place that a man should ever want to get into it?" A week into his term, he suspected the rest would be spent doing little more than ladling out jobs. It was enough to make him pine to be returned to the House. "I have heretofore [as a congressman] been treating of the fundamental principles of government, and here I am considering all day whether A or B should be appointed to this or that office," Garfield grumbled to a friend. His diary entries read depressingly:

> I must resist a very strong tendency to be dejected and unhappy by the prospect which is offered by the work before me . . . I love to deal with doctrine and events. The contests of men and about men I greatly dislike.[27]

How ironic, then, that his presidency was being overrun by the settlement of such contests, from the cabinet level to that of a local post office. Garfield decided future administrations needed to be freed of them. Such power could not be worth the hassle of dispensing it. "Some civil service reform will come by necessity," Garfield wrote, "after the wearisome years of wasted Presidents have paved the way for it." He did not have much free time for such reflections, though: when news arrived that a Baltimore postmaster had died, Garfield sighed to an aide that the whole city would be upon them by sunrise.[28]

Relief came again in the form of afternoon coach rides with Crete. She, too, was having a tough time adjusting to the White House; a First Lady's public functions each require as much finesse as a foreign summit, but Crete's innocent miscues had already made bylines. Still, she showed no signs of being cowed by these early ordeals. "Crete grows up to every new emergency with fine tact and faultless taste," the president marveled after one of their escapes around the city.[29]

He hardly knew the half of it; office-seekers were pestering the First Lady, too. At a White House event, one had even cornered Crete to say he had helped elect her husband—apparently, via a speech given in New York, titled "Garfield against Hancock." Crete nodded politely. The man took this to mean she was thrilled by their acquaintance.[30]

The staff nearby needed no introduction to him, nor would they have wished one on anybody else. He was already infamous among them as a "continuous" occupant of the White House's foyers and hoarder of its stationery. He had sent a note to the president that, bizarrely, demanded a prime diplomatic appointment ("I think I prefer Paris to Vienna"). Efforts to inform him that the Department of State handled such things had no effect; those to stop him using the mansion's letterhead only made him irate. "Don't you know who I am?" he would shout. "I am one of the men that made Garfield President."[31]

Such eccentricities were not unheard-of among the White House's callers. The man was permitted to keep visiting for a while, not quite indistinguishable from thousands of other supplicants and sycophants.

The self-assurance of a certain cabinet member around the White House drew more notice than the unruliness of any office-seeker. James Blaine was spotted entering the mansion at all hours of the day—almost as though he had been the one elected to it the previous winter. In corners of the District, it was being supposed that (in practice, at least), he had been; men pointed out that Half-Breeds put Garfield over the top in Chicago, and now heard Stalwarts complain of being inexplicably cut off from promised cabinet spoils. These observations were added, almost alchemically, to the old political reputations of Blaine and Garfield (one a boss infamously covetous of the presidency, the other an irresolute, wonky legislative leader who had not even sought it). It was more than enough to stir whispers in Washington that the country now had two presidents.

The idea permeated the city by mid-March. More jobseekers flocked to the Department of State for Blaine's endorsement than to the White House for Garfield's. Gossip columns cast the secretary as a clam burbling happily at high tide; a hand with fingers in every pie baking at the White House; a potter, shaping pliant presidential clay; a shadowy python, coiled about the new administration. The caricatures both reflected and reinforced perspectives, as caricatures do. "The impression is abroad in the land that he [Blaine] is the power near the throne," declared one writer.[32]

It found a credible audience in Congress. Friends there warned Garfield to keep Blaine confined to affairs of state, as one might a mischievous monkey to a cage. "If you can only restrain his immense activity and keep him from meddling in other Departments, you will have a brilliant Secretary," John Sherman implored the president.[33]

Garfield made noises that sounded like agreement. He ordered his gathered secretaries to stick to their own departments (to best preserve "our harmony") and assured friends "no member of the Cabinet behaves with more careful respect to the rights of his brother . . . than Blaine." But views from Pennsylvania Avenue told a different story; Blaine was seen slipping into the White House ahead of cabinet meetings, leaving out a backdoor, then reentering alongside other secretaries. And the only person Garfield took more evening coach rides with than his wife was his secretary of State.[34]

Had the president opened a copy of *Puck* over one of these excursions, he would have seen the scene re-created in print—albeit with Blaine dressed as a chauffeur, whip-in-hand, telling Garfield, "Don't be afraid— *I'm* the driver."[35]

It was, ironically, an accurate depiction of their real relationship. Garfield knew where he wanted his administration to go, but he was honestly open-minded on how best to steer it there: which turns to take, which to avoid. Each presidency is conducted with an eye to the errors of the last, and, starting his own, Garfield could still recall diagnosing his predecessor's fatal flaw; Hayes had suffered "that worst infirmity, the fear of being influenced by men of his own Party who are larger than he." The result had been an entire term of gridlock.

So Garfield deemed it wise to tolerate Blaine's intrusions—nodding as the secretary of State suggested men for judgeships, questioned decisions made in other parts of the administration, dictated the time of their carriage rides, and even lectured the president on a proper executive schedule ("Take care of yourself and see nobody after lunch"). Sometimes Garfield happily heeded Blaine's advice. At others he politely overruled it. The balanced composition of the cabinet should have proved that enough to the American public—as well as those skeptical senators perched on Capitol Hill.[36]

But, Garfield had to admit, it also felt good to have a cabinet comrade in whom he could truly confide. The presidency is a lonely post—perhaps the loneliest in the universe—and fate did Garfield a favor by letting him deal an old friend in as secretary of State. He and Blaine had entered Congress simultaneously nearly two decades before, wheeling and dealing through the postwar Republican ranks in tandem; Garfield saw terrific poetry in the fact that they were able to cross the White House's transom together. "With the love of comradeship of 20 years, and with faith in the next four," he had written Blaine on Inauguration Day morning. In the weeks afterward, their notes only became longer and more affectionate. The president would open his with "my dear Blaine," and receive extended replies signed off by "your devoted friend, personally and politically."[37]

The ritual carriage rides at dusk continued in between these exchanges. As the two statesmen clopped past teeming parlors, spectators would openly discuss, over brandy, coffee, and brandied coffee, the route taken by the "Blaine-Garfield" administration thus far.[38]

On March 13, the secretary's focus was returned to where it technically belonged by the murder of Tsar Alexander II. The Russian had been the rare enlightened monarch, yet an anarchist bomb had slain him anyway. Consuls in Saint Petersburg were left to wonder if the "late Czar's reforms" might be helped or hurt by his martyrdom.[39]

In Washington, Harriet Blaine expressed pity for how long the wounded Tsar had clung to life. A few rooms over, her husband and the president jointly decided to send a letter of sympathy to Russia, "making allusion to our own loss in the death of Lincoln." Meanwhile, the American press predicted another royal would soon meet the same fate. "Uneasy lies the head that wears a crown," snarked one front page.[40]

The White House should have kept such commenters humble. It was in shoddy condition—with carpets so ratty that its last tenants had been forced to arrange furniture over the most glaring holes. This only drew attention to the manor's uninspired decor. "The place is now full of modern abominations in upholstery and garish gilding," judged a visitor as the Garfields moved in. Vermin scurried noisily behind the walls. More embarrassingly, wooden plumbing made farting sounds echo around the mansion during wet weather. The odor was also flatulent—courtesy of sewage and tidal bogs dotting the Potomac less than a mile away.[41]

Presidents were supposed to dip into personal funds to keep the White House operating, both structurally and socially. Yet Garfield had always kept a closer eye on public spending than his own. His existing finances were already stretched very thin at Lawnfield; keeping the lights on and soirees going at the White House would surely deplete them further. Now cut off from the handsome legal fees that had (barely) permitted him to purchase the home on I Street and a hundred-acre farm as a congressman, Garfield faced the prospect of a pauper presidency.

Only the intervention of Congress and his predecessor helped him keep up appearances. In a "burst of generosity," the government diverted funds to fix the White House's worst damage, while Hayes graciously lent his own carriage to the new president, saving Garfield from having to travel to functions on foot. It seems all Garfield had to suffer in exchange was a lecture on the dangers of letting the White House serve liquor again. He politely heard Hayes out and (out of habit) refused to commit to a decision on the matter. This prompted Hayes, once again, to decide his friend lacked the "grit to face fashionable ridicule."[42]

Other hand-me-downs nonetheless passed between the two. Harriet Blaine took friends to tour the White House, where (she later blathered) they "saw the Garfields, and the Hayes' china."[43]

The new First Family had no complaints about their new home, however. Abram and Irvin zipped down its corridors on bicycles, passing interminable lines of office-seekers. Their elder brothers studied for college, while Mollie began walking unescorted to a school across Lafayette Square. Crete single-handedly took on the task of refurbishing the White House—for a first step, asking her husband to borrow books on decoration from the Library of Congress. Turkish sofas and Japanese silks began to dance about her thoughts.[44]

Only the president's mother confined herself to actual inactivity in a second-floor bedroom. Its trio of windows offered Eliza a vibrant triptych: a pastel driveway, verdant executive lawns, the State and War departments in steely, imperial gray. Peering across these scenes, "Grandma Garfield" enjoyed a strange celebrity among the people in them—the product of an election campaign that had lionized her widowhood and culminated in a kiss from her son upon his assumption of the presidency. His old promise (to care for her, as she once did him) had now been magnificently fulfilled before the whole country.

She seemed to brighten with her upgraded surroundings. "An intelligent observer, and a keen, but kindly critic of persons and events, she finds life as full of interest for her as it is devoid of worry and care," reported a new admirer.[45]

In compliance with the power presumably arranging all this, she continued to accompany her son and daughter-in-law to the District's Disciple Church on Vermont Avenue. Its popularity had grown markedly (if not mysteriously) in recent weeks. Described by one rude newcomer as a "Campbellite shanty," it still overfilled each Sunday that March.[46]

Garfield brooded over this in a pew on March 20; even at worship, he could not escape the masses angling for a piece of him:

It gives me a sorry view of human nature to see a little church filled to double its usual attendance by the accident of one of its frequenters . . . [being] elected to a high office.[47]

At the White House, the president saw another poor specimen of humanity fishing for influence that Sunday; Senator Roscoe Conkling had dropped by to discuss, as Garfield couched to him in writing, "what can be done for Jacobins" in New York. The prospect of lasting party peace shimmered, mirage-like, between the two as they talked.[48]

The visit went smoothly. Lord Roscoe listed the men he wanted tapped to each federal post in his state. The president nodded for nearly three hours. Only once did he stop—to say that those non-Stalwart New Yorkers who had helped nominate him at the convention needed recognition. The senator suggested they might enjoy exotic positions overseas; Garfield sensed Conkling was angling to have personal enemies floated out of the country on an ice floe. "I will go as far as I can to keep the peace," the president replied, "but I will not abandon the New York Protestants."[49]

Conkling still departed the White House "in a very good humor," certain the next nominations due in the Senate for confirmation would please him. Only one New York job had gone undiscussed (the customs collectorship, Arthur's old post) but Garfield assured the senator, on his way out the door, that they would talk it over soon.[50]

On Tuesday, the White House formally nominated a gang of Stalwarts to become New York's next cohort of district attorneys and marshals. Word reached the Senate then pulsed up to Albany: reformists heard the news, howled that this traitor president was handing the Empire State over to corruptionists, then fled for bed, saying they didn't care to be in politics anymore, anyway.[51]

The sun set. Writers rushed to revise earlier assessments of this administration. They still hesitated to credit its actions to the president. "If anybody wants to know who is the real power under Garfield, such anxious inquirer has only to learn how to spell two words to answer his own question," opined one. "Those two words are 'Roscoe Conkling.'"[52]

As these words slugged into print, Secretary Blaine rose in the dark on Fifteenth Street as if from the dead. A migraine had kept him in bed for days; pangs of jaw pain hinted at an imminent abscess. This was the cruel twist of Blaine's nature that negated the rest at vital moments—a proclivity for ill-timed illness, to be suffered amid a presidential convention, or (as in this case) when vital political moments were going on without him. Friends guessed it was really a neurosis. "His life was a hand-to-hand contest with imaginary diseases, which is itself a disease," one would write. Americans prefer stoic, steady people for president. Unluckily for Blaine, and his ambition, he was a hypochondriac hummingbird. But if anything could snap his symptoms (even momentarily) it was news that Roscoe Conkling was about to get what he wanted.[53]

The First Family looked up from dinner to see the secretary's sickly face manifest in their doorway. The president left the table to join Blaine in another room, only to come back alone and looking ashen himself. Crete only got her husband to say why after dessert. "I have broken Blaine's heart with the appointments I have made today," he confessed. "He regards me as having surrendered to Conkling . . ." The First Lady heard Garfield mutter something about needing to administer a "very thorough antidote," for the good of the party.[54]

Blaine returned at half-past ten o'clock, staying until midnight to brew it with the president.[55]

Portly, tailored, "strikingly handsome . . . in the chair," the vice president looked comfy presiding over the Senate the next day. This poise then crumpled as Arthur opened a new note from the White House. His eyes drew to a listing of his old job—the collectorship—then bulged at the name beside it. He had the paper whisked to the real power in the room. Conkling read it, turned pink, then got up to whisper to New York's other senator, Thomas Platt. The Easy Boss was heard asking what this meant. "I don't know," Conkling hissed. Confused murmurs spread in the Chamber.[56]

They were answered when the message was read aloud: the president was moving to award New York's collectorship not to a Stalwart, but rather to an independent named William Robertson. To facilitate this, Garfield had set up a line of other clerical dominoes—suggesting the shuffling of a few Grant-appointed diplomats to new posts, which would make room for the current collector to be shipped abroad. In sum, it was—as another has written—a game of ambassadorial musical chairs, all arranged to bestow a reformer the crown jewel of New York's patronage.[57]

The effect around the nation was barometric. All air left the Senate, as did Conkling, Platt, and the vice president ("the three Senators from New York"), leaving the new nominees in limbo. The men remaining in the Chamber could only quip the sun now shone on an opposite branch of the Republican Party as it had the day before. In Albany, reformist legislators' hats flew skyward, "in entire disregard of the chances of damage to chandeliers," while their owners rushed to correct statements made to reporters last night; the men now wanted it known that they admired this president's "determined effort . . . to give adequate recognition to both wings of the Republican Party in this State." Only a handful of Stalwarts offered quotes—mumbling about patronage being dispensed "without consultation."[58]

Garfield took their silence to mean the matter was settled. "Foreseeing the difficulties which attend the affairs of NY and determined not to be classed as the friend of one faction only, I carried out a plan," he doodled happily. "This brings the contest to an early close, and fully recognizes the minority element [of New York Republicans]." Like all peacemakers, the president felt handing everyone a half-victory added up to a full one for himself. For comfort in this (and to imagine he came up with it alone) he could review a new message from the secretary of State.

"Your work of today created a splendid impression . . . [that you] *treat both sides fairly*," Blaine's latest letter gushed. Reformist articles in the morning said the same thing; that Garfield, "as President of the United States . . . [finds] Party divisions impolitic, unwise, and impracticable."[59]

Other forecasters knew to be wary when Conkling went quiet. Allies said, "when he was maddest he was the most silent." A Stalwart paper called the political skies overcast; another wrote of seeing a cloud on the horizon, "portentous with smothered thunder."[60]

It might as well have been pouring from Conkling's ears. When the Stalwart boss broke his silence that night, it was to seethe about betrayal. "All we ask is to be allowed to win in New York," he hissed to Platt. "And it is hard enough to do that." The Stalwarts' power hinged on their ability to reward loyalists with lucrative public posts; around the District, type was now being set on pieces explaining the place of the collectorship above all others. "It dwarfs every other office in the Empire State, and if used as a political machine is a power," read one such draft.[61]

To have the customhouse ripped away again, after the lean years of Hayes and being deprived the Treasury by Garfield, was therefore more than an insult to Conkling. This was an existential threat—a knife-thrust at the heart of his machine, an entity that the Republican Party depended on to keep the Empire State out of Democratic hands. Anything other than total control of all New York's spoils cast doubt on Conkling's ability to award any of it, and thus jeopardized his whole operation.

The senator could only snort; he had not wanted to kill an administration again, but this "trickster of Mentor" gave him no choice. Conkling informed loyalists in the press he would block the Robertson nomination, and he told those in the administration to sabotage it.

Senator Platt suggested another course, but even Conkling had his limits. "Young man," he chided, "do not be too hasty about this matter!"[62]

Within days, as spring sleet pooled in neglected nooks of the White House, the administration sprang leaks, too. Its caller list was slipped to the public (thus exposing Blaine's incriminating visits the night before the Robertson nomination) while cabinet members lined up to protest the collectorship nomination. A pair even made moves to resign; Postmaster James, on behalf of Stalwarts everywhere, and Attorney General MacVeagh, over a creeping certainty that Secretary Blaine was truly calling shots in this administration. Garfield soothed the men but soon found cabinet meetings poorly attended anyway.[63]

The vice president only visited to drop off written protests by New York's senators and offer advice on how to fix everything. Other Conkling mouthpieces in the press gave the same half-threats to Garfield: "If the nomination shall be withdrawn, no harm will have been done," read one Stalwart column. Another ominously observed it had been four years (almost to the week) since Hayes fell out with Conkling.[64]

On that note, a final Stalwart writer opined, no one wanted to see the "curious spectacle of a friendless President" again. Garfield had to face a bleak truth: "It is simply impossible for a man in his position to please all factions or to keep everybody his friend."[65]

Unfortunately for the Stalwarts, the president agreed. Clearly, he could not placate all parts of his party after all—for one was not only insatiable, but under the delusion it could publicly dictate terms to (even threaten!) the administration. Conkling had confused candidate with president; gone was the nominee who needed approval from all his party's blocs— nods from these bosses, those editors; he had won his race and all the power that came with it. Garfield jotted that to himself, as if in reminder:

> The President is authorized to nominate and did so. A Senator considers it a personal affront that he was not previously told. I stand joyfully on that issue—let who will, fight me."[66]

Further steeling Garfield's spine was the fact he had gone to great lengths to accommodate his party's spoilsmen—picking a Stalwart as vice president, giving another control of a patronage-rich cabinet spot, and politely ignoring rudeness from Conkling, warnings from Blaine, and complaints by reformists along the way. Garfield had even elevated a list of Conkling loyalists to "almost every place in New York, so that no one failed to see they were generously treated." The president could now take that most invigoratingly righteous of stances: that of a spurned compromiser. "Of course I deprecate war," he told Whitelaw Reid. "But if it is brought to my doorstep the bringer will find me at home."[67]

Indeed, when Platt came by to repeat Conkling's demand that the offending nomination be taken back, the president refused. At this point, Garfield claimed to not care if the confirmation process killed its subject. "Robertson may be carried out of the Senate head first or feet first," he said. "I shall never withdraw him."[68]

Thus, quite accidentally, and after at least two administrations' worth of fits and starts, the Republican factions entered a decisive confrontation with one another. "The War of the Roses has now begun in good earnest," trumpeted bylines.[69]

Across the country, the contest became a proxy for all the sleeping dogs of the political system. Where John Hay believed it would decide which individual truly wielded the power in this government ("If he [Garfield] surrenders now, Conkling is President"), Garfield thought it would settle a larger question for many administrations, past and future. "President Grant surrendered New York patronage to Mr. Conkling . . . President Hayes . . . made a constant petty warfare between himself and Mr. Conkling in which both sides became unduly irritated," Garfield explained to Burke Hinsdale. His failed effort to pursue a middle course on the matter with Conkling had raised its stakes considerably. "This brings on the contest . . . and will settle the question whether the President is the registering clerk of the Senate, or the Executive of the nation."[70]

It was a phrase Garfield would repeat throughout the ensuing weeks, while Conkling showed a similar understanding of the situation—frothing behind closed doors ("like a bull of Bashan," a witness thought) about a senator's rights to be "consulted" on federal appointments in their state.[71]

Reformists rubbed their hands, in prayer and anticipation, that those rights might at last be killed. Their view of the standoff's significance was even grander than Garfield's. New York, E. L. Godkin pointed out, was the fattest patronage fief in the country, "the State which places the largest number of offices at the disposal of the [politicians] . . . the State in which 'the spoils system' has been brought to greatest perfection," the state run by "the greatest of all the Bosses, and the most exacting." Hayes had tried and failed to break the Stalwart machine's hold over it. If Garfield could, then presidential precedent would be set and bosses in any state could tremble.[72]

Yet this hope went slightly marred by the parallel belief that Garfield was still not a real disciple of reform. The serving collector was a Hayes appointee and an independent; his term had years left to run. A truly reformist executive would have refrained from trying to remove such a man in such a manner. Garfield thus seemed to be aiming to commandeer the spoils system from the Senate, rather than do away with it entirely. This raised Godkin's doubts as to who was really behind the customhouse conflict:

> For the present, however much Judge Robertson's nomination may be due to Mr. Blaine's selfishness . . . we do not yet believe that the President is prepared to make a mockery of the reform sentiment of the country.[73]

Columns of visiting senators at the White House suspected the same thing. Their number amazed one onlooker—he noted that hardly any congressmen (of either party) ever called on Hayes. "But the new President, who has always been personally one of the most popular public men who ever came to Washington, is called upon daily by the most distinguished of the Democrats, and many of them with no axes to grind, but simply to testify their respect and regard." Such were the yields of having been militantly polite to everyone in Washington for years.[74]

Garfield was now telling all such callers, regardless of party, that their vote on Robertson's confirmation will be a "test of friendship or hostility to the Administration." John Sherman agreed to take charge of pushing it—warming to the idea of forever curbing the "interference of Senators in appointments to office," and thus avenging what had befallen the Hayes administration.[75]

But Sherman also felt miffed that this reprisal was really coming "from Garfield or rather from Blaine." It was a correction being uttered often around the city, by Republicans bemused their party's tensions had all come to boil so quickly. "What a muss Garfield has already made of it," another wrote. "Or rather what a muss Blaine has made of it."[76]

Temperatures climbed by the end of March, but the Senate stayed in stalemate; the perfect balance of power between Republicans and Democrats in it meant a lone dissenter could slow proceedings to a glacial pace. Still, observers thought they could see Garfield's case gaining momentum. "The strength of the nomination grows more and more apparent the longer it is considered."[77]

Some of the president's other appointment decisions proved reformers were right to deem him not a full devotee to their cause. Bothered to no end by the chore of handing out patronage to strangers, Garfield also managed to give old comrades sinecures. Charles Henry, student-turned-soldier-turned-political agent, was made marshal of the District of Columbia. Other veterans of the Forty-Second Ohio became judges and territorial governors. Burke Hinsdale would soon be offered the enviable spot of envoy to the Kingdom of Hawaii—a nicer place to work than Hiram. "The salary is $7,500, and the cost of living comparatively light," the president wrote. Such favors measure innocuously amid an age of runaway political machines, bar one: Garfield arranged for another friend, David Swaim, to be made judge advocate general of the Army. Even the most lenient of reviewers can't help but wonder if Swaim would have gotten the job, had he not supplied the loan that built Garfield's house on I Street.[78]

In short, though the president knew parts of the spoils system demanded overhaul, he was also not ignorant of its advantages, which extended to the practical business of political dealmaking. Garfield was given a unique chance to demonstrate these in the first month of his administration: during the last election, a biracial alliance of Virginians had elected a new party to power. Calling themselves the "Readjusters," these citizens were (confusingly) committed to contesting not only Virginia's onerous Reconstruction debts, but also its poll taxes and lack of public schooling. This platform appealed to poor whites and Blacks alike (uniting them under the view that class, not race, was the real divider of Americans) and had a fittingly unusual figurehead—ex–Confederate General William Mahone, who, as of Garfield's presidency, had assumed one of Virginia's Senate seats.

Mahone was an eccentric presence in the chamber. He weighed a hundred pounds, wore flared pants (making parts of him look "exceedingly feminine" from an angle) and spoke in a falsetto pitch past a waist-length beard. Both parties wanted him in their caucus anyway. Bouquets were left on Mahone's desk; Ben Hill of Georgia tried to convince him Readjusters were really just Democrats. The Virginian loudly rebuffed such outreach (squeaking of his state's "instincts of independence") then scurried over to the White House to tell Garfield his real price: he would vote Republican as long as he could control Virginia's federal patronage.[79]

Briefly, the president expressed dismay that Black Virginians could abuse their hard-won (and endangered) suffrage by sending such a scoundrel to the Senate. He could deal with an ex-rebel. But a repudiator of public debt, running a party founded on that principle? Outrageous.[80]

However, Garfield's better instincts soon won out. He met the Readjusters halfway—telling Virginian Republicans to leave some patronage aside, and Senate friends to give Mahone committee posts "until he is reasonably satisfied." In exchange, Garfield could look ahead to not only another ally in the Senate, but also (as he phrased it) the "open door to larger consequences in the South." Indeed, the haul was sufficient for Mahone to shore up in Virginia what historians would eulogize as the "most successful political coalition of whites and Blacks organized in the South between Reconstruction and the 1960s."[81]

• • •

In April, a train steamed toward the distant town of "Independenceville." The president hung off its stack, an engineer's cap flying off his head as he waved at an obstacle down the line. A glance there revealed a giant steer with "Stalwartism" branded on its haunch. Its face was that of Roscoe Conkling—his hair curled into horns, his eyes crossed with rage at the challenge implied by the oncoming engine.

Typewriter keys meteored through the clouds, stamping a caption under the scene: "IT LOOKS BAD FOR THE BULL." Of course, any collision would not exactly benefit the train either.[82]

The administration made other discreet overtures to Black Americans, in the form of giving jobs to a handful of prominent ones. Blanche Bruce, the nation's first elected Black senator, had just lost his seat representing Mississippi after one term; Garfield appointed him register of the Treasury to make up for it. Former congressman Robert Elliott was made an agent of the same department. Frederick Douglass, too, was awarded a federal post—that of recorder of deeds for the District of Columbia. It was technically a demotion from marshalship, but, as Douglass wrote, he found much to savor in the new assignment:

> This office was, in many respects, more congenial to my feelings . . . [requiring] no social duties whatever, and therefore neither fettered my pen nor silenced my voice in the cause of my people. . . . I was the first colored man who held the office, and like all innovations on established usage, my appointment did not meet with the approval of the conservatives and old-time rulers of the country, but, on the contrary, met with resistance from both these and the press as well as from the street corners. . . . [Yet] Having, so to speak, broken the ice by giving to the country the example of a colored man at the head of that office, it has become the one special office to which, since that time, colored men have aspired.[83]

Thus, while such gestures by Garfield were somewhat superficial, there was also significance in that superficiality. They would, in this administration and beyond, help inoculate all Americans to the spectacle of Black men in places of public power. Such appointments would also set a norm for how future presidents could tip their cap to racial justice, without going over electorally dangerous lines (either in voters' minds, or that of Mason-Dixon).

And yet, Garfield also leaned over them, pushing for progress. A few weeks into the administration, Douglass received a summons to "talk over matters pertaining to the cause of my people" with the president—specifically, their presence, or lack thereof, in embassies overseas. "In this conversation," Douglass recalled, "he referred to the fact that his Republican predecessors . . . had never sent colored men to any of the white nations." Garfield had invited the abolitionist to the White House for advice on which Black Americans might represent the nation well as diplomats in Europe.

The president instructed him to follow up with Blaine. Upon learning the secretary was aboard the initiative, Douglass felt confident it might really happen.[84]

As March merged into April, then April became May, most other chances for meaningful work slipped through the president's hands like grains of sand. He supported a probe into where, exactly, Stephen Dorsey had gotten all those funds for last summer's campaign ("Go ahead regardless of where and whom you hit," Garfield would tell investigators). He heard a petition from a nurse that the previous four presidents had ignored, deciding they had all erred; the country had no reason to abstain from the International Committee of the Red Cross. Garfield referred Clara Barton to Secretary Blaine, putting into motion an American chapter of the organization.[85]

With that, the president was stuck facing two opposite wellsprings of unproductivity: the deadlock trapping the Robertson appointment in the Senate, and the never-ending hordes of office-seekers invading the White House. He began to fear neither would resolve satisfactorily;

Conkling might be able to confirm only the Stalwart appointments, then leave Robertson's untouched so that it would die at the end of Congress's session. Even more dreadful to Garfield was the thought that the job-seekers would never stop ambushing him. Their thirst for office seemed vampiric. "These people would take my very brain, flesh, and blood if they could!" the president exclaimed.[86]

For advice, he could (as ever) turn to his secretary of State. Blaine was infinitely creative in the application of executive power and had concocted a way to force an end to Conkling's obstructionism all the way back in March. He had pled for Garfield to deploy it:

I know by inspiration that it will work like a charm. . . . If you take the step I urge he [Conkling] is stripped at one stroke of every opportunity to even annoy you. You are in the twinkling of an eye master of the whole situation.[87]

Garfield had evidently hesitated to accept such advice, but time was running out for Conkling to see reason. The congressional recess loomed.

The president could also commiserate with Blaine about office-seekers. One had proven particularly disruptive—a waif-like man who was insistent on getting a European consular post (preferably in Paris) as reward for a campaign speech titled "Garfield against Hancock." Blaine could not shake the intruder, who visited the secretary an estimated twenty-five times to personally press this ludicrous claim. Soon Blaine completely lost his patience. "Never speak to me about the Paris consulship again," he would snap at the interloper.[88]

The brush-off persuaded the man to stop calling at the Department of State and start seeing its secretary as the most insidious of villains. He dashed off a warning to the president. Blaine was a "vindictive politician and an evil genius, and you will have no peace till you get rid of him," the man wrote Garfield, quoting what he claimed to be gossip in Washington. "I will see you in the morning if I can and talk with you."[89]

But, unbeknownst to this man, the White House staff had already put his name on a list of those banned from the building.[90]

Circumstance finally forced the president to try to break the Senate logjam on May 5. In the morning, rumor reached him that Conkling, indeed, wanted to confirm the Stalwart nominations to New York's patronage, while leaving Robertson's to wither on the legislative vine as Congress went into recess. To avoid that, Garfield finally activated Blaine's plan—withdrawing every appointment due for Senate approval ahead of Robertson's, and thus making a vote on his confirmation inevitable. "It may end in his defeat," the president admitted. "But it will prevent me from being finessed out of a test."[91]

A flurry of senators came by, begging Garfield to let the issue drop and the party settle for a stalemate. But he would not have it—insisting, with a bit of atypical fist-pounding, that Conkling was the instigator of this conflict. Then the president said any senator who did not vote in favor of Robertson would hereafter require letters of introduction to be let into the White House. "Amiably Obstinate," was how a report generously described Garfield's demeanor. "He simply wished his administration to be treated at least with respect," another stated.[92] Correspondents now entertained the possibility that the lily-livered man in the White House had a spine after all. "The papers that have been putting it this way: 'President (?) Garfield,' can now drop the interrogation point," the District's *Evening Star* decreed.[93]

The president read the response differently. "The withdrawals of the NY appts . . . I think show that the public do not desire the continuance of boss rule in the Senate," Garfield wrote. Then he turned to a dearer concern; Crete had just fallen badly ill with fever.[94]

In another part of Washington, Conkling paced, much as he had for weeks. As pressure had gradually built around his obstruction of the Robertson appointment, the senator was reduced to ranting for hours about his grievances with Garfield—or rather, the man surely pulling the president's strings. Hands behind his back, hair locks quivering, Conkling strode in circles and told the universe that his nemesis must be behind all this:

> It was Blaine who had pestered the President day and night about the necessity of crushing Conkling, and who had infused backbone into the President. . . . It was Blaine who had talked Garfield into nominating Robertson for Collector.

A witness to one such episode was confronted by Conkling's finger being shoved in his face, "as if, for the moment, its owner fancied me one of the hated triumvirate of Blaine, Robertson, and Garfield."[95]

This was the paranoia of a boss feeling his back being pressed against a wall. Conkling's position had been eroding since Robertson's name was first sent to the Senate. The very day after the nomination, New York's legislature had even passed a motion urging its confirmation. Now, with the president's latest move, those Stalwarts who had been on the cusp of inheriting federal positions only had their boss's behavior to blame for losing them. An even greater humiliation was imminent—the almost certain confirmation of Robertson by the Senate over Conkling's dissent.[96]

Simply imagining this was sufficient for him to consider the once-unthinkable. Platt's earlier suggestion slithered, snakelike, into Conkling's flustered mind.

Their new plan was (quite literally) political suicide. The two Stalwarts went through with it together on May 16—quitting their Senate seats and leaving long, self-pitying notes to be read aloud to surviving friends in the chamber, protesting the president's violation of their rights. As a flushed Chester Arthur handed these to a clerk, Platt and Conkling's remaining colleagues, stunned, asked over and over again for them to be reread.[97]

Meanwhile, the two now ex-senators prepared to leave Washington for the higher, happier realm of their home state. They expected loyalists in Albany to be enamored by their martyrdom—so much so as to instantly reelect both to the Senate. Then Conkling and Platt could return to their old places, having pulled off the astounding political feat of self-destruction, then resurrection, in between which the Robertson issue could be conveniently resolved in their absence. It would be a stunning display of Stalwart power—not only over New York, but the usual laws of public life.

Platt only felt jealous that Conkling was being credited with the idea. Early coverage of the plot cast the Easy Boss as only an accomplice to it, rather than its inventor. He could look forward to many years under a grating new nickname: "Me Too" Platt.[98]

Back in the District, and beyond earshot of the two fleeing Stalwarts, mirth broke out on the National Mall. Garfield had predicted as much upon hearing the news at Crete's bedside. "A very weak attempt at the heroic—if I do not mistake it will be received with guffaws of laughter," he wrote of the resignations.[99]

Such noise filled the very chamber the New Yorkers had just quit. "Conkling has made a fool of himself," chuckled a senator from Missouri. The same term and its synonyms were repeated between snorts: "childish." Henry Dawes of Massachusetts elaborated—describing Conkling as a "big baby, boo-hooing because he can't have all the cake, and refusing to play any longer, runs home to his mother."[100]

Sometimes it is difficult to distinguish powerful political acts from petty ones, even for veteran statesmen. Steaming up to Albany, Conkling and Platt thought they had made a heroic protest on behalf of senatorial rights. Only on reaching Manhattan did they realize everyone else was interpreting it as an infantile tantrum. "It seems ridiculous, too much like boy's play," said an incredulous Stalwart. Once New Yorkers realized reports of the resignations were true, the majority view became that Conkling and Platt had likely made a terminal error. "If it will only end the rule of Bossism in this State," a New York Republican was heard wishing aloud.[101]

Such were the unique perils of running a political machine; keeping it operating and intact relied on a boss's ability to continue renting the allegiance of its component parts. For the first time, Conkling was returning to Albany with a satchel empty of spoils, and himself to blame—minus his pout over the collectorship, his cronies would have been able to help themselves to almost every other piece of federal patronage in New York. No longer; and thus, Platt and Conkling were returning to a power base that was starting to spin apart in discontent.

At least one follower remained faithful. Arthur was seen heading to Albany to help make the ex-senators' case for reappointment personally. Commenters sarcastically praised the vice president's "skill and energy in all subterranean politics."[102]

Cartoonists jockeyed for how best to depict the Stalwarts' spectacular self-sabotage. One drew Conkling bursting like a balloon over the Senate floor as other senators danced a happy ring-around-the-rosy below. "A Harmless Explosion," read the caption. Another New York artist sketched up a pair of tombstones. The first was dedicated to "R. CONKLING—Statesman, Perished fighting for office." The smaller one simply declared "me too[,] t. platt."[103]

The president barely noticed when Robertson was finally confirmed. It should have been a moment of triumph for Garfield—the appointment's success was quietly era-defining. The executive branch had not only reestablished its authority over the Senate bosses, but, unexpectedly, purged the most infamous of them from power. Reformists clinked glasses in honor of their unlikely hero in the White House; his strange zigzagging on their cause had bagged its biggest adversary. "Roscoe is finished," John Hay crowed to Whitelaw Reid. "That Olympian brow will never again garner up the thunders of yore."

Yet Garfield was preoccupied with worry for the First Lady, whose condition had plummeted in the previous fortnight—whether from malaria or exhaustion, no nurse could say for sure. "Hard to think of business with any shadow of doubt hanging over the light of my life," read one of the president's diary entries in this period.[104]

He spent most of May trying to disperse it, keeping vigil by his wife's sickbed. "I was made tearfully proud by the fact that she told the Dr. I was much the best nurse she had had," he reported after one sleepless night. Callers went spurned; misadventures by the Garfield kids (twisted ankles, voyages out to army forts) tactfully unreported to their mother. Only after weeks of such handling was the First Lady well enough to come to the dinner table—albeit only when carried by her husband and eldest son.[105]

Throughout Crete's convalescence, the president kept only a passing eye on faraway events in Albany, where Conkling and Platt continued struggling to persuade the legislature to give them their Senate seats back. A few rank-and-file Stalwarts openly voiced little interest in reelecting the two—invoking "horse-sense" when asked why. That Garfield had renominated some Stalwarts to federal posts after Robertson's confirmation offered further proof that the president was a reasonable, magnanimous man—and the ex-senators were not. Arthur's presence in town, on the other hand, was just embarrassing everyone.[106]

When Conkling lost a ballot for reappointment in June (scratching together just a third of Republican votes in the legislature), the president penned a eulogy for the Stalwart's career:

> Conkling, who was always inclined to think someone was trying to "humiliate" him . . . succeeded in inflicting measureless humiliation on himself. Suicide is the chief mode of political death, after all.[107]

Even deeper disgrace awaited poor Platt. One night, a group of Half-Breeds used a stepladder to peer through his hotel room window in Albany. They watched on as, therein, the married Stalwart and a "lady of the town" got intimate. Soon it was reported in the legislature, on good authority, that Platt could be counted on to pull out of the Senate contest, too.[108]

. . .

The first month of summer passed coolly and quickly for the administration. That did not mean it was pleasant for the president; Garfield was only happy when he felt useful, but the end of the Senate drama drew his mind to the other bane of his efficiency: the ongoing siege of the White House by jobseekers. His diary entries hit ever-deeper notes of mournfulness:

> My day is pittered away by the personal seeking of people. . . . What might not a vigorous thinker do, if he could be allowed to use the opportunities of a Presidential term in vital, useful activity? Some civil service reform will come by necessity, after the wearisome years of wasted Presidents have paved the way for it.[109]

An escape was in order; halfway through June, the president took Crete and his secretaries to Elberon, a town on the New Jersey shoreline. Cabinet meetings were held beside the azure-blue Atlantic. "The worry and work of Washington seems very far away . . . I have always felt that the ocean was my friend," Garfield mused.[110]

The only hostile presence in Elberon happened to be one of his predecessors. Ulysses Grant had taken the customhouse saga as poorly as possible—seeing it, from a distance, as a deliberate assault on his allies by a president under the sway of other forces. Grant even sent a letter saying so; Garfield opened this note to find himself directly accused of "giving the Administration over to the settlement of *other people's* private grievances," and deliberately humiliating Stalwarts "for no other crime than their friendship and support" of Grant.[111]

The subtext bled through: Grant believed Garfield was letting himself be puppeted by Secretary Blaine and the Half-Breeds. Nor did Grant keep this accusation private. As Senate Stalwarts buckled, the former president had dusted off an old critique to a reporter: "Garfield is a man without backbone."[112]

Columnists tutted at Grant's breach of etiquette, and Garfield did too. "I am quite certain he injures himself more than he does me," the president wrote. Their interactions on the Jersey shoreline were predictably uncomfortable. Grant could be seen sulking along the beach, lifting his hat in brief acknowledgment when the president or First Lady was in eyesight. Garfield discussed the matter with his cabinet and decided that his predecessor simply missed power.[113]

Before leaving Washington, Garfield made an appearance that drew little notice but meant much to him. He attended the graduation of Howard University's newest class of law students. The school's founder was a friend, and its cause meant much to the president; public education, he had recently predicted to Burke Hinsdale, would with time become the "final cure for the 'solid south'"—the means for Black Americans to solve their repression by seizing enlightenment for themselves. It would be especially liberating in the old Confederacy, where wealth and power was particularly concentrated in the hands of a few privileged whites. As the president elaborated to Hinsdale:

> The way to make the majority always powerful over the minority is to make its members as trained and intelligent as the minority itself.[114]

Garfield had the honor of handing each newly minted lawyer their Howard diploma. He noticed, with satisfaction, that one of them was his barber.[115]

Garfield returned to the District at the end of June, invigorated by his time on the seashore. On the night of July 1, Harriet Blaine looked out her bay window on Fifteenth Street to see the president bounding up her steps. "It was a very handsome and happy-looking man who sat down with me," she would recall, his pink corsage and gray summer suit burning themselves brightly into her memory. Secretary Blaine came downstairs to join Garfield on a loop around the block.[116]

A stranger followed their stroll from the opposite side of the street.

He had been stalking each for a while: attending the president's church on Vermont Avenue; reading the movements of both in the papers. The sight of the two friends walking that night, "in the most delightful and cozy mood possible," laughing with heads together like schoolgirls, verified his worst fears—that "Mr. Garfield had sold himself body and soul to Blaine, and that Blaine was using Garfield to destroy the Stalwart element of this nation . . . and disrupt the Republican Party and cause a civil war."

Reaching in his pocket, the man brushed past application papers and fingered a revolver he had bought a few days before. He was not ready to give up on the Paris consulship, though; perhaps if events the next day went according to plan, a grateful country might bestow it on him.[117]

On the morning of July 2, the president impressed his eldest sons with a gymnastic routine; somersaulting over Jim's bed, then springing across the floor on all fours, flexing his fingers and toes for propulsion. The boys couldn't replicate it and would later say this display was their father's way of showing them a feat to strive for. Then the three readied to head for the railway station together; as anyone could read in the papers, the president was due to take a train to his college reunion at Williams.[118]

A State Department coach pulled up at three minutes past nine to ferry them to the depot. Blaine was waiting within—he could never pass up a chance to talk business with the president, even for a few moments. Their carriage trotted six blocks to the Baltimore and Potomac station on Sixth and B streets. On arrival, Garfield turned to say goodbye to Blaine. But the secretary insisted on escorting him to the platform, where other cabinet members were waiting.[119]

Arm in arm, the pair moved up the steps in tandem while Jim and Hal Garfield followed. The president asked a policeman at the entrance for the time. It was nine-twenty.[120]

Blaine had crossed two-thirds of the station's waiting room when a bang erupted behind him, followed by another. He flinched and reached over to Garfield in instinct, only to feel the president rear up and shout, "My God!

What is this?" A figure rushed past as screams and the tang of burned gunpowder filled the room. Still acting off reflex, the secretary of State moved in pursuit—only to hear calls of "we have caught him" come from the exit beyond. Turning back, he saw Garfield facedown and vomiting. The president lost consciousness as the secretary reached him again.[121]

Blood pooled below both men as commuters closed in overhead. Blaine watched the hems of their clothes start to stain red.[122]

The cop who had told the president the time less than a minute before was now arresting his shooter outside the station. The assailant put up little fight—not even raising the warm pistol in his hand. Onlookers surged forth at the detainee: twisting his wrist; seizing his neck; knocking his hat off. A flying wedge of officers bundled him to a nearby jail through a back route.[123]

This likely saved the assassin's life. A baggage-handler later swore that the gunman would have swung from the station's rafters "then and there" if the police hadn't arrived in force.[124]

When asked what "in God's name, man," was his motive for shooting Garfield, the gunman answered, "I am a Stalwart, and want Arthur for President."[125]

The stricken president had since been hauled on a hay-and-horsehair mattress to the station's second floor. Opening his eyes, he beheld a strange collection of faces: his sons', weeping; his cabinet's, stunned. Few were paler than that of Secretary Lincoln, who had witnessed the attack from about forty feet away, then sprinted to the station's telegraph room to summon troops and doctors to the scene. That done, the secretary of War had realized how ironic his presence was.[126]

"My god," Lincoln was soon saying aloud. "How many hours of suffering I have passed in this town."[127]

Garfield's were only beginning. His right arm stung; in his back throbbed a deeper ache; his feet prickled with electric, nervous pain. But, not five minutes after the shooting, worse discomfort started coming from an outside source: his doctors. The first to arrive poured brandy and ammonia salts down the president's throat, then turned him over for what established practice deemed a necessity. Flicking aside a clot on the small of the patient's back, the physician sank a finger into the gunshot wound to try tracing the path of the slug still within.[128]

As new medics reached the depot, each insisted on repeating the torture. Grimy digits, attached to men who did not yet believe in washing their hands, tunneled past shattered ribs to burrow into the president. Metal probes followed, but got hooked on bone shards at a depth of three inches. Pushing down on Garfield's sternum was necessary to free these instruments. Coating them, imperceptible to the naked eye (and fictional, to many of those in the American medical community) were millions of living microbial poisons, now seeded across the president's abdomen.[129]

He braved it all with nips of brandy and clenches of the jaw. Lincoln was impressed; Garfield seemed the "coolest man in the room," answering all questions in a steady, strong voice.[130]

When the president's ambulance was at last ready to bear him to the White House, the doctors agreed he was mortally wounded. None of their probing had found the bullet, but its angle of entry pointed ominously to the liver. Garfield's vitals, "almost pulseless," hinted at severe internal hemorrhage. Attempts to tell him the wound wasn't serious stirred skeptical shakes of the head. "I thank you doctor," Garfield replied, "but I am a dead man."[131]

It was the right conclusion—tacitly reached by everyone—but it would take a while for them to realize they had reached it erroneously. As Garfield's coach galloped cruelly over bumpy avenues, those who had seen his injury guessed he would finish bleeding to death in hours. Yet by the time the president returned to the White House, another deadly process was just kindling in him, beyond the sight or comprehension of his doctors. Secretly, silently, an infection had taken root.[132]

28

"Like as the waves make towards the pebbled shore,
So do our minutes hasten to their end."

—Shakespeare's "Sonnet 60," as quoted in Garfield
diary entry for November 25, 1878

The president struggled to look stoic as his stretcher was lifted to an upstairs room on the southeast corner of the White House. One moment, his right arm hung nerveless over his head. The next, he was giving a hearty wave to the passing figure of Harriet Blaine. Garfield asked her to stay close until Crete reached him; lying on the depot floor, the president had managed to dictate a telegram to be flashed to his wife in New Jersey, explaining he was "seriously hurt, how serious I cannot yet say. . . . I send my love to her."[1]

His caregivers thought they might just solve that question if they could only find out where the bullet had gone. William Tecumseh Sherman appeared beside the president to assist on this matter. Garfield leaned forward to expose a deceptively small red hole four inches to the right of his spine, now barely oozing enough blood to stain a pillow. Sherman then asked for the coat Garfield had been wearing. Together the general and the president studied an opening punched above its tail with a shared, almost scholarly curiosity. Silently, though, Sherman was making grim calculations. "A terrible wound," he admitted to a friend upon leaving the mansion. He would not have been shocked if the president had keeled over right there beside him.[2]

Garfield hung on as the hours passed. He vomited sporadically, only to drift into spells of sleep that were broken by hot pain knifing in his feet. His pulse faded almost into imperceptibility. Soon the doctors who had shepherded him from the station could only hope "that the illustrious sufferer might again see the face he loved so well." Indeed, this was the one thing the president looked nervous about when awake. He asked several times what might be keeping Crete—"extremely anxious," a physician later recalled, "lest she should be too late for an intelligent interview."[3]

Carriage wheels rolled over an outside driveway at twenty minutes to seven, creating a crunching noise that stirred the president. "That's my wife!" he beamed. The First Lady had also endured ordeals that day: the most terrible of all telegrams; an audience with a tearful, repentant Ulysses Grant, saying he had seen weaker men survive worse; a breakdown of the train spiriting her and Mollie down to Washington.[4]

Once Crete finally entered the White House, Harriet Blaine thought she looked "fatigued, desperate, but firm and quiet and full of purpose to save." The First Lady was granted five minutes with her clearly dying husband. "The words of love, hope and cheer given . . . known only to themselves and to God," an exiled attendant wrote.[5]

Whatever they were, though, the effect was miraculous. Garfield rallied within the hour. His vitals steadied, indicating any internal bleeding had "spontaneously arrested." The doctors were encouraged—one, enough so to flip the president and once again wiggle a dirty finger ("with difficulty") into the wound. The slug still hid within, under muscle, broken ribs, and admittedly more fat than the patient would prefer to own. He was given a glass of champagne to take the edge off.[6]

Beyond, silence reigned. Mixed throngs of laborers, gowned ladies, and newsboys, white and Black, softly clung to the White House's iron fencing, while for thousands of miles around, the nation stilled upon hearing of the shooting. Forges cooled in Pittsburgh; trades were halted midtransaction on New York's exchanges. Southern mayors and officials gathered citizens to break word of the tragedy as gently as possible.[7]

It hit with great force elsewhere: one person in Albany vomited at the news of the president's shooting, while in another part of the country, an old man died of shock upon hearing it. Even impassive Jay Gould was stunned into showing bona fide emotion. "Garfield has been shot!" the magnate breathed, ashen-faced and trembling, to a relative. "President Garfield has been shot!" The news halted a younger and more dynamic American in his tracks across an ocean: "A frightful calamity for America," Theodore Roosevelt, Jr., wrote from vacation in Europe. He decided the bullet fired into Garfield "means work in the future for those who mean their country well."[8]

Meanwhile, an awful déjà vu flourished back across the Atlantic. "Nothing since the death of Lincoln has so stirred the populace," a man said in Chicago. Identical remarks (almost to the word) were made in Albany, New Orleans, and Detroit. Other commenters in other cities opined that this assassination carried "more importance to the country than that of Abraham Lincoln," for it had occurred in peacetime. Implied was a fear that the killing of presidents in America was now normalized. The general shock was compounded in both parties by the fact that Garfield, of all statesmen, could be the target of such a malicious attack. As one column declared, speaking for many:

> No matter how much certain Republicans may have opposed Mr. Garfield politically, everybody esteemed him personally.[9]

For a while, many assumed the attempt on his life had succeeded. Bells tolled out Garfield's death in arid Californian valleys. Flags drooped at half-mast along the eastern seaboard. Merchants and editors fringed their storefronts and extra editions with dark mourning sashes. The common cry made coast-to-coast once it was learned the president still lived was the same, as uttered from pulpits, before newsstands, and in state legislatures: "Thank God!"[10]

Among those spared from this early whiplash of rumor were those most vulnerable to it—the oldest and youngest members of the president's family. Eliza Garfield was with relatives in Cleveland. They hid the news of her son's shooting, for fear of adding to the day's death toll. Another vacuum of information was created around the littlest Garfields—Irvin and Abe—on a train ride to Mentor. Papers were confiscated from depots along their route; conductors banned mention of the shooting in the cars; people coming aboard became discreetly included in the conspiracy.[11]

By the following day, it had been established everywhere that the president was not dead but critically injured—hardly good news, but good enough to finally share with his mother, at least.[12]

The day after went into record books as the quietest Fourth of July ever seen. From Newport to Cheyenne, Portland to Fort Wayne, Brooklyn to San Francisco, pyrotechnic celebrations were postponed in favor of a new national pastime: gathering before giant bulletin boards to read the latest updates dispatched from the president's sickroom. Party differences appeared forgotten amid the throngs.[13]

"It is not James A. Garfield that lies gasping for breath," said the leader of one such crowd in New York. "It is the American Republic." It was perhaps suitable, then, that other watchers expressed surprise when reminded it was Independence Day.[14]

The stillness in Washington was rigorously enforced. Authorities feared any clatter reaching the president might be enough to tip him over the brink. People caught using fireworks were fined based on their proximity to the White House. "No steam and other whistles have been heard in the city," noted a wanderer. "Bells have ceased to toll; men walk about as though shod in soft slippers, and talk with bated breath." The correspondent rode for miles, hearing hardly a sound except for the occasional crying policeman.[15]

A crowd remained glued to the White House's fence, eyes on the manor's windows at all hours. A breeze off the Potomac sometimes lifted the odd curtain to reveal pacing cabinet members.[16]

James Blaine remained completely out of sight—sifting somewhere through urgent telegrams from abroad. Queen Victoria was "most anxious" to hear the president's condition; King Alfonso XII had written with similar concern from a palace in Madrid. Head-down in composing replies, the secretary of State hid a tear-stained face from all but the closest friends.[17]

"We are hopeful, but there is great anxiety," he said to one. "We hope."[18]

The only turbulence left in the country whirled about the Stalwarts like a hurricane. It kicked up as soon as Roscoe Conkling and the vice president reached Manhattan on July 2 (fresh from another fruitless trip to Albany) to hear the president had been shot. The rumor literally felled Arthur, who folded into a chair at its impact. "It can't be true," he moaned.[19]

The pair made haste for the Fifth Avenue Hotel, only to hear the news not just confirmed but made far worse for them in particular. The gunman had sworn allegiance to Stalwartism (and the vice president!) at the scene of the crime. This fact, combined with the political chaos of the previous three months, were all many Americans needed to decide that the shooting had been part of a Stalwart conspiracy to seize the presidency. The deputy attorney general declared himself a believer. Even Prime Minister William Gladstone told the British Parliament that the theory could not be ruled out.[20]

Reports of the prisoner's backstory and his conduct behind bars would soon refute these suspicions. The American public were to gradually realize the assassin was both vile and unhinged in equally vast measure—hardly the type to be included as a critical part of a political plot. Many citizens would pass time before the bulletin boards discussing inventive ways to execute him. A Black woman in New York wanted the would-be assassin hanged. Another man proposed having him thrown under the train "which was to have carried President Garfield away." A Midwestern industrialist asked for the shooter to instead be delivered to his foundry, "so I could throw him into a boiling hot kettle of molten iron."[21]

This did not mean the Stalwarts were off the hook, though. Platt joined Arthur and Conkling at the Fifth Avenue Hotel on the day of the shooting to find "evidence of insanity among others than . . . [the shooter] manifested": an angry mob had gathered in front of the building; threats had been passed to clerks that the vice president and other Stalwart guests hiding within "would pay the penalty" for the attack on Garfield. One note prescribed the time and manner of this precisely:

Gens. We will hang Conkling and Co. at nine PM sharpe. THE COMMITTEE.[22]

Policemen (uniformed and not) arrived on time to thwart any such retribution, but the point was clear; despite the shooter's increasingly evident insanity, many Americans had already decided that, directly involved or not, Conkling and the rest of the Stalwarts bore at least some responsibility for the attack on the president.[23]

This case was conveniently laid out by the national media. Heated Stalwart rhetoric against Garfield during the late customhouse brawl was reprinted in newspapers; editors around the country shook their heads at what now seemed obvious. Southern papers declared that the "intrigues of Conkling and the slanders of Grant" had evidently "wrought up the miserable assassin to the pitch of regarding the death of the President as a political necessity." Northern writers agreed that the shooting would never have transpired, "but by the spirit which a political faction has begotten and nursed."[24]

In sum, the nation stood ready to blame Conkling not only for inflaming partisan polarization, but also for what such rhetoric had prompted an "ill-balanced" mind to do. It was a remarkable (and remarkably quick-developing) incidence of the American public collectively punishing a political bloc for divisiveness.[25]

That the shooter had been a frustrated office-seeker brought further condemnation not simply on the Stalwarts, but the corrupt machinery their faction (and others) had been built upon. On the first Sunday after Garfield's wounding, American ministers mounted their pulpits to pile holy scorn on the spoils system. "Is not the commission of the crime largely due to the abuse of those very institutions which we enjoy and esteem as our strength?" a Methodist in New York asked his flock.

> Every position is in the market for sale, and almost every office . . . it is a sad commentary on the political condition of the country when two-thirds of the time of officials is spent in the distribution of patronage.[26]

A Unitarian priest just down the street struck similar tones. "Is it not a new argument for putting the spoils of office out of party politics when madness, suicide, and murder wait upon its inspiration?" From Conkling's hometown of Utica to as far off as Germany, secular observers also blamed Garfield's shooting on a "political system of corruption" in desperate need of reform. Editors at *The Nation* expressed wonder that the civil service reform cause could grow so popular, so quickly:

> We do not think we have taken up a newspaper during the last ten days which has not in some manner made the crime the product of "the spoils system." . . . It has fallen on a mass of popular indignation all ready to explode.[27]

Other contributing factors to the tragedy were considered; a Canadian offered that no president could be safe "in times of excitement" as long as Americans carried their "love of liberty so far as to allow the wickedest classes the liberty of carrying deadly weapons." But another editorial wrapped all the guilty parties and factors into a cohesive whole:

> For though the murderer was obviously of a disordered mind, it is impossible to ignore the causes which led immediately to this act. . . .

He was a disappointed office-seeker, and he linked the bitterness of his present disappointment with the passionate animosity of a faction. His resentment was inflamed and intensified by the assaults upon the President which have been common in too many circles for the past few months.[28]

And yet Conkling (now nestled on Fifth Avenue) seemed poised to profit immensely from Garfield's shooting all the same. Though the boss's odds of returning to the Senate had guttered out, his longtime crony was probably going to inherit the most powerful post on the continent. The same thought almost simultaneously dawned on an old nemesis hundreds of miles away. "Arthur for President!" Rutherford Hayes wrote in despair into his diary. "Conkling the power behind the throne, superior to the throne!"[29]

The former senator was tight-lipped with most of the reporters in his hotel. He simply told one that the president's shooting was, indeed, "the most terrible incident in our country since the death of Lincoln." Then the boss retreated into his suite, as crowds outside kept shouting his guilt.[30]

The gunman was, sadly, not forgotten. In an instant he had become a figure of morbid curiosity to regular citizens—his behavior behind bars, only intensifying the public's twin feelings of revulsion and fascination for him. He reenacted the president's reaction to being shot; he preened for photos; he ate heartily of the prison food; he planned a speaking tour; he waxed lyrical to journalists about his life, lashing out when cut off for a question. "His vanity is literally nauseating," a reporter wrote. The prisoner appeared to believe the "civilized world is holding its breath to hear of the minutest detail of his career."[31]

Sadly, he was right to think so; articles about the shooter had swiftly filled the country's major newspapers after his crime (with one lengthy piece literally titled "The Assassin's Career"). Journalists held interviews with anyone who had even remotely known him. Nothing such sources reported was admiring: everyone in the prisoner's life universally remembered him as a "shyster," "fraud," "deadbeat," or "vicious, wild character." But this only roused readers' appetites for more. Correspondents traced his ancestry—which, to the relief of German-Americans, led to France. His infamous campaign speech ("Garfield against Hancock") reached a far larger audience than its author could have ever dreamed of, if only because the public wished to read how "crack-brained" and "ridiculous" it was.[32]

Amid this nationwide obsession, someone thought to ask Robert Ingersoll what could have moved such a person to shoot the president. The orator did not have to think hard:

> His motive? Oh, the man was soured and embittered against the whole world. His life was a failure. There was nothing in the past or the present as an augury of hope for the future. He was ready to die, and he determined, with the malignity of a fiend, to drag someone down with him, and he did it.[33]

It was a shrewd sketch of a certain type of person destined to repeat in society: a lost soul who, with little left to live for, commits an atrocity simply for the sake of attention and notoriety. By shooting Garfield, this one attained not only voluminous press coverage and interest from his contemporary countrymen, but a place in future archives, history books, and biographies. His name was Charlie Guiteau, though perhaps it would have been better if everyone had simply agreed not to identify him at all.

Much of the immediate coverage of the president's shooting made it easy to forget he still lived. His assailant was referred to as "the murderer." Reverends quoted Old Testament passages that an absent-minded congregant could easily misinterpret ("How are the mighty fallen!"). Midsentence, journalists stopped themselves from accidentally reporting the worst. "Garfield dies—if he dies—a martyr to the spoils," wrote a reformist editor in New York.[34]

The updates telegrammed several times daily from the president's bedside not only kept reminding the country the president was alive, but soon shared remarkable news of his apparent recovery. His sleep turned "tranquil," his temperature "normal." Brief flutters in Garfield's pulse went dismissed as the result of changes in bedding and body position. Most inspiring were reports of the patient's resurgence of appetite; he expressed dissatisfaction with the tepid chicken broth being spooned to him every couple hours. "The President calls for a beefsteak," declared one cheerful byline on July 7.[35]

At the one-week mark, the doctors' bulletin confirmed the "condition of the President continues to be favorable." Cabinet members abandoned once-gloomy vigils to provide their own encouraging quotes to the press. The secretary of the Navy said Garfield seemed "halfway over the bridge." Postmaster General James borrowed a different idiom. "Out of the woods," he told a journalist.[36]

These expressions were much more useful to the average American than was the medical jargon packing official reports. Multitudes peered at public bulletin boards in blazing heat and rain, bemusedly rereading every scrap of scientific lingo forwarded by Garfield's doctors—with creased brows, "striving hard to decipher the true inwardness of tympanitis and peritonitis." They walked away looking reassured by the obscurity of the language, pleased to be told of the "peritoneum," of the "Parenchymatous organs," of "traumatic lesions," etc., etc. "These words are impressive, although they may not convey any particular definite meaning," a witness wrote.[37]

Few yet suspected that the authors of these updates did not truly understand what they were describing either. The membership of the team treating the president had solidified swiftly after his shooting—and, to be sure, they ranked as an elite medical group per all measures of the era. They had been drawn from across academia, military service, public health administration, and private practice to collaborate on the most important case of their time. Upon hearing their names, even the president (in an apt turn of phrase) called the list "eminently satisfactory."[38]

Regrettably, though, a modern reader must conclude that this

eminence did not really count for much. None of Garfield's doctors exemplified the immature, underdeveloped state of their profession better
than their leader, Willard Bliss—the rare physician to have, by middle
age, earned the esteem of statesmen and poets: Lincoln had appointed
him to be a division surgeon in the Army of the Potomac during the Civil
War, while Walt Whitman (impressed by Bliss's skill with a bonesaw)
described him as "one of the best surgeons in the Army." Bliss also possessed that most invaluable and timeless of medical traits: an immaculate
bedside manner. His peers had never seen another doctor be so attentive
to patients.[39]

The exile did not last long, though, for the entire field of American
And yet, Bliss's mastery of the tactile aspects of his craft was countered by a curious faith in metaphysics and pseudoscience. Deft at fixing torn arteries, Bliss also had a near-irrepressible curiosity for quack
treatments, which he mistook for scientific breakthroughs. The intangible
inner processes of the body remained in great part a mystery to him—so
much so, that he did not understand how little he knew about them. Bliss
had spent years promoting an Andean herb as the cure for "cancer, syphi-
lis, ulcers . . . and all chronic blood diseases." This belief helped get him
booted, briefly, from the District of Columbia Medical Society.[40]

The exile did not last long, though, for the entire field of American
medicine was also in a state of flux—oscillating, like much of the rest of
the country, between rational and irrational forces by the end of the nineteenth century. The nation was mechanizing, but its doctors still often
conducted their work as if it were the dark ages. Bloodletting and blistering remained in use—the same treatments that had hastened the death
of Garfield's father, Abram, a half-century before. More "fashionable surgeons" in other wards looked down on such outdated ideas, but still used
animal sinew instead of thread to sew up incisions.[41]

As for the fluids seeping from such cuts, many American doctors
(Bliss included) still subscribed to an idea that had persisted since ancient Greece: that "humors" like blood and bile filled a sort of hydraulic
function in the body, regulating mental and physical health. And within
this "humoral system," pus occupied an esteemed place as a sign of good

healing. "Hence the aim of many was to hasten the formation of this 'laudable' pus," a doctor writing in a more advanced age would snark.[42]

The odor produced by it was, by extension, also mistakenly welcome. As sommeliers might whiff a good vintage, or affineurs savor sharp cheddar, physicians in the United States during the Garfield administration still appreciated the "good old surgical stink" of their wards.[43]

Enlightenment glimmered in far-off corners of the profession. A British surgeon named Dr. Joseph Lister had theorized that bodily infections were not due to internal fluid imbalances, but rather tiny invisible organic invaders entering patients from without. Lister's experiments dousing cuts, operating theaters, and scalpels with carbolic acid promptly cut rates of "paennia, hospital gangrene, or erysipelas" in his wards to near-zero. Afterward, he shared his findings (and new revulsion for pus and "putrid exhalations") with medical societies in Britain and overseas. Yet America's ruling class of doctors had tutted in dismissive disdain. "In order to successfully practice Mr. Lister's antiseptic method," one sniffed, declining even to give the Brit his due title, "it is necessary that we should believe, or act as if we believed, the atmosphere to be loaded with germs."[44]

A few more open-minded American practitioners did, albeit imperfectly or half-heartedly. They would flick acid over a patient's wound, only to then sneeze into their hands and spit onto their needles before setting to work. Others tried to innovate upon Lister's idea. One man in Missouri even invented a custom antiseptic solution named in the doctor's honor. "Listerine" would sell middlingly, however, until sellers learned to market it as a way to clean mouths instead of wounds.[45]

The treatments applied by Garfield's doctors straddled the split worlds of their profession. They injected the president with morphine to soothe his pain, then prescribed doses of milk, liquor, and lime water to do the same for his stomach. Token antiseptic washes were made of his wound, only for surgeons to continue forcing in unsanitized probes to try solving the pivotal question of the case. "The attending and consulting surgeons state that it is impossible to predict a final result of the shot without locating the ball," explained a reporter.[46]

Toward the middle of the month, yellow discharge began to leak out of Garfield. Its viscosity and volume became a staple of the updates issued to the public, in ever-cheerier tones as the quantity grew. "There is now a free discharge of healthy pus," Dr. Bliss happily reported on the night of July 17.[47]

New York finished picking its new senators on July 22—and (predictably by this point) neither turned out to be Stalwarts. "I am glad it is over," the president said from bed. Then he uttered a peace offering: "I am sorry for Conkling. He has made a great mistake. . . . I will offer him any favor he may ask, or any appointment he may desire." Garfield's instinct to conciliate simply could not be killed, whether by bad manners or gunshot.[48]

If Conkling ever received this overture, though, he did not act on it. Perhaps the boss still suspected Arthur would soon be able to do better.

Bliss, meanwhile, could not have asked for a better-behaved patient. The president was compliant and cheerful in his sickbed, staying sunny through all sorts of rough treatment. Garfield had to be vigorously rolled up to a hundred times daily to prevent bedsores; his wound needed rebinding every few hours; and, more painfully for the president's pride, he could no longer go to the bathroom by himself. His attendants would sift through "every passage of his bowels and urine" for clues to his health, as parents might for a newborn. Perhaps most frustratingly (particularly to a biographer) Garfield had been reduced to a passive character in his own story. His days of writing were over, his pen almost completely stilled; no more could he scrawl out reflections on the events swirling about him, now more dramatically than ever.[49]

Based on what others heard in his sickroom, though, Garfield was determined to face his new predicament as he had old ones—with good-natured grit. A clear "thank you, gentlemen" always came from the president whenever orderlies finished attending to him. "Here comes old temperature again," he would quip if one returned with a thermometer. In-between bouts of sleep and vomiting, Garfield joked about dodging bullets in battle only to have caught one in peacetime.[50]

He also tried to buck up his family. "It is only the hull that is staved in," Garfield promised one of the boys. "The upper works are unharmed." The First Lady proved harder to assuage; Crete was the most stubborn presence at her husband's bedside. Garfield kept awake as long as she stayed near, but also encouraged her to go out on coach rides for fresh air. "She is absolutely unstampedable," he would boast to doctors after she left.[51]

Yet an undercurrent of distress ebbed through as July continued. The president quietly conceded that his feet felt as though they were stuck in a roaring fireplace, his spine like it might not be there anymore. "*Strangulatus pro Republica*," Garfield scribbled on a scrap of paper in the middle of the month.[52]

Another crack emerged once Garfield heard what seemed, at first, to be heartwarming news: members of the New York Chamber of Commerce had started up a public collection fund to benefit Crete and the children. Donations amounted to tens of thousands of dollars within days. "How kind and thoughtful!" the wounded president said upon learning this. "What a generous people!" Then a doctor watched him realize what contingency the fund was created for: "He was then silent and absorbed for a long time . . . I never heard him allude to the subject afterward."[53]

The American people were certainly now thoughtful—compulsively thoughtful—about his well-being. Kids asked their parents, "How is the President tonight?" while being tucked into bed, before praying for the Lord to "not let any more naughty men shoot him." Upon waking, they would rush out to empty predawn streets to ask newsboys for updates.[54]

Adults, on the other hand, tacked a new chapter to the Garfield mythology that had been circulated nationwide during his presidential campaign. It showed signs of gaining devotees across party lines; a Democrat in Albany stood up and practically announced this to his state's legislature:

When we see a boy driving a horse on a canal; when we see him going from the towpath to college, sawing wood and doing chores in order to obtain an education; when we see that boy graduated with distinguished honors; when we see him going to the defence of his country; when we see that man in Congress, serving there for twenty years, a bright star . . . when we see that man taken out of Congress and elected to the highest office in the land; when we see that man shot down by the hands of an assassin, there is no condemnation too great for the Democrats . . . to express their abhorrence of the crime or of the men who have incited it, if it was incited.[55]

Some Americans confident in the president's recovery began quantifying the political boost generated by surviving assassination. "Garfield will arise from his bed the most popular man in America," wrote a commentator. "This worship will make him all-powerful if he lives," agreed one politician.[56]

Many citizens were not willing to merely pray for the president. Reading of his condition in newspapers and bulletins, thousands imagined they might actually hold the key to his recovery. Surgeons and soldiers forwarded treatment ideas to the White House, citing personal experience with gunshot injuries. A few gems of advice glinted unheeded in this pile. "Do not allow probing of the wound," urged one doctor in Kansas. "Saturate everything with carbolic acid. . . . Probing generally does more harm than the balls."[57]

Other citizens did not let a lack of medical expertise stop them from trying to be of assistance. They also wrote in, but a few were so eager to help heal the president that they showed up to the White House in person. A lady presented herself at its gates wearing a bathing suit and bearing a vial of unknown liquid she promised would cure Garfield. One visitor swore to the guards that God had sent him to save the president. Another eluded security entirely—slipping over the mansion's fence in the dead of night, then knocking on its door to insist on seeing Garfield.

These callers were all (with varying degrees of delicacy) turned away, their snake oil pocketed by Joseph Stanley Brown for inclusion in a collection he was putting together. An authorized visitor snuck a peek at it:

> There is a closet in the private secretary's office which has been con-
> verted into a curiosity shop. In it have been deposited all the patent
> medicines, salves and things. . . . The closet looks now as if somebody
> had thoroughly mixed the contents of three apothecary shops and let
> them stay mixed.[58]

The quantity of such confiscations underlined a lesson many had taken from Garfield's shooting: the time had probably come for America's leaders to be better protected from its people. "Presidents have driven about Washington like other people and travelled over the country as unguarded and uncontained as any private citizen," pointed out one editorial.

> All this, we fear, must come to an end now . . . the President must be
> a slave of his office, the prisoner of forms and restrictions, for he will
> have reason to fear an assassin in every crowd that presses about him
> and in every stranger who seeks to approach him.[59]

Not all callers were turned away. A few citizens approached the White House staff in early July with ideas on how Garfield's room might be artificially cooled—no small feat in a Washington summer. A machine shop staffed by naval engineers started droning away in the cellar to cobble their designs together. After some trial and error—necessary steps in invention—they produced a fan-powered apparatus that forced ambient air through fabric saturated with ice and salt. Garfield's doctors switched it on to find the device cooled their space by almost thirty degrees. It was the first air-conditioner.[60]

Other members of the public pondered the issue Garfield's doctors had now-infamously not been able to solve: the location of the bullet. Though the question had long since been deemed clinically irrelevant by the medical team, they received a storm of proposals on how to find the wayward slug. Some were delightfully simple. One man somberly advised dangling the president upside-down like a wet towel until the projectile fell out. Competing (and more compelling) suggestions drew on emerging technology. A supple probe was sent in from Boston with an inbuilt incomplete circuit—the idea being that the circuit would light up upon making contact with the metal ball. "Another [man] sent a drawing of a machine composed of a rubber tube and an air-pump," one of Garfield's physicians recounted. "The rubber tube was to be introduced into the wound until it came in contact with the bullet . . . and by suction the bullet removed."[61]

However, the most intriguing idea for finding the bullet could only be heard, rather than read of, by mid-July—in *pop-thwacks*, in front of what had lately been a stable on Connecticut Avenue. Though the smell of dung still filled that space, it now served as a workshop for none other than Alexander Graham Bell. Several years before, Bell had made himself a household name around the globe by inventing the telephone; reports of the trouble tracing the ball in Garfield had fired his prodigious imagination again. "I cannot possibly persuade him to sit, just these days," his wife complained. "He is hard at work day and night . . . for the President's benefit."[62]

This work currently consisted of shooting bits of wood and sacks of wet bran, then passing what looked like coils of wire over the targets. Bell and a colleague soon decided slabs of raw beef would be a better, meatier stand-in for Garfield's back.[63]

On the morning of July 21, a wad of fiber fell out of the president. A closer inspection revealed it to be a piece of Garfield's coat that had been forced into his body by the bullet. An even larger bundle, matted with fluid and pulverized bone, surfaced the next day. Bliss insisted there remained nothing to be worried about. His bulletins assured the public that the wound "is looking very well," having "discharged several ounces of healthy pus."[64]

It continued to flow freely throughout July 23. Chills shook the rest of Garfield's body, and by midmorning his skin was "drenched with a profuse perspiration." A reexamination of the bullet hole revealed that a three-inch deep abscess (or "superficial pus-sac," per Bliss's opinion) had formed in the opening. The doctors decided to cut a new hole in the patient's back to better drain it. Bliss's account of this procedure featured an observation of the president's remarkable fortitude: "Without an anasthetic, and without a murmur, or a muscular contraction by the patient, the incision was made."[65]

Afterward, the physician again informed reporters all was well. "The obstruction has been completely overcome," Bliss said. "Should other complications arise, no reason exists why we should not be able to deal with them. . . . The President is again on a fair way to recovery." Yet discord now murmured audibly in the ranks; a navy doctor on the team told a journalist that the American people "have never known how seriously the President has been hurt," and that his danger period had not, in fact, passed.[66]

Bliss was not one to take kindly to dissent. His captainship of Garfield's medical team had already seen barely suppressed conflict: Bliss had loudly kicked one doctor off the case after a disagreement over who, exactly, was in charge.[67]

Here he exemplified another enduring facet of his profession: its propensity to attract big egos. The glory of healing a president beckoned to Bliss's. "If I can't save him, no one can," he had said.[68]

Alexander Graham Bell got to evaluate Garfield's status personally on July 26. He and a colleague entered the White House as the president slept that day, hauling with them a medusoid mass of wires, plates, batteries, and a solitary cone-shaped earpiece. The inventors told the doctors this contraption was an "induction balance," but essentially it represented an iteration on Bell's telephonic technology. In theory, placing metal near a current created across the machine's wires would disrupt the flow of electrons within, creating audible clicking in the receiver. Bell and his partner had heard a tell-tale crackle when passing their device over bullets lodged in all sorts of simulation material. They had thereby invented the first-ever metal detector—all for the sake of saving Garfield.[69]

His appearance briefly took Bell aback. An "ashen grey color" saturated the president's skin, reminding Bell of a corpse. Shaking free of this thought, the inventor draped wires over Garfield and began scanning for the bullet—only to hear a weak, strange splutter from the receiver. The sound was totally novel; its appearance now, of all times, quite humiliating, as Bell could make little sense of it. He departed the White House embarrassed to find reporters adding his name to a list of "nostrum inventors," the equivalent of snake oil salesmen.[70]

Bell returned on August 1 to again try out his invention on the president, only to find his repairs over the last few days had apparently done nothing of use. Now just a light static could be heard through his "induction balance bullet detector," no matter where its sensor plate rested on the president. Bell shuffled away defeated—not suspecting that Garfield's bed still sat on a layer of metal springs, perfectly placed to add interference to Bell's device.[71]

By the time the inventor realized this, the president's doctors had stopped up their ears to him. The value of any further visits was dismissed. "I feel all the more mortified because I feel that I have really accomplished a great work," Bell lamented to his wife.[72]

Regardless of whether one trusted the upbeat bulletins leaving the White House, it could not be denied that Garfield was now incapable of filling the duties of his office. A cursory cabinet meeting was held by his bedside; extradition papers were presented for his shaky signature; but these did not stop awkward Constitutional questions from arising. Americans had seen a president shot dead before, and experienced a couple more expiring from sudden illness. An incapacitated executive, though, was a new spectacle entirely. "What kind of a government are we living under now?" a Democrat editor asked. "Is the executive power suspended? Or is it exercised by . . . a number of officers unknown to the Constitution, or unauthorized by any law to act in any contingency?"[73]

Luckily, like a speeding bicycle removed of its rider, the federal government had passed some invisible operational threshold beyond which it could spin on without active steering for a while. The cabinet simply went about its work. "Every man running his own Department, and thinking he is doing so well alone that he may be President some day," Robert Todd Lincoln wrote happily. The secretary of War missed the regular "hand-strengthening" shakes he had received in cabinet meetings with the president, but consoled himself with the faith that these would resume soon.[74]

His colleague atop the State Department could not be so sure. Blaine looked like he had aged years in a matter of days—his youthful, jumpy style of movement slowing into the tottering stride of a much older man. With Arthur ensconced in New York and Garfield bedbound, the Plumed Knight was now the most powerful man in Washington and closer than ever to practically being president. Yet (contrary to what enemies might assume) Blaine evidenced little pleasure in this arrangement. Anxiety for Garfield's well-being instead consumed the secretary. In between official duties, he became Arthur's primary source for goings-on in Washington, a regular caller at the presidential sickroom (Blaine's visiting privileges matched that of the president's family and doctors), and even a skeptic of Bliss's care.[75]

Friends worried Blaine was again taking on more duties than he could (or should) handle, but something about the president's treatment gnawed at the secretary. As his assistant would recall:

> Mr. Blaine, in the privacy of his home, declared that the surgeons were probing for the ball in the wrong direction. Having been himself exactly in the line of fire. . . . he insisted that the ball had passed his good ear and must consequently have entered the President's body at a different angle from what the doctors assumed in their diagnosis. With the aid of a dummy he demonstrated his opinion to the attendants. Perhaps it was unprofessional. . . .[76]

More universally unwelcome were the office-seekers—finally emerging in Washington again after spending a few weeks in embarrassed hiding. Their reappearance invited scorn from all corners. "The hungry army of office-seekers are reported to be again prowling around the White House, seeking the first opportunity to urge their 'claims,'" described the District's *Evening Star*. "Fellows of this sort should be promptly hustled over to the Insane asylum, or to the jail . . ."[77]

Indeed, elected Republicans and Democrats had begun to discuss getting rid of this class of men, in tones that finally boded well for meaningful bipartisan action on reform. "No one can altogether escape responsibility for the existing state of things," pronounced a Republican senator from New England. "It is upon us, and stares the most earnest and thoughtful statesmanship in the face . . . to inquire how it can be done away with."[78]

Another reformer calculated that the president's shooting had advanced the cause by ten years.[79]

The vice president, secluded in his four-story manor on Lexington Avenue, was determined to avoid as many further stares as possible. Only once had Chester Arthur left New York since Garfield's shooting. That trip (to the capital, on July 3) had been at every step an awkward affair. Repeatedly denied entry to the president's sickroom, Arthur settled for giving tearful condolences to a silent First Lady.[80]

His return to Manhattan coincided with reports detailing the scale to which the Americans were still not only blaming Stalwarts for the crime, but expressing a violent animosity toward him as the main beneficiary of it: men in Ohio threatened to march on Washington with guns to stop any possible inauguration of Arthur; a Department of War clerk drunkenly volunteered to shoot the vice president before it came to that; a New York prison inmate killed another with an ax over the very idea of an Arthur administration. Those not invoking (or provoking) bloodshed at the thought of Arthur in the White House gasped at it, including his friends. "'Chet' Arthur, President of the United States!" one reportedly exclaimed. "Good God!"[81]

Arthur appealed to the same power when given the chance. "God knows I do not want the place I was never elected to," he blurted to a dignitary. It was an unfortunate reminder that Arthur had never been elected to any place before the vice presidency, and that should Garfield slip away his successor would objectively be the least-qualified executive Americans had ever known. But many citizens did not presume Arthur would be actually running his own administration, anyhow. "Arthur nominally will be President; Conkling will be the real President," a banking executive predicted to one paper.[82]

Every morning that summer, the vice president could open the dailies to see black-and-white columns of print filled with such dismissals and damnations of him. He read them all with bloodshot eyes set in a face pale in distress—for Arthur, too, had no faith in his abilities should the worst transpire, and no desire to test them. The very thought of being president terrified him. Confidantes could barely get him to talk. No one had seen him in such a state since Nell died.[83]

What words Arthur did manage to get out expressed earnest wishes for Garfield's recovery. "If it were possible for me to be with the President," he told one reporter, "I would not only offer him my sympathy, I would ask that I might remain by his bedside." On dark-edged stationery, the vice president scrawled a prayer. "My heart is full of deep anxiety. May God in his infinite goodness bring us safely out of this great peril, and my faith is strong that He will." The good news still coming from Washington buoyed this hope. "As the President gets better I get better," Arthur assured another journalist.[84]

Fireworks saved from canceled Independence Day festivities at last lit up Brooklyn on the night of August 4 to honor the president's reported recovery. "The news from Washington regarding General Garfield's condition continues to be favorable," affirmed the city's *Daily Eagle* the following morning. An adjacent article wondered what business Garfield would prioritize on resuming his official duties.[85]

Yet the symptoms presenting within the White House told a rather different story. Pus now came from the president in a volume no longer measured by his doctors in drams but ounces. They plugged a drainage tube into Garfield to facilitate this flow (as one might tap a maple for sap) and insisted the torrent to be a favorable sign. "Profuse and laudable in character," read a report of the discharge on August 3.[86]

By mid-August, however, the declining condition of the president could not be denied any longer. His condition was plainly terrible. As pus continued pouring out of him, Garfield's diet switched to almost exclusively liquids (beef extract, wine, rum, milk, brandy, and lime water)—and even these he struggled to keep down. Dr. Bliss soon thought it better to feed the president via enema instead. Various recipes were then cycled through in attempts to solve for "annoying and offensive flatus" as Garfield's fever climbed.[87]

An even worse sign appeared on the evening of August 17. The president felt pain on the right side of his face, a little in front and below his ear. A closer look revealed his parotid gland had begun to swell. It fell and inflated, balloon-like, during the next few days, eventually becoming engorged enough to fill Garfield's mouth with mucus and require drainage. A slit was cut into the president's face without anesthetic; pus escaped; the patient endured a subsequent spritz of carbolic acid into the incision.[88]

More fluid kept seeping from the original wound, still striking the surgeons as "laudable in character." A piece of dead flesh fell out on August 19, which they exploited by pushing the drainage tube farther into the patient. The depth it reached betrayed a gruesome change that had occurred within the president's body. Back on the train station floor, a metal probe could not be forced more than a few inches past Garfield's wound; now, a month and a half later, a hose could be comfortably slid a whole foot into him. The bullet hole had become a cavity.[89]

Bliss and the medical team's attempt to optimistically describe this latest development met ridicule. "No ill wind ever blows to the President's doctors," sniped a Democrat. "When the tube will penetrate his wound only three or four inches, they are happy . . . that the wound is rapidly healing. When the tube will go in over a foot, they rejoice because it drains the wound better. . . ."[90]

But reality had, in fact, begun to reach the doctors. "A feeling of uneasiness prevailed today," one wrote on August 22.[91]

As the last weeks of summer ebbed away, the press corps asked cabinet secretaries if Garfield's doctors had been lying to the public this whole time. Citizens reverted to the habit of looking up forlornly at flagpoles—checking if any flew at half-mast. Those returning from vacations in the countryside reported a "widespread belief that the President is dying, or that the chances against his recovery are much stronger than those in favor." At least two women were institutionalized at the start of September, being judged "insane on the subject of the President's illness."[92]

Garfield tried his best to soothe another. He took up a pen to write a note to Eliza—still in Ohio, shielded from her son's decline by heartening press reports and encouraging telegraphs from her grandchildren. The president's letter, in weak handwriting, attempted to bolster the protective bubble holding around his mother:

Dear Mother,

Don't be disturbed by conflicting reports about my condition. It is true I am still weak . . . but I am gaining every day, and need only time and patience to bring me through.

Give my love to all the friends and relatives and especially sisters Hitty and Mary. Your loving son,

James A. Garfield[93]

Friends thought Eliza was coping with the strain better than any other Garfield (she was accustomed to tragedy, after all), but her spirit seemed to crumple by month's end. Folding and unfolding a handkerchief, she was heard uttering a prayer, "May the Lord help me to be resigned."[94]

Back in Washington, boils the size of peas bubbled on Garfield's back. Pus was also spotted leaking into his ear canal. "These were evidently due to the septic condition of the President's system," one of his doctors would write in hindsight.[95]

When Garfield dreamed, either awake or in fitful sleep, he imagined being home—a place far away now, beyond a confounding stretch of space and time. He was a toddler again in the Orange cabin with Eliza, Thomas, Hitty, and Mary; the taste of squirrel soup drifted under his nose; imaginary biscuits broke between his teeth. Then the soft, rich sod of the Western Reserve was giving way under his boots, and suddenly he was in Cleveland, greeting friends not seen in years.[96]

The president blinked and found himself back in the White House. He asked Bliss if it might be possible to move somewhere else. "If we can't go to Mentor, I want to go down the [Potomac] River." He was refused on account of his condition. "It's all right now," Garfield pled. "I want to get away."[97]

He repeated the request throughout the next few days even as his parotid gland resurged with infection and his fever soared. At one point the president became delusional—unable to say where nor who he was anymore. Perhaps, for a moment, Garfield was back at Lawnfield.[98]

Newspapers soon reported this "mental disturbance" had cleared, like fog carried off by the breeze. Bliss told a journalist that the president was sure to recover soon. The swollen parotid gland certainly did not merit concern. "It is doing very well . . . suppurating most satisfactor[il]y. That is a very good sign."[99]

The same pseudoscience Bliss and many of his brethren still preached convinced them to eventually permit the president's removal from Washington. Gas from marshes near the city was the suspected cause of seasonal malaria surges in its people—the same imperfect logic that had held when Garfield caught "the ague" on the Ohio Canal almost forty years prior. A bump in cases among White House staff in the summer of 1881 added urgency to the perceived threat. "It is said that since the President was shot no less than ten persons employed in the Executive Mansion have succumbed to malarious influences," reported a source in the District.[100]

Yet Mentor was too distant for the sick president to be moved safely, while a boat trip down the Potomac hardly offered a viable escape from contagious swamp fumes. The beachside at Elberon therefore seemed a sounder destination for Garfield's evacuation. Fond memories from his brief time on its shores remained with the president, as did an older affection the sea had long conjured in him. "I have always felt that the ocean was my friend," Garfield had written two weeks before being shot.[101]

On August 27, Rutherford Hayes awoke in Ohio to find the songbird that had regaled his family in the White House had passed away. "His death is unimportant of course," Hayes mused, "but one feels a foolish presentiment that the death of the bird presages that of President Garfield." He looked ahead, sadly and hesitantly, to what might transpire as a result. "The less Arthur has to do with Conkling the better for his Administration, if he is to form one."[102]

Arthur remained too terrified by the thought of his own presidency to even consider such questions. Garfield's decline had dragged the vice president's mood to new depths, and the man himself into deeper hiding. The avenue outside his Manhattan townhome had turned into a no-man's-land—journalists lined up on one side, Arthur entrenched behind curtains on the other, and every caller crossing the street being a joint figure of interest. Conkling's almost-daily visits drew particular notice. Reformists could only assume the worst.[103]

Unseen, however, another person—a complete stranger—had managed to reach the besieged Arthur via letter. Julia Sand was merely a citizen anxious to have her vice president know the true feeling of the nation for him. Unfortunately, it was not a positive one:

The hours of Garfield's life are numbered. . . . The people are bowed in grief; but—do you realize it?—not so much because he is dying, but because *you* are his successor. What President ever entered office under circumstances so sad! The day he was shot, the thought arose in a thousand minds that *you* might be the instigator of the foul act. Is not that a humiliation which cuts deeper than any bullet can pierce?

It is a wonder the vice president kept reading after this opener. But read on he did, to find Sand meant the best in writing so plainly:

Great emergencies awaken generous traits which have lain dormant half a life. If there is a spark of true nobility in you, now is the occasion to let it shine. Faith in your better nature forces me to write to you—but not to beg you to resign. Do what is more difficult and brave. Reform! It is not the proof of highest goodness never to have done wrong—but it is a proof of it, sometime in one's career, to pause and ponder, to recognize the evil, to turn resolutely against it and devote the remainder of one's life to that only which is pure and exalted. . . . Your name now is on the annals of history. You cannot slink back into obscurity if you would. A hundred years hence, school boys will recite your name in the list of Presidents. . . . And what shall posterity say? It is for you to choose whether your record shall be written in black or in gold. For the sake of your country, for your own sake and for the sakes of all who have ever loved you, let it be pure and bright.[104]

Arthur flipped the letter to read its return address before stashing the note for future reference.

A few nights later, as the last hours of August petered out, the vice president broke his seclusion by going out for a liberating sail on the dark expanse of New York Bay. He let the press know he had no plans to go to Washington, "until he was notified of the President's death or the absolute impossibility of his recovery." It was Arthur's way of announcing he had not abandoned hope.[105]

•   •   •

Washington broiled when Garfield left it for the last time, "the air seeming like a furnace" on the morning of September 5. The atmosphere in his train stayed cool and comfortable—the entire locomotive having been renovated to insulate its passenger from as much of the outside world as possible. A fifteen-inch-thick mattress balanced beneath the president on springy planks suspended over the floor. Large curtains hung around his bed to protect him against unwanted light, while the roof above had been hollowed to enable better circulation throughout the car.

The engine itself burned anthracite coal to minimize exhaust fumes, while wire netting placed over the train's windows stopped what smoke was produced from bothering the president.[106]

A signal car ran ahead to intercept other trains—thus hastening and quieting Garfield's trip. "No sound of bell or whistle was heard," reported a witness along the tracks. In fact, the most distinct noise heard between Washington and Elberon came from crying crowds of men and women at each passing station.[107]

The engine sheared north at up to seventy miles per hour. Bliss bent to ask the president if the vibrations thrumming through the car at this velocity hurt him at all. "He smiled and said, 'Let them go,' evidently meaning to quiet any anxiety I might feel," the doctor later reported. Garfield also declined the suggestion of stopping to bathe an hour before Elberon. "Let us reach the end of our journey first," he replied. "That is most important."[108]

"This is delightful," he said from a reclining chair angled above the Atlantic. Garfield was on the second-floor balcony of a cottage, his gaze fixed on a vista soothingly shaded in blues—the lapis of the ocean buttressing the softer pastels of the sky, a thin haze smudging them all together at the horizon. The president vastly preferred this perch to his bed, where nothing could distract him from a smothering tide of pus and mucus rising in his throat.[109]

His doctors appreciated the view, too. Together they all studied tiny silhouettes of boats that speckled the sea surface. The president made a game of considering each vessel's speed and direction, then guessing where it was heading.[110]

He asked if anything had been heard from his eldest sons. Hal and Jim had begun their college studies at Williams after spending the previous two months repeating (and apparently believing) rosy reports from their father's surgeons. A letter from Hal indeed reached Elberon, revealing to the president that his boys still expected to hear the best from him imminently:

> We are so thankful and happy to know that you are improving and that the change is really going to be a benefit.[111]

Other family members knew better by now. While Garfield's two youngest sons remained in a world of their own at Mentor, Crete and Mollie were at the president's bedside at Elberon, where they saw the direness of his situation firsthand.

The First Lady's vigil was particularly agonizing. Dr. Bliss asked her late one evening if she would not like to retire for bed to avoid the "danger of too great fatigue." She replied that standing in her husband's presence was, for her, a form of rest.[112]

The family's closest intimates were also in attendance. One night, Crete took aside Joseph Stanley Brown to ask, in confidence, "just what *you* think the chances are for the General's recovery?" The aide would long remember his ensuing failure of courage:

> One look in the anguished face of that wonderful woman and I threw truthfulness to the winds, and lied and lied as convincingly and consolingly as I could. As soon as decency permitted I excused myself, but once beyond the door all restraint gave way and I was an utterly shattered and broken secretary.[113]

Dr. Bliss continued issuing cheery platitudes from the sickroom discordant with both the mood in the cottage and reality. He said Garfield was sure to recover—the patient's "only unfavorable symptom" being minor lung congestion. There was "no abscess, no pus, no pyaemia."[114]

Bliss's remarks were provided to cabinet secretaries, who did not insult the public by pretending to believe them. "God knows his statements are misstatements of facts," Attorney General MacVeagh told a journalist.[115]

The president awoke on September 16 coughing up a river of "purulent material" and lung tissue, then spent much of the day hallucinating. As his mind wandered, telegrams shot down to marble department hallways in Washington, as well as north to a certain townhome on New York's Lexington Avenue. A train bearing cabinet members was soon speeding to Elberon.[116]

As the sun set the following night, Garfield found lucidity again and turned to an attendant. "Doctor, am I not critically ill?" he asked. Getting an affirmative nod, the president sighed. "I thought so."[117]

On September 18, he called over Almon Rockwell (an old army comrade) to answer something for him. Garfield looked up to ask, "Do you think my name will have a place in human history?" Rockwell balked before replying; this was the question of a man meditating on a finished life:

Yes, a grand one, but a grander one in human hearts. You must not talk in that way. You have a great work to perform.

Silence. Then came a reply not quite curt enough to hide its sadness: "No, my work is done." It was a decidedly uncharacteristic answer.[118]

At ten o'clock the next night, Garfield called out, "Oh, my!" to an almost empty room. Crete was missing for once, but the president spotted a friend. "Swaim, what a pain I have right here," Garfield complained, gesturing over his heart. The pulse within was immeasurable and Swaim called for help; Bliss rushed in to see the president's eyes roll as their owner faded into sleep. The doctor's words for Crete (the next person through the door) at last betrayed an awareness of his patient's situation. "Madame, he is dying."[119]

Mollie Garfield, other doctors, and further friends of the family entered but none said a word. A steady breathing from the president filled their ears. Several of those present would remember it for as long as they lived. It weakened during the next thirty minutes as Crete moved closer to her husband's side. She would not budge from this spot for hours.[120]

Outside, waves crashed rhythmically under an ink-black sky. Garfield's breath drifted in and out of tempo. When the end finally came, it did so gently enough that almost no one watching noticed.[121]

EPILOGUE

"Let us not burden our remembrance with a heaviness that's gone."

—Shakespeare's *The Tempest*, as quoted in

Garfield diary entry for January 9, 1878

Sunlight pierces the fleecy cloudbanks that encircle Cleveland on Memorial Day, 1890, pouring warmth and illumination over scenes of preparation throughout the city below. Flags snap above a three-mile stretch of Euclid Avenue; hundreds of thousands of people teem on its intersections, finding that prime viewing spots for the day's events had been occupied overnight. Uniformed troops straighten plumages that shimmer in scarlet and midnight, ocher and cotton gray. Trees in springtime bloom offer a green ceiling over the parade route ahead.[1]

A trumpet blast sends twenty-five thousand men marching at one o'clock. Veterans wheeze out old war songs on fifes, only for the notes to be lost in continual applause that carries unbroken for hours. Women rip flowers from bouquets to throw over the procession. Men on tiptoes glimpse the bobbing tips of bayonets. It takes almost two hours for the points to pass any given spot on the avenue.[2]

Their ultimate destination is visible from everywhere in Cleveland; a spire peeks up on the city's horizon, crowning an almost two-hundred-foot-tall structure built atop a hill in Lake View Cemetery. It had taken nine years and more than a hundred thousand dollars to be completed, and every marcher can see why once they begin reaching its base by mid-afternoon. Metal-studded oak doors and buttressed balconies lend the building a passing resemblance to a huge castle turret. But churchlike elements also draw the eye: stained-glass windows and neogothic arches; angel mosaics and terracotta reliefs.[3]

Spectators today are therefore right to describe this monument—the final resting place of a politician—with religious reverence. It is, one writes, "a beautiful memorial . . . erected to perpetuate the fame of the martyred President."[4]

The presiding officer of the afternoon's dedication ceremony is Rutherford Hayes, head of the Garfield Memorial Association. The former president is a characteristically uninspiring sight today: gray of beard, black of attire, wincingly sunburned of skin. But the applause Hayes receives upon standing is generous, his speech generously brief.[5]

The next president to speak to the assembly is the serving one, and mercifully Benjamin Harrison can stir real enthusiasm in an audience. No sooner does his inexpressive, ruddy face pop into view against the Garfield Memorial, then the masses cheer full-throatedly. The voting public marvels at Harrison's ability to stay "Sphinx-like" amid any popular excitement. His speech today delves appropriately deep, connecting the significance of the structure being unveiled with that of the man it venerates:

> This monument, so imposing and tasteful, fittingly typifies the grand and symmetrical character of him in whose honor it has been builded. His was the "arduous greatness of things done." No friendly hand constructed and placed for his ambition a ladder upon which he might climb. His own brave hands framed and nailed the cleats upon which he climbed to the heights of public usefulness and fame.[6]

Not long after Harrison finishes, the crowd begs another attendee to address them extempore. Congressman William McKinley hesitates until he can no longer rightfully resist the popular will. He rises to say, simply, that no one "since Washington, Lincoln, or Grant, has ever been closer to the hearts of the people than General Garfield." His remarks close the speaking portion of the service as well as an invisible loop: now Republican presidents past, present, and future have spoken in remembrance of one of their own.[7]

Another is missing, albeit for good cause: Chester Arthur had died of kidney disease shortly after serving the remainder of Garfield's term. His administration had gone surprisingly well, chiefly on account of its leader's single-minded fixation on getting people to like him. Washington's glitterati agreed the White House had never known a more gracious occupant. After a tasteful six-month mourning period for his predecessor, Arthur, with waves of his cane, had the executive mansion renovated with expensive Tiffany decor and ordered its doors thrown open for what seemed like an infinite cycle of social events. "There was no talk of Temperance," a historian has written. Dry old Rutherford Hayes could only despair from afar: "Nothing like it ever before in the Executive Mansion—liquor, snobbery, and worse."[8]

All those invited inside were charmed by the dapper bachelor holding court. "He was one of the most delightful of our Presidents . . . all who met him learned not only to respect but love him," a veteran reporter recalled. The affection grew after the press discovered "our good King Arthur" followed the daily ritual of putting fresh flowers before a mystery woman's portrait. Gossip swirled, then turned into tearful awe once it was learned the picture depicted his deceased wife, Nell. Mailed proposals of marriage had flooded in to the president from the nation's single womenfolk, but these Arthur let pile up.[9]

He preferred trying on clothes to doing work—reportedly, donning up to twenty pairs of pants before selecting one to wear. "President Arthur never did today what he could put off until tomorrow," an aide sighed. But whenever he did turn to political battles, he took care to pick a popular side. This course led Arthur to sign the Chinese Exclusion Act of 1882; it reached a crucible when the Civil Service Reform Act landed on his desk in early 1883.[10]

The lattermost act had sailed through Congress on a groundswell of bipartisan support, its clauses conjuring nightmares in the minds of bosses: the legislation called for federal civil service jobs to be awarded based on merit; a quarter of all offices to be given to top scorers on competitive exams, regardless of party; bureaucrats to be exempted from giving "time or money" to political campaigns; the bolstering of a permanent presidential commission to oversee the implementation of such rules.[11]

These items were a long-standing reformist wish list, but they had been lent new political strength by Arthur's murdered predecessor. The Reform Act's author (a Democrat) branded Garfield's killing a product of the spoils system and the inspiration for the new legislation; pro-reform posters lionizing Garfield as a casualty to machine politics plastered most every post office in the country; Democrats and Republicans in Congress who voted for the Act admitted the president's slaying "gave impulse" to its passage.[12]

In the interest of making Garfield a better martyr, reformist campaigners brushed over the real man's blemishes on their cause—his softness on specifics, his preference for meeting bosses halfway rather than antagonizing them. Henry Adams wrote out his revulsion:

> The cynical impudence with which the reformers have tried to manufacture an ideal statesman out of the late shady politician beats anything in novel-writing.

But most reformists (like their new idol) saw the importance of being pragmatic. As a historian of their cause has written, "Garfield dead proved more valuable . . . than Garfield alive."[13]

Arthur surprised many by not hesitating to sign the Reform Act into law. With a pen stroke, he dealt a lasting blow to the corrupt structures that enabled his own rise to power—one from which they would never recover. Old allies were left to grumble about treachery. "Arthur has deserted us," Platt lamented. "He has done less for us than Garfield, or even Hayes," exclaimed another Stalwart boss.[14]

Most aggrieved was Roscoe Conkling—the man many once assumed would be pulling this president's strings. Instead, he had been reduced to skulking the courthouses of Manhattan as a corporate attorney. His hair grayed, its trademark locks denaturing with age as its owner continued to boil with volcanic energy. "He . . . does not glow with love for the human race," an acquaintance judged. Much of the former senator's rage was focused on his onetime crony, now installed in the White House ("His Accidency," as Conkling preferred to call Arthur). The boss even slapped down a most generous olive branch from the president—a Supreme Court seat—citing only "reasons you would not fail to appreciate."[15]

Lord Roscoe would also go to his death defiantly. Refusing to be trapped overnight in his office during the great blizzard of 1888, he walked alone through a New York City throttled with ice. Conkling reached home only after striding through an eye-depth snowbank, thereby catching the sickness that many believed killed him. His passing marked the end of a grim (and grimly entertaining) era of American politics. "There would be other political bosses," a writer later opined, "but he was the last of a type."[16]

A warmer fate befell Arthur. The reformed spoilsman died in 1886 having won a place in the hearts of many who once hated him. "No man ever entered the Presidency so profoundly and widely distrusted, and no one ever retired . . . more generally respected," eulogized a journalist. Before passing on, Arthur had managed to visit Ms. Julia Sand's home to thank her for seeing the best in him when no one else would.[17]

Blaine is also missing from the consecration of the Garfield Memorial. He does not have as good an excuse as Arthur or Conkling, for the Plumed

Knight is alive (at least technically speaking). But he is dead politically, a fate that Blaine could blame only himself and his own irrepressible ambition for. In the previous decade, he had quit Arthur's cabinet, launched two further failed presidential campaigns, and barely managed to be made secretary of State again—only to find Harrison justifiably reluctant to trust him.[18]

Thus, Blaine's halcyon days had been at Garfield's side. He once reflected out loud on them to an assembled Congress, his closing words conjuring the setting of the president's last hours: a salt breeze blowing off the Atlantic; waves rolling pale under noonday sun; cherry-red clouds hanging low at dusk; the tranquility Garfield must surely have felt before it all. "Great in life," Blaine mused, "he was surpassingly great in death."[19]

The Garfield family is also unheard from during the Memorial's dedication, despite being in remarkably complete attendance: Crete ("her gray locks stirring in the breeze") and the president's children are seated in a pair of rows behind the speaker's podium; even Eliza is present, albeit only in the tower's burial crypt.[20]

But bright futures are now ahead of all the president's children. Hal and Jim share a law partnership and would each fill positions in great future administrations (those of Woodrow Wilson and Theodore Roosevelt, respectively). Mollie now goes by Mollie Stanley Brown, having married her father's former secretary. Irvin would soon graduate from Harvard Law School. Abram is set for a career behind an architect's desk, designing buildings that would be placed on the National Register of Historic Places.[21]

Crete, meanwhile, would spend the rest of her life only a few miles away, converting Lawnfield into a site perpetuating her husband's memory for the public. It is on its way to becoming, in practice, the first-ever Presidential Memorial Library.

•   •   •

Rain falls as the ceremony finishes. A fireworks show planned for the evening is canceled on account of sudden thunderstorms, but this does little to dull the moods of the celebrants. A feeling prevails that the day's bleak ending could not mar the happy events that preceded it. "As it is," a participant writes, ". . . the final scene has been played in the great drama that began fifty-eight years ago in a rude house on a half-cleared forest farm in the old Western Reserve."[22]

Almost two thousand miles away, in an arid Arizona valley, a humbler memorial bakes in the desert sun—a small, four-sided cairn alone against the elements. It had been built for free rather than with thousands of donated dollars; not from quarried marble, but stone scrounged from the surrounding hills; by a famous Black cavalry regiment (the "Buffalo Soldiers") instead of a council of white businessmen and politicians.

Each rock in this monument's surface bears the name of the rider who placed it. Some of their signatures loop elegantly, as if handwritten. Others are stamped in blocky type. Symbols of crossed sabers and chain-links further embellish the stonework. But the largest and centermost slab offers only the following to the empty scrubland beyond:

IN

MEMORY OF

JAS A.

GARFIELD

It is the only hint as to the mound's purpose. Any answers to further questions (like why this structure stands here, and why it places this president's name among those of these men) are lost once its builders leave the valley, never to be asked such things.

Winds wear its edges down; children scamper over its shelves; people steal bricks for use as doorstops; a new century arrives, and decades later a local couple tentatively take the surviving stones home. Thus, blow by blow, the work is reduced to fragments literal and figurative—the pieces scattered not only in a nearby fireplace, but across sepia-drenched photos and fleeting scraps of memory.

These are still enough to lend the original a form of immortality. One day they would be put together again, by Americans hoping to return life to an era, story, and people few once thought worth remembering.[23]

Acknowledgments

Two people who began this journey with me (who made it all possible) were sadly not able to witness its end. I owe immense debts of gratitude to Alice Mayhew and Mike Hoogland; they each heard an unusual book idea about an unusual American president from an unusual author, and with terrific respective courage decided to say yes. Then they were each called away. I hope somewhere, somehow, they know I'm grateful.

A pair of icons from the publishing world arrived on time to oversee this work's completion. To the first, Bob Bender, I am thankful for the best editing a biographer could hope for. Jane Dystel, on the other hand, was the worldly agent who kept everything running according to schedule—not letting a single detail slip notice, anchoring this writer to the real world. Furthermore, I am very grateful to Johanna Li, Kate Lapin, Adrian James, Joan Shapiro, and Phil Metcalf for helping shape this work into its final form.

I also express heartfelt thanks to the following people: Alison and Roger Rankin, for becoming the Cleveland family of one perpetually sleep-deprived, underdressed author; Janet Vogel, Terri Foy, and Chris Schmidt, for making a stranger feel at home at Hiram College; Dr. John Gaddis, for his patience as a reader and willingness to treat a guest (and their clothes) to beer in New Haven; Dr. Jerry Rushford, for his superhuman abundance of knowledge, character, and enthusiasm; Dr. Todd Arrington, for his great work—in the historical plane and the physical one—preserving the Garfield legacy; Kathleen Burger, for rousing emails sent every Sunday without fail; the congregation of the National City Christian Church, for giving a lapsed Catholic a taste of life as a Disciple of Christ; Peter and Lynne Morgan, for useful research material sent through the mail; Ann Sindelar, for expert assistance rendered at the Western Reserve Historical Society; Susan Bowditch, for sharing how Garfield is remembered by his descendants; Helen and Abram Garfield, for telling me how James Rudolph Garfield got the nickname "Bum"; Maureen Geck, for opening the Garfield birthplace cabin on behalf of an off-season visitor—and gifting him a commemorative plate that he still has on display; Patrick Davis, for guiding a tourist over and through forgotten battlefields in frigid east Kentucky; Stanley McChrystal, Robin West, Charlie Hill, Will Goodyear, Phil Kaplan, Ugonna Eze, and Haley Adams for their editorial comments.

I am also deeply in debt to Dr. Maury Klein, Dr. Richard Franklin Bensel, Dr. Greg Downs, Dr. Nicolas Parrillo, Dr. Michael Holt, Thompson Smith, Larry Daniel, and especially Dr. Adam Rowe for their help correcting errors of fact and judgment.

Dr. Allan Peskin is the monolith of modern Garfield scholarship, on whose work all current and future ones must be built.

Finally, I must express my heartfelt appreciation to Edmund Morris—for doing an embarrassingly starstruck young biographer the courtesy of telling him how hard this work would be.

Select Bibliography

This bibliography, for the sake of conciseness, lists only the research resources cited most frequently throughout this work. Full citations of all other relevant archival collections, books, journals, magazines, and newspapers are provided where necessary in the endnotes.

PAPERS AND ARCHIVAL COLLECTIONS

JAG—LC   James A. Garfield Papers, Library of Congress
LG—LC   Lucretia Garfield Papers, Library of Congress
JAG—HC   James A. Garfield Papers, Hiram College
SG—WRHS   Swaim–Garfield Letters, Western Reserve Historical Society
JAG—WRHS   James Garfield Collection, Western Reserve Historical Society

GOVERNMENT PUBLICATIONS

Congressional Globe.

Congressional Record.

Report of the Select Committee to Investigate the Alleged Credit Mobilier Bribery. Washington, D.C.: House of Representatives (42nd Congress, Session III, Report No. 77), February 18, 1873.

Ex Parte Milligan, U.S. Supreme Court; Transcript of Record with Supporting Pleadings. U.S. Supreme Court, 1866.

Investigation into the Causes of the Gold Panic. Washington, D.C.: House of Representatives (41st Congress, Session II, Report No. 31), March 1, 1870.

Proceedings of the Electoral Commission and of the Two Houses of Congress in Joint Meeting. Washington, D.C.: Government Printing Office, 1877.

Proceedings of the Republican National Convention. Chicago: The JNO. B. Jeffrey Printing and Publishing House, 1881.

Report of the Proceedings in the Case of the United States vs. Charles J. Guiteau (3 vols). Washington, D.C.: Government Printing Office, 1882.

The War of the Rebellion: A Compilation of the Official Records of the Union and Confederate Armies. Washington, D.C.: Government Printing Office, 1880.

BOOKS/THESES

Ackerman, Kenneth D. *Dark Horse: The Surprise Election and Political Murder of President James A. Garfield* (Falls Church, Virginia: Viral History Press, 2011).

———. *The Gold Ring: Jim Fisk, Jay Gould, and Black Friday, 1869* (New York: Carroll & Graf, 2005).

Adams, Charles F., and Henry Adams. *Chapters of Erie, and Other Essays* (Boston: James R. Osgood and Company, 1871).

Adams, Henry. *The Letters of Henry Adams (1858–1891)* (Cambridge, Massachusetts: The Riverside Press, 1930).

———. *The Education of Henry Adams: An Autobiography* (New York: Modern Library paperback edition, 1999).

Ames, Oakes. *Oakes Ames: A Memoir* (Cambridge, Massachusetts: Riverside Press, 1884).

Arrington, B. T. *The Last Lincoln Republican: The Presidential Election of 1880* (Lawrence, Kansas: University Press of Kansas, 2020).

Avery, Elroy. *A History of Cleveland and Its Environs: The Heart of New Connecticut* 3 vols. (Chicago and New York: The Lewis Publishing Company, 1918).

Balch, William Ralston, ed. *Garfield's Words: Suggestive Passages From The Public And Private Writings of James Abram Garfield* (Boston: Houghton, Mifflin and Company, 1881).

———. *The Life of James Abram Garfield* (Philadelphia: J. C. McCurdy & Co., 1881).

Beale, Harriet S. Blaine, ed. *Letters of Mrs. James G. Blaine* 2 vols. (New York: Duffield and Company, 1908).

Benedict, Michael Les. *A Compromise of Principle: Congressional Republicans and Reconstruction, 1863-1869*, 1st ed. (New York: Norton, 1974).

Benjamin, Samuel Greene Wheeler. *The Life and Adventures of a Free Lance* (Burlington, Vermont: Free Press Company, 1914).

Bensel, Richard Franklin. *Yankee Leviathan: The Origins of Central State Authority in America, 1859-1877* (Cambridge, England; New York: Cambridge University Press, 1990).

Bernstein, Peter L. *Wedding of the Waters: The Erie Canal and the Making of a Great Nation* (paperback ed.) (New York: Norton, 2006).

Bierce, Ambrose. *The Collected Works of Ambrose Bierce* 12 vols. (New York: The Neale Publishing Company, 1909).

Blaine, James. *Eulogy on the Late President Garfield* (Philadelphia: Hubbard Brothers, 1882).

———. *Twenty Years Of Congress: From Lincoln to Garfield* 2 vols. (Norwich, Connecticut: The Henry Bill Publishing Company, 1886).

Blight, David W. *Frederick Douglass: Prophet of Freedom*, first Simon & Schuster hardcover edition (New York: Simon & Schuster, 2018).

Blumenthal, Sidney. *All The Powers of the Earth* (New York: Simon & Schuster, 2019).

Bond, Otto, ed. *Under the Flag of the Nation: Diaries and Letters of a Yankee Volunteer in the Civil War* (Columbus, Ohio State University Press, 1961).

Booraem, Hendrik. *The Road to Respectability: James A. Garfield and His World, 1844-1852*, A Western Reserve Historical Society Publication (Lewisburg, Pennsylvania: Bucknell University Press, 1988).

Boutwell, George S. *Reminiscences of Sixty Years in Public Affairs* 2 vols. (New York: Mc-Clure, Phillips & Co., 1902).

Bradford, Gamaliel. *American Portraits, 1875–1900* (New York: Houghton Mifflin Company, 1923).

Brands, H. W. *American Colossus: The Triumph of Capitalism, 1865–1900* (New York: Anchor Books, 2011).

———. *The Zealot and the Emancipator: John Brown, Abraham Lincoln and the Struggle for American Freedom,* first edition (New York: Doubleday, 2020).

Brisbin, James S. *The Early Life and Public Career of James A. Garfield,* edited by Paul Rich (Westphalia Press, 2013).

Brodie, Fawn M. *Thaddeus Stevens: Scourge of the South* (New York: The Norton Library, 1966).

Brooks, Noah, and Herbert Mitgang. *Washington, D.C., in Lincoln's Time* (Athens: University of Georgia Press, 1989).

Brown, David S. *The Last American Aristocrat: The Brilliant Life and Improbable Education of Henry Adams* (New York: Scribner, 2020).

Bundy, J. M. *The Life of James A. Garfield* (New York: A.S. Barnes & Co., 1881).

Burrows, Edwin G., and Mike Wallace. *Gotham: A History of New York City to 1898,* first issued as paperback (New York: Oxford University Press, 2000).

Caldwell, Robert. *James A. Garfield: Party Chieftain* (Hamden, Connecticut: Archon Books, 1965).

Carpenter, C. S., ed. *James A. Garfield: His Speeches at Home* (C.S. Carpenter, 1880).

Chernow, Ron. *Grant* (New York: Penguin Press, 2017).

———. *The House of Morgan: An American Banking Dynasty and the Rise of Modern Finance* (New York: Atlantic Monthly Press, 1990).

———. *Titan: The Life of John D. Rockefeller, Sr.* (New York: Random House, 1998).

Clancy, Herbert. *The Presidential Election of 1880* (Chicago: Loyola University Press, 1958).

Clayton, Mary Black. *Reminiscences of Jeremiah Sullivan Black* (St. Louis, Missouri: Christian Publishing Company, 1887).

Clemenceau, Georges. *American Reconstruction: 1865–1870* (New York: Da Capo Press, 1969).

Cohen, Jared. *Accidental Presidents: Eight Men Who Changed America* (New York: Simon & Schuster, 2019).

Cohen, Max. *Garfield Souvenirs and "Gems" of Press and Pulpit* (Washington, D.C.: 1881).

Coleman, Charles H. *The Election of 1868: The Democratic Effort to Regain Control* (New York: Octagon Books, 1971).

Conkling, Alfred. *The Life and Letters of Roscoe Conkling: Orator, Statesman, Advocate* (New York: Charles L. Webster & Company, 1889).

Cornog, Evan. *The Birth of Empire: DeWitt Clinton and the American Experience, 1769–1828* (New York: Oxford University Press, 1998).

Cortissoz, Royal. *The Life of Whitelaw Reid* 2 vols. (London: Thornton Butterworth Limited, 1921).

Cox, Jacob Dolson. *Military Reminiscences of the Civil War* 2 vols. (New York: Charles Scribner's Sons, 1900).

Cox, Samuel S. *Three Decades of Federal Legislation, 1855 to 1885* (Occidental Publishing Co., 1885).

Cronon, William. *Nature's Metropolis: Chicago and the Great West* (New York: Norton, 1992).

Crook, William H. *Through Five Administrations*, ed. Margarita Spalding Gerry (New York: Harper & Brothers, 1910).

Crowe-Carraco, Carol. *The Big Sandy*, paperback edition (Lexington: The University Press of Kentucky, 2009).

Dana, Charles. *Recollections of the Civil War: With the Leaders at Washington and in the Field in the Sixties* (New York: D. Appleton and Company, 1909).

Daniel, Larry J. *Days of Glory: The Army of the Cumberland, 1861–1865*, paperback edition (Baton Rouge: Louisiana State University Press, 2006).

Doenecke, Justus D. *The Presidencies of James A. Garfield & Chester A. Arthur* (Lawrence: Regents Press of Kansas, 1981).

Donald, David Herbert. *Lincoln,* first edition (New York: Touchstone, 1996).

Douglass, Frederick. *Life and Times of Frederick Douglass* (Boston: DeWolfe, Fiske, & Co., Publishers, 1892).

Downs, Gregory P. *After Appomattox: Military Occupation and the Ends of War* (Cambridge, Massachusetts: Harvard University Press, 2015).

Du Bois, William E. B. *Black Reconstruction in America: 1860–1880* first edition (New York: The Free Press, 1998).

Eaton, Clement. *A History of the Southern Confederacy* paperback edition (New York: First Free Press, 1965).

Ely, William. *The Big Sandy Valley* (Catlettsburg, Kentucky: Central Methodist, 1887).

Emerson, Jason. *Giant in the Shadows: The Life of Robert T. Lincoln* (Carbondale: Southern Illinois University Press, 2012).

Feis, Ruth Stanley-Brown. *Mollie Garfield in the White House* (New York: Rand McNally & Company, 1963).

Fish, Carl Russell. *The Civil Service and The Patronage* (Longmans, Green, and Co., 1905).

Flick, Alexander. *Samuel Jones Tilden: A Study in Political Sagacity* (Westport, Connecticut: Greenwood Press, 1939).

Foner, Eric. *Reconstruction: America's Unfinished Revolution, 1863–1877* first edition (New York: Harper & Row, 1988).

———. *The Second Founding: How the Civil War and Reconstruction Remade the Constitution* first edition (New York: W.W. Norton & Company, 2019).

Foster, Douglas A. *A Life of Alexander Campbell* (Grand Rapids, Michigan: William B. Eerdmans Publishing Company, 2020).

Fuller, Corydon. *Reminiscences of James A. Garfield, with Notes Preliminary and Collateral* (Cincinnati: Standard Publishing Co., 1887).

Garfield, James. *Life and Character of Almeda A. Booth* (Washington, D.C.: Henry L. Rose, 1877).

———. *The Diary of James A. Garfield*, edited by Frederick Williams and Harry Brown, 4 vols. (1967).

———. *The Works of James A. Garfield*, edited by Burke Hinsdale, 2 vols. (Boston: James R. Osgood and Company, 1882).

Garfield, James, and Lucretia Garfield. *Crete and James*, edited by John Shaw (East Lansing: Michigan State University Press, 1994).

Grant, Ulysses S. *Personal Memoirs of U.S. Grant* (New York: Barnes & Noble Books, 2003).

Gray, Charlotte. *Alexander Graham Bell: The Reluctant Genius and His Passion for Invention* (New York: Arcade Publishing, 2021).

Green, Constance McLaughlin. *Washington: A History of the Capital, 1800–1950* (Princeton Univ. Press, 1976).

Green, Francis Marion. *A Royal Life, or the Eventful History of James A. Garfield: Twentieth President of the United States* (Chicago: Central Book Concern, 1882).

———. *Hiram College and Western Reserve Eclectic Institute—Fifty Years of History, 1850–1900* (Cleveland: The O.S. Hubbell Printing Company, 1901).

Hancock, Almira Russell. *Reminiscences of Winfield Scott Hancock* (New York: C.L. Webster & Company, 1887).

Hayden, A. S. *Early History of the Disciples in the Western Reserve, Ohio; with Biographical Sketches of the Principal Agents in Their Religious Movement* (Cincinnati: Chase & Hall Publishers, 1875).

Hayes, H. G., and C. J. Hayes. *A Complete History of the Life and Trial of Charles Julius Guiteau* (Hubbard Brothers, 1882).

Hazen, William. *A Narrative of Military Service* (Boston: Ticknor and Company, 1885).

Henry, Frederick A. *Captain Henry of Geauga: A Family Chronicle* (Cleveland: The Gates Press, 1942).

Hinman, Wilbur F. *The Story of the Sherman Brigade* (Alliance, Ohio: Daily Review, 1897).

Hinsdale, Burke. *President Garfield and Education* (Boston: James R. Osgood and Company, 1882).

———. *The Republican Text-Book for the Campaign of 1880* (New York: D. Appleton and Company, 1880).

Hirshon, Stanley. *Farewell to the Bloody Shirt: Northern Republicans and the Southern Negro* paperback (Quadrangle Books, Inc., 1968).

Hoar, George. *Autobiography of Seventy Years*, 2 volumes (New York: Charles Scribner's Sons, 1903).

Hollister, Ovando James. *Life of Schuyler Colfax* (New York: Funk & Wagnalls, 1886).

Holt, Michael F. *By One Vote: The Disputed Presidential Election of 1876* (Lawrence: University Press of Kansas, 2008).

———. *The Rise and Fall of the American Whig Party: Jacksonian Politics and the Onset of the Civil War* (New York: Oxford University Press, 1999).

Hoogenboom, Ari. *Outlawing the Spoils: A History of the Civil Service Reform Movement, 1865–1883* (Urbana: University of Illinois Press, 1961).

———. *Rutherford B. Hayes: Warrior & President* (Lawrence: University Press of Kansas, 1995).

Howe, Daniel Walker. *What Hath God Wrought: The Transformation of America, 1815–1848*; *The Oxford History of the United States*, David M. Kennedy, general ed.; volume 5 (New York: Oxford University Press, 2009).

Hudson, William C. *Random Recollections of an Old Political Reporter* (New York: Cupples and Leon Company, 1911).

Ingalls, John. *A Collection of the Writings of John James Ingalls: Essays, Addresses, and Orations* (Hudson Kimberly Publishing Co., 1902).

Jordan, David M. *Roscoe Conkling of New York: Voice in the Senate* (Ithaca, NY: Cornell University Press, 1971).

Julian, George. *The Life of Joshua R. Giddings* (Chicago: A.C. McClurg and Company, 1892).

Klein, Maury. *The Life and Legend of Jay Gould* (Baltimore: Johns Hopkins University Press, 1986).

———. *Union Pacific: Birth of a Railroad, 1862–1893*, first ed. (Garden City, New York: Doubleday, 1987).

Koontz, Hilda E., and Peter M. Morgan. *Miracles in the Cathedral: A History of the National City Christian Church* (National City Christian Church, 2005).

Lamers, William M. *The Edge of Glory: A Biography of General William S. Rosecrans, U.S.A.* paperback edition (Baton Rouge: Louisiana State University Press, 1999).

Leech, Margaret. *The Garfield Orbit*, edited by Harry Brown (New York: Harper & Row, Publishers, 1978).

Logan, Rayford Whittingham. *The Betrayal of the Negro, from Rutherford B. Hayes to Woodrow Wilson* (New York: Da Capo Press, 1997).

Mason, F. H. *The Forty-Second Ohio Infantry: A History of the Organization and Services of That Regiment in the War of the Rebellion; with Biographical Sketches of Its Field Officers and a Full Roster of the Regiment* (Chicago: Andrews & Co., 1876).

Mathews, Alfred. *Ohio And Her Western Reserve: With A Story of Three States* (New York: D. Appleton and Company, 1902).

McClure, Alexander. *Recollections of Half a Century* (Salem, Massachussetts: The Salem Press Company, 1902).

McCulloch, Hugh. *Men and Measures of Half a Century: Sketches and Comments* (New York: Charles Scribner's Sons, 1889).

McCullough, David G. *The Pioneers: The Heroic Story of the Settlers Who Brought the American Ideal West* (New York: Simon & Schuster, 2019).

McElroy, Robert. *Levi Parsons Morton: Banker, Diplomat, and Statesman* (New York, London: G.P. Putnam's Sons, 1930).

McPherson, James M. *Battle Cry of Freedom: The Civil War Era*, volume 6 of *The Oxford History of the United States*, David M. Kennedy, general editor. (Oxford: Oxford University Press, 2003).

Middlekauff, Robert. *The Glorious Cause: The American Revolution, 1763–1789*, revised and expanded edition of *The Oxford History of the United States*, C. Vann Woodward, general ed., volume 3 (Oxford: Oxford University Press, 2007).

Millard, Candice. *Destiny of the Republic: A Tale of Madness, Medicine and the Murder of a President* (New York: Anchor Books, 2012).

Mills, William Stowell. *The Story of the Western Reserve of Connecticut* (New York: Brown & Wilson Press, 1900).

Mitchell, Robert B. *Congress and the King of Frauds: Corruption and the Credit Mobilier Scandal at the Dawn of the Gilded Age*, first edition (Roseville, Minnesota: Edinborough Press, 2018).

Morgan, H. Wayne. *From Hayes to McKinley: National Party Politics, 1877–1896* (Syracuse University Press, 1969).

Morris, Edmund. *Edison*, first edition (New York: Random House, 2019).

———. *The Rise of Theodore Roosevelt*, Modern Library paperback edition (New York: Modern Library, 2010).

———. *Theodore Rex*, paperback edition (New York: The Modern Library, 2010).

Morris, Roy. *Fraud of the Century: Rutherford B. Hayes, Samuel Tilden, and the Stolen Election of 1876* (New York: Simon & Schuster, 2004).

Muzzey, David Saville. *James G. Blaine: A Political Idol of Other Days* (Kennikat Press, 1963).

Nasaw, David. *Andrew Carnegie* (London: Penguin, 2007).

Nevins, Allan. *The Emergence of Modern America, 1865–1878* (New York: The Macmillan Company, 1927).

Niven, John. *Salmon P. Chase: A Biography* (New York, Oxford: Oxford University Press, 1995).

Parrillo, Nicholas R. *Against the Profit Motive: The Salary Revolution in American Government, 1780–1940* (New Haven, Connecticut: Yale University Press, 2013).

Peskin, Allan. *Garfield* (Kent, Ohio: Kent State University Press, 1999).

Platt, Thomas Collier. *The Autobiography of Thomas Collier Platt*, edited by Louis Lang (New York: B.W. Dodge & Company, 1910).

Polakoff, Keith Ian. *The Politics of Inertia: The Election of 1876 and the End of Reconstruction* (Baton Rouge: Louisiana State University Press, 1973).

Poore, Ben Perley. *Perley's Reminiscences of Sixty Years in the National Metropolis*, 2 volumes (Philadelphia: Hubbard Brothers, 1886).

Prokopowicz, Gerald J. *All for the Regiment: The Army of the Ohio, 1861–1862* (Chapel Hill: University of North Carolina Press, 2001).

Reeves, Thomas C. *Gentleman Boss: The Life of Chester Alan Arthur* (Newtown, Connecticut: American Political Biography Press, 2019).

Rehnquist, William H. *Centennial Crisis: The Disputed Election of 1876* (New York: Vintage Books, 2005).

Reid, Whitelaw. *After the War: A Southern Tour* (Cincinnati, Ohio: Moore, Wilstach & Baldwin, 1866).

———. *Ohio In the War: Her Statesmen, Generals, and Soldiers* 2 volumes (Columbus, Ohio: Eclectic Publishing Company, 1868).

Remini, Robert Vincent. *The House: The History of the House of Representatives* (New York: Smithsonian Books, in association with HarperCollins, 2006).

Reyburn, Robert. *Clinical History of the Case of President James Abram Garfield* (Chicago: American Medical Association, 1894).

Rice, Harvey. *Pioneers of the Western Reserve* (Boston: Lee and Shepard, 1883).

Riddle, Albert Gallatin. *Recollections of War Times: Reminiscences of Men and Events in Washington, 1860–1865* (New York: G.P. Putnam's Sons, 1895).

Ridpath, John Clark. *The Life and Work of James A. Garfield* (Jones Brothers & Company, 1881).

Ronan, Peter. *Historical Sketch of the Flathead Indian Nation* (Helena, Montana: Journal Publishing Co., 1890).

Rushford, Jerry. "Political Disciple: The Relationship between James A. Garfield and the Disciples of Christ," *Churches of Christ Heritage Center* (1977).

Rutkow, Ira M. *James A. Garfield*, first edition (New York: Times Books, 2006).

Sandburg, Carl. *Abraham Lincoln: The Prairie Years*, Sangamon Edition, two volumes (New York: Charles Scribner's Sons, 1926).

———. *Abraham Lincoln: The War Years*, Sangamon Edition, four volumes (New York: Charles Scribner's Sons, 1939).

Schmiel, Eugene D. *Citizen-General: Jacob Dolson Cox and the Civil War Era* (Athens: Ohio University Press, 2014).

Schurz, Carl, Frederic Bancroft, and William Dunning. *The Reminiscences of Carl Schurz*, three volumes (New York: The McClure Company, 1908).

Seale, William. *The President's House: A History*, second edition, two volumes (Baltimore, Washington, D.C.: Johns Hopkins University Press, in association with White House Historical Association, 2008).

Sherman, John. *Recollections of Forty Years in the House, Senate and Cabinet*, two volumes (Akron, Ohio: The Werner Company, 1895).

Sherman, Thomas H. *Twenty Years with James G. Blaine: Reminiscences by His Private Secretary* (New York: The Grafton Press, 1928).

Shields-West, Eileen. *The World Almanac of Presidential Campaigns* (New York: World Almanac, 1992).

Smith, Theodore Clark. *The Life and Letters of James Abram Garfield*, two volumes (New Haven, Connecticut: Yale University Press, 1925).

Stahr, Walter. *Seward: Lincoln's Indispensable Man*, first hardcover edition (New York: Simon & Schuster, 2012).

———. *Stanton: Lincoln's War Secretary* (New York: Simon & Schuster, 2017).

Stanley, D. S. *Personal Memoirs of Major-General D. S. Stanley, U.S.A.* (Cambridge, Massachusetts: Harvard University Press, 1917).

Stiles, T. J. *The First Tycoon: The Epic Life of Cornelius Vanderbilt*, first edition, [Nachdr.] (New York: Vintage Books, 2010).

Swanberg, W. A. *Jim Fisk: The Career of an Improbable Rascal* (New York: Charles Scribner's Sons, 1959).

———. *Sickles the Incredible* (Gettysburg, Pennsylvania: Stan Clark Military Books, 1991).

Taliaferro, John. *All the Great Prizes: The Life of John Hay, from Lincoln to Roosevelt*, first hardcover edition (New York: Simon & Schuster, 2013).

Taylor, George Rogers. *The Transportation Revolution, 1815–1860* (White Plains, New York: M.E. Sharpe, 1951).

Trefousse, Hans L. *The Radical Republicans: Lincoln's Vanguard for Racial Justice*, Louisiana Paperbacks, L-71 (Baton Rouge: Louisiana State University Press, 1975).

———. *Andrew Johnson: A Biography*, Reissued (New York: Norton, 1997).

Trelease, Allen W. *White Terror: The Ku Klux Klan Conspiracy and Southern Reconstruction*, paperback edition (Baton Rouge: Louisiana State University Press, 1995).

Tucker, Glenn. *Chickamauga: Bloody Battle in the West* (New York: Smithmark Publishers, 1994).

Tucker, William Edward, and Lester G. McAllister. *Journey in Faith: A History of the Christian Church (Disciples of Christ)* (Saint Louis: CBP Press, 1989).

Upton, Harriet Taylor. *History of the Western Reserve*, three volumes (The Lewis Publishing Company, 1910).

Vermilya, Daniel. *James Garfield and the Civil War* (Charleston, South Carolina: The History Press, 2015).

White, Andrew Dickson. *Autobiography of Andrew Dickson White*, two volumes (New York: The Century Company, 1905).

White, Richard. *Railroaded: The Transcontinentals and the Making of Modern America*, first edition (New York: W.W. Norton & Co, 2011).

———. *The Republic for Which It Stands: The United States during Reconstruction and the Gilded Age, 1865–1896*, the Oxford History of the United States (New York: Oxford University Press, 2017).

White, Ronald C. *American Ulysses: A Life of Ulysses S. Grant*, first edition (New York: Random House, 2016).

Wiley, Bell Irvin. *The Life of Johnny Reb: The Common Soldier of the Confederacy*, updated edition (Baton Rouge: Louisiana State University Press, 2017).

Williams, Charles Richard, ed. *Diary and Letters of Rutherford Birchard Hayes: Nineteenth President of the United States*, four volumes (Columbus: The Ohio State Archaeological and Historical Society, 1925).

Williams, Frederick, ed. *The Wild Life of the Army: Civil War Letters of James A. Garfield* (East Lansing: Michigan State University Press, 1964).

Woods, Terry K. *Ohio's Grand Canal: A Brief History of the Ohio & Erie Canal* (Kent, Ohio: Kent State University Press, 2008).

Woodward, C. Vann. *Reunion and Reaction: The Compromise of 1877 and the End of Reconstruction* (New York, Oxford: Oxford University Press, 1991).

Work, David. *Lincoln's Political Generals* (Urbana: University of Illinois Press, 2009).

MAGAZINES, JOURNALS

The Atlantic Monthly; The Century Magazine; Cosmopolitan; Harper's Weekly; The Nation; The North American Review; Puck.

NEWSPAPERS

The Anti-Slavery Bugle; Ashtabula Weekly Telegraph; The Baltimore Sun; The Boston Globe; The Brooklyn Union; Chicago Tribune; The Cincinnati Enquirer; Cincinnati Gazette; Cleveland Daily Leader; Cleveland Plain Dealer; The Daily Cleveland Herald; The Daily Ohio Statesman; Detroit Free Press; Evening Star; Inter Ocean; New York Herald; The New York Times; The New York Sun; New-York Tribune; Portage County Democrat; Portage Sentinel; The Star Tribune; The Summit County Beacon; Western Reserve Chronicle.

Notes

PROLOGUE

1. "The Weather," *Chicago Tribune*, June 10, 1880; "The Tribune's Boom," *Chicago Tribune*, June 9, 1880; "Garfield En Route For Home," *New-York Tribune*, June 10, 1880; "After the Nominations," *The New York Times*, June 9, 1880.

2. "Garfield En Route For Home," *New-York Tribune*, June 10, 1880; "Gen Garfield's Departure," *Inter Ocean*, June 10, 1880.

3. "Phrenological Character of James A. Garfield," May 14, 1864, JAG—LC; "General Garfield's Departure," *Inter Ocean*, June 10, 1880.

4. "General Garfield's Departure," *Inter Ocean*, June 10, 1880; "Garfield En Route for Home," *New-York Tribune*, June 10, 1890; "The Levee," *Chicago Tribune*, June 9, 1880.

5. "Homeward Bound," *Chicago Tribune*, June 10, 1880; "How It Was Done," *Inter Ocean*, June 9, 1880.

6. "Sequels to the Convention," *New-York Tribune*, June 10, 1880.

7. "The Man," *Chicago Tribune*, June 9, 1880; "Lives of the Candidates," *The New York Times*, June 9, 1880; "The Man," *Chicago Tribune*, June 9, 1880.

8. "Clipping," *Chicago Tribune*, June 9, 1880; "The Republican Nominees," *Manhattan Enterprise*, June 18, 1880.

9. James Garfield to Burke Hinsdale, February 17, 1861, JAG—LC; "Confiscation of Rebel Property," January 28, 1864; James Garfield, *The Works of James A. Garfield*, ed. Burke Hinsdale, vol. 1, 1882; "Lives of the Candidates," *The New York Times*, June 9, 1880.

10. James Garfield, "The National Bureau of Education: Speech Delivered in the House of Representatives," June 8, 1866.

11. Blaine, James. *Eulogy on the Late President Garfield* (Philadelphia: Hubbard Brothers, 1882), pages 23–24.

12. James Blaine to James Garfield, January 13, 1878, JAG—LC; James Garfield to Halsey Hall, July 1876, JAG—LC; Andrew Dickson White. *Autobiography of*

Andrew Dickson White, volume 1 (New York: The Century Company, 1905), page 187.

13. James Garfield to Whitelaw Reid, September 2, 1880, JAG—LC; A handy list of Garfield's legal cases can be found in JAG—LC; "A Century in Congress," *The Atlantic Monthly*, April 1877; "The Currency Conflict," *The Atlantic Monthly*, February 1876; James Garfield et al., "Ought the Negro to Be Disfranchised? Ought He to Have Been Enfranchised?" *The North American Review*, March 1879.

14. "Pons Asinorum," *The New England Journal of Education*, volume 3, no. 14, April 1, 1876, page 161.

15. "An Expert Opinion," *The New York Sun*, June 9, 1880; "Garfield and the Fraud of '76," *The New York Sun*, June 10, 1880.

16. "A Democratic View of Garfield," *New-York Tribune*, June 11, 1880; "From A Democratic Point of View," *New-York Tribune*, July 5, 1881.

17. John Ingalls. *A Collection of the Writings of John James Ingalls: Essays, Addresses, and Orations* (Hudson Kimberly Publishing Co., 1902), page 401.

18. Ari Hoogenboom. *Rutherford B. Hayes: Warrior & President* (Lawrence: University Press of Kansas, 1995), page 431.

19. "Next President," *Inter Ocean*, June 10, 1880; "Gath on Garfield," *The Cincinnati Enquirer*, June 10, 1880; William H. Crook. *Through Five Administrations*, ed. Margarita Spalding Gerry (New York: Harper & Brothers, 1910), page 257; Ingalls, John James. *A Collection of the Writings of John James Ingalls: Essays, Addresses, and Orations* (Kansas City, Missouri: Hudson-Kimberly Publishing Co., 1902), page 398.

20. "Homeward Bound," *Chicago Tribune*, June 10, 1880; Allan Peskin. *Garfield* (Kent, Ohio: Kent State University Press, 1978), page 143.

21. "Garfield En Route for Home," *New-York Tribune*, June 10, 1880; "Next President," *Inter Ocean*, June 10, 1880; "Homeward Bound," *Chicago Tribune*, June 10, 1880.

22. "What They Say," *Cincinnati Enquirer*, June 10, 1880; "Ethan Allen on Garfield's Strength," *New-York Tribune*, June 10, 1880.

23. James Blaine. *Twenty Years Of Congress: From Lincoln to Garfield.*, vol. 2 (Norwich, Connecticut: The Henry Bill Publishing Company, 1886), pages 674–675; Richard White. *The Republic for Which It Stands: The United States during Reconstruction and the Gilded Age, 1865-1896*, The Oxford History of the United States (New York: Oxford University Press, 2017), pages 219–220; Allan Nevins. *The Emergence of Modern America, 1865–1878* (New York: The Macmillan Company, 1927), page 31.

24. Frederick Douglass. *Life and Times of Frederick Douglass* (Boston: DeWolfe, Fiske, & Co., Publishers, 1892), page 611.

25. Nevins, *The Emergence of Modern America, 1865–1878*, page 385.

26. Richard White, *The Republic for Which It Stands*, page 333; James Blaine to James Garfield, March 4, 1881, JAG—LC.

27. H. Wayne Morgan. *From Hayes to McKinley: National Party Politics, 1877–1896* (Syracuse University Press, 1969), page 69; Ari Hoogenboom. *Outlawing the Spoils: A History of the Civil Service Reform Movement, 1865–1883* (Urbana: University of

Illinois Press, 1961), page 107; Henry Adams. *The Letters of Henry Adams (1858–1891)* (Cambridge, Massachusetts: The Riverside Press, 1930), page 319.

28. Samuel Clemens and Charles Dudley Warner. *The Gilded Age: A Tale of To-Day* (Hartford, Connecticut: American Publishing Company, 1874).

29. "Homeward Bound," *Chicago Tribune*, June 11, 1880.

30. Francis Marion Green. *Hiram College and Western Reserve Eclectic Institute—Fifty Years of History, 1850–1900* (Cleveland, Ohio: The O.S. Hubbell Printing Company, 1901), page 163; Diary entry for February 5, 1879, JAG—LC.

31. James Garfield to Jacob Dolson Cox, July 20, 1877, JAG—LC; James Garfield to Burke Hinsdale, September 10, 1877, JAG—LC; James Garfield to Charles Whittlesey, September 14, 1874. JAG—WRHS.

32. Thomas Collier Platt. *The Autobiography of Thomas Collier Platt*, ed. Louis Lang (New York: B.W. Dodge & Company, 1910), page 125; John Sherman. *Recollections of Forty Years in the House, Senate and Cabinet.*, vol. 2 (The Werner Company, 1895), page 807; Ruth Stanley-Brown Feis. *Mollie Garfield in the White House* (Rand McNally & Company, 1963), page 29; "From A Democratic Point of View," *New-York Tribune*, July 5, 1881.

33. Frederick Douglass. *Life and Times of Frederick Douglass*, pages 633–634; Ron Chernow. *Grant* (New York: Penguin Press, 2017), page 909; H. Wayne Morgan, *From Hayes to McKinley: National Party Politics, 1877–1896*, page 86; Carl Schurz. *The Reminiscences of Carl Schurz* volume 3 (New York: The McClure Company, 1908), page 395; David M. Jordan. *Roscoe Conkling of New York: Voice in the Senate* (New York: Cornell University Press, 1971), page 348.

34. H. Wayne Morgan. *From Hayes to McKinley: National Party Politics, 1877–1896*, page 86; James Garfield to Burke Hinsdale, September 10, 1877, JAG—LC.

35. H. Wayne Morgan. *From Hayes to McKinley: National Party Politics, 1877–1896*, page 86; Richard White, *Autobiography of Andrew Dickson White*, volume 1, page 188.

36. "Gath on Garfield," *Cincinnati Enquirer*, June 10, 1880.

37. "Next President," *Inter Ocean*, June 10, 1880; "Homeward Bound," *Chicago Tribune*, June 10, 1880.

38. James Garfield to Corydon and Mary Fuller, January 5, 1856, JAG—LC; "General Garfield in Cleveland," *New-York Tribune*, June 11, 1880.

39. "Garfield At Hiram," *Chicago Tribune*, June 11, 1880.

40. "Garfield at Hiram," *Chicago Tribune*, June 11, 1880; Albion Tourgee. *Figs and Thistles: A Romance of the Western Reserve* (New York: Fords, Howard & Hulbert, 1879), page 21.

41. "Some Incidents In the Life of James A. Garfield, from those who knew him" (typescript), c. 1931, JAG—HC; Frederick A. Henry. *Captain Henry of Geauga: A Family Chronicle* (Cleveland, Ohio: The Gates Press, 1942), page 192.

42. "Honors to the Candidate," *The New York Times*, June 11, 1880; "Garfield at Hiram," *Chicago Tribune*, June 11, 1880; James Garfield to Lucretia Garfield, June 15, 1875, JAG—LC; James Garfield to Lucretia Garfield, June 6, 1880, JAG—LC; William Ralston Balch, ed. *Garfield's Words: Suggestive Passages From The Public And Private*

Writings of James Abram Garfield (Boston: Houghton, Mifflin and Company, 1881), pages 338–340.

43. "Garfield at Hiram," *Chicago Tribune*, June 11, 1880; Hinsdale, *President Garfield and Education*, pages 104–105.

44. Robert Reyburn. *Clinical History of the Case of President James Abram Garfield* (Chicago: American Medical Association, 1894), page 94.

45. Jared Cohen. *Accidental Presidents: Eight Men Who Changed America* (New York: Simon & Schuster, 2019), page 383; Painting of "Chief James Garfield Velarde," The Metropolitan Museum of New York, https://www.metmuseum.org/art/collection.

46. Entry for "Garfield Lupine," www.wildflowersearch.org; Robert Van Tress, "History of Hippecoris Garfieldii," *Herbertia*, 1936, http://bulbnrose.x10.mx/Amaryllis/HIPPECOR.htm; "Mister Garfield," https://www.youtube.com/watch?v=tuucpkMEFVM; Gerrad Hall, "The Cat's Meow," *CNN*, October 26, 2000, http://archives.cnn.com/2000/fyi/student.bureau/10/24/jim.davis/.

CHAPTER 1

1. Margaret Leech. *The Garfield Orbit*, ed. Harry Brown (New York: Harper & Row, Publishers, 1978), page 12; Eliza Garfield, "Genealogical Notes," 1869, JAG—LC; Harriet Taylor Upton. *History of the Western Reserve*, vol. 1 (The Lewis Publishing Company, 1910), page 31, 382; Charles Dickens. *American Notes for General Circulation* (Carlisle, Massachusetts: Applewood Books, 2007), pages 133–134; James S. Brisbin. *The Early Life and Public Career of James A. Garfield*, ed. Paul Rich (Westphalia Press, 2013), page 51.

2. John Clark Ridpath. *The Life and Work of James A. Garfield* (Philadelphia: P.W. Ziegler & Co., 1881), page 15; J. M. Bundy. *The Life of James A. Garfield* (New York: A.S. Barnes & Co., 1880), page 3; Russell Conwell. *The Life, Speeches, and Public Services of James A. Garfield, Twentieth President of the United States* (Boston: B.B. Russell, 1881), pages 32–33; Eliza Garfield, "Genealogical Notes," 1869, JAG—LC; Theodore Clark Smith. *The Life and Letters of James Abram Garfield*, volume 1 (New Haven, Connecticut: Yale University Press, 1925), page 2.

3. Eliza Garfield, "Genealogical Notes," 1869, JAG—LC; Albion Tourgee. *Figs and Thistles: A Romance of the Western Reserve* (New York: Fords, Howard & Hulbert, 1879), page 19; Alexis de Tocqueville, Eduardo Nolla, and James T. Schleifer. *Democracy in America*, English edition, volume 1 (Indianapolis: Liberty Fund, 2012).

4. Eliza Garfield, "Genealogical Notes," 1869, JAG—LC.

5. Kevin F. Kern and Gregory S. Wilson. *Ohio: A History of the Buckeye State* (Malden, Massachusetts: Wiley Blackwell, a John Wiley & Sons, Inc. Publication, 2014), page 112; David G. McCullough. *The Pioneers: The Heroic Story of the Settlers Who Brought the American Ideal West*, first Simon & Schuster hardcover edition (New York: Simon & Schuster, 2019), page 7.

6. Harriet Taylor Upton. *History of the Western Reserve*, volume 1 (The Lewis Publishing Company, 1910), pages 30, 465–466; William Stowell Mills. *The Story of the Western Reserve of Connecticut* (New York: Brown & Wilson Press, 1900), page 103.

7. Elroy McKendree Avery. *A History of Cleveland and Its Environs: The Heart of New Connecticut*, vol. 1 (The Lewis Publishing Company, 1918), pages 53–54; Harriet Taylor Upton, *History of the Western Reserve*, pages 45–47; Scott M. Steiger et al., "Lake-Effect Thunderstorms in the Lower Great Lakes," *Journal of Applied Meteorology and Climatology* 48, no. 5: 889–902.

8. William Stowell Mills, *The Story of the Western Reserve of Connecticut*, pages 101–102.

9. Edwin G. Burrows and Mike Wallace, *Gotham*, pages 334–335; Daniel Walker Howe. *What Hath God Wrought: The Transformation of America, 1815–1848*, The Oxford History of the United States, volume 5, David M. Kennedy, general ed. (Oxford: Oxford University Press, 2007), page 548; T. J. Stiles. *The First Tycoon: The Epic Life of Cornelius Vanderbilt* first edition (New York: Vintage Books, 2010), page 33.

10. George Rogers Taylor. *The Transportation Revolution, 1815–1860* (White Plains, New York: M.E. Sharpe, 1951), pages 32–33; Evan Cornog. *The Birth of Empire: DeWitt Clinton and the American Experience, 1769–1828* (New York: Oxford University Press, 1998), pages 6, 159; Peter L. Bernstein. *Wedding of the Waters: The Erie Canal and the Making of a Great Nation*, first paperback edition (New York: Norton, 2006), pages 206, 343.

11. Bernstein, pages 343, 346; Cornog, *The Birth of Empire*, page 163.

12. David Nasaw. *Andrew Carnegie* (London: Penguin, 2007), pages 28–29.

13. Harvey Rice. *Pioneers of the Western Reserve* (Boston: Lee and Shepard, 1883), pages 92–93; Kevin F. Kern and Gregory S. Wilson. *Ohio: A History of the Buckeye State* (Malden, Massachusetts: Wiley Blackwell, a John Wiley & Sons, Inc. Publication, 2014), page 169; Harriet Taylor Upton, *History of the Western Reserve*, pages 72–73.

14. Terry K. Woods. *Ohio's Grand Canal: A Brief History of the Ohio & Erie Canal* (Kent, Ohio: Kent State University Press, 2008), pages 12–13; Kern and Wilson, *Ohio: A History of the Buckeye State*, page 172.

15. Theodore Clark Smith, *The Life and Letters of James Abram Garfield*, page 3; Peskin, *Garfield*, page 5; J. M. Bundy, *The Life of James A. Garfield*, page 6; Eliza Garfield, "Genealogical Notes," 1869, JAG—LC.

16. Hendrik Booraem, *The Road to Respectability: James A. Garfield and His World, 1844–1852*, A Western Reserve Historical Society Publication (Lewisburg, Pennsylvania: Bucknell University Press, 1988), page 29.

17. William Ralston Balch. *The Life of James Abram Garfield* (Philadelphia: J.C. McCurdy & Co., 1881), page 31; J. M. Bundy, *The Life of James A. Garfield*, page 10; Peskin, *Garfield*, pages 5–6; Eliza Garfield, "Genealogical Notes," 1869, JAG—LC.

18. Eliza Garfield, "Genealogical Notes," 1869, JAG—LC; Eliza Garfield to James Garfield, November 19, 1871, JAG—LC.

19. Eliza Garfield, "Genealogical Notes," 1869, JAG—LC; Thomas Garfield, "Recollections of the Life of James A. Garfield," circa 1882, JAG—LC.

20. Harriet Taylor Upton, *History of the Western Reserve*, page 73; Woods, *Ohio's Grand Canal*, page 5; Tocqueville, Nolla, and Schleifer, *Democracy in America*, volume 1; Elroy McKendree Avery, *A History of Cleveland and Its Environs: The Heart of New*

Connecticut, page 169; Kevin F. Kern and Gregory S. Wilson. *Ohio: A History of the Buckeye State*, page 175.

21. Woods, *Ohio's Grand Canal*, pages 87–90; Margaret Leech. *The Garfield Orbit*, ed. Harry Brown (New York: Harper & Row, Publishers, 1978), page 21.

22. Howe, *What Hath God Wrought*, pages 532–535, 543–544; Christopher Clark. *Social Change in America: From the Revolution through the Civil War* (Chicago: Ivan R. Dee, 2006), page 211.

23. Robert Middlekauff. *The Glorious Cause: The American Revolution, 1763–1789*, revised and expanded edition, The Oxford History of the United States, C. Vann Woodward, general ed., volume 3 (Oxford: Oxford University Press, 2007), page 666.

24. Sidney Blumenthal. *All The Powers of the Earth* (New York: Simon & Schuster, 2019), page 4; Howe, *What Hath God Wrought*, pages 148, 154.

25. Thomas Jefferson. *Notes on the State of Virginia* (Boston: Lilly and Wait, 1832), page 170.

26. J. M. Bundy. *The Life of James A. Garfield*, pages 9–10.

27. J. M. Bundy, *The Life of James A. Garfield*, page 9.

28. J. M. Bundy, *The Life of James A. Garfield*, page 10; Eliza Garfield, "Genealogical Notes," 1869, JAG—LC.

29. Hendrik Booraem, *The Road to Respectability*, page 22; Burke Hinsdale and H. R. Cooley, "Eliza Ballou Garfield, Mother of President James A. Garfield: Addresses Made at Her Burial" (Leader Printing Company, 1888), JAG—LC.

30. Eliza Garfield, "Genealogical Notes," 1869, JAG—LC.

31. J. M. Bundy, *The Life of James A. Garfield*, page 10; Hendrik Booraem, *The Road to Respectability*, pages 35–36; Thomas Garfield, "Recollections of the Life of James A. Garfield," c. 1882, JAG—LC.

32. Eliza Garfield, "Genealogical Notes," 1869, JAG—LC; Eliza Garfield to James Garfield, April 24, 1873, JAG—LC.

33. Thomas Garfield to James Garfield, April 15, 1854, JAG—LC.

34. Hendrik Booraem, *The Road to Respectability*, page 35; Thomas Garfield, "Recollections of the Life of James A. Garfield."

35. Eliza Garfield, "Genealogical Notes," 1869, JAG—LC.

36. Theodore Clark Smith, *The Life and Letters of James Abram Garfield*, 1925, page 12; Diary entry for May 25, 1875, JAG—LC.

37. James Garfield to J. H. Rhodes, November 19, 1862, Frederick Williams, *The Wild Life of the Army: Civil War Letters of James A. Garfield*.

38. James Garfield to H. B. Perkins, November 7, 1871, JAG—LC.

CHAPTER 2

1. Harriet Taylor Upton, *History of the Western Reserve*, pages 461, 480–482, 510; Harvey Rice, *Pioneers of the Western Reserve*, pages 127–128.

2. Harriet Taylor Upton, *History of the Western Reserve*, page 377; William Ralston Balch, *The Life of James Abram Garfield*, page 38.

3. Diary entries for February 8 and 28, March 7, April 7 and 15, 1848, James Garfield,

The Diary of James A. Garfield, ed. Frederick Williams and Harry Brown, volume 1; Hendrik Booraem, *The Road to Respectability*, page 44.

4. Hendrik Booraem, *The Road to Respectability*, page 43; Thomas Garfield, "Recollections of the Life of James A. Garfield," JAG—LC.

5. Hendrik Booraem, *The Road to Respectability*, page 43; H. W. Everest, as quoted in Hinsdale, *President Garfield and Education*, page 32; Thomas Garfield, "Recollections of the Life of James A. Garfield," JAG—LC.

6. Hendrik Booraem, *The Road to Respectability*, page 43; James Garfield to Eliza Garfield, November 19, 1855, JAG—LC.

7. Harriet Taylor Upton, *History of the Western Reserve*, page 146.

8. Harriet Taylor Upton, *History of the Western Reserve,* pages 146–147.

9. Diary entries for January 31, February 1, 1848, Garfield, *The Diary of James A. Garfield*, volume 1.

10. J. M. Bundy, *The Life of James A. Garfield*, page 11; Thomas Garfield, "Recollections of the Life of James A. Garfield," JAG—LC.

11. Margaret Leech, *The Garfield Orbit*, page 15.

12. William Ralston Balch, *The Life of James Abram Garfield*, page 37.

13. Hendrik Booraem, *The Road to Respectability*, page 43; Thomas Garfield, "Recollections of the Life of James A. Garfield," circa 1882, JAG—LC; J. M. Bundy, *The Life of James A. Garfield*, pages 13–14.

14. George Taylor, *The Transportation Revolution, 1815–1860*, page 46; Terry Woods, *Ohio's Grand Canal*, page 91; Edmund Morris. *Edison*, first edition (New York: Random House, 2019), page 618.

15. Biographical interview of James Garfield, 1880, JAG—LC;

16. Allan Peskin, *Garfield*, page 12.

17. Diary entries for April 16, May 4, May 25, 26, 1848. Garfield, *The Diary of James A. Garfield* volume 1; James Brisbin, *The Early Life and Public Career of James A. Garfield*, page 50.

18. Diary entries for August 17, 30, 1848, James Garfield, *The Diary of James A. Garfield*, ed. Frederick Williams and Harry Brown, volume 1, 1867.

19. Theodore Clark Smith, *The Life and Letters of James Abram Garfield*, 1925, page 24; Biographical Interview of James Garfield, 1880, JAG—LC; Peskin, *Garfield*, page 12.

20. Biographical interview of James Garfield, 1880, JAG—LC.

21. Biographical interview of James Garfield, 1880, JAG—LC; Diary entry for August 30, 1848, Garfield, *The Diary of James A. Garfield*, volume 1.

22. Biographical interview of James Garfield, 1880, JAG—LC.

23. Biographical interview of James Garfield, 1880, JAG—LC; James Garfield to the Geauga Seminary Board of Trustees, May 8, 1867, Corydon Fuller. *Reminiscences of James A. Garfield, with Notes Preliminary and Collateral* (Cincinnati: Standard Publishing Co., 1887), page 2.

24. Hendrik Booraem, *The Road to Respectability*, page 99; Allan Peskin, *Garfield*, page 15.

25. James Garfield to Eliza and Thomas Garfield, March 31, 1849, JAG—LC.

26. Hendrik Booraem, *The Road to Respectability*, page 103.

27. Diary entries for July 9, 28, August 2, 3, 7, 1849. Garfield, *The Diary of James A. Garfield*, volume 1; James Garfield to Thomas Garfield, August 16, 1849, JAG—LC.

28. Theodore Clark Smith, *The Life and Letters of James Abram Garfield*, 1925, pages 28–29; Margaret Leech, *The Garfield Orbit*, pages 24–26.

29. Diary entries for March 20, 21, 1849. Garfield, *The Diary of James A. Garfield*, volume 1.

30. Daniel Howe, *What Hath God Wrought*, pages 798–799, 804.

31. Daniel Howe, *What Hath God Wrought*, page 799; James M. McPherson, *Battle Cry of Freedom: The Civil War Era*, new edition, The Oxford History of the United States, David M. Kennedy, general ed., volume 6 (Oxford: Oxford University Press, 1988), page 51.

32. Michael F. Holt, *The Rise and Fall of the American Whig Party: Jacksonian Politics and the Onset of the Civil War* (New York: Oxford University Press, 1999), page 251; Walter Stahr, *Seward: Lincoln's Indispensable Man*, first Simon & Schuster hardcover edition (New York: Simon & Schuster, 2012), page 128.

33. Corydon Fuller, *Reminiscences of James A. Garfield, with Notes Preliminary and Collateral*, page 24; Sidney Blumenthal, *All the Powers of Earth*, page 69; George Julian. *The Life of Joshua R. Giddings* (Chicago: A.C. McClurg and Company, 1892), page 65.

34. David W. Blight. *Frederick Douglass: Prophet of Freedom*, first Simon & Schuster hardcover edition (New York: Simon & Schuster, 2018), page 187; Alfred Mathews. *Ohio and Her Western Reserve: With a Story of Three States* (New York: D. Appleton and Company, 1902), page 175; Albion Tourgee. *Figs and Thistles: A Romance of the Western Reserve* (New York: Fords, Howard & Hulbert, 1879), page 21; Laura J. Gorretta and Chagrin Falls Historical Society. *Chagrin Falls: An Ohio Village History* (Chagrin Falls, Ohio: Chagrin Falls Historical Society, 2004), pages 54–56.

35. Paul Finkelman, ed. *His Soul Goes Marching On: Responses to John Brown and the Harpers Ferry Raid* (Charlottesville: University Press of Virginia, 1995), pages 4–5.

36. Diary entry for August 21, 31, 1849. Garfield, *The Diary of James A. Garfield*, volume 1.

37. Diary entry for March 20, 1849. Garfield, *The Diary of James A. Garfield*, volume 1.

38. Diary entry for September 6, 1850. Garfield, *The Diary of James A. Garfield*, volume 1.

39. Diary entry for August 22, 1849, JAG—LC; Diary entry for September 25, 1849, JAG—LC.

40. Diary entry for September 30, 1849. Garfield, *The Diary of James A. Garfield*, volume 1.

41. Diary entries for November 10, 23, December 12, 19, 20, 24, 1849, January 4, 1850. Garfield, *The Diary of James A. Garfield*, volume 1.

42. Diary entry for February 28, 1850. Garfield, *The Diary of James A. Garfield*, volume 1. Diary entries for December 31, 1849, and January 1, February 28, 1850, JAG—LC; Diary entry for March 2, 1850, JAG—LC.

43. Diary entries for March 2, 3, 4, and 8, 1850, JAG—LC.

44. Jerry Rushford, "Political Disciple: The Relationship between James A. Garfield and the Disciples of Christ," 1977, page 1; James Garfield to S. R. Galbraith (Letterbook Copy), August 5, 1868, JAG—LC.

45. William Edward Tucker and Lester G. McAllister. *Journey in Faith: A History of the Christian Church (Disciples of Christ)* (Saint Louis: CBP Press, 1989), pages 25–26; Jerry Rushford, "Political Disciple: The Relationship between James A. Garfield and the Disciples of Christ," 1977, pages 1–2; D. Duane Cummins. *The Disciples: A Struggle for Reformation* (St. Louis, Missouri: Chalice Press, 2009), page 1.

46. Jerry Rushford, "Political Disciple: The Relationship between James A. Garfield and the Disciples of Christ," pages 9–11.

47. Jerry Rushford, "Political Disciple: The Relationship between James A. Garfield and the Disciples of Christ," page 3; D. Duane Cummins, *The Disciples*, page 83; A. S. Hayden. *Early History of the Disciples in the Western Reserve, Ohio; with Biographical Sketches of the Principal Agents in Their Religious Movement* (Cincinnati: Chase & Hall Publishers, 1875), page 144.

48. Diary entry for April 12, June 1, 1850; Garfield, *The Diary of James A. Garfield*, volume 1.

49. Diary entry for April 2, 1850, JAG—LC.

50. Diary entry for June 25, July 2, 1850; Garfield, *The Diary of James A. Garfield*, volume 1.

51. Diary entry for July 6, 1850; Garfield, *The Diary of James A. Garfield*, volume 1.

CHAPTER 3

1. James McPherson. *Battle Cry of Freedom: The Civil War Era*, new edition, The Oxford History of the United States, David M. Kennedy, general ed., volume 6 (Oxford: Oxford University Press, 1988), pages 70–71, 75; David Herbert Donald. *Lincoln*, first edition (New York: Touchstone, 1996), page 167.

2. James M. McPherson, *Battle Cry of Freedom: The Civil War Era*, page 80; Hans L. Trefousse. *The Radical Republicans: Lincoln's Vanguard for Racial Justice*, Louisiana Paperbacks; L-71 (Baton Rouge: Louisiana State University Press, 1975), page 52.

3. David Blight, *Frederick Douglass*, page 241; H. W. Brands. *The Zealot and the Emancipator: John Brown, Abraham Lincoln and the Struggle for American Freedom*, first edition (New York: Doubleday, 2020), page 35; George Washington Julian, *The Life of Joshua R. Giddings*, page 304.

4. Diary entry for October 2, 1850. Garfield, *The Diary of James A. Garfield*, volume 1.

5. Jerry Rushford, "Political Disciple: The Relationship between James A. Garfield and the Disciples of Christ," 1977, pages 4–5.

6. William Edward Tucker and Lester G. McAllister. *Journey in Faith: A History of the Christian Church (Disciples of Christ)* (Saint Louis: CBP Press, 1989), pages 197–198.

7. Diary entry for September 6, 13, 29, 1850. Garfield, *The Diary of James A. Garfield*, volume 1; "Address on War," *Millennial Harbinger*, July 1848, page 384.

8. Diary entries for February 15, February 26, March 27, May 1, May 2, May 3, 1851. Garfield, *The Diary of James A. Garfield*, volume 1.

9. Diary entries for April 17, May 2, 5, 31, June 2, 1851. Garfield, *The Diary of James A. Garfield*, volume 1.

10. Diary entry for August 23, 1851. Garfield, *The Diary of James A. Garfield*, volume 1. Corydon Fuller, *Reminiscences of James A. Garfield, with Notes Preliminary and Collateral*, pages 25–26.

11. F. M. Green. *Hiram College and Western Reserve Eclectic Institute—Fifty Years of History, 1850–1900* (Cleveland, Ohio: The O.S. Hubbell Printing Company, 1901), pages 4–5; Margaret Leech, *The Garfield Orbit*, page 21.

12. Diary entry for June 23, 1854; Garfield, *The Diary of James A. Garfield*, volume 1; Corydon Fuller, *Reminiscences of James A. Garfield, with Notes Preliminary and Collateral*, pages 29, 115.

13. Burke Hinsdale, *President Garfield and Education*, page 15.

14. Corydon Fuller, *Reminiscences of James A. Garfield, with Notes Preliminary and Collateral*, pages 26–27; F. M. Green, *Hiram College and Western Reserve Eclectic Institute—Fifty Years of History, 1850–1900*, pages 19–25, 30.

15. F. M. Green, *Hiram College and Western Reserve Eclectic Institute—Fifty Years of History, 1850–1900*, pages 19–20; Corydon Fuller, *Reminiscences of James A. Garfield, with Notes Preliminary and Collateral*, pages 26–27, 31.

16. Burke Hinsdale, *President Garfield and Education*, pages 24–26; Corydon Fuller, *Reminiscences of James A. Garfield, with Notes Preliminary and Collateral*, page 31.

17. Burke Hinsdale, *President Garfield and Education*, pages 20–24.

18. Burke Hinsdale, *President Garfield and Education*, pages 26–27; Corydon Fuller, *Reminiscences of James A. Garfield, with Notes Preliminary and Collateral*, pages 31–32.

19. James Garfield. *Life and Character of Almeda A. Booth* (Washington, D.C.: Henry L. Rose, 1877), pages 17–18; Diary entry for August 25, 26, 1851, Garfield, *The Diary of James A. Garfield*, volume 1.

20. Burke Hinsdale, *President Garfield and Education*, page 26; F. M. Green, *Hiram College and Western Reserve Eclectic Institute—Fifty Years of History, 1850–1900*, page 35.

21. Diary entry for October 13, 1851, Garfield, *The Diary of James A. Garfield*, volume 1.

22. Diary entry for September 24, 1850, Garfield, *The Diary of James A. Garfield*, volume 1; Burke Hinsdale, *President Garfield and Education*, page 32; Corydon Fuller, *Reminiscences of James A. Garfield, with Notes Preliminary and Collateral*, page 32.

23. Burke Hinsdale, *President Garfield and Education*, page 32; Diary entry for September 5, 26, 1851, Garfield, *The Diary of James A. Garfield*, volume 1.

24. Diary entry for October 17, September 2, 1851, Garfield, *The Diary of James A. Garfield*, volume 1.

25. Diary entry for October 10, 1851, Garfield, *The Diary of James A. Garfield*, volume 1.

26. Corydon Fuller, *Reminiscences of James A. Garfield, with Notes Preliminary and Collateral*, pages 32, 36–37.

27. Corydon Fuller, *Reminiscences of James A. Garfield, with Notes Preliminary and Collateral,* page 42; Diary entry for January 7, 1852, Garfield, *The Diary of James A. Garfield,* volume 1.

28. Corydon Fuller, *Reminiscences of James A. Garfield, with Notes Preliminary and Collateral,* page 46.

29. Corydon Fuller, *Reminiscences of James A. Garfield, with Notes Preliminary and Collateral,* pages 41–43.

30. Diary entry for April 21, 27, 28, 1852, Garfield, *The Diary of James A. Garfield,* volume 1.

31. James Garfield to Burke Hinsdale, May 11, 1875, JAG—LC; Diary entry for April 16, May 1, 1852, Garfield, *The Diary of James A. Garfield,* volume 1; James Garfield to Burke Hinsdale, May 11, 1875, JAG—LC.

32. Corydon Fuller, *Reminiscences of James A. Garfield, with Notes Preliminary and Collateral,* pages 55–59.

33. F. M. Green, *Hiram College and Western Reserve Eclectic Institute—Fifty Years of History, 1850–1900,* page 41; Diary entry for June 24, 1854, volume 1.

34. Charles Wilber to James Garfield, January 10, 1854, JAG—LC; Burke Hinsdale, *President Garfield and Education,* page 37.

35. Diary entry for June 25, 1853, Garfield, *The Diary of James A. Garfield,* volume 1; Thomas Garfield, "Recollections of the Life of James A. Garfield," JAG—LC.

36. Diary entry, October 9, 1853, Garfield, *The Diary of James A. Garfield,* volume 1.

37. Diary entry, January 1, 1853, Garfield, *The Diary of James A. Garfield,* volume 1.

38. Theodore Clark Smith, *The Life and Letters of James Abram Garfield,* 1925, page 67; Diary entry for September 28, 1850, Garfield, *The Diary of James A. Garfield,* volume 1.

39. James Garfield to Thomas Garfield, November 5, 1871, JAG—LC; James Garfield to Burke Hinsdale, January 5, 1871, JAG—LC.

40. James Garfield to Lucretia Garfield, November 16, 1853. James Garfield and Lucretia Garfield, *Crete and James,* ed. John Shaw (East Lansing: Michigan State University Press, 1994).

41. Corydon Fuller, *Reminiscences of James A. Garfield, with Notes Preliminary and Collateral,* page 57; Lucretia Garfield to James Garfield, December 31, 1855, JAG—LC.

42. Diary entry for May 22, 1852, May 14, 1853, Garfield, *The Diary of James A. Garfield,* volume 1; Photo available in JAG—LC.

43. William Ralston Balch. *The Life of James Abram Garfield* (Philadelphia: J.C. McCurdy & Co., 1881), pages 338–339; Corydon Fuller, *Reminiscences of James A. Garfield, with Notes Preliminary and Collateral,* pages 55–57.

44. Diary entry for December 31, 1853, Garfield, *The Diary of James A. Garfield,* volume 1; Garfield and Garfield, *Crete and James,* page 12.

45. Lucretia Garfield to James Garfield, January 26, 1854. Garfield and Garfield, *Crete and James.*

46. James Garfield to Lucretia Garfield, January 28, 1854. Garfield and Garfield, *Crete and James.*

47. Scrap sent from Providence, Rhode Island, to JAG, May 1, 1854, JAG—LC; Diary entry for June 23, 1854, Garfield, *The Diary of James A. Garfield*, volume 1.
48. Diary entry for June 23, 1854, Garfield, *The Diary of James A. Garfield*, volume 1.
49. Corydon Fuller to James Garfield, May 24, 1854, JAG—LC; Diary entry for June 23, 1854, Garfield, *The Diary of James A. Garfield*, volume 1.
50. Diary entry for June 23, 1854, Garfield, *The Diary of James A. Garfield*, volume 1.
51. Diary entries for June 23, June 24, 1854, Garfield, *The Diary of James A. Garfield*, volume 1.
52. Diary entry for June 29, 1854, Garfield, *The Diary of James A. Garfield*, volume 1.
53. Diary entry for July 1, July 5, 1854, Garfield, *The Diary of James A. Garfield*, volume 1.
54. Corydon Fuller, *Reminiscences of James A. Garfield, with Notes Preliminary and Collateral*, pages 119–120.

CHAPTER 4

1. James Garfield to Corydon Fuller, July 16, 1854, November 20, 1855, JAG—LC; James Garfield to Corydon and Mary Fuller, January 5, 1856, JAG—LC; James Garfield to Corydon Fuller, July 30, 1854, JAG—LC.
2. James Garfield to Corydon Fuller, July 30, 1854, JAG—LC; Diary entry for July 22, 1854, Garfield, *The Diary of James A. Garfield*, volume 1; James Garfield to Corydon Fuller, July 30, 1854, JAG—LC.
3. Jerry Rushford, "Political Disciple: The Relationship between James A. Garfield and the Disciples of Christ," page 59; John Ingalls, *A Collection of the Writings of John James Ingalls: Essays, Addresses, and Orations*, page 398; James Garfield to Mary Fuller, January 12, 1856, JAG—LC.
4. John Ingalls, *A Collection of the Writings of John James Ingalls: Essays, Addresses, and Orations*, page 398; "Speech of the Backwoodsman," JAG—LC; Samuel Greene Wheeler Benjamin. *The Life and Adventures of a Free Lance* (Burlington, Vermont: Free Press Company, 1914), page 142.
5. Samuel Greene Wheeler Benjamin, *The Life and Adventures of a Free Lance*, page 142; Jonas Bundy, *The Life of James A. Garfield*, page 34.
6. John Ingalls, *A Collection of the Writings of John James Ingalls: Essays, Addresses, and Orations*, page 397; Jonas Bundy, *The Life of James A. Garfield*, page 33; "Speech on Literary Societies," October 10, 1855, JAG—LC.
7. Allan Peskin, *Garfield*, page 37.
8. Samuel Greene Wheeler Benjamin, *The Life and Adventures of a Free Lance*, page 140.
9. H. W. Brands, *The Zealot and the Emancipator*, page 42; James McPherson, *Battle Cry of Freedom*, pages 121–122.
10. James McPherson, *Battle Cry of Freedom*, page 125; H. W. Brands, *The Zealot and the Emancipator*, page 43.
11. H. W. Brands, *The Zealot and the Emancipator*, pages 48–53.
12. Diary entry for November 2, 1855, Garfield, *The Diary of James A. Garfield*, volume 1.

13. Untitled oration at Williams College, September 27, 1854, JAG—LC.

14. James Garfield to Mary Fuller, September 16, 1854, Corydon Fuller, *Reminiscences of James A. Garfield, with Notes Preliminary and Collateral;* James Garfield to Eliza Garfield, September 30, 1854, JAG—LC.

15. James Garfield to Corydon Fuller, June 19, 1855, JAG—LC; James Garfield to Eliza Garfield, June 18, 1855, JAG—LC.

16. William Ralston Balch, *The Life of James Abram Garfield,* page 79.

17. Diary entry for September 10, 1855, Garfield, *The Diary of James A. Garfield,* volume 1; James Garfield to Lucretia Garfield, July 7, 1855, Lucretia Garfield to James Garfield, April 14, 1855, Garfield and Garfield, *Crete and James.*

18. Diary entry for September 10, 1855, Garfield, *The Diary of James A. Garfield,* volume 1.

19. Diary entry for September 11, 1855, Garfield, *The Diary of James A. Garfield,* volume 1; Lucretia Garfield to James Garfield, September 12, 1855, Garfield and Garfield, *Crete and James.*

20. James Garfield to Lucretia Garfield, March 16, 1856, JAG—LC.

21. James Garfield to Lucretia Garfield, November 10, 1855, JAG—LC.

22. James Garfield to Corydon Fuller, February 11, 1856, JAG—LC.

23. Amos Sutton Hayden, *Early History of the Disciples in the Western Reserve, Ohio; with Biographical Sketches of the Principal Agents in Their Religious Movement,* page 265; Corydon Fuller, *Reminiscences of James A. Garfield, with Notes Preliminary and Collateral,* page 64; F. M. Green, *Hiram College and Western Reserve Eclectic Institute—Fifty Years of History, 1850–1900,* page 90; James Garfield to Corydon Fuller, February 11, 1856, JAG—LC.

24. James Garfield to Corydon Fuller, February 11, 1856, JAG—LC; Theodore Clarke Smith, *The Life and Letters of James Abram Garfield,* 1925, page 103.

25. Diary entry for November 19, 1855, Garfield, *The Diary of James A. Garfield,* volume 1.

26. James Garfield to Corydon Fuller, June 17, 1856, JAG—LC; James Garfield to Corydon Fuller, February 11, 1856, JAG—LC.

27. Burke Hinsdale, *President Garfield and Education,* page 37.

28. Theodore Clarke Smith, *The Life and Letters of James Abram Garfield,* 1925, page 111; James Garfield to Corydon Fuller, November 9, 1856; Corydon Fuller, *Reminiscences of James A. Garfield, with Notes Preliminary and Collateral,* page 240; Burke Hinsdale, *President Garfield and Education,* pages 58–60.

29. Burke Hinsdale, *President Garfield and Education,* page 127.

30. Burke Hinsdale, *President Garfield and Education,* pages 61–64.

31. F. M. Green, *Hiram College and Western Reserve Eclectic Institute—Fifty Years of History, 1850–1900,* page 93.

32. Burke Hinsdale, *President Garfield and Education,* page 47; James Garfield to Corydon Fuller, August 30, 1857, Corydon Fuller, *Reminiscences of James A. Garfield, with Notes Preliminary and Collateral.*

33. "Clipping," *Portage Sentinel,* June 25, 1857.

34. "The Hiram Institute," *Western Reserve Chronicle,* February 24, 1858.

CHAPTER 5

1. Burke Hinsdale, *President Garfield and Education*, page 56; F. M. Green, *Hiram College and Western Reserve Eclectic Institute—Fifty Years of History, 1850–1900*, pages 156–157; C. C. Smith, "The Old Days at Hiram," *The Ohio Work*, March 1946; Diary entry for October 2, 1857, Garfield, *The Diary of James A. Garfield*, volume 1; Allan Peskin, *Garfield*, page 58.

2. Frederick Henry, *Captain Henry of Geauga: A Family Chronicle*, page 76; Burke Hinsdale, *President Garfield and Education*, page 55; James Garfield to Harmon Austin, November 9, 1857, JAG—LC; F. M. Green, *Hiram College and Western Reserve Eclectic Institute—Fifty Years of History, 1850–1900*, page 167.

3. Burke Hinsdale, *President Garfield and Education*, pages 64–65; Frederick Henry, *Captain Henry of Geauga: A Family Chronicle*, page 97.

4. Burke Hinsdale, *President Garfield and Education*, pages 66–67.

5. F. M. Green, *Hiram College and Western Reserve Eclectic Institute—Fifty Years of History, 1850–1900*, page 103.

6. James Garfield, *The Diary of James A. Garfield*, ed. Frederick Williams and Harry Brown, volume 1, 1867; Diary entry for December 31, 1858, "The Journal of William and Henry Boynton, 1854–1864," The Henry Boynton Papers, Western Reserve Historical Society.

7. James Garfield to Corydon Fuller, March 23, 1858, Corydon Fuller, *Reminiscences of James A. Garfield, with Notes Preliminary and Collateral*; Smith, *The Life and Letters of James Abram Garfield*, 1925, pages 113–114; Jonas Bundy, *The Life of James A. Garfield*, page 46.

8. Diary entry for October 3, 1857, Garfield, *The Diary of James A. Garfield*, volume 1.

9. Diary entry for October 13, 1857, Garfield, *The Diary of James A. Garfield*, volume 1; Jerry Rushford, "Political Disciple: The Relationship between James A. Garfield and the Disciples of Christ," page 130.

10. "Reception to Gen. Fremont," *The New York Times*, August 5, 1880; Fawn M. Brodie. *Thaddeus Stevens: Scourge of the South* (The Norton Library, 1966), page 130; Hans Trefousse, *The Radical Republicans*, page 105.

11. Jerry Rushford, "Political Disciple: The Relationship between James A. Garfield and the Disciples of Christ," pages 126–127; James Garfield to Harmon Austin, March 30, 1859, JAG—LC.

12. James Garfield to Henry Boynton, March 21, 1856, "Henry Boynton Papers," Western Reserve Historical Society; James Garfield to Corydon Fuller, March 23, 1858, JAG—LC.

13. Jerry Rushford, "Political Disciple: The Relationship between James A. Garfield and the Disciples of Christ," page 127; Diary entry for October 6, 1857, Garfield, *The Diary of James A. Garfield*, volume 1.

14. James Garfield to Corydon Fuller, January 16, 1858, Corydon Fuller, *Reminiscences of James A. Garfield, with Notes Preliminary and Collateral*.

15. James Garfield to J. Harry Rhodes, April 15, 1859, JAG—LC.

16. "Warren and Braceville Plank Road Co.," *Western Reserve Chronicle*, January 17, 1855; H. Z. Williams. *History of Trumbull and Mahoning Counties, with Illustrations*

and Biographical Sketches, vol. 1 (Cleveland, Ohio: H.Z. Williams & Bro., 1882), page 306; "Trumbull Agricultural Society," *Western Reserve Chronicle*, June 1, 1859; Harmon Austin to James Garfield, October 25, 1858, JAG—LC.

17. Harmon Austin to James Garfield, March 3, 1859, JAG—LC.
18. Harmon Austin to James Garfield, March 29, 1859, JAG—LC; James Garfield to Harmon Austin, March 30, 1859, JAG—LC.
19. Harmon Austin to James Garfield, May 29, 1859, JAG—LC.
20. Lucretia Garfield to James Garfield, May 18, 1858; Lucretia Garfield to James Garfield, May 18, 1858; Lucretia Garfield to James Garfield, June 27, 1858, Garfield and Garfield, *Crete and James.*
21. James Garfield to Lucretia Garfield, June 29, 1858, Garfield and Garfield, *Crete and James*; Diary entry for April 14, 1858, Garfield, *The Diary of James A. Garfield*, volume 1.
22. Lucretia Garfield to James Garfield, August 19, 1858, Garfield and Garfield, *Crete and James*; Diary entry for November 11, 1858, Garfield, *The Diary of James A. Garfield*, volume 1.
23. James Garfield to Harmon Austin, May 21, 1859, JAG—LC; Jerry Rushford, "Political Disciple: The Relationship between James A. Garfield and the Disciples of Christ," page 132; Theodore Clarke Smith, *The Life and Letters of James Abram Garfield*, 1925, page 131.
24. Allan Peskin, *Garfield*, page 58.
25. James Garfield to J. H. Rhodes, June 20, 1859, JAG—LC.
26. Diary entry for August 22, 1859, Garfield, *The Diary of James A. Garfield*, volume 1.
27. Diary entry for August 23, 1859, Garfield, *The Diary of James A. Garfield*, volume 1.
28. "The Republican Candidates on our State, Senatorial and County Tickets," *Republican Democrat*, September 7, 1859.
29. "Communications," *Anti-Slavery Bugle*, October 15, 1859; "Clipping," *Portage Sentinel*, September 21, 1859.
30. Corydon Fuller, *Reminiscences of James A. Garfield, with Notes Preliminary and Collateral*, pages 286–287.
31. Frederick Douglass, *Life and Times of Frederick Douglass*, page 340.
32. James M. McPherson, *Battle Cry of Freedom: The Civil War Era*, page 206.
33. Diary entry for December 2, 1859, Garfield, *The Diary of James A. Garfield*, volume 1.
34. James Garfield to A. G. Riddle, December 5, 1859, JAG—LC.

CHAPTER 6

1. Allan Peskin, *Garfield*, page 67; James McPherson, *Battle Cry of Freedom*, page 714.
2. James Garfield to J. H. Rhodes, January 1, 1860, JAG—LC.
3. James Garfield to J. H. Rhodes, January 1, 1860, JAG—LC; Jacob Dolson Cox, "The Youth and Early Manhood of General James A. Garfield," *Society of the Army of the Cumberland, Fourteenth Reunion* (Cincinnati: Robert Clarke & Company, 1888), page 96.
4. James Garfield to J. H. Rhodes, January 9, 1860, JAG—LC; Allan Peskin, *Garfield*, page 69.

5. Hans Trefousse, *The Radical Republicans*, page 132; David Herbert Donald. *Charles Sumner and the Coming of the Civil War* (Naperville, Illinois: Sourcebooks, 2009), pages 258–259.

6. Seating map of Ohio Senate Chamber found in JAG—LC; William Ralston Balch, *The Life of James Abram Garfield*, page 105; Theodore Clarke Smith, *The Life and Letters of James Abram Garfield*, 1925, page 153; Clipping, *The Daily Empire*, January 26, 1860.

7. William Ralston Balch, *The Life of James Abram Garfield*, page 107; "The Legislative Spree," *Anti-Slavery Bugle*, February 11, 1860.

8. "Extracts from Columbus Letters," *Republican Democrat*, February 15, 1860; "The Military Invasion Bill," *Portage County Democrat*, March 7, 1860.

9. "Senator Garfield Preaching to the Convicts," *Western Reserve Chronicle*, March 7, 1860.

10. "Report of Meetings," *Anti-Slavery Bugle*, August 18, 1860; "Senator Garfield," *Summit County Beacon*, January 19, 1860.

11. Diary entries for August 9, August 26, 1860, Garfield, *The Diary of James A. Garfield*, volume 1; Frederick Henry, *Captain Henry of Geauga: A Family Chronicle*, page 97.

12. Lucretia Garfield to James Garfield, January 1, 1860. Garfield and Garfield, *Crete and James*.

13. James Garfield to Lucretia Garfield, March 14, 1860, JAG—LC; Allan Peskin, *Garfield*, page 75.

14. Allan Peskin, *Garfield,* page 75.

15. James Garfield to Lucretia Garfield, February 5, 1860, JAG—LC; James Garfield to Corydon Fuller, October 3, 1860, Corydon Fuller, *Reminiscences of James A. Garfield, with Notes Preliminary and Collateral*; James Garfield to Lucretia Garfield, January 13, 1861, Garfield and Garfield, *Crete and James*.

16. Allan Peskin, *Garfield*, page 76.

17. James Garfield to Lucretia Garfield, July 25, 1860, JAG—LC.

18. Carl Sandburg. *Abraham Lincoln: The Prairie Years*, The Sangamon Edition, volume 1 (New York: Charles Scribner's Sons, 1926), page 302; F. M. Brodie, *Thaddeus Stevens: Scourge of the South*, page 187; David Blight, *Frederick Douglass*, page 321.

19. David Herbert Donald, *Lincoln*, page 241; James McPherson, *Battle Cry of Freedom*, page 227; Hans Trefousse, *The Radical Republicans*, page 134.

20. James McPherson, *Battle Cry of Freedom*, pages 228–229; Sidney Blumenthal, *All The Powers of the Earth*, page 628.

21. David Herbert Donald, *Lincoln*, page 257; James McPherson, *Battle Cry of Freedom*, pages 244, 264.

22. James Garfield to Burke Hinsdale, February 17, 1861, JAG—LC; Carl Sandburg, *Abraham Lincoln: The Prairie Years*, volume 2, page 389.

23. "Grand Pole Raising at Hiram," *Western Reserve Chronicle*, September 5, 1860; Theodore Clarke Smith, *The Life and Letters of James Abram Garfield*, 1925, page 154.

24. James Garfield to Burke Hinsdale, January 15, 1861, JAG—LC; James Garfield to Burke Hinsdale, February 17, 1861, JAG—LC.

25. James Garfield to Burke Hinsdale, February 17, 1861, JAG—LC.
26. James Garfield to Lucretia Garfield, January 13, 1861, JAG—LC.

CHAPTER 7

1. Carl Sandburg, *Abraham Lincoln: The War Years,* volume 1, pages 206–210; James McPherson, *Battle Cry of Freedom,* page 274.
2. James McPherson, *Battle Cry of Freedom,* page 274; Hans Trefousse, *The Radical Republicans,* page 168.
3. James Garfield to J. H. Rhodes, April 13, 1861, JAG—LC; James Garfield to Lucretia Garfield, April 14, 1861, Garfield and Garfield, *Crete and James.*
4. Carl Sandburg, *Abraham Lincoln: The War Years,* volume 1, page 221; James Garfield to Lucretia Garfield, April 28, 1861, Garfield and Garfield, *Crete and James.*
5. Carl Sandburg, *Abraham Lincoln: The War Years,* 1939, volume 1, page 215; Edmund Morris. *The Rise of Theodore Roosevelt,* Modern Library paperback edition (New York: Modern Library, 2010), pages 9–10.
6. J. M. Atwater to James Garfield, April 19, 1861, JAG—LC; F. A. Williams to James Garfield, February 23, 1861, JAG—LC.
7. James McPherson, *Battle Cry of Freedom,* page 313; David Work. *Lincoln's Political Generals* (Urbana: University of Illinois Press, 2009), pages 6–7; Carl Sandburg, *Abraham Lincoln: The War Years,* 1939, volume 1, page 221; David Herbert Donald, *Lincoln,* page 297.
8. F. H. Mason. *The Forty-Second Ohio Infantry: A History of the Organization and Services of That Regiment in the War of the Rebellion; with Biographical Sketches of Its Field Officers and a Full Roster of the Regiment* (Cleveland: Cobb, Andrews & Co., 1876), page 7.
9. James McPherson, *Battle Cry of Freedom,* pages 328–329.
10. James Garfield to J. H. Rhodes, April 13, 1861, JAG—LC; James Garfield to Lucretia Garfield, April 14, 1861, Garfield and Garfield, *Crete and James.*
11. James Garfield to J. H. Rhodes, April 17, 1861, JAG—LC; "The Reserve in Awake," *Cleveland Daily Herald,* April 22, 1861; Allan Peskin, *Garfield,* page 89.
12. James Garfield to Lucretia Garfield, April 14, 1861, Frederick Williams, editor, *The Wild Life of the Army: Civil War Letters of James A. Garfield.*
13. James Garfield to J. H. Rhodes, April 17, 1861, JAG—LC; Jacob Dolson Cox. *Military Reminiscences of the Civil War,* volume 1 (New York: Charles Scribner's Sons, 1900), page 29; James Garfield to J. H. Clapp, June 8, 1861, Frederick Williams, editor, *The Wild Life of the Army: Civil War Letters of James A. Garfield;* James Garfield to Burke Hinsdale, June 14, 1861, JAG—LC; W. J. Bascom to James Garfield, June 6, 1861, JAG—LC.
14. James Garfield to Burke Hinsdale, June 14, 1861, JAG—LC; Eugene D. Schmiel. *Citizen-General: Jacob Dolson Cox and the Civil War Era* (Athens: Ohio University Press, 2014), page 25; James Garfield to J. H. Rhodes, April 17, 1861, JAG—LC; James Garfield to William Dennison, May 3, 1861, JAG—LC.
15. James Garfield to Lucretia Garfield, April 14, 1861, Garfield and Garfield, *Crete and James.*

16. James Garfield to William Dennison, June 18, 1861, JAG—LC; "Mr. Garfield Declines," *Western Reserve Chronicle*, June 28, 1861; James Garfield to Harmon Austin, June 28, 1861, JAG—LC.

17. Carl Sandburg, *Abraham Lincoln: The War Years*, 1939, volume 1, pages 301–302.

18. James McPherson, *Battle Cry of Freedom*, page 345.

19. Walter Stahr, *Seward*, page 299; James McPherson, *Battle Cry of Freedom*, page 348.

20. Daniel Vermilya. *James Garfield and the Civil War* (Charleston, South Carolina: The History Press, 2015), pages 44–45; James Garfield to William Dennison, August 7, 1861, JAG—LC; James Garfield to Lucretia Garfield, August 14, 1861, Frederick Williams, editor, *The Wild Life of the Army: Civil War Letters of James A. Garfield*.

21. James Garfield to Hiram Friends, August 31, 1861, JAG—LC; James Garfield to Lucretia Garfield, August 31, 1861, JAG—LC.

22. Frank Mason, *The Forty-Second Ohio Infantry: A History of the Organization and Services of That Regiment in the War of the Rebellion; with Biographical Sketches of Its Field Officers and a Full Roster of the Regiment*, page 43; Frederick Henry, *Captain Henry of Geauga: A Family Chronicle*, page 101; W. H. H. Monroe, "Reminiscences of James A. Garfield," JAG—HC.

23. Frank Mason, *The Forty-Second Ohio Infantry: A History of the Organization and Services of That Regiment in the War of the Rebellion; with Biographical Sketches of Its Field Officers and a Full Roster of the Regiment*, pages 43–46; Frederick Henry, *Captain Henry of Geauga: A Family Chronicle*, page 106; James Garfield to J. H. Rhodes, October 2, 1861, JAG—LC.

24. James Garfield to Hiram Friends, August 31, 1861, JAG—LC; James Garfield, "My Campaign In East Kentucky," ed. Edmund Kirke, *North American Review* 143, no. 361 (December 1886): 526; W. H. H. Monroe, "Autobiography of W. H. H. Monroe's Service in Co. A, the 42nd Ohio Regiment in the War of the Rebellion," JAG—HC; J. H. Rhodes to James Garfield, October 16, 1861, JAG—LC.

25. James Garfield to J. H. Rhodes, October 2, 1861, JAG—LC; James Garfield to Lucretia Garfield, November 4, 1861, Frederick Williams, editor, *The Wild Life of the Army: Civil War Letters of James A. Garfield*; James Garfield to Lucretia Garfield, November 23, 1861, Frederick Williams, editor, *The Wild Life of the Army: Civil War Letters of James A. Garfield*.

26. Lucretia Garfield to James Garfield, October 27, 1861, Garfield and Garfield, *Crete and James*; J. H. Rhodes to James Garfield, November 26, 1861, JAG—LC.

27. James Garfield to Luther Day, August 30, 1861, JAG—LC; F. H. Mason, *The Forty-Second Ohio Infantry: A History of the Organization and Services of That Regiment in the War of the Rebellion; with Biographical Sketches of Its Field Officers and a Full Roster of the Regiment*, page 46; "Sword Presentation," *Cleveland Daily Herald*, November 12, 1861.

CHAPTER 8

1. James M. McPherson and David M. Kennedy. *Battle Cry of Freedom: The Civil War Era*, New ed., The Oxford History of the United States, David M. Kennedy,

general ed.; volume 6 (Oxford: Oxford University Press, 1988), pages 348–349; Hans Trefousse, *The Radical Republicans*, pages 180–181.

2. Carl Sandburg, *Abraham Lincoln: The War Years*, 1939, volume 1, page 271; Gerald J. Prokopowicz. *All for the Regiment: The Army of the Ohio, 1861–1862*, Civil War America (Chapel Hill: University of North Carolina Press, 2001), pages 65–67.

3. Daniel Vermilya, *James Garfield and the Civil War*, page 49, pages 67–68.

4. Frederick Henry, *Captain Henry of Geauga: A Family Chronicle*, page 110.

5. James Garfield to J. H. Rhodes, December 17, Frederick Williams, ed., *The Wild Life of the Army: Civil War Letters of James A. Garfield*; James Garfield to J. H. Rhodes, December 17, 1861.

6. Frank Mason, *The Forty-Second Ohio Infantry: A History of the Organization and Services of That Regiment in the War of the Rebellion; with Biographical Sketches of Its Field Officers and a Full Roster of the Regiment*, pages 48–49.

7. James Garfield to Lucretia Garfield, December 16, 1861, Garfield and Garfield, *Crete and James*; James Garfield to J. H. Rhodes, December 17, 1861, JAG—LC.

8. "The War in East Kentucky," *The New York Times*, January 12, 1862; "Affairs in Kentucky," *The New York Times*, October 11, 1861; Carol Crowe-Carraco. *The Big Sandy*, paperback edition (Lexington: The University Press of Kentucky, 1979), page 36.

9. James Garfield to J. H. Rhodes, December 17, 1861, Frederick Williams, *The Wild Life of the Army: Civil War Letters of James A. Garfield*.

10. Frederick Henry, *Captain Henry of Geauga: A Family Chronicle*, page 111; Frank Mason, *The Forty-Second Ohio Infantry: A History of the Organization and Services of That Regiment in the War of the Rebellion; with Biographical Sketches of Its Field Officers and a Full Roster of the Regiment*, pages 49–50.

11. William Ely. *The Big Sandy Valley* (Catlettsburg, Kentucky: Central Methodist, 1887), page 18.

12. William Ely, *The Big Sandy Valley*, page 19; James Garfield to Eliza Garfield, January 26, 1862. Frederick Williams, *The Wild Life of the Army: Civil War Letters of James A. Garfield*; Frederick Henry, *Captain Henry of Geauga: A Family Chronicle*, page 111; Frank Mason, *The Forty-Second Ohio Infantry: A History of the Organization and Services of That Regiment in the War of the Rebellion; with Biographical Sketches of Its Field Officers and a Full Roster of the Regiment*, pages 52–55.

13. James Garfield to Lucretia Garfield, January 26, 1862. Frederick Williams, *The Wild Life of the Army: Civil War Letters of James A. Garfield*; Frederick Henry, *Captain Henry of Geauga: A Family Chronicle*, page 118; Allan Peskin, *Garfield*, page 123; Frank Mason, *The Forty-Second Ohio Infantry: A History of the Organization and Services of That Regiment in the War of the Rebellion; with Biographical Sketches of Its Field Officers and a Full Roster of the Regiment*, pages 88–89.

14. Otto Bond, ed. *Under the Flag of the Nation: Diaries and Letters of a Yankee Volunteer in the Civil War* (Columbus: Ohio State University Press, 1961), pages 14–16.

15. Frank Mason, *The Forty-Second Ohio Infantry: A History of the Organization and Services of That Regiment in the War of the Rebellion; with Biographical Sketches of Its Field Officers and a Full Roster of the Regiment*, page 57.

16. Frank Mason, *The Forty-Second Ohio Infantry: A History of the Organization and Services of That Regiment in the War of the Rebellion; with Biographical Sketches of Its Field Officers and a Full Roster of the Regiment*, pages 57–58; James Garfield to Lucretia Garfield, January 1, 1862, Frederick Williams, *The Wild Life of the Army: Civil War Letters of James A. Garfield.*

17. James Garfield to Don Carlos Buell, December 26, 1861, *The War of the Rebellion: A Compilation of the Official Records of the Union and Confederate Armies*, series 1, volume 7 (Government Printing Office, 1882), page 25; Don Carlos Buell to James Garfield, December 28, 1861, JAG—LC.

18. Garfield, "My Campaign In East Kentucky"; Frederick Henry, *Captain Henry of Geauga: A Family Chronicle*, page 112.

19. Frank Mason, *The Forty-Second Ohio Infantry: A History of the Organization and Services of That Regiment in the War of the Rebellion; with Biographical Sketches of Its Field Officers and a Full Roster of the Regiment*, pages 58–59; James Garfield to Lucretia Garfield, December 25, 1861, Garfield and Garfield, *Crete and James*; Garfield, "My Campaign In East Kentucky," JAG—LC.

20. Frederick Henry, *Captain Henry of Geauga: A Family Chronicle*, pages 112–113; Garfield, "My Campaign In East Kentucky," JAG—LC.

21. W. H. H. Monroe, "Reminiscences of James A. Garfield," JAG—HC; Frank Mason, *The Forty-Second Ohio Infantry: A History of the Organization and Services of That Regiment in the War of the Rebellion; with Biographical Sketches of Its Field Officers and a Full Roster of the Regiment*, pages 62–63; James Garfield to Lucretia Garfield, January 13, 1862, Frederick Williams, *The Wild Life of the Army: Civil War Letters of James A. Garfield.*

22. James Garfield to J. B. Fry, January 8, 1862, *The War of the Rebellion: A Compilation of the Official Records of the Union and Confederate Armies*, series 1, volume 7, page 28.

23. Clement Eaton. *A History of the Southern Confederacy*, paperback edition (New York: The Free Press, 1965), page 95; Humphrey Marshall to Sidney Johnson, December 30, 1861, *The War of the Rebellion: A Compilation of the Official Records of the Union and Confederate Armies*, series 1, volume 7, 1882, page 43; Allan Peskin, *Garfield*, page 107.

24. Humphrey Marshall to Sidney Johnston, January 14, 1862, *The War of the Rebellion: A Compilation of the Official Records of the Union and Confederate Armies*, series 1, volume 7, 1882, page 49.

25. Humphrey Marshall to Sidney Johnston, January 14, 1862, *The War of the Rebellion: A Compilation of the Official Records of the Union and Confederate Armies*, series 1, volume 7, 1882, page 43; Allan Peskin, *Garfield*, page 107.

26. *The War of the Rebellion: A Compilation of the Official Records of the Union and Confederate Armies*, series 1, volume 7, 1882, page 28; James Garfield to Lucretia Garfield, January 13, 1862, Frederick Williams, *The Wild Life of the Army: Civil War Letters of James A. Garfield.*

27. James Garfield to Lucretia Garfield, January 13, 1862, Frederick Williams, *The Wild Life of the Army: Civil War Letters of James A. Garfield*; Frank Mason, *The*

Forty-Second Ohio Infantry: A History of the Organization and Services of That Regiment in the War of the Rebellion; with Biographical Sketches of Its Field Officers and a Full Roster of the Regiment, pages 67–68; Garfield, "My Campaign In East Kentucky."

28. Frank Mason, *The Forty-Second Ohio Infantry: A History of the Organization and Services of That Regiment in the War of the Rebellion; with Biographical Sketches of Its Field Officers and a Full Roster of the Regiment*, page 69; James Garfield to Lucretia Garfield, January 13, 1862, Frederick Williams, *The Wild Life of the Army: Civil War Letters of James A. Garfield*; Daniel Vermilya, *James Garfield and the Civil War*, page 64.

29. Frederick Henry, *Captain Henry of Geauga: A Family Chronicle*, page 114; Daniel Vermilya, *James Garfield and the Civil War*, page 64; James Garfield to Eliza Garfield, January 26, 1862, Frederick Williams, *The Wild Life of the Army: Civil War Letters of James A. Garfield*.

30. William Ely, *The Big Sandy Valley*, page 299; Frank Mason, *The Forty-Second Ohio Infantry: A History of the Organization and Services of That Regiment in the War of the Rebellion; with Biographical Sketches of Its Field Officers and a Full Roster of the Regiment*, pages 71–72.

31. Frederick Henry, *Captain Henry of Geauga: A Family Chronicle*, pages 113–114.

32. James Garfield to Eliza Garfield, January 26, 1862, Frederick Williams, *The Wild Life of the Army: Civil War Letters of James A. Garfield*; Frank Mason, *The Forty-Second Ohio Infantry: A History of the Organization and Services of That Regiment in the War of the Rebellion; with Biographical Sketches of Its Field Officers and a Full Roster of the Regiment*, page 76.

33. Frederick Henry, *Captain Henry of Geauga: A Family Chronicle*, page 114; James Garfield to Lucretia Garfield, January 13, 1862, Frederick Williams, *The Wild Life of the Army: Civil War Letters of James A. Garfield*.

34. Frank Mason, *The Forty-Second Ohio Infantry: A History of the Organization and Services of That Regiment in the War of the Rebellion; with Biographical Sketches of Its Field Officers and a Full Roster of the Regiment*, page 76.

35. "General Garfield's Victory Over Marshall," *The Evening Star*, February 11, 1862; "Further of the Affair at Paintsville," *Detroit Free Press*, January 15, 1862; "Important from Kentucky—Humphrey Marshall's Rebel Force Disbanded," *Hartford Courant*, January 13, 1862; "The Battle of Prestonburg, Kentucky," *New England Farmer*, February 1, 1862; "Gallantry of Colonel Garfield," *The Indiana Herald*, January 29, 1862; "Latest Eastern News," *Petaluma Argus*, January 21, 1862; Clipping, *The New York Times*, January 22, 1862; "Col. Garfield's Victory," *The New York Times*, January 21, 1862.

36. "Col. J. A. Garfield," *Western Reserve Chronicle*, February 5, 1862.

37. "Col. Garfield's Victory," *Cleveland Morning Leader*, January 13, 1862; "Col. Garfield," *Summit County Beacon*, January 30, 1862; J. H. Rhodes to James Garfield, January 20, 1862, JAG—LC.

38. William Hazen to James Garfield, January 24, 1862, JAG—LC; *The War of the Rebellion: A Compilation of the Official Records of the Union and Confederate Armies*, series 1, volume 7, 1882, pages 24–25.

39. Frederick Henry, *Captain Henry of Geauga: A Family Chronicle*, page 115.

40. Frank Mason, *The Forty-Second Ohio Infantry: A History of the Organization and Services of That Regiment in the War of the Rebellion; with Biographical Sketches of Its Field Officers and a Full Roster of the Regiment*, pages 78–79; "The Indomitable Energy of Col. Garfield—How He Piloted a Steamer and Saved his Men from Starvation," *Cleveland Daily Leader*, February 7, 1862.

41. James Garfield to Lucretia Garfield, February 23, 1862, JAG—LC; Frank Mason, *The Forty-Second Ohio Infantry: A History of the Organization and Services of That Regiment in the War of the Rebellion; with Biographical Sketches of Its Field Officers and a Full Roster of the Regiment*, pages 82–83.

42. James Garfield to Lucretia Garfield, February 23, 1862, JAG—LC; James Garfield to Lucretia Garfield, March 10, 1862, Frederick Williams, *The Wild Life of the Army: Civil War Letters of James A. Garfield*.

43. James Garfield to Lucretia Garfield, March 10, 1862, Frederick Williams, *The Wild Life of the Army: Civil War Letters of James A. Garfield*.

44. James Garfield to J. H. Rhodes, February 12, 1862, Frederick Williams, *The Wild Life of the Army: Civil War Letters of James A. Garfield*.

45. Frank Mason, *The Forty-Second Ohio Infantry: A History of the Organization and Services of That Regiment in the War of the Rebellion; with Biographical Sketches of Its Field Officers and a Full Roster of the Regiment*, pages 80–81; Garfield, "My Campaign In East Kentucky."

46. Frederick Henry, *Captain Henry of Geauga: A Family Chronicle*, pages 123–124; Frank Mason, *The Forty-Second Ohio Infantry: A History of the Organization and Services of That Regiment in the War of the Rebellion; with Biographical Sketches of Its Field Officers and a Full Roster of the Regiment*, pages 86–87; Frederick Henry, *Captain Henry of Geauga: A Family Chronicle*, page 124; James Garfield to Lucretia Garfield, March 19, 1862, Frederick Williams, *The Wild Life of the Army: Civil War Letters of James A. Garfield*.

47. James Garfield to Lucretia Garfield, March 19, 1862, Frederick Williams, *The Wild Life of the Army: Civil War Letters of James A. Garfield*; Frederick Henry, *Captain Henry of Geauga: A Family Chronicle*, page 120; James Garfield to "My Dear Wall," February 14, 1863, Frederick Williams, *The Wild Life of the Army: Civil War Letters of James A. Garfield*; James Garfield to J. H. Rhodes, March 3, 1862, JAG—LC.

48. Frank Mason, *The Forty-Second Ohio Infantry: A History of the Organization and Services of That Regiment in the War of the Rebellion; with Biographical Sketches of Its Field Officers and a Full Roster of the Regiment*, pages 89–90; Biographical interview of James Garfield, 1880, JAG—LC.

CHAPTER 9

1. James Garfield to Augustus Williams, April 16, 1862, JAG—HC; Gerald J. Prokopowicz, *All for the Regiment: The Army of the Ohio, 1861–1862*, Civil War America (Chapel Hill: University of North Carolina Press, 2001), pages 98–99; Ambrose Bierce, *The Collected Works of Ambrose Bierce*, volume 1 (New York: The Neale

Publishing Company, 1909), pages 236–237; James McPherson, *Battle Cry of Freedom*, page 409; Ulysses S. Grant. *Personal Memoirs of U.S. Grant* (New York: Barnes & Noble Books, 2003), page 202.

2. James McPherson, *Battle Cry of Freedom*, page 405; Ron Chernow, *Grant*, pages 199, 201; Bierce, *The Collected Works of Ambrose Bierce*, page 242.

3. James Garfield to Augustus Williams, April 16, 1862, JAG—HC; James Garfield to Lucretia Garfield, April 21, 1862, JAG—LC; James Garfield to Lucretia Garfield, April 9, 1862, JAG—LC.

4. Ulysses S. Grant, *Personal Memoirs of U.S. Grant*, pages 206, 233; James Garfield to Lucretia Garfield, April 21, 1862, JAG—LC.

5. James Garfield to Eliza Garfield, May 8, 1862. Frederick Williams, *The Wild Life of the Army: Civil War Letters of James A. Garfield*; Bierce, *The Collected Works of Ambrose Bierce*, pages 237–238, 250; Gerald Prokopowicz, *All for the Regiment*, pages 115–117.

6. Bierce, *The Collected Works of Ambrose Bierce*, page 237; Ulysses S. Grant, *Personal Memoirs of U.S. Grant*, page 200; James Garfield to J. H. Rhodes, May 19, 1862, JAG—LC.

7. James Garfield to J. H. Rhodes, May 19, 1862, JAG—LC.

8. James Garfield to Almeda Booth, May 20, 1862, JAG—LC.

9. James Garfield to J. H. Rhodes, May 1, 1862, JAG—LC; James Garfield to Lucretia Garfield, February 23, 1862, Frederick Williams, *The Wild Life of the Army: Civil War Letters of James A. Garfield*; James Garfield to J. H. Rhodes, May 1, 1862, JAG—LC.

10. James McPherson, *Battle Cry of Freedom*, pages 352–354.

11. James Garfield to J. H. Rhodes, May 1, 1862, JAG—LC.

12. James Garfield to Harmon Austin, May 28, 1862, JAG—LC; James Garfield to J. H. Rhodes, May 19, 1862, JAG—LC.

13. J. H. Rhodes to James Garfield, May 3, 1862, JAG—LC; George Washington Julian, *The Life of Joshua R. Giddings*, page 353; Allan Peskin, *Garfield*, page 140.

14. "From Garfield's Brigade," *Summit County Beacon*, April 10, 1862; "Our Military Correspondence," *The Jeffersonian Democrat*, April 11, 1862; "From the 64th Regiment," *Summit County Beacon*, May 22, 1862; "From Corinth Before the Evacuation," *Cleveland Daily Leader*, June 6, 1862.

15. J. H. Rhodes to James Garfield, May 9, 1862, JAG—LC; J. H. Rhodes to James Garfield, May 26, 1862, JAG—LC.

16. William Hazen. *A Narrative of Military Service* (Boston: Ticknor and Company, 1885), pages 28–36, 47; James Garfield to J. H. Rhodes, May 28, 1862, JAG—LC.

17. James Garfield to J. H. Rhodes, May 19, 1862, JAG—LC; James Garfield to J. H. Rhodes, May 28, 1862, JAG—LC; Gerald J. Prokopowicz, *All for the Regiment: The Army of the Ohio, 1861–1862*, page 117; James Garfield to J. H. Rhodes, May 28, 1862, JAG—LC; James Garfield to J. H. Rhodes, June 10, 1862, JAG—LC; J. H. Rhodes to James Garfield, May 26, 1862, JAG—LC.

18. James Garfield to J. H. Rhodes, June 10, 1862, JAG—LC.

19. James Garfield to Lucretia Garfield, June 7, 1862, Frederick Williams, *The Wild Life of the Army: Civil War Letters of James A. Garfield.*

20. James Garfield to Lucretia Garfield, June 14, 1862; Wilbur F. Hinman. *The Story of the Sherman Brigade* (Alliance, Ohio: Daily Review, 1897), pages 218–220; James Garfield to Harmon Austin, June 25, 1862, Frederick Williams, ed., *The Wild Life of the Army: Civil War Letters of James A. Garfield.*

21. James Garfield to Lucretia Garfield, June 14, 1862.

22. James Garfield to Lucretia Garfield, June 14, 1862; James Garfield to Lucretia Garfield, June 23, 1862. Frederick Williams, *The Wild Life of the Army: Civil War Letters of James A. Garfield.*

23. James Garfield to Harmon Austin, June 25, 1862, JAG—LC.

24. Whitelaw Reid. *Ohio In the War: Her Statesmen, Generals, and Soldiers,* vol. 1 (Columbus: Eclectic Publishing Company, 1868), page 762.

25. P. R. Spencer to James Garfield, July 7, 1862, JAG—LC.

26. James Garfield to J. H. Rhodes, July 24, 1862, JAG—LC; J. H. Rhodes to James Garfield, May 26, 1862, JAG—LC; J. H. Rhodes to James Garfield, July 26, 1862, JAG—LC.

27. Lucretia Garfield to James Garfield, July 20, 1862, Garfield and Garfield, *Crete and James.*

28. James Garfield to Lucretia Garfield, July 17, 1862, Frederick Williams, *The Wild Life of the Army: Civil War Letters of James A. Garfield*; James Garfield to David Swaim, July 9, 1862, SG—WRHS.

29. James Garfield to J. H. Rhodes, July 10, 1862, JAG—LC.

30. James Garfield to David Swaim, July 9, 1862, SG—WRHS.

31. Orders granting Garfield sick leave, dated July 30, 1862, JAG—LC; J. H. Rhodes to James Garfield, August 1, 1862, JAG—LC.

32. James Garfield to Lucretia Garfield, February 15, 1862, Frederick Williams, *The Wild Life of the Army: Civil War Letters of James A. Garfield*; Lucretia Garfield to James Garfield, July 20, 1862, Garfield and Garfield.

33. James Garfield to Corydon Fuller, September 5, 1862, JAG—LC; James Garfield to Eliza Garfield, September 2, 1862, Frederick Williams, *The Wild Life of the Army: Civil War Letters of James A. Garfield*; Lucretia Garfield to James Garfield, September 18, 1862, Garfield and Garfield, *Crete and James*; James Garfield to Lucretia Garfield, September 17, 1862, JAG—LC.

34. Clipping, *Jeffersonian Democrat,* August 8, 1862; "For Congress," *Western Reserve Chronicle,* August 6, 1862; "General Garfield," *Cleveland Daily Leader,* August 14, 1862.

35. James Garfield to Horace Beebe, August 15, 1862, JAG—LC.

36. James Garfield to Eliza Garfield, September 2, 1862, Frederick Williams, *The Wild Life of the Army: Civil War Letters of James A. Garfield.*

37. "Nineteenth Congressional District," *Cleveland Daily Leader,* September 2, 1862.

38. James Garfield to Corydon Fuller, September 5, 1862, JAG—LC.

CHAPTER 10

1. James Garfield to J. H. Rhodes, September 22, 1862, Frederick Williams, *The Wild Life of the Army: Civil War Letters of James A. Garfield*; James Garfield to Burke Hinsdale, September 12, 1862, JAG—LC; James Garfield to Lucretia Garfield, September 17, 1862, Frederick Williams, *The Wild Life of the Army: Civil War Letters of James A. Garfield.*

2. Constance McLaughlin Green. *Washington: A History of the Capital, 1800–1950*, volume 1 (Princeton, New Jersey: University Press, 1976), pages 246–247; Thomas H. Sherman. *Twenty Years with James G. Blaine: Reminiscences by His Private Secretary* (New York: The Grafton Press, 1928), pages 1–2; Robert Vincent Remini. *The House: The History of the House of Representatives* (New York: Smithsonian Books, in association with HarperCollins, 2006), page 178.

3. James Garfield to Lucretia Garfield, September 20, 1862, Frederick Williams, *The Wild Life of the Army: Civil War Letters of James A. Garfield*; Walter Stahr. *Stanton: Lincoln's War Secretary* (New York: Simon & Schuster, 2017), page 134; John Niven. *Salmon P. Chase: A Biography* (New York, Oxford: Oxford University Press, 1995), page 79.

4. James Garfield to Harmon Austin, September 25, 1862, Frederick Williams, *The Wild Life of the Army: Civil War Letters of James A. Garfield.*

5. James Garfield to Lucretia Garfield, September 27, 1862, Frederick Williams, *The Wild Life of the Army: Civil War Letters of James A. Garfield*; James Garfield to Lucretia Garfield, November 16, 1862, JAG—LC; James Garfield to Lucretia Garfield, October 12, 1862, Frederick Williams, *The Wild Life of the Army: Civil War Letters of James A. Garfield.*

6. James Garfield to J. H. Rhodes, May 1, 1862, JAG—LC.

7. James McPherson, *Battle Cry of Freedom*, page 533; James Garfield to J. H. Rhodes, October 5, 1862, Frederick Williams, *The Wild Life of the Army: Civil War Letters of James A. Garfield.*

8. James Garfield to Burke Hinsdale, October 30, 1862, Frederick Williams, *The Wild Life of the Army: Civil War Letters of James A. Garfield*; James Garfield to J. H. Rhodes, October 5, September 26, 1862, Frederick Williams, *The Wild Life of the Army: Civil War Letters of James A. Garfield.*

9. James Garfield to J. H. Rhodes, September 26, December 7, 1862, Frederick Williams, *The Wild Life of the Army: Civil War Letters of James A. Garfield.*

10. James Garfield to Lucretia Garfield, September 20, 1862, Frederick Williams, *The Wild Life of the Army: Civil War Letters of James A. Garfield*; Diary entry of Salmon Chase for September 25, 1862, Salmon P. Chase, *The Diary and Correspondence of Salmon P. Chase, as Provided in the Annual Report of the American Historical Association for the Year 1902*, vol. 2 (Washington, D.C.: Government Printing Office, 1903).

11. Richard Franklin Bensel. *Yankee Leviathan: The Origins of Central State Authority in America, 1859–1877* (Cambridge, England; New York: Cambridge University Press, 1990), pages 239–248; John Niven, *Salmon P. Chase: A Biography*, page 297; Carl Sandburg, *Abraham Lincoln: The War Years*, 1939, volume 1, page 652; "Richard Cole," Historic Photograph of Salmon P. Chase Donated to the Treasury, U.S.

Department of the Treasury, *Treasury Notes* (blog), December 26, 2013, https://www.treasury.gov/connect/blog/Pages/Salmon-Chase-Photo.aspx.

12. James Garfield to J. H. Rhodes, November 2, 1862, Frederick Williams, *The Wild Life of the Army: Civil War Letters of James A. Garfield.*

13. James Garfield to Lucretia Garfield, February 1, 1863, Frederick Williams, *The Wild Life of the Army: Civil War Letters of James A. Garfield.*

14. James McPherson, *Battle Cry of Freedom*, page 358.

15. Hans Trefousse, *The Radical Republicans*, pages 1–2; F. M. Brodie, *Thaddeus Stevens: Scourge of the South*, page 196.

16. Carl Sandburg, *Abraham Lincoln: The War Years*, 1939, volume 1, page 396; Noah Brooks and Herbert Mitgang. *Washington, D.C., in Lincoln's Time*, The Journalist's Lincoln (Athens: University of Georgia Press, 1989), page 27; Carl Sandburg, *Abraham Lincoln: The War Years*, 1939, volume 1, page 398.

17. Carl Sandburg, *Abraham Lincoln: The War Years*, 1939, volume 1, pages 393, 395, 399.

18. F. M. Brodie, *Thaddeus Stevens: Scourge of the South*, page 159.

19. James M. McPherson and David M. Kennedy. *Battle Cry of Freedom: The Civil War Era*, new ed., The Oxford History of the United States, David M. Kennedy, general ed., volume 6 (Oxford: Oxford University Press, 1988), page 557.

20. James M. McPherson and David M. Kennedy, *Battle Cry of Freedom: The Civil War Era*, pages 356, 500; Abraham Lincoln, et al., *The Writings of Abraham Lincoln, Rethinking the Western Tradition* (New Haven; London: Yale University Press, 2012), page 395.

21. Lincoln, et al., *The Writings of Abraham Lincoln, Rethinking the Western Tradition*, page 396.

22. James Garfield to Lucretia Garfield, September 27, 1862, Frederick Williams, *The Wild Life of the Army: Civil War Letters of James A. Garfield.*

23. James Garfield to Lucretia Garfield, January 2, 1863, JAG—LC; James Garfield to J. H. Rhodes, September 26, 1862, Frederick Williams, *The Wild Life of the Army: Civil War Letters of James A. Garfield.*

24. Lucretia Garfield to James Garfield, December 28, 1862, JAG—LC; Lucretia Garfield to James Garfield, January 2, 1863, JAG—LC; Lucretia Garfield to James Garfield, November 16, 1862, JAG—LC.

25. James Garfield to Lucretia Garfield, October 3, 1862, Frederick Williams, *The Wild Life of the Army: Civil War Letters of James A. Garfield*; James Garfield to Lucretia Garfield, January 6, 1863, Garfield and Garfield, *Crete and James.*

26. James Garfield to Lucretia Garfield, January 20, 1863, JAG—LC.

27. Allan Peskin, *Garfield*, page 160.

CHAPTER 11

1. James Garfield to Lucretia Garfield, January 25, 1863. Frederick Williams, *The Wild Life of the Army: Civil War Letters of James A. Garfield*; James Garfield to J. H. Rhodes, January 27, 1863, Frederick Williams, *The Wild Life of the Army: Civil War Letters of James A. Garfield.*

2. William M. Lamers. *The Edge of Glory: A Biography of General William S. Rosecrans, U.S.A*, Louisiana paperback edition (Baton Rouge: Louisiana State University Press, 1999), page 245; Carl Sandburg, *Abraham Lincoln: The War Years*, volume 2, page 6.

3. James Garfield to Lucretia Garfield, January 26, 1863, Garfield and Garfield, *Crete and James*; Glenn Tucker. *Chickamauga: Bloody Battle in the West* (New York: Smithmark Publishers, 1994), page 43.

4. James Garfield to Lucretia Garfield, January 25, 1863, Frederick Williams, *The Wild Life of the Army: Civil War Letters of James A. Garfield*; James Garfield to J. H. Rhodes, February 14, 1863, Frederick Williams, *The Wild Life of the Army: Civil War Letters of James A. Garfield*; Larry J. Daniel. *Days of Glory: The Army of the Cumberland, 1861–1865*, Louisiana paperback edition (Baton Rouge: Louisiana State University Press, 2006), page 217.

5. James Garfield to J. H. Rhodes, February 14, 1863. Frederick Williams, *The Wild Life of the Army: Civil War Letters of James A. Garfield*.

6. James Garfield to Salmon Chase, February 15, 1863, Frederick Williams; Salmon Chase to James Garfield, February 24, 1863, JAG—LC.

7. James Garfield to Lucretia Garfield, February 26, 1863, Frederick Williams, *The Wild Life of the Army: Civil War Letters of James A. Garfield*.

8. James R. Gilmore (Edmund Kirke). *Personal Recollections of Abraham Lincoln and the Civil War* (Boston: L.C. Page and Company, 1898), page 118; Allan Peskin, *Garfield*, page 174.

9. James Garfield to Salmon Chase, April 12, 1863, Frederick Williams, *The Wild Life of the Army: Civil War Letters of James A. Garfield*.

10. James Garfield to Salmon Chase, April 12, 1863, JAG—LC; Larry Daniel, *Days of Glory*, page 253; James Garfield to Salmon Chase, April 12, 1863, Frederick Williams, *The Wild Life of the Army: Civil War Letters of James A. Garfield*.

11. Larry Daniel, *Days of Glory*, page 254; James Garfield to Lucretia Garfield, April 25, 1863, James Garfield to Eliza Garfield, March 22, 1863, Frederick Williams, *The Wild Life of the Army: Civil War Letters of James A. Garfield*.

12. James Garfield to Lucretia Garfield, April 25, 1863, JAG—LC.

13. Glenn Tucker, *Chickamauga*, page 43; William Lamers, *The Edge of Glory*, page 253.

14. William Lamers, *The Edge of Glory*, page 252; Allan Peskin, *Garfield*, page 181; Larry Daniel, *Days of Glory*, page 257; Ulysses S. Grant, *Personal Memoirs of U.S. Grant*, page 257.

15. James Garfield to Lucretia Garfield, January 26, 1863, Frederick Williams, *The Wild Life of the Army: Civil War Letters of James A. Garfield*; James Garfield to J. H. Rhodes, June 11, 1863, Frederick Williams, *The Wild Life of the Army: Civil War Letters of James A. Garfield*.

16. James Garfield to William Rosecrans, June 12, 1863, Frederick Williams, *The Wild Life of the Army: Civil War Letters of James A. Garfield*.

17. Glenn Tucker, *Chickamauga*, page 46; D. S. Stanley. *Personal Memoirs of Major-General D.S. Stanley, U.S.A* (Cambridge, Massachusetts: Harvard University Press, 1917), pages 131, 158.

18. James Garfield to William Rosecrans, June 12, 1863, Frederick Williams, *The Wild Life of the Army: Civil War Letters of James A. Garfield*; James Garfield to Lucretia Garfield, June 14, 1863, Frederick Williams, *The Wild Life of the Army: Civil War Letters of James A. Garfield*.

19. James Garfield to Lucretia Garfield, June 24, 1863, Frederick Williams, *The Wild Life of the Army: Civil War Letters of James A. Garfield*.

20. Whitelaw Reid. *Ohio In the War: Her Statesmen, Generals, and Soldiers*, volume 1 (Columbus: Eclectic Publishing Company, 1868), page 756; James Garfield to Lucretia Garfield, June 24, 1863, JAG—LC.

21. James McPherson, *Battle Cry of Freedom*, page 669; Larry Daniel, *Days of Glory*, page 273; William Lamers, *The Edge of Glory*, pages 286–288.

22. Reid, *Ohio In the War: Her Statesmen, Generals, and Soldiers*, page 756; Larry Daniel, *Days of Glory*, page 275; James McPherson, *Battle Cry of Freedom*, page 669.

23. James McPherson, *Battle Cry of Freedom*, pages 636–638, 664–665.

24. William Lamers, *The Edge of Glory*, page 291.

25. *The War of the Rebellion: A Compilation of the Official Records of the Union and Confederate Armies*, series 1, volume 23 (Government Printing Office, 1889), page 409.

26. James Garfield to Salmon Chase, July 27, 1863, Frederick Williams, *The Wild Life of the Army: Civil War Letters of James A. Garfield*.

27. William Lamers, *The Edge of Glory*, page 292; James Garfield to Lucretia Garfield, September 6, 1863, Frederick Williams, *The Wild Life of the Army: Civil War Letters of James A. Garfield*.

28. James McPherson, *Battle Cry of Freedom*, page 670; Glenn Tucker, *Chickamauga*, page 29.

29. Glenn Tucker, *Chickamauga*, pages 122–123; James McPherson, *Battle Cry of Freedom*, page 671; Larry Daniel, *Days of Glory*, page 305.

30. Glenn Tucker, *Chickamauga*, pages 122–123.

31. Glenn Tucker, *Chickamauga*, page 123; Larry Daniel, *Days of Glory*, page 317.

32. James Garfield to Harmon Austin, March 8, 1875, JAG—LC.

33. Charles Dana. *Recollections of the Civil War: With the Leaders at Washington and in the Field in the Sixties* (New York: D. Appleton and Company, 1909), page 114; "Chattanooga," *New York Herald*, September 29, 1863; Larry Daniel, *Days of Glory*, pages 318, 323. William Lamers, *The Edge of Glory*, page 336.

34. Charles Dana, *Recollections of the Civil War: With the Leaders at Washington and in the Field in the Sixties*, pages 115–117; Jacob Dolson Cox. *Military Reminiscences of the Civil War*, vol. 2 (New York: Charles Scribner's Sons, 1900), page 9.

35. James McPherson, *Battle Cry of Freedom*, page 672.

36. Charles Dana, *Recollections of the Civil War: With the Leaders at Washington and in the Field in the Sixties*, pages 115–118.

37. Charles Dana, *Recollections of the Civil War*, page 118; Jacob Dolson Cox, *Military Reminiscences of the Civil War*, page 10.

38. William Lamers, *The Edge of Glory*, pages 354–355.

39. James Garfield to Eliza Garfield, October 13, 1863, Frederick Williams, *The Wild Life of the Army: Civil War Letters of James A. Garfield*.

40. Glenn Tucker, *Chickamauga*, page 359.

41. James McPherson, *Battle Cry of Freedom*, page 674; "The Battles At Chickamauga," *New York Herald*, September 27, 1863; Theodore Clarke Smith, *The Life and Letters of James Abram Garfield*, page 338.

42. Carl Sandburg, *Abraham Lincoln: The War Years*, volume 2, pages 426, 434.

43. William Lamers, *The Edge of Glory*, pages 408–409.

44. James Garfield to Eliza Garfield, October 13, 1863, Frederick Williams, *The Wild Life of the Army: Civil War Letters of James A. Garfield*; General Orders No. 231, Department of the Cumberland, October 10, 1863, JAG—LC.

45. William Lamers, *The Edge of Glory*, page 411; James Garfield to David Swaim, November 16, 1863, SG—WRHS.

46. James Garfield to Lucretia Garfield, October 30, 1863, JAG—LC; "Local Matters," *The Baltimore Sun*, October 29, 1863.

47. "The Great Union Meeting at Baltimore," *Cleveland Daily Herald*, November 2, 1863.

48. James Garfield to Harmon Austin, December 1, 1863 (first note on that date), Frederick Williams, *The Wild Life of the Army: Civil War Letters of James A. Garfield*; James Garfield to Harmon Austin, December 1, 1863 (second note on that date), Frederick Williams, *The Wild Life of the Army: Civil War Letters of James A. Garfield*; Lucretia Garfield to James Garfield, December 6, 1863, Garfield and Garfield, *Crete and James*.

49. Margaret Lord to Lt. George Hurlbut, December 13, 1863, James A. Garfield Collection, JAG—HC.

50. James Garfield to Lucretia Garfield, December 6, 1863, Garfield and Garfield, *Crete and James*; James Garfield to David Swaim, December 15, 1863, SG—WRHS.

CHAPTER 12

1. Noah Brooks, *Washington, D.C., in Lincoln's Time*, pages 20–21; "Local News," *The Evening Star*, December 2, 1863.

2. Bell Irvin Wiley. *The Life of Johnny Reb: The Common Soldier of the Confederacy*, updated edition (Baton Rouge: Louisiana State University Press, 2017), page 136; James McPherson, *Battle Cry of Freedom*, page 721.

3. Hans Trefousse, *The Radical Republicans*, page 283; James McPherson, *Battle Cry of Freedom*, page 700.

4. James McPherson, *Battle Cry of Freedom*, pages 699–700; Carl Sandburg, *Abraham Lincoln: The War Years*, 1939, volume 2, page 484; David Herbert Donald, *Lincoln*, page 472; James McPherson, *Battle Cry of Freedom*, pages 704–705.

5. Hans Trefousse, *The Radical Republicans*, page 284; Carl Sandburg, *Abraham Lincoln: The War Years*, volume 4, page 189.

6. Fawn M. Brodie, *Thaddeus Stevens: Scourge of the South*, page 207; Michael Les Benedict. *A Compromise of Principle: Congressional Republicans and Reconstruction, 1863–1869*, first edition (New York: Norton, 1974), page 76.

7. Xi Wang. *The Trial of Democracy: Black Suffrage and Northern Republicans, 1860–1910*, Studies in the Legal History of the South (Athens: University of Georgia

Press, 1997), page 15; Hans Trefousse, *The Radical Republicans*, page 287; Fawn M. Brodie, *Thaddeus Stevens: Scourge of the South*, page 208.

8. Robert Remini, *The House*, pages 157–158.

9. Noah Brooks, *Washington, D.C., in Lincoln's Time*, page 30.

10. James Garfield to Lucretia Garfield, December 6, 1863, Frederick Williams, *The Wild Life of the Army: Civil War Letters of James A. Garfield*.

11. Albert Gallatin Riddle, *Recollections of War Times: Reminiscences of Men and Events in Washington, 1860–1865* (G.P. Putnam's Sons, 1895), page 253; Robert C. Schenck, *Draw: Rules for Playing Poker* (Brooklyn, New York: privately printed, 1880).

12. James Garfield to Lucretia Garfield, December 21, 1863, JAG—LC.

13. *Congressional Globe*, 38th Congress, Session I, pages 127, 1290, 2772.

14. James Garfield to Lucretia Garfield, December 21, 1863, JAG—LC.

15. Lucretia Garfield to James Garfield, January 22, 1864, Garfield and Garfield, *Crete and James*; James Garfield to Lucretia Garfield, April 17, 1864, JAG—LC.

16. James Garfield to Burke Hinsdale, February 18, 1864, JAG—LC.

17. Noah Brooks, *Washington, D.C., in Lincoln's Time*, page 30; Carl Sandburg, *Abraham Lincoln: The War Years*, 1939, volume 2, page 558; Speech of General Garfield, *Cleveland Daily Herald*, April 16, 1864.

18. Ari Hoogenboom, *Rutherford B. Hayes: Warrior & President*, page 192; "Mr. Pendleton's Record," *Indianapolis Star*, October 3, 1864.

19. "Northern Ohio Sanitary Fair," *Cleveland Daily Leader*, February 24, 1864; "Speech on Confiscation of Rebel Property," January 28, 1864; Garfield, *The Works of James A. Garfield*, 1882.

20. *Congressional Globe*, 38th Congress, Session I, page 213; *Congressional Globe*, 38th Congress, Session I, page 1504.

21. Eric Foner. *The Second Founding: How the Civil War and Reconstruction Remade the Constitution*, first edition (New York: W.W. Norton & Company, 2019), page 19; "Enrolling and Calling Out the National Forces," June 25, 1864, Garfield, *The Works of James A. Garfield*, 1882.

22. James Garfield to Lucretia Garfield, May 29, 1864, JAG—LC; James Garfield to J. H. Rhodes, April 28, 1864, JAG—LC; James Garfield to William Cooper Howells, June 18, 1864, Margaret Leech, *The Garfield Orbit*.

23. Eugene Schmiel, *Citizen-General: Jacob Dolson Cox and the Civil War Era*, pages 167–168; *Congressional Globe*, 38th Congress, Session I, page 1505.

24. Biographical interview of James Garfield, 1880, JAG—LC.

25. James Garfield to David Swaim, August 13, 1864, SG—WRHS.

26. Fawn Brodie, *Thaddeus Stevens: Scourge of the South*, page 208; "To The Supporters of the Government," *New-York Tribune*, August 5, 1864.

27. Salmon P. Chase and John Niven. *The Salmon P. Chase Papers* (Kent, Ohio: Kent State University Press, 1993), page 477; James Garfield to David Swaim, August 13, 1864, SG—WRHS.

28. Allan Peskin, *Garfield*, page 242; Albert Riddle, *Recollections of War Times: Reminiscences of Men and Events in Washington, 1860—1865*, pages 304–305.

29. Allan Peskin, *Garfield*, page 243.

30. James McPherson, *Battle Cry of Freedom*, page 714; John Niven, *Salmon P. Chase: A Biography*, pages 346–347; Milton C. Canfield to James Garfield, February 9, 1864, JAG—LC.

31. Carl Sandburg, *Abraham Lincoln: The War Years*, 1939 volume 2, pages 628, 640.

32. James Garfield to J. H. Rhodes, April 28, 1864, JAG—LC; James Garfield to J. H. Rhodes, May 9, 1864, JAG—LC; Theodore Clarke Smith, *The Life and Letters of James Abram Garfield*, 1925, page 377; John Niven, *Salmon P. Chase: A Biography*, page 357.

33. Theodore Clarke Smith, *The Life and Letters of James Abram Garfield*, 1925, pages 375–376.

34. Diary entry for June 3, 1874. JAG—LC; James Garfield to Harmon Austin, April 26, 1879, JAG—LC; James Garfield to Burke Hinsdale, January 5, 1881, JAG—LC; Diary entry for November 30, 1873 and February 5, 1879, JAG—LC.

35. James McPherson, *Battle Cry of Freedom*, page 715; John Niven, *Salmon P. Chase: A Biography*, pages 365–366.

36. Lucretia Garfield to James Garfield, April 14, 1864, JAG—LC; Lucretia Garfield to James Garfield, May 29, 1864, JAG—LC.

37. James Garfield to Lucretia Garfield, May 8, 1864, Garfield and Garfield, *Crete and James*; Lucretia Garfield to James Garfield, May 8, 1864, JAG—LC; Allan Peskin, *Garfield*, page 160.

38. James Garfield to Lucretia Garfield, June 12, 1864, Garfield and Garfield, *Crete and James*.

39. Lucretia Garfield to James Garfield, June 16, 1864, Garfield and Garfield, *Crete and James*; James Garfield to Lucretia Garfield, June 19, 1864, Garfield and Garfield, *Crete and James*.

40. Lucretia Garfield to James Garfield, July 3, 1864, JAG—LC; James Garfield to Lucretia Garfield, September 23, 1864, Garfield and Garfield, *Crete and James*.

41. Biographical interview of James Garfield, 1880, JAG—LC; William Ralston Balch, *Garfield's Words: Suggestive Passages From The Public And Private Writings of James Abram Garfield*, page 340.

42. "Abolition of Slavery—Speech of General Garfield," *Cleveland Daily Herald*, January 19, 1865.

43. James McPherson, *Battle Cry of Freedom*, pages 839–840; David Blight, *Frederick Douglass*, page 454.

44. James Garfield to Burke Hinsdale, February 5, 1865, JAG—LC; David Herbert Donald, *Lincoln*, page 555.

45. David Herbert Donald, *Lincoln*, page 558.

46. James Garfield to Lucretia Garfield, April 17, 1865, JAG—LC.

47. "Suffrage and Safety," July 4, 1865, Garfield, *The Works of James A. Garfield*, 1882.

48. James Garfield to J. H. Rhodes, October 5, 1862, JAG—LC; Noah Brooks, *Washington, D.C., in Lincoln's Time*, page 98.

49. "Suffrage and Safety," July 4, 1865, Garfield, *The Works of James A. Garfield*, 1882.

50. "Gen. Garfield Sun-Struck," *Daily Ohio Statesman*, July 7, 1865.

CHAPTER 13

1. "Gen. Garfield Sun-Struck," *Daily Ohio Statesman,* July 7, 1865; James Garfield to David Swaim, September 23, 1865, SG—WRHS.
2. Clement Eaton, *A History of the Southern Confederacy,* pages 230, 239; James McPherson, *Battle Cry of Freedom,* page 856.
3. Georges Clemenceau. *American Reconstruction: 1865–1870* (New York: Da Capo Press, 1969), page 40.
4. Richard White, *The Republic for Which It Stands,* pages 31–32; Gregory P. Downs. *After Appomattox: Military Occupation and the Ends of War* (Cambridge, Massachusetts: Harvard University Press, 2015), pages 32–33.
5. Gregory Downs, *After Appomattox,* pages 97–98.
6. Richard White, *The Republic for Which It Stands,* page 181.
7. William Crook, *Through Five Administrations,* pages 81–83; Carl Sandburg, *Abraham Lincoln: The War Years,* 1939, volume 1, page 391.
8. Hans Trefousse, *The Radical Republicans,* page 183.
9. Eric Foner, *Reconstruction: America's Unfinished Revolution, 1863–1877,* first edition, The New American Nation Series (New York: Harper & Row, 1988), page 177.
10. Hans Trefousse, *The Radical Republicans,* page 313.
11. Richard White, *The Republic for Which It Stands,* pages 37–38; Hans Trefousse, *Andrew Johnson,* page 217.
12. David Blight, *Frederick Douglass,* page 474.
13. Eric Foner, *Reconstruction,* page 180.
14. Georges Clemenceau, *American Reconstruction: 1865–1870,* page 39.
15. Hans Trefousse, *The Radical Republicans,* page 317; Eric Foner, *Reconstruction,* page 235.
16. Georges Clemenceau, *American Reconstruction: 1865–1870,* page 60; Fawn Brodie, *Thaddeus Stevens: Scourge of the South,* page 224.
17. Whitelaw Reid. *After the War: A Southern Tour* (Cincinnati, Ohio: Moore, Wilstach & Baldwin, 1866), pages 304–305.
18. Whitelaw Reid, *After the War: A Southern Tour,* pages 310–311, 352, 577–578.
19. Brenda Wineapple. *The Impeachers: The Trial of Andrew Johnson and the Dream of a Just Nation,* first edition (New York: Random House, 2019), page 69.
20. James Garfield to Corydon Fuller, October 3, 1865, Corydon Fuller, *Reminiscences of James A. Garfield, with Notes Preliminary and Collateral.*
21. James Garfield to David Swaim, September 23, 1865, SG—WRHS.
22. James Garfield to David Swaim, April 27, 1865, SG—WRHS.
23. "Opening of the Campaign—Senator Sherman and Generals Garfield and Geiger at Ravenna," *Western Reserve Chronicle,* September 6, 1865.
24. James Garfield to Corydon Fuller, October 3, 1865, Corydon Fuller, *Reminiscences of James A. Garfield, with Notes Preliminary and Collateral.*
25. James Garfield to David Swaim, September 23, 1865, SG—WRHS.
26. Eugene Schmiel, *Citizen-General: Jacob Dolson Cox and the Civil War Era,* pages 186–188.

27. Eugene Schmiel, *Citizen-General: Jacob Dolson Cox and the Civil War Era*, pages 176, 186–187; Eric Foner, *Reconstruction*, page 223.

28. Eugene Schmiel, *Citizen-General: Jacob Dolson Cox and the Civil War Era*, page 189; Harmon Austin to James Garfield, August 6, 1865, JAG—LC.

29. James Garfield to Jacob Dolson Cox, August 5, 1865, JAG—LC.

30. James Garfield to Jacob Dolson Cox, August 5, 1865, JAG—LC.

31. Jacob Cox to James Garfield, July 21, 1865, JAG—LC.

32. James Garfield to Jacob Dolson Cox, August 5, 1865, JAG—LC; "Opening of the Campaign—Senator Sherman and Generals Garfield and Geiger at Ravenna," *Western Reserve Chronicle*, September 6, 1865; "The Cox Meeting at Warren," *Daily Ohio Statesman*, August 19, 1865.

33. James Garfield to Harmon Austin, August 6, 1865, JAG—LC.

34. Lucretia Garfield to James Garfield, July 4, 1865, JAG—LC.

35. James Garfield to Lucretia Garfield, December 3, 1865, Garfield and Garfield, *Crete and James*; Lucretia Garfield to James Garfield, December 10, 1865, JAG—LC.

36. James Garfield to Eliza Garfield, March 24, 1864, JAG—LC.

37. James Garfield to Burke Hinsdale, December 11, 1865, JAG—LC; James Garfield to Harmon Austin, December 13, 1865, JAG—LC.

38. Diary entry of Rutherford Hayes for December 1, 1865, Charles Richard Williams, ed., *Diary and Letters of Rutherford Birchard Hayes: Nineteenth President of the United States*, volume 3 (The Ohio State Archaeological and Historical Society, 1925).

39. James Garfield to Harmon Austin, December 13, 1865, JAG—LC.

40. James Garfield to Harmon Austin, December 13, 1865, JAG—LC.

41. Schuyler Colfax to James Garfield, April 8, 1865, JAG—LC.

42. Biographical interview of James Garfield, 1880, JAG—LC.

43. Biographical interview of James Garfield, 1880, JAG—LC; James Garfield to Harmon Austin, December 13, 1865, JAG—LC.

44. Biographical interview of James Garfield, 1880, JAG—LC.

45. "Scenes in Congress—Grouping of Members in the Allotment of Seats," *Kansas Daily Tribune*, December 31, 1865; James Garfield to Lucretia Garfield, December 10, 1865, JAG—LC.

46. James Garfield to Lucretia Garfield, December 17, 1865, JAG—LC.

47. H. Wayne Morgan, *From Hayes to McKinley: National Party Politics, 1877–1896*, page 33; Whitelaw Reid, *After the War: A Southern Tour*, page 431.

48. James Garfield, "Speech on the Restoration of the Southern States," February 1, 1866, Garfield, *The Works of James A. Garfield*, 1882.

49. Clipping, *Cleveland Daily Leader*, February 7, 1866; "From Washington," *Cincinnati Enquirer*, February 7, 1866.

50. James Garfield to Burke Hinsdale, February 13, 1866, JAG—LC; James Garfield to Corydon Fuller, February 15, 1866, Corydon Fuller, *Reminiscences of James A. Garfield, with Notes Preliminary and Collateral*.

51. "Congressional Differences of Opinion," *Cleveland Daily Herald*, February 8, 1866.

52. Hans Trefousse, *Andrew Johnson*, pages 242–243; James Garfield to David Swaim,

March 10, 1866, SG—WRHS; Lucretia Garfield to Harmon Austin, February 26, 1866, JAG—LC.

53. James Garfield to David Swaim, February 20, 1866, SG—WRHS; James Garfield to N. L. Chaffee, March 24, 1866, JAG—WRHS.

54. Hans Trefousse, *Andrew Johnson*, page 244.

CHAPTER 14

1. William E. B. Du Bois. *Black Reconstruction in America: 1860–1880*, first edition (New York: The Free Press, 1998), page 281; Hans Trefousse, *Andrew Johnson*, page 245.

2. Du Bois, *Black Reconstruction in America*, pages 282–284.

3. James Garfield to David Swaim, April 9, 1866, JAG—WRHS.

4. James Garfield to Burke Hinsdale, April 12, 1866, JAG—LC.

5. Eric Foner, *The Second Founding*, page 68; Hans Trefousse, *Andrew Johnson*, page 252.

6. Eric Foner, *The Second Founding*, page 84; James Garfield to W. C. Howells, May 15, 1866, JAG—LC.

7. *Congressional Globe*, 39th Congress, Session I, page 2462; James Garfield to W. G. Howells, May 15, 1866, JAG—LC.

8. James Garfield, "The Tariff Bill of 1866," Speech delivered in the House of Representatives, July 10, 1866, Garfield, *The Works of James A. Garfield*, 1882.

9. James Garfield, "The Public Debt and Specie Payments," March 16, 1866, Garfield.

10. Allan Peskin, *Garfield*, pages 292–293; James Garfield to Burke Hinsdale, April 15, 1866, JAG—LC.

11. Allan Peskin, "The Short, Unhappy Life of the Federal Department of Education," *Public Administration Review* 33, no. 6 (December 1973).

12. James Garfield, "The National Bureau of Education," June 8, 1866, Garfield, *The Works of James A. Garfield*, 1882.

13. James Garfield, "The National Bureau of Education," June 8, 1866, Garfield, *The Works of James A. Garfield*, 1882.

14. *Congressional Globe*, 40th Congress, Session II, page 1141.

15. *Congressional Globe*, 40th Congress, Session II, page 1141.

16. James Garfield to John Eaton, May 16, 1870 JAG—LC.

17. Allan Peskin, "The Short, Unhappy Life of the Federal Department of Education," *Congressional Globe*, 40th Congress, Session II, page 1141.

18. *Congressional Globe*, 40th Congress, Session II, page 1140.

19. *Congressional Globe*, 39th Congress, Session I, page 3270.

20. George Abbott to James Garfield, February 7, 1868, JAG—LC; Allan Peskin, *Garfield*, pages 295–296.

21. John Niven, *Salmon P. Chase: A Biography*, page 404; Mary Black Clayton. *Reminiscences of Jeremiah Sullivan Black* (St. Louis, Missouri: Christian Publishing Company, 1887), page 137.

22. Mary Black Clayton, *Reminiscences of Jeremiah Sullivan Black,* pages 135–136.

23. Biographical interview of James Garfield, 1880, JAG—LC.

24. James Garfield to Burke Hinsdale, March 6, 1866, JAG—LC.
25. "The Case of Col. L.P. Milligan," *Plymouth Democrat*, February 8, 1866; *Milligan, Ex Parte U.S. Supreme Court; Transcript of Record with Supporting Pleadings* (U.S. Supreme Court, 1866), pages 5–18.
26. "From Indianapolis," *Chicago Tribune*, June 7, 1865; Clipping, *Evansville Daily Journal*, May 19, 1865.
27. Biographical interview of James Garfield, 1880, JAG—LC.
28. "The Congressional Question," *Western Reserve Chronicle*, July 11, 1866.
29. Theodore Clarke Smith, *The Life and Letters of James Abram Garfield*, page 395.
30. Jeremiah Black to James Garfield, April 11, 1865, JAG—LC.
31. James Garfield to Burke Hinsdale, January 20, 1867, JAG—LC; James Garfield to Lucretia Garfield, August 22, 1865, JAG—LC; Allan Peskin, *Garfield*, pages 248–250.
32. James Garfield to Lucretia Garfield, May 31, 1865, JAG—LC.
33. Robert B. Mitchell, *Congress and the King of Frauds: Corruption and the Credit Mobilier Scandal at the Dawn of the Gilded Age*, first edition (Roseville, Minnesota: Edinborough Press, 2019), page 12; J. H. Rhodes to James Garfield, December 20, 1866, JAG—LC.
34. James Garfield to Lucretia Garfield, April 10, 1865, JAG—LC.
35. Biographical interview of James Garfield, 1880, JAG—LC.
36. Theodore Clark Smith, *The Life and Letters of James Abram Garfield*, volume 2 (New Haven: Yale University Press, 1925), page 827.
37. *Milligan, Ex Parte U.S. Supreme Court; Transcript of Record with Supporting Pleadings*.
38. John Niven, *Salmon P. Chase: A Biography*, pages 405, 408.
39. Fawn Brodie, *Thaddeus Stevens: Scourge of the South*, page 291.
40. Ibid.
41. "Why Union men should not favor the renomination of Gen. Garfield—Hutchins Forever!" *Western Reserve Chronicle*, July 18, 1866; James Garfield to Burke Hinsdale, January 1, 1867, JAG—LC; James Garfield to Burke Hinsdale, July 18, 1866, JAG—LC; James Garfield to Burke Hinsdale, June 11, 1866, JAG—LC.
42. "The Congressional Question," *Western Reserve Chronicle*, July 25, 1866; "Gen. Garfield and his Professional Practice," *Ashtabula Weekly Telegraph*, July 21, 1866.
43. "Coming Right Along!" *The States and Union*, September 26, 1866; Diary entry for October 5, 1866, Garfield, *The Diary of James A. Garfield* volume 1; Eric Foner, *Reconstruction*, page 333.
44. Diary entry for August 31, 1866, Garfield, *The Diary of James A. Garfield* volume 1; James Garfield to J. H. Rhodes, July 26, 1866, JAG—LC; James Garfield to Harmon Austin, August 18, 1866, JAG—HC; Diary entry for October 5, 1866, Garfield, *The Diary of James A. Garfield* volume 1; Diary entry for September 25, 1866, Garfield, *The Diary of James A. Garfield* volume 1; Diary entry for September 18, 1866, Garfield, *The Diary of James A. Garfield*, volume 1.
45. Diary entry for August 16, 1866, Garfield, *The Diary of James A. Garfield*, volume 1; Clipping, *Gallipolis Journal*, October 25, 1866.
46. James Garfield to Burke Hinsdale, January 1, 1867, JAG—LC.

47. Gregory Downs, *After Appomattox*, pages 154–155; Georges Clemenceau, *American Reconstruction: 1865–1870*, page 83.

48. Hans Trefousse, *The Radical Republicans*, page 359; Fawn Brodie, *Thaddeus Stevens: Scourge of the South*, page 291; Hans Trefousse, *Andrew Johnson*, page 290.

49. "Reconstruction: Remarks Made in the House of Representatives on Various Occasions," Garfield, *The Works of James A. Garfield*, 1882.

50. Hans Trefousse, *The Radical Republicans*, pages 276–277.

51. James Garfield to Harmon Austin, February 15, 1867, JAG—LC.

52. James Garfield to Harmon Austin, March 20, 1867, JAG—HC; James Garfield to Frederick Kinsman, January 31, 1867, JAG—WRHS.

53. James Garfield to David Swaim, February 23, 1867, SG—WRHS.

CHAPTER 15

1. James Garfield to W. D. Howells, May 5, 1867, JAG—LC; James Garfield to Burke Hinsdale, July 12, 1867, JAG—LC.

2. Lucretia Garfield to James Garfield, July 7, 1867, and James Garfield to Lucretia Garfield, July 8, 1867, Garfield and Garfield, *Crete and James*.

3. Diary entry for July 14, 1867, Garfield, *The Diary of James A. Garfield* volume 1.

4. Diary entry for July 24, 1867, Diary entry for July 25, 1867, Diary entry for July 26, 1867, Garfield, *The Diary of James A. Garfield*, volume 1.

5. Diary entry for August 1, 1867, Diary entry for August 7, 1867, Diary entry for August 2, 1867, Diary entry for August 5, 1867, Garfield, *The Diary of James A. Garfield*, volume 1.

6. James Garfield to Burke Hinsdale, August 2, 1867, JAG—LC; James Garfield to Eliza Garfield, August 2, 1867, JAG—LC.

7. "Gen. Garfield's Early Student Life," *Western Reserve Chronicle*, July 31, 1867.

8. Diary entry for October 6, 1867, Garfield, *The Diary of James A. Garfield* volume 1.

9. Diary entry for October 5, 1867, Garfield, *The Diary of James A. Garfield* volume 1.

10. Diary entry for November 6, 1867, Garfield, *The Diary of James A. Garfield* volume 1.

11. James Garfield to J. H. Rhodes, November 25, 1867, JAG—LC.

12. Hans Trefousse, *The Radical Republicans*, pages 366–369; 380–382.

13. Hans Trefousse, *Andrew Johnson*, page 300; James Garfield to J. H. Rhodes, November 25, 1867, JAG—LC.

14. "Washington," *New-York Tribune*, November 23, 1867.

15. James Garfield to Lucretia Garfield, November 24, 1867, JAG—LC.

16. James Garfield to J. H. Rhodes, November 25, 1867, JAG—LC; James Garfield to Harmon Austin, December 13, 1865, JAG—LC.

17. Ovando James Hollister. *Life of Schuyler Colfax* (New York: Funk & Wagnalls, 1886), page 315.

18. James Garfield to Burke Hinsdale, December 5, 1867, JAG—LC; James Garfield to J. H. Rhodes, December 6, 1867, JAG—LC.

19. James Garfield to J. H. Rhodes, April 28, 1868, JAG—LC; Hans Trefousse, *Andrew Johnson*, page 318; James Garfield to B. F. Hoffman, May 4, 1868, JAG—LC.

20. James Garfield to Burke Hinsdale, May 3, 1868, JAG—LC.

21. *Congressional Globe*, 40th Congress, Session II, page 1560.

22. John Niven, *Salmon P. Chase: A Biography*, page 423.

23. James Garfield to J. H. Rhodes, May 7, 1868, JAG—LC.

24. John Niven, *Salmon P. Chase: A Biography*, pages 421, 423.

25. Fawn Brodie, *Thaddeus Stevens: Scourge of the South*, page 339; Hans Trefousse, *The Radical Republicans*, page 383.

26. Gideon Welles. *Diary of Gideon Welles*, ed. John T. Morse Jr., volume 3 (New York: Houghton Mifflin Company, 1911), page 294.

27. Hans Trefousse, *Andrew Johnson*, page 326; James Garfield to J. H. Rhodes, May 20, 1868, JAG—LC; James Garfield to L. W. Hall, May 20, 1868, JAG—LC.

28. James Garfield to Harmon Austin, April 26, 1879; Eliza Garfield to James Garfield, June 14, 1868, JAG—LC.

29. James Garfield to Harmon Austin, April 20, 1868, JAG—HC.

30. Hans Trefousse, *The Radical Republicans*, page 344.

31. James Blaine, *Twenty Years Of Congress: From Lincoln to Garfield* volume 2, page 355.

32. George Hoar. *Autobiography of Seventy Years* volume 1 (New York: Charles Scribner's Sons, 1903), pages 239–240.

CHAPTER 16

1. Ron Chernow, *Grant*, pages 102–103, 545–547; H. Wayne Morgan, *From Hayes to McKinley: National Party Politics, 1877–1896*, page 57.

2. Charles Coleman, *The Election of 1868*, page 368.

3. Charles Coleman, *The Election of 1868*, pages 362–363; Eric Foner, *Reconstruction*, page 342.

4. James Blaine, *Twenty Years Of Congress: From Lincoln to Garfield* volume 2, page 408.

5. James Garfield to David Swaim, May 21, 1864, SG—WRHS; "Political Issues of 1868," August 28, 1868, Garfield, *The Works of James A. Garfield*, 1882.

6. Clipping, *Ashtabula Weekly Telegraph*, August 29, 1868; "Political Issues of 1868," August 28, 1868, Garfield, *The Works of James A. Garfield*, 1882.

7. "Political Issues of 1868," August 28, 1868. Garfield, *The Works of James A. Garfield*.

8. James Garfield to L. Gould, November 9, 1868, JAG—LC; James Garfield to Hon. D. R. Tilden, February 12, 1869, JAG—LC.

9. W. E. B. Du Bois, *Black Reconstruction in America*, page 373.

10. James Garfield to Richard Brown, January 30, 1869, JAG—LC.

11. James Garfield to Lionel Sheldon, December 17, 1868, JAG—LC.

12. H. Wayne Morgan, *From Hayes to McKinley: National Party Politics, 1877–1896*, page 66; Gamaliel Bradford. *American Portraits, 1875–1900* (New York: Houghton Mifflin Company, 1923), page 116.

13. H. Wayne Morgan, *From Hayes to McKinley*, page 66; Gamaliel Bradford, *American Portraits, 1875–1900*, page 126.

14. Gamaliel Bradford, *American Portraits, 1875–1900*, pages 126–127.

15. H. Wayne Morgan, *From Hayes to McKinley: National Party Politics, 1877–1896*, page 68.

16. John Ingalls, *A Collection of the Writings of John James Ingalls: Essays, Addresses, and*

Orations, page 404; Gamaliel Bradford, *American Portraits, 1875–1900,* page 117; Ron Chernow, *Grant,* page 901.

17. Allan Peskin, *Garfield,* page 246.

18. James Blaine to James Garfield, November 19, 1868, JAG—LC.

19. James Garfield to James Blaine, March 11, 1869, JAG—LC.

20. James Blaine to James Garfield, circa March 11, 1869, JAG—LC.

21. Albert Riddle, *Recollections of War Times: Reminiscences of Men and Events in Washington, 1860–1865,* pages 249–250.

22. Dr. Carl Russell Fish. *The Civil Service and The Patronage* (London: Longman, Green, and Co., 1904), page 14.

23. Ari Hoogenboom, *Outlawing the Spoils: A History of the Civil Service Reform Movement, 1865–1883,* page 1; Nicholas R. Parrillo. *Against the Profit Motive: The Salary Revolution in American Government, 1780–1940,* Yale Law Library Series in Legal History and Reference (New Haven: Yale University Press, 2013), pages 139, 221.

24. Ari Hoogenboom, *Outlawing the Spoils: A History of the Civil Service Reform Movement, 1865–1883,* page 1.

25. Thomas C. Reeves. *Gentleman Boss: The Life of Chester Alan Arthur* (Newtown, Connecticut: American Political Biography Press, 1991), page 47.

26. David Saville Muzzey. *James G. Blaine: A Political Idol of Other Days* (Kennikat Press, 1963), pages 60–61.

27. H. Wayne Morgan, *From Hayes to McKinley: National Party Politics, 1877–1896,* page 71.

28. Don Pardee to James Garfield, March 20, 1865, JAG—LC.

29. James Garfield to A. J. Dyers, December 22, 1873, JAG—LC; James Garfield to Harmon Austin, June 16, 1865, JAG—LC.

30. James Garfield to Charles Henry, November 3, 1869, JAG—LC; Frederick Henry, *Captain Henry of Geauga: A Family Chronicle,* pages 218, 224.

31. Ari Hoogenboom, *Outlawing the Spoils: A History of the Civil Service Reform Movement, 1865–1883,* page 12.

32. James Garfield to Harmon Austin, June 7, 1869, JAG—LC.

33. Theodore Clarke Smith, *The Life and Letters of James Abram Garfield,* 1925, page 829; James Garfield to Burke Hinsdale, December 14, 1869, JAG—LC.

34. "Report of the Select Committee to Investigate the Alleged Credit Mobilier Bribery," pages 128–129.

35. James Garfield to Lucretia Garfield, May 30, 1869, JAG—LC.

36. Harry Garfield, "Speech By Dr. Harry Augustus Garfield," *Bulletin of Hiram College,* November 19, 1931, JAG—HC.

37. James Garfield to Jeremiah Black, July 24, 1869, JAG—LC; Allan Peskin, *Garfield,* page 306; "The Ninth Census," December 16, 1869, Garfield, *The Works of James A. Garfield,* 1882.

38. Henry Adams. *The Letters of Henry Adams (1858–1891)* (Cambridge, Massachusetts: The Riverside Press, 1930), pages 162–163.

39. "Elements of Success," as delivered June 29, 1869, typescript, JAG—HC.

40. James Garfield to David Swaim, August 10, 1868, SG—WRHS.

CHAPTER 17

1. Richard Bensel, *Yankee Leviathan*, pages 171, 249, 260–261, 265–266; James McPherson, *Battle Cry of Freedom*, page 443; Charles R. Geisst. *Wall Street: A History* updated edition (New York: Oxford University Press, 2018), page XIII.

2. J. W. Schuckers. *The Life and Public Services of Salmon Portland Chase* (New York: D. Appleton and Company, 1874), page 219; Richard Bensel, *Yankee Leviathan*, page 258; James Garfield to James Ward, Harris Blackord, Thomas Carter, December 29, 1869, JAG—LC; Kenneth D. Ackerman. *The Gold Ring: Jim Fisk, Jay Gould, and Black Friday, 1869* (New York: Carroll & Graf, 2005), page 46.

3. Kenneth Ackerman, *The Gold Ring*, pages 105–106; Edmund Morris, *Edison*, page 609; "Wall Street," *New York Herald*, September 25, 1869.

4. "The Gold Excitement," *The Baltimore Sun*, September 27, 1869; Edmund Morris, *Edison*, pages 608–610.

5. Kenneth Ackerman, *The Gold Ring*, pages 109–112; "Wall Street," *New York Herald*, September 25, 1869.

6. James Garfield to Burke Hinsdale, February 2, 1868, JAG—LC; James Garfield to H. N. Eldridge, December 24, 1869, JAG—LC; James Garfield, "The Currency," May 15, 1868; *The Works of James A. Garfield*, Burke Hinsdale ed., vol. 1 (James R. Osgood and Company, 1882).

7. Kenneth Ackerman, *The Gold Ring*, page 183; "Josie Mansfield in California," *San Francisco Call*, December 1, 1901; Charles F. Adams and Henry Adams. *Chapters of Erie, and Other Essays* (Boston: James R. Osgood and Company, 1871), pages 106–107; W. A. Swanberg. *Jim Fisk: The Career of an Improbable Rascal* (New York: Charles Scribner's Sons, 1959), page insert, page 18.

8. Charles F. Adams and Henry Adams, *Chapters of Erie, and Other Essays*, page 115; W. A. Swanberg, *Jim Fisk: The Career of an Improbable Rascal*, pages 126–127; "Wall Street," *New York Herald*, September 30, 1869.

9. Kenneth Ackerman, *The Gold Ring*, page 191.

10. Maury Klein. *The Life and Legend of Jay Gould* (Baltimore: Johns Hopkins University Press, 1986), page 112; James Garfield, "'Investigation into the Causes of the Gold Panic,' 41st Congress, Session II, Report No. 31," March 1, 1870, page 15; Kenneth Ackerman, *The Gold Ring*, pages 196–198, 200.

11. Edmund Morris, *Edison*, page 610.

12. Kenneth Ackerman, *The Gold Ring*, pages 266, 267; "The Week," *The Nation*, September 30, 1869.

13. James Garfield to Burke Hinsdale, November 15, 1869, JAG—LC; Kenneth Ackerman, *The Gold Ring*, page 227.

14. "Facts Already Ascertained about the Gold Combination," *New York Sun*, October 11, 1869; Richard White, *The Republic for Which It Stands*, page 247; Ron Chernow, *Grant*, page 678; Henry Adams. *The Education of Henry Adams: An Autobiography*, 1999 Modern Library paperback edition (New York: Modern Library, 1999), page 271.

15. Clipping, *Cleveland Plain Dealer*, January 11, 1870; Henry Adams to James Garfield, December 30, 1869, JAG—LC; James Garfield to Burke Hinsdale, January 10, 1870, JAG—LC.

16. James Garfield to Irvin McDowell, December 24, 1869, JAG—LC; Clipping, *The Evening Star*, January 11, 1870.
17. *Congressional Globe*, 41st Congress, Session II, page 367.
18. "The Twin Financial Heroes," *Cleveland Daily Herald*, January 31, 1870.
19. "The Twin Financial Heroes," *Cleveland Daily Herald*, January 31, 1870; "Black Friday," *The Buffalo Commercial*, January 25, 1870.
20. Clipping, *Evening Star*, January 27, 1870.
21. Maury Klein, *The Life and Legend of Jay Gould*, page 19.
22. Diary entry for November 4, 1866, Garfield, *The Diary of James A. Garfield* volume 1; Charles F. Adams and Henry Adams, *Chapters of Erie, and Other Essays*, page 103.
23. Kenneth Ackerman, *The Gold Ring*, pages 70–71; Ron Chernow, *Grant*, pages 674–675.
24. James Garfield, "'Investigation into the Causes of the Gold Panic,' 41st Congress, Session II, Report No. 31," page 173; Kenneth Ackerman, *The Gold Ring*, pages 272–274.
25. James Garfield to Irvin McDowell, January 18, 1870, JAG—LC; James Garfield to Halsey Hall, January 25, 1870, JAG—LC; "The September Panic," *The New York Times*, January 24, 1870; "Washington," *The New York Times*, January 31, 1870.
26. James Garfield to J. H. Rhodes, January 25, 1870, JAG—LC; James Garfield, "'Investigation into the Causes of the Gold Panic,' 41st Congress, Session II, Report No. 31," pages 342—346.
27. "'Investigation into the Causes of the Gold Panic,' 41st Congress, Session II, Report No. 31," James Garfield, page 474; James Garfield to J. H. Rhodes, January 25, 1870, JAG—LC.
28. James Garfield to J. H. Rhodes, January 28, 1870, JAG—LC.
29. George S. Boutwell. *Reminiscences of Sixty Years in Public Affairs*, vol. 2 (New York: McClure, Phillips & Co., 1902), pages 211–212.
30. Ron Chernow, *Grant*, pages 675–677.
31. James Garfield, "'Investigation into the Causes of the Gold Panic,' 41st Congress, Session II, Report No. 31," page 474; Jacob Dolson Cox to James Garfield, February 1, 1870, JAG—LC.
32. James Garfield, "'Investigation into the Causes of the Gold Panic,' 41st Congress, Session II, Report No. 31," page 474.
33. James Garfield to Alvah Udall, March 5, 1870, JAG—LC.
34. James Garfield, "'Investigation into the Causes of the Gold Panic,' 41st Congress, Session II, Report No. 31," pages 1–23, 461–479.
35. "Washington," *New York Times*; "The Gold Conspiracy," *Evening Star*; "Washington," *Chicago Tribune*, all March 2, 1870.
36. Kenneth Ackerman, *The Gold Ring*, page 275; "The Week," *The Nation*, March 3, 1870.
37. Henry Adams, *The Education of Henry Adams*, page 271.
38. H. W. Brands, *American Colossus*, page 42; Richard White, *The Republic for Which It Stands*, page 205.

39. Ron Chernow, *Grant*, pages 679–680; Henry Adams, *The Education of Henry Adams*, page 271.

40. "Whitewash for Grant," *New York Sun*, December 27, 1871.

41. James Garfield to Alvah Udall, March 5, 1870, JAG—LC.

42. James Garfield to Hon. William Ritizel, June 20, 1870, JAG—LC.

43. James Garfield to M. A. Quetetet, May 21, 1870, JAG—LC.

44. *Congressional Globe*, 41st Congress, Session II, page 4186.

45. James Garfield to "My Dear Colonel," March 23, 1870, JAG—LC.

46. Eric Foner, *The Second Founding*, pages 95–96, 105.

47. James Garfield to Robert Folger, April 16, 1870, JAG—LC.

48. James Garfield to M. A. Quetetet, May 21, 1870, JAG—LC.

CHAPTER 18

1. Ron Chernow, *Grant*, page 729; Hugh McCulloch. *Men and Measures of Half a Century: Sketches and Comments* (New York: Charles Scribner's Sons, 1889), pages 355–356; David S. Brown, *The Last American Aristocrat: The Brilliant Life and Improbable Education of Henry Adams*, 2020, page 111.

2. "Civil Service Reform: Remarks Made in the House of Representatives," March 14, 1870, James Garfield, *The Works of James A. Garfield*, Burke Hinsdale, ed., vol.1 (James R. Osgood and Company, 1882).

3. Eugene Schmiel, *Citizen-General: Jacob Dolson Cox and the Civil War Era*, page 205.

4. Eugene Schmiel, *Citizen-General: Jacob Dolson Cox and the Civil War Era*, pages 213, 218; Ron Chernow, *Grant*, page 730.

5. James Garfield to L. W. Hall, October 21, 1870, JAG—LC.

6. Jacob Cox to James Garfield, October 24, 1870, JAG—LC.

7. James Garfield to J. D. Cox, October 26, 1870, JAG—LC.

8. Eugene Schmiel, *Citizen-General: Jacob Dolson Cox and the Civil War Era*, pages 218–220.

9. Diary entry for November 28, 1872, JAG—LC.

10. "Garfield's Speech—The Cut Direct," *Cleveland Plain Dealer*, November 25, 1870.

11. Clipping, *Cleveland Plain Dealer*, May 31, 1870; James Garfield to A. W. Stiles, May 23, 1870, JAG—LC; James Garfield to R. M. Stinson, January 7, 1871. JAG—LC.

12. James Garfield to William Ritizel, December 22, 1870, JAG—LC; James Garfield to R. M. Stinson, January 7, 1871, JAG—LC.

13. James Garfield to Harmon Austin, January 21, 1871, JAG—LC.

14. Ari Hoogenboom, *Outlawing the Spoils: A History of the Civil Service Reform Movement, 1865–1883*, pages 79–85.

15. James Garfield to M. C. Hendren, March 18, 1871, JAG—LC; Ron Chernow, *Grant*, page 702; David Blight, *Frederick Douglass*, page 523.

16. "The Problem At the South," *The Nation*, March 23, 1871; Ron Chernow, *Grant*, pages 702, 703; Richard White, *The Republic for Which It Stands*, page 189.

17. Ron Chernow, pages 701–704; James Garfield to M. C. Hendren, March 18, 1871, JAG—LC; Eric Foner, *Reconstruction*, page 454.

18. Ron Chernow, *Grant*, page 705; Eric Foner, *Reconstruction*, page 455.

19. Carl Schurz, *The Reminiscences of Carl Schurz* volume 3, pages 331–332.

20. James Garfield to Burke Hinsdale, March 23, 1871, JAG—LC.

21. Allen W. Trelease. *White Terror: The Ku Klux Klan Conspiracy and Southern Recon-struction*, Louisiana paperback edition (Baton Rouge: Louisiana State University Press, 1995), page 387; James Garfield to Burke Hinsdale, March 30, 1871, JAG—LC; James Garfield to W. C. Howells, March 18, 1871, JAG—LC; Allen Trelease, *White Terror*, page 387.

22. James Garfield to Jacob Dolson Cox, March 23, 1871, JAG—LC; Ron Chernow, *Grant*, page 705.

23. James Garfield to Burke Hinsdale, March 30, 1871, JAG—LC.

24. James Garfield to Burke Hinsdale, March 30, 1871, JAG—LC.

25. Ron Chernow, *Grant*, page 704; Eric Foner, *Reconstruction*, page 456.

26. James Garfield to Samuel Bowles, March 31, 1871, JAG—LC; James Garfield to Harmon Austin, March 24, 1871, JAG—LC.

27. "The Last Pacific Railroad," *Chicago Tribune*, February 17, 1871; James Garfield to W. C. Howell, March 30, 1871, JAG—LC; James Garfield to Samuel Bowles, March 31, 1871, JAG—LC.

28. James Garfield to Burke Hinsdale, March 14, 1871, JAG—LC.

29. Speeches by Morton, Butler, and Garfield, *Chicago Tribune*, April 5, 1871.

30. "The Ku-Klux Act: Speech Delivered in the House of Representatives," April 4, 1871, Garfield, *The Works of James A. Garfield*, 1882.

31. "Congressional Summary," *Des Moines Register*, April 5, 1871; James Garfield to Harmon Austin, April 11, 1871, JAG—LC.

32. Silas Smith to James Garfield, April 5, 1871, JAG—LC; James Garfield to Jacob Dolson Cox, April 8, 1871, JAG—LC; James Garfield to James Reed, April 13, 1871, JAG—LC; James Garfield to Cyrus F. Smith, April 8, 1871, JAG—LC.

33. Jacob Cox to James Garfield, April 11, 1871, JAG—LC.

34. James Garfield to Isaac Demmon, April 8, 1871, JAG—LC.

35. James Garfield to Virgil Kline, July 21, 1871, JAG—LC.

36. Eric Foner, *Reconstruction*, page 457; Ron Chernow, *Grant*, page 708; Allen Trelease, *White Terror*, page 409.

37. Eric Foner, *Reconstruction*, pages 455, 459; Ron Chernow, *Grant*, page 710.

CHAPTER 19

1. Diary entries for August 13–16, 1872, JAG—LC; James Garfield to Lucretia Gar-field, August 14, 1872, JAG—LC.

2. "The House Committees," *Cleveland Daily Herald*, December 9, 1867; Clipping, *Chicago Tribune*, December 6, 1871.

3. "General Garfield," *Delaware Gazette,* March 24, 1871; Diary entry for February 17, 1872, JAG—LC; Harry Garfield, "Speech by Dr. Harry Augustus Garfield," *Bulletin of Hiram College*, November 19, 1931, JAG—HC.

4. "General Garfield," *Delaware Gazette*, March 24, 1871; "New York Correspon-dence," *The Pacific Commercial Advertiser*, January 1, 1870.

5. Diary entry for June 12, 1872, JAG—LC; James Garfield to Burke Hinsdale, February 22, 1872, JAG—LC; James Garfield to Halsey Hall, December 26, 1871, JAG—LC.

6. James Garfield to Whitelaw Reid, October 7, 1871, JAG—LC.

7. Robert W. Cherny. *American Politics in the Gilded Age, 1868–1900*, The American History Series (Wheeling, Illinois: Harlan Davidson, 1997), page 53; Ron Chernow, *Grant*, page 742; Eric Foner, *Reconstruction*, page 503.

8. Eric Foner, *Reconstruction*, page 504; James Garfield to John Q. Smith, August 8, 1872, JAG—LC; Diary entry for April 27, 1872, JAG—LC; James Garfield to W. C. Howells, July 11, 1872, JAG—LC.

9. James Garfield to Lyman Hall, April 6, 1872, JAG—LC; James Garfield to Jerome Burrows, July 29, 1872, JAG—LC; "The Liberal Republican Movement," *New-York Tribune*, March 18, 1872.

10. Diary entry for August 9, 1872, JAG—LC; Diary entry for August 20, 1872, JAG—LC.

11. "Hon. James A. Garfield," *Helena Weekly Herald*, August 22, 1872.

12. James Garfield to Secretary of Interior Delano, August 17, 1872; Margaret Leech, *The Garfield Orbit*; Memoranda titled "Flathead Removal," found in JAG—LC; "Montana Confederated Salish & Kootenai Tribes of the Flathead Reservation, Salish-Pend d'Oreille Culture Committee, and Mont. (Elders Cultural Advisory Council) Confederated Salish & Kootenai Tribes of the Flathead Reservation," *The Salish People and the Lewis and Clark Expedition*, 2018, pages 113–114.

13. Diary entry for August 22, 1872, JAG—LC; Diary entry for August 24, 1872, JAG—LC.

14. Peter Ronan, *Historical Sketch of the Flathead Indian Nation*, page 64; James Garfield to Columbus Delano, September 7, 1872, JAG—LC.

15. "Reflection and Conclusion on 'American Indians,'" May 1856, JAG—LC; "Indian Affairs: Remarks made in the House on Various Occasions," January 25, 1871, Garfield, *The Works of James A. Garfield*, 1882.

16. Peter Ronan, *Historical Sketch of the Flathead Indian Nation*, pages 62–64; Montana Confederated Salish & Kootenai Tribes of the Flathead Reservation, Salish-Pend d'Oreille Culture Committee, and Mont. (Elders Cultural Advisory Council) Confederated Salish & Kootenai Tribes of the Flathead Reservation, *The Salish People and the Lewis and Clark Expedition*, 2018, page 116.

17. Diary entries for August 27, 29, 30, and September 3, 1872, JAG—LC.

18. "Civilizing the Indians," *New-York Tribune*, January 1, 1873.

19. Diary entry for February 24, 1874, JAG—LC.

20. Diary entry for September 7, 1872, JAG—LC; "The King of Frauds," *New York Sun*, September 4, 1872.

21. Diary entry for September 19, 1872, JAG—LC.

CHAPTER 20

1. Richard White, *The Republic for Which It Stands*, page 119; Allan Nevins, *The Emergence of Modern America, 1865–1878*, page 51; Samuel S. Cox. *Three Decades of Federal Legislation, 1855 to 1885* (Occidental Publishing Co., 1885), page 694.

2. Richard Bensel, *Yankee Leviathan*, pages 252, 308; Hugh McCulloch, *Men and Measures of Half a Century: Sketches and Comments*, page 508; Allan Nevins, *The Emergence of Modern America, 1865–1878*, page 37.

3. "The Future of the Republic: Its Dangers and Hopes," July 2, 1873; James Garfield. *The Works of James A. Garfield*, ed. Burke Hinsdale, volume 2 (James R. Osgood and Company, 1882).

4. Maury Klein. *Union Pacific: Birth of a Railroad, 1862–1893* first edition (Garden City, New York: Doubleday, 1987), pages 17, 27–28, 32–33; Richard White. *Railroaded: The Transcontinentals and the Making of Modern America*, first edition (New York: W.W. Norton & Co, 2011), page 22; Richard White, *The Republic for Which It Stands*, pages 258–259.

5. Maury Klein, *Union Pacific: Birth of a Railroad, 1862–1893*, page 16.

6. Oakes Ames. *Oakes Ames: A Memoir* (Cambridge, Massachusetts: Riverside Press, 1884), pages 5–6; Robert Mitchell, *Congress and the King of Frauds*, pages 16–17.

7. Oakes Ames, *Oakes Ames: A Memoir*, pages 8–9; Robert Mitchell, *Congress and the King of Frauds*, pages 18–19.

8. "Report of the Select Committee to Investigate the Alleged Credit Mobilier Bribery," 1873, page 5.

9. Maury Klein, *Union Pacific: Birth of a Railroad, 1862–1893*, pages 191–194; Robert Mitchell, *Congress and the King of Frauds*, pages 35–38, "Report of the Select Committee to Investigate the Alleged Credit Mobilier Bribery," 1873, page 10.

10. Oakes Ames, *Oakes Ames: A Memoir*, page 8; Maury Klein, *Union Pacific: Birth of a Railroad, 1862–1893*, pages 194–195.

11. "The King of Frauds," *New York Sun*, September 4, 1872.

12. Oakes Ames, *Oakes Ames: A Memoir*, page 14.

13. Diary entry for September 9, 1872, JAG—LC; Diary entry for September 10, 1872, JAG—LC; "The Credit Mobilier Slander," *The New York Times*, September 16, 1872.

14. J. S. Black to James Garfield, September 12, 1872, JAG—LC; Allan Peskin, *Garfield*, page 356.

15. Allan Peskin, *Garfield*, pages 356–357.

16. Robert Mitchell, *Congress and the King of Frauds*, pages 61, 64.

17. Richard White, *The Republic for Which It Stands*, page 211; James Garfield to David Swaim, September 30, 1872, SG—WRHS.

18. James Garfield to Frank Mason, November 13, 1872, JAG—LC.

19. Diary entry for December 1, 1872, JAG—LC.

20. James Blaine to James Garfield, November 26, 1872, JAG—LC.

21. Diary entry for December 1, 1872, JAG—LC; Theodore Clarke Smith, *The Life and Letters of James Abram Garfield*, page 531.

22. Robert Mitchell, *Congress and the King of Frauds*, pages 71–72.

23. "Report of the Select Committee to Investigate the Alleged Credit Mobilier Bribery," pages 1–2; "Speaker Blaine and the Credit Mobilier," *Brooklyn Union*, December 4, 1872.

24. Robert Mitchell, *Congress and the King of Frauds*, page 75; "Report of the Select Committee to Investigate the Alleged Credit Mobilier Bribery," pages 21, 23–24.

25. James Garfield to J. P. Robison, January 9, 1873, JAG—LC.

26. "General Garfield, You are Wanted," *Cincinnati Enquirer*, September 17, 1872; "Report of the Select Committee to Investigate the Alleged Credit Mobilier Bribery," pages 128–129.

27. Diary entry for January 14, 1873, JAG—LC.

28. James Garfield to Jeremiah Black, September 16, 1872, JAG—LC; "Will Gen. Garfield Speak Out?" *Daily Gazette*, October 2, 1872.

29. James Garfield to David Swaim, September 30, 1872, SG—WRHS.

30. Diary entry for January 14, 1873, JAG—LC; James Garfield to Harmon Austin, February 17, 1873, JAG—LC.

31. Robert Mitchell, *Congress and the King of Frauds*, page 74; Maury Klein, *Union Pacific: Birth of a Railroad, 1862–1893*, page 296.

32. Oakes Ames, *Oakes Ames: A Memoir*, page 19; James Garfield to Jeremiah Black, January 25, 1873, JAG—LC; Robert Mitchell, *Congress and the King of Frauds*, page 111.

33. "Report of the Select Committee to Investigate the Alleged Credit Mobilier Bribery," pages 443–461; Allan Peskin, *Garfield*, page 359.

34. Diary entry for January 22, 1873, JAG—LC.

35. James Garfield to Burke Hinsdale, January 27, 1873, JAG—LC; Diary entry for February 9, 1873, JAG—LC; James Garfield to David Swaim, January 6, 1873, SG—WRHS; "New Political Definitions," *Detroit Free Press*, January 25, 1873.

36. James Garfield to Harmon Austin, February 17, 1873, JAG—LC; Diary entry for February 9, 1873, JAG—LC.

37. James Garfield to W. C. Howells, February 17, 1873, JAG—LC.

38. Neil Rolde. *Continental Liar from the State of Maine: James G. Blaine* first edition (Gardiner, Maine: Tilbury House Publishers, 2006), page 151; Clipping, *Cleveland Plain Dealer*, February 18, 1873.

39. Harriet Blaine to Walker Blaine, May 15, 1872, Harriet S. Blaine Beale, ed., *Letters of Mrs. James G. Blaine*, volume 1 (New York: Duffield and Company, 1908).

40. "Report of the Select Committee to Investigate the Alleged Credit Mobilier Bribery," VII, VIII, XIX; Maury Klein, *Union Pacific: Birth of a Railroad, 1862–1893*, page 296; Jack Beatty, *Age of Betrayal: The Triumph of Money in America, 1865–1900* first Vintage Books edition (New York: Vintage Books, 2008), page 229; H. W. Brands, *American Colossus*, page 360.

41. "Garfield's Obituary by Gen. Butler," *New York Sun*, February 6, 1873; "Credit Mobilier in the House," *New York Sun*, March 1, 1873.

42. Whitelaw Reid to James Garfield, March 11, 1873, JAG—LC.

43. Charles Henry to James Garfield, February 18, 1873, JAG—LC; Robert Mitchell, *Congress and the King of Frauds*, page 115.

44. Allan Peskin, *Garfield*, pages 378–380.

45. Diary entry for June 13, 1872, JAG—LC.

46. James Garfield to Lucretia Garfield, March 9, 1873, JAG—LC; Allan Peskin, *Garfield*, page 367; Diary entry for March 28, 1873, JAG—LC; Allan Peskin, *Garfield*, page 367; James Garfield to David Swaim, April 1, 1873, SG—WRHS.

47. George S. Boutwell, *Reminiscences of Sixty Years in Public Affairs* volume 2, pages 11–12; Robert Cherny, *American Politics in the Gilded Age, 1868–1900*, page 54; Thomas Sherman, *Twenty Years with James G. Blaine: Reminiscences by His Private Secretary*, page 33.

48. James Garfield to David Swaim, April 1, 1873, SG—WRHS; Francis Marion Green, *A Royal Life, or the Eventful History of James A. Garfield: Twentieth President of the United States* (Chicago: Central Book Concern, 1882), pages 310–312.

49. Diary entry for April 2, 1873, JAG—LC.

50. James Garfield to Harmon Austin, April 2, 1873, JAG—LC; James Garfield to W. C. Howells, April 3, 1873, JAG—LC.

51. Lucretia Garfield to James Garfield, September 25, 1872, JAG—LC; Lucretia Garfield to James Garfield, April 26, 1873, JAG—LC; James Garfield to Lucretia Garfield, April 19, 1873, JAG—LC.

52. Diary entry for April 19, 1873, JAG—LC; Eliza Garfield to Phebe Clapp, December 7, 1873, JAG—LC.

53. James Garfield to W. C. Howells, April 3, 1873, JAG—LC; Diary entry for April 16, 1873, JAG—LC; Diary entry for April 15, 1873, JAG—LC.

54. "To the Republican Voters of the 19th District," April 21, 1873, JAG—LC.

55. James Garfield to David Swaim, April 2, 1873, SG—WRHS; "To the Republican Voters of the 19th District," April 21, 1873, JAG—LC.

56. "Review of the Transactions of the Credit Mobilier Company," May 8, 1873, JAG—LC.

57. "To the Republican Voters of the 19th District," April 21, 1873, JAG—LC; "Review of the Transactions of the Credit Mobilier Company," May 8, 1873, JAG—LC.

58. Diary entry for April 21, 1873, JAG—LC.

59. Diary entry for April 12, 1873, JAG—LC.

60. James Garfield to Harmon Austin, May 13, 1873, JAG—LC; Diary entry for May 18, 1873, JAG—LC.

61. Clipping, *The Nation*, May 1, 1873; Theodore Clarke Smith, *The Life and Letters of James Abram Garfield*, page 546.

62. James Garfield to Harmon Austin, June 3, 1873, JAG—LC.

63. Jack Beatty, *Age of Betrayal*, page 229; John Ingalls, *A Collection of the Writings of John James Ingalls: Essays, Addresses, and Orations*, page 341; Charles F. Adams and Henry Adams, *Chapters of Erie, and Other Essays*, page 408.

64. Ron Chernow, *Grant*, page 754.

65. "The Speaker's Strategy," *New York Sun*, March 1, 1873.

66. H. W. Brands, *American Colossus*, page 89; H. W. Brands. *The Money Men: Capitalism, Democracy, and the Hundred Years' War over the American Dollar* (New York, London: W.W. Norton, 2007), pages 161–162; Ronald C. White. *American Ulysses:*

A Life of Ulysses S. Grant, first edition (New York: Random House, 2016), page 542; Jack Beatty, *Age of Betrayal*, page 232; John Sherman. *Recollections of Forty Years in the House, Senate and Cabinet*, volume 1 (The Werner Company, 1895), pages 488–489; Richard White, *Railroaded*, page 47; Eric Foner, *Reconstruction*, pages 512–513.

67. David Nasaw, *Andrew Carnegie*, pages 153–154; David Blight, *Frederick Douglass*, pages 546–549; Eric Foner, *Reconstruction*, page 535.

68. Eric Foner, *Reconstruction*, pages 529–530.

69. Richard White, *The Republic for Which It Stands*, pages 279–280; Ron Chernow, *Grant*, page 759.

70. Ron Chernow, *Grant*, page 759.

71. Diary entry for January 13, 1873, JAG—LC.

72. Diary entry for May 24, 1873, JAG—LC.

73. Diary entry for December 31, 1873, JAG—LC; "A Talk With Gen. Garfield," *New-York Tribune*, November 17, 1873.

74. Diary entry for December 31, 1873, JAG—LC.

75. Diary entry for December 5, 1873, JAG—LC. .

76. H. W. Brands, *American Colossus*, page 360.

CHAPTER 21

1. David Saville Muzzey, *James G. Blaine: A Political Idol of Other Days*, pages 159–160; H. W. Brands, *American Colossus*, pages 89–90; James Garfield to Burke Hinsdale, March 26, 1874, JAG—LC.

2. James Garfield to Burke Hinsdale, March 26, 1874, JAG—LC; Diary entry for March 23, 1874, JAG—LC; Ron Chernow, *Grant*, page 780; Diary entry for April 23, 1874, JAG—LC; James Garfield to Burke Hinsdale, April 23, 1874, JAG—LC.

3. James Garfield to Charles Henry, February 19, 1874, JAG—HC; "Hon. Dawes and Garfield Control Expenditures," *Chicago Tribune*, February 23, 1874.

4. "The Army Bill . . . The Appropriations Committee Sustained in their Effort to Reduce the Rank and File of the Army," *New-York Tribune*, February 4, 1874; "Current Topics at the Capital," *New-York Tribune*, April 16, 1874; Diary entry for February 25, 1874, JAG—LC; James Garfield to Jacob D. Cox, March 20, 1874, JAG—LC; "The Sundry Civil Service Bill in the House," *New-York Tribune*, June 23, 1874.

5. "Remarks on Civil Service Reform," June 12, 1874, Garfield, *The Works of James A. Garfield*, 1882.

6. James Garfield to Harmon Austin, July 12, 1873, JAG—LC; James Garfield to Harmon Austin, December 14, 1873, JAG—LC; James Garfield to Charles Henry, September 26, 1873, JAG—HC; "Garfield's District," Cleveland Plain Dealer, August 6, 1874, JAG—LC.

7. "Gen. Garfield: Thoughts from his sick bed," *Chicago Tribune*, August 16, 1875; James Garfield to Burke Hinsdale, January 4, 1875, JAG—LC.

8. Diary entry for November 19, 1874, JAG—LC.

9. Diary entry for February 23, 1874, JAG—LC.

10. James Garfield to Charles Henry, November 4, 1874, JAG—HC; Robert Cherny, *American Politics in the Gilded Age, 1868–1900*, page 56.

11. Diary entry for November 12, 1874, JAG—LC; Theodore Clarke Smith, *The Life and Letters of James Abram Garfield*, page 521.

12. Richard White, *The Republic for Which It Stands*, page 286; Theodore Clarke Smith, *The Life and Letters of James Abram Garfield*, page 520.

13. Diary entry for January 7, 1875, JAG—LC; James Garfield to W. B. Hazen, November 18, 1874, JAG—LC.

14. H. Wayne Morgan, *From Hayes to McKinley: National Party Politics, 1877–1896*, page 59; Thomas Sherman, *Twenty Years with James G. Blaine: Reminiscences by His Private Secretary*, page 61.

15. Thomas Sherman, *Twenty Years with James G. Blaine*, page 39; Carl Schurz, *The Reminiscences of Carl Schurz*, volume 3, page 366.

16. George Hoar, *Autobiography of Seventy Years* volume 2, page 200.

17. Diary entry for May 4, 1874, JAG—LC; Diary entry for March 28, 1875, JAG—LC; Diary entry for March 16, 1875, JAG—LC.

18. James Garfield to Burke Hinsdale, April 4, 1876, JAG—LC; Diary entry for March 15, 1875, JAG—LC.

19. Diary entry for March 3, 1876, JAG—LC.

20. Diary entry for March 17, 1875, JAG—LC; Theodore Clarke Smith, *The Life and Letters of James Abram Garfield*, page 600.

21. Lucretia Garfield to James Garfield, April 25, 1875, Garfield and Garfield, *Crete and James*.

22. Lucretia Garfield to James Garfield, March 9, 1876, JAG—LC; Ron Chernow, *Grant*, page 735.

23. David Saville Muzzey, *James G. Blaine: A Political Idol of Other Days*, page 83.

24. Diary entry for March 16, 1875, JAG—LC.

25. John Taliaferro. *All the Great Prizes: The Life of John Hay, from Lincoln to Roosevelt* first Simon & Schuster hardcover edition (New York: Simon & Schuster, 2013), page 170.

26. Ari Hoogenboom, *Rutherford B. Hayes: Warrior & President*, page 260; Whitelaw Reid, *Ohio In the War: Her Statesmen, Generals, and Soldiers*, page 849; H. Wayne Morgan, *From Hayes to McKinley: National Party Politics, 1877–1896*, pages 8–11; Ari Hoogenboom, *Rutherford B. Hayes: Warrior & President*, page 176.

27. David Jordan, *Roscoe Conkling of New York: Voice in the Senate*, page 243.

28. Ari Hoogenboom, *Rutherford B. Hayes: Warrior & President*, page 260; Henry Adams. *The Letters of Henry Adams (1858–1891)* (Cambridge, Massachusetts: The Riverside Press, 1930), page 288.

29. James McPherson, *Battle Cry of Freedom*, page 796.

30. David Saville Muzzey, *James G. Blaine: A Political Idol of Other Days*, pages 76–78.

31. Carl Schurz, *The Reminiscences of Carl Schurz*, volume 3, page 365; *Congressional Record*, 44th Congress, Session I, pages 326–329.

32. Carl Schurz, *The Reminiscences of Carl Schurz*, volume 3, page 365.

33. Diary entry for January 12, 1876, JAG—LC; Allan Peskin, *Garfield*, page 393.

34. "Second Amnesty Debate," *New-York Tribune*, January 13, 1876.

35. Diary entry for January 13, 1876, JAG—LC.

36. David Saville Muzzey, *James G. Blaine: A Political Idol of Other Days*, pages 83–84; Diary entry for June 1, 1876, JAG—LC.

37. Thomas Sherman, *Twenty Years with James G. Blaine: Reminiscences by His Private Secretary*, page 53; David Saville Muzzey, *James G. Blaine: A Political Idol of Other Days*, pages 93–95.

38. Diary entry for June 5, 1876, JAG—LC.

39. Diary entry for June 8, 1876, JAG—LC.

40. John Ingalls, *A Collection of the Writings of John James Ingalls: Essays, Addresses, and Orations*, page 423; David Saville Muzzey, *James G. Blaine: A Political Idol of Other Days*, page 100; Diary entry for June 11, 1876, JAG—LC.

41. Diary entry for February 10, 1876, JAG—LC; Neil Rolde, *Continental Liar from the State of Maine*, page 187; Carl Schurz, *The Reminiscences of Carl Schurz* volume 3, page 367.

42. Diary entry for June 11, 1876, JAG—LC; Diary entry for June 12, 1876, JAG—LC.

43. David Saville Muzzey. *James G. Blaine: A Political Idol of Other Days* (Kennikat Press, 1963), page 113.

44. Thomas Platt, *The Autobiography of Thomas Collier Platt*, page 76; Keith Ian Polakoff. *The Politics of Inertia: The Election of 1876 and the End of Reconstruction* (Baton Rouge: Louisiana State University Press, 1973), page 56.

45. Charles Williams ed., *Diary and Letters of Rutherford Birchard Hayes: Nineteenth President of the United States*, page 324; Keith Ian Polakoff. *The Politics of Inertia: The Election of 1876 and the End of Reconstruction* (Baton Rouge: Louisiana State University Press, 1973), page 56.

46. John Ingalls, *A Collection of the Writings of John James Ingalls: Essays, Addresses, and Orations*, page 426; Neil Rolde, *Continental Liar from the State of Maine*, page 185.

47. John Ingalls, *A Collection of the Writings of John James Ingalls: Essays, Addresses, and Orations*, page 425; David Saville Muzzey, *James G. Blaine: A Political Idol of Other Days*, pages 111–112.

48. Hugh McCulloch, *Men and Measures of Half a Century: Sketches and Comments*, page 413; Ari Hoogenboom, *Rutherford B. Hayes: Warrior & President*, page 263.

49. Diary entry for June 16, 1876, JAG—LC; Ari Hoogenboom, *Rutherford B. Hayes: Warrior & President*, page 263.

50. James Garfield to Harmon Austin, February 9, 1876, JAG—LC.

51. Diary entry for July 7, 1876, JAG—LC; James Garfield to Rutherford Hayes, June 30, 1876, JAG—LC.

52. Richard White, *The Republic for Which It Stands*, page 327; William H. Rehnquist. *Centennial Crisis: The Disputed Election of 1876* (New York: Vintage Books, 2005), page 71; Keith Polakoff, *The Politics of Inertia*, page 71.

53. Hugh McCulloch, *Men and Measures of Half a Century: Sketches and Comments*, pages 413–414; Michael F. Holt. *By One Vote: The Disputed Presidential Election of 1876* (Lawrence: University Press of Kansas, 2008), pages 98–99.

54. Rutherford Hayes to James Garfield, July 8, 1876, JAG—LC.

55. Rutherford Hayes to James Garfield, August 5, 1876, JAG—LC; Rutherford Hayes to James Garfield, August 6, 1876, JAG—LC.

56. Rutherford Hayes to James Garfield, July 8, 1876, JAG—LC; Keith Polakoff, *The Politics of Inertia*, page 116; Thomas Platt, *The Autobiography of Thomas Collier Platt*, page 76.

57. Allan Peskin, *Garfield*, page 404; Theodore Clarke Smith, *The Life and Letters of James Abram Garfield*, pages 611–613; James Garfield to Lucretia Garfield, September 3, 1876, JAG—LC; "Gen. Garfield To-Night!" *Bangor Daily Whig and Courier*, September 4, 1876.

58. Keith Polakoff, *The Politics of Inertia*, page 153; James Garfield to Halsey Hall, July 1876, JAG—LC.

59. "The Democratic Party and the Government," August 4, 1876, Garfield, *The Works of James A. Garfield*, 1882.

60. Diary entry for September 19, 1876, JAG—LC.

61. James Garfield to Lucretia Garfield, September 20, 1876, JAG—LC.

62. "The Currency Conflict," *The Atlantic Monthly*, February 1876; "Pons Asinorum," *The New England Journal of Education* volume 3, no. 14 (April 1, 1876), 161.

63. Diary entry for May 15, 1874, JAG—LC; Diary entry for November 28, 1874, JAG—LC.

64. Allan Peskin, *Garfield*, page 431; Diary entry for October 31, 1876, JAG—LC.

65. Diary entry for October 21, 1876, JAG—LC; Diary entry for October 25, 1876, JAG—LC.

66. Eliza Garfield to Alpha Boynton, November 19, 1876, JAG—LC.

67. Diary entry for November 3, 1876, JAG—LC; Diary entry for November 6, 1876, JAG—LC.

68. Diary entry for November 5, 1876, JAG—LC.

CHAPTER 22

1. Eric Foner, *Reconstruction*, page 571; Thomas Reeves, *Gentleman Boss*, page 103; Keith Polakoff, *The Politics of Inertia*, page 156.

2. Roy Morris. *Fraud of the Century: Rutherford B. Hayes, Samuel Tilden, and the Stolen Election of 1876* (New York: Simon & Schuster, 2004), page 162.

3. Charles Williams ed., *Diary and Letters of Rutherford Birchard Hayes: Nineteenth President of the United States*, page 372.

4. Charles Williams ed., *Diary and Letters of Rutherford Birchard Hayes*, page 376.

5. James Garfield to Corydon Fuller, November 9, 1876, Corydon Fuller, *Reminiscences of James A. Garfield, with Notes Preliminary and Collateral*; David Saville Muzzey, *James G. Blaine: A Political Idol of Other Days*, page 119.

6. Keith Polakoff, *The Politics of Inertia*, page 201.

7. W. A. Swanberg. *Sickles the Incredible* (Gettysburg, Pennsylvania: Stan Clark Military Books, 1991), pages 54, 64–67, 216–225.

8. Roy Morris, *Fraud of the Century*, page 12.

9. Michael Holt, *By One Vote*, page 173; H. Wayne Morgan, *From Hayes to McKinley: National Party Politics, 1877–1896*, page 144.

10. William Rehnquist, *Centennial Crisis*, page 97.

11. Charles Williams ed., *Diary and Letters of Rutherford Birchard Hayes: Nineteenth President of the United States*, page 376; Keith Polakoff, *The Politics of Inertia*, pages 202, 205; Roy Morris, *Fraud of the Century*, page 164; C. Vann Woodward. *Reunion and Reaction: The Compromise of 1877 and the End of Reconstruction* (New York, Oxford: Oxford University Press, 1991), page 18.

12. Michael Holt, *By One Vote*, page 175.

13. Diary entry for November 8, 1876, JAG—LC; Diary entry for November 9, 1876, JAG—LC; Diary entry for November 10, 1876, JAG—LC.

14. Ronald White, *American Ulysses*, pages 572, 578; Michael Holt, *By One Vote*, page 178.

15. Michael Holt, *By One Vote*, page 178.

16. "The New Republican Leader," *Star Tribune*, December 6, 1876.

17. Diary entry for November 11, 1876, JAG—LC.

18. Diary entry for November 11, 1876, JAG—LC; James Garfield to Burke Hinsdale, November 11, 1876, JAG—LC.

19. James Garfield to Lucretia Garfield, November 14, 1876, JAG—LC; Diary entry for November 12, 1876, JAG—LC.

20. Don Pardee to James Garfield, October 11, 1863, JAG—LC.

21. James Garfield to the Garfield children, November 19, 1876, JAG—LC.

22. James Garfield to the Garfield children, November 19, 1876, JAG—LC; James Garfield to Lucretia Garfield, November 20, 1876, JAG—LC.

23. Michael Holt, *By One Vote*, pages 194–195.

24. James Garfield to Lucretia Garfield, November 24, 1876, JAG—LC; Michael Holt, *By One Vote*, page 182; James Garfield to Lucretia Garfield, November 16, 1876, Garfield and Garfield, *Crete and James*; Diary entry for November 10, 1876, JAG—LC.

25. "The Bulldozers," *Kansas Daily Tribune*, December 5, 1876.

26. Allan Peskin, *Garfield*, page 410; James Garfield to Eliza Garfield, November 29, 1876, JAG—LC.

27. James Garfield to Eliza Garfield, November 29, 1876, JAG—LC; James Garfield to Lucretia Garfield, November 27, 1876, JAG—LC.

28. Diary entry for December 2, 1876, JAG—LC; James Garfield to Burke Hinsdale, December 4, 1876, JAG—LC.

29. Diary entry for December 5, 1876, JAG—LC; Ari Hoogenboom, *Rutherford B. Hayes: Warrior & President*, page 278.

30. Michael Holt, *By One Vote*, pages 191–192; C. Vann Woodward, *Reunion and Reaction*, page 19; Michael Holt, *By One Vote*, page 196.

31. Ari Hoogenboom, *Outlawing the Spoils: A History of the Civil Service Reform Movement, 1865–1883*, page 147; Ari Hoogenboom, *Rutherford B. Hayes: Warrior & President*, page 284.

32. "Tilden and Reform," *San Francisco Examiner*, November 3, 1876; C. Vann Woodward, *Reunion and Reaction*, page 20; Roy Morris, *Fraud of the Century*, page 173; Michael Holt, *By One Vote*, page 184.

33. "The Political Situation," *The New York Times*, December 5, 1876; "Bayonet Practice in the South," *The Baltimore Sun*, December 5, 1876.

34. Michael Holt, *By One Vote*, page 184.

35. H. Wayne Morgan, *From Hayes to McKinley: National Party Politics, 1877–1896*, page 3; Ronald White, *American Ulysses*, page 579.

36. Samuel Cox, *Three Decades of Federal Legislation, 1855 to 1885*, pages 636–637.

37. James Garfield to Harmon Austin, December 7, 1876, JAG—LC; James Garfield to Charles Henry, December 8, 1876, JAG—HC.

38. "Angry Threats in Washington," *New-York Tribune*, December 7, 1876.

39. Diary entry for December 7, 1876, JAG—LC.

40. "The Great Muddle," *Evening Star*, December 9, 1876; Theodore Clarke Smith, *The Life and Letters of James Abram Garfield*, page 624.

41. Ari Hoogenboom, *Rutherford B. Hayes: Warrior & President*, page 283; James Garfield to Rutherford Hayes, December 13, 1876, JAG—LC.

42. James Garfield to Rutherford Hayes, December 13, 1876, JAG—LC.

43. James Garfield to Rutherford Hayes, December 13, 1876, JAG—LC.

44. Rutherford Hayes to James Garfield, December 16, 1876, JAG—LC.

45. Diary entry for December 18, 1876, JAG—LC.

46. Diary entry for January 1, 1877, JAG—LC; James Garfield to Burke Hinsdale, December 18, 1876, JAG—LC; James Garfield to Burke Hinsdale, January 4, 1877, JAG—LC.

47. "D.P. At the Capital," *Cincinnati Enquirer*, December 20, 1876.

48. James Garfield to Rutherford Hayes, January 19, 1877, JAG—LC.

49. Eric Foner, *Reconstruction*, page 579; C. Vann Woodward, *Reunion and Reaction*, page 150.

50. James Garfield to Rutherford Hayes, January 19, 1877, JAG—LC; Ari Hoogenboom, *Rutherford B. Hayes: Warrior & President*, page 285.

51. David Jordan, *Roscoe Conkling of New York: Voice in the Senate*, page 254; Alfred Conkling. *The Life and Letters of Roscoe Conkling: Orator, Statesman, Advocate* (New York: Charles L. Webster & Company, 1889), page 524; David Jordan, *Roscoe Conkling of New York: Voice in the Senate*, page 259; "The Question of the Hour," *The New York Times*, January 25, 1877.

52. Diary entry for January 24, 1877, JAG—LC; "The Question of the Hour," *The New York Times*, January 26, 1877.

53. "The Bill Approved," *Chicago Tribune*, January 30, 1877; Ron Chernow, *Grant*, pages 848–849.

54. William Rehnquist, *Centennial Crisis*, page 115; C. Vann Woodward, *Reunion and Reaction*, page 150; Roy Morris, *Fraud of the Century*, page 216.

55. Diary entry for January 27, 1877, JAG—LC; "The Louisiana Frauds Clearly Established," *New York Sun*, February 1, 1877; "The House and Senate Members of the Tribunal," *Brooklyn Daily Eagle*, January 30, 1877.

56. Diary entry for January 29, 1877, JAG—LC; Diary entry for January 30, 1877, JAG—LC; "It Is a Law," *Chicago Tribune*, January 30, 1877.

57. Ari Hoogenboom, *Rutherford B. Hayes: Warrior & President*, page 287; C. Vann

Woodward, *Reunion and Reaction*, pages 153–154; Ari Hoogenboom, *Rutherford B. Hayes: Warrior & President*, page 286.

58. "The Formality in Congress," *New-York Tribune*, January 31, 1877.

59. *Harper's Weekly* XXI, no. 1051, February 17, 1877.

60. "The Counting of the Vote," *The New York Times*, February 2, 1877.

61. "Proceedings of the Electoral Commission" (Washington, D.C.: Government Printing Office, 1877), pages 28–29; "Counting the Vote," *New-York Tribune*, February 3, 1877.

62. Diary entry for February 16, 1877, JAG—LC; Michael Holt, *By One Vote*, page 226; "Proceedings of the Electoral Commission," page 100; "Slow but Sure," *Chicago Tribune*, February 4, 1877.

63. Diary entry for February 3, 1877, JAG—LC; Diary entry for February 6, 1877, JAG—LC.

64. Theodore Clarke Smith, *The Life and Letters of James Abram Garfield*, page 637; "Smash the Electoral Tribunal!" *Cincinnati Enquirer*, February 13, 1877.

65. Roy Morris, *Fraud of the Century*, page 225.

66. "The Moral Ruin of Garfield," *New York Sun*, February 12, 1877.

67. Diary entries for February 10, 13, 15, 1877, JAG—LC.

68. "A Century in Congress," *The Atlantic Monthly*, April 1877.

69. James Garfield to W. C. Howells, February 17, 1877, JAG—LC; Diary entry for February 13, 1877, JAG—LC.

70. James Garfield to Harmon Austin, February 16, 1877, JAG—LC; James Garfield to W. C. Howells, February 17, 1877, JAG—LC.

71. Diary entry for February 26, 1877, JAG—LC; James Garfield to Harmon Austin, February 22, 1877, JAG—LC.

72. Carol W. Gelderman. *A Free Man of Color and His Hotel: Race, Reconstruction, and the Role of the Federal Government* first edition (Washington, D.C.: Potomac Books, 2012), page 21; "Stories of James Wormley," *The Evening Star*, November 15, 1890; Donet Graves, "Wormley Hotel," January 22, 2016.

73. C. Vann Woodward, *Reunion and Reaction*, page 196; Roy Morris, *Fraud of the Century*, page 233.

74. Diary entry for February 26, 1877, JAG—LC.

75. Roy Morris, *Fraud of the Century*, pages 223–227; "The Count Goes On," *New York Herald*, February 25, 1877.

76. C. Vann Woodward, *Reunion and Reaction*, page 193.

77. Diary entry for February 26, 1877, JAG—LC; Michael Holt, *By One Vote*, page 239.

78. James Garfield to Rutherford Hayes, December 13, 1876, JAG—LC.

79. Diary entry for February 25, 1877, JAG—LC.

80. Diary entry for February 26, 1877, JAG—LC.

81. Diary entry for February 26, 1877, JAG—LC.

82. David Jordan, *Roscoe Conkling of New York: Voice in the Senate*, page 263; W. E. B. Du Bois, *Black Reconstruction in America*, page 692; Margaret Leech, *The Garfield Orbit*, page 169.

83. Diary entry for February 28, 1877, JAG—LC.

84. Ari Hoogenboom, *Rutherford B. Hayes: Warrior & President*, page 293.

85. "En Route," *Cincinnati Enquirer*, March 2, 1877; Clipping, *Cincinnati Enquirer*, March 2, 1877; "Off for Washington," *Cincinnati Daily Star*, March 1, 1877.

86. "At Last," *Chicago Tribune*, March 2, 1877; Roy Morris, *Fraud of the Century*, page 235; "Southern Democrats for Order," *New-York Tribune*, March 2, 1877.

87. Diary entry for March 1, 1877, JAG—LC; Alexander Flick. *Samuel Jones Tilden: A Study in Political Sagacity* (Westport, Connecticut: Greenwood Press, 1939), page 396.

88. H. Wayne Morgan, *From Hayes to McKinley: National Party Politics, 1877–1896*, page 2; "Gov. Hayes's Arrival," *New-York Tribune*, March 3, 1877.

89. Ron Chernow, *Grant*, page 850; C. Vann Woodward, *Reunion and Reaction*, page 10.

90. Ari Hoogenboom, *Rutherford B. Hayes: Warrior & President*, page 295.

91. Michael Holt, *By One Vote*, Appendix B.

92. "Arrival of the Dignitaries," *The Times*, March 6, 1877.

93. Diary entry for March 5, 1877, JAG—LC.

94. Ari Hoogenboom, *Rutherford B. Hayes: Warrior & President*, page 299.

95. "Arrival of the Dignitaries," *The Times*, March 6, 1877.

96. "The New Regime," *Boston Globe*, March 5, 1877.

97. Diary entries for March 4, 5, 1877, JAG—LC.

98. David Blight, *Frederick Douglass*, page 583; Roy Morris, *Fraud of the Century*, pages 247–248.

99. H. W. Brands, *American Colossus*, page 388; Roy Morris, *Fraud of the Century*, page 256.

100. "The Electoral Count Bill," *San Francisco Examiner*, February 2, 1887.

CHAPTER 23

1. Alexander Flick, *Samuel Jones Tilden: A Study in Political Sagacity*, pages 396–397; Samuel Cox, *Three Decades of Federal Legislation, 1855 to 1885*, page 656; Richard White, *The Republic for Which It Stands*, page 333.

2. H. Wayne Morgan, *From Hayes to McKinley: National Party Politics, 1877–1896*, page 10.

3. Ari Hoogenboom, *Rutherford B. Hayes: Warrior & President*, page 301; "Washington," *Chicago Tribune*, March 9, 1877; David Jordan, *Roscoe Conkling of New York: Voice in the Senate*, pages 265–266.

4. Stanley Hirshon. *Farewell to the Bloody Shirt: Northern Republicans and the Southern Negro* paperback edition (Quadrangle Books, Inc., 1968), page 39; "Mr. Hayes in the South," *Boston Globe*, September 21, 1877.

5. Stanley Hirshon, *Farewell to the Bloody Shirt: Northern Republicans and the Southern Negro*, page 39; Charles Williams ed., *Diary and Letters of Rutherford Birchard Hayes: Nineteenth President of the United States*, page 444.

6. Ben Perley Poore, *Perley's Reminiscences of Sixty Years in the National Metropolis*, volume 2 (Hubbard Brothers, 1886), page 349.

7. Theodore Clark Smith, *The Life and Letters of James Abram Garfield*, volume 2

(New Haven, Connecticut: Yale University Press, 1925), page 653; Diary entry for March 8, 1877, JAG—LC; Diary entry for March 11, 1877, JAG—LC.

8. Thomas Platt, *The Autobiography of Thomas Collier Platt*, page 67; Alfred Conkling, *The Life and Letters of Roscoe Conkling: Orator, Statesman, Advocate*, page 538.

9. Diary entry for March 7, 1877, JAG—LC; James Garfield to Burke Hinsdale, March 10, 1877, JAG—LC; Diary entry for March 6, 1877, JAG—LC.

10. Theodore Clark Smith. *The Life and Letters of James Abram Garfield* volume 2 (New Haven: Yale University Press, 1925), page 653; Diary entry for March 11, 1877, JAG—LC; James A. Garfield to W. C. Howells, April 2, 1877, JAG—LC.

11. Diary entry for March 27, 1877, JAG—LC; Diary entry for November 19, 1878, JAG—LC.

12. Theodore Clarke Smith, *The Life and Letters of James Abram Garfield*, page 654.

13. Diary entry for March 7, 1877, JAG—LC; Diary entry for March 8, 1877, JAG—LC.

14. Diary entry for March 9, 1877, JAG—LC; Clipping, *Ashtabula Weekly Telegraph*, March 9, 1877.

15. James Garfield to Harmon Austin, March 28, 1877, JAG—LC; "Garfield Declines," *Cleveland Plain Dealer*, March 12, 1877.

16. "Garfield Declines," *Cleveland Plain Dealer*, March 12, 1877; "Gen. Garfield's Self-Sacrifice," *Chicago Tribune*, March 12, 1877; "The Leadership of the House," *New-York Tribune*, March 12, 1877.

17. James Garfield to Harmon Austin, March 28, 1877, and James Garfield to Charles Henry, March 13, 1877, JAG—HC; Allan Peskin, *Garfield*, page 421.

18. Rutherford Hayes to James Garfield, December 25, 1877, JAG—LC.

19. Thomas Reeves, *Gentleman Boss*, page 62; Nicholas R. Parrillo. *Against the Profit Motive: The Salary Revolution in American Government, 1780–1940*, Yale Law Library Series in Legal History and Reference (New Haven: Yale University Press, 2013), page 223; Kenneth Ackerman, *Dark Horse*, pages 136–137; Thomas Reeves, *Gentleman Boss*, page 62; David Jordan, *Roscoe Conkling of New York: Voice in the Senate*, pages 209–210.

20. David Jordan, *Roscoe Conkling of New York*, pages 271–272; Ari Hoogenboom, *Outlawing the Spoils: A History of the Civil Service Reform Movement, 1865–1883*, pages 152–153; Ari Hoogenboom, *Rutherford B. Hayes: Warrior & President*, page 352; Thomas Platt, *The Autobiography of Thomas Collier Platt*, page 83.

21. Alfred Conkling, *The Life and Letters of Roscoe Conkling: Orator, Statesman, Advocate*, pages 540–541.

22. H. Wayne Morgan, *From Hayes to McKinley: National Party Politics, 1877–1896*, page 33; Thomas Reeves, *Gentleman Boss*, pages 42, 57; H. W. Brands, *American Colossus*, page 393.

23. Ari Hoogenboom, *Rutherford B. Hayes: Warrior & President*, page 483; David Jordan, *Roscoe Conkling of New York: Voice in the Senate*, page 282; Charles Williams ed., *Diary and Letters of Rutherford Birchard Hayes: Nineteenth President of the United States*, page 449.

24. Ari Hoogenboom, *Rutherford B. Hayes: Warrior & President*, pages 355–356.

25. Edmund Morris, *The Rise of Theodore Roosevelt*, page 125.
26. H. Wayne Morgan, *From Hayes to McKinley: National Party Politics, 1877–1896*, page 34; David Saville Muzzey, *James G. Blaine: A Political Idol of Other Days*, page 144; Ari Hoogenboom, *Rutherford B. Hayes: Warrior & President*, page 296.
27. Theodore Clarke Smith, *The Life and Letters of James Abram Garfield*, pages 658–659.
28. William McKinley to James Garfield, April 10, 1877, JAG—LC.
29. Diary entry for October 15, 1877, JAG—LC; Diary entry for November 19, 1877, JAG—LC.
30. Biographical interview of James Garfield, 1880, JAG—LC.
31. "A Talk With Gen. Garfield," *New-York Tribune*, August 11, 1877.
32. William Balch, *The Life of James Abram Garfield*, pages 262–263.
33. William Balch, *The Life of James Abram Garfield*, page 332; William Brisbin, *The Early Life and Public Career of James A. Garfield*, pages 334–337; Allan Peskin, *Garfield*, page 428.
34. John Ingalls, *A Collection of the Writings of John James Ingalls: Essays, Addresses, and Orations*, page 398.
35. William Brisbin, *The Early Life and Public Career of James A. Garfield*, page 243; Carl Schurz, *The Reminiscences of Carl Schurz* volume 3, page 395; John Sherman, *Recollections of Forty Years in the House, Senate and Cabinet* volume 2, page 807; Allan Peskin, *Garfield*, page 440; "Why He is Called De Golyer Garfield," *New York Sun*, April 13, 1879; Clipping, *Cleveland Plain Dealer*, June 28, 1873.
36. Allan Peskin, *Garfield*, page 441; "Demoralized Democrats," *New York Sun*, February 14, 1878.
37. James Garfield to Burke Hinsdale, June 23, 1879, JAG—LC.
38. Allan Peskin, *Garfield*, page 441.
39. Theodore Clarke Smith, *The Life and Letters of James Abram Garfield*, pages 659–662; Clipping, *Buffalo Morning Express*, November 19, 1877.
40. Ari Hoogenboom, *Rutherford B. Hayes: Warrior & President*, pages 392–393.
41. Diary entry for March 24, 1879, JAG—LC; Allan Peskin, *Garfield*, pages 438–439.
42. Theodore Clarke Smith, *The Life and Letters of James Abram Garfield*, pages 679–680.
43. "Garfield on the Army Bill," *New-York Tribune*, March 31, 1879; "The Struggle In Congress," *The Evening Star*, March 31, 1879.
44. Allan Peskin, "Garfield and Hayes: Political Leaders of the Gilded Age," *Ohio History* 77, no. 1, 2, 3: 111–124, 195–97, 119; Ari Hoogenboom, *Rutherford B. Hayes: Warrior & President*, pages 399–402.
45. Allan Peskin, *Garfield*, page 440.
46. James Garfield to Burke Hinsdale, September 10, 1877, JAG—LC; Allan Peskin, *Garfield*, pages 426, 430; James Garfield to W. C. Howells, March 1, 1878.
47. Rutherford Hayes to James Garfield, February 9, 1879, JAG—LC; Rutherford Hayes to James Garfield, February 23, 1879, JAG—LC; Allan Peskin, *Garfield*, page 423; Diary entry for October 13, 1877, JAG—LC.

48. James Garfield to W. C. Howells, March 1, 1878, JAG—LC; James Garfield to Harmon Austin, March 3, 1878, JAG—LC.

49. Diary entry for October 30, 1878, JAG—LC.

50. James Blaine to James Garfield, January 13, 1878, JAG—LC; James Blaine to James Garfield, August 28, 1878, JAG—LC; James Blaine to James Garfield, July 20, 1879, JAG—LC.

51. James Garfield to Burke Hinsdale, September 10, 1877, JAG—LC.

52. James Garfield to Lucretia Garfield, June 4, 1877, Garfield and Garfield, *Crete and James*.

53. Diary entry for September 23, 1879, JAG—LC.

54. Diary entry for November 30, 1874, JAG—LC; Lucretia Garfield to James Garfield, June 10, 1877, JAG—LC; Lucretia Garfield to James Garfield, June 8, 1877, Garfield and Garfield, *Crete and James*; James Garfield to Garfield children, June 10, 1877, JAG—LC; Ruth Feis, *Mollie Garfield in the White House*, pages 37–40.

55. Ruth Feis, *Mollie Garfield in the White House*, page 25; Harry Garfield, "Speech By Dr. Harry Augustus Garfield," *Bulletin of Hiram College*, November 19, 1931, JAG—HC.

56. Diary entry for August 24, 1875, JAG—LC.

57. Lucretia Garfield to James Garfield, November 26, 1876, JAG—LC; Lucretia Garfield to James Garfield, May 31, 1877, JAG—LC; Lucretia Garfield to James Garfield, June 8, 1877.

58. Lucretia Garfield to James Garfield, November 29, 1876, JAG—LC; Lucretia Garfield to James Garfield, June 5, 1877, Garfield and Garfield, *Crete and James*.

59. William Balch, *The Life of James Abram Garfield*, pages 314–320; James Garfield to Burke Hinsdale, May 13, 1877, JAG—LC; Ruth Feis, *Mollie Garfield in the White House*, page 35; James Garfield to Henry Boynton, May 24, 1877, Henry Boynton Papers, Western Reserve Historical Society.

60. James Garfield to Harmon Austin, April 3, 1880, JAG—LC; Clipping, *Cleveland Plain Dealer*, August 5, 1878.

61. Eliza Garfield to James Garfield, June 4, 1879, JAG—LC.

62. William Balch, *The Life of James Abram Garfield*, pages 319, 341.

63. Ronald White, *American Ulysses*, page 617; Ari Hoogenboom, *Rutherford B. Hayes: Warrior & President*, pages 402, 423.

64. David Saville Muzzey, *James G. Blaine: A Political Idol of Other Days*, page 158; Ron Chernow, *Grant*, pages 883–884; John Sherman, *Recollections of Forty Years in the House, Senate and Cabinet* volume 2, page 767; H. Wayne Morgan, *From Hayes to McKinley: National Party Politics, 1877–1896*, page 40.

65. B. T. Arrington. *The Last Lincoln Republican: The Presidential Election of 1880*, American Presidential Elections (Lawrence: University Press of Kansas, 2020), page 65.

66. James Garfield to R. P. Harmon, April 16, 1875, JAG—LC.

67. Diary entry for April 14, 1880, JAG—LC; James Garfield to Lucretia Garfield, August 6, 1876, JAG—LC.

68. Allan Peskin, *Garfield*, page 444; Benjamin Arrington, *The Last Lincoln Republican*, page 52.

69. James Garfield to Harmon Austin, May 13, 1879, JAG—LC; James Garfield to Charles Henry, February 22, 1879, JAG—HC.

70. James Garfield to W. C. Howells, January 27, 1879, JAG—LC.

71. Allan Peskin, *Garfield*, page 445; William Kerr. *John Sherman: His Life and Public Services* volume 2 (Boston: Sherman, French & Company, 1908), page 49.

72. Allan Peskin, *Garfield*, page 446; "Data of Garfield's Senatorial Canvass," circa 1879, JAG—LC.

73. "A Talk with Gen. Garfield," *New-York Tribune*, August 11, 1877; "The Garfield Movement," *Cleveland Plain Dealer*, July 5, 1877.

74. Allan Peskin, *Garfield*, pages 446–447; James Garfield to Harmon Austin, January 11, 1880, JAG—LC.

75. Frederick Henry, *Captain Henry of Geauga: A Family Chronicle*, page 291.

76. Benjamin Arrington, *The Last Lincoln Republican*, page 63.

77. "Garfield and Sherman," *Cincinnati Enquirer*, January 29, 1880; James Garfield to Harmon Austin, April 16, 1880, JAG—LC.

78. "Honoring Garfield," *National Republican*, January 23, 1880.

79. "Public Opinion," *New-York Tribune*, March 22, 1878; Diary entry for July 23, 1878, JAG—LC.

80. Diary entry for February 5, 1879, JAG—LC.

81. H. Wayne Morgan, *From Hayes to McKinley: National Party Politics, 1877–1896*, page 55.

82. Ron Chernow, *Grant*, page 886; H. Wayne Morgan, *From Hayes to McKinley: National Party Politics, 1877–1896*, page 71; Henry Adams. *The Letters of Henry Adams (1858–1891)* (Cambridge, Massachusetts: The Riverside Press, 1930), page 319.

83. Theodore Clarke Smith, *The Life and Letters of James Abram Garfield*, pages 950–951; Diary entry for February 11, 1880, JAG—LC.

84. Diary entry for April 24, 1880, JAG—LC.

CHAPTER 24

1. "Our Library," *Chicago Tribune*, January 2, 1873; William Cronon. *Nature's Metropolis: Chicago and the Great West* (New York: Norton, 1992), page 346; Elias Colbert and Everett Chamberlain. *Chicago and the Great Conflagration* (New York: C.F. Vent, 1872), page 445.

2. Ron Chernow, *Grant*, pages 872–873.

3. H. Wayne Morgan, *From Hayes to McKinley: National Party Politics, 1877–1896*, page 71.

4. "Chicago!" *The Evening Star*, June 3, 1880; "The Streets and Corridors," *New-York Tribune*, June 2, 1880.

5. "Chicago!" *The Evening Star*, June 3, 1880; "The Streets and Corridors," *New-York Tribune*, June 2, 1880; "The National Convention," *The New York Times*, June 3, 1880; "The Convention and Its Work," *The New York Times*, June 3, 1880.

6. "Some of the Incidents," *The New York Times*, June 2, 1880.

7. "The Exposition Building," *Chicago Tribune*, May 19, 1873; "The Convention and Its Work," *The New York Times*, June 3, 1880.

8. "The National Convention," *The New York Times*, June 3, 1880; "From The Galleries," *The Inter Ocean*, June 3, 1880; "At Work," *Chicago Tribune*, June 3, 1880.

9. Jas. S. Brisbin, *The Early Life and Public Career of James A. Garfield*, page 376.

10. "From the Galleries," *The Inter Ocean*, June 3, 1880; Robert McElroy. *Levi Parsons Morton: Banker, Diplomat, and Statesman* (New York; London: G.P. Putnam's Sons, 1930), pages 99–100; "Some of the Incidents," *The New York Times*, June 2, 1880; Harriet Blaine to Margaret Blaine, May 15, 1880; Mrs. Blaine, *Letters of Mrs. James G. Blaine*.

11. Kenneth Ackerman, *Dark Horse*, pages 49–51; Benjamin Arrington, *The Last Lincoln Republican*, page 71.

12. Diary entry for June 1, 1880, JAG—LC; "Telegrams to the Star," *Evening Star*, June 1, 1880.

13. James Garfield to Charles Henry, January 26, 1880, JAG—HC; Diary entry for March 4, 1880, JAG—LC.

14. Diary entry for May 31, 1880, JAG—LC; James Garfield to Lucretia Garfield, June 2, 1880, JAG—LC; "General," *The Inter Ocean*, May 31, 1880.

15. Thomas Reeves, *Gentleman Boss*, page 169; David Saville Muzzey, *James G. Blaine: A Political Idol of Other Days*, page 167; "The Eve of the Contest," *New-York Tribune*, June 2, 1880.

16. "From the Galleries," *The Inter Ocean*, June 3, 1880; "The Fight Against Grant," *New York Sun*, June 1, 1880; "General," *The Inter Ocean*, May 31, 1880.

17. Wharton Barker, "The Secret History of Garfield's Nomination," *Pearson's Magazine*, no. XXXV (May 1916), page 440.

18. "The Field of Action," *Chicago Tribune*, June 3, 1880; "Third-termer's Second Choice," *New-York Tribune*, June 1, 1880.

19. James Garfield to Lucretia Garfield, May 31, 1880, Garfield and Garfield, *Crete and James*.

20. "Excitement at Chicago," *New-York Tribune*, June 1, 1880; Allan Peskin, *Garfield*, page 458.

21. "The Presidency At Stake," *The New York Times*, May 31, 1880; James Garfield to Lucretia Garfield, June 2, 1880, JAG—LC.

22. "The Convention Called to Order," *New York Sun*, June 3, 1880; "The First Skirmish," *New York Sun*, June 3, 1880.

23. "At Work," *Chicago Tribune*, June 3, 1880; "Inside the Hall," *Chicago Tribune*, June 3, 1880; "Trouble and Turmoil," *Cincinnati Enquirer*, June 3, 1880.

24. "The Contest of the Morning," *New-York Tribune*, June 4, 1880; *Proceedings of the Republican National Convention* (Chicago: The JNO. B. Jeffrey Printing and Publishing House, 1881), page 15; "The Field of Action," *Chicago Tribune*, June 4, 1880.

25. "The Contest of the Morning," *New-York Tribune*, June 4, 1880.

26. "Skirmishing," *The Inter Ocean*, June 4, 1880; "The Contest of the Morning," *New-York Tribune*, June 4, 1880.

27. Kenneth Ackerman, *Dark Horse*, page 23; "General," *The Inter Ocean*, June 3, 1880.

28. *Proceedings of the Republican National Convention*, pages 17–19, 23; "The First Round," *Chicago Tribune*, June 4, 1880.

29. *Proceedings of the Republican National Convention*, page 23; "The First Round," *Chicago Tribune*, June 4, 1880.

30. "The First Round," *Chicago Tribune*, June 4, 1880.

31. *Proceedings of the Republican National Convention*, page 23.

32. "The Field of Action," *Chicago Tribune*, June 4, 1880; "An Outsider," *Chicago Tribune*, June 4, 1880; "Bubble, Bubble, Toil and Trouble, at Chicago," *Detroit Free Press*, June 4, 1880; "The Contest of the Morning," *New-York Tribune*, June 4, 1880.

33. James Garfield to Lucretia Garfield, June 3, 1880, JAG—LC; Allan Peskin, *Garfield*, pages 464.

34. "An Anti-Grant Victory," *New-York Tribune*, June 4, 1880; "The Struggle at Chicago," *The New York Times*, June 4, 1880; "Bubble, Bubble, Toil and Trouble, at Chicago," *Detroit Free Press*, June 4, 1880; "An Anti-Grant Victory," *New-York Tribune*, June 4, 1880; *Proceedings of the Republican National Convention*, page 29.

35. "The Second Round," *Chicago Tribune*, June 5, 1880; "The President-Makers," *The New York Times*, June 5, 1880; Barker, "The Secret History of Garfield's Nomination."

36. *Proceedings of the Republican National Convention*, pages 34–39; Benjamin Arrington, *The Last Lincoln Republican*, page 74.

37. *Proceedings of the Republican National Convention*, page 40; "The Great Contest Renewed," *New-York Tribune*, June 5.

38. "The Great Contest Renewed," *New-York Tribune*, June 5, 1880; *Proceedings of the Republican National Convention*, pages 40–41.

39. "The Great Contest Renewed," *New-York Tribune*, June 5, 1880; "Second Round," *Chicago Tribune*, June 5, 1880; "The Great Contest Renewed," *New-York Tribune*, June 5, 1880; *Proceedings of the Republican National Convention*, page 41; "The Great Contest Renewed," *New-York Tribune*, June 5, 1880.

40. "Chicago," *Star Tribune*, June 5, 1880; H. Wayne Morgan, *From Hayes to McKinley: National Party Politics, 1877–1896*, page 33.

41. Alfred Conkling, *The Life and Letters of Roscoe Conkling: Orator, Statesman, Advocate*, page 592; Roscoe Conkling to James Garfield, June 4, 1880, JAG—LC.

42. *Proceedings of the Republican National Convention*, page 44; "Real Work Begun," *New York Sun*, June 5, 1880.

43. H. Wayne Morgan, *From Hayes to McKinley: National Party Politics, 1877–1896*, page 90; Barker, "The Secret History of Garfield's Nomination," pages 441–442; "Chicago!" *Evening Star*, June 5, 1880.

44. *Proceedings of the Republican National Convention*, page 125; J. W. Hogan, et al. to James Garfield, June 4, 1880, JAG—LC; "Playing for Time," *Chicago Tribune*, June 5, 1880; "Details of the Morning Session," *New-York Tribune*, June 5, 1880; "Bedlam!" *The Evening Star*, June 5, 1880; "Stuck," *Cincinnati Enquirer*, June 5, 1880; "Second Round," *Chicago Tribune*, June 5, 1880.

45. Lucretia Garfield to James Garfield, June 4, 1880, JAG—LC.

46. "Gath's Gossip," *Cincinnati Enquirer*, June 5, 1880.

47. James Garfield to Lucretia Garfield, June 6, 1880, JAG—LC.

48. *Proceedings of the Republican National Convention,* page 175; "An Anxious Day," *Chicago Tribune,* June 6, 1880.

49. *Proceedings of the Republican National Convention,* page 175; "The Candidates Proposed," *New-York Tribune,* June 6, 1880; Candice Millard. *Destiny of the Republic: A Tale of Madness, Medicine and the Murder of a President* (New York: Anchor Books, 2012), page 43; "Who Will Be Nominated," *The New York Times,* June 7, 1880.

50. *Proceedings of the Republican National Convention,* page 176; "The Candidates Proposed," *New-York Tribune,* June 6, 1880.

51. "A Magnificent Occasion," *The Inter Ocean,* June 7, 1880; "Presenting the Candidates," *The New York Times,* June 6, 1880; David Jordan, *Roscoe Conkling of New York: Voice in the Senate,* page 334.

52. "The Candidates Proposed," *New-York Tribune,* June 6, 1880; *Proceedings of the Republican National Convention,* pages 180–182.

53. Royal Cortissoz. *The Life of Whitelaw Reid* volume 2 (London: Thornton Butterworth Limited, 1921), page 24; Kenneth Ackerman, *Dark Horse,* page 74; "The Candidates Proposed," *New-York Tribune,* June 6, 1880.

54. *Proceedings of the Republican National Convention,* page 182; Thomas Platt, *The Autobiography of Thomas Collier Platt,* page 111; "In the Stables," *Cincinnati Enquirer,* June 7, 1880.

55. Diary entry for May 25, 1880, JAG—LC.

56. James Garfield to Lucretia Garfield, June 6, 1880, JAG—LC; "Progress of the Contest," *The New York Times,* June 6, 1880.

57. "Progress of the Contest," *The New York Times,* June 6, 1880; Candice Millard, *Destiny of the Republic,* page 44; *Proceedings of the Republican National Convention,* pages 178–184.

58. "By Gaslight," *The Inter Ocean,* June 7, 1880; "Not Yet," *The Inter Ocean,* June 7, 1880.

59. *Proceedings of the Republican National Convention,* pages 185–186.

60. Candice Millard, *Destiny of the Republic,* page 46; George Hoar, *Autobiography of Seventy Years* volume 2, page 393; "Not Yet," *The Inter Ocean,* June 7, 1880; "The Candidates Proposed," *New-York Tribune,* June 6, 1880; "The Oratorical Tournament," *Chicago Tribune,* June 7, 1880.

61. "Before the Battle," *Chicago Tribune,* June 6, 1880; John Sherman, *Recollections of Forty Years in the House, Senate and Cabinet* volume 2, page 774.

62. "The Events of Saturday," *The New York Times,* June 7, 1880; "Hotel Hash," *Cincinnati Enquirer,* June 7, 1880; *Proceedings of the Republican National Convention,* pages 184–186; "After the Battle," *Cincinnati Enquirer,* June 10, 1880; "Blaine Still Leading," *New-York Tribune,* June 7, 1880.

63. Clipping, *New-York Tribune,* June 7, 1880.

64. "A Magnificent Occasion," *The Inter Ocean,* June 7, 1880.

65. Alfred Conkling, *The Life and Letters of Roscoe Conkling: Orator, Statesman, Advocate,* page 604.

66. James Garfield to Lucretia Garfield, June 6, 1880, Garfield and Garfield, *Crete and*

James; Allan Peskin, *Garfield*, page 470; Theodore Clarke Smith, *The Life and Letters of James Abram Garfield*, 1925, page 978.

67. "Points," *The Inter Ocean*, June 7, 1880.

68. "The Balloting," *Detroit Free Press*, June 8, 1880; "The Balloting Begun," *New-York Tribune*, June 8, 1880.

69. *Proceedings of the Republican National Convention*, page 198; Allan Peskin, *Garfield*, pages 471.

70. Barker, "The Secret History of Garfield's Nomination"; "Still Unsettled," *Chicago Tribune*, June 8, 1880.

71. Clipping, *Chicago Tribune*, June 8, 1880; *Proceedings of the Republican National Convention*, pages 250–251.

72. H. Wayne Morgan, *From Hayes to McKinley: National Party Politics, 1877–1896*, page 93; "Gen. Garfield Nominated," *New York Sun*, June 9, 1880.

73. Allan Peskin, *Garfield*, page 474.

74. "Garfield," *The Inter Ocean*, June 9, 1880; *Proceedings of the Republican National Convention*, page 269.

75. George Hoar, *Autobiography of Seventy Years* volume 2, pages 395, 397, 401–402.

76. "Garfield," *The Inter Ocean*, June 9, 1880; "Garfield for President," *New-York Tribune*, June 9, 1880.

77. Kenneth Ackerman, *Dark Horse*, page 94.

78. "Garfield," *The Inter Ocean*, June 9, 1880; "Garfield and Arthur," *The New York Times*, June 9, 1880; "Gen. Garfield Nominated," *New York Sun*, June 9, 1880.

79. "The Sixth Day," *Boston Globe*, June 9, 1880; Kenneth Ackerman, *Dark Horse*, page 95.

80. Theodore Clarke Smith, *The Life and Letters of James Abram Garfield*, page 983; "Congress and Chicago," *The Evening Star*, June 8, 1880; Benjamin Arrington, *The Last Lincoln Republican*, page 95.

81. James Blaine to James Garfield, June 8, 1880, JAG—LC.

82. "The Sixth Day," *Boston Globe*, June 9, 1880.

83. "The Trying Moment," *The Inter Ocean*, June 9, 1880.

84. James Garfield to Lucretia Garfield, June 8, 1880, Garfield and Garfield, *Crete and James*.

85. "Garfield for President," *New-York Tribune*, June 9, 1880; Alexander McClure, *Recollections of Half a Century*, pages 109–110; "On the Outside," *Chicago Tribune*, June 9, 1880.

86. "After the Battle," *Inter Ocean*, June 9, 1880; Frederick Henry, *Captain Henry of Geauga: A Family Chronicle*, page 296.

87. Harry and James Garfield to James Garfield, June 8, 1880, JAG—LC; Kenneth Ackerman, *Dark Horse*, page 106; Alexander McClure, *Recollections of Half a Century*, page 110.

88. Allan Peskin, *Garfield*, page 477; "Arthur for Vice-President," *New-York Tribune*, June 9, 1880.

89. Candice Millard, *Destiny of the Republic*, page 52; Kenneth Ackerman, *Dark Horse*, page 97; "Garfield and Arthur," *New York Sun*, June 9, 1880.

90. Kenneth Ackerman, *Dark Horse*, page 98; Theodore Clarke Smith, *The Life and Letters of James Abram Garfield*, page 985; Alfred Conkling, *The Life and Letters of Roscoe Conkling: Orator, Statesman, Advocate*, pages 608–609; Thomas Platt, *The Autobiography of Thomas Collier Platt*, pages 115–119.

91. Kenneth Ackerman, *Dark Horse*, page 107.

92. Ron Chernow, *Grant*, pages 902–904.

93. *Proceedings of the Republican National Convention*, page 276; Kenneth Ackerman, *Dark Horse*, page 97; Alexander McClure, *Recollections of Half a Century*, page 110.

94. Ari Hoogenboom, *Outlawing the Spoils: A History of the Civil Service Reform Movement, 1865–1883*, page 182.

95. James Garfield to W. C. Howells, December 12, 1871, JAG—LC.

96. De Alva Stanwood Alexander. *A Political History of the State of New York* volume 3 (New York: Henry Holt and Company, 1909), pages 443–444.

97. H. Wayne Morgan, *From Hayes to McKinley: National Party Politics, 1877–1896*, page 143.

98. Thomas Reeves, *Gentleman Boss*, pages 16, 37, 55, 72, 84; Thomas Platt, *The Autobiography of Thomas Collier Platt*, page 182.

99. Ari Hoogenboom, *Rutherford B. Hayes: Warrior & President*, page 370; Thomas Reeves, *Gentleman Boss*, pages 158–159.

100. "The Great Joy of Dr. Bellows," *New-York Tribune*, June 10, 1880.

101. De Alva Stanwood, *A Political History of the State of New York*, page 444.

102. William C. Hudson. *Random Recollections of an Old Political Reporter* (New York: Cupples and Leon Company, 1911), pages 97–98.

103. T. B. Connery, "The Secret History of the Garfield-Conkling Tragedy," *The Cosmopolitan* XXIII, no. 2 (June 1897): 152.

104. *Proceedings of the Republican National Convention*, pages 287, 294.

105. "The Levee," *Chicago Tribune*, June 9, 1880.

106. "Reception of the Nominees," *The Inter Ocean*, June 9, 1880; Kenneth Ackerman, *Dark Horse*, page 112; Thomas Reeves, *Gentleman Boss*, page 182.

107. *Proceedings of the Republican National Convention*, page 297.

108. "Next President," *The Inter Ocean*, June 10, 1880; "Welcoming Gen. Garfield," *The New York Times*, June 10, 1880.

109. "Homeward Bound," *Chicago Tribune*, June 10, 1880.

110. Frederick Henry, *Captain Henry of Geauga: A Family Chronicle*, page 297.

111. Kenneth Ackerman, *Dark Horse*, page 107; H. Wayne Morgan, *From Hayes to McKinley: National Party Politics, 1877–1896*, pages 94–95; Thomas Reeves, *Gentleman Boss*, page 183.

112. John Ingalls, *A Collection of the Writings of John James Ingalls: Essays, Addresses, and Orations*, page 402; "Joel W. Mason's Confidence," *New-York Tribune*, June 10; Thomas Reeves, *Gentleman Boss*, page 184.

113. H. Wayne Morgan, *From Hayes to McKinley: National Party Politics, 1877–1896*, page 95; David Saville Muzzey, *James G. Blaine: A Political Idol of Other Days*, page 172.

114. Clipping, *The Nation*, June 17, 1880.

115. Candice Millard, *Destiny of the Republic*, pages 64–65; H. G. Hayes and C. J. Hayes.

A Complete History of the Life and Trial of Charles Julius Guiteau (Hubbard Brothers, 1882), page 66.

CHAPTER 25

1. "Our New President," *The Daily Commonwealth*, June 9, 1880; Clipping, *The Daily Commonwealth*, June 9, 1880; James Garfield to Blymer Manufacturing Company, November 11, 1875.
2. "Ratification Meeting at Key West," *The Evening Star*, June 9, 1880; "The Full Ticket," *The Pacific Bee*, June 12, 1880; "Michigan," *Chicago Tribune*, June 9, 1880; "Dark Horse," *The Record-Union*, June 9, 1880; James Blaine, *Twenty Years Of Congress: From Lincoln to Garfield* volume 2, page 667; "The Great Joy of Dr. Bellows," *New-York Tribune*, June 10, 1880.
3. "The Nominee," *Boston Globe*, June 9, 1880; "The Candidates," *The Inter Ocean*, June 9, 1880; "General Burnett Much Gratified," *New-York Tribune*, June 9, 1880; "The Candidates," *New-York Tribune*, June 9, 1880; "The Man," *Chicago Tribune*, June 9, 1880; "Gath on Garfield," *Chicago Tribune*, June 12, 1880; "The Man," *Chicago Tribune*, June 9, 1880.
4. "The Candidates," *The Inter Ocean*, June 9, 1880.
5. "Lives Of The Candidates," *The New York Times*, June 9, 1880.
6. "Action of the Union League Club," *The New York Times*, June 11, 1880.
7. Clipping, *The Daily News*, June 9, 1880; "The Republican Candidate For The Presidency," *The Daily News*, June 10, 1880; "European Comment," *The Inter Ocean*, June 10, 1880.
8. "Reminiscential," *Chicago Tribune*, June 9, 1880; Ari Hoogenboom, *Rutherford B. Hayes: Warrior & President*, page 431; Allan Peskin, *Garfield*, page 493.
9. "Honors to the Candidate," *The New York Times*, June 11, 1880.
10. Royal Cortissoz, *The Life of Whitelaw Reid*, volume 2, page 35; Rutherford Hayes to James Garfield, July 26, 1880, JAG—LC.
11. Charles Emory Smith, "How Conkling Nixed Nominating Blaine," *Saturday Evening Post*, June 8, 1901; William Hudson, *Random Recollections of an Old Political Reporter*, page 98; *Puck* VIII, No. 170, June 9, 1880; Allan Peskin, *Garfield*, page 485; Thomas Platt, *The Autobiography of Thomas Collier Platt*, page 125; Herbert Clancy. *The Presidential Election of 1880* (Chicago: Loyola University Press, 1958), page 168.
12. Ron Chernow, *Grant*, pages 902, 904.
13. Allan Peskin, *Garfield*, page 482.
14. Lucretia Garfield to James Garfield, June 15, 1880, Garfield and Garfield, *Crete and James*; Theodore Clarke Smith, *The Life and Letters of James Abram Garfield*, page 996.
15. "Arrival of General Garfield," *The Evening Star*, June 15, 1880; "Gen. Garfield in Washington," *The Evening Star*, June 16, 1880; Clipping, *The Evening Star*, June 17, 1880; David Jordan, *Roscoe Conkling of New York: Voice in the Senate*, page 347; Alfred Conkling, *The Life and Letters of Roscoe Conkling: Orator, Statesman, Advocate*, page 611.

16. Chester Arthur to James Garfield, June 18, 1880, JAG—LC.

17. Diary entry for April 19, 1880, JAG—LC; Diary entry for January 24, 1879, JAG—LC; Diary entry for September 25, 1879, JAG—LC.

18. Diary entry for January 24, 1879, JAG—LC; James Garfield to Whitelaw Reid, June 29, 1880, JAG—LC; James Garfield to James Blaine, June 29, 1880, JAG—LC.

19. James Garfield to Carl Schurz, July 6, 1880, JAG—LC; James Garfield to Whitelaw Reid, June 29, 1880, JAG—LC; James Garfield to James Blaine, June 29, 1880, JAG—LC; James Garfield to Chester Arthur, June 29, 1880, JAG—LC.

20. James Blaine to James Garfield, July 4, 1880, JAG—LC.

21. James Garfield to Chester Arthur, July 3, 1880, JAG—LC; James Garfield to Chester Arthur, July 8, 1880, JAG—LC; Chester Arthur to James Garfield, June 28, 1880, JAG—LC; Chester Arthur to James Garfield, July 1, 11, 1880, JAG—LC.

22. Margaret Leech, *The Garfield Orbit*, page 211.

23. James Blaine to James Garfield, July 4, 1880, JAG—LC; James Garfield to James Blaine, June 29, 1880, JAG—LC.

24. Edmund Morris, *The Rise of Theodore Roosevelt*, page 405; Carl Fish, *The Civil Service and The Patronage*, page 216.

25. Rayford Whittingham Logan. *The Betrayal of the Negro, from Rutherford B. Hayes to Woodrow Wilson*, first Da Capo Press edition (New York: Da Capo Press, 1997), pages 34–35; Frederick Douglass, *Life and Times of Frederick Douglass*, page 634.

26. Allan Nevins, *The Emergence of Modern America, 1865–1878*, pages 386–391; Margaret Leech. *In the Days of McKinley* (New York: Harper & Row, 1959), page 451.

27. P. W. Dooner. *Last Days of the Republic* (San Francisco: Alta California Publishing House, 1880), page 256; Richard White, *The Republic for Which It Stands*, page 381.

28. Leon Burr Richardson. *William E. Chandler, Republican* (New York: Dodd, Mead & Company, 1940), page 257; Benjamin Arrington, *The Last Lincoln Republican*, page 103.

29. *Harper's Weekly* XXIV, no. 1231 (July 31, 1880); *Harper's Weekly* XXIV, no. 1233 (August 14, 1880).

30. *Puck* VII, No. 172, June 23, 1880; Herbert Clancy, *The Presidential Election of 1880*, page 231; Candice Millard, *Destiny of the Republic*, page 69.

31. C. S. Carpenter, ed., *James A. Garfield: His Speeches at Home* (C.S. Carpenter, 1880).

32. James Garfield to W. C. Howells, August 23, 1880, JAG—LC.

33. James Garfield to Harry Garfield and James R. Garfield, June 16, 1880, JAG—LC; Harry Garfield to James Garfield, June 13, 1880, JAG—LC.

34. Benjamin Arrington, *The Last Lincoln Republican*, page 150; Alan Gephardt, Debbie Weinkamer, and Joan Kapsch, "The Front Porch Campaign," A Fickle Current, https://www.nps.gov/jaga/a-fickle-current-podcast.htm.

35. H. Wayne Morgan, *From Hayes to McKinley: National Party Politics, 1877–1896*, pages 105–106; "Garfield At Mentor," *The Inter Ocean*, July 24, 1880.

36. James Blaine. *Eulogy on the Late President Garfield* (Philadelphia: Hubbard Brothers, 1882), page 27.

37. H. Wayne Morgan, *From Hayes to McKinley: National Party Politics, 1877–1896*, pages 105–106; C. S. Carpenter, *James A. Garfield: His Speeches at Home.*

38. "Presidential," *Chicago Tribune*, June 14, 1880; Ruth Feis, *Mollie Garfield in the White House*, page 44; Joseph Stanley Brown, "My Friend Garfield," *American Heritage* XXII, no. 5 (August 4, 1971): 48–53, 100–101.

39. "Gath," *Brooklyn Daily Eagle*, June 22, 1880; James Brisbin, *The Early Life and Public Career of James A. Garfield*, pages 341–342.

40. Kenneth Ackerman, *Dark Horse*, page 138; "Gath," *Brooklyn Daily Eagle*, June 22, 1880; William Balch, *Garfield's Words: Suggestive Passages From The Public And Private Writings of James Abram Garfield*, pages 338–340.

41. "A Pilgrimage," *Cincinnati Enquirer*, September 24, 1880; William Balch, *Garfield's Words: Suggestive Passages From The Public And Private Writings of James Abram Garfield*; Corydon Fuller, *Reminiscences of James A. Garfield, with Notes Preliminary and Collateral*, pages 430–431; Thomas Garfield, "Recollections of the Life of James A. Garfield," JAG—LC; Kenneth Ackerman, *Dark Horse*, page 164; Gephardt, Weinkamer, and Kapsch, "The Front Porch Campaign."

42. A. F. Rockwell, "From Mentor to Elberon," *Century Magazine*, 1882.

43. James Garfield to Harmon Austin, August 23, 1880, JAG—LC; Whitelaw Reid to James Garfield, August 13, 1880, JAG—LC; Diary entry for August 22, 1880, JAG—LC.

44. Burke Hinsdale. *The Republican Text-Book for the Campaign of 1880* (New York: D. Appleton and Company, 1880), pages 150–152.

45. David Jordan, *Roscoe Conkling of New York: Voice in the Senate*, page 348; John Sherman to James Garfield, July 19, 1880, JAG—LC; Carl Schurz to James Garfield, July 20, 1880, JAG—LC; Ari Hoogenboom, *Rutherford B. Hayes: Warrior & President*, page 434.

46. James Garfield to Carl Schurz, July 22, 1880, JAG—LC; James Garfield to Burke Hinsdale, July 25, 1880, JAG—LC.

47. Henry Adams. *The Letters of Henry Adams (1858–1891)* (Cambridge, Massachusetts: The Riverside Press, 1930), page 324.

48. James Blaine to James Garfield, July 4, 1881, JAG—LC; B. A. Hinsdale, *The Republican Text-Book for the Campaign of 1880*, pages 151–152.

49. Diary entry for July 28, 1880, JAG—LC; "Garfield," *The Inter Ocean*, August 4, 1880.

50. Herbert Clancy, *The Presidential Election of 1880*, pages 169–170; "Marshall Jewell," *Chicago Tribune*, February 18, 1883; Allan Peskin, *Garfield*, page 487.

51. Stephen Dorsey to James Garfield, July 24, 1880, JAG—LC; Marshall Jewell to James Garfield, July 21, 1880, JAG—LC.

52. James Garfield to J. W. Dorsey, July 28, 1880, JAG—LC.

53. Diary entry for July 30, 1880, JAG—LC; Diary entry for July 31, 1880, JAG—LC.

54. "Gen. Garfield Welcomed," *The New York Times*, August 5, 1880; "From Buffalo to Albany," *New-York Tribune*, August 5, 1880.

55. "From Buffalo to Albany," *New-York Tribune*, August 5, 1880; "Down the Hudson," *New-York Tribune*, August 5, 1880.

56. "Garfield in New York," *New-York Tribune*, August 5, 1880; "Gen. Garfield Welcomed," *The New York Times*, August 5, 1880.

57. James Garfield to Lucretia Garfield, August 4, 1880, Garfield and Garfield, *Crete and James*; "The Greeting In This City," *The New York Times*, August 5, 1880; "Reception to Gen. Fremont," *The New York Times*, August 5, 1880.

58. James Garfield to James Blaine, July 30, 1880, JAG—LC; James Garfield to James Blaine, July 30, 1880 (2), JAG—LC.

59. "Garfield in New York," *New-York Tribune*, August 5, 1880.

60. "Report of the Proceedings in the Case of the *United States vs. Charles J. Guiteau*," (Washington, D.C.: Government Printing Office, 1882), pages 2209–2210, 2157.

61. Kenneth Ackerman, *Dark Horse*, page 149; Diary entry for August 5, 1880, JAG—LC.

62. John Sherman, *Recollections of Forty Years in the House, Senate and Cabinet*, volume 2, page 780; Thomas Platt, *The Autobiography of Thomas Collier Platt*, page 129.

63. Edmund Morris, *The Rise of Theodore Roosevelt*, page 394.

64. *Harper's Weekly* XLI, no. 2129 (October 9, 1897), page 534; Thomas Platt, *The Autobiography of Thomas Collier Platt*, pages 129–131.

65. Alfred Conkling, *The Life and Letters of Roscoe Conkling: Orator, Statesman, Advocate*, page 612; Thomas Platt, *The Autobiography of Thomas Collier Platt*, page 132.

66. "Incidents of the Journey," *The New York Times*, August 8, 1880.

67. Herbert Clancy, *The Presidential Election of 1880*, page 200.

68. Thomas Reeves, *Gentleman Boss*, page 194; Alfred Conkling, *The Life and Letters of Roscoe Conkling: Orator, Statesman, Advocate*, page 614; Royal Cortissoz, *The Life of Whitelaw Reid* volume 2, page 38.

69. Thomas Platt, *The Autobiography of Thomas Collier Platt*, page 131; "Incidents of the Journey," *The New York Times*, August 8, 1880; "Garfield At Chautauqua," *The New York Times*, August 9, 1880; Diary entry for August 10, 1880, JAG—LC.

70. Diary entry for August 10, 1880, JAG—LC; Ulysses Grant to James Garfield, August 5, 1880, JAG—LC.

71. Diary entry for August 9, 1880, JAG—LC.

72. Kenneth Ackerman, *Dark Horse*, page 150.

73. Diary entry for August 5, 1880, JAG—LC.

74. Allan Peskin, *Garfield*, page 493; *Garfield and Arthur Campaign Songbook* (Republican National Committee, 1880), pages 3, 4, 5, and 17.

75. Jas. Brisbin. *The Early Life and Public Career of James A. Garfield*, ed. Paul Rich (Westphalia Press, 2013); Horatio Alger, Jr. *From Canal Boy to President* (DeWolfe, Fiske & Co., 1881); William Thayer. "From Log-Cabin to the White House," (James H. Earle, 1881); J. M. Stewart, "Garfield At The Helm," June 8, 1880, JAG—LC; "W.E.C.," "Nail It Down," circa summer 1880, JAG—LC.

76. *Garfield and Arthur Campaign Songbook*, page 21; Anonymous, *A Record of the Statesmanship and Political Achievements of Gen. Winfield Scott Hancock*, 1880.

77. Eileen Shields-West, *The World Almanac of Presidential Campaigns* (New York: World Almanac, 1992), page 108; Images of these products were posted on the

Instagram page of the National Parks Service—Mentor on the following dates: June 22, 2020, May 9, 2020, and September 13, 2020.

78. "The Great Grant Parade," *The New York Times*, October 6, 1880; Thomas Reeves, *Gentleman Boss*, page 196; David Jordan, *Roscoe Conkling of New York: Voice in the Senate*, pages 152–153.

79. Thomas Platt, *The Autobiography of Thomas Collier Platt*, page 133.

80. Jerry Rushford, "Political Disciple: The Relationship between James A. Garfield and the Disciples of Christ," 1977, pages 265–267.

81. Frederick Douglass, *Life and Times of Frederick Douglass*, pages 633–634; "Freedmen For Garfield," *The New York Times*, October 26,1880.

82. Kenneth Ackerman, *Dark Horse*, page 136.

83. Thomas Reeves, *Gentleman Boss*, pages 199, 200–201; Kenneth Ackerman, *Dark Horse*, page 160; Ari Hoogenboom, *Outlawing the Spoils: A History of the Civil Service Reform Movement, 1865–1883*, page 185.

84. Robert McElroy, *Levi Parsons Morton: Banker, Diplomat, and Statesman*, pages 112–113; Ari Hoogenboom, *Outlawing the Spoils: A History of the Civil Service Reform Movement, 1865–1883*, pages 205–206.

85. David Blight, *Frederick Douglass*, page 618; Robert Caldwell. *James A. Garfield: Party Chieftain* (Hamden, Connecticut: Archon Books, 1965), insert between Pages 304–305; "Pithy Political Paragraphs," *San Francisco Examiner*, September 20, 1880.

86. Thomas Platt, *The Autobiography of Thomas Collier Platt*, page 132.

87. Diary entry for August 13, 1880, JAG—LC; Diary entry for August 14, 1880, JAG—LC; Susan B. Anthony to James Garfield, August 16, 1880, JAG—LC; James Garfield to Jay Hubbell, August 22, 1880, JAG—LC; James Garfield to Chester Arthur, August 31, 1880, JAG—LC.

88. Jay Hubbell to James Garfield, July 8, 1880, JAG—LC; Stephen Dorsey to D. Swaim, September 1, 1880, JAG—LC; Allan Peskin, *Garfield*, page 496.

89. Diary entry for August 6, 1880, JAG—LC; James Garfield to Amos Townsend, September 2, 1880, JAG—LC; Ron Chernow. *Titan: The Life of John D. Rockefeller, Sr.* (New York: Random House, 1998), pages 210–221; Allan Peskin, *Garfield*, page 503.

90. Allan Peskin, *Garfield*, page 497; Ron Chernow, *Titan*, pages 210–221.

91. Allan Peskin, *Garfield*, page 496; James Garfield to Burke Hinsdale, July 25, 1880, JAG—LC.

92. Diary entry for August 31, 1880, JAG—LC.

93. James Blaine to James Garfield, September 14, 1880, JAG—LC; Herbert Clancy, *The Presidential Election of 1880*, page 193; Diary entry for September 14, 1880, JAG—LC; H. Wayne Morgan, *From Hayes to McKinley: National Party Politics, 1877–1896*, page 116.

94. Herbert Clancy, *The Presidential Election of 1880*, page 195; "The Battle Begun," *Harrisburg Daily Independent*, September 16, 1880; James Garfield to Albert Riddle, September 15, 1880, Albert Gallatin Riddle Papers, Western Reserve Historical Society.

95. William Hudson, *Random Recollections of an Old Political Reporter*, page 112.

96. Ron Chernow, *Grant*, page 905; "Grand Rally At Warren," *The New York Times*, September 29, 1880.

97. "A Grand Republican Plea," *The New York Times*, September 18, 1880; David Jordan, *Roscoe Conkling of New York: Voice in the Senate*, page 356.

98. James Garfield to Chester Arthur, September 13, 1880, JAG—LC.

99. "It Was Grant," *Cincinnati Enquirer*, September 29, 1880.

100. "Grand Rally at Warren," *The New York Times*, September 29, 1880; Diary entry for September 28, 1880, JAG—LC.

101. Thomas Platt, *The Autobiography of Thomas Collier Platt*, page 135; "Grand Rally at Warren," *The New York Times*, September 29, 1880.

102. James Garfield to Harmon Austin, October 6, 1880, JAG—LC.

103. James Garfield to James Blaine, September 30, 1880, JAG—LC.

104. Herbert Clancy, *The Presidential Election of 1880*, page 233.

105. "California Ours," *Boston Globe*, October 21, 1880; "Undone," *Detroit Free Press*, October 21, 1880; "Latest Telegraph," *Times-Picayune*, October 21, 1880; "Chinese Cheap Labor," *Cincinnati Enquirer*, October 21, 1880.

106. "The Republican Campaign—Callers on General Garfield," *New-York Tribune*, August 7, 1880; Diary entry for October 20, 1880, JAG—LC; Benjamin Arrington, *The Last Lincoln Republican*, page 158; Lucretia Garfield to James R. Garfield, October 24, 1880, JAG—LC; James Garfield to Marshall Jewell, October 20, 1880, JAG—LC; "The Case of the Alleged Forger," *New York Sun*, October 30, 1880.

107. James Garfield to Marshall Jewell, October 23, 1880, JAG—LC; Lucretia Garfield to Harry Garfield, October 24, 1880, JAG—LC.

108. James Garfield to Marshall Jewell, October 23, 1880, JAG—LC; Lucretia Garfield to Harry Garfield, October 11, 1880, JAG—LC.

109. "Pacific Coast Items," *The Record-Union*, October 30, 1880; "Politics," *The Record-Union*, October 30, 1880.

110. Benjamin Arrington, *The Last Lincoln Republican*, page 155; Stanley Brown, "My Friend Garfield," *American Heritage,* August 1971.

111. C. S. Carpenter, *James A. Garfield: His Speeches at Home;* James Garfield to William Cooper Howells, June 18, 1864; Margaret Leech, *The Garfield Orbit.*

112. Garfield et al., "Ought the Negro to Be Disfranchised? Ought He to Have Been Enfranchised?" page 248.

113. James Garfield to David Swaim, August 10, 1868, SG—WRHS.

114. "Addressing The Boys in Blue," *The New York Times*, August 7, 1880.

115. Stanley Brown, "My Friend Garfield," "Colored Jubilee Singers"; C. S. Carpenter, *James A. Garfield: His Speeches at Home.*

116. C. S. Carpenter, "The Future of Colored Men."

117. Diary entry for January 25, 1881, JAG—LC.

118. Diary entry for November 1, 1880, JAG—LC; Diary entry for November 2, 1880, JAG—LC.

119. Theodore Roosevelt, Jr., diary entry for November 3, 1880, "Theodore Roosevelt Papers," Library of Congress.

120. Patty Mays to James R. Garfield, Harry Garfield, November 2, 1880, JAG—LC; Diary entry for November 2, 1880, JAG—LC.

121. Edmund Morris, *Edison*, page 388.

122. Diary entries for November 3, 4, 5, 1880, JAG—LC.

123. James Garfield to Harmon Austin, November 16, 1880, JAG—LC; Allan Peskin, *Garfield*, pages 510–512; Herbert Clancy, *The Presidential Election of 1880*, page 240.

124. Clipping, *The Inter Ocean*, November 4, 1880; Allan Peskin, *Garfield*, page 512.

125. James Garfield to Burke Hinsdale, November 17, 1880, JAG—LC.

126. Lucretia Garfield and James A. Garfield to James R. Garfield, December 2, 1880, JAG—LC.

127. Herbert Clancy, *The Presidential Election of 1880*, page 242.

128. Almira Russell Hancock. *Reminiscences of Winfield Scott Hancock* (New York: C.L. Webster & Company, 1887), pages 174–175.

129. "Indiana's October Vote," *The New York Times*, February 12, 1881.

130. Harriet Blaine to Walker Blaine, October 27, 1880, Beale, *Letters of Mrs. James G. Blaine*.

131. Theodore Clarke Smith, *The Life and Letters of James Abram Garfield*, page 1049; James Blaine to James Garfield, December 16, 1880, JAG—LC; Diary entry for December 12, 1880, JAG—LC; Harriet Blaine to Walker Blaine, January 16, 1881, Beale, *Letters of Mrs. James G. Blaine*.

132. James Blaine to James Garfield, December 16, 1880, JAG—LC; James Blaine to James Garfield, December 13, 1880, JAG—LC.

133. James Garfield to James Blaine, December 19, 1880, JAG—LC.

134. Diary entry for November 27, 1880, JAG—LC; Robert McElroy, *Levi Parsons Morton: Banker, Diplomat, and Statesman*, pages 124–125; Roscoe Conkling to James Garfield, February 8, 1881, JAG—LC; H. Wayne Morgan, *From Hayes to McKinley: National Party Politics, 1877–1896*, page 124.

135. David Saville Muzzey, *James G. Blaine: A Political Idol of Other Days*, pages 180–181.

136. Allan Peskin, *Garfield*, page 680; Diary entry for January 21, 1880, JAG—LC.

CHAPTER 26

1. "Gath's Views," *Cincinnati Enquirer*, March 5, 1881; "The Street Decorations," *The New York Times*, March 5, 1881; "The Crowds and The Decorations," *New-York Tribune*, March 5, 1881; "Visitors," *The Inter Ocean*, March 5, 1881; "Inauguration Day," *The Evening Star*, March 4, 1881; "Washington," *San Francisco Examiner*, March 5, 1881; "Street Decorations," *The Inter Ocean*, March 5, 1881.

2. "The Crowds and The Decorations," *New-York Tribune*, March 5, 1881; "Inaugural Ceremonies," *New-York Tribune*, March 5, 1881.

3. Diary entry for January 17, 1881, JAG—LC.

4. Diary entry for March 3, 1881, JAG—LC.

5. Diary entry for March 2, 1881, JAG—LC; Diary entry for March 3, 1881,

JAG—LC; Kenneth Ackerman, *Dark Horse*, pages 218–219; Diary entry for March 4, 1881, JAG—LC.

6. Diary entry for March 4, 1881, JAG—LC.

7. "A New Chief Magistrate," *The New York Times*, March 5, 1881; "Inauguration Day," *The Evening Star*, March 4, 1881.

8. Allan Peskin, *Garfield*, page 538; H. Wayne Morgan, *From Hayes to McKinley: National Party Politics, 1877–1896*, page 125.

9. "The Great Fraud of 1876," *New York Sun*, March 5, 1881.

10. "Washington," *Chicago Tribune*, March 5, 1881; Allan Peskin, *Garfield*, page 537.

11. "Washington," *Chicago Tribune*, March 5, 1881; "Presto!" *Cincinnati Enquirer*, March 5, 1881; "At the Capitol," *The Evening Star*, March 4, 1881.

12. "Presto!" *Cincinnati Enquirer*, March 5, 1881; Frederick Douglass, *Life and Times of Frederick Douglass*, page 627.

13. "The Inaugural Ceremonies," *The Inter Ocean*, March 5, 1881; "Presto!" *Cincinnati Enquirer*, March 5, 1881.

14. Candice Millard, *Destiny of the Republic*, page 91; "On the Capitol Steps," *New-York Tribune*, March 5, 1881.

15. "Inaugural Address," Garfield, *The Works of James A. Garfield*, 1882; "How The Address Was Received," *The New York Times*, March 5, 1881.

16. Frederick Douglass, *Life and Times of Frederick Douglass*, page 629; "How The Address Was Received," *The New York Times*, March 5, 1881.

17. "Garfield President," *New-York Tribune*, March 5, 1881.

18. "Presto!" *Cincinnati Enquirer*, March 5, 1881.

19. "A Royal Welcome," *The Inter Ocean*, March 5, 1881.

20. Candice Millard, *Destiny of the Republic*, page 90.

21. "Going Out and In," *National Republican*, March 5, 1881; Allan Peskin, *Garfield*, page 541.

22. James Blaine to James Garfield, March 4, 1881, JAG—LC.

23. "Presto!" *Cincinnati Enquirer*, March 5, 1881; "A Reception at the White House," *The New York Times*, March 5, 1881.

24. "Comments of the Press," *New-York Tribune*, March 5, 1881; "Press Comment," *Chicago Tribune*, March 5, 1881.

25. "Press Comment," *Chicago Tribune*, March 5, 1881.

26. Allan Peskin, *Garfield*, page 541; "Inauguration Ball," *The Evening Star*, March 5, 1881; "The Inauguration Ball," *New-York Tribune*, March 5, 1881.

27. "The Inauguration Ball," *New-York Tribune*, March 5, 1881; "The Fire Works," *The Evening Star*, March 4, 1881.

28. Diary entry for March 4, 1881, JAG—LC.

29. "Street Decorations," *The Inter Ocean*, March 5, 1881; "The Inauguration," *The Evening Star*, March 5, 1881.

30. "Mr. Hayes's Lucky Escape," *The New York Times*, March 6, 1881.

CHAPTER 27

1. "The Week," *The Nation*, March 10, 1881; Clipping, *Chicago Tribune*, March 3, 1881; Justus D. Doenecke. *The Presidencies of James A. Garfield & Chester A. Arthur*, American Presidency Series (Lawrence: Regents Press of Kansas, 1981), page 33; Clipping, *Cincinnati Enquirer*, March 4, 1881.

2. Justus D. Doenecke, *The Presidencies of James A. Garfield & Chester A. Arthur*, page 33; "Eli Perkins on the new Postmaster-General," *Chicago Tribune*, March 6, 1881.

3. Jason Emerson. *Giant in the Shadows: The Life of Robert T. Lincoln* (Carbondale: Southern Illinois University Press, 2012), pages 216–217; Fred Rosen. *Murdering the President: Alexander Graham Bell and the Race to Save James Garfield* (Lincoln: Potomac Books, an imprint of the University of Nebraska Press, 2016), page xviii.

4. "What They Say," *Cincinnati Enquirer*, March 6, 1881.

5. "The New Administration," *New York Sun*, March 6, 1881; "Seven Up," *Cincinnati Enquirer*, March 6, 1881.

6. "The Cabinet," *Cincinnati Enquirer*, March 6, 1881; John Ingalls, *A Collection of the Writings of John James Ingalls: Essays, Addresses, and Orations*, page 436.

7. David Jordan, *Roscoe Conkling of New York: Voice in the Senate*, page 373.

8. Theodore Clarke Smith, *The Life and Letters of James Abram Garfield*, pages 1016–1017, 1047.

9. Alexander McClure, *Recollections of Half a Century*, page 112.

10. Henry Dawes, "Garfield and Conkling," *Century Magazine*, January 1894.

11. Alexander McClure, *Recollections of Half a Century*, page 112.

12. Alfred Conkling, *The Life and Letters of Roscoe Conkling: Orator, Statesman, Advocate*, page 632; "Roscoe's Wrath," *The Philadelphia Times*, March 27, 1881.

13. "Beginning the Term," *National Republican*, March 7, 1881; Diary entry for March 5, 1881, JAG—LC.

14. James Blaine. *Eulogy on the Late President Garfield* (Philadelphia: Hubbard Brothers, 1882), page 29.

15. "The Passing Crowd," *National Republican*, March 5, 1881.

16. Royal Cortissoz, *The Life of Whitelaw Reid* volume 2, page 58; Carl Fish, *The Civil Service and The Patronage*, page 109; "The 'Orifice' Seekers," *The Evening Star*, March 9, 1881.

17. "Washington," *Chicago Tribune*, March 8, 1881.

18. "The 'Orifice' Seekers," *The Evening Star*, March 9, 1881; "A Glance At The White House," *New-York Tribune*, March 18, 1881; "The Raid for the Marshalships," *The Evening Star*, March 21, 1881.

19. "The 'Orifice' Seekers," *The Evening Star*, March 9, 1881; Clipping, *The Evening Star*, March 8, 1881.

20. Royal Cortissoz, *The Life of Whitelaw Reid* volume 2, page 58.

21. Diary entry for March 8, 1881, JAG—LC.

22. "Gall," *Cincinnati Enquirer*, March 25, 1881; Stanley Brown, "My Friend Garfield."

23. "Official Hunger," *San Francisco Examiner*, March 22, 1881.

24. Ibid.

25. Diary entry for March 8, 1881, JAG—LC.

26. Diary entry for February 5, 1879, JAG—LC; Diary entry for April 24, 1880, JAG—LC.

27. Thomas Sherman, *Twenty Years with James G. Blaine: Reminiscences by His Private Secretary*, page 78; Diary entry for March 14, 1881, JAG—LC.

28. Diary entry for June 13, 1881, JAG—LC; Stanley Brown, "My Friend Garfield."

29. "Capital Chips," *Star Tribune*, March 18, 1881; Diary entry for March 10, 1881, JAG—LC.

30. H. H. Alexander and Edward Easton. *Report of the Proceedings in the Case of the United States vs. Charles J. Guiteau*, volume 1 (Washington, D.C.: Government Printing Office, 1882), pages 664–665.

31. Charles Guiteau to James Garfield, March 8, 1881, JAG—LC; Alexander and Easton, *Report of the Proceedings in the Case of the* United States vs. Charles J. Guiteau, page 208; Candice Millard, *Destiny of the Republic*, page 123.

32. "One Who Knows," *New York Herald*, April 8, 1881; "Various Comments," *National Republican*, March 31, 1881; "Blaine Wins," *Boston Post*, March 25, 1881; Justus Doenecke, *The Presidencies of James A. Garfield & Chester A. Arthur*, page 54; "The 'Orifice' Seekers," *The Evening Star*, March 9, 1881.

33. David Saville Muzzey, *James G. Blaine: A Political Idol of Other Days*, page 187.

34. Diary entry for March 11, 1881, JAG—LC; James Garfield to Thomas Nichol, May 29, 1881, JAG—LC; Allan Peskin, *Garfield*, page 554; Diary entry for June 13, 1881, JAG—LC; James Blaine to James Garfield, March 13, 1881, JAG—LC; Diary entry for April 19, 1881, JAG—LC.

35. "Garfield's Quandary," *Puck*, Volume IX, No. 214, April 13, 1881.

36. James Garfield to Harmon Austin, March 3, 1878, JAG—LC; James Blaine to James Garfield, April 1, 1881, JAG—LC; James Blaine to James Garfield, circa April 1881, JAG—LC; Allan Peskin, *Garfield*, page 554.

37. James Garfield to James Blaine, March 4, 1881, JAG—LC; James Garfield to James Blaine, March 17, 1881, JAG—LC; James Blaine to James Garfield, circa March 1881, JAG—LC.

38. Frederick Henry, *Captain Henry of Geauga: A Family Chronicle*, pages 532.

39. "Affairs at St. Petersburg," *New-York Tribune*, March 17, 1881.

40. Harriet Blaine to Margaret Blaine, March 14, 1881, Harriet Beale, *Letters of Mrs. James G. Blaine*; Diary entry for March 19, 1881, JAG—LC; *Puck*, Volume IX, No. 217, May 4, 1881.

41. Allan Peskin, *Garfield*, page 544; "A Glance At The White House," *New-York Tribune*, March 18, 1881; Edmund Morris. *Theodore Rex*, paperback edition (New York: The Modern Library, 2010), page 174; Candice Millard, *Destiny of the Republic*, page 206.

42. William Seale. *The President's House: A History* second edition, volume 1 (Baltimore, Washington, D.C.: Johns Hopkins University Press, In association with White House Historical Association, 2008), pages 497–499; Ari Hoogenboom, *Rutherford B. Hayes: Warrior & President*, page 458.

43. Harriet Blaine to Margaret Blaine, March 24, 1881, Harriet Beale, *Letters of Mrs. James G. Blaine*.

44. "A President's Daily Life," *New-York Tribune*, March 20, 1881; Ruth Feis, *Mollie Garfield in the White House*, page 60; Diary entry for March 14, 1881, JAG—LC; William Seale, *The President's House*, page 497.

45. "A President's Daily Life," *New-York Tribune*, March 20, 1881.

46. "The President and His Little Church Around the Corner," *The Baltimore Sun*, March 7, 1881; Hilda E. Koontz and Peter M. Morgan. *Miracles in the Cathedral: A History of the National City Christian Church* (National City Christian Church, 2005), page 4.

47. Diary entry for March 20, 1881, JAG—LC.

48. James Garfield to Roscoe Conkling, March 20, 1881, JAG—LC.

49. Diary entry for March 20, 1881, JAG—LC.

50. T. B. Connery, "The Secret History of the Garfield-Conkling Tragedy"; David Jordan, *Roscoe Conkling of New York: Voice in the Senate*, page 381.

51. Diary entry for March 22, 1881, JAG—LC; Allan Peskin, *Garfield*, page 558; "What Is Said At Albany," *The New York Times*, March 23, 1881; "The Sentiment at Albany," *The New York Times*, March 24, 1881.

52. "Washington," *Chicago Tribune*, March 24, 1881.

53. James Blaine to James Garfield, circa March 1881, JAG—LC; John Ingalls, *A Collection of the Writings of John James Ingalls: Essays, Addresses, and Orations*, page 427.

54. Lucretia Garfield diary entry for March 22, 1881, Lucretia Garfield Papers, LoC.

55. Diary entry for March 22, 1881, JAG—LC.

56. "Roscoe's Wrath," *The Philadelphia Times*, March 27, 1881; Thomas Reeves, *Gentleman Boss*, page 223; H. Wayne Morgan, *From Hayes to McKinley: National Party Politics, 1877–1896*, page 132.

57. "Distributing the Offices," *The New York Times*, March 24, 1881; H. Wayne Morgan, *From Hayes to McKinley: National Party Politics, 1877–1896*, page 132.

58. "Washington," *Chicago Tribune*, March 24, 1881; "Distributing the Offices," *The New York Times*, March 24, 1881; "The Sentiment at Albany," *The New York Times*, March 24, 1881; "Town Talk," *Brooklyn Daily Eagle*, March 24, 1881; "The President's Policy," *New-York Tribune*, March 24, 1881.

59. Diary entry for March 23, 1881, JAG—LC; James Blaine to James Garfield, March 23, 1881, JAG—LC; "Washington," *Chicago Tribune*, March 24, 1881.

60. "Washington," *Chicago Tribune*, March 24, 1881; "A Cloud Which is Gathering," *National Republican*, March 24, 1881.

61. H. Wayne Morgan, *From Hayes to McKinley: National Party Politics, 1877–1896*, page 132; "The Bomb-shell in the Conkling Camp," *The Evening Star*, March 24, 1881.

62. David Jordan, *Roscoe Conkling of New York: Voice in the Senate*, page 342; Thomas Platt, *The Autobiography of Thomas Collier Platt*, page 151.

63. Candice Millard, *Destiny of the Republic*, page 205; Diary entry for March 30, 1881, JAG—LC; Diary entry for March 26, 1881, JAG—LC; Diary entry for April 1, 1881, JAG—LC; Diary entry for March 28, 1871, JAG—LC.

64. Thomas Reeves, *Gentleman Boss*, page 227; "The New York Collectorship," *National Republican*, March 26, 1881; "Two Bosses," *Cincinnati Enquirer*, March 26, 1881.

65. "The President's Nominations," *The Inter Ocean*, March 25, 1881.
66. Diary entry for March 27, 1881, JAG—LC.
67. James Garfield to Whitelaw Reid, March 30, 1881, JAG—LC; James Garfield to Whitelaw Reid, April 18, 1880, JAG—LC.
68. Diary entry for April 5, 1881, JAG—LC; Royal Cortissoz, *The Life of Whitelaw Reid* volume 2, page 61.
69. "Blaine Wins," *Boston Post*, March 25, 1881.
70. Royal Cortissoz, *The Life of Whitelaw Reid* volume 2, page 60; James Garfield to Burke Hinsdale, April 4, 1881, JAG—LC; James Garfield to J. Q. Smith, April 29, 1881.
71. Ari Hoogenboom, *Outlawing the Spoils: A History of the Civil Service Reform Movement, 1865–1883*, page 204.
72. "The President's New York Appointments," *The Nation*, March 31, 1881.
73. Ibid.
74. "Telegraphic News," *The Baltimore Sun*, March 26, 1881.
75. Diary entry for April 2, 1881, JAG—LC; John Sherman, *Recollections of Forty Years in the House, Senate and Cabinet*, volume 2, pages 817.
76. Ari Hoogenboom, *Outlawing the Spoils: A History of the Civil Service Reform Movement, 1865–1883*, page 206; Ari Hoogenboom, *Rutherford B. Hayes: Warrior & President*, page 468.
77. "The Situation At The Capital," *New-York Tribune*, March 31, 1881.
78. Frederick Henry, *Captain Henry of Geauga: A Family Chronicle*, page 308; Allan Peskin, *Garfield*, page 551; James Garfield to Burke Hinsdale, June 16, 1881, JAG—LC; James Garfield to Rutherford Hayes, December 16, 1880, JAG—LC.
79. Richard White, *The Republic for Which It Stands*, page 364; "Mahone, Virginia," *The Evening Star*, March 15, 1881; Nelson Morehouse Blake. *William Mahone of Virginia: Soldier and Political Insurgent* (Richmond: Garrett & Massie, 1935), pages 248–249; "Telegraphic Summary," *The Baltimore Sun*, March 16, 1881; Nelson Blake, *William Mahone of Virginia: Soldier and Political Insurgent*, page 210.
80. Stanley Hirshon, *Farewell to the Bloody Shirt: Northern Republicans and the Southern Negro*, page 95.
81. Allan Peskin, *Garfield*, page 567; Diary entry for March 15, 1881, JAG—LC; Justus Doenecke, *The Presidencies of James A. Garfield & Chester A. Arthur*, page 51.
82. *Puck*, Volume IX, No. 213, 1881.
83. "From Washington," *The Baltimore Sun*, May 20, 1881; Justus Doenecke, *The Presidencies of James A. Garfield & Chester A. Arthur*, page 49; Frederick Douglass, *Life and Times of Frederick Douglass*, page 631.
84. Frederick Douglass, *Life and Times of Frederick Douglass*, pages 636–639.
85. Justus Doenecke, *The Presidencies of James A. Garfield & Chester A. Arthur*, page 47; William Barton. *The Life of Clara Barton* volume 2 (Boston: Houghton Mifflin Company, 1922), pages 147–153.
86. Diary entry for May 4, 1881, JAG—LC; Kenneth Ackerman, *Dark Horse*, page 286.
87. James Blaine to James Garfield, March 29, 1881, JAG—LC.

88. Alexander and Easton, *Report of the Proceedings in the Case of the* United States vs. Charles J. Guiteau, page 122; Candice Millard, *Destiny of the Republic*, page 125.

89. Charles Guiteau to James Garfield, May 23, 1880, JAG—LC.

90. William Crook, *Through Five Administrations*, page 267.

91. Diary entry for May 5, 1881, JAG—LC.

92. Justus Doenecke, *The Presidencies of James A. Garfield & Chester A. Arthur*, page 45; "The President Amiably Obstinate," *The Evening Star*, May 6, 1881; "The New York Nominations," *New-York Tribune*, May 7, 1881.

93. Clipping, *The Evening Star*, May 6, 1881.

94. Diary entry for May 6, 1881, JAG—LC.

95. T. B. Connery, "The Secret History of the Garfield-Conkling Tragedy."

96. David Jordan, *Roscoe Conkling of New York: Voice in the Senate*, pages 384–385.

97. "A Sensation In Politics," *The New York Times*, May 17, 1881.

98. "Indignant but not Frightened," *New-York Tribune*, May 17, 1881; Thomas Platt, *The Autobiography of Thomas Collier Platt*, page 150.

99. Diary entry for May 16, 1881, JAG—LC.

100. "A Sensation in Politics," *The New York Times*, May 17, 1881; "Indignant but not Frightened," *New-York Tribune*, May 17, 1881; H. Wayne Morgan, *From Hayes to McKinley: National Party Politics, 1877–1896*, page 135.

101. "Discussion Among Politicians," *New-York Tribune*, May 17, 1881.

102. Thomas Reeves, *Gentleman Boss*, page 235.

103. *Puck*, Volume IX, No. 220, 1881.

104. John Taliaferro, *All the Great Prizes*, pages 203–204; Diary entry for May 13, 1881, JAG—LC.

105. Diary entry for May 11, 1881, JAG—LC; Diary entry for May 28, 1881, JAG—LC; Diary entry for June 12, 1881, JAG—LC.

106. "Under Conkling's Thumb," *The New York Times*, June 19, 1881; Diary entry for May 19, 1881, JAG—LC.

107. Diary entry for June 9, 1881, JAG—LC.

108. David Jordan, *Roscoe Conkling of New York: Voice in the Senate*, page 405; William Hudson, *Random Recollections of an Old Political Reporter*, page 98.

109. Diary entry for June 13, 1881, JAG—LC.

110. James Garfield to Levi Morton, June 17, 1881, JAG—LC.

111. Diary entry for June 19, 1881, JAG—LC; Ulysses Grant to James Garfield, April 24, 1881, JAG—LC.

112. Ron Chernow, *Grant*, page 909.

113. Diary entry for June 24, 1881, JAG—LC; Diary entry for June 22, 1881, JAG—LC.

114. Stanley Hirshon, *Farewell to the Bloody Shirt: Northern Republicans and the Southern Negro*, pages 90–92.

115. Diary entry for June 1, 1881, JAG—LC.

116. Thomas Sherman, *Twenty Years with James G. Blaine: Reminiscences by His Private Secretary*, pages 80–81.

117. Alexander and Easton, *Report of the Proceedings in the Case of the* United States vs. Charles J. Guiteau, pages 692–696.

118. Harry Garfield, "Speech By Dr. Harry Augustus Garfield," *Bulletin of Hiram College*, November 19, 1931, JAG—HC.

119. Alexander and Easton, *Report of the Proceedings in the Case of the* United States vs. Charles J. Guiteau, page 121.

120. "The Story of the Crime," *New-York Tribune*, July 3, 1881.

121. Alexander and Easton, *Report of the Proceedings in the Case of the* United States vs. Charles J. Guiteau, page 121.

122. "Assassination! The President Shot," *The Evening Star*, July 2, 1881.

123. Alexander and Easton, *Report of the Proceedings in the Case of the* United States vs. Charles J. Guiteau, pages 186–187.

124. Candice Millard, *Destiny of the Republic*, page 158.

125. "The Story of the Crime," *New-York Tribune*, July 3, 1881.

126. Jason Emerson, *Giant in the Shadows*, page 228.

127. "A Great Nation In Grief," *The New York Times*, July 3, 1881.

128. Robert Reyburn, *Clinical History of the Case of President James Abram Garfield*, page 10; Alexander and Easton, *Report of the Proceedings in the Case of the* United States vs. Charles J. Guiteau, page 231; Ira M. Rutkow. *James A. Garfield* first edition, The American Presidents Series (New York: Times Books, 2006), pages 84–85.

129. Robert Reyburn, *Clinical History of the Case of President James Abram Garfield*, page 10; Ira Rutkow, *James A. Garfield*, page 86.

130. Jason Emerson, *Giant in the Shadows*, page 228.

131. Robert Reyburn, *Clinical History of the Case of President James Abram Garfield*, pages 10–11; Ira Rutkow, *James A. Garfield*, page 85; Kenneth Ackerman, *Dark Horse*, page 336.

132. "The President Shot," *New-York Tribune*, July 3, 1881; "3rd Extra," *The Evening Star*, July 2, 1881.

CHAPTER 28

1. Thomas Sherman, *Twenty Years with James G. Blaine: Reminiscences by His Private Secretary*, pages 84–85; William Balch, *The Life of James Abram Garfield*, page 597.

2. Robert Reyburn, *Clinical History of the Case of President James Abram Garfield*, page 7; Thomas Sherman, *Twenty Years with James G. Blaine: Reminiscences by His Private Secretary*, pages 86–87; James L. McDonough, *William Tecumseh Sherman: In the Service of My Country: A Life*, page 695.

3. Alexander and Easton, *Report of the Proceedings in the Case of the* United States vs. Charles J. Guiteau, page 251; Robert Reyburn, *Clinical History of the Case of President James Abram Garfield*, pages 13–14.

4. Candice Millard, *Destiny of the Republic*, page 174; Robert Reyburn, *Clinical History of the Case of President James Abram Garfield*, page 14; Ron Chernow, *Grant*, page 910; Kenneth Ackerman, *Dark Horse*, page 352.

5. Harriet Blaine to Margaret Blaine, July 3, 1881, Harriet Beale, *Letters of Mrs. James G. Blaine*, page 211; Robert Reyburn, *Clinical History of the Case of President James Abram Garfield*, page 14.

6. Robert Reyburn, *Clinical History of the Case of President James Abram Garfield*, page 14; Ira Rutkow, *James A. Garfield*, page 91.

7. "The Popular Sympathy," *The Evening Star*, July 3, 1881; "Scenes in and about Wall Street," *New-York Tribune*, July 4, 1881; "Throughout the Country," *The Baltimore Sun*, July 3, 1881.

8. "Died from the Shock," *The Evening Star*, July 3, 1881; "At Albany," *Boston Globe*, July 3, 1881; Maury Klein, *The Life and Legend of Jay Gould*, page 217; Edmund Morris, *The Rise of Theodore Roosevelt*, page 128.

9. "Throughout the Country," *The Baltimore Sun*, July 3, 1881; "Voice of the Press," *New-York Tribune*, July 4, 1881; Clipping, *Detroit Free Press*, July 3, 1881; "At The State Capital," *New-York Tribune*, July 3, 1881; "What Men Say," *Detroit Free Press*, July 3, 1881; "At The Fifth Avenue Hotel," *The New York Times*, July 3, 1881.

10. "The Interior Speaks," *San Francisco Examiner*, July 4, 1881; "In New York," *Boston Globe*, July 3, 1881; "Tolling the Bells in Albany," *The Baltimore Sun*, July 3, 1881; "A Rumor of Death," *The New York Times*, July 5, 1881; "Sorrow in the City," *New-York Tribune*, July 3, 1881; "Later," *Detroit Free Press*, July 3, 1881; "Still voting for Senators," *The New York Times*, July 3, 1881.

11. "The President's Aged Mother," *New York Sun*, July 4, 1881; Allan Peskin, *Garfield*, page 598.

12. "The President's Aged Mother," *New York Sun*, July 4, 1881.

13. "The Celebration," *San Francisco Examiner*, July 3, 1881; "Indiana," *The Inter Ocean*, July 4, 1881; "Newport's Festivities Given Up," *The New York Times*, July 5, 1881; "No Celebration in Portland," *The New York Times*, July 5, 1881; "Decorations Taken Down," *The New York Times*, July 5, 1881; "No Party Difference Known," *The New York Times*, July 4, 1881.

14. "A Great City's Anxiety," *The New York Times*, July 4, 1881; "The City still on the Rack," *New-York Tribune*, July 5, 1881.

15. "Local News," *The Evening Star*, July 5, 1881; "The Gloom At the Capital," *The New York Times*, July 5, 1881.

16. "Watching and Waiting," *New York Sun*, July 5, 1881.

17. "Inquiries and Messages from Abroad," *The Baltimore Sun*, July 4, 1881

18. "Secretary Blaine and the President," *The Evening Star*, July 5, 1881.

19. "The Vice-President," *National Republican*, July 4, 1881.

20. Alexander and Easton, *Report of the Proceedings in the Case of the* United States vs. Charles J. Guiteau, page 206; "Deputy Attorney-General Cook's Belief to a Conspiracy," *New York Sun*, July 5, 1881; "What Gladstone Said," *Detroit Free Press*, July 8, 1881.

21. Kenneth Ackerman, *Dark Horse*, page 359; Candice Millard, *Destiny of the Republic*, page 213; "Guiteau in Jail," *The Evening Star*, July 3, 1881; Thomas Reeves, *Gentleman Boss*, page 240; "Great Relief to All Hearts," *New-York Tribune*, July 7, 1881; Candice Millard, *Destiny of the Republic*, page 191; "The Wounded Chief," *Detroit Free Press*, July 3, 1881.

22. Thomas Platt, *The Autobiography of Thomas Collier Platt*, page 163.

23. "Scenes At the Fifth Avenue Hotel," *New-York Tribune*, July 5, 1881.

24. "Opinions of the Press," *The New York Times*, July 3, 1881; "Faction's Latest Crime," *New-York Tribune*, July 3, 1881.

25. "Three Facts About Guiteau," *New-York Tribune*, July 11, 1881.

26. "Sentiments of Dr. Newman," *New-York Tribune*, July 4, 1881.

27. "Views of the Rev. Dr. Bellows," *New-York Tribune*, July 4, 1881; "The Spoils Alone," *Buffalo Weekly Express*, July 7, 1881; "In the Old World," *New York Sun*, July 4, 1881; Ari Hoogenboom, *Outlawing the Spoils: A History of the Civil Service Reform Movement, 1865–1883*, page 209.

28. "The Feeling Abroad," *The Evening Star*, July 4, 1881; "The New York Press on the Murderous Deed," *The Evening Star*, July 3, 1881.

29. Ari Hoogenboom, *Rutherford B. Hayes: Warrior & President*, page 470.

30. "Effect of the News," *Detroit Free Press*, July 3, 1881; "Mr. Conkling Under Police Protection," *New-York Tribune*, July 5, 1881.

31. Candice Millard, *Destiny of the Republic*, pages 213–215; "Guiteau in Jail," *The Evening Star*, July 3, 1881.

32. "The Assassin's Career," *New-York Tribune*, July 3, 1881; "Not a German," *The Evening Star*, July 3, 1881; "More of Guiteau's Career," *New York Sun*, July 4, 1881; "Guiteau's Political Fancies," *New-York Tribune*, July 3, 1881.

33. "The Assassin's Career," *New-York Tribune*, July 3, 1881.

34. "The New York Press on the Murderous Deed," *The Evening Star*, July 3, 1881; "The Rev. Dr. Macarthur's Thoughts," *New-York Tribune*, July 4, 1881; "The Spoils Alone," *Buffalo Weekly Express*, July 7, 1881.

35. Robert Reyburn, *Clinical History of the Case of President James Abram Garfield*, pages 19, 26; "Hope Alive," *The Evening Star*, July 6, 1881.

36. Robert Reyburn, *Clinical History of the Case of President James Abram Garfield*, page 25; "The First Danger Period Passed," *New-York Tribune*, July 7, 1881; "The President's Life," *New-York Tribune*, July 9, 1881; "The President," *San Francisco Examiner*, July 15, 1881.

37. "Great Relief To All Hearts," *New-York Tribune*, July 7, 1881; Clipping, *New-York Tribune*, August 5, 1881.

38. Ira Rutkow, *James A. Garfield*, pages 91, 94; Robert Reyburn, *Clinical History of the Case of President James Abram Garfield*, page 16.

39. Ira Rutkow, *James A. Garfield*, page 85; Robert Reyburn, *Clinical History of the Case of President James Abram Garfield*, page 17.

40. Candice Millard, *Destiny of the Republic*, pages 163–164.

41. Ira Rutkow, *James A. Garfield*, page 99; "Sunbeams," *New York Sun*, September 17, 1881.

42. Joseph Lister. *The Collected Papers of Joseph Baron Lister* volume 1 (Oxford: Clarendon Press, 1909), page xxiii.

43. Candice Millard, *Destiny of the Republic*, page 184.

44. Joseph Lister, "On the Antiseptic Principle in the Practice of Surgery," *The British Medical Journal*, September 21, 1867, page 248; Candice Millard, *Destiny of the Republic*, page 184.

45. Ira Rutkow, *James A. Garfield*, page 105, https://web.archive.org/web/20160712 170405/http://www.chemheritage.org/discover/online-resources/thanks-to -chemistry/listerine.aspx.

46. Robert Reyburn, *Clinical History of the Case of President James Abram Garfield*, pages 20, 22; Ira Rutkow, *James A. Garfield*, page 95; "Letters From the People," *New-York Tribune*, July 11, 1881.

47. Robert Reyburn, *Clinical History of the Case of President James Abram Garfield*, pages 28–35.

48. David Jordan, *Roscoe Conkling of New York: Voice in the Senate*, page 408; "The Story of President Garfield's Illness," Doctor Willard Bliss, *Century Magazine*, 1881, page 302.

49. Robert Reyburn, *Clinical History of the Case of President James Abram Garfield*, pages 18, 29.

50. A. F. Rockwell, "From Mentor to Elberon," page 437; Robert Reyburn, *Clinical History of the Case of President James Abram Garfield*, page 17; Max Cohen. *Garfield Souvenirs and "Gems" of Press and Pulpit* volume 1 (Washington, D.C., 1881), page 11.

51. A. F. Rockwell, "From Mentor to Elberon," page 437; Cohen, *Garfield Souvenirs and "Gems" of Press and Pulpit*, page 10.

52. Cohen, *Garfield Souvenirs and "Gems" of Press and Pulpit*, pages 13, 15; Almon Rockwell, "An Autograph of President Garfield," *Century Magazine*, 1881, page 300.

53. "For Mr. Garfield's Family," *New York Sun*, July 8, 1881; Doctor Willard Bliss, "The Story of President Garfield's Illness," *Century Magazine*, 1881, page 301.

54. "A Little Child's Prayer," *Star-Tribune*, July 24, 1881; Clipping, *New-York Tribune*, July 14, 1881.

55. "At The State Capital," *New-York Tribune*, July 3, 1881.

56. Allan Peskin, *Garfield*, page 600.

57. "Voluntary Medical Advisers All Over the Country," *The Evening Star*, July 5, 1881; Kenneth Ackerman, *Dark Horse*, page 363.

58. "A Visitor Calling in a Bathing Suit," *New York Sun*, August 21, 1881; "Strange Characters At The Capital," *New-York Tribune*, July 7, 1881; "Incidents," *The Evening Star*, July 6, 1881; "The White House Patient," *The Evening Star*, July 19, 1881.

59. "A Blow At Republicanism," *New-York Tribune*, July 3, 1881.

60. William Balch, *The Life of James Abram Garfield*, page 646; Robert Reyburn, *Clinical History of the Case of President James Abram Garfield*, page 29.

61. William Balch, *The Life of James Abram Garfield*, page 647; Robert Reyburn, *Clinical History of the Case of President James Abram Garfield*, page 23.

62. Charlotte Gray, *Alexander Graham Bell: The Reluctant Genius and His Passion for Invention*, page 217; Candice Millard, *Destiny of the Republic*, pages 187–188.

63. Charlotte Gray, *Alexander Graham Bell*, page 219; Candice Millard, *Destiny of the Republic*, page 189.

64. Robert Reyburn, *Clinical History of the Case of President James Abram Garfield*, pages 38–39.

65. Robert Reyburn, *Clinical History of the Case of President James Abram Garfield*, pages

40–41; Doctor Willard Bliss, "The Story of President Garfield's Illness," *Century Magazine*, 1881, page 301.

66. "The President's Relapse," *The New York Times*, July 25, 1881.

67. Candice Millard, *Destiny of the Republic*, pages 180–181.

68. Ira Rutkow, *James A. Garfield*, page 93.

69. Charlotte Gray, *Alexander Graham Bell*, pages 219–220; Ira Rutkow, *James A. Garfield*, page 118.

70. Charlotte Gray, *Alexander Graham Bell*, page 220.

71. Charlotte Gray, *Alexander Graham Bell*, page 220.

72. Ira Rutkow, *James A. Garfield*, page 119.

73. Allan Peskin, *Garfield*, page 603; "If He Could Speak," *New York Sun*, August 21, 1881.

74. Jason Emerson, *Giant in the Shadows*, pages 229–230.

75. James Blaine to Chester Arthur, July 2, 1881, Chester A. Arthur Papers, LoC; "Anxiety in the City," *The New York Times*, July 24, 1881; "Watching and Waiting," *New York Sun*, July 5, 1881; "Still Growing Stronger," *The New York Times*, July 23, 1881.

76. Kenneth Ackerman, *Dark Horse*, page 369; Thomas Sherman, *Twenty Years with James G. Blaine: Reminiscences by His Private Secretary*, page 88.

77. Clipping, *The Evening Star*, July 22, 1881.

78. "Civil Service Reform," *The New York Times*, July 22, 1881.

79. "Civil Service Reform," *New-York Tribune*, July 24, 1881.

80. Thomas Reeves, *Gentleman Boss*, page 244; Kenneth Ackerman, *Dark Horse*, pages 357–358.

81. Kenneth Ackerman, *Dark Horse*, page 349; "Strange Characters At the Capital," *New-York Tribune*, July 7, 1881; Jared Cohen, *Accidental Presidents*, page 166; Andrew White, *Autobiography of Andrew Dickson White*, volume 1, page 193.

82. Jared Cohen, *Accidental Presidents*, page 163; "Scenes In and About Wall Street," *New-York Tribune*, July 3, 1881.

83. Thomas Reeves, *Gentleman Boss*, page 242.

84. Thomas Reeves, *Gentleman Boss*, page 242; H. Wayne Morgan, *From Hayes to McKinley: National Party Politics, 1877–1896*, page 140.

85. Clipping, circa late summer, 1881, JAG—HC; "Condition of the President," *Brooklyn Daily Eagle*, August 5, 1881; Clipping, *Brooklyn Daily Eagle*, August 5, 1881.

86. Robert Reyburn, *Clinical History of the Case of President James Abram Garfield*, pages 48, 50.

87. Doctor Willard Bliss. *Feeding Per Rectum: As Illustrated in the Case of the Late President Garfield, and Others* (Washington, D.C., 1882), pages 9–10; Robert Reyburn, *Clinical History of the Case of President James Abram Garfield*, pages 53–59.

88. Robert Reyburn, *Clinical History of the Case of President James Abram Garfield*, pages 61–68.

89. Robert Reyburn, *Clinical History of the Case of President James Abram Garfield*, pages 61–63.

90. "No Ill Wind," *New York Sun*, August 22, 1881.

91. Robert Reyburn, *Clinical History of the Case of President James Abram Garfield*, page 66.

92. "Domestic News," *San Francisco Examiner*, August 15, 1881; Clipping, *New-York Tribune*, August 27, 1881; "The Croakers And Their Influence," *New-York Tribune*, August 12, 1881; "Insane About President Garfield," *New-York Tribune*, September 3, 1881.

93. Harry Garfield to Eliza Garfield, August 12, 1881, JAG—LC; James Garfield to Eliza Garfield, August 11, 1881, JAG—LC.

94. "The President's Mother," *The New York Times*, August 23, 1881; "Mother Garfield Happy Again," *The Evening Star*, September 2, 1881.

95. Robert Reyburn, *Clinical History of the Case of President James Abram Garfield*, pages 70, 75.

96. Allan Peskin, *Garfield*, page 601; Robert Reyburn, *Clinical History of the Case of President James Abram Garfield*, page 67.

97. Robert Reyburn, *Clinical History of the Case of President James Abram Garfield*, page 68.

98. Robert Reyburn, *Clinical History of the Case of President James Abram Garfield*, pages 69–70.

99. "Glad Tidings," *The Evening Star*, August 28, 1881.

100. "The President's Condition—Cause for Anxiety," *New York Sun*, August 14, 1881.

101. Diary entry for June 19, 1881, JAG—LC.

102. Charles Richard Williams, ed. *Diary and Letters of Rutherford Birchard Hayes: Nineteenth President of the United States* volume 4 (The Ohio State Archaeological and Historical Society, 1925), pages 32–33.

103. "General Arthur and the President," *New-York Tribune*, August 25, 1881; "Vice-President Arthur," *New York Sun*, August 26, 1881; "General Arthur Still In New York," *New-York Tribune*, August 28, 1881.

104. Julia Sand to Chester Arthur, August 27, 1881, Chester A. Arthur Papers, LoC.

105. "The Proposed Removal of the President," *The Evening Star*, September 2, 1881.

106. "Preparations for the Removal," *New-York Tribune*, September 6, 1881; "The Removal of the President," *The Evening Star*, September 5, 1881; "A Petulant Patient," *The Inter Ocean*, September 6, 1881; Allan Peskin, *Garfield*, page 605.

107. Doctor Willard Bliss, "The Story of President Garfield's Illness," *Century Magazine*, 1881, page 303.

108. Ibid.

109. Robert Reyburn, *Clinical History of the Case of President James Abram Garfield*, pages 89–92.

110. "A Day Almost Without Incident," *New-York Tribune*, September 14, 1881.

111. "A Day Almost Without Incident," *New-York Tribune*, September 14, 1881; James Rudolph Garfield to Eliza Garfield July 23, 1881, JAG—LC; Harry Garfield to Eliza Garfield, August 30, 1881, JAG—LC; Harry Garfield to Eliza Garfield, September 5, 1881, JAG—LC; Harry Garfield to James Garfield, September 13, 1881, JAG—LC.

112. Theodore Clarke Smith, *The Life and Letters of James Abram Garfield*, page 1199;

Doctor Willard Bliss, "The Story of President Garfield's Illness," *Century Magazine*, 1881, page 304.

113. Stanley Brown, "My Friend Garfield."

114. "Some of Dr. Bliss's Recent Statements Compared," *New York Sun*, September 15, 1881; Candice Millard, *Destiny of the Republic*, page 263.

115. "Some of Dr. Bliss's Recent Statements Compared," *New York Sun*, September 15, 1881.

116. Robert Reyburn, *Clinical History of the Case of President James Abram Garfield*, pages 92–93.

117. Robert Reyburn, *Clinical History of the Case of President James Abram Garfield*, page 93.

118. Robert Reyburn, *Clinical History of the Case of President James Abram Garfield*, page 94.

119. Robert Reyburn, *Clinical History of the Case of President James Abram Garfield*, pages 95–96.

120. Stanley Brown, "My Friend Garfield"; Doctor Willard Bliss, "The Story of President Garfield's Illness," *Century Magazine*, 1881, pages 303–305.

121. Robert Reyburn, *Clinical History of the Case of President James Abram Garfield*, page 96.

EPILOGUE

1. "Garfield's Tomb," *Cincinnati Enquirer*, May 31, 1890; "Harrison in Ohio," *Cincinnati Enquirer*, May 30, 1890; "The Day of the Dead," *The Evening Star*, May 30, 1890; "At Garfield's Tomb," *Chicago Tribune*, May 31, 1890; "To the Honor of Garfield," *New-York Tribune*, May 31, 1890.

2. "The Day of the Dead," *The Evening Star*, May 30, 1890; "At Garfield's Tomb," *The Tribune*, June 6, 1890; "At Garfield's Tomb," *Chicago Tribune*, May 31, 1890.

3. "At Garfield's Tomb," *Chicago Tribune*, May 31, 1890; Elizabeth McClelland, "A Time For Preservation: Restoring the Garfield Monument," *Western Reserve Magazine*, May 1985, page 42, JAG—HC.

4. "Garfield," *Summit County Beacon*, June 4, 1890.

5. "At the Tomb of Garfield," *Detroit Free Press*, June 2, 1890; "To the Honor of Garfield," *The New York Tribune*, May 31, 1890.

6. "To the Honor of Garfield," *The New York Tribune*, May 31, 1890.

7. "Garfield," *Summit County Beacon*, June 4, 1890.

8. Poore, *Perley's Reminiscences of Sixty Years in the National Metropolis*, volume 2, page 452; H. Wayne Morgan, *From Hayes to McKinley: National Party Politics, 1877–1896*, page 146; Thomas Reeves, *Gentleman Boss*, page 271.

9. Alexander McClure, *Recollections of Half a Century*, page 121; Thomas Reeves, *Gentleman Boss*, page 276; H. Wayne Morgan, *From Hayes to McKinley: National Party Politics, 1877–1896*, page 148.

10. Kenneth Ackerman, *Dark Horse*, page 387; Justus Doenecke, *The Presidencies of James A. Garfield & Chester A. Arthur*, page 79.

11. Edmund Morris, *The Rise of Theodore Roosevelt*, page 405; Ari Hoogenboom,

Outlawing the Spoils: A History of the Civil Service Reform Movement, 1865–1883, page 217.

12. Ari Hoogenboom, *Outlawing the Spoils: A History of the Civil Service Reform Movement, 1865–1883*, pages 213–217; Samuel Cox, *Three Decades of Federal Legislation, 1855 to 1885*, page 676.

13. Ari Hoogenboom, *Outlawing the Spoils: A History of the Civil Service Reform Movement, 1865–1883*, pages 212–215.

14. Thomas Platt, *The Autobiography of Thomas Collier Platt*, page 181; Justus Doenecke, *The Presidencies of James A. Garfield & Chester A. Arthur*, page 76.

15. David Jordan, *Roscoe Conkling of New York: Voice in the Senate*, pages 416, 422; Alfred Conkling, *The Life and Letters of Roscoe Conkling: Orator, Statesman, Advocate*, page 677.

16. Alfred Conkling, *The Life and Letters of Roscoe Conkling: Orator, Statesman, Advocate*, pages 701–702; H. Wayne Morgan, *From Hayes to McKinley: National Party Politics, 1877–1896*, page 142.

17. Candice Millard, *Destiny of the Republic*, page 291; Thomas Reeves, *Gentleman Boss*, page 296.

18. David Saville Muzzey. *James G. Blaine: A Political Idol of Other Days* (Kennikat Press, 1963), pages 462–463.

19. James Blaine, "Eulogy on the Late President Garfield."

20. "To the Honor of Garfield," *New-York Tribune*, May 31, 1890; "Description of the Building," *Chicago Tribune*, May 31, 1890.

21. "At Garfield's Tomb," *Chicago Tribune*, May 31, 1890.

22. "To the Honor of Garfield," *New-York Tribune*, May 31, 1890.

23. "Description of Garfield Monument at Bonita Canyon," JAG—HC.

Photo Credits

1. Wikimedia Commons
2. Western Reserve Historical Society
3. Library of Congress, Prints and Photographs Division
4. Library of Congress, Prints and Photographs Division
5. Library of Congress, Prints and Photographs Division
6. Library of Congress, Geography and Map Division
7. Library of Congress, Prints and Photographs Division
8. Library of Congress, Prints and Photographs Division
9. National Portrait Gallery
10. Library of Congress, Prints and Photographs Division
11. National Archives and Records Administration
12. Library of Congress, Prints and Photographs Division
13. Library of Congress, Prints and Photographs Division
14. Library of Congress, Prints and Photographs Division
15. Wikimedia Commons
16. Wikimedia Commons
17. Wikimedia Commons
18. Library of Congress, Prints and Photographs Division

Index